SPORTS AND ATHLETICS PREPARATION, PERFORMANCE, AND PSYCHOLOGY

GREEK ATHLETIC SPORTS AND FESTIVALS

SPORTS AND ATHLETICS PREPARATION, PERFORMANCE, AND PSYCHOLOGY

Additional books and e-books in this series can be found
on Nova's website under the Series tab.

SPORTS AND ATHLETICS PREPARATION, PERFORMANCE, AND PSYCHOLOGY

GREEK ATHLETIC SPORTS AND FESTIVALS

EDWARD NORMAN GARDINER

Copyright © 2020 by Nova Science Publishers, Inc.

All rights reserved. No part of this book may be reproduced, stored in a retrieval system or transmitted in any form or by any means: electronic, electrostatic, magnetic, tape, mechanical photocopying, recording or otherwise without the written permission of the Publisher.

We have partnered with Copyright Clearance Center to make it easy for you to obtain permissions to reuse content from this publication. Simply navigate to this publication's page on Nova's website and locate the "Get Permission" button below the title description. This button is linked directly to the title's permission page on copyright.com. Alternatively, you can visit copyright.com and search by title, ISBN, or ISSN.

For further questions about using the service on copyright.com, please contact:
Copyright Clearance Center
Phone: +1-(978) 750-8400   Fax: +1-(978) 750-4470   E-mail: info@copyright.com.

NOTICE TO THE READER

The Publisher has taken reasonable care in the preparation of this book, but makes no expressed or implied warranty of any kind and assumes no responsibility for any errors or omissions. No liability is assumed for incidental or consequential damages in connection with or arising out of information contained in this book. The Publisher shall not be liable for any special, consequential, or exemplary damages resulting, in whole or in part, from the readers' use of, or reliance upon, this material. Any parts of this book based on government reports are so indicated and copyright is claimed for those parts to the extent applicable to compilations of such works.

Independent verification should be sought for any data, advice or recommendations contained in this book. In addition, no responsibility is assumed by the Publisher for any injury and/or damage to persons or property arising from any methods, products, instructions, ideas or otherwise contained in this publication.

This publication is designed to provide accurate and authoritative information with regard to the subject matter covered herein. It is sold with the clear understanding that the Publisher is not engaged in rendering legal or any other professional services. If legal or any other expert assistance is required, the services of a competent person should be sought. FROM A DECLARATION OF PARTICIPANTS JOINTLY ADOPTED BY A COMMITTEE OF THE AMERICAN BAR ASSOCIATION AND A COMMITTEE OF PUBLISHERS.

Additional color graphics may be available in the e-book version of this book.

Library of Congress Cataloging-in-Publication Data

ISBN: 978-1-53616-878-5

Published by Nova Science Publishers, Inc. † New York

To F. E. Thompson
In grateful acknowledgment of all that the author
in common with many another Marlburian
owes to his teaching, his sympathy and his friendship

Contents

List of Figures		ix
List of Abbreviations		xv
Preface		xvii
Part 1.	A History of Greek Athletics and Athletic Festivals from the Earliest Times to 393 A.D.	1
Chapter 1	Introductory	3
Chapter 2	Athletics in Homer	7
Chapter 3	The Rise of the Athletic Festival	19
Chapter 4	The Age of Athletic Festivals, Sixth Century B.C.	41
Chapter 5	The Age of the Athletic Ideal, 500-440 B.C.	57
Chapter 6	Professionalism and Specialization, 440-338 B.C.	79
Chapter 7	The Decline of Athletics, 338-146 B.C.	95
Chapter 8	Athletics under the Romans	107
Chapter 9	The Olympic Festival	127
Chapter 10	The Pythian, Isthmian, and Nemean Festivals	139
Chapter 11	The Athletic Festivals of Athens	153
Part 2.	The Athletic Exercises of the Greeks with an Account of Their Stadia and Gymnasia	169
Chapter 12	The Stadium	171
Chapter 13	The Foot-Race	183
Chapter 14	The Jump and Halteres	201
Chapter 15	Throwing the Diskos	215
Chapter 16	Throwing the Javelin	235

Chapter 17	The Pentathlon	**251**
Chapter 18	Wrestling	**261**
Chapter 19	Boxing	**285**
Chapter 20	The Pankration	**309**
Chapter 21	The Hippodrome	**321**
Chapter 22	The Gymnasium and the Palaestra	**333**
Bibliography		**363**
Index		**371**
Index of Greek Words		**379**
Related Nova Publications		**383**

LIST OF FIGURES

Figure 1.	Fragment of Steatite Pyxis. Cnossus.	8
Figure 2.	Scene from Clazomenae Sarcophagus in British Museum.	15
Figure 3.	Amphiaraus Vase. Berlin, 1655.	20
Figure 4.	Dipylon Vase. Copenhagen.	20
Figure 5.	Plan of Olympia.	24
Figure 6.	Statue of Girl Runner. Vatican. Copy of fifth-century original. (From a photograph by Alinari).	32
Figure 7.	Apollo, found at Tenea. Munich.	58
Figure 8.	Statue by an Argive Sculptor. Delphi. (*Greek Sculpture*, Figure 134.)	58
Figure 9.	Choiseul-Gouffier Apollo. British Museum.	60
Figure 10.	Figure from E. pediment at Aegina. Munich. (*Greek Sculpture*, Figure 41.)	61
Figure 11.	Bronze Statuette from Ligourio. Berlin. (*Greek Sculpture*, Figure 39.)	61
Figure 12.	Bronze Statuette of Hoplitodromos. Tübingen.	62
Figure 13.	Myron's Diskobolos (from a bronzed cast made in Munich, combining the Vatican body and the Massimi head).	63
Figure 14.	Doryphoros, after Polycleitus. Naples. (*Greek Sculpture*, Figure 74.)	63
Figure 15.	Diadumenos from Vaison, after Polycleitus. British Museum. (*Greek Sculpture*, Figure 75.)	64
Figure 16.	Bronze head of ephebos. Munich, Glyptothek, 457. (From a photograph by Bruckmann.)	67
Figure 17.	R.-f. kylix. Munich, 795.	68
Figure 18.	Charioteer. Delphi. (*Greek Sculpture*, Figure 138.)	72
Figure 19.	Apoxyomenos. Rome, Vatican.	79
Figure 20.	Statue of Agias by Lysippus. Delphi. (*Greek Sculpture*, Figure 141.)	81
Figure 21.	Farnese Heracles, by Glycon. Naples. (*Greek Sculpture*, Figure 125.)	96
Figure 22.	Athletics under the Romans. From a mosaic found at Tusculum.	115
Figure 23.	Professional boxer, from mosaic in Thermae of Caracalla. Lateran.	124
Figure 24.	Staters of Elis, in British Museum (enlarged). Fifth century. (*a*) Head of nymph Olympia. (*b*) Victory seated, with palm; olive twig below.	127
Figure 25.	R.-f. kylix. Bibliothèque Nationale, 532.	135
Figure 26.	R.-f. kylix. Canino Coll.	136

Figure 27.	Imperial coins of Delphi, in British Museum (enlarged). (*a*) Prize table. (*b*) Crown of bay leaves.	139
Figure 28.	Imperial coin of Corinth, in British Museum (enlarged).	143
Figure 29.	Silver Vase. Bibliothèque Nationale. Imperial period.	147
Figure 30.	Scene from Silver Vase (Figure 29).	148
Figure 31.	Imperial coin of Argos, in British Museum (enlarged).	149
Figure 32.	Small Panathenaic(?) amphora, in British Museum, B. 188. Sixth century.	156
Figure 33.	B.-f. kylix, in British Museum, B. 80.	156
Figure 34.	Votive Relief. Acropolis Museum. Hellenistic period.	160
Figure 35.	Relief on monument of Atarbus. Acropolis Museum. Fourth century.	162
Figure 36.	Relief on Stele. Athens, National Museum, 3300. Imperial period.	163
Figure 37.	Panathenaic amphora, in British Museum, B. 144. Sixth century.	164
Figure 38.	Panathenaic amphora, in British Museum, B. 138. Sixth century.	165
Figure 39.	Panathenaic (?) amphora from Camirus. Bibliothèque Nationale, 243.	166
Figure 40.	Marble chair of judge at Panathenaea. Imperial period.	166
Figure 41.	Portion of starting lines at Olympia.	172
Figure 42.	The Stadium of Epidaurus, S.E. corner, showing the starting lines and rectangular end. (From a photograph by Mr. Emery Walker.)	174
Figure 43.	Stadium of Epidaurus.	175
Figure 44.	Stadium of Delphi.	176
Figure 45.	The starting lines at Delphi. (From a photograph by Mr. Emery Walker.)	177
Figure 46.	The Stadium of Delphi.	178
Figure 47.	R.-f. Amphora. Louvre.	185
Figure 48.	R.-f. kylix. Formerly at Naples.	187
Figure 49.	R.-f. kylix. Chiusi.	187
Figure 50.	Panathenaic amphora. Sixth century. (*Mon. d. I.* I. xxii. 7 b.)	189
Figure 51.	Panathenaic amphora, in British Museum, B. 609. Archonship of Niceratus, 333 B.C.	190
Figure 52.	Panathenaic amphora. Munich, 498. Sixth century.	191
Figure 53.	Panathenaic amphora. Fourth century. (Stephani, *C. R. Atlas*, 1876, Pl. i.)	192
Figure 54.	R.-f. kylix ascribed to Euphronius. Paris, Bibliothèque Nationale, 523.	194
Figure 55.	R.-f. kylix. Formerly in Berlin. (*J.H.S.* xxiii. p. 278.)	195
Figure 56.	R.-f. kylix. Berlin, 2307.	196
Figure 57.	R.-f. kylix. British Museum, E. 818.	197
Figure 58.	Panathenaic amphora. British Museum, B. 608. Archonship of Pythodelus, 336 B.C.	197
Figure 59.	R.-f. kylix. Munich, 1240.	198
Figure 60.	Leaden halter found at Eleusis. Athens, National Museum, 9075.	203
Figure 61.	Halteres in the British Museum. (*a*) Cast of halter found at Olympia, L. 11-1/2 in. (*b*) Limestone halter found at Camirus, L. 7-1/2 in. (*c*) Leaden halter, L. 8 in.	203
Figure 62.	Stone halter found at Corinth (10 inches).	204
Figure 63.	R.-f. pelike, in British Museum, E. 427.	205
Figure 64.	R.-f. krater. Copenhagen (?). (*Annali*, 1846, M.)	206

List of Figures

Figure 65.	R.-f. kylix. Bologna. (Jüthner, *Ant. Turn.* 16.)	207
Figure 66.	R.-f. kylix. Bourguignon Coll. (*Arch. Zeit.*, 1884, xvi.)	208
Figure 67.	B.-f. amphora. British Museum, B. 48.	209
Figure 68.	R.-f. kylix. (Klein, *Euphronius*, p. 306.)	210
Figure 69.	R.-f. pelike, belonging to Dr. Hauser. (*J.H.S.* xxiii. p. 272.)	211
Figure 70.	R.-f. oinochoe. British Museum, E. 561.	213
Figure 71.	B.-f. amphora, in British Museum, B. 271.	216
Figure 72.	Bronze diskos found at Aegina. Berlin.	216
Figure 73.	Diskos of Exoïdas. British Museum, 3207.	218
Figure 74.	(*a*) R.-f. kylix. Chiusi. (*b*) R.-f. kylix. Würzburg, 357, A.	220
Figure 75.	The Standing Diskobolos. Vatican. Copy of fifth-century original. (From a photograph by Anderson.)	221
Figure 76.	R.-f. kylix, in *British Museum*, E. 6. 1. The diskobolos holds the diskos in front of him in both hands (Figure 76). 2. He holds the diskos flat in his right hand which is turned outwards so that the diskos rests against the forearm. The left hand is usually raised above the head.	222
Figure 77.	B.-f. kelebe. British Museum, B. 361.	222
Figure 78.	R.-f. krater of Amasis. Corneto.	223
Figure 79.	R.-f. pelike, in British Museum, E. 395.	224
Figure 80.	Interior of Figure 66.	225
Figure 81.	Fifth-century bronze. (*J.H.S.* xxvii. p. 18.)	225
Figure 82.	B.-f. lekythos, in British Museum, B. 576.	226
Figure 83.	Bronze statuette. New York.	227
Figure 84.	Bronze diskobolos, in British Museum, 675.	228
Figure 85.	R.-f. kylix. Louvre.	229
Figure 86.	Coins of Cos, in British Museum (enlarged).	230
Figure 87.	Panathenaic amphora. Naples, Racc. Cum. 184.	231
Figure 88.	B.-f. hydria. British Museum, E. 164.	232
Figure 89.	R.-f. kylix. Boulogne.	232
Figure 90.	B.-f. hydria. Vienna, 318.	233
Figure 91.	R.-f. kylix. Würzburg, 432.	236
Figure 92.	Various methods of attaching the amentum. (*J.H.S.* xxvii. p. 250.)	237
Figure 93.	B.-f. kylix. British Museum, B. 380.	237
Figure 94.	François vase. Florence.	238
Figure 95.	Illustrations of the use of the throwing-thong. *a*, *b*, Jüthner, Figures 47, 48. Reconstruction of throw. *c*, Detail from *B.M. Vases*, B. 134. *d*, The ounep of New Caledonia.	239
Figure 96.	R.-f. psykter. Bourguignon Coll.	241
Figure 97.	B.-f. stamnos. Vatican.	242
Figure 98.	B.-f. vase. Acropolis, Athens, 606.	242
Figure 99.	R.-f. amphora, in British Museum, E. 256.	243
Figure 100.	R.-f. kylix. Munich, 562 A.	244
Figure 101.	R.-f. kylix. Berlin, 3139 inv.	244
Figure 102.	R.-f. kylix. Torlonia, 270 (148).	245
Figure 103.	R.-f. amphora. Munich, 408.	245

Figure 104.	R.-f. kylix. Rome(?) (Jüthner, *Ant. Turn.* Figure 43.)	**246**
Figure 105.	R.-f. kylix. Berlin, 2728.	**248**
Figure 106.	Panathenaic amphora. British Museum.	**249**
Figure 107.	Panathenaic amphora, in British Museum, B. 134. Sixth century.	**252**
Figure 108.	Panathenaic amphora. Leyden. Sixth century.	**252**
Figure 109.	Wrestling types on coins, in British Museum. *a, b, c,* Aspendus, fifth and fourth centuries. *d,* Heraclea in Lucania, fourth century. *e, f,* Syracuse, *circa* 400 B.C. *g,* Alexandria, Antoninus Pius. (*J.H.S.* xxv. p. 271.)	**262**
Figure 110.	One of a pair of bronze wrestling boys, generally known as Diskoboloi. Naples. (Photograph by Brogi.)	**267**
Figure 111.	Panathenaic amphora, in British Museum, B. 603. Archonship of Polyzelus, 367 B.C.	**267**
Figure 112.	R.-f. kylix, in British Museum, E. 84.	**268**
Figure 113.	Group from British Museum amphora, B. 295 (Figure 143).	**269**
Figure 114.	R.-f. kylix, in British Museum, E. 94.	**270**
Figure 115.	R.-f. kylix. Paris. (Interior of Figure 54.)	**270**
Figure 116.	R.-f. amphora. Berlin, 2159.	**271**
Figure 117.	R.-f. krater. Oxford, Ashmolean, 288.	**272**
Figure 118.	Reverse of Figure 143. British Museum, B. 295.	**272**
Figure 119.	B.-f. amphora. Munich, 584.	**273**
Figure 120.	Panathenaic amphora. Boulogne, Musée Municipale, 441.	**274**
Figure 121.	B.-f. amphora. Munich, 1336.	**274**
Figure 122.	R.-f. kylix. Philadelphia.	**275**
Figure 123.	B.-f. amphora. Munich, 495.	**275**
Figure 124.	R.-f. kylix. British Museum, E. 48.	**277**
Figure 125.	B.-f. kylix, in British Museum, E. 36.	**277**
Figure 126.	Metope of Theseum. Theseus and Cercyon. (*Greek Sculpture*, Figure 66.)	**278**
Figure 127.	Bronze wrestling group. Paris.	**279**
Figure 128.	B.-f. amphora. Vatican.	**279**
Figure 129.	Bronze group, in the British Museum.	**280**
Figure 130.	Bronze. St. Petersburg.	**281**
Figure 131.	Bronze. Constantinople.	**282**
Figure 132.	R.-f. kylix, in British Museum, E. 63.	**286**
Figure 133.	R.-f. kylix, in British Museum, E. 39.	**287**
Figure 134.	Interior of Figure 151. British Museum, E. 78.	**288**
Figure 135.	Panathenaic amphora, in British Museum, B. 607. Archonship of Pythodelus, B.C. 336.	**288**
Figure 136.	Boxer. Terme Museum, Rome. (From a photograph by Anderson.)	**289**
Figure 137.	Right hand of boxer, from Sorrento. Naples.	**290**
Figure 138.	Caestus, from mosaic in the Thermae of Caracalla. Lateran Museum.	**291**
Figure 139.	Bronze situla. Watsch.	**292**
Figure 140.	Fragment of b.-f. situla, in British Museum, B. 124.	**293**
Figure 141.	B.-f. amphora, in British Museum, B. 271.	295
Figure 142.	B.-f. stamnos. Bibliothèque Nationale, 252.	**296**

List of Figures

Figure 143.	B.-f. amphora, in British Museum, B. 295.	297
Figure 144.	Panathenaic amphora. Berlin, 1831. Sixth century.	299
Figure 145.	Panathenaic amphora. Campana. Sixth century (?).	300
Figure 146.	R.-f. kylix of Pamphaeus. Corneto.	300
Figure 147.	Panathenaic amphora. Louvre, F. 278.	301
Figure 148.	Panathenaic amphora, in British Museum, B. 612. Fourth century.	301
Figure 149.	Marble head of boxer, with ear-lappets.	306
Figure 150.	B.-f. hydria, in British Museum, B. 326.	307
Figure 151.	R.-f. kylix. British Museum, E. 78.	310
Figure 152.	R.-f. kylix. Baltimore.	311
Figure 153.	R.-f. kylix. Berlin.	311
Figure 154.	Panathenaic amphora. Sixth century. (*Mon. d. I.* I. xxii.)	313
Figure 155.	Panathenaic amphora. Sixth century. (*Mon. d. I.* I. xxii.)	313
Figure 156.	B.-f. hydria. Munich, 114.	315
Figure 157.	Panathenaic amphora, in British Museum, B. 604. Fourth century. Signed by the artist "Kittos."	315
Figure 158.	Panathenaic amphora, in British Museum, B. 610. Archonship of Nicetes, 332 B.C.	316
Figure 159.	Panathenaic amphora. Lamberg Coll.	316
Figure 160.	Heracles and Triton. B.-f. amphora, in British Museum, B. 223.	318
Figure 161.	Herakles and Antaeus. R.-f. kylix. Athens.	318
Figure 162.	Graeco-Roman gems in British Museum.	319
Figure 163.	Group of pankratiasts. Uffizi Palace, Florence. (From a photograph by Brogi.)	319
Figure 164.	Aphesis at Olympia. (After Weniger.)	322
Figure 165.	Panathenaic amphora found at Sparta. Sixth century.	325
Figure 166.	Panathenaic amphora, in British Museum, B. 132. Sixth century.	327
Figure 167.	Silver tetradrachm and gold stater of Philip II. of Macedon, in the British Museum (enlarged).	327
Figure 168.	Silver tetradrachm of Rhegium, in British Museum (enlarged). Early fifth century.	328
Figure 169.	Panathenaic amphora, in British Museum, B. 133. Sixth century.	328
Figure 170.	Silver staters of Tarentum, in the British Museum (enlarged).	329
Figure 171.	Silver tetradrachms of Catana, in the British Museum (enlarged). Fifth century.	331
Figure 172.	Decadrachm of Agrigentum, 413-406 B.C. Decadrachm of Syracuse, 400-360 B.C.	331
Figure 173.	R.-f. kylix. Canino Coll.	337
Figure 174.	R.-f. kylix. Munich, 515.	338
Figure 175.	R.-f. kylix. Copenhagen.	338
Figure 176.	R.-f. krater. Berlin, 2180.	340
Figure 177.	Bronze cista. Vatican.	340
Figure 178.	R.-f. amphora. St. Petersburg, Hermitage, 1611.	340
Figure 179.	Ficoroni cista. Kirchner Museum, Rome. Third century B.C.	341
Figure 180.	B.-f. hydria. Leyden, 7794b.	342
Figure 181.	Scene on r.-f. vase. (Tischbein, i. 58).	342

Figure 182.	R.-f. kylix. British Museum, E. 83.	343
Figure 183.	Strigil, in British Museum, inscribed κέλων. Fifth century.	343
Figure 184.	Plan of gymnasium at Delphi. (*B.C.H.*)	344
Figure 185.	Plan of palaestra at Olympia.	346
Figure 186.	Stele of Diodorus. Prusa. (Imperial period.)	348
Figure 187.	Plan of lower gymnasium, Priene. (*Priene*, Figure 271.)	350
Figure 188.	Bathroom in gymnasium at Priene. (*Priene*, Figure 278.)	352
Figure 189.	Plan of gymnasia at Pergamum. (Simplified from *Ath. Mitth.*)	353
Figure 190.	Stele representing victorious crew. Athens. (Hellenistic period?)	360

LIST OF ABBREVIATIONS

Arch. Zeit	Archäologische Zeitung.
Ath. Mitth.	Mittheilungen des Deutschen Arch. Inst., Athenische Abtheilung.
B.C.H.	Bulletin de Correspondance hellénique.
Berl. Vas.	Furtwängler, Beschreibung der Vasensammlung zu Berlin.
B.M. Bronzes	British Museum Catalogue of Bronzes.
B.M.C.	British Museum Catalogue of Greek Coins.
B.M. Vases	British Museum Catalogue of Vases, 1893, etc.
B.S.A.	Annual of the British School at Athens.
C.I.G.	Corpus Inscriptionum Graecarum.
C.R.	Comptes rendus de l'Académie des Inscriptions.
Dar.-Sagl.	Daremberg-Saglio, Dictionnaire des antiquités.
Ditt. *Syll.*	Dittenberger, Sylloge Inscriptionum Graecarum.
Ἐφ. Ἀρχ.	Ἐφημερὶς Ἀρχαιολογική.
Gerhard, *A. V.*	Gerhard, Auserlesene Vasenbilder.
Greek Sculpture	E. A. Gardner, Handbook of Greek Sculpture.
I.G.	Inscriptions Graecae.
Jahrb.	Jahrbuch des Deutschen Archäologischen Instituts.
J.H.S.	Journal of Hellenic Studies.
Krause, *Gym.*	J. H. Krause, Die Gymnastik und Agonistik der Hellenen.
Mon. d. I.	Monumenti dell' Instituto.
Ol.	Olympia. Die Ergebnisse der Ausgrabung.
Ol. Ins.	Die Inschriften von Olympia = Textb. v. of "Die Ergebnisse."
Ox. Pap.	Grenfell and Hunt, Oxyrhynchus Papyri.
Rev. Arch.	Revue Archéologique.
Röm. Mitth.	Mittheilungen des Deutschen Archäologischen Instituts, Römische Abtheilung.

PREFACE*

It is my hope that the present volume may prove of interest to the general reader as well as to the student of the past. For though its subject may seem at first sight purely archaeological, many of the problems with which it deals are as real to us to-day as they were to the Greeks. The place of physical training and of games in education, the place of athletics in our daily life and in our national life, are questions of present importance to us all, and in considering these questions we cannot fail to learn something from the athletic history of a nation which for a time at least succeeded in reconciling the rival claims of body and of mind, and immortalized this result in its art.

This is my first and perhaps my chief justification for the length of this volume. My second is that there is no existing work in English on the subject, nor even in the extensive literature which Germany has produced is there any work of quite the same scope. The *Gymnastik u. Agonistik* of J. H. Krause is a masterpiece of erudition, accuracy and judgment. But this work was published in 1841, and since that date excavation and the progress of archaeology have brought to light such a mass of new material as to change entirely our outlook on the past. The excavations at Olympia have for the first time enabled us to trace the whole history of the festival and to treat Greek athletics historically.

In the first part of this work I have endeavoured to write a continuous history of Greek athletics. The attempt is an ambitious one, perhaps too ambitious for one whose occupation has left him little time for continuous study. The long period covered involves a multitude of difficult and disputed problems, which it is impossible within the limits of this work to discuss fully. In all these cases I have endeavoured to sift the evidence for myself, and to form an independent judgment. Many of the details may be obscure, and many of my conclusions are doubtless open to criticism. Yet the general outline of the story is clear, and I venture to think that it has a more than passing interest and importance.

The second part is more technical, though it may perhaps appeal to those who are actively interested in athletics. It consists of a number of chapters, each complete in itself, dealing with the details of Greek athletics. Many of the chapters are taken from articles published by me in the *Journal of Hellenic Studies*. The chapters on the Stadium, the Gymnasium, the Hippodrome and Boxing are entirely new. In the first two of these chapters will be found the

---

* This is an edited, augmented and reformatted version of "Greek Athletic Sports and Festivals" by E. Norman Gardiner, MA, originally published by Macmillan and Co., dated 1910.

latest results of excavations at Delphi, Epidaurus, Priene and Pergamum, results which are not readily accessible to the English reader.

The arrangement of the work has involved a certain amount of repetition, and the introduction separately and in their historical order of certain details which it would be clearer perhaps, and certainly more picturesque, to group together. But it seemed to me worth while to sacrifice something of clearness and effect in order to bring out the historical aspect of the subject, an aspect which is completely obscured in most of our text-books. Further, I have endeavoured clearly to distinguish between what is certain and what is conjectural. The words "perhaps" and "possibly" recur, I am only too ixconscious, with monotonous persistence. But where the evidence is too inadequate or too contradictory to admit of certainty, the only safe and honest course is to confess ignorance and to hope that the discovery of some new manuscript may dispel our doubts. The neglect of this distinction between the conjectural and the certain has been a fertile source of error.

Great importance has been attached to the evidence of contemporary monuments, and illustrations have been given of the principal monuments described. In their selection preference has been given *ceteris paribus* to objects in the British Museum, because these are likely to be most accessible to the majority of readers. In the case of vases the interpretation often depends on the composition, and whole scenes have as far as possible been reproduced rather than single figures. Museum references are appended to the illustrations wherever available, and also some indication of the date of the objects illustrated. Literary references will be found in the list of illustrations.

Many of the illustrations have been prepared expressly for this book, and for these I am indebted to the careful and excellent work of Mr. Emery Walker. A large number are reproduced from articles by myself and others which have appeared in the *Journal of Hellenic Studies*, and in expressing my thanks to the Council of the Hellenic Society for permission to reproduce them I should like to render testimony to the value of the Library of that Society to any one who, like myself, does not live in the vicinity of any great Library. But for the generous facilities which this Society affords for borrowing books, any work which I have been able to do would have been almost impossible.

In spelling, consistency appears to be unattainable, and I xhave in the main adopted the compromise recommended in the *Journal of Hellenic Studies*. In the case of proper nouns, names of places, people, buildings, festivals, the Latin spelling has been adopted, in the case of other Greek words the Greek spelling, except where the Latin form is so familiar that any other form would be pedantic. Names of months are treated as purely Greek words. With regard to ει, *ei* has been kept where it occurs in the stem of a word, *e* is employed *usually* in terminations.

It is impossible to mention here the many authors whose works I have laid under contribution. Many of my debts are acknowledged in the notes. But I cannot omit to mention three—Dr. J. H. Krause, of whose work I have already spoken; Dr. Ernst Curtius, the writer of the chapter on the history of Olympia in the great work which he edited with Dr. Adler; and Dr. Julius Jüthner, whose *Antike Turngeräthe* and edition of Philostratus' *Gymnastike* published only last year are indispensable to any student of the subject. To Dr. Jüthner I must also express my thanks for his generous permission to make use of the illustrations in his work.

Among the many friends who have helped me I should like especially to thank Professor E. A. Gardner, Mr. G. F. Hill, and Mr. H. B. Walters for their constant readiness to advise me and to give me the benefit of their special knowledge of Greek sculpture, coins and vases. Many of the illustrations of sculpture are taken from Professor E. A. Gardner's *Handbook of Greek Sculpture*, and the coins have been especially selected for me by Mr. G. F. Hill. Nor must I omit to mention Louis Dyer, whose death occurred while I was working on the early history of Olympia. He had himself projected a work on Olympia, to which I hoped to refer in confirmation of my views. His minute and accurate knowledge, his readiness to impart his xiknowledge, his enthusiastic and unselfish sympathy made his death an irreparable loss to me. Many corrections are due to the conscientious care of another of my friends, Herbert Awdry, who was engaged in reading my proofs almost up to the day of his death.

It is a fitting circumstance that this book should have been produced under the auspices of Professor Percy Gardner, seeing that he was unconsciously the originator of it. My interest in the subject was first aroused by the chapter on Olympia in his *New Chapters from Greek History*, which I read on my return from a cruise in the "Argonaut," in the course of which I had visited Olympia. Professor Percy Gardner has read the book both in manuscript and in proof, and many improvements are due to his suggestions. He is, however, in no wise responsible for the views expressed, much less for any errors which I may have committed.

E. Norman Gardiner
Epsom College, Surrey.

Part 1. A History of Greek Athletics and Athletic Festivals from the Earliest Times to 393 A.D.

Chapter 1

INTRODUCTORY

The recent revival of the Olympic games is a striking testimony to the influence which ancient Greece still exercises over the modern world, and to the important place which athletics occupied in the life of the Greeks. Other nations may have given equal attention to the physical education of the young; other nations may have been equally fond of sport; other nations may have produced individual athletes, individual performances equal or superior to those of the Greeks, but nowhere can we find any parallel to the athletic ideal expressed in the art and literature of Greece, or to the extraordinary vitality of her athletic festivals. The growth of this ideal, and the history of the athletic festivals, are the subject of the following chapters.

The athletic ideal of Greece is largely due to the practical character of Greek athletics. Every Greek had to be ready to take the field at a moment's notice in defence of hearth and home, and under the conditions of ancient warfare his life and liberty depended on his physical fitness. This is especially true of the earlier portion of Greek history, but is more or less true of the whole period with which we are concerned. Greece was never free from war—wars of faction, wars of state against state, wars against foreign invaders—and ancient warfare made no distinction between combatants and non-combatants. Every citizen was a soldier, physical fitness was a necessity to him, and his athletic exercises were admirably calculated to produce this fitness. Running and jumping made him active and sound of wind; throwing the diskos and the spear trained hand and eye for the use of weapons; wrestling and boxing taught him to defend himself in hand-to-hand warfare.

The practical value of these exercises explains their importance in Greek education. They constituted what the Greeks described as "gymnastic," the term "athletics" being properly confined to competitions. Gymnastic trained the body as music trained the mind. There was no artificial separation, no antagonism between the two such as has disfigured much of our modern education. The one was the complement of the other: together they comprised the whole of Greek education. An ill-trained body was as much a sign of an ill-educated man as ignorance of letters, and the training of the body by athletic exercises distinguished the Greek from the barbarian. The training began often as early as seven, but it did not end at the age when boys leave school. The Greek did not consider his education finished at the age of sixteen or seventeen, and he continued the training of body and mind till middle age or later, daily resorting to the gymnasium for exercise and recreation.

Music and gymnastic reacted on one another. The tone and manly vigour which athletic exercises gave saved the Greek from the effeminacy and sensuality to which the artistic temperament is prone. At the same time the refining influence of music saved him from the opposite faults of brutality and Philistinism. The Greek carried the artist's love of beauty into his sports. Mere strength and bulk appealed to him no more in the human body than they did in art. Many of his exercises were performed to music, and he paid as much attention to the style in which he performed as to the result of his performance. This love of form refined even his competitions. Hence, in spite of his love of competition, the Greek was no record-breaker. In this we have one of the principal differences which distinguished Greek from modern athletics, in which the passion for records is becoming more and more prevalent.

The Greek did not care for records, and he kept no records. It is futile, therefore, to try to compare the performances of Greek athletes and of modern. But of the effect which athletic training produced on the national physique in the fifth century, we can judge from the art which it inspired. The sculptors of this period portrayed the most perfect types of physical development, of strength combined with grace, that the world has ever seen. The athletic art of Greece is the noblest tribute to the results of Greek education at its best.

A further difference between modern and Greek athletics results from the practical character of the latter. The Greek regarded athletics as an essential part of his education and life; we usually regard them as recreation or play, and it is only of late years that their educational value has been realized. Consequently in England athletic games have to a large extent superseded athletics proper. In some respect games have a decided advantage; their interest is more varied, there is more scope for combination, and they are undoubtedly superior as a training of character. On the other hand, they do not produce the same all-round development as an athletic system like that of the Greeks produced. In many cases the benefit derived from them is confined to the skilled players. They tend to become too scientific, and when this is the case require an expenditure of time and an amount of organization which put them beyond the reach of most men when they have left school.

The interest which is somewhat wanting in pure athletics was provided in Greece by innumerable competitions. The love of competition was characteristic of the Greek. In whatever he did, he sought to excel his fellows, and the rivalry between cities was as keen as that between individuals. On the table on which the prizes were placed at Olympia, the figure of Agon or Competition was represented side by side with that of Ares. There were competitions in music, poetry, drama, recitation. At some places there were beauty competitions for men, or boys, or women. We hear of competitions in drinking and in keeping awake. Strangest of all was a competition in kissing, which took place at the Dioclea at Megara. But no competitions were so numerous or so popular as athletic and equestrian competitions. The Greek was always competing or watching competitions; yet, strange to say, among all the evils produced by over-competition, betting was not found.

Competitions were from an early time associated with religious Festivals. And it is to this association with religion that Greek athletics owed their wonderful vitality. The connexion between sport and religion dates from the early custom of celebrating a chieftain's funeral with a feast and games. Sometimes the chieftain's tomb became a religious and political centre for the neighbouring tribes, where a festival was held in his honour at stated periods. Some of these festivals retained their local character, others gradually extended their influence till they became national meeting-places for the whole Greek race.

These Panhellenic festivals played an important part in the politics of Greece. They appealed to those two opposite principles which determine the whole history of Greece, the love of autonomy and the pride of Hellenism. The independent city states felt that they were competing in the persons of their citizens, whose fortunes they identified with their own. At the same time, the gathering of citizens from every part of the Greek world quickened the consciousness of common brotherhood, and kept them true to those traditions of religion and education which distinguished Greek from barbarian.

Enough has been said to show the importance of athletics in the whole life of the Greeks, and their intimate connection with their education, their art, their religion, and their politics. It is by virtue of this many-sided interest that the subject deserves the attention of all who are interested in the life and thought of Greece.

At the same time, it must be borne in mind that the athletic ideal which we have described was only realized during a short period of the fifth century, under the purifying influence of the enthusiasm evoked by the war with Persia. Even then, perhaps, it was only partially realized. We must not close our eyes to the element of exaggeration inherent in all such ideals. Before the close of the fifth century the excessive prominence given to bodily excellence and athletic success had produced specialization and professionalism. From this time sport, over-developed and over-specialized, became more and more the monopoly of a class, and consequently ceased to invigorate the national life. The old games, in which all competed in friendly and honourable rivalry, gave place to professional displays, in which victory was too often bought and sold, where an unathletic crowd could enjoy the excitement of sport by proxy. Yet in spite of specialization, professionalism, corruption, in spite of all the vicissitudes through which Greece passed, the athletic festivals survived. The athletic ideal, often and long obscured, but never wholly lost, reappeared from time to time in different parts of the Greek world, till, under the patronage of the Antonines, the Panhellenic festivals recovered some semblance at least of their olden glory.

The extraordinary vitality of those festivals gives interest to the attempt to trace their history. This history extends over some 1200 years. We are apt to limit our conceptions of Greek history to the few centuries comprised in the curricula of our universities and schools, and to forget that Greek history does not end with the death of Alexander, or even with the loss of Greek independence, but that, under the rule of Rome, the life of Greece, its institutions and festivals, went on, to a great extent, unchanged, acquiring more and more hold over her conquerors, till the whole Roman world was Hellenized, and with the founding of Constantinople the centre of the empire itself was transferred to Greek soil. To such a narrow conception of history it is a wholesome corrective to trace the story of one branch of Greek activity from beginning to end. And nowhere can the continuity of Greek life be traced more clearly than in the history of her athletic festivals. That we are able to do so is chiefly due to the excavations conducted at Olympia under the auspices of the German government, which are still being continued by Dr. Dörpfeld. It is for this reason that in the following chapters the history of Olympia forms the basis of the history of Greek athletics.

The story of Greek athletics has a peculiarly practical interest in the present day in view of the development of athletics which has taken place in the last fifty years, and of the revival of the Olympic games. There are striking resemblances between the history of modern athletics and of Greek. The movement began in the sports of our public schools and universities, spread rapidly through all English-speaking lands, and is now extending to the Continent. Athletics are as popular among us as they were in Greece, and for us, as for the

Greeks, they have been a great instrument of good. Unfortunately the signs of excess are no less manifest to-day than they were in the times of Xenophanes and Euripides. History repeats itself strangely. We have seen the same growth of competition, the same hero-worship of the athlete, the same publicity and prominence given to sport out of all proportion to its deserts, the same tendency to specialization and professionalism. Sport has too often become an end in itself. The hero-worship of the athlete tempts men to devote to selfish amusement the best years of their lives, and to neglect the true interests of themselves and of their country. The evil is worse with us, because our games have not the practical value as a military training which Greek sports had. Still more grievous than this waste of time and energy is the absorbing interest taken by the general public in the athletic performances of others. The crowds which watch a professional football match, the still larger crowds of those who think and read of little else, the columns of the daily press devoted to accounts of such matches, are no proof of an athletic nation, but rather of the reverse. They are merely a sign of an unhealthy love of excitement and amusement, and of the absence of all other interests. Of the evils of professionalism this is no place to speak. They are well known to anyone who has followed the history of boxing, wrestling, or football. The history of football during the last two years is ominous. On the one hand we see the leading amateur clubs revolting from the tyranny of a Football Association conducted in the interests of various joint-stock companies masquerading as Football Clubs; on the other hand we see the professional players forming a trades-union to protect themselves against the tyranny of this same commercialism. The Rugby Union has struggled manfully to uphold the purity of the game, and has often received but scanty encouragement for its efforts. Fortunately there are signs that public opinion is changing, and is beginning to appreciate the efforts of the amateur bodies controlling various sports. The very existence of these bodies proves how real the danger is. Under these circumstances the history of the decline of Greek athletics is an object-lesson full of instruction.

What has been said above explains perhaps why the revival of the Olympic games has not been received in England with any great amount of enthusiasm. The promoters of these games were inspired by the ideal of ancient Greece, and wished to establish a great international athletic meeting which would be for the nations of the world what Olympia was for Greece. We must all sympathize with their aspirations. Unfortunately they do not seem to have realized the full lesson of Greek athletics, nor did they realize the dangers of competition on so vast a scale under the more complicated conditions of modern life. In England, where athletics have already developed to an extent unknown on the Continent, we have begun to realize the dangers of over-competition. The experience of recent years has taught us that international competitions do not always make for amity, and do not always promote amateur sport. The events of the last Olympic games, and the subsequent performances of some of the victors of these games, particularly of the fêted heroes of the so-called Marathon race, have gone far to justify the forebodings of those who feared that one of the chief results of such a competition would be an increase in professionalism.

Chapter 2

ATHLETICS IN HOMER

Greek civilization is regarded by modern authorities as the result of a fusion between two races—a short, dark, highly artistic race belonging to that Eurafrican stock which seems at one time to have peopled not only the Aegean, but all the coasts of the Mediterranean, and a tall, fair-haired, athletic race the branches of which penetrated by successive invasions into the southern extremities of Europe, while their main body spread over central Europe westwards as far as our own islands. It was to the physical vigour and restless energy of the latter race that the Greeks owed their colonial activity and their love of sport. And it is perhaps no mere accident that these same characteristics have been so marked in our own history. But if the Greeks owed to the fair-haired invaders from the North the athletic impulse, the development and persistence of Greek athletics is largely due to the artistic temperament of the original inhabitants.

The practical character of Greek sports indicates a nation of warriors. The chariot-race and foot-race, boxing, wrestling, throwing the stone and the spear, were as naturally the outcome of the Homeric civilization as the tournament and the archery meeting were of the conditions of fighting in the middle ages, or the rifle meeting of those of our own day. Moreover, the myths with which Greek fancy invested the origin of their sports point to an age of fighting and conquest. Olympia, as we shall see, stood on the highway of the northern invaders, and at Olympia the institution of the games is connected with such tales as the conquest of Cronus by Zeus, of Oenomaus by Pelops, of Augeas by Heracles, and the return of the Heracleidae, tales which clearly had their rise in the struggles of rival races and religions. Again, Greek athletics were chiefly, though not entirely, the product of the Peloponnese. Three of the four great festivals were in the Peloponnese, including the Olympic festival, the prototype of all the rest; the athletic school of sculpture originated in the Peloponnese, and physical training was carried to its highest point in Sparta. Now it was in the Peloponnese that the invading races established themselves most strongly; the fair-haired Achaeans made themselves masters of the Mycenaean world, and their Dorian successors preserved their own characteristics in their greatest purity at Sparta. These considerations justify us in ascribing the athletic impulse to the northern invaders.

Figure 1. Fragment of Steatite Pyxis. Cnossus.

Excavations on Mycenaean and pre-Mycenaean sites furnish some testimony, chiefly negative, in favour of this view. The civilization disclosed by the excavations at Cnossus and other Cretan sites is an Aegean product influenced possibly by Egypt and the East, but certainly not by the mainland of Greece, though its own influence was probably extensive. Cretan civilization, like Egyptian, seems so much a thing apart that it hardly comes into our subject. In Egypt, indeed, we find depicted in the tombs of Beni-Hassan a varied array of athletic sports and games, including a most wonderful series of over 300 wrestling groups, but even Herodotus does not venture to ascribe Greek athletics to the Egyptians. At Cnossus the favourite sport seems to have been a sort of bull-baiting.[1] A fresco discovered by Dr. Evans represents a girl toreador in a sort of cowboy costume in the act of being tossed by a bull, while a youth appears to be turning a somersault over the animal's back into the arms of a girl who stands behind the bull. Sometimes on gems a youth is depicted "springing from above, and seizing the bull's horns in cowboy fashion." The latter scene has also been found in a fresco at Tiryns, and a similar sport known as ταυροκαθαψία survived in historical times in Thessaly.[2] These purely acrobatic feats have nothing distinctively athletic about them, any

---

[1] *B.S.A.* vii. p. 94; viii. pp. 74, 77; ix. p. 56; x. p. 41. R. M. Burrows, *Discoveries in Crete*, Pl. i.
[2] The ταυροκαθαψία proper is a feat rather of the hunting-field than of the circus, and should be connected rather with the bull-snaring scenes on the Vaphio cups, *vide* E. Gardner, *Greek Sculpture*, p. 61, or with the feat known as βοῦς αἴρεσθαι depicted in Tischbein ii. 3, and referred to in inscriptions relative to the Epheboi. The only representation that I know of this sport is on a late relief from Smyrna in the Ashmolean Museum at Oxford, No. 219. The performers are represented pursuing bulls on horseback, leaping on to their backs, and seizing their horns, by twisting which they throw them on to the ground. The Greek bull was clearly a small

more than dancing, another favourite Minoan spectacle, for which possibly was intended a square theatre surrounded by rows of seats at the north-west of the palace. Indeed, such scenes are the very reverse of athletic; for history has shown that the peoples who find pleasure in such performances have ceased to be, even if they ever have been, themselves athletic. The only form of true athletics represented is boxing, which occurs on some clay sealings, on a steatite relief (Figure 1), and in conjunction with a bull-hunting scene on a steatite rhyton found at Hagia Triada.[3] The boxers are muscular and athletic-looking, their attitude is decidedly vigorous. They wear, according to Dr. Evans, a kind of glove or caestus, but the illustrations do not enable us to determine its character, and I do not feel sure that any such covering is intended. Anyhow, the Minoan boxer has a distinctly gladiatorial look, which is quite in harmony with the bull-baiting scenes. We shall probably not be far wrong in assuming that Minos, like oriental despots, kept his own prize-ring, and that his courtiers preferred to be spectators of the deeds of others rather than to take any active part in sports themselves. Sports and games, of course, existed in Crete as in all countries, but there is no evidence in Crete of anything from which Greek athletics could have developed. The unathletic character of the Aegean people is confirmed by the absolute absence of anything athletic at Mycenae and Tiryns, if we except the bull scenes, a fact which certainly supports the modern view that the Mycenaean civilization was due chiefly to the conquered inhabitants, and not to the Achaean conquerors, whom we know from Homer to have been skilled in all games.

In Homer we find ourselves at once in an atmosphere of true sport, of sport for the simple love of the physical effort and the struggle. The wrestling and boxing may be "distressful," but just as every sportsman finds a "hard game" the most enjoyable, so the struggle in Homer is a joy to the young man who makes trial of his strength, a joy to the veteran who, as he watches, revives in memory the triumphs of his youth, and a joy too to the poet.[4] It is this feeling that makes the description of the games of Patroclus a perpetual delight to anyone who has ever felt himself the joy of sport, and that almost justifies the words of Schiller, that he who has lived to read the 23rd *Iliad* has not lived in vain. The joy is never quite the same afterwards. Even in Pindar it is no longer unalloyed. With the stress of competition other feelings and motives have entered in, and something of the heroic courtesy is lost: side by side with the joy of victory we are conscious of the bitterness of defeat. In Homer we feel only the joy, the joy of youth.

The description of the games in the *Iliad* could only have been written by a poet living among an athletic people with a long tradition of athletics, and such are the Achaeans. Sports are part of the education of every Achaean warrior, and distinguish him from the merchant. "No, truly, stranger," says Euryalus to Odysseus, "nor do I think thee at all like one that is skilled in games whereof there are many among men, rather art thou such an one as comes and goes in a benched ship, a master of sailors that are merchantmen, one with a memory for his freight, or that hath the charge of a cargo homeward bound, and of greedily gotten gains; thou seemest not a man of thy hands."[5]

---

    animal, but must still have been a formidable opponent. The records of the gladiatorial shows afford abundant proof that man could by the aid of skill triumph over the strongest animal. The principles of jiu-jitsu could be applied against animals as easily as against men.

[3] *B.S.A.* vii. p. 95, Figure 31; ix. p. 57, Figure 35.
[4] *Od.* iv. 626, xvii. 168, 174; *Il.* ii. 774.
[5] *Od.* viii. 153 sq. (Butcher and Lang's translation).

Euryalus is a Phaeacian, and the Phaeacians, be it remarked, are not Achaeans. Who they are we know not—whether, as Victor Bérard assures us, Phoenicians, or a branch of that Aegean folk whose wondrous civilization has been revealed to us at Cnossus, or a creation of the poet's brain. In Homer they are a mysterious folk, and this is not the place to try and solve the mystery. One thing is certain: they are not true Achaeans, and though the poet ascribes to them much of the manners of the Achaeans, including their games, he lets us know with a delightful humour that they are not quite the real thing. Their love of sport is assumed, and consequently somewhat exaggerated. "There is no greater glory for a man," says Laodamas, "than that which he achieves by hand and foot."[6] We can hardly imagine such a sentiment from one of the heroes of the *Iliad*, or from the Odysseus of the *Odyssey*. The Phaeacian, however, is somewhat of a braggart, and wishes to pose as a sportsman before a stranger, who is no longer young, and whom he certainly does not suspect of being an athlete. "Let us make trial," says Alcinous, "of divers games, that the stranger may tell his friends when home he returneth how greatly we excel all men in boxing and wrestling, and leaping and speed of foot"[7]—a harmless boast and safe apparently. But Odysseus, stung by their taunts, picks up a diskos larger than the Phaeacians ever threw and hurls it far beyond their marks, and then in his anger challenges any of the Phaeacians to try the issue in boxing, or in wrestling, or any sport except running, for which, after his buffeting in the sea, he is not quite in condition. At once the tune changes, and Alcinous confesses that after all the Phaeacians are no perfect boxers nor wrestlers, but (a safe boast after what Odysseus has said!) speedy runners and the best of seamen. And then the truth comes out: "Dear to us ever is the banquet, and the harp and the dance, and changes of raiment, and the warm bath and love and sleep!" Clearly the Phaeacians are no sportsmen, nor Achaeans, and we have really no concern with them; but I may be pardoned for dwelling on this delightful scene, because through it all we can trace the truth that to the poet every warrior is a sportsman, a man of his hands, and that the sportsman is not occupied with "greedily gotten gains."

The same scene tells us, too, that sports are no new thing among the Achaeans. Odysseus, when challenging the Phaeacians, recalls the prowess of his youth, just as in the *Iliad* the aged Nestor recalls his victories in the games which the Epeans held at Buprasium at the funeral of Amarynces. But there is a yet remoter past in which heroes and gods contended. "There were giants in those days" is always the theme of the aged sportsman, and Odysseus, though more than a match for all his contemporaries, confesses that with the men of old he would not vie, with Heracles and Eurytus, "who contended with the immortal gods."

But though the Achaeans were an athletic race with a long tradition of athletes, we must beware of the common fallacy of introducing into Homer the ideas and arrangements of later Greek athletics. Homeric tradition undoubtedly influenced Greek athletics, but to talk of the Homeric gymnasium, the Homeric stadium, the Homeric pentathlon, or solemnly to explain Homer in the light of these institutions, is as ridiculous as to talk of King Arthur's school of physical training or Robin Hood's shooting gallery. The Homeric Greek had no gymnasium, no race-course, no athletic meeting. There was nothing artificial about his sports: they were the natural product of a warlike race, part of the daily life of the family. They were the education of the boys, the recreation of the men, and even the elders took their share in teaching and encouraging the younger. For physical vigour and skill in military exercises

---

[6] *Od.* viii. 147.
[7] *Od.* viii. 100.

were indispensable to the chieftain in an age when battles were won by individual prowess. No elaborate arrangements were necessary; the courtyard would serve for a wrestling ring, the open country for a race-course, and when sports were to be held on a larger scale a suitable space could be quickly cleared. For though there were no athletic meetings, there were friendly gatherings for sports in plenty. On the occasion of any gathering, whether to entertain a distinguished guest, to offer a sacrifice, or to pay the last rites to a departed chieftain, sports formed part of the programme. Sometimes prizes were offered—a victim or an ox-hide for the foot-race, a woman or a tripod for the chariot-race. Particularly was this the case in the funeral sports, when the prizes were rich and numerous.

The value of the prizes seems intended to mark the generosity of the giver of the games, and to show honour to the dead rather than to attract or reward competitors. That they were rather gifts, mementoes of the dead, than prizes, is clear from the fact that at the games of Patroclus every competitor receives a prize, in one case even without a competition. Sometimes, as in the days of the tournament, a weighty issue might be decided by an athletic contest. Instances of this are frequent in the legends of the Greeks: in Homer we have the fatal contest with the bow of Odysseus by which Penelope proposed to decide between her importunate suitors. But whatever the occasion, the Homeric games differed entirely from the athletic festival or meeting. They were impromptu, almost private entertainments, in which only the invited guests, or, in the case of a prince's funeral, the neighbouring princes or leaders of the army took part. When Odysseus, disguised as a beggar, craved leave to try the bow, the request was met with a storm of protest from the suitors.

From what has been said it is clear that the Homeric games were chiefly aristocratic: it was the sceptred kings and their families who excelled in all games, and who alone entered for competitions, though, as we shall see, the common soldiers too had their sports.

In considering the different events of the Homeric sports, it will be convenient to follow the description of the funeral games of Patroclus in the *Iliad*. First in order of time and of honour comes the chariot-race, the most aristocratic of all the events, the monopoly of chieftains who went to war in chariots. Too important an event for casual gatherings, it was especially connected with great funeral games. Here, as we have noticed, rich prizes were offered, and the possession of a fine stud of horses was a source of considerable profit. Thus Agamemnon enumerates among the gifts with which he hopes to appease Achilles twelve "prize-winning" steeds who have already won him no small fortune.

In the *Odyssey* we have no mention of the chariot-race; and naturally so, for Ithaca (wherever it be) is no land "that pastureth horses," nor does it possess "wide courses or meadow-land." In the *Iliad* it is otherwise; the plains of Thessaly and Argos, the homes of Achilles and the Atreidae, were always famed for their horses, and in the plain of Troy the Greek charioteers found ample scope. It is interesting, too, to note that, except at Troy, the only other chariot-races mentioned in the *Iliad* are in spacious Elis,[8] which was in Homeric times the land of the Epeans, where the lords of Ithaca kept studs of horses, and in historic times the scene of the Olympic festival. It was at Buprasium in Elis that Nestor competed at the funeral games of Amarynces; and on a former occasion his father Neleus had gone to war with Augeas because the latter had seized four horses which he had sent to Elis to compete in the games for a tripod. The mention of four horses is suspicious, for the chariot in which the Achaean heroes raced was the two-horse war-chariot. There are also other reasons for

---

[8] *Il.* xi. 697, xxiii. 630.

supposing the passage to be a late interpolation subsequent to the institution of the Olympic chariot-race.

For the chariot-race Achilles provides five prizes—"for the winner a woman skilled in fair handiwork and a tripod, for the second a six-year-old mare in foal, for the third a goodly caldron untouched by the fire, for the fourth two talents of gold, for the fifth a two-handled urn." For the five prizes there are five competitors. On the details of the competitors and of their horses we must not linger, nor on the lecture on the art of driving which the aged Nestor reads to his son Antilochus. Critics complain that it interrupts the narrative; but the rambling, prosy speech is delightfully characteristic of the garrulous old sportsman, and so human! Its point seems to consist in certain information which he gives about the course; for it is no regular race-course, like the later hippodrome. It is a natural course selected for the occasion like that of a point-to-point race, save that in this case the chariots after rounding the goal return to the starting point. On such a course local knowledge is invaluable. The point selected for the goal is a withered tree-stump with a white stone on either side of it—a monument of some dead man, or a goal for the race set up by men of old—and round it is smooth driving ground. At this point, which is just visible from the start, the two tracks meet—not necessarily parallel tracks, for chariots cannot take a bee-line from point to point, but must follow the lie of the ground. Here Achilles places an umpire, godlike Phoenix, "to note the running and tell the truth thereof"; for though the goal is just visible, the track is sometimes lost to the spectators' view, and as the chariots round the mark they disappear from sight for a time. The track, like Greek roads in general, is not of the smoothest, and in one part has been partially washed away by a torrent, so that there is no room for two chariots to pass. Possibly the road in this part, as is often the case, passed along the actual bed of the winter torrent.

The charioteers draw lots for their places, and then the chariots take their place in a line. Commentators gravely debate whether the Greek means "in a line" or "in file," like a row of hansom cabs! But there is no subject wherein commentators are so rampant as in athletics, and there is no athletic absurdity which they do not father upon the Greeks, who, after all, really did know a little about sports. We are not told how the horses were started—we must hurry on with the poet to the finish. How Apollo made Tydeides drop his whip, and how Athene restored it to him and then made the leader's horses run off the course and wreck his chariot; how Antilochus when they came to the broken part of the course "bored" Menelaus and deprived him of the place; how the spectators quarrelled as to which chariot was leading, and Idomeneus offered to bet Aias a caldron or a tripod; how Antilochus apologised for his youthful impetuosity and Menelaus generously forgave him; how every man received his prize, even he whose chariot was broken,—all this is known to every reader of Homer; to retell it would be sacrilege. Particularly charming is the scene where Achilles presents Nestor with a prize which has been left over as a "memorial of Patroclus' burying." In recalling his youthful victories at Buprasium the old man mentions that he was defeated in the chariot-race by the two sons of Actor, one of whom held the reins while the other plied the whip. Here apparently we have a hint of an earlier form of the chariot-race, where, as in war, the chieftain was accompanied by his charioteer. In Achilles' time there is already a difference between the sport and the reality.

The next two events—the boxing and the wrestling matches—are described as ἀλεγεινός, "hard" or "distressful," an epithet which, as before observed, seems rather a recommendation than otherwise. Indeed these two sports, which are always mentioned together, already held the position of pre-eminence which they held at the time of Pindar, and they formed the chief part of the Achaean chieftain's athletic education. For boxing and wrestling are essentially exercises of skill. The child and the savage hit, kick, tear, scratch, bite, and from this primitive rough-and-tumble the Greek in later time developed the scientific pankration; it is only the civilised man who distinguishes boxing and wrestling, who uses the fist to strike and conducts a fight by rules. In Homer both wrestling and boxing are already arts, and though in their rougher form popular sports, the science of them seems to have been the monopoly of the chieftains, perhaps, like the Japanese jiu-jitsu, jealously handed down from father to son. The importance of the art of self-defence in those unsettled times is obvious from the many legends of robbers and bullies who challenged strangers to a bout of wrestling or boxing, till their career of murder was cut short by a Heracles, a Theseus, or a Polydeuces, in whose victories later art and story represented the triumph of science and Hellenism over brute force and barbarism. Such a victory Odysseus himself is said to have won in Lesbos over Philomeleides, whom he threw mightily, and all the Achaeans rejoiced.[9] In Homer, Polydeuces is already "the boxer," and Odysseus "of many counsels" wins glory both as boxer and wrestler.

For the boxing Achilles offers two prizes. Epeius at once advances and claims the first prize. In his somewhat brutal arrogance, and his admission that, though superior to all in boxing, he falls short in actual warfare, we have perhaps a foretaste of the later professional boxer. But mock modesty is no characteristic of the Greeks, and poetic nemesis was not to be meted out; moreover, his boastfulness is atoned for by his courtesy in his victory. Still, in the contrast between real war and the sport we seem to see the poet's judgment that athletics are man's recreation, not his business. The challenge of Epeius is accepted by Euryalus, who came of a boxing stock; for his father Mecisteus had formerly defeated all the Cadmeans at the burial of Oedipodes. Their friends help to gird them, and bind on the well-cut thongs of oxhide. The loin-belt was, as we shall see, discarded later on, but the thongs remained unchanged till the fifth century, when we shall find them constantly depicted on the vases. Then the two "lifted up stalwart hands and fell to. And noble Epeius came on, and as the other cast a glance around, smote him on the cheek, nor could he much more stand, for his fair limbs straightway failed under him, and as when beneath the north wind's ripple a fish leapeth on a tangle-covered beach, and then the black wave hideth it, so leapt Euryalus at that blow. But the great-hearted Epeius took him in his hands and set him upright, and his dear comrades stood around him and led him through the ring with trailing foot, spitting out clotted blood, drooping his head awry, and they set him down in his swoon among them." The description is perfectly clear. Epeius forced the fighting, and catching his opponent off his guard knocked him out in orthodox, or, as some purists would say, unorthodox, fashion with a swinging uppercut on the point of the jaw.

A yet better description of a fight with a similar finish occurs in the *Odyssey*.[10] Odysseus, returning to his home disguised as a beggar, finds installed there the professional beggar Irus, who at once picks a quarrel with him. The suitors, delighted and amused at the prospect of a fight between a pair of beggars, form a ring round the pair and egg them on, promising to the winner a haggis that is cooking at the fire. But when the beggars strip and gird up their rags they see that they are mistaken in one of their men. Odysseus strips like an athlete, clean and

---

[9] *Od.* iv. 341 sq.
[10] *Od.* xviii. 15 sq.

big of limb, and the suitors marvel. Irus too, despite his bulk, marvels, and would fain withdraw. But it is too late: the suitors will not be baulked of their fun, and the fight starts. Of course it is a foregone conclusion, and Odysseus himself knows it. He knows, too, what he can do; his only doubt is whether he shall kill the braggart outright, or strike him lightly to the earth. He decides on the latter course, and proceeds to dispose of him in most artistic fashion. Irus leads off with a clumsy left-hander at Odysseus' right shoulder, and Odysseus cross-counters with a blow on the neck below the ear which knocks him out. Fights of this sort were doubtless common occurrences, and a little science must have been a very useful possession. That the Achaeans did possess something of the science is clear from the two fights described in Homer, though their science seems rather of the unconventional American type, and does not commend itself to staunch supporters of the orthodox English school.

For wrestling also two prizes are offered, a tripod valued at twelve oxen, and a "woman skilled in all manner of work" valued only at four oxen. For the two prizes there are two competitors, no less persons than Odysseus and Ajax, the types respectively of cleverness and strength. The match is conducted under definite rules, the rules of what was called "upright wrestling," in which, the object being to throw the opponent, ground wrestling was not allowed. Girding themselves the two advanced "into the midst of the ring, and clasped each the other in his arms with stalwart hands like gable rafters of a lofty house." The attitude is identical with that adopted by Westmorland and Cumberland wrestlers to-day. Then came the struggle for a closer grip; but when after much striving neither could gain an advantage, Ajax suggested an expedient that each in turn should allow the other to obtain a fair grip and try to throw him by lifting him off the ground. There is here no suggestion of unfairness, but undoubtedly the advantage is with the heavier man. Odysseus, however, was equal to the occasion, and as Ajax lifted him, not forgetful of his art, he struck him with his foot behind the knee, in technical language "hammed" him, and so brought him to the ground, falling heavily upon him. As both wrestlers fell together the bout was inconclusive. Next came Odysseus' turn: unable to lift his bulky opponent off the ground "he crooked his knee within the other's, and both fell sideways." The chip employed was apparently "the hank" or "the inside click" of the modern wrestler. But the fall was what is known as a dog-fall, and inconclusive. The two were proceeding to the third bout when Achilles put an end to the contest, and awarded to each an equal prize.

Futile efforts have been made to explain the verdict by showing that Odysseus won the first bout and Ajax the second; the explanation given above rests on the simple supposition that when both wrestlers fell, no fall was scored. If each had won one bout, the excitement would have been too intense for the contest to be stopped, but two inconclusive bouts were naturally tedious to the spectators.

The foot-race need not detain us long. There were three prizes and three competitors; among them, in spite of his recent exertions, the veteran Odysseus. The course was of the same impromptu type described for the chariot-race, round some distant mark and back to the starting place, where the ground was wet and slippery with the blood of the oxen slaughtered for sacrifice. It was a great race. Ajax, the son of Oeleus, led, while Odysseus followed closely in his track amid the cheers of the Achaeans. As they neared the finish Odysseus prayed to Athene, who "made his limbs feel light, both feet and hands"—a delightful description of the spurt; but not content with such legitimate aid, she caused Ajax, just as they reached the prize, to slip in the victim's blood. But in Homer there is no ill-feeling at such incidents; the defeated rivals merely comment good-humouredly on the interference of the goddess, just as the modern sportsman, not always so good-humouredly, on his opponent's luck. "Friends, ye will bear me witness when I say that even herein the immortals favour elder men." What the moderns ascribe to luck, the Achaeans, like all the ancients, ascribed to the direct action of the gods: it is a later age that makes fortune a goddess.

Of the four remaining events, three at least—the single combat between Ajax and Diomede, throwing the solos, and the contest with the bow—are admitted even by the most conservative critics to be a late interpolation; the fourth event—throwing the spear—is usually assigned to the earlier account of the games, though one of the arguments adduced, that spear-throwing formed part of the Homeric pentathlon, seems singularly weak! There is no suggestion in Homer of any such thing as the pentathlon, a competition consisting of five events in which the same competitors competed, and to talk of the Homeric pentathlon merely because Nestor happens to mention five events in the games at Buprasium is quite unhistorical and most misleading. It would be more to the point to urge that spear-throwing, throwing the solos or diskos, and archery go together, because these same three events are mentioned together in the 2nd *Iliad*.[11] But this is no place for the details of Homeric criticism. For our present purpose we can learn nothing from the passage about Homeric spear-throwing, for the simple reason that the competition never came off, Achilles out of courtesy to his leader assigning the first prize to Agamemnon without a contest.

Figure 2. Scene from Clazomenae Sarcophagus in British Museum.

It is unnecessary to consider in detail the confused and lifeless descriptions of these events, but a word must be said of the events themselves. The combat between armed men is depicted on a sixth-century sarcophagus from Clazomenae, now in the British Museum (Figure 2).[12] Here, among chariots in full course, or preparing for the race, we see pairs of warriors fighting. They are armed with helmet, spear, and shield, and between each pair stands a youth playing the pipes to show the nature of the fight. At either end stands a pillar bearing a bowl for the prize, while against the pillar rests a naked figure leaning dejectedly upon a staff, the spirit apparently of the dead man in whose honour the games were held. The armed combat was alien, however, to the spirit of the Greeks; we hear of it, indeed, in later times at Mantinea and at Cyrene, but it found no place in any of the great Greek festivals.[13] It

---

[11] *Il.* ii. 774.
[12] Murray, *Sarcophagi in British Museum*, Pl. ii., iii.
[13] Athenaeus, pp. 153, 154. The true Hoplomachia, as described in Homer and practised apparently by the Mantineans and Cyrenaeans, must not be confounded with the later so-called Hoplomachia, competitions in which were held at the Athenian Thesea between boys of all ages as well as men, and which was regularly taught in the gymnasia by officials known as Hoplomachoi. The latter was merely a military training in the use of arms, and the competitions therein were probably as harmless as modern fencing competitions. The Spartans at all events regarded the Hoplomachia as unpractical and useless for a nation of soldiers, and Plato, though he recommends the armed combat between men in heavy or light armour as preferable to the

was probably connected exclusively with funeral rites, a substitute for human sacrifices. In the earlier part of the book Achilles slays twelve Trojan captives upon the pyre of his friend; in the latter part armed warriors fight in his honour. The one scene is but the later doublet of the other.

The description of the archery competition is simply ludicrous. The first prize is for the man who hits a dove fastened by a cord to the top of a mast, while the second prize is for the man who performs the infinitely harder feat of severing the cord. The choice of ten double axes for the first prize and ten single axes for second suspiciously suggests a reminiscence of the more serious competition with Odysseus' bow in the *Odyssey*, where the twelve axe-heads to be shot for are part of the treasures that Odysseus had once won as prizes.[14] In the *Odyssey* the bow holds an honourable place, but in the *Iliad*, though a few heroes are famed for their skill in archery, the bow is rather the weapon of the soldiery, and especially of the Trojans, and skill with it is regarded by the Achaean noble who fought in his chariot with the same not unnatural dislike and contempt, not unmingled with fear, as it was by the chivalry of France in the days of Agincourt.[15]

Archery was regarded with the same contempt by the Greek hoplite of the fifth century, and though it formed part of the training of the Athenian Epheboi, it never entered largely into Greek sports. The diskos, however, was always and in all places a favourite exercise. Odysseus, as we have seen, to prove his strength to the Phaeacians, hurled far beyond all their marks a diskos larger than his hosts themselves ever threw.[16] The word diskos means nothing more than a "thing for throwing," and the object thrown by Odysseus was a stone. Whether the artificial diskos of later times was known to the poet may be doubted, although the words "diskos" and "a diskos' throw" are of frequent occurrence. In the later gymnasium there was no doubt always a supply of diskoi of various weights and sizes, like the supply of dumbbells in our own gymnasia. But we should hardly expect to find such a stock of athletic implements in the agora of the Phaeacians hard by the ships where these impromptu after-dinner sports took place. It seems more likely that the diskoi were merely the large round pebbles of the seashore, such as the Phaeacian fisher-folk used for holding down their nets and tackle laid out to dry in the agora, and such as every visitor to the seaside instinctively picks up and throws. A stone, a lump of metal, or a tree-trunk provides for early man a natural weapon in time of war, a test of strength in time of peace. From such simple forms are derived the weight, the hammer, and the caber of our modern sports. In Homer stones still played no small part in actual warfare. Even heroes use them. Diomedes hurls at Aeneas a "handful such as two men, as men now are, could scarcely lift,"[17] and with a similar rock, which he wields as lightly as a shepherd waves a fleece, Hector himself bursts in the gate of the Achaean wall.[18] But stones are more especially the weapon of the common soldiery, and when the fight grows general round the body of Cebriones the stones fly fast.[19] Naturally, then, throwing the

---

pankration for his ideal state, yet has no great regard for the fashionable exponents and teachers of the art in his time. Plato, *Laches* 182, *Gorg.* 456, *Leg.* 834. Cp. Dar.-Sagl, *s.v.* "Hoplomachia."

[14] *Od.* xxi. 4, 61.
[15] *Il.* xi. 385.
[16] *Od.* viii. 186 sq.
[17] *Il.* v. 302.
[18] *Il.* xii. 445.
[19] *Il.* xvi. 774. In Professor Furtwängler's reconstruction of the Aegina pediment one of the fallen warriors holds a stone which he is about to hurl. Stone-throwing by hand and with the sling is mentioned as part of the peltast's training by Plato, *Leg.* 834 A.

stone forms a part of the Achaean sports. From the use of the term κατωμαδίοιο,[20] "thrown from the shoulder," it has been supposed that the Achaeans put the weight from the shoulder. They may have done so; but "the whirl" with which Odysseus hurled the stone, and the distance that he threw it, clearly indicate an underhand throw.

The weight hurled at the games of Patroclus was no stone but an unwrought metal of mass, probably the contents of one of the open-hearth furnaces of the Mediterranean world. This "pig of iron," which had been taken by Achilles from Eetion of Thebes, is not only the weight to be thrown but the prize, and contrary to the courteous Achaean custom the only prize, although there are four competitors. "The winner's shepherd, or ploughman," says Achilles, "will not want for iron for five years." But in spite of its weight Polypoetes hurls it as far as a herdsman flings the *bola*[21] "when it flieth whirling through the herds of kine." The word *solos* occurs only in this passage and in later imitators of Homer; the passage is, as has been said, a very late one, so late that the writer seems to be consciously archaizing, and I believe that, wishing to give the description a primitive appearance, he substituted the solos for the athlete's diskos, with which he was undoubtedly familiar. The word seems to be connected with the Semitic *sela*, a rock, but at an early date to have been used to describe the pigs of iron produced on the island of Elba and elsewhere. In late writers it is sometimes a poetical synonym for the diskos.

The chariot-race and the strictly athletic events, such as boxing, wrestling, and running, were essentially the sports of the nobles; but though the latter excelled the common soldiery in throwing the spear, heaving the weight, and shooting with the bow, as they did in everything else, there is in these three events a distinctly popular element. The bow, the javelin, and the stone were the weapons of all alike, and so, when Achilles was sulking in his tent, his folk, we read, "sported with diskos, with casting of spears, and archery." The diskos and the spear were also the favourite recreation of the suitors of Penelope, who had, we may suppose, no taste for more strenuous exercises. Their popular character is clearly indicated by the use of the terms "a diskos throw" or "a spear throw" as measures of distance.[22]

Jumping, which was an important event in the later pentathlon, is in Homer only mentioned as one of the sports in which the nimble Phaeacians excelled. Among these we meet with ball-play, a favourite amusement of the Greeks in all ages. Not only do Nausicaa and her maidens disport themselves with the ball on the seashore, but all her brothers give a display of their skill before Odysseus, and in both cases the players, as they toss the ball from one to another, move in a sort of rhythmic dance to the strains of music in a way which would have delighted the heart of some modern professors of physical culture.[23] Dance and song were always dear to the Greeks. We have also hints of acrobatic shows that remind us of the Cretan scenes. On the shield of Achilles was wrought "a dancing place like unto that which once in wide Cnossus Daedalus wrought for Ariadne of the fair tresses ... and among the dancers as the minstrel played two tumblers whirled."[24] "Verily," says Patroclus to Meriones, as smitten by a stone he falls from his chariot, "verily there are tumblers among the Trojans

---

[20] *Il.* xxiii. 431; but cp. *Od.* viii. 189; *Il.* xxiii. 840.
[21] For this interpretation of καλαῦροψ, and for the discussion of the terms diskos and solos, *vide infra*, p. 313.
[22] *Il.* xxiii. 431, 529; xvi. 589.
[23] *Od.* vi. 100, viii. 370.
[24] *Il.* xviii. 605 (= *Od.* iv. 18).

too."[25] Still more suggestive of the circus is the comparison of Ajax rushing over the plain to a man driving four horses and leaping from horse to horse as they fly along.[26]

With the origin of the Homeric poems we are not here concerned. Whether we regard them as the work of a single poet or as evolved by a series of poets, whether as a contemporary picture of the Mycenaean age or as based upon tradition, it is generally agreed that the state of society described is separated by a long interval from any of which we have historical knowledge in Greece, and that, despite slight discrepancies, this description is in its general features consistent. Of this society the games are the natural product. Just as in the Homeric polity we can trace the elements from which the various later institutions were evolved, and yet the polity as a whole is distinct from all later developments, so in athletics the events are the same as are found in the later festivals, but the spirit that pervades them is purely Homeric and separated by a wide interval from the spirit of the Olympic games. Critics tell us that the chief passages referring to the sports are comparatively late, later than the founding of the Olympic games in 776 B.C. If this is so, the poet must have followed closely traditions of a much earlier date. Otherwise we can hardly explain the contrast between the Homeric and the Olympic games, and the absence, with one doubtful exception, of any allusion to the latter. This silence is especially remarkable when we remember the large part played in the games of the *Iliad* by Nestor and the Neleidae, who lived in the neighbouring Pylos, and the close connection in the *Odyssey* between Elis and Ithaca.

The distinctive character of the Homeric games may be summed up in two words—they are aristocratic and spontaneous. They are spontaneous as the play of the child, the natural outlet of vigorous youth. There is no organized training, no organized competition, and sport never usurps the place of work. They are aristocratic because, though manly exercises are common to all the people, excellence in them belongs especially to the nobles; and when sports are held on an elaborate scale at the funeral of some chieftain, it is the nobles only who compete.

---

[25] *Il.* xvi. 742, 750.
[26] *Il.* xv. 679.

Chapter 3

THE RISE OF THE ATHLETIC FESTIVAL

The athletic meeting was unknown to Homer: in historic times it is associated with religious festivals celebrated at definite periods at the holiest places in Greece. If the growth of the athletic festival was due to the athletic spirit of the race, its connexion with religion may be traced to those games with which the funeral of the Homeric chieftain was celebrated. Though the origin of the great festivals is overgrown with a mass of late and conflicting legends in which it is difficult to distinguish truth from fiction, there is no reason for discrediting the universal tradition of their funeral origin, confirmed as it is by survivals in the ritual of the festivals, by the testimony of the earliest athletic art, and by later custom.[27] So we may conjecture that these games, originally celebrated at the actual funeral, tended like other funeral rites to become periodical, and as ancestor-worship developed into hero-worship became part of the cult of heroes, which seems to have preceded throughout Greece the worship of the Olympian deities. When the latter superseded the earlier heroes, they took over these games together with the sanctuaries and festivals of the older religion.

The custom of celebrating funerals with games and contests is not confined to Greece. Among the funeral scenes that decorate the walls of Etruscan tombs we see depicted chariot-races, horse-races, boxing, wrestling, and other athletic sports, together with contests of a more brutal nature.[28] From the Etruscans the custom spread to the Romans, who borrowed from the same people their gladiatorial games, which were likewise possibly of funeral origin. Funeral games are found in Circassia, in the Caucasus, among the Khirgiz, and yet further afield in Siam and in North America.[29] But the most instructive example for our purpose is furnished by the old Irish fairs, which lasted from pagan times down to the beginning of the last century.[30] These fairs, founded in memory of some departed chieftain, took place at stated intervals commonly in the neighbourhood of the ancient burial-place. Thus the triennial fair of Carman, near Wexford, was instituted in fulfilment of the dying charge of Garman "as a fair of mourning to bear his name forever." These fairs, which lasted several days, and to which people of all classes flocked from every part of Ireland, and even from Scotland,

---

[27] Frazer, *Pausanias*, i. 44, 8; Rouse, *Greek Votive Offerings*, pp. 4, 10; Körte, "Die Entstehung der Olympionikenliste," *Hermes*, xxxix., 1904, pp. 224 ff.; Krause, *Die Pythien, Nemeen, und Isthmien*, pp. 9, 112, 171.

[28] Dennis, *Cities and Cemeteries of Etruria*, 2nd Ed. i. 374; ii. 323, 330.

[29] Frazer, *loc. cit.*

[30] P. W. Joyce, *Social History of Ireland*, ii. pp. 435 ff.

furnished an opportunity for the transaction of a variety of business public and private. Laws were promulgated, councils and courts were held, marriages were arranged and celebrated.

There was, of course, buying and selling of every sort, but the principal business of these gatherings was the holding of sports and competitions. Of these there was an endless variety—horse-races, athletic exercises, games, pastimes, special sports for women, competitions in music, in the recitation of poems and tales. There were shows and performances by jugglers, clowns, acrobats, circus-riders, and for everything there were prizes, "for every art that was just to be sold, or rewarded or exhibited or listened to." Like the sacred month of the Olympic festival, the time of the fairs was "one universal truce," during which all quarrels and strife were repressed, no distraint for debt, no vengeance was allowed, and the debtor might enjoy himself with impunity. "The Gentile of the Gael," says an old writer, "celebrated the fair of Carman without breach of law, without crime, without violence, without dishonour." On the introduction of Christianity the Church took over the old pagan fairs; the pagan rites were abolished, each day began with a religious service, and the fair concluded with a grand religious ceremonial. In every detail the history of these fairs bears an extraordinary resemblance to that of the Greek athletic festivals.

Figure 3. Amphiaraus Vase. Berlin, 1655.

Figure 4. Dipylon Vase. Copenhagen.

In Greek lands there is everywhere evidence of the existence of funeral games at all periods, from the legendary games of Pelias to those celebrated at Thessalonica in the time of Valerian, or perhaps in his honour.[31] The games of Pelias and those celebrated by Acastus in honour of his father were represented respectively on the two most famous monuments of early decorative art—the chest of Cypselus dedicated in the Heraeum at Olympia, and the throne of Apollo at Amyclae. Both works are lost, and known to us only from the descriptions of Pausanias, but the manner in which the games of Pelias were represented can be judged from the similar scene on a sixth-century vase, the Amphiaraus vase in Berlin (Figure 3).[32] A still earlier representation of funeral games occurs on a geometric cup from the Acropolis, possibly dating from the eighth century (Figure 4).[33] On one side are two naked men, with one hand holding each other by the arm, and with the other preparing to stab one another with swords, a mimic fight perhaps rather than a real one, but one which, like the Pyrrhic dance depicted on the other side, may recall more sanguinary funeral contests. On the reverse stand two boxers in the centre between a group of warriors, and a group of dancers; an armed dancer leaping off the ground to the accompaniment of a four-stringed lyre, and two others holding possibly castanets. A similar scene occurs on a silver vase from Etruria, said by Furtwängler to be of Cyprian origin; while the wide distribution of funeral games is further shown by the Clazomenae sarcophagus already described, and by a fragment of a sixth-century vase manufactured at Naucratis (Figure 140).[34] The games depicted on these monuments are very similar to those described in Homer. The prizes are generally tripods and bowls which stand between the combatants or at the finish of the course. The contests were not confined to athletics and chariot-races. Hesiod tells us that he was present at Chalcis at the games held in honour of Amphidamas by his sons, and himself won a tripod as a prize for a "hymn."[35] At Delphi, too, the only contests previous to the sixth century were musical.

Of periodical games in memory of the dead the earliest example, apart from the great festivals, is furnished by the games of Azan in Arcadia, where, according to Pausanias, the chariot-race was the oldest event.[36] At Rhodes the festival of the Heliea seems to have originated in the funeral games of Tlepolemus.[37] In more historical times we frequently find the memory of generals and statesmen kept alive by games founded in their honour by their countrymen, or those whom they had benefited. Miltiades was honoured by games in the Chersonese, Leonidas and Pausanias at Sparta, Brasidas at Amphipolis, Timoleon at Syracuse, Mausolus at Halicarnassus. Kings and tyrants followed the example: Alexander instituted games in honour of his friend Hephaestion. Those, too, who had fallen in war were often commemorated by their states with athletic festivals. The Pythia were reorganized by the Amphictions as a funeral contest in honour of those who fell in the first Sacred war, in memory of which the victors received crowns of bay cut in the Vale of Tempe, and the Eleutheria at Plataea were established by the victorious Greeks to commemorate those who had died in battle against the Persians. At Athens, too, a festival was held in the Academy

---

[31] *C.I.G.* 1969, ἀγὼν ἐπιτάφιος θεματικός.
[32] *Berl. Vas.* 1665. *Mon. d. I.* X. Pl. iv., v.
[33] *Arch. Zeit.*, 1885, Pl. viii. The vase is now at Copenhagen. The silver cup referred to below is in the Uffizi Palace, and is reproduced in Schreiber's *Atlas*, xiii. 6, and Inghirami, *Mon. Etr.* iii. 19, 20.
[34] *B.M. Vases*, B. 124.
[35] Hesiod, *Op.* 654.
[36] Paus. viii. 4, 5.
[37] Pindar, *Ol.* vii. 77-80.

under the direction of the polemarch in memory of those citizens who had died for their country.[38]

The origin of funeral games is too difficult a question to be discussed here. Many explanations have been offered. Roman critics held the Etruscan combats, from which their own gladiatorial games were borrowed, to have been originally a substitute for human sacrifice; and this explanation has been suggested above in connexion with the armed fight in the games of Patroclus. This view receives some support from the occurrence of the armed fight, whether real or mimic, and of the armed Pyrrhic dance, which was certainly a mimicry of battle, on some of the monuments representing funeral games, perhaps, too, from the prominence in these games of boxing, which may be regarded as a further modification of the more brutal combats. Plutarch suggests apologetically that in early days such fights took place even at Olympia,[39] and the lads of the Peloponnese, we are told, every year lashed themselves upon the grave of Pelops till the blood ran down. But the significance of the latter rite is doubtful. Another view connects these contests with those fights for succession with which Dr. Frazer's *Golden Bough* has made us familiar. In support of this we may cite the famous chariot-race between Pelops and Oenomaus for the hand of Hippodameia, or such later myths as the wrestling match by which Zeus won from Cronus the sovereignty of heaven. Connected with the idea of succession is the credit and popularity accruing to the heirs from the magnificence of the games with which they celebrated their dead predecessor. The costly prizes offered must assuredly have caused no less pleasure to the living than to the dead. Comparatively late is the idea that the dead man somehow assisted as spectator and enjoyed the games held in his honour.[40] In all these views there is probably some truth, the amount of which varied in different places; but whatever truth there is in any or all of them as applied to the Greeks, they afford no adequate explanation of the variety and importance of Greek funeral games unless full account be taken also of the intense love of competition and the strong athletic spirit of the race. But whatever the origin of funeral games, there can be no doubt that they adequately account for the close connexion between athletics and religion; nor is this view discredited by doubts as to the particular funeral legends which later invention attached to particular festivals.

The athletic festival required for its growth fairly settled conditions of life, and during the troubled period which intervened between the time of Nestor and the first Olympiad no progress was possible. Long before the Homeric poems were composed, love of adventure, quickened perhaps by pressure from the North, had driven the Achaeans and other kindred tribes forth from the mainland of Greece to find fresh homes in the islands and on the eastern shores of the Aegean. Other tribes, Aeolians, Ionians, Dorians, followed, and for centuries the stream of colonization flowed eastwards, carrying Greek civilization to every part of the Aegean. This civilization gathered fresh life from contact with the East. There, while Greece itself was paralyzed by wars and migrations, great cities grew and flourished, cities great not only in material prosperity but in art and literature and science. Of the history of these cities unfortunately we know nothing; we can only judge of their greatness by the results which we

---

[38] Frazer, *Paus.* i. 29, 30.
[39] Plut. *Quaest. Symp.* v. 2.
[40] Unless we accept Mr. Myers' translation of Pindar, *Ol.* i. 94, "And from afar off he beholdeth the glory of the Olympian games in the courses called of Pelops." Most modern editors translate κλέος τηλόθεν δέδορκε, "his glory shineth from afar," which, in view of the words which follow, ἐν δρόμοις Πέλοπος, seems decidedly preferable to making Pelops the subject.

find in the seventh and sixth centuries when the rise of the Lydian and Persian empires first brought them into conflict with these powers. But of one thing we may be sure—the Greek settlers brought with them their love of sport. This must be a truism to all who hold that the 23rd *Iliad* was composed in the Eastern Aegean; it is confirmed by the many victories gained in later days at Olympia by athletes from the cities and islands of the East, and by the numerous athletic festivals existing in those parts in historical times.

Under the settled and luxurious conditions of Eastern life it is probable that the athletic festival developed at an early date,[41] though owing to the same conditions athletics never attained in the East to the position which they occupied in the Peloponnese, and the athletic business was often secondary to the other business of the festivals. This at least is suggested by the history of the Delian festival. The antiquity of this festival is vouched for by the Homeric *Hymn to Apollo*. At a time when Olympia was still little more than a local gathering, the long-robed Ionians were already flocking to Apollo's isle with their children and their wives. Even from the mainland of Greece choirs came with hymns to Apollo. We still possess a fragment of Eumelus, a Bacchiad of Corinth, said by Pausanias to have been written for the Messenian choir sent to Delos in the eighth century.[42] "There when the games are ordered they rejoice to honour Apollo with boxing and dance and song." The picture in the *Hymn to Apollo* is full of joy and grace: the fair ships drawn up by the water's edge, the costly merchandise spread out upon the shore, the throng of long-robed men and fair-girdled women, and in the background the slopes of Mount Cynthus, halfway up which stands out the rocky archway of Apollo's ancient shrine. A fair scene truly, and typical no doubt of many another festival where men of kindred race gathered together for sacrifice and song, for sport and traffic. But in this joyous festival of the jovial Delians we feel that athletics hold but a secondary place. For the more serious business of athletics we must go to the sterner, more strenuous festivals of the Peloponnese—above all to Olympia.

"Best of all is water and gold as a flaming fire in the night shineth eminent amid lordly wealth: but if of prizes in the games thou art fain, O my soul, to tell, then as for no bright star more quickening than the sun must thou search in the void firmament by day, so neither shall we find any games greater than the Olympic whereof to utter our voice."[43] The sanctity of Olympia and its festival go back to days far earlier than the coming of the Dorians, perhaps of any Greek race; but the growth of the festival dates from the time when, after the Dorian invasion, the movements of the peoples ceased and the land became settled, and its greatness is largely due to the athletic ideal and the genius for organization which characterized that race. "It is not the least of the many debts which we owe to Heracles," says Lysias in his *Panegyric*, "that by instituting the Olympic games he restored peace and goodwill to a land torn asunder by war and faction and wasted by pestilence." Pausanias uses similar language of the restoration of the games by Iphitus and Lycurgus, whose action another tradition ascribes to the advice of the Delphic oracle. But though we can hardly credit the founders of the games, whoever they were, with this far-sighted Panhellenic policy at so early a date, the

---

[41] It is perhaps no accident that in our imperfect records of the Olympic games the earliest victor outside the Peloponnese is Onomastus of Smyrna, who in *Ol.* 23 won the boxing, an event said to have been then introduced for the first time. He is said to have drawn up rules for boxing which were adopted at Olympia. Again, no family was more distinguished in the history of Greek athletics than the Diagoridae of Rhodes, whose victories in boxing and the pankration were immortalized by Pindar. The prominence of boxing in the East reminds us of Minoan times, and perhaps the tradition may have survived from these days.

[42] Paus. iv. 4, 1; iv. 33, 2.

[43] Pindar, *Ol.* i. (E. Myers' translation).

tradition is founded upon facts: the first Olympiad does mark the settlement of Greece, and the festival did promote the unity of Greece. Its growth, though not its origin, was due to the Dorians.

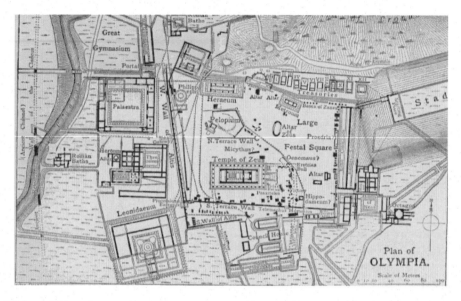

Figure 5. Plan of Olympia.

Olympia lies about ten miles from the sea on the northern bank of the Alpheus, at the point where its valley spreads out into a wide and fertile plain. In an angle formed by this river with its tributary the Cladeus, which rushes down from the mountains of Elis between steep banks formerly shaded with plane-trees, at the foot of the pine-clad hill of Cronus, stood the grove of wild olive-trees, brought there according to tradition by Heracles from the land of the Hyperboreans, the sacred grove from which the Altis took its name. The slopes of the neighbouring hills were covered with a variety of trees, and in the rich undergrowth of flowering shrubs the wild boar, deer, and other game found cover. It was to Scillus, only a few miles distant, that the veteran Xenophon retired to spend his old age in literature and sport. In old days the vegetation was far more luxuriant than now; besides the olive groves, the white poplars, from which alone the wood for the sacrifice to Zeus and Pelops might be cut, and even the palm-tree flourished there. The rich well-watered plain was covered with vines and crops, while its meadows afforded abundant pasturage for horses and for cattle.[44]

To the modern traveller Olympia seems too much out of the way to be the scene of a great national gathering; even to the Greek of the fifth century it must have seemed to stand outside the busy centres of Greek life, and perhaps it was this very remoteness, combined with its ancient sanctity, that saved Olympia, like Delphi, from being the battle-ground between the rival states of Greece. But it had not been so always. The flat, rich, alluvial plains of the western Peloponnese had not formerly lagged behind the rest of Greece. The long, almost unbroken curves of sandy shore offered little harbourage for the triremes of a later day. But the earlier mariner or trader from the East who coasted around Greece had no love for deep land-locked harbours; all he wanted was a sandy shore where he could beach his

---

[44] Vide Bötticher, *Olympia*, ch. i.

ships sheltered by some convenient headland as at Triphylian Pylos, or at the open mouth of some river like the Alpheus. Hence there is no reason to doubt the traditions that connect Cretans and Phoenicians with Olympia.[45] The coastline has advanced considerably since those days, and the small boats of these ancient mariners could advance up the river with perfect safety through the flat open plain as far as Olympia. This accessibility of Olympia by sea had yet more important consequences at a later age when the festival attracted men from the great colonies of Italy and Sicily. Olympia may even have been associated with the founding of these colonies; for the coast road round Elis and the shores of the gulf of Corinth connected it with Sicyon, Corinth, and Megara. May we not suppose that, as the colonists sailed down the gulf of Corinth, many of them would turn aside before they bade farewell to their native shores to visit the venerable grove of Olympia and consult its ancient oracle?

Again, Olympia stood full in the way of the Achaean tribes as they pressed southwards from their first settlement at Dodona. In speaking of the Achaeans we are using the word provisionally for convenience' sake to denote the pre-Dorian Greeks of the Peloponnese as opposed to the original inhabitants and the later Dorians. In the *Odyssey* they have spread over the islands, over Pleuron by the sea and rocky Calydon, over Elis and Messenia. So close was the connexion between the islands and Elis, then the land of the Epeans, that the princes of Ithaca used its broad plains for breeding cattle and horses. The narrow straits offered no obstacle to this adventurous people, and for centuries before the passage of Oxylus, the one-eyed Aetolian from Naupactus, the Achaeans and others had been crossing over in larger or smaller companies till they had spread over the whole Peloponnese. Hence for the Achaeans in the Peloponnese Olympia stood in the same position as Dodona in northern Greece. The Dorians, indeed, seem to have failed in their attempt to follow in the same course; but legend connected with the return of the Heracleidae the invasion of their Aetolian allies under Oxylus, who dispossessed the Epean lords of Elis. The quarrel between these newcomers and the earlier settlers for the possession of Olympia lasted for centuries, but through all the changes of population, though many fresh cults were added by the invaders, the superstition with which all newcomers in those days regarded the gods and sanctuaries of the earlier inhabitants preserved the old cults inviolate, so that in the buildings and altars of Olympia, and the ritual of its festival, all the various strata of its history are plainly visible.

Lastly, though remote from the struggles of later history, no place in the Peloponnese was more accessible to other parts. Besides the coast-route that connected it with Messenia and the gulf of Corinth, the valleys of the Alpheus and its tributaries afforded a natural means of communication with all parts of the interior, and it was to the athletic character of the inhabitants of the Peloponnese that the athletic fame of the festival in the first place was due. Without this native talent it could never have attracted competitions from northern Greece or from the colonies of the West, nor could it ever have acquired its peculiar sanctity but for the position it had held in the earlier migrations.

It is unnecessary here to discuss the various myths which Greek imagination wove about the beginnings of Olympia, and the perplexing problems which they raise. Two propositions may be regarded as fairly established. In the first place, Olympia was a holy place before the Achaeans came to the Peloponnese. In the second place, the beginning of the games was earlier than the Dorian invasion, but later probably than the coming of the Achaeans.

---

[45] For the history of Olympia *vide* Curtius, "Entwurf einer Geschichte von Olympia," in *Ol.* Text. i. pp. 16-68.

The antiquity of Olympia is proved by the presence there of those elements of primitive religion which preceded the worship of the Olympian deities. The altar of Cronus on the hill top which bore his name recalled a sovereignty earlier than that of Zeus. An ancient oracle of earth preceded the oracle of Zeus. Of the worship of the powers of the underworld there is abundant evidence at Olympia, as in the rest of the Peloponnese; the priestess of Demeter Chamyne, for example, was exempted from the rule that excluded women from Olympia, and had her place of honour in the stadium opposite the seats of the Hellanodicae. In Hera, whose worship at Olympia was earlier than that of Zeus, we may probably recognize a Hellenized form of the great Mother Goddess of the Aegean world. Lastly, that Pelops claimed precedence of Zeus is clear from the fact that the athletes sacrificed to Pelops first and then to Zeus. At his tomb within the Altis, originally a barrow, only afterwards enclosed in a shrine, he was worshipped with all the ceremonial due to the dead, and every year the youths of the Peloponnese lashed themselves upon his grave till the blood ran down.[46] Yet it does not follow that the cult of Pelops was pre-Achaean. We cannot clearly draw the line between what belonged to the Achaeans and what to the original inhabitants. There was no violent breach, but rather a gradual fusion of the races, in the course of which the Achaeans made their own much of the earlier civilization. Certainly the cult of heroes continued all through Greek history; in later days even noted athletes were canonized.

The ancient writings of the Eleans, according to Pausanias, ascribed the institution of the games to the Idaean Heracles, one of the Cretan Curetes to whom the infant Zeus was entrusted. But to Pindar and Bacchylides the games are associated with the tomb of Pelops. Pelops, as the story goes, came to Olympia as a suitor for the hand of Hippodameia, whose father Oenomaus challenged all her suitors to a chariot-race, and slew with his spear all whom he defeated. Thirteen suitors had been slain when Pelops came and, by the aid of Myrtilus, the charioteer of Oenomaus, who removed the lynch-pins from his master's chariot wheels, slew him and won his bride and kingdom. This story, afterwards represented on the chest of Cypselus and on the pediments of the temple of Zeus, was commemorated by the earliest monuments of the Altis. Besides the tomb of Pelops himself, there was an ancient wooden pillar said to be the only remnant of the house of Oenomaus, which was struck by lightning,[47] and also the Hippodamium, apparently a funeral mound, surrounded afterwards by a wall, where the women of Elis every year offered sacrifice.

It was at the ancient tomb of Pelops, Pindar tells us, that Heracles the son of Zeus, returning from his victory over Augeas, founded the Olympian games. There "he measured a sacred grove for the Father, and having fenced round the Altis marked the bounds thereof. There he set apart the choicest of the spoil for an offering from the war and sacrificed and ordained the fifth year feast." "In the foot-race down the straight course was Likymnius' son Oeonus first, from Nidea had he led his host; in the wrestling was Tegea glorified by Echemus; Doryclus won the prize of boxing, a dweller in the city of Tiryns, and with the four-horse chariot Samos of Mantinea, Halirrhothius' son; with the javelin Phrastor hit the mark; in distance Eniceus beyond all others hurled the stone with a circling sweep, and all the warrior company thundered a great applause."[48]

---

[46] For the cult of Pelops *vide* Paus. v. 13, 2; Schol. to Pindar, *Ol.* i. 146, 149.
[47] The latest excavations show that this site had been inhabited in prehistoric days. Traces of six buildings have been discovered below the geometric stratum; they are characterized by a semicircular apsidal ending. *Ath. Mitth.* xxxiii. 185; *Year's Work in Classical Studies*, 1908, p. 12.
[48] Pindar, *Ol.* xi. 64.

The poet has glorified into a Peloponnesian festival what can have been no more than a local gathering in which the neighbouring chieftains took part, and the introduction of Heracles may have been an invention of the Eleans; for, according to Pausanias, it was Iphitus who first induced the Eleans, or, as he should have said, the Pisatans, to sacrifice to Heracles whom they had before regarded as their enemy. Yet there is probably some truth in the connexion of the games with Pelops' grave, a tradition which we find also in Pindar's great rival Bacchylides. But who was Pelops? Was he god, man, or hero? Like the oracle of Delphi when asked a similar question about Lycurgus, we may well doubt. Yet in spite of certain modern authorities, who see local gods in most of the heroes of legend, it is perhaps safer to accept the universal belief of the Greeks that he was a man, some chieftain who after his death was worshipped as a hero. Moreover, the tradition of his Phrygian origin is a strong argument against the view that he was a native pre-Achaean god of the Peloponnese, though it is by no means incompatible with his connection with the Achaeans in view of the original kinship of the latter with the Phrygians. At all events Pelops is pre-Dorian, and the victors in these games, according to Pindar, are pre-Dorians.

The existence of the games in pre-Dorian times agrees entirely with the athletic character of the Achaeans in the Peloponnese as described in Homer; and if we find in the poet no mention of Olympia, his silence is easily explained by the simple, local character of the festival at this time. It will be remembered that in the funeral games of the north-western Peloponnese chariot-racing played a prominent part. The antiquity of this sport at Olympia is confirmed by the discovery of a number of very early votive offerings, many of them models of horses or chariots, found in a layer that extends below the foundations of the Heraeum. This temple was founded, it is said, by the people of Scillus some eight years after the coming of Oxylus; and even if we cannot go so far as Dr. Dörpfeld, who assigns it to the tenth or eleventh centuries, there is no doubt of its great antiquity, and that the Scilluntines were of an Arcadian, not a Dorian stock.

Before the building of the Heraeum we must picture Olympia as a sacred grove surrounded by a hedge interspersed with open spaces where stood the barrow of Pelops and sundry earth altars, such as the great altar of Zeus, or the six double altars at which the competitors offered sacrifice. Thither the country-folk resorted to inquire of the future from the ancient earth oracle, or perhaps, as at Dodona, from the rustling of the leaves. These oracles were interpreted by certain hereditary families, the Iamidae and Clytidae, who maintained their privileges even when Dorian influence had prevailed. Thither at set times the neighbouring tribes flocked to take part in the games held at the tomb of Pelops. The sanctuary and festival of Olympia were in the territory of the Pisatae, a tribal group of village communities possibly nine in number situated on either side of the Alpheus valley, and loosely bound together by the common worship of the hero Pelops.[49] They took their name from the village of Pisa, perhaps on account of its nearness to Olympia.

The Pisatae were one of many such tribal groups, or amphictyonies in the Peloponnese, in parts of which this form of life continued into the fifth century or later. Such were the groups of nine cities mentioned in the catalogue of the ships in the *Iliad*, the nine Arcadian cities grouped round the tomb of Aepytus, the nine Pylian cities of Nestor's kingdom, the nine Argive cities under Diomed, the nine Lacedaemonian cities under Sparta. Such, too, were the

---

[49] Cp. Louis Dyer, "The Olympian Council House," in *Harvard Classical Studies*, 1908, where a full account of these Peloponnesian leagues will be found.

Caucones, a wandering tribe whose hero Caucon was in later times supposed to be buried near Lepreum; such were the Epeans of Elis; while the Eleans who supplanted them retained this form of government till the founding of the city-state of Elis in the fifth century. Like all such clans these leagues were intensely aristocratic: the chieftains were regarded with superstitious reverence, and the tribal centre was often the tomb of some departed hero-chief. Of cities, properly speaking, there were none in the western Peloponnese. A few strong fortresses served as residences for powerful chieftains and as refuge for their followers in danger; but most of the people lived in unwalled villages like the Scotch Highlanders. Their wealth consisted largely in horses and cattle, which they bartered with the islanders or with Cretan or Phoenician traders who landed at Pylos or sailed up the Alpheus to Olympia. In search of pasturage they ranged in winter over the lowland plains, retiring in summer to the sheltered upland valleys. The constant pressure of newcomers kept them constantly on the move, southwards and eastwards. This shifting of the tribal centres may be traced in the places that bore the name of Pylos. Settling originally in Elean Pylos, the gateway of the netherworld, these Pylians, united by some netherworld cult, were forced to move first to Triphylian Pylos, probably the Pylos of Nestor, and at a later stage to Messenian Pylos. Of their raids and cattle-lifting, their feuds and their reprisals, we have a vivid picture in the *Odyssey*. Such, we may suppose, was the life of the Pisatae and their neighbours, the pre-Dorian inhabitants of Elis, Triphylia, Arcadia and Messenia. The Pisatae perhaps enjoyed a position more established than the rest, thanks to the superstitious reverence which alone saved the rich valley of Olympia from attack, but under these unsettled conditions the real development of the festival was impossible, though the prestige which it had already acquired is shown in the building of the Heraeum by the Scilluntines.

The coming of the Dorians brought order into the Peloponnese, but only after a long and bitter struggle. The settling of Oxylus and his Aetolians in Elis checked the stream of migration from the north-west, and the power of the Dorians prevented further aggression from other quarters. Meanwhile such of the earlier inhabitants as clung to their independence were driven into the mountains of Arcadia and Achaea, or into Messenia. In the south-west the civilization, of which we have a glorified picture in Nestor's kingdom, lasted perhaps till the final conquest of the country by the Spartans; in the mountains the inhabitants developed into a race of hardy mountaineers and shepherds, fond of sport and war, clinging tenaciously to their ancient customs and manner of government, but playing no part in the history of Greece save as mercenaries in the pay of more progressive states.

In the long struggle that preceded the final settlement even Olympia was involved. The Eleans—as we may call the newcomers from Aetolia—strove hard to wrest from the Pisatans the control of the sanctuary; but the latter doggedly maintained their rights, which had been recently vindicated by the building of the Heraeum, and religious feeling was on their side. Still, the prestige of the festival suffered to such an extent that the games, it is said, were neglected and forgotten. At length, weary of incessant strife and a pestilence that followed it, the contending factions, on the advice, according to one story, of the Delphic oracle, resolved to re-establish the Olympic games as a means of restoring goodwill and unity to the land. This work was ascribed to Iphitus, king of Elis, a descendant of Oxylus, to Cleosthenes, king of Pisa, and to Lycurgus of Sparta. The ordinance regulating the festival was engraved on a diskos preserved in the temple of Hera down to the time of Pausanias, on which the names of

Iphitus and Lycurgus were still legible in the days of Aristotle.[50] The antiquity of the diskos is unquestionable, but it may well be doubted if it was contemporary with the event described. More probably it dated from the seventh century, when Sparta, as we shall see, took an active part in the games. The introduction of Sparta and Lycurgus at this early date is certainly suspicious. Be this as it may, the organization of the festival by Iphitus and Cleosthenes may be regarded as the first definite historical fact in its history.

From this date the festival was held every fourth year until its abolition by the emperor Theodosius at the close of the fourth century A.D. It took place at the time of the second or third full moon after the summer solstice in the Elean months Apollonios and Parthenios, which correspond approximately to August and September. For the sacred month (ἱερομηνία) in which the festival took place, a holy truce (ἐκεχειρία) was proclaimed beforehand by the truce-bearers of Zeus (σπονδοφόροι). During this truce there was to be peace throughout the land, no one was permitted to bear arms within the sacred territory, and all competitors, embassies, and spectators travelling to Olympia were regarded as under the protection of Zeus and sacrosanct. The effect of this truce, at first purely local, spread with the growth of the festival to all the states taking part in it till the whole Greek world felt its influence. Any violation of the truce, any wrong inflicted on the pilgrims of Zeus, was punished by a heavy fine to Olympian Zeus. The Spartans at the time of the Peloponnesian war, having entered the sacred territory during the truce under arms, were condemned to pay a fine of two minae for every hoplite; on their refusal to pay they were excommunicated. Even Alexander condescended to apologize and make restitution to the Athenian Phrynon, who had been seized and robbed by some of his mercenaries on his way to Olympia.[51]

By the truce of Iphitus the control of the festival seems to have been divided between the Eleans and Pisatans, vested probably at an early date in a joint council representing the various village communities. The council certainly existed in later days as a final court of appeal, and the fact that the earliest building under the new régime was the council-house, part of which dates from the middle of the sixth century, points to the antiquity of such a body. The dual control was recognized in the appointment of two executive officials, the Hellanodicae. The royal robes of purple worn by these officials indicate that they were originally the kings of the respective tribes. One of them, according to Elean tradition the only one, was always a descendant of Oxylus; but the official position of the Pisatae survived in later times in the priestly families of the Iamidae and Clytidae. As was to be expected, the dual control did not work smoothly. The Pisatae, mindful of their ancient rights, and jealous of the interference of the Eleans, made repeated but futile efforts to regain the sole control. But the superior might of the Eleans, supported at first at all events by the Spartans, prevailed more and more, till shortly after the Persian wars the Eleans laid waste the revolting cities of Triphylia, destroyed Pisa itself, and remained henceforth sole masters of Olympia, save for a spasmodic effort of the Pisatans and Arcadians in Ol. 104 (364 B.C.).

The view of Olympian history taken above differs considerably from the orthodox view taken from Pausanias and Strabo, and based on "the ancient writings of the Eleans." This priestly fiction may be summarized as follows. The games originally established by Oxylus were refounded by Iphitus and Lycurgus, and were under the management of the Eleans. In

---

[50] Paus. v. 20, 1; Plut. *Lycurgus* 1, 1. The part taken by Cleosthenes is vouched for by Phlegon, *Frag. Hist. Gr.* p. 602, and in a scholion on Plato's *Republic*, 465 D. Vide Dyer, *l.c.* pp. 40 ff.

[51] Thuc. v. 49; Demosth. *De fals. leg.*, ὑπόθ. p. 335.

Ol. 8 the Pisatans called in Pheidon, king of Argos, and with his help dispossessed the Eleans, but lost their control in the next Olympiad. In Ol. 28 Elis, being at war with Dyme, allowed the Pisatans to celebrate the games. In Ol. 34 Pantaleon, king of Pisa, celebrated the games at the head of an army. According to one account the Pisatans had control of the festival for twenty-two successive Olympiads, from the 30th to the 51st. Finally, somewhere between Ols. 48 and 52, the Eleans defeated the rebellious Pisatans, destroyed Pisa, laid waste Triphylia, and henceforth held undisputed control of Olympia with the exception of Ol. 104, which was celebrated by the Arcadians and Pisatans. In consequence this Olympiad, together with the 8th and 34th, were expunged from the register and reckoned as Anolympiads. Till Ol. 50 there was only one Hellanodicas, a descendant of Oxylus; at this date a second was appointed, and both were chosen by lot from the whole number of the Eleans.

This story is obviously a pious fraud invented by the priests of Elis to justify their usurpation by asserting a prior claim, a claim contradicted by all the evidence, and expressly denied by Xenophon.[52] For the same reason the part played by Cleosthenes in the truce of Iphitus is omitted by Pausanias, though fortunately preserved in another account. It is only possible to point out briefly some of the inconsistencies and absurdities in the priestly story. Elis is represented throughout as in control of Olympia, which is situated outside its boundaries in Pisatis, an independent state with a king of its own, and this independent state is represented as continually trying to usurp what is its own. The story of the Anolympiads is discredited by the fact that in the Olympic register, a document of at least equal value, these Olympiads were reckoned and the names of the victors were given. The part played by Pheidon is involved in all the obscurity that surrounds that most tantalizing character, but that the great tyrant, whenever he lived, did try to increase his prestige by seizing control of the Olympia, is rendered probable by the connection of similar tyrants with Olympia and the other festivals. The story of the addition of the second Hellanodicas in Ol. 50, at the very time when Pisa is said to have been destroyed, is a manifest absurdity. The two Hellanodicai represent a dual monarchy, and a dual monarchy represents a union of races. Assuming, what is now generally admitted, the pre-Dorian origin of the festival, the original Hellanodicas must have been a Pisatan, the second must have been added when Elis secured a share in the government. Moreover, the selection of the two officials by lot, a thoroughly democratic institution, is unthinkable in Elis, at that time an oligarchy of oligarchies, though it may well have been introduced when the democrats of Elis obtained the mastery. Lastly, the date of the final destruction of Pisa, about which Pausanias is obviously confused, is contradicted by the direct statement of Herodotus, who speaks of the war in which it took place as "in my days" (ἐπ' ἐμέο).[53] The earlier date has been supported by reference to a sixth-century inscription at Olympia recording a treaty for mutual defence between Elis and Heraea, by the terms of which either party failing to help the other is liable in case of need to a fine of a talent of silver to Olympian Zeus.[54] Too much, perhaps, has been made of this inscription, which is probably one of many such local treaties, the record of which has perished. Moreover, it seems highly probable that Heraea, so far from being opposed to Pisa, was a member of the early Pisatan league. The original claims of Pisa are admitted by all modern historians; all further difficulties vanish on the supposition of a subsequent dual control, in which Elis

---

[52] *Hell.* iii. 2, 31; vii. 4, 28.
[53] Hdt. iv. 148.
[54] *C.I.G.* 11; Roberts's *Greek Epigraphy*, 291.

gradually became the predominant partner until, in the fifth century, she ousted Pisa completely.

The regulations for competitors may be traced back to the earliest times. No one in later days was allowed to compete who was not of pure Greek parentage on both sides, or who had neglected to pay any penalty incurred to Olympian Zeus, or who had incurred ceremonial pollution by manslaughter, committed, we may suppose, in the sacred territory. These restrictions had their origin in a religious festival that formed a bond of union between neighbouring communities, which was gradually extended through the sacred truce-bearers till it embraced the whole Greek race. That this local or tribal exclusiveness grew into a Panhellenic exclusiveness, was due partly to the influence of the Dorians, partly to the close connexion of the colonies with Olympia. In the fifth century Alexander, the son of Amyntas, was not allowed to compete at Olympia until he had first satisfied the Hellanodicae that he was of Greek descent.

Similarly, the exclusion of women from Olympia was doubtless due to some religious taboo rather than to any sense of modesty or decorum. Such a feeling cannot have existed in these times. Certainly the Ionian women attended the festival of Delos, and Spartan girls took part in all athletic exercises with the boys. Pausanias in one passage tells us that the restriction did not extend to unmarried girls, but the truth of his statement is at least doubtful. We never hear of any unmarried women being present at the festival, and Olympia can have afforded little or no accommodation for them. The only certain exception is in the case of the priestess of Demeter, Chamyne, a exception that is quite consistent with the idea of an ancient taboo. Otherwise no woman was allowed to cross the Alpheus during a stated number of days. The penalty for so doing was death, the transgressor being thrown from the Typaean rock. Only one instance is recorded of this rule being broken. Pherenice, a member of the famous family of the Diagoridae, in her anxiety to see her son Peisirodus compete in the boys' boxing, accompanied him to Olympia disguised as a trainer. In her delight at his victory she leapt over the barrier and so disclosed her sex. The Hellanodicae, however, pardoned her in consideration for her father and brothers and son, all of them Olympic victors, but they passed a decree that henceforth all trainers should appear naked.[55]

Yet, though personally excluded from the games, women were allowed to enter their horses for the chariot-race, and even to set up statues for their victories. They had also their own festival at Olympia, the Heraea.[56] Every four years a peplos was woven for Hera by sixteen women of Elis, and presented to the goddess. At the festival there were races for maidens of various ages. Their course was 500 feet, or one-sixth less than the men's stadium. The maidens ran with their hair down their backs, a short tunic reaching just below the knee, and their right shoulder bare to the breast. The victors received crowns of olive and a share of the heifer sacrificed to Hera. They had, too, the right of setting up their statues in the Heraeum. There is in the Vatican a copy of a fifth-century statue of one of these girl victors, represented just as Pausanias describes them (Figure 6). She seems to be just on the point of starting. Unfortunately the arms of the statue are restored, and we cannot feel certain of the motive. The Heraea were said to have been instituted by Hippodameia in gratitude for her marriage with Pelops. Of their real origin and history we are unfortunately ignorant. According to Curtius the Heraea were the prototype of the Olympia, and races for maidens

---

[55] Paus. v. 6, 7.
[56] Paus. v. 16.

were earlier than those for men, but this is most improbable. The weaving of the peplos reminds us, of course, of the similar ceremony at the Panathenaea, while the races for maidens suggest Dorian influence. Certainly we can hardly make the Dorians responsible for the exclusion of women from Olympia, which may be safely referred to the earlier non-Greek race.

Figure 6. Statue of Girl Runner. Vatican. Copy of fifth-century original. (From a photograph by Alinari).

In early days athletes wore the loin-cloth which Cretan excavations have shown to have been worn generally in the Mediterranean world. The Homeric Greeks girded themselves for sports, and on some of the earliest athletic vases the loin-cloth is depicted (Figures 128, 142). Generally, however, the Greek athletes were absolutely naked. This custom is ascribed to an accident. Orsippus of Megara, in Ol. 15, 720 B.C., accidentally or on purpose dropped his loin-cloth in the race. The advantage which he gained thereby produced such an impression that from this date all runners discarded the loin-cloth. This story was commemorated by an epigram, written possibly by Simonides, which was inscribed on his tomb. The practice does not seem to have been adopted by all athletes till a later date, for Thucydides states that the abandonment of the loin-cloth even at Olympia dated from shortly before his own time.[57]

The prizes were originally tripods and other objects of value. It was in Ol. 7 that the crown of wild olive was first introduced on the advice of the Delphic oracle. The branches of which the crowns were made were cut from the sacred olive-trees with a golden sickle, by a boy whose parents were both living. This was henceforth the only prize given at Olympia. Of the rewards and honours bestowed by the victor's countrymen, and of other details connected with the games, we shall speak in another chapter. Our knowledge is not sufficient for a description of the festival at this early period.

The athletic records of Olympia date from the year 776 B.C., the 28th Olympiad from the organization of the games by Iphitus. This Olympiad, in which Coroebus of Elis won the foot-race, is counted as the first Olympiad in the Olympic register,[58] and from this date we have a complete list of winners in this race copied by Eusebius from the work of Julius Africanus, who brought the register down to the year 217 A.D. The register was originally compiled by Hippias of Elis at the close of the fifth century. It was revised and brought up to date by various writers from Aristotle and Philochorus down to Phlegon of Tralles in the time of Hadrian and Julius Africanus in the third century A.D. A list of victors was set up at Olympia by Paraballon, an Olympic victor, and the father of the boy victor Lastratidas, whose date is fixed by Hyde in the first half of the fourth century B.C.[59] It was not till the third century B.C. that the Olympic register was used as a means of reckoning dates, the year being dated by the number of the Olympiad and the name of the winner of the stade-race. Hence the preservation by Eusebius of the names of the winners of this race. The earlier lists, as we know from fragments of Phlegon and a fragment recently found on an Oxyrhynchus papyrus, contained the names of winners in other events.

The value of the early portions of the register has been called in question by Mahaffy, Busolt, and Körte, who, starting from Plutarch's sceptical remark that Hippias had no sure basis for his work, contend that no credit should be attached to the records previous to the sixth century. They have proved that the register was imperfect—it could hardly have been otherwise; that the task of compiling it was difficult—men like Hippias and Aristotle would not otherwise have devoted their time to it. But we can hardly believe that Hippias could have imposed a purely fictitious list of victors on the critical Greek world at the end of the fifth century, or that Aristotle would have revised it without some evidence for his work. What sort of record was kept by the priests of Olympia, and when it began, we cannot say. The use of writing at Olympia is proved for the seventh century by the diskos of Iphitus and the decrees or Φράτραι of the Eleans with regard to the sacred truce. The official register of Athenian archons dates from 683 B.C., if not earlier, and recent discoveries as to the antiquity of writing in Crete make us hesitate to deny the existence of written records for the eighth century. Besides official lists there must have been many local lists of victors, family records, genealogies, besides inscriptions on monuments. Of the first sixteen victors in the register four at least are connected by Pausanias with monuments or inscriptions, possibly not contemporary with the people commemorated but yet valuable as evidence. If you set up a monument to your great-grandfather, it may be of great importance to a future antiquarian in

---

[57] Paus. i. 44; *Anth. Pal.* App. 272; Thuc. i. 6.
[58] For a full discussion of the register, its history and its sources, *vide* Jüthner, *Philostratus*, pp. 60-70.
[59] *De Olympionicarum Statuis*, p. 36.

making out your genealogy. Most people in the present day have no knowledge of their great-grandfathers, or prefer to forget their existence; but in a tribal society with intense respect for birth it is very different, especially in a poetical race. Their only history is the history of the family and clan; family traditions and genealogies are remembered and handed down with a care and accuracy unknown to our cosmopolitan civilization. Such were the sources from which the sophist must have collected material for his register in his travels, and though his list may have been imperfect and often inaccurate, it is yet sufficiently accurate to afford valuable indications of the growth and development of the festival.

In two points we may certainly reject the evidence of the register, and of Elean tradition. During the period of war and confusion preceding Iphitus, they said, the games had been forgotten. For many Olympiads the only competition was the stade-race, but gradually, as the memory of the old games came back to them, one event after another was added. In Ol. 14 the double race (δίαυλος) was added, in Ol. 15 the long race (δολιχός), in Ol. 18 the pentathlon and wrestling, in Ol. 23 boxing, in Ol. 25 the four-horse chariot-race, in Ol. 33 the pankration and the horse-race, in Ol. 37 the first events for boys, the foot-race and wrestling, in Ol. 38 the pentathlon for boys, which, however, was not repeated, in Ol. 41 the boys' boxing, in Ol. 65 the race in armour. After this date various events for horses and mules were introduced at different times, competitions for heralds and trumpeters, and in Ol. 145 the pankration for boys.

The first part of this account is obviously absurd in view of the evidence given above for funeral games. There can be no doubt that in the first Olympiad the programme included at least all the events described by Pindar, the foot-race, the diskos, the spear, boxing, wrestling, and the chariot-race. If the Olympic games did develop from a single event, it was probably not from the foot-race, but from the armed fight or the chariot-race. Probably the compiler dated the introduction of each new event from the first occasion on which he found a mention of it. This may explain the number of first events won by Sparta, a state particularly well known to Hippias, one, too, where we should expect athletic records to be kept with especial care. On the other hand, there is no doubt that the programme received many additions, variations of the foot-race such as the double race and the long race, complicated events such as the pentathlon and pankration, especially boys' events, and there is no valid reason for doubting the date of such additions.

Connected with this story of the evolution of the games is the precedence given to the stade-race, the winner of which gave his name to the Olympiad. This custom, as we have seen, is not earlier than the third century, and arose not from the excessive importance of that event, but from the mere accident of its coming first on the programme and also on the list of victors. The Greek sportsman had doubtless long been in the habit of dating the years by reference to the victory of some famous athlete, especially if he were a fellow-countryman. Thucydides twice quotes in dates Olympic victories, each time victories in the pankration, an event very popular at Athens. In the earliest inscription that uses the Olympiads for chronology the pankration is also the event mentioned.[60] Hence one is inclined to suspect the completeness of the list of winners in the stade-race. Possibly early records and traditions often stated the fact of a victory without mentioning the event in which it was won, and the compiler of the register, having adopted his theory of development, assumed that all such victories were won in the foot-race.

---

[60] Thuc. iii. 8, v. 49; Ditt. *Syll.*, 2nd Ed., 256.

In 776 B.C. Olympia itself had as yet changed but little. The only building was the Heraeum, a long, low, narrow temple built originally of wood. One of the wooden pillars was still standing in the time of Pausanias. As the wooden pillars decayed they were replaced by stone pillars. Hence the pillars, many of which are still standing, differed in size, in material, in their fluting and their capitals, the earliest belonging in style to the seventh or sixth centuries, the latest to the Roman period. The temple was a treasure-house. There was kept the diskos of Iphitus, and at a later period the chest of Cypselus, and the table of ivory and gold on which the crowns for the victors were placed. Of the wealth of votive offerings and statues that once adorned this temple nearly all have perished; but there, at the exact spot described by Pausanias, the German excavators found the Hermes of Praxiteles, which represents the most perfect type of that physical beauty and harmonious development that Greek athletics produced.

The number of altars had no doubt grown. The altar of Zeus already rivalled, if it did not eclipse, the earlier altar of Hera and the tomb of Pelops. This altar stood on a double elliptical base of stone, the lower base 125 feet, the upper 32 feet in circumference. The altar itself was built up of the ashes of the victims which were brought once every year by the seers from the Prytaneum, kneaded with water from the Alpheus and deposited on the altar. In the time of Pausanias it had reached a height of 22 feet.

There was as yet no race-course at Olympia. The races and games must have taken place in the open space that stretched from the altar of Zeus and tomb of Pelops, below the slopes of the hill of Cronus, from which the spectators doubtless looked on. The races probably finished at the altar, and there, under the immediate protection of Zeus, the victors were crowned. The race, according to a tradition related by Philostratus,[61] originated in a torch-race, in which the competitors, starting from the distance of a stade, raced with lighted torches to the altar, the one who arrived first and lighted the fire receiving the prize; similarly for the double race or diaulos, the runners raced from the altar to summon to the sacrifice the deputations from Greek states and then raced back to the altar; while the long race originated in the practice of the heralds whose office it was to carry declarations of war to different parts of Greece. Of such ceremonial races we shall find examples in many parts of Greece, but the tradition deriving from them the races at Olympia may be rejected as a late invention, which perhaps had its origin in the fact that before the stadium was constructed the races did finish at the altar. Certainly in Pindar's time boxing and similar events still took place there, and it is doubtful whether they were ever transferred to the stadium.

For the first half-century Olympia remained the local festival of the Elean and pre-Dorian countryfolk of the West. The first victor was Coroebus of Elis,[62] whose tomb appropriately marked the boundary between Elis and Heraea, a symbol of the truce between the two races. Yet the Eleans could not appeal to their athletic records in support of their claims. Of the first eleven victors only one other was an Elean, while the older race was represented by seven Messenians, one Achaean from Dyme, and one native of Dyspontium, a town near the mouth of the Alpheus that belonged to the Pisatan league. According to a scandalous tradition quoted by Athenaeus, Coroebus was a cook, but the scanty records which we possess of these earlier victors prove that the games still maintained their aristocratic character, and the

---

[61] *Gym.* 4.
[62] Paus. v. 8, 6; viii. 26, 3; Athen. ix. 382 B. Details with regard to the various victors mentioned in this and the following chapters may be found under their names in Krause, *Olympia*, H. Förster, *Olympische Sieger*, and W. Hyde, *De Olympionicarum Statuis*, in all of which full references are given.

tradition may be set aside as the invention of the enemies of Elis, or the anti-athletic party of a later age.

After Ol. 11 only one Messenian victory is chronicled till the restoration of Messenia in the fourth century. Hypenos, who won the double race on its introduction in Ol. 15, was a Pisatan, though Elis tried to claim him. With these exceptions the old stock disappears, and the Eleans are too supine, or too much occupied with feuds with Argos, to take their place. Yet the athletic vigour of the old race reappears afterwards from other quarters in families like the Diagoridae of Rhodes who were descended from a daughter of the Messenian patriot Aristomenes, in colonies like Achaean Croton, in the late successes of Arcadia at a time when athletics had become a sufficiently lucrative profession to tempt from their poor homes these hardy mountaineers and shepherds. Perhaps the long roll of Spartan successes owed something to the Messenians whom they had conquered. The records of their ancient successes were doubtless jealously treasured by those who had left their homes, and we may well suppose that from such records the early part of the Olympic register was compiled.

The eclipse of the "home counties," as we may call them, was partly due to the growing importance of the festival, partly to the pressure of Argos and Sparta. Of the part played by Argos we know but little; what we do know is that Pheidon of Argos, whenever he lived, like other tyrants tried to exploit the festival for the extension of his own dominion, that he espoused the cause of the Pisatans, and that there was a feud between the Eleans and the Argives,[63] which perhaps explains the complete absence of Argos in the list of early victors. Elis found a natural ally in Sparta. The valleys of the Eurotas and the Alpheus form a direct means of communication between Sparta and Olympia, and the control of this route by Sparta after the conquest of Messenia gave her a natural advantage over her rival.

The influence of Olympia spread first along the northern coast of the Peloponnese, secondly to Sparta. In the second half-century, Ol. 13-25, Corinth, Megara, Epidaurus, Sicyon, Hyperesia, Athens, Thebes, figure in the list of victors, and yet farther east, Smyrna. All these places communicate with Olympia by the Gulf of Corinth. It is significant that this extension of its influence eastwards coincides with the founding of the first Greek colonies in Italy and Sicily. The Corinthians, passing along the north coast of the gulf to Corcyra, crossed over and founded Syracuse 734 B.C. Six years later the Megarians founded a new Megara beside the hills of Hybla, and a century later the two Megaras combined to colonize Selinus. The Achaeans, making a stepping-stone of Zacynthos, founded the rich cities of Sybaris and Croton, and later Metapontum, and built on the Lacinian promontory south of Croton a temple of Hera, which became a centre of worship for the Greeks of Italy. Even the Eastern Greeks of the islands took part in this movement. Gela was colonized by settlers from Rhodes and Crete. All these colonies and many others played a great part in the history of Olympia, the importance of which we can see, not only in their list of victories, but in the remains of the so-called treasuries which they built there, and it is hardly fanciful to suppose that their connexion with Olympia dated from the time when the settlers were leaving the shores of Greece.

The victory of Onomastus of Smyrna in Ol. 23 is no less significant of the full communication existing between the mainland and the East at the commencement of the seventh century.[64] Eastern despots sent offerings to Delphi; poets from the islands and Asia

---

[63] Paus. v. 2 and 3.
[64] Bury, *History of Greece*, p. 110.

Minor brought into Greece the Phrygian and Aeolian modes of music; even the alphabet came from the East. At Olympia, when the victors' friends held revel in their honour in the evening, they sang down to the time of Pindar the triumphal song of Heracles composed by Archilochus of Paros.[65] Smyrna, at that time the foremost city of the Eastern coast, was closely connected with the Peloponnese. The poet Mimnermus tells us that his race had come from Neleian Pylos to Colophon first, and had then dispossessed the Aeolian inhabitants of Smyrna.[66]

The first appearance of Thebes is on the occasion of the introduction of the chariot-race in Ol. 25. As we have seen, the chariot-race seems to have been one of the earliest, if not the earliest, event at the Olympia, and one is inclined to suspect that the innovation consisted in the substitution of the four-horse chariot for the older two-horse chariot, which was revived at Olympia in later times.

Thus we see that within a century of the first Olympiad, Olympia had become a centre to which competitors came not only from the Peloponnese, but from Athens, Thebes, and even from the East.

The long list of Spartan successes begins in Ol. 15 (720 B.C.), and continues till Ol. 50 (576 B.C.), from which date they cease almost entirely. During most of this period the superiority of Sparta is undisputed. This superiority may be partially explained by the careful records of athletic victories kept in that most methodical of states, whereas the records of other states were less careful and less accessible to the historian. Yet making full allowance for our imperfect knowledge of other states, the Spartan successes are sufficiently remarkable, and their sudden cessation hardly less so. Aristotle has given us the explanation of these facts.[67] Sparta was the first Greek state to introduce a systematic physical and military training, which for a time made her unrivalled in sport and war; when other states followed her example, her superiority disappeared. Moreover, in the seventh century Sparta was still a progressive, enlightened state, fond of poetry and music, taking an energetic part in all the manifold activities of Greek life; only the good effects of her system were yet apparent; its iron rule had not yet produced that narrow spirit of exclusiveness which was fatal to progress.[68] Hence Spartan participation in the Olympic festival not only raised the prestige of the festival, but gave a new importance and seriousness to athletics. Hitherto they had been a diversion of the nobles; henceforth they were to be part of the education of the people. The physical education of Greece was largely due to Spartan example. At the beginning of the sixth century we find Solon making laws for the palaestrae and gymnasia, and we may suspect that most important cities possessed these institutions.

Sparta is credited with no less than five victories in events said to be introduced for the first time—the long race in Ol. 15, wrestling and the pentathlon in Ol. 18, the boys' wrestling in Ol. 37, and the boys' pentathlon in Ol. 38. The latter event was abolished in the next Olympiad owing to Elean jealousy at the success of the Spartan boy Eutelidas. Perhaps the various events for boys were introduced for the benefit of the home counties which had been

---

[65] Pindar, *Ol.* ix. The date of Archilochus is fixed by Hauvette in the first half of the seventh century. *Cl. Rev.* xxi. p. 143.
[66] Mimnermus, *Fr.* 9 (Bergk).
[67] Aristot. *Politics*, v. 4.
[68] The recent excavations at Sparta prove that the decline of athletics coincided with the decline of art. Mr. R. M. Dawkins, writing in last report of the *B.S.A.*, vol. xiv. p. 2, says: "In every case we have the remarkable result that the finest works belong to the seventh century, and that the sixth already shows the beginning of the decline which is so marked in the very poor character of the finds of the fifth century."

ousted by increased competition from without, and if so we can understand a certain feeling of soreness at the Spartan success, especially as Eutelidas won the boys' wrestling in the same Olympiad. The statue in his honour at Olympia was the oldest of all the statues of athletes; it seems to have stood originally on the site occupied by the temple of Zeus, and on the building of the temple to have been moved to the south.[69] Special notice is due to Hipposthenes, the victor in the boys' wrestling in Ol. 37, who subsequently won five more victories in wrestling at Olympia, and who had a temple built in his honour at Sparta. His son almost equalled his father's record, winning five victories in wrestling.[70] Another equally famous athlete was Chionis, who won four victories in the stade-race and three in the double race, besides victories in other sports, Ols. 28-31. He is said to have taken part with Battus in the colonization of Cyrene, and his exploits were commemorated at a later date by his countrymen on stone pillars at Sparta and at Olympia, where they also set up in his honour a statue, the work of Myron.

Meanwhile, during the period of Spartan pre-eminence, the influence of Olympia had been steadily spreading, especially among the colonies of the West. In Ol. 33 two new events were added—the riding race, which was won by a Thessalian from Crannon, and the pankration, a combination of boxing and wrestling, which was won by Lygdamis of Syracuse, who was said to have had the proportions of Heracles, his foot, like that of the hero, being exactly an Olympic foot. The various events for boys were introduced between Ol. 37 and Ol. 41, and in the boys' boxing the first winner came from Sybaris. Croton had already begun her victorious career. From Miletus in Ol. 46 came the boy runner Polymnestor, who, as a shepherd boy, was said to have captured hares by speed of foot; while from Samos came the effeminate-looking Pythagoras with his long hair and purple robes. Rejected from the boys' boxing as a weakling, he entered for the men's competition and won it. So rapid was the progress of the colonies, and so keen their participation in the Olympic festival, that from Ol. 50 they outstripped the mother country, and the following century may be described as the colonial period of Olympia. The first attempt made by any Greek state to secure for itself a local habitation at Olympia was the building of a treasury by the Geloans at the close of the seventh century. Before the close of the sixth their example had been followed by Metapontum, Selinus, Sybaris, Byzantium and Cyrene, the only representatives of the Peloponnese being the Megarians. Nothing indicates more clearly the predominance of the colonies than this line of treasuries, or rather communal houses,[71] standing on a terrace at the foot of the hill of Cronus between the Heraeum and the entrance of the later stadium, and commanding a view of the Altis, of the altars, and the games. One wonders if the Spartans indulged in lamentations over the decay of Spartan athletics. I think not, for that reserved and silent people had too much pride and dourness; moreover athletics to them were but a means to an end, the training of soldier citizens. Certainly from this date they ceased to figure in the victors' lists, engrossed perhaps in more serious contests and schemes of aggrandizement, or else estranged from the festival by the new democratic, Panhellenic spirit introduced there by the colonies, and unwilling to suffer defeat at the hands of upstarts.

The influence of the colonies was great. Their competition gave a fresh impulse to that wave of athleticism which reached its height in the sixth century. To Olympia they gave a

---

[69] Hyde, *op. cit.* p. 56.
[70] Paus. iii. 13, 9.
[71] For the treasuries at Olympia *vide* Louis Dyer, in *J.H.S.* vols. xxv. and xxvi.

Panhellenic character as a meeting-place for all the scattered members of the Greek race, and thereby tended to preserve and strengthen that feeling of unity which contact with other nations had already quickened into life. No foreigner could enter as a competitor at Olympia, no barbarous potentates sent offerings to its shrines or consulted its oracle. Olympia remained throughout its history purely and exclusively Hellenic. Again, the colonies brought Olympia into touch with the democratic spirit of the age, and broke down the barriers of Elean and Spartan exclusiveness. The colonial claimed admission purely by virtue of his Greek birth, and no distinctions of rank or caste or wealth were known in the Olympic games. Sport, especially national sport, is a great leveller of social distinctions.

The political importance of such a festival, which drew competitors and spectators from all quarters of the Greek world, could not escape the notice of the clear-sighted and ambitious tyrants and nobles of the seventh century. But the sanctity of the place and the new democratic spirit of the festival were too strong for them. Pheidon of Argos had tried to make himself master of Olympia by force of arms. Other tyrants tried more peaceful means, seeking to win popularity among the assembled crowds and influence with the powers of Olympia by victories in the chariot-race, or by sumptuous offerings to Olympian Zeus. In the middle of the seventh century Myron of Sicyon won a victory in the chariot-race and commemorated his success by dedicating two treasure-chests of solid bronze, one of which weighed 500 talents. These treasure-chests were afterwards placed in the treasure-house of the Sicyonians, built in the fifth century possibly in the place of some more ancient structure. The excavations of Olympia have revealed the solid floor intended to bear the weight of these treasure-chests. His grandson Cleisthenes, himself a victor, took advantage of the festival to proclaim the famous competition for the hand of his daughter Agariste, which Herodotus describes. Cypselus of Corinth, too, dedicated at Olympia a golden statue of Zeus made in the style of the early metal-workers, of beaten gold plates riveted together. His son Periander was victor in the chariot-race, and gave to Olympia the famous chest of Cypselus in which, according to the story, the infant Cypselus had been hidden by his mother from the assassins sent by the oligarchs of Corinth to murder him. From Athens came the would-be tyrant Cylon, who won the diaulos race in Ol. 35; and in the next generation the chariot-race was won by Alcmaeon, the son of that Megacles who was responsible as archon for the death of Cylon and the consequent pollution of the Alcmaeonidae, and the father of Megacles, the successful suitor of Agariste. Yet, in spite of their victories and their offerings, no tyrant secured influence at Olympia, no building there bore a tyrant's name. The so-called treasuries were the communal houses of states, that of the Megarians, which dates about this time, being set up probably not by the tyrant Theagenes but by the people after his fall, and before their power was weakened by the successes of Athens.

Thus at the beginning of the sixth century Olympia had acquired a unique position as the national festival of Hellas. Competitors and spectators of all classes gathered there from every part of Greece. The sacred truce-bearers proclaimed the month of peace throughout the Greek world, and in response, cities of Asia and of Sicily vied with one another in the splendour of the official embassies (θεωρίαι) sent to represent them at the festival. The old aristocratic character survived in the chariot-race and horse-race, which afforded to tyrants and nobles an opportunity of displaying their riches and their power. The athletic programme was now practically complete, the only important innovation of later times being the race in full armour introduced 520 B.C., and this programme was truly democratic. In athletic events noble and peasant met on equal terms. The aristocratic prejudice against these popular contests did not yet exist; and though the honour of the Olympic crown was open to the poorest citizen of Greek birth, such was the prestige of the festival that it was coveted even by the highest. The representative character of Olympia was due to a variety of causes. The geographical position of the place, its ancient sanctity, the athletic vigour of the pre-Dorian Greeks, the discipline and training of the Spartans, the enthusiastic patriotism of the colonies, the ambition of tyrants, the new spirit of democracy,—these and other causes contributed to the result, and the importance of the result was recognized by the founding within the next half-century of three other Panhellenic festivals at Delphi, at Nemea, and at the Isthmus, and of many another festival which, like the Panathenaea, aspired to but never attained Panhellenic dignity.

Yet, despite the growth of the festival and the development of athletics, there was little change in the appearance of the Altis or the organization of the games. Some of the wooden pillars of the Heraeum were perhaps replaced by stone, but no fresh building appeared till the treasuries, the earliest of which date from the close of the seventh century. The games still took place near the altar, where a course could be easily measured and marked out before each meeting. The new events added were merely variations of those which we find in Homer. Popularity and competition had no doubt improved the standard of performance, but athletic training did not yet exist. In the towns, indeed, gymnasia and palaestrae were already springing up; but these were educational rather than athletic, intended to train and discipline the young as useful soldiers rather than to produce champion athletes. The bulk of the population living an open-air country life in which war, hunting, and games played a considerable part, had no need of training. Thus, though athletics had become popular, they still maintained the spontaneity and joy of the Homeric age: they were still pure recreation.

Chapter 4

THE AGE OF ATHLETIC FESTIVALS, SIXTH CENTURY B.C.

The sixth century is the age of organized athletics. The rise of Sparta and her success in sport and war gave to the Greek world an object lesson on the value of systematic training, and henceforth the training of the body was an essential part of Greek education. Palaestrae and gymnasia were established everywhere, and Solon found it necessary to lay down laws for their conduct. These institutions were originally intended for the training of the young, but the growth of athletic competition soon called into being a new and specialized form of training, the training of competitors for the great games. An art of training sprung up, and in the time of Pindar the professors of the new art, besides reaping a rich harvest from their pupils, received honour scarcely inferior to that of the victors themselves. The rapid development of the Olympic festival had shown the value of athletics as a bond of union between Greeks throughout the world, and the general yearning after a unity which was destined never to be realized found expression in the establishment of other festivals for which Olympia served as a model.

At Delphi, the Isthmus, and Nemea, local festivals and competitions had long existed.[72] The oracle of Delphi had already acquired a Panhellenic, almost a cosmopolitan importance, rivalling that of Olympia. The Pythian festival was said to have been founded to commemorate Apollo's victory over the Python. To expiate the death of the dragon, Apollo had been condemned to nine years of exile, and the festival was therefore held every ninth year, or, according to our reckoning, once in eight years. Later legend asserted that there had been athletic games at Delphi, and various heroes were named as victors in these sports. But it seems probable that the original competitions at Delphi were purely musical, and in the hymn for Apollo Delphusa expressly commends Delphi as the home for the god on the ground that there his altar will be undisturbed by the "whirling of fair chariots or the sound of swift-footed steeds." The innate ambition of the Greek and his desire to outshine his fellows found vent in competitions of every sort. Musical competitions were specially connected with the worship of Apollo at Delos and at Sparta; at Delphi a prize was given for a hymn to Apollo chanted to the accompaniment of the cithara.

---

[72] The legends connected with these festivals are collected in Krause, *Pythien*, and the various articles on them in Dar.-Sagl.

Such the festival remained till the outbreak of the first Sacred war. The war was due to the impious conduct of the Crisaeans, who, having command of the plain and the harbour of Cirrha, had enriched themselves at the expense of the Delphians and Apollo, by levying exorbitant tolls on the pilgrims who landed at Cirrha on their way to the oracle. The Delphians appealed to their natural protectors, the Amphictyonic League at Thermopylae, who straightway proclaimed a sacred war. The command of the expedition was given to the Thessalian Eurylochus; the Athenians, on the advice of Solon, sent a contingent under Alcmaeon, while Cleisthenes, the ambitious tyrant of Sicyon, eagerly embraced the opportunity of posing as a champion of Greek religion. The festival was restored and reorganized in 590 B.C. New musical events were added, a solo on the flute and a song accompanied by the flute; athletic and equestrian competitions also were introduced on the model of those at Olympia; but since Delphi as yet had no stadium, the games were held in the plain of Crisa below. The chariot-race for some reason or other was omitted, but two additional athletic events found a place, a long race and a diaulos race for boys.

The war, however, broke out afresh and lasted for six years, at the end of which, in 582, the festival was finally reorganized out of the spoil of Crisa as a pentaëteris, and placed under the control of the Amphictyons. The year 582 dates as the first Pythiad, and from this time the festival was held every fourth year, in the August of the third year of each Olympiad. The valuable prizes which had been offered of old were abolished, and in their place was substituted a crown of bay leaves plucked from the Vale of Tempe. The somewhat scanty details which we possess as to the festival and its history will be discussed in a later chapter. For the present it is sufficient to note one significant fact: the chariot-race which had been omitted in 590 was introduced in 582, and the first victor was Cleisthenes of Sicyon himself. The plains of Sicyon were admirably adapted for breeding horses, a pursuit which afforded its tyrants a ready means of increasing and displaying their wealth. Myron had already gained a victory in the chariot-race at Olympia, and his grandson Cleisthenes, shortly after his Pythian success, secured the same honour on the occasion when he issued his invitation to the suitors for the hand of Agariste. At Sicyon itself he commemorated the part which he had played in the Sacred war by a splendid colonnade built out of the spoils of Cirrha, and at the same time he reorganized as a local Pythia an ancient festival connected with the Argive hero Adrastus, whose memory he delighted to insult.[73] We may therefore safely regard the introduction of the chariot-race at Delphi as due to the tyrant's influence, and the remodelling of the festival as part of his pushing Panhellenic policy.

Almost at the same time, perhaps in the same year, 582 B.C., the Isthmian festival was reorganized. This festival, which claimed an antiquity greater even than that of Olympia, was celebrated at the sanctuary of Poseidon, which stood in a grove of pine-trees at the south-east of the Isthmus, a little to the south of the eastern end of the present Corinth canal. The various legends of its origin are all connected directly or indirectly with the worship of Poseidon. The wreath of dry celery leaves, which in the time of Pindar was the prize, recalled the story that the games were first founded in honour of the luckless Melicertes at the spot to which his dead body was carried by a dolphin. According to another legend they were instituted by the Attic hero Theseus, when he had freed the land from the terror of the robber Sinis. This story points to the close connexion of the Isthmia with Athens. The Athenian envoys enjoyed the

---

[73] The victory of Chromius of Aetna, celebrated by Pindar, *Nem.* ix., was won not at Nemea but at the Sicyonian Pythia.

privilege of precedence (προεδρία) at this festival, and a space was reserved for them, as much as could be covered by the sail of the ship which brought them to the Isthmus. No other festival was so conveniently situated for the Athenians. Athens and Corinth had much in common, and were on most friendly terms before the relations between them were embittered by commercial rivalry, and their friendship was especially close in the period following the fall of the Cypselidae. Another version of the Theseus legend represents him as founding the Isthmia in rivalry of Heracles, who had founded the Olympic games; and here we may trace a certain jealousy existing between the two festivals.[74] We know on good authority that the Eleans were not allowed to compete at the Isthmia. This ban, which Elean tradition represented as a self-denying ordinance imposed by the curse of Molione, may well have originated in this rivalry. We can imagine that the Elean authorities regarded with no favour the rise of a rival festival on a site so central, the meeting-place of the trade of East and West. Yet, after all, Olympia had no reason to fear its rival. The central position of Corinth involving her in all the feuds and wars of Greek history, prevented the Isthmia from ever acquiring that unique independence which characterized the more remote Olympia. There can be little doubt, too, that from the first the festival reflected the luxurious commercial character of Corinth. There the joyous life of the Ionian race found vent in a sort of cosmopolitan carnival which contrasted strangely with the more strenuous Dorian festival of remote Olympia.

The remodelled festival was a trieteris, held in the spring of the second and fourth years of each Olympiad. The programme was a varied one, including, besides athletics and horse-races, musical competitions, and possibly a regatta. The presidency of the festival belonged to the Corinthians. Whether its establishment as a Panhellenic festival was due to the tyrant Periander or expressed the joy of the people at their liberation from his rule, the evidence does not allow us to determine. The latter seems to me more probable. The great tyrant, laid by his victory in the chariot-race at Olympia, and by costly offerings to Olympia and Delphi, tried to win the support of the authorities at these places, and it may well be that the founding of a rival festival marked the popular reaction against his policy. Be this as it may, the establishment of the Isthmia is another sign of the great national movement towards unity. Tyrants recognized and tried to utilize the movement for their own advantage. But Panhellenism was independent of tyrants; it was a spontaneous movement of the people, and it need cause no surprise that one Panhellenic festival should owe its origin to a tyrant, another to the people.

A similar doubt attaches to the last of the Greek festivals, the Nemea. The cypress grove of Nemea, where stood the temple of the Nemean Zeus, lay in a secluded valley among the hills, half-way between Phlius and Cleonae. Here under the presidency of the latter state local games had long been celebrated. They were said to have been founded by Adrastus as funeral games in honour of the child Opheltes, who, having been left by his nurse in the grove, had been devoured by a serpent. According to another story, they were founded by Heracles after his slaying of the Nemean lion, and by him dedicated to Zeus. They were reorganized in the year 573 B.C. as a trieteris, and took place like the Isthmia in the second and fourth year of each Olympiad, probably at the very beginning of the Olympic year in July. The prize was a

---

[74] The existence of such rivalry is suggested by the quarrel recorded by Pausanias v. 2, 3, with regard to the colossal statue set up by Cypselus at Olympia, and in the account given by Herodotus ix. 81 of the distribution of the Persian spoils. A statue of Zeus 10 cubits high is set up at Olympia, while that of Poseidon at the Isthmus is only 7 cubits high. So Pindar, *Ol.* xiii. 25, prays that Zeus may not be jealous if he sings the praise of Corinth.

wreath of fresh celery, but was said to have been originally a wreath of olive. As at Olympia, the managers of the games bore the title of Hellanodicae. As at Olympia, the contests were until later times purely athletic and equestrian. The striking resemblances to Olympia are clearly due to Dorian influence, and may perhaps help us to understand how it was that, within a few years of the founding of the Isthmia, a second Panhellenic festival was established in its immediate neighbourhood.

The little town of Cleonae, which held the presidency of the Nemea down to the time of Pindar, could certainly never have raised its festival unaided to Panhellenic dignity. Cleonae seems to have been for a time under the dominion of Cleisthenes of Sicyon; yet it seems hardly likely that the tyrant, who had already helped in establishing the Pythia at Delphi, besides a local Pythia at Sicyon, and whose policy was so markedly anti-Dorian, should have founded a second Panhellenic festival of so purely Dorian a type. Moreover, it seems that Cleonae had already thrown off the yoke of Cleisthenes, whose power was on the decline. Argos, too, was on the decline, and though Argos in the year 460 B.C. usurped the presidency of the games, we find similar claims put forward by Corinth and by Mycenae. The fact that so many states claimed the presidency of the festival suggests that its re-establishment was not the work of any one state but of the Dorians of the north-eastern Peloponnese generally. If we are right about the jealousy felt by the authorities of Olympia towards the newly-founded Isthmia, and the character of the latter festival, we may perhaps see in the founding of the Nemea the protest of Dorian puritanism against innovations which seemed to degrade the serious business of athletics. Scandalized by the laxness of the new festival, with its traffic and its pleasures and its multitude of entertainments, the Dorians of Argolis conceived the idea of founding at Cleonae an eastern counterpart of Olympia. The strenuousness of athletics in Argolis is surely indicated in the strength and severity characterizing the athletic school of sculpture which had its origin in Sicyon and Argos, half-way between which places appropriately lay Cleonae. The view suggested above is of course hypothetical, but it accords with what we know of the Isthmia and the Nemea, and satisfactorily explains the Panhellenic character of the latter.

Olympiad.	B.C.				
55. 1	560/559		560	Late Summer	Olympia.
2	559/8	{	559	Summer	Nemea.
		{	558	Spring	Isthmia.
3	558/7		558	August	Pythia.
4	557/6	{	557	Summer	Nemea.
		{	556	Spring	Isthmia.
56. 1	556/5		556	Late Summer	Olympia.

Thus by the year 570 the four Panhellenic festivals were established. They were distinctively the sacred meetings (ἱεροὶ ἀγῶνες) and the games of the crown (στεφανῖται), so called to distinguish them from the numerous games where prizes of value were given (θεματικοί). It is no little proof of the true athletic feeling of the Greeks that in their four greatest festivals no prize was given but the simple crown of leaves. The cycle of these festivals will be best understood by a glance at the following table, which shows the order of the festivals during a single Olympiad.[75] It must be remembered that the Greek year began with the summer solstice, and consequently belongs half to one, half to the next year, according to our reckoning.

Thus we see that in the even years there were two Panhellenic festivals, in the odd years one.

The competition of other Panhellenic festivals threatened the supremacy of Olympia, and forced the easy-going conservative authorities of that place into activity. Hitherto they had allowed the festival to develop from without; they had allowed Gela and Megara to build treasuries overlooking the Altis, and so to establish some sort of claim to a share in the management; content with their traditional customs they had made no attempt to provide adequate organization for an athletic meeting of such importance. Now they saw that if they were to maintain their position they must set their house in order. A significant story is told by Herodotus.[76] In the reign of Psammetichus II. (594-589 B.C.) some Elean ambassadors visited Egypt to see if the Egyptians could suggest any improvement in the rules for the Olympic games, which they boasted were the fairest and best that could be devised. The Egyptians, after considering a while, asked if they allowed their own citizens to compete. The Eleans replied that the games were open to all Greeks, whether they belonged to Elis or any other state. To this the Egyptians, with true commercial instinct, answered that the rules were far from just, for that it was impossible but that they would favour their own countrymen and deal unfairly with foreigners; if, therefore, they wished to manage the games with fairness they must confine the games to strangers and allow no native of Elis to compete. It is to the credit of the Greeks that no such self-denying ordinance was introduced or found to be necessary, and that the Greeks themselves never raised any such objection till a much later date. It is only when sport becomes too competitive and too lucrative and the professional and commercial spirit enters in that elaborate safeguards are required against unfairness.

This story is valuable evidence that the Eleans were at this time seeking to improve their arrangements. What the improvements were we do not know, but that some sort of reorganization took place is rendered probable by the tradition recorded above, that in Ol. 50 a second Hellanodicas was first appointed. Possibly the Olympic Council was remodelled. We find this Council in the fourth century acting as a court of appeal, and in Imperial times it is mentioned in inscriptions as authorizing the setting up of honorific statues.[77] The Hellanodicae were its executive officers, and from their history and numbers it seems probable that the Council represented the various tribes which formed a sort of amphictyony originally controlling the festival. Their existence in the sixth century is proved by the remains of their Council-house. This building lay below the south wall of the Altis. It consists of two long buildings, terminated at the west end by an apse, parallel to each other, and united by a square chamber between them. The northern wing of the building dates from the middle of the sixth century at the latest. The apsidal chamber at the end was divided by a partition, and served probably for the storage of archives and treasure, while the rest of the building formed the business quarters of the Council and the Hellanodicae. There the competitors had to appear and take an oath before the altar of Zeus Horkios that they had observed, and would observe the conditions of the festival. Another building connected with the permanent

---

[75] Adapted from Jebb's *Bacchylides*.
[76] Hdt. ii. 160.
[77] Louis Dyer, "The Olympic Council" in *Harvard Studies*, 1907, p. 36; Paus. vi. 3, 7; *Ol. Ins.* 372-486 *passim*.

management of the festival was the Prytaneum, also built about the same time. In it was the altar of Hestia, on which the sacred fire was kept always burning. The ashes from this altar, collected and mixed with the water of the Alpheus, were used to build up the great altar of Zeus. Here, when the games were ended, distinguished guests and victors were feasted, and songs of victory were chanted in their honour.

The Council must have exercised a control over all new buildings erected at Olympia. In the second half of the sixth century fresh treasuries were built by the states of Selinus, Sybaris, Byzantium, and Cyrene, a list which sufficiently illustrates the widespread influence of the festival. The planning and alignment of these buildings clearly implies the supervision of some local authority.

Significant of the new energy of these authorities and of their desire to render Olympia itself worthy of the festival, was a practice, which began in this century, of allowing victors to commemorate their victories by votive statues. The earliest of these statues, according to Pausanias, were those of Praxidamas of Aegina, who won the boxing in Ol. 59, and of Rhexibius of Opus who won the pankration two Olympiads later. These statues were of wood, and we may, therefore, suspect that those seen by Pausanias were not really the first but only the oldest which had survived. Certainly there were statues of earlier victors. Some of these, like that of the Lacedaemonian Chionis, or that of the famous pankratiast Arrhichion, at his native home Phigalia, were set up by their countrymen many years after their death. Others, like that of the Spartan boy Eutelidas, who won the boys' wrestling and the boys' pentathlon, may have been contemporary. The first sculptors of athletic statues, whose names we know, are Chrysothemis and Eutelidas of Argos, who made the statues for the Heraean Damaretus, who won the race in armour in Ols. 65, 66, and for his son Theopompus, who won two victories in the pentathlon. On the inscriptions beneath these statues the artists claimed to have learnt their art from former artists. Argos and Sicyon, the homes of the earliest athletic sculpture, were, as we have seen, closely connected with the newly organized Panhellenic festivals, in addition to which there were a number of minor local festivals throughout that district. We may, therefore, safely connect the rise of the athletic school of art with the athletic movement that produced these festivals. These early statues were, of course, not portrait statues. We learn from Pliny that the right of setting up a portrait statue was confined to winners of a triple victory. The accuracy of this statement is open to doubt; certainly it cannot have been true before the fourth century, previous to which portrait statues were practically unknown. The early artists must have contented themselves with type statues, representing the various events in which victory had been gained.

Towards the close of the century certain additions were made to the programme. In Ol. 65 (520 B.C.) the race in heavy armour was introduced at Olympia, and in 498 B.C. at Delphi. This innovation was clearly due to the growing importance of the heavy-armed infantry in Greek warfare. Greek sports were, as we have seen, in their origin practical and military, but with changed conditions of warfare they had lost their military character and become purely athletic. The chieftain no longer went to war in his chariot; his men no longer threw stones or light javelins. Individual warfare was giving place to the manœuvring of masses of heavy-armed troops. The introduction of the race in armour was an attempt to restore to athletics their practical character. The race was a diaulos, i.e., up the stadium and back to the starting-point, a distance of about four hundred yards. The men wore helmets, greaves, and round shields. At a later time the greaves were discarded, perhaps as a concession to athletes who regarded such a race as a spurious sort of athletics. Certainly the race never attained to the same prestige as the other events.

In Ol. 70 (500 B.C.) a mule chariot-race (ἀπήνη) was introduced, and in the next Olympiad a riding race for mares (κάλπη), in which the riders dismounted in the last lap and ran with their steeds. In both these events, which were discontinued after a short trial in Ol. 84, we may see the influence of the Elean nobility, whose wealth and power were derived largely from their horses and cattle. The introduction of mule chariot-races may have been partly due to the influence of the Lords of Sicily; the victory of Anaxilas is commemorated on the coins of Rhegium and Messana (Figure 168). The κάλπη is of especial interest. Helbig has shown that the Hippeis of Athens and other Greek states in the sixth century were not cavalry soldiers in the strict sense of the word, but mounted infantry, the true successors of the Homeric chieftains.[78] Just as the latter went to war in their chariots, but dismounted in order to fight, leaving the chariot in charge of the charioteer, and remounting for flight or for pursuit, so the Hippeis of the sixth century merely used their horses for advance or for retreat, dismounting when they came into close contact with the foe, and leaving their horses with their squires, who accompanied them, either mounted behind them *en croupe*, or on horses of their own. The Homeric custom survived only in sports, in the ἀποβατής, whom we see represented on the frieze of the Parthenon in the act of dismounting; the later custom was represented for a brief time only by the κάλπη. As we have seen in discussing the race in armour, the system of individual warfare was passing away. Sparta had shown the superiority of masses of armed infantry. Previous to the Persian wars, Thessalian cavalry had already been employed by Peisistratus, and these served in the fifth century as the model on which corps of cavalry proper were organized in Athens and other states. But in 500 B.C. there were no cavalry in the Peloponnese, and the conservative nobles may well have regarded with jealousy a change which threatened to put them on a level with the ordinary foot-soldier. The introduction of the κάλπη then was an attempt to stimulate and encourage the older style of fighting. But the attempt was doomed to failure; the progress of military tactics was not to be checked by the Eleans, and while the hoplite race survived as long as the festival itself, the κάλπη was ignominiously abandoned in 444 B.C.

Besides the four great festivals of the Crown there were countless local festivals where competitions of various sorts were held.[79] The prizes offered were often tripods, and bowls of silver or of bronze; sometimes articles of local manufacture, such as a cloak at Pellene, a shield at Argos, vases of olive-oil at Athens; sometimes a portion of the victim sacrificed, or the victim to be sacrificed. The British Museum possesses a bronze caldron[80] of about the sixth century, which was found at Cyme in Italy, and was given as a prize at some local games founded by, or held in honour of, a certain Onomastus. It bears the inscription, "I was a prize at the games of Onomastus." Many of these festivals were connected with the cults of local heroes, and had existed for generations. Sometimes the competitions themselves bore a distinctly ritual character; thus the torch-race, which we meet with in many parts of Greece, was connected with the primitive custom of periodically distributing new and holy fire from the sacred hearth where it had been kindled. Sometimes the competitions were musical, as at the Spartan Carnea; more frequently they were purely athletic. The athletic competitions

---

[78] W. Helbig, *Les Hippeis athéniens.*
[79] Pindar, *Ol.* ix, xiii. etc.
[80] *B.M. Bronzes*, 135.

acquired fresh life from the stimulus given to athletics by the growth of the Panhellenic festivals. At first purely local, even these minor gatherings in Pindar's time drew competitors from various parts of Greece. Many fresh festivals were added, and old ones reorganized during the sixth century, especially in the eastern parts of Greece, but of most of these we know little besides the names. The greatest of all was the Panathenaic Festival.

Athenian nobles had won distinction at Olympia in the seventh century. Four Athenian victories are chronicled in the stade-race. Cylon, as already mentioned, won a victory in the diaulos in Ol. 35 (640 B.C.), a victory which perhaps cost him dear. Having consulted the Delphic oracle as to the success of his plot to make himself master of Athens, he was advised to carry out his plan at the greatest festival of Zeus. The former Olympic victor naturally concluded that the oracle meant the Olympia, and not the Athenian Diasia, and this mistake is said to have led to his failure and his death. Another prominent Athenian victor was Phrynon, who in the Olympiad after Cylon's victory won the pankration, an event in which the Athenians seem to have excelled. He was general in the Athenian expedition to Sigeum, where he fell in single combat against Pittacus of Mitylene, who, according to later tradition, arraying himself as a fisherman, entangled Phrynon in his net and then ran him through with his trident in true gladiatorial style. Early in the sixth century we find Hippocrates, the father of Peisistratus, present as one of the Athenian envoys to Olympia. It was on this occasion, says Herodotus,[81] that he had a dream respecting the birth of Peisistratus, which dream was explained to him by the Spartan Ephor Chilon. Chilon, who was reckoned among the seven wise men of Greece, is said to have died some years later at Olympia from joy at the victory of his son Damagetus in boxing.[82] During the sixth century we have no record of Athenian successes in athletic contests, but many of the rival nobles won victories in the chariot-race. Peisistratus himself was proclaimed victor under strange circumstances. Cimon, the half-brother of Miltiades, the tyrant of the Chersonnese, himself a victor, had been banished from Athens by Peisistratus. This Cimon had a remarkable record. He won the chariot-race with the same team of mares at three successive Olympiads. At the second he agreed with Peisistratus that if he proclaimed the tyrant winner, he should be recalled from exile.[83] In spite of this he was put to death by the thankless sons of Peisistratus shortly after his last victory. Curtius ascribes to Peisistratus an inscription on the altar of the twelve gods at Athens recording the distance from Athens to Olympia.[84]

The value of athletics and their political importance had been realised by Solon. Besides making rules for the conduct of gymnasia he offered a public reward of 500 drachmae to each Olympian victor, 100 to each Isthmian victor, and so on to the victors in other games. This measure is sometimes misrepresented as an attempt on the part of Solon to check the extravagant rewards lavished on athletes. Such a view is utterly false. There is no evidence that athletes did receive extravagant rewards in Solon's time: and 500 drachmae, though perhaps a trivial sum to the professional athletes of a later and degenerate age, was then a considerable amount.[85] Rather we may see in this measure an attempt to encourage athletics

---

[81] Hdt. i. 59.
[82] Hermipp. *Fr.* 14. The story is suspicious, because the Spartans are said not to have been allowed to compete in boxing.
[83] Hdt. vi. 103.
[84] Hdt. ii. 7.
[85] At a later time a drachma was a day's pay for a sailor, hoplite, or artisan, and in Pericles' time a juryman received only two obols. In Solon's time, owing to the scarcity of money, the value of a drachma must have been considerably higher.

among the people, and perhaps to counteract the growing love of chariot-racing among the aristocracy.

It is tempting to ascribe to Solon's influence and policy the founding of the Panathenaea, or rather the remodelling of the old Athenaea, under this name. This event is assigned to the year 566 B.C., about the time when Athens, by the efforts of Solon and Peisistratus, finally made herself mistress of Salamis, and thus, by securing the control of the bay of Eleusis, was at last enabled to develop, unchecked, her maritime and commercial policy. The founding of the Panathenaea is attributed to Peisistratus, who certainly encouraged athletics and developed the festival; but, if the date 566 B.C. is correct, the festival was founded six years before he became tyrant, and while he was still the trusted friend of Solon, and, owing to his success in war, the hero of the people. The name Panathenaea seems significant, both of that unity of the Athenian people, which Solon tried with somewhat chequered success to promote, and also of that dream of expansion which Athens, freed from the rivalry of Megara, was now beginning to cherish. At the same time we can see in the name why the Panathenaea could never become truly Panhellenic. Olympia, Delphi, Nemea were fitted to become Panhellenic by virtue of the political insignificance of the states that controlled them; even the Isthmia, though held under the presidency of Corinth, was by its name dissociated from that power, and Corinth herself was in her own way a Panhellenic centre where politics were as yet subordinate to commerce. In such places the national desire for unity found a natural expression. But the Panathenaic festival was in the first place the festival of the union of Attica in the worship of Athene, and the only unity which it could offer to the rest of Greece was unity beneath the Aegis of Athene. Thus, while at the Panhellenic festivals all events were open to the whole of Greece, at Athens, besides such open events, we find others confined to her own citizens.

The Panathenaea were said to have been founded, or perhaps refounded, by Theseus, who, according to legend, united into one state the village communities of Attica. Certainly there existed an ancient yearly festival in honour of Athene, though we cannot say if it bore the name Panathenaea. This festival continued to be celebrated every year after the founding of the greater festival, and was called the Little Panathenaea.[86] The Great Panathenaea were a pentaëteris, and were held in the third year of each Olympiad in the month of Hekatombaion or about the end of July. The programme of the festival was even more varied than that of the Isthmia. The great event of the festival, the procession that bore the peplos to the temple of Athene on the Acropolis, afforded an opportunity for the display of all the forces of Athens. The competitions included, besides athletics and horse-races, musical contests, recitations, torch-races, Pyrrhic dances, a regatta, and even a competition for good looks. For most of the events the prizes consisted in jars of Attic oil. Olive-oil was the most valuable product of Attica: the olive trees were under the control of the state, and the export of olive-oil was a state monopoly. As many as 1300 amphorae of oil were distributed as prizes, the winner in the chariot-race receiving as many as 140 amphorae. As even at a later period an amphora of oil was worth 12 drachmae, it is clear that the prizes had a considerable commercial value. Some of the jars containing the oil were ornamented with scenes representing the various competitions. It is probable that only one such painted vase was given for each victory. The manufacture and painting of vases was already an important industry at Athens, and the prize vase full of oil represented, therefore, the chief natural product and the chief industry of early

---

[86] On the Panathenaea *vide* A. Mommsen, *Feste der Stadt Athen*.

Attica. These prize vases must have been greatly cherished. Numbers of them have been found in Italian tombs and elsewhere, and the variety of the subjects depicted throws no little light on the events of the festival. But details must be reserved for another chapter.

The multiplication of athletic festivals and the valuable prizes offered at them must have been a source of no small profit to the successful athlete. The victor at the Panhellenic games, it is true, received no other reward from the authorities than the wreath of leaves;[87] but at the lesser festivals, where he would be a welcome and an honoured guest, he was sure of a rich harvest of prizes. Moreover, he received substantial rewards at the hands of his grateful fellow-citizens. For in these games the individual was regarded as the representative of his state: the herald who proclaimed his victory proclaimed, too, the name of his state, and in his success the whole state shared and rejoiced. Hence we can understand the righteous indignation of the people of Croton in Ol. 75, when their famous fellow-countryman, Astylus, who had already won the stade-race and the diaulos in two successive Olympiads, on the third occasion entered himself as a Syracusan in order to ingratiate himself with the tyrant Hieron. Such an act was felt to be almost a sacrilege, and the Crotoniats in their wrath destroyed the statue of Astylus, which they had erected in the precinct of Lacinian Hera, and converted his house, perhaps the house which they had given him, into a common prison.[88]

The representative character of the Panhellenic athlete and the connexion of the games with the national religion explain the honours paid to him by his fellow-citizens.[89] His homecoming was an occasion of public rejoicing. The whole city turned out to welcome him and escort him in triumph to his home and to the chief temples of the city, where he offered thanksgiving and paid his vows to the gods and heroes to whom he owed his victory. Songs were composed expressly for the occasion by the greatest poets of the age, and sung by choirs of youths and maidens before the temples or before his house. His exploits were recorded on pillars of stone, and his statue was set up in some public place, or even in the sanctuary of the gods, to serve as an incentive to posterity. He received, too, more substantial rewards. We have seen how Solon granted considerable sums of money to the victors in the great games, and we may be sure that the example of Athens was followed by other states. At Athens and elsewhere the victor had the privilege of a front seat at all public festivals, and sometimes, too, the right of free meals in the Prytaneum. At a later time he was exempted from taxation. At Sparta, which seems to have stood somewhat aloof from the athletic movement, he was rewarded characteristically with the right of fighting in battle next to the king and defending his person. In the rich cities of the West the adulation of the victor, at a somewhat later date, took the most extravagant forms. Exaenetus of Agrigentum, who won the foot-race at Olympia in Ol. 92, was drawn into the city in a four-horse chariot, attended by three hundred of the chief citizens, each riding in a chariot drawn by a pair of white horses. Sometimes, it seems, a breach in the city walls was made for the victor's entry. It is in Italy that we first hear of the worship of the athlete as a hero. Philippus of Croton, an Olympic victor, renowned as the handsomest man in Greece, was worshipped as a hero after his death.[90] Euthymus of Locri Epizephyrii, who won three Olympic victories in boxing in Ols. 74, 76, 77, was even

---

[87] The palm branch as a symbol of victory does not occur till the close of the fifth century. Mr. F. B. Tarbell traces its origin to Delos, and derives its popularity from the restoration of the Delian festival by Athens in 426 B.C. "The Palm of Victory" in *Classical Philology*, vol. iii. pp. 264 ff.

[88] Paus. vi. 13, 1. Hieron is apparently a mistake for Gelon.

[89] Krause, *Olympia*, pp. 195-201.

[90] Hdt. v. 47.

said to have been so worshipped during his lifetime. It was perhaps a righteous retribution for such impiety that his statues at Locri and Olympia were, according to the story, struck by lightning on the same day.[91] Theagenes of Thasos and Polydamas of Scotussa were also worshipped as heroes, and the statue of Theagenes was credited with the power of healing fevers.[92] But these extravagances, if true, belong to a later period, and must have been repugnant to the religious feeling and sound sense of the Peloponnese before the Persian wars.

Of all these honours the most significant are the hymn of victory and the statue. It was not merely that the greatest artists and poets were employed to immortalise the victor, and that they demanded a high price for their services. The statue and the hymn were honours confined originally to gods and heroes, and, bestowed on mortal athletes, did literally lift these "lords of earth to the gods." "Not even the mighty Polydeuces nor the iron son of Alcmene could hold up their hands against him." So wrote Simonides of Ceos, the earliest writer of epinikia, of the famous boxer Glaucus of Carystus, language which, as the late Sir Richard Jebb remarks, would have sounded very like an impiety to Alcman. The words are significant of the changed attitude towards athletics, and the hero-worship founded by the artist and the poet was perhaps largely responsible for the extravagances of a later age. But the influence of athletics on art and literature, and that of art and literature on athletics, are subjects that belong chiefly to the fifth century, and will be dealt with in the next chapter.

The growing popularity of athletics and the excessive honours showered upon physical excellence could hardly escape criticism. In that age of intense intellectual activity there must have been many far-sighted observers who resented the predominance of athletics, though perhaps they feared to express their feelings. One at least there was who knew no such fear, and fortunately his protest has survived. The bold and original thinker, Xenophanes of Colophon, was exactly contemporary with the movement which we have been describing. Born at Colophon about the year 576 B.C. he was forced to leave his native place at the age of twenty-five, and for sixty-five years travelled about the cities of Greece and Sicily, finally settling at Elea in Italy, where he became the founder of the Eleatic school of philosophy, and died in the year 480 B.C. A fearless critic of the current ideas about the gods, denying that the godhead could be like unto man, he may well have been scandalized at the representation of gods and heroes as athletes, and at the offering of divine honours to victors in the games; and his wide experience of men and cities showed him clearly the danger of the growing worship of athletics. After enumerating the honours shown to the athlete he continues: "Yet is he not so worthy as I, and my wisdom is better than the strength of men and horses. Nay, this is a foolish custom, nor is it right to honour strength more than excellent wisdom. Not though there were among the people a man good at boxing, or in the pentathlon, or in wrestling, nay, nor one with swiftness of foot which is most honoured in all contests of human strength—not for his presence would the city be better governed. And small joy would there be for a city should one in contests win a victory by the banks of Pisa. These things do not make fat the dark corners of the city."

Less than a century later the words of Xenophanes are echoed by Euripides, but the object of the protest is no longer the same. The class of professional athletes whom Euripides denounces did not exist in the days of the older poet. It is against the excessive importance

---

[91] Pliny, *H. N.* vii. 47. Strabo, vi. 255.
[92] Paus. vi. 11, 9; Lucian, *Deor. Concilium*, 12.

attached to athletics, the false and one-sided ideal, that Xenophanes protests. In his wanderings through the cities of Greece he has learnt by bitter experience the evils that exist, evils of tyranny and party strife, extremes of luxury and poverty, and he feels that the energies of his countrymen are being misdirected. It is not a little curious that foreign writers, deceived by the glamour of Olympia, are wont to treat the protest of Xenophanes as the captious utterance of a soured and peevish cynic. Yet the fragments of his writings which exist show him to have been a man of wide experience and sympathies; and in England, where we have witnessed a similar wave of athleticism, his wisdom is generally recognized. Let us pause to consider what was the state of athletics in the time of Xenophanes.

The popularity of athletics, the growth of competition, and the rewards lavished on successful athletes completely changed the character of athletics in the sixth century. The actual events remained the same, but a change came over the attitude of performers and spectators. It was a change which will be readily understood by anyone familiar with the history of our own sports and games during the last century, the change from spontaneous to organized sport. The change brought with it both good and evil; the standard of performance was greatly improved, but athletics ceased to be pure recreation, and something of the old Homeric joy was lost; and though the spirit of sport survived for a century more, even in the sixth century we can trace signs of the evils which over-competition inevitably brings in its train.

In every Greek state all boys, whatever their station, received a thorough physical training. Sometimes, as in Sparta, this training was extended to girls. This training consisted partly in the traditional exercises of the public games, partly in dances which corresponded to our musical drill in which the performers went through the various movements of the palaestra or of actual war to the accompaniment of music. Thus every boy was trained to take his part in athletic competitions. Local festivals provided the promising athlete with an opportunity of testing his strength and skill from early boyhood. At Olympia there had been only two classes of competition, for boys and for men. In the festivals of the sixth century we find a third class added for those betwixt the age of boy and man, the beardless (ἀγένειοι). In local festivals of a later date we find three or even four classes for boys only, sometimes confined to local competitors; and perhaps, if we had details of the local festivals of the sixth century, we should find the same. These boys' events were clearly intended to foster local talent. The youth who won success in his home festival would try his luck in the neighbouring competitions, and if still successful would go farther afield and perhaps enter for the Panhellenic games. Hence the competitors, especially at the Olympia, represented the picked athletes of all the states. The prizes offered at the various festivals enabled many to compete, who in a previous age could not have afforded the necessary time or money; and we may be sure that the emulation of the various states would not have allowed any citizen to lose his chance of the crown for lack of funds. The popular character of athletics is illustrated by a fragment of an epigram ascribed to Simonides on an Olympic victor "who once carried fish from Argos to Tegea."[93] At the same time the noble families which had for generations been famed in athletics exerted themselves to their utmost to maintain their hereditary prestige. All classes caught the athletic mania. It was at the close of the century that Alexander, the son of Amyntas, king of Macedon, competed in the foot-race at Olympia.

---

[93] Simonides, 163 (Bergk). Quoted by Aristotle, *Rhet.* i. 7 and 9.

Competition naturally raised the standard of athletics. Natural ability and ordinary exercise were no longer sufficient to secure success without long and careful training. Hence there arose a class of professional trainers. These men, who were often old athletes, acquired considerable repute, and doubtless were handsomely rewarded by the rich individuals or states that employed them. In their hands athletics became scientific; instead of being regarded as a recreation and a training for war they became an end in themselves. One state alone, Sparta, held aloof from the new athletics and competitions. At Sparta the one object was to produce a race of hardy soldiers, and the new science, which aimed at producing athletes, could find no place there. No Spartan was allowed to employ a trainer in wrestling. Boxing was said to have been introduced by the Spartans, but though they recognized the value of boxing as a sport, they realized the dangers of it as a competition, and forbade their citizens to take part in competitions for boxing or the pankration, on the ground that it was disgraceful for a Spartan to acknowledge defeat. Hence the disappearance of Sparta from the list of the Olympic victors which has already been noticed. Sparta in athletics fell behind the rest of Greece, and Philostratus, comparing them with the more scientific athletics, describes them as somewhat boorish.[94] Yet perhaps the Spartans and Xenophanes were right.

The new training required no little expenditure of time and money. The would-be victor at Olympia must have lived in a constant state of training and competition, which left time for little else. Theagenes of Thasos, who lived at the time of the Persian wars, is said to have won no less than fourteen hundred crowns.[95] To such men athletics were no longer a recreation, but an absorbing occupation. The professional amateur is but a short step removed from the true professional. For a time wealth and leisure gave a great advantage to the wealthy individual, and the wealthy city. In the sixth century the most successful states are the rich cities of Sicily and Italy. The sons of noble families still figure prominently in the epinikia of Pindar and Bacchylides. But the increase of rich prizes was soon to put the poor man on a level with the rich. Before the close of the fifth century we shall find athletics left to the professional, while princes and nobles compete only in the chariot-races and horse-races. For this result states like Sybaris and Croton were hugely responsible. They thought to encourage athletics by offering large money prizes; in reality they killed the spirit of sport. Sybaris indeed—or, according to another account, Croton—endeavoured to outshine Olympia by holding a festival of her own at the same time as the Olympia, and attracting away the pick of the athletes by the magnificence of the prizes.[96] When such an attempt was possible, professionalism was near at hand.

These evils, however, did not yet exist in the sixth century, though implied already in that excessive love of athletics which aroused the indignation of Xenophanes. The nation had become a nation of athletes, and not the least important characteristic which distinguished the Greek from the barbarian was henceforth his athletic training. The result was a standard of athletic excellence never again perhaps equalled. Most of the athletes whose names were household words for centuries, belong to the sixth and the first half of the fifth centuries. Such were Milo of Croton, Glaucus of Carystus, Theagenes of Thasos. Though we occasionally

---

[94] The attitude of the Spartans towards athletics is expressed in a poem of Tyrtaeus (Bergk, No. 12), in which he declares that he would set no store by speed of foot or skill in wrestling, apart from warlike might. Later their contempt of training and skill degenerated into sheer brutality. Phil. *Gym.* 9 and 58; Plutarch, *Apophthegm. Lac. Var.* 25 (233 E); *Anth. Plan.* i. 1.
[95] Paus. vi. 11, 5.
[96] Athenaeus, 522, 523.

find distinguished runners, such as Phanas of Pellene, who, by winning three races at Olympia in one day, won the title of triple victor (τριαστής), or a little later Astylus of Croton, of whom we have heard already, the typical athlete of the sixth century was the strong man—the boxer, the wrestler, or the pankratiast. The object of the old gymnastic was to produce strength only, says Philostratus,[97] contrasting the ancient athletes with their degenerate successors, and the success of the old training was shown in the fact that these old athletes maintained their strength for eight or even nine Olympiads. There was nothing artificial or unnatural about their training: the careful dieting, the elaborate massage, the rules for exercise and sleep introduced by later trainers were unknown. The trainers of those days confined themselves to actual athletics, to the art of boxing or wrestling especially, and the athletes owed their strength to a healthy, vigorous, out-of-door life.

This fact is illustrated by the legends that sprang up about the famous athletes of this age, which, amid much invention and exaggeration, probably contain some substratum of truth. The father of Glaucus discovered his son's strength from seeing him one day hammer a ploughshare into the plough with his naked fist. Theagenes first displayed his strength at the age of nine in a youthful escapade. Taking a fancy to a certain bronze statue in the market-place, he one day shouldered it and carried it off. The exploits of Samson with wild beasts find many parallels in the stories of Greek athletes; but the most characteristic exercise of the sixth century was weight-lifting. Milo practised weight-lifting on most scientific principles with a young bull calf, which he lifted and carried every day till it was fully grown. A still more famous weight-lifter was Titormus, a gigantic shepherd who lived in Aetolia, and did not, as far as we know, compete in any competitions. Challenged by Milo to show his strength, he took him down to the river Euenus, threw off his mantle, and seized a huge boulder which Milo could hardly move. He first raised it to his knees, then on to his shoulders, and after carrying it sixteen yards, threw it.[98] He next showed his strength and courage by seizing and holding fast by the heels two wild bulls.

These stories of weight-lifting have been strangely confirmed by discoveries in Greece. At Olympia a block of red sandstone was found, bearing a sixth-century inscription to the effect that one Bybon with one hand threw it over his head.[99] The stone weighs 143-1/2 kilos (315 lbs.), and measures 68 × 33 × 38 cms. A one-handed lift of such an object is clearly impossible, and I can only suggest that Bybon lifted the weight with both hands in the manner described above, then balanced it on one hand and threw it. At Santorin another such block has been found, a mass of black volcanic rock, weighing 480 kilos. The inscription on it, which belongs to the close of the sixth century, runs as follows: "Eumastas the son of Critobulus lifted me from the ground." To lift such a weight from the ground, though possible, is quite a good performance.

Swimming, too, was a favourite exercise, and Philostratus tells us that Tisander, a boxer of Naxos, who lived, on a promontory of the island, kept himself in training by swimming out to sea. These old athletes, says the same author, hardened themselves by bathing in the rivers, and sleeping in the open air on skins or heaps of fodder. Living such a life they had healthy appetites, and were not particular about their food, living on porridge and unleavened bread, and such meat as they could get. The strong man is naturally a large eater, and all sorts of

---

[97] *Gym.* 43.
[98] Aelian, *V.H.* xii. 22.
[99] *Ol. Ins.* 717. This and the Santorin stone (*I.G.* xiii. 449) are discussed in *J.H.S.* xxvii. p. 2.

tales were current as to the voracity of these athletes. Milo, according to an epigram, after carrying a four-year-old heifer around the Altis, ate it all on the same day; and a similar feat is ascribed to Titormus and Theagenes.[100] These tales are clearly the invention of a later age, when the strong man trained on vast quantities of meat; and as Milo excelled all men in strength, it followed that he must also have excelled them in voracity. But whatever the truth of these stories, it is certain that the athletes of those times were healthy and free from disease, preserved their strength, and lived long. If athletic training did occupy an undue share of their time, it did not unfit them for the duties of ordinary life and military service. Many of them won distinction as soldiers and generals, while the effects of athletic training on the nation were shown in the Persian wars.

When we turn to the records of art we still find strength the predominant characteristic of the period. We see this in those early nude statues, so widely distributed throughout Greece and the islands, which are generally classed under the name of Apollo. In all we see the same attempt to render the muscles of the body, whether we regard the tall spare type of the Apollo of Tenea, or the shorter heavier type of the Argive statues. It is in the muscles of the trunk rather than of the limbs that real strength lies, and it is the careful marking of these muscles that distinguishes early Greek sculpture from all other early art, and the sculpture of the Peloponnese in particular from the softer school of Ionia. Perhaps the most characteristic figure of the sixth century is that of the bearded Heracles, not the clumsy giant of later days, but the personification of endurance and trained strength, a man, as Pindar says, short of stature, but of unbending soul. So we see him on many a black-figured vase of the sixth century, and the type survives in the pediments of Aegina or the Metopes of Olympia in the next century. Matched against giants and monsters he represents the triumph of training and endurance over mere brute force. If we compare the figures of athletes on these vases with those on the red-figured vases of the next century, we find the same result; the ideal of the fifth century is the grace of athletic youth, that of the sixth is the strength of fully developed manhood; the hero of the former is Theseus, of the latter Heracles. Finally, if we would realise the true greatness of sixth-century athletics, let us remember that it was this century which rendered possible and inspired the athletic ideal of Pindar in the next.

"For if a man rejoice to suffer cost and toil, and achieve god-builded excellence, and therewithal fate plant for him fair renown, already at the farthest bonds of bliss hath such an one cast anchor."

---

[100] Athenaeus, 412 D, E.

Chapter 5

THE AGE OF THE ATHLETIC IDEAL, 500-440 B.C.

Though the Greeks of the sixth and fifth centuries attained a remarkable standard of athletic excellence, it is probable that in individual performance the modern athlete could at least have held his own with them. Yet despite our modern athleticism it is certain that no other nation has ever produced so high an average of physical development as the Greeks did in this period. This result was due largely to the athletic ideal which found its highest expression in the athletic poetry and art of the fifth century. The ideal is unique in the history of the world, nor are the circumstances which produced it ever likely to occur again. Due, in the first place, to the early connection of athletics with religion, it owed its development in the fifth century to two causes, firstly, to the growth of athletic art and poetry, secondly, to the intense feeling of Panhellenic unity produced by the struggle with Persia. It was this ideal that checked the growth of those evils which inevitably result from the excessive popularity of athletics, and maintained their purity till the short-lived unity of Greece was shattered by the Peloponnesian war. To understand this ideal we must briefly trace the history of athletic art and literature, and then note how the national feeling found expression in the Panhellenic and especially in the Olympic games.

Without athletics, says the late Professor Furtwängler,[101] Greek art cannot be conceived. The skill of the Greek artist in representing the forms of the naked body is due in the first instance to the habit of complete nudity in athletic exercises, a habit which, even if it were, as Thucydides says, not introduced into all athletic competitions at Olympia till shortly before his own time, must certainly, if we may judge from the evidence of the black-figured vases, have been almost universal in the palaestra of the sixth century. Besides the unrivalled opportunities that this habit afforded the sculptor of studying the naked body in every position of activity, it must have served as a valuable incentive to the youths of Greece to keep themselves in good condition. The Greek, with his keen eye for physical beauty, regarded flabbiness, want of condition, imperfect development as a disgrace, a sign of neglected education, and the ill-trained youth was the laughing-stock of his companions. Hence every Greek learnt to take a pride in his physical fitness and beauty. This love of physical beauty is strikingly illustrated in one of the war-songs of Tyrtaeus:[102] "It is a shame," he says, "for an old man to lie slain in the front of the battle, his body stripped and exposed." Why? Because an old man's body cannot be beautiful. "But to the young," he continues, "all things are

---

[101] A. Furtwängler, *Die Bedeutung der Gymnastik in der griechischen Kunst.*
[102] x. ll. 21 ff. (Bergk).

seemly as long as the goodly bloom of lovely youth is on him. A sight for men to marvel at, for women to love while he lives, beautiful, too, when fallen in the front of the battle."

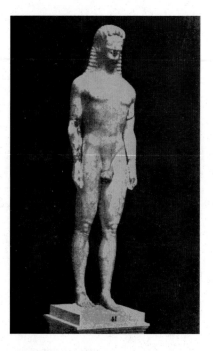

Figure 7. Apollo, found at Tenea. Munich.

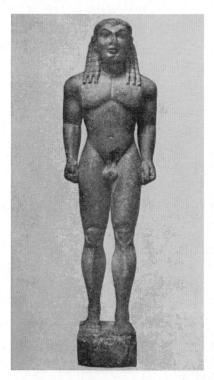

Figure 8. Statue by an Argive Sculptor. Delphi. (*Greek Sculpture*, Figure 134.)

We have seen how there arose in the sixth century a demand for athletic statues, and how the early artists endeavoured to express trained strength by the careful treatment of the muscles of the body, especially those of the chest and abdomen. The early athletic statues must have been of the type of those archaic figures which are rightly or wrongly classed under the name of Apollo, and which, whether they represent a god or a man, are certainly inspired by athletics. Though we see in all the same evident desire to express strength yet we find considerable variety of physical type, far more so, in fact, than we find in the fifth century, which was dominated by a more or less definite ideal of physical beauty and proportion. In the sixth century the artists were experimenting, and therefore we may suppose were influenced more by local or individual characteristics. Thus the slim, long-limbed Apollo of Tenea (Figure 7), with his well-formed chest, spare flanks, and powerful legs is the very type of the long-distance runner. These long, lean, wiry runners are often depicted on Panathenaic vases, and suggest inevitably these day-runners (ἡμεροδρόμοι), who acted as scouts or couriers in the Persian wars. Quite different is the type of the early Argive statues found at Delphi (Figure 8). Square and thickset, with powerful limbs and massive heads, they seem naturally to lead up to the type of the Ligourio bronze and of Polycleitus, and suggest that such a build was characteristic of Argolis. Between the two extremes comes an extensive series of statues from Boeotia, one of which shows strong signs of Aeginetan influence.[103] In the fifth century we look in vain for such divergences of type, and the reason is that Greek art was tending more and more towards an ideal, and neither the typical runner nor the typical strong man quite fulfils the artist's ideal. Vase paintings afford an interesting illustration of this change. The wrestling groups on the black-figured vases show far greater variety and originality, a more realistic imitation of the manifold positions of wrestling than we find on the red-figured vases of the fifth century, where only such types are preserved as commended themselves to the more highly-trained artistic sense of the later craftsmen.

In the early part of the fifth century we still find a variety of physical type. On the one hand we have the Choiseul-Gouffier Apollo (Figure 9) with his broad square shoulders, powerful chest and back—essentially a big man, and therefore identified by Dr. Waldstein with the boxer Euthymus, though recent evidence tends to show that the statue really represents the god and no mortal athlete. At the other extreme we have the neat, small, sinewy forms of the warriors on the Aeginetan pediments (Figure 10). Between the two come a number of types. Unfortunately we have no extant examples of the great Argive school. The bronze in which the Argive sculptor worked was too valuable to escape the ravages of the plunderer, and a certain monotony, which must have characterized purely athletic sculpture, prevented the later copyist from reproducing these works. But if we may argue from the Ligourio bronze (Figure 11), the Argive type was short like the Aeginetan but heavier and more fleshy. On the other hand, the statues which are recognized as copies of the famous group of Critias and Nesiotes[104] representing Harmodius and Aristogeiton show a taller, larger-boned type, more approaching that of the Choiseul-Gouffier Apollo, which may perhaps be recognized as Athenian.[105] But in all this diversity of physical type we ask ourselves in vain what class of athlete is represented in any particular statue, whether a boxer, a wrestler, a pentathlete, or a runner. The reason seems to be that in all these statues the ideal

---

[103] *Greek Sculpture*, Figure 25; cp. *B.C.H.*, 1907, p. 187.
[104] *Greek Sculpture*, Figures. 34, 35, 36.
[105] Cp. a fine archaic bronze diskobolos in the Metropolitan Museum of New York, published in the *Museum Bulletin*, iii. p. 33; *vide infra* Figure 83.

element is strong; there is a difference of build, but each build is shown with the fullest all-round development of which it is capable. Certainly there is not in this period a single figure that represents a typical runner so clearly as does the Apollo of Tenea. Perhaps the nearest type to that of the runner is the Aeginetan; but unfortunately we know that the events in which Aegina won most distinction were wrestling and the pankration, winners in which we should expect to find characterized by a heavier build. The fact is that the real specialization of the athlete was only just beginning, and the universal athletic training had produced in the first half of the fifth century so uniform a standard of development that, runners perhaps excepted, it must have been difficult to distinguish between the representatives of other events, in all of which strength was more important than pace. Hence the earlier sculptors, in order to indicate an athlete's victory, were forced to attach to his statue some special attribute, a diskos, or a pair of jumping weights for a pentathlete, a boxing thong for a boxer.[106] As their technical skill increased they began to represent the athlete in some characteristic position. Glaucias of Aegina showed the famous boxer Glaucus of Carystos sparring with an imaginary opponent.[107] At Athens Pausanias saw a statue of Epicharinus by Critius in the attitude of one practising for the hoplite race, perhaps in the attitude of the well-known Tübingen bronze, which represents a hoplitodromos practising starts[108] (Figure 12).

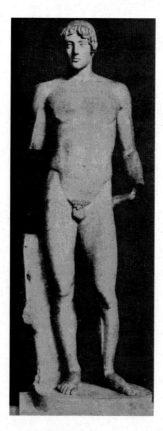

Figure 9. Choiseul-Gouffier Apollo. British Museum.

---

[106] Such attributes are common in bronzes, cp. Pausanias v. 26, 3; 27, 12; vi. 3, 9; 10, 4; 13, 7.
[107] Paus. vi. 10, 1-3.
[108] Paus. i. 23, 9.

Figure 10. Figure from E. pediment at Aegina. Munich. (*Greek Sculpture*, Figure 41.)

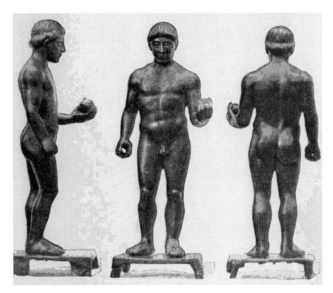

Figure 11. Bronze Statuette from Ligourio. Berlin. (*Greek Sculpture*, Figure 39.)

The last-named statues at once suggest the Diskobolos of Myron (Figure 13). This statue marks a new departure in athletic art. It is not, as far as we know, a statue in honour of any particular victor, but a study in athletic genre. To the same class belong the Doryphoros and Diadumenos of Polycleitus.[109] The earlier statues had been ideal in as far as they were not portrait statues, but statues of athletic types connected with the name of some victor, and many such statues are assigned to Myron and Polycleitus. But the statues of which we are speaking were avowedly and professedly ideal studies in athletic art. Myron undertook to represent the athlete in motion. He chose that most difficult, yet most characteristic moment

---

[109] Cp. Walter Pater, *Greek Studies*, pp. 281 ff.

in the swing of the diskobolos, which alone combines the idea of rest and that of motion, when the diskos has been swung back to its full extent, and the momentary pause suggests stability, while the insecurity of the delicate balance implies the strong movement which has preceded it, and the more violent movement which is to follow. No other moment could give the same idea of force and swiftness. If we look at the countless representations of the diskobolos on vases and in bronzes, we see that the fixing of any other moment in the swing destroys at once all idea of motion. The movement is checked at an unnatural point, and the result is lifeless. Only at the close of the swing backward does the brief pause give the artist an excuse for fixing it in bronze. It is a magnificent conception, and in spite of minor defects magnificently executed. Unfortunately we know the statue only through more or less late and inaccurate marble copies. Perhaps the truest idea of the grace of the original bronze can be obtained from the bronzed cast in the Ashmolean Museum at Oxford, from which our illustration is taken. The diskobolos is, as has been said, a study of athletic action, and it is therefore difficult to form a true idea of his proportions, nor was the artist concerned so much with proportions as with movement. Yet if we can imagine the diskobolos standing at rest, he might well take his place besides the glorious youths of the Parthenon frieze, tall like the Tyrannicides, yet of somewhat lighter build, taller and lighter likewise than the type of Polycleitus.

Figure 12. Bronze Statuette of Hoplitodromos. Tübingen.

The Age of the Athletic Ideal, 500-440 B.C. 63

Figure 13. Myron's Diskobolos (from a bronzed cast made in Munich, combining the Vatican body and the Massimi head).

Figure 14. Doryphoros, after Polycleitus. Naples. (*Greek Sculpture*, Figure 74.)

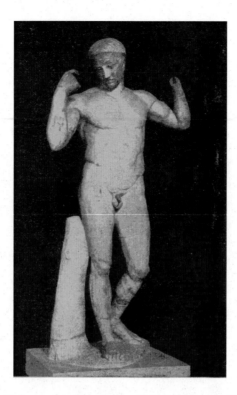

Figure 15. Diadumenos from Vaison, after Polycleitus. British Museum. (*Greek Sculpture*, Figure 75.)

In the Doryphoros (Figure 14), and Diadumenos (Figure 15), we have another type of athletic genre. These statues are studies of the athlete at rest, studies in proportion. The Doryphoros indeed was called the canon, because in it the artist was said to have embodied his ideal of the proportions of the human body. If we consider what such a canon implies, we shall understand why the old diversity of type tended to disappear. The artist of this period was seeking an ideal of human proportion. Such an ideal is not to be found in any extremes of type, in strength or beauty by itself, but only in a combination of the two, in the golden mean, that avoidance of all excess which dominated Greek life and thought. The influence of athletic training had impressed upon him the value of physical strength systematically trained and developed; his artistic sense taught him that no subject was fitting for his art which did not present beauty of outline and proportion. Hence that union of strength and beauty which characterizes the athletic art of this period.

Other circumstances contributed to produce uniformity of type. The three great sculptors of the age, Myron, Pheidias and Polycleitus, whom we now know to have been almost contemporaries, and in the full activity of their art in the middle of the century, were all, according to traditions, pupils of the Argive sculptor Ageladas. In the stern, manly discipline of the Argive school they acquired their consummate knowledge of the human body. The influence of these artists was increased by the concentration at this period of all art at Athens. Polycleitus indeed remained at Argos; but Myron and Pheidias worked at Athens, and through Pheidias the art of Athens spread over the Greek world. The school in which these artists had been trained had devoted itself to the study of athletic proportion, and it was therefore only natural that a similar athletic ideal should prevail generally,—a similar but not quite the same ideal. Polycleitus remained true to the Argive tradition of a somewhat thickset, massive type, with square-jawed, powerful head. At Athens the influence of the softer Ionian art, perhaps, too, the prevalence of other characteristics in the population, produced a slighter, taller, more graceful type. Both schools combined strength and beauty. In both it is impossible to decide in what event any particular athlete had excelled; but while strength continued to be the prevalent idea of Polycleitus, Athenian art was rather dominated by the idea of beauty.

This union of strength and beauty belongs especially to the time of full-grown youth and opening manhood. It is the age when the Greek youth began to undertake some of the duties of citizenship, and when the state took upon itself his training. In most Greek cities somewhere between the ages of sixteen and eighteen the youths were enrolled in corps, and for two years were subject to a strict military discipline under officers appointed by the state. They learnt to use their weapons and to ride; they hardened their bodies by athletic exercises and hunting; they gained practical experience in war by acting as police patrols on the frontiers. This time of life was especially devoted to athletics and physical training. At many of the games there were special competitions for youths of this age—the beardless or ἀγένειοι. To the same age belong these romantic boy friendships which figure so largely in Greek life, from the time of Harmodius and Aristogeiton or earlier. That these friendships did at times lead to serious abuse cannot, unfortunately, be denied. But the charge of immorality brought against them seems to me greatly exaggerated,[110] at least as far as regards the fifth century and the most enlightened states. These friendships arose on the one side from the natural hero-worship of youth, on the other from an intense appreciation of bodily beauty.

This strong artistic feeling is illustrated by the practice which arose among the vase painters of inscribing on their cups the name of some popular youth with the word καλός, or sometimes the more general inscription καλὸς ὁ παῖς, "the boy is fair." The term "love names" applied to these inscriptions is somewhat unfortunate. The word καλός implies none of that modern maudlin sentimentality so often mistaken for love, but rather the artist's sense of the beautiful, sometimes his admiration for some popular youth, sometimes, perhaps, merely his satisfaction in the form he has himself created. The point, however, which interests us here is that the beauty which appealed to the Greek of the latter half of the fifth century was not the beauty of woman, nor even of the mature man, but the beauty of manly youth, and the art of the Periclean age has been well described as the glorification of the ephebos.

The growing preference for the younger type can be traced in the lists of athletic statues at Olympia recorded by Pausanias. There is a steady increase during the fifth century of the proportion of boy victors as compared with men, and the increase is more than maintained during the fourth century. The change is perhaps connected with a change in the character of athletics. There can be no doubt that athletics were already becoming more specialized, and the specialized athlete did not appeal to the artist of the fifth century. In the following age we find an increasing diversity of type, but in the Periclean age the ideal of athletic youth dominates all treatment of the human figure. We can see it in the figures of children and young boys which, despite their small stature, have the proportions and muscular development of men, or in the figures of women which, whether undraped or, as was more usual, draped, differ little in framework and proportion from the figures of graceful youths. In the Periclean age, we cannot distinguish between the athlete and the ephebos. Every educated youth is an athlete, and every athlete is an educated youth and a citizen of a free state. Of the

---

[110] Vide Krause, *Gym.* pp. 943 ff., a criticism of the exaggerated view put forward in Becker's *Charicles*.

strictly athletic statues unfortunately we possess only marble copies, which in the transference from bronze have lost much of the grace of the originals. But the ephebos is known to us from many a grave relief, and above all from the sculptures of the Parthenon. The grave reliefs are at least originals, though we do not know the artists' names, while the Parthenon sculptures were executed under the direction of Pheidias. A truer idea of the athletic youth of this age can be formed from the Theseus of the pediment, or the epheboi of the frieze, than from late copies of Polycleitus.

In all these figures the prevailing impression is one of a perfect harmony, an absence of all exaggeration. Beauty of line is not exaggerated into softness, nor strength into coarseness. There is, too, a graceful ease of movement and of action which tells of an education in which music goes hand in hand with gymnastic. Musical drill and dances formed an important part of Greek education; even at the great festivals the competitors in the pentathlon performed to the accompaniment of the flute. The influence of music is especially suggested by the rhythmic movement and poise of the Diadumenos. Hence these harmonious shapes produce an effect deeper than that of mere physical beauty, they seem to be the outward expression of the spirit within. καλὸς καὶ ἀγαθός—beauty and goodness—are inseparable to the Greek. The heads, too, are in perfect harmony with the body; somewhat passionless perhaps, they seem to denote a mind well ordered as the body. They are not the heads of students or philosophers, much less of mere athletes, but the heads of healthy, vigorous youths, to whom all activity whether of mind or body is a joy. In the clear-cut, strong features we read courage and resolution, endurance and self-control. The expression is calm and dignified, yet without a trace of arrogance or pride. The face is often turned slightly downwards, and the downcast eyes produce an impression of modesty which is most marked in those statues which, like the Diadumenos binding the victor's fillet round his head, expressly represent victory. Such is the beautiful bronze head of the ephebos shown in Figure 16. This combination of dignity and modesty is part of what the Greeks called αἰδώς,[111] a word which we shall see is the keynote of Pindar's athletic ideal, and which expresses more than any other the spirit of these statues.

The influence of athletics is equally plain in the lesser arts. On coins and gems it is seen chiefly in the nude figures of gods and heroes. Sometimes, however, we find a purely athletic type. On the coins of Aspendus in Pamphylia we have a long series of wrestling groups (Figure 109), and on the other side a naked slinger, a punning allusion it seems to the name Aspendus. On the coins of Cos occurs a most interesting figure of the diskobolos, a crude attempt to represent the very moment selected by Myron (Figure 86). Both series date from the early fifth century. On gems of a later date we have frequent copies of the actual work of Myron. In Sicily we find no representations of the athlete proper, but the close connexion of Sicily with Olympia, and the successes of its cities and tyrants in the chariot and horse races are commemorated by numerous coins bearing a horseman or a chariot.[112]

---

[111] Cp. Aristoph. *Nub.* 995—
 ἄλλο τε μηδὲν
 αἰσχρὸν ποιεῖν, ὅ τι τῆς Αἰδοῦς μέλλει τἄγαλμ' ἀναπλήσειν.
 The Spartans considered Αἰδώς a goddess, Xen. *Symp.* 8, 36.
[112] *Vide infra*, Figures. 167 ff.

Figure 16. Bronze head of ephebos. Munich, Glyptothek, 457. (From a photograph by Bruckmann.)

These, however, are but isolated examples; the art which above all other was influenced by athletics was that of the vase painter. Athletic scenes are among the earliest on the vases. This may be partly due to the connexion of games with funeral rites, for which many of the painted vases were made. But there is another and more general reason for the vase painter's preference. Athletic scenes were especially adapted for the spaces which he wished to fill, whether it were a long band running round the whole vase, or an oblong panel. In the former case, the foot-race or the horse-race, or a series of athletes engaged in various sports, offered an effective variation of the procession of men or animals so common on early vases, while nothing could be better adapted for a panel than a boxing or a wrestling match with umpires or friends looking on. So effective was the latter scheme found that it was applied to mythological subjects. The contests of Heracles with giants or with monsters become a wrestling match or pankration in which gods and goddesses take the place of umpires. So in the fifth century, on the red-figured cups the exploits of Theseus in ridding the world of monsters and bullies are depicted as events in the palaestra. To Theseus was ascribed the invention of scientific wrestling: he appears on the vases as a graceful youth triumphing by trained skill over the brute force of his opponents.

The story of athletic types follows the same course on the vases as in sculpture, though, as the development of the simpler art was more rapid, the changes took place earlier. The bearded athletes of the black-figure vases disappear at the beginning of the fifth century, and on the red-figure vases, from the time of the Persian wars, the ephebos is ubiquitous. Moreover, it is not so much the actual competitions that we see as the daily life and training of the palaestra. Strigils, oil-flasks, and jumping-weights hang upon the walls; picks and javelins are planted in the ground. Trainers in their long mantles and naked assistants stand about and watch the practice of the youths. Sometimes with outstretched hands they instruct them; sometimes they correct them with their long forked rods. The youths themselves run, leap, wrestle, throw the diskos or the javelin; some look on and chat, others prepare for exercise, anointing their bodies with oil, binding on the boxing thongs, or fitting the cord to the javelin; others having finished their work scrape themselves with strigils, or standing round a basin empty vessels of water over each other. All the varied life of the palaestra is before us.

The vases on which these scenes abound belong chiefly to the middle of the century, the period of the "fine style," as it is called. But, as I have noted before, the actual athletic types have already become somewhat conventional, and we feel that the artist's interest in them has become secondary. It is rather the variety of the life, with its possibilities of grouping and composition, that appeals to him. At Athens, at least, a change is beginning in the attitude of the people towards athletics. The fine period of vase painting ends about the year 440 B.C., and in the vases of the decline this change is more marked. We still see the palaestra; but it is indicated sketchily by an occasional pair of halteres on the wall; and the youths stand about idly gossiping and arguing, but take no part in manly exercise. This disappearance of athletics from the vases is significant: the sculptor could still work out his own ideals, but the vase painter was dependent for his trade on the popular taste, and the vases are therefore a true index of the feeling of the time. If we compare one of these later vases with such a vase as the Panaetius kylix in Munich (Figure 17), we cannot help being reminded of the contrast drawn by Aristophanes in the *Clouds* between the old education of the men who fought at Marathon and the education of his day. The vases enable us to date the change about the year 440, and we shall find other indications that confirm this date.

Figure 17. R.-f. kylix. Munich, 795.

There is, however, in this athletic art something more than mere beauty or mere strength. The outward harmony is but the expression of that harmonious development of mind and body which it was the aim of Greek education to produce by means of music and gymnastic. For the interpretation of this spirit we can turn to the living word—a surer guide than merely subjective impressions. Athletic poetry arose like athletic sculpture in the sixth century, but while the athletic ideal continued to influence Greek art during the whole of its history, the hymn of victory, like the athletic painting on the vase, disappears abruptly before the Peloponnesian wars. The earliest writer of the epinikion, Simonides of Ceos, was born in the year 556 B.C.; his nephew Bacchylides, born at Iulis in the same island, lived till the year 428 B.C.[113] His great Theban rival, Pindar, born a few years earlier, had died in 443 B.C. With Pindar and Bacchylides the epinikion almost ceased to exist. We have indeed a fragment of a hymn written some years later by Euripides to celebrate the triumphs of Alcibiades in the chariot-race at Olympia. But this is a mere accident, and it is, we may mark, in honour not of an athletic event but of a chariot-race. Euripides, we shall see, was little inclined to hymn the athletes of his day. The last of Pindar's Odes, the 8th Pythian, was written in honour of a victory in wrestling won by Aristomenes of Aegina in 446 B.C., and the latest odes of Bacchylides which we can date are six years earlier. The agreement of these dates with the evidence of the vase paintings can hardly be an accidental coincidence.

Particularly noticeable are the number and importance of those odes which belong to the years immediately following the Persian wars. The writer of epinikia, like the sculptor of athletic statues, was by the very nature of his art Panhellenic. His muse, as Pindar tells us, was a hireling. He wrote for those who could pay him best, for the wealthy nobles of Thessaly or Aegina, or the princes of Sicily. Neither in Ceos nor in Thebes could a poet find sufficient scope for his genius. The little island of Ceos, famed for its athletes and its music, lay somewhat outside the main currents of Greek life. Thebes had fallen from her legendary greatness, and played but an inglorious part in the Persian wars. Hence, though the poets turned with special tenderness and pride to sing of the victors of their native cities, they spent much of their lives at the courts of powerful patrons, and found their highest inspiration in that burst of Panhellenic feeling that the Persian wars produced, and which for the moment united in the service of Hellas tyrant and oligarch and people. If Theban Pindar could not, like Simonides, sing of those who fell at Thermopylae or Salamis, his patriotism found vent in no less than six odes in honour of the victors in the great national celebration at Olympia in 476 B.C.

The defeat of Persia not only gave a fresh impulse to the Panhellenic festivals: it raised athletic training into a national duty. The consciousness of a great danger safely past arouses a nation to a sense of its military and physical needs. We can remember only a few years ago the growth of rifle clubs, the cry for military and physical training that followed the Boer war. The danger, it is felt at such times, may occur again, and it behoves every citizen to be ready to play his part. Among the Greeks this feeling gathered force not from any consciousness of their own shortcomings, but from a consciousness of their superiority. At Marathon the Greeks of the mainland had for the first time found themselves face to face with the Orientals, and for the first time realized the gulf that separated them from themselves. Their triumph was the triumph of freedom and law over slavery and despotism. A handful of free citizens had defeated a horde of slaves, and this result was due in no small degree to their athletic

---

[113] For the following sections *vide* Jebb's *Bacchylides*, Introduction.

training. Witness the famous charge of Marathon. Critics may throw doubt on its truth: it is sufficient that Herodotus supposed it possible. An army charging a distance of eight furlongs over ground that would try any cross-country runner! No wonder the Persians regarded the Greeks as madmen. The mere existence of such a story is proof enough of the athletic training of the nation. Moreover, the sight of the long-haired, effeminate Persians, whose bodies were not hardened by exercise and tanned by exposure to the air, seems to have impressed itself indelibly on the national imagination. Hence the extraordinary popularity during the years that followed of all those military and athletic exercises which we see so constantly depicted on the red-figured vases. We must remember that at Athens this training was for the most part voluntary. It was only during the two years' training of the epheboi that the state undertook the education of its members. Yet from this time the palaestra and gymnasium became the resort of all classes and all ages. And what was true of Athens, was true, we may feel sure, of the rest of Greece. For a time Athenian influence prevailed everywhere. The old Spartan pre-eminence had passed away, and even in athletics Athens had become the school of Greece. If Athens produced few victors in the games, she at least set an example in physical training. "Meet is it that from Athens a fashioner of athletes come," says Pindar of the Athenian Menander who trained Pytheas of Aegina for a Nemean victory, won probably in 481 or 479 B.C.[114] The effect of this national athletic movement is seen in the great games. The lists of the victors at Olympia, or the lists of those for whom Bacchylides and Pindar sang, are representative of the length and breadth of Greece from Rhodes to Agrigentum, from Cyrene to Thasos.[115] Finally, the national rejoicing over the victory of Plataea could find no fitter expression than the founding, at that city, of a new athletic festival, the Eleutheria.

Before we consider the individual writers of epinikia two points may be noticed which are common to all poems of this class. In the first place, the epinikion was essentially Panhellenic in its theme and also in its structure. The hymn itself consisted of three parts—an allusion to the victory, a legend suggested by the victor's home or lineage, or by the locality of the festival, and some moral reflections or advice. The heroes and gods of the legends had for the most part lost their local character and become the common property of the race, and the poet, by coupling the present with the past, thereby proclaimed the continuity and unity of Hellas. Secondly, the epinikion was aristocratic. The victors whom the poet praised were princes and nobles, who competed for pure love of sport, and for whom athletics were in no sense a profession, nor even the chief occupation of their lives. Life was not all sport in Greece at this period, and these men did not shirk their duties, but played their part with honour in the more serious contests of war and politics.

Of the epinikia of Simonides only a few fragments survive. To these we may add several epigrams of somewhat doubtful authenticity. Little more was known of Bacchylides till a few years ago the discovery of an Egyptian papyrus by Drs. Grenfell and Hunt restored to us, besides other poems, large portions of thirteen of his epinikia. Bacchylides came from an island of athletes: his own family seems to have been athletic, his grandfather is said to have been distinguished as an athlete, and his uncle was the poet Simonides. He dwells with intense delight on the details of the games, the light foot and strong hands of the victor, the

---

[114] Pindar, *N.* v. 49.
[115] *Vide* the list of Olympic victors for Ol. 75-83 found on an Oxyrhyncus papyrus. Grenfell and Hunt, *Ox. Pap.* ii. 222; C. Robert, *Hermes*, xxxv. pp. 141 ff.

whirlwind rush of the chariots, the cheers of the spectators, the triumphal rejoicings at the victor's home. But of the deeper meaning, the spirit of the games, we learn little from him.

With Pindar it is different. He is a prophet with a theory of life which he applies to everything of which he sings, to the stories of gods and heroes, or to the deeds of men. He has, too, a high conception of the poet's office, which is to give to all excellence that immortal fame which should be the chief incentive to all noble deeds. It has been said that to be an athlete and the father of athletes is for Pindar the highest reach of human ambition. The criticism is unfair for two reasons. In the first place, it takes account only of a portion of Pindar's work. He is said to have written poems of ten different classes, most of them connected with the worship of the gods. Of nine of these classes we possess but a few fragments; only the epinikia have survived. In the epinikia the poet's theme is necessarily the praise of winners at the games, in other words the praise of youth, and early manhood. But Pindar himself recognizes clearly that every age has its own excellence. The virtues of the old are good counsel and prudence, those of youth are courage and endurance. "By trial is the issue manifest,"[116] and the virtues of youth are proved in battle,[117] or in the peaceful contests of the games, which are, as we have seen, the training of the citizen for the sterner contests of war. Secondly, the word "athlete" is ambiguous. It suggests too much the professional athlete of a later age, the man who, from selfish and mercenary motives, devoted his whole life to athletics and who, as Euripides tells us, was after his prime "useless as a worn-out coat." But the well-born youths and princes for whom Pindar sang were actuated by no mercenary motives, but by that pure love of physical effort and of competition which is natural to all healthy youth. "The shepherd, and the ploughman, the fowler, and he whom the sea feedeth, strive but to keep fierce famine from their bellies; but whoso in the games or in war hath won delightful fame, receiveth the highest of rewards in fair words of citizens and of strangers."[118]

What then are the qualities of Pindar's athlete? They are summed up in that most typical of all his athletic odes, the 11th *Olympian*, in honour of Agesidamus of Epizephyrian Locri, the winner of the boys' boxing match in the great Ol. 76. "If one be born with excellent gifts, then may another who sharpeneth his natural edge, speed him, God helping, to an exceeding weight of glory. Without toil there have triumphed a very few."

Firstly and above all the athlete must be born "with excellent gifts." Strength and beauty are the gifts of Zeus, of the graces, of fate. They are bestowed especially on members of ancient and honourable families, and Pindar as a true aristocrat delights to enumerate the great deeds of the victor's ancestors in war and sport. He has, too, to the full, the artist's appreciation of physical beauty, and he never tires of describing it. But physical beauty must be matched by beautiful deeds; the athlete must not shame his beauty. Natural gifts imply the duty of developing them, and excellence can only be attained, God helping, by "cost and toil."[119] Here, as Professor Gildersleeve has well said, Pindar gives a moral dignity to athletics; for the cost and toil are undertaken not by compulsion or for selfish motives but for fame. Even the desire for fame is not selfish. Victory is a delight and honour to the victor's city, to his family, even to his dead ancestors. Moreover, the true sportsman "delights" in the toil and cost.

---

[116] *N.* iii. 70.
[117] *P.* ii. 63.
[118] *I.* i. 47 ff.
[119] *I.* i. 42, iv. 57, v. 10.

Figure 18. Charioteer. Delphi. (*Greek Sculpture*, Figure 138.)

The expense of competing in the chariot and horse races was naturally far heavier than that of competing in athletic events; yet even the latter involved considerable sacrifice of time and money, and the services of the famous trainers mentioned by the poets must have been dearly bought. The toil, too, was not unaccompanied by risk. More than two-thirds of Pindar's victors won their crowns in wrestling, boxing, or the pankration, events which involved no little danger to limb, if not to life. The chariot-race had been equally dangerous in days when the owners drove their own chariots. In Pindar's time this was no longer the rule. We could hardly expect a Hieron or a Gelon to compete in person, any more than we could expect to find one of our own horse owners riding his own horse in the Derby. Yet we still find the owner occasionally acting as charioteer,[120] and more frequently still some son or younger member of his family.[121] Such, it seems likely, was the aristocratic youth whose bronze statue has been recently discovered by the French at Delphi[122] (Figure 18). The element of risk must always add a zest to sport, and it certainly does in Pindar's eyes. "Deeds of no risks," he says, "are honourless whether done among men or among hollow ships."[123] It follows then that the most necessary qualities for an athlete are courage and endurance. On the latter virtue Pindar, like his countrymen generally, insists even more than on courage, perhaps because the Greeks felt the need of it more. Heracles for example, Pindar's ideal athletic hero, is a "man of unbending spirit." Yet neither physical strength nor endurance is sufficient without skill, and skill can only be obtained by constant practice under skilful teachers.

---

[120] Herodotus of Thebes, *I*. i.
[121] Thrasybulus, *P*. vi.; *I*. ii.
[122] *Greek Sculpture*, Figure 138. The identification of this statue is uncertain. It has been suggested that the word "Polyzalos" on the basis is an adjective, and that the victory recorded is that of Arcesilas of Cyrene. This view has been assailed in *Ath. Mitth.* xxxiv. by A. D. Keramopoullos, who believes that the statue was vowed by Gelon and actually set up by Polyzalos.
[123] *O*. vi. 9.

In the old days athletic skill had been handed down in noble families from father to son; such families still existed. Lampon of Aegina, the father of two athletes, Phylacidas and Pytheas,[124] is described as a "whetstone among athletes," bestowing practice on all that he does, and exhorting his sons to follow the precept of Hesiod, "Practice perfects the deed." His son Phylacidas, too, is commended for his training of his younger brother Pytheas. More often, however, the services of a professional trainer were called in. Thus Pytheas owed his victory largely to the Athenian trainer Menander. But though training can help to develop natural gifts, without natural gifts it can do little. "The natural," says Pindar, "is ever best."[125]

But when athlete and trainer have done their best, the issue still rests in the hands of the gods. Pindar, like Aeschylus, is deeply religious, and regards the gods as the moral rulers of the world. Every good gift of mind or body, every excellence comes from the gods, and victory is bestowed on those who are pleasing to them. Man wins their favour partly by piety, by observance of their festivals and offerings at their altars, but still more by such conduct as averts their jealousy. Their jealousy is excited by all excess, by pride and insolence; it is appeased by that attitude of mind which is expressed by that untranslatable and indefinable word αἰδώς. Aidos is the direct opposite of ὕβρις or insolence; it is the feeling of respect for what is due to the gods, to one's fellowmen, to oneself, a feeling that begets a like feeling towards oneself in others. It is the spirit of reverence, of modesty, of courtesy. Above all it is the sense of honour, and as such inspires the athlete and the soldier, distinguishing them from the bully and the oppressor. Strength may tempt its owner to abuse it; success may engender "braggart insolence."[126] But aidos puts into men's hearts "valour and the joy of battle."[127] Aidos, mark, not passion, aidos, the child of forethought, and therefore the true man feels for his might "aidos," which prevents him from abusing it.[128] Hence while the bully inspires terror and loathing, the warrior and the athlete win in the sight of citizens and strangers grace and honour (αἰδοία χάρις).[129]

In sport aidos is that scrupulous sense of honour and fairness, which is of the essence of that much abused word "a sportsman." No sports demand so high a sense of honour as boxing and wrestling, the events which, with the pankration, were most popular in Greece, and no sports are therefore so liable to abuse and corruption. It is aidos which makes a man a "straight fighter," εὐθυμάχας, the epithet with which Pindar describes the boxer Diagoras of Rhodes, "who walks in the straight path that abhors insolence."[130] The commercial spirit is incompatible with this feeling. "Aidos is stolen away by secret gains,"[131] says Pindar in his praise of Chromius of Aetna. Was he thinking of the scandal aroused a few years before by Astylus of Croton when for the sake of gain he proclaimed himself a Syracusan? It is tempting to suppose so. The resentment that this conduct caused was at least a healthy sign. Further, aidos is akin to and includes the principle of self-control, σωφροσύνη, which is implied in Pindar's favourite doctrine of the mean,[132] and which plays so important a part in

---

[124] *I.* iv., v.; *N.* v.
[125] *O.* ix. 100.
[126] *O.* i. 56, xiii. 10; *N.* i. 65; *I.* iii. 2.
[127] *O.* vii. 44.
[128] *P.* iv. 173.
[129] *O.* vii. 89; cp. vi. 76, where χάρις is αἰδοία as the giver of αἰδώς.
[130] *O.* vii. 15, 90.
[131] *N.* ix. 33.
[132] σωφροσύνη does not occur in Pindar; σώφρων only twice: *P.* iii. 63, of Cheiron; *I.* vii. 27, of the sons of Aeacus. For the meaning of αἰδώς cp. Gilbert Murray, *The Rise of the Greek Epic*, p. 88.

the philosophy of the next century. The self-control of the athlete was a commonplace, but aidos is something more subtle, more indefinable, more effective than any rule or principle; and the comprehension of it helps us to understand how even sports which seem at first sight brutal are yet under the special patronage of those fair-haired graces who, in Professor Gildersleeve's expressive phrase, "give and grace the victory," "from whom come unto men all pleasant things and sweet, and the wisdom of man and his beauty and the splendour of his fame."[133]

Such an ideal could not fail to exercise a lasting influence on athletics. Literature and art increased the popularity of athletics by appealing not merely with new force to the old motives of patriotism and religion but also to the growing aesthetic feeling of the race. To this may be ascribed the importance which the Greeks ascribed to style and grace. It was not sufficient, for example, to throw an opponent in wrestling, it had to be done in style and with skill. The cult of style grew sometimes, it would seem, almost into affectation. Aelian tells a story of a trainer, Hippomachus, who hearing the crowd applaud a pupil of his for throwing his opponent, at once chastised him, saying that he must have done something wrong, for the people would never have cheered a scientific throw.[134] We do not know the date of Hippomachus, but the story undoubtedly illustrates a tendency which actually existed.

The same love of beauty must have helped to check the growth of specialization with its exaggerated and one-sided development, and also to preserve the purity of sport against the influence of professionalism. Thanks largely to this ideal Olympia maintained her prestige, and to a great extent her high standard of athletic honour, long after the liberty of Greece had become a memory, and her gods a laughing-stock of the satirist. An inscription of the reign of Hadrian, discovered at Olympia, is a striking illustration of this vitality. It records a decree in honour of T. Claudius Rufus, a pankratiast of Smyrna, who, though matched in the final heat of the pankration with an opponent who had drawn a bye in the preceding heat, fought on till nightfall, and left the contest drawn.[135] The decree relates how he had resided at Olympia for the necessary course of training so that his σωφροσύνη was recognized by all men, how he had trained according to the traditional customs of the games, and had in the stadium given an exhibition worthy of Olympian Zeus, and of his own training and reputation, in recognition of which the Eleans had voted him the right of erecting his statue in the Altis. The decree is perhaps somewhat fulsome, and suggests that such examples of σωφροσύνη must have been exceptional at the time. Yet it shows that the memory at least of the old ideal survived even under the empire and was still cherished at Olympia.

We have already seen what an impulse was given to athletics and to the Panhellenic festivals by the Persian wars. No festival was more Panhellenic than that of Olympia, and no place felt more keenly than Elis the invigorating effects of the new spirit of unity and of freedom. Elis had played an inglorious part in the national struggle. The narrow and unprogressive oligarchy showed the same lack of energy and initiative which they had shown in the management of the Olympic festival during the sixth century. The Elean contingent arrived at Plataea too late to take part in the battle. Returning home full of bitter self-reproach they at once determined to put an end to the old régime, and banished the leaders who had been responsible for the fiasco. This was the beginning of the Synoecism of Elis which was

---

[133] *O.* xiv. 5.
[134] Aelian, *V.H.* ii. 6.
[135] *Ol. Ins.* 54.

not finally completed till 471 B.C., when the government of the scattered, unwalled villages was for the first time centred in the newly founded city state of Elis. The change was facilitated by the eclipse of Spartan prestige in the Peloponnese, while the growing influence of Athens was clearly shown both in these political changes and in the outburst of artistic activity at Olympia which followed the founding of Elis. But the new order could not fail to excite violent opposition, especially among the conservative folk of Pisatis and Triphylia, and their opposition culminated in a civil war which only ended about the year 470 or 469 with the devastation of the whole district by the Eleans.

The opposition of Pisatis was due partly to the transference of the political centre to Elis, perhaps in a greater degree to the new régime inaugurated at Olympia. The old dual control of the festival by Elis and Pisatis was, as we have seen already, passing away; possibly its death-blow was given by the banishment of the aristocrats, some of whom may have had hereditary connexion with the festival. At all events, from the time of Plataea the two Hellanodicae who represented the dual control were replaced by a board of nine,[136] and permanent quarters were provided for the new administration by the enlargement of the Bouleuterion, the south wing of which was added about this time. The increase in the number of officials may have been rendered desirable by the increasing strenuousness of the competitions. The nine were divided into three groups of three each, in charge respectively of the horse-races, the pentathlon, and the other athletic events, an excellent arrangement which at once commends itself to the modern athletic mind. Yet it seems more likely that the number nine was dictated by political considerations, and the fact that there were nine tribes of the Eleans. It was a change to a sort of popular representation, and its popular character is further marked by the fact that these officials were elected by lot, a democratic institution which can hardly have belonged to the earlier régime.

This change first took effect in Ol. 76, and possibly was introduced in view of that great national Olympiad. It was on this occasion, according to a popular story, that Themistocles himself appeared and received such an ovation from the crowd that the athletes themselves were neglected. The national character of this Olympiad assured the success of the new order. In the following festival the competition was so great that the pankration could not be decided before nightfall, and it was decided from this date to extend and rearrange the festival. In the 77th Olympiad, too, a tenth Hellanodicas was added apparently to represent the newly conquered district of Triphylia. This number remained unchanged till Ol. 103, when, the number of tribes having been raised to twelve in consequence of a still further extension of territory southwards, a corresponding change was made in the number of the Hellanodicae. The war with Arcadia which ensued reduced the number for a time to eight, but in Ol. 108 the number was restored to ten and no further change was made. These Hellanodicae must be regarded as the executive officers of the Elean Council, to whom in case of doubt or dissatisfaction there was a right of appeal.

The intimate connexion between the political changes in Elis and the Olympic festival can be best realized from Pausanias' account of the new city.[137] Everything in Elis seems to have been planned purely and simply with a view to the festival. The agora was nothing more or less than a training-ground for horses, it was a large open square or oblong surrounded by colonnades with no other ornaments than a few altars to Zeus and other gods, and even these

---

[136] Paus. v. 9, 5.
[137] vi. 23.

so constructed as to be easily removable. Close to this agora, appropriately called the hippodrome, were no less than three gymnasia with running tracks, and rings for boxing or wrestling, and conveniently connected with agora and gymnasium was the Hellanodiceon, or headquarters of the Hellanodicae. Here the latter had to reside for ten months before the festival, receiving instruction in all the ancient usages of the games from the Guardians of the Lavs (Nomophylakes). During the last month before the games they themselves were engaged in superintending the practice of the athletes, who spent the last thirty days of their training at Elis, and in classifying men and horses according to age, a matter of no little difficulty when no registers of births were kept. The principal buildings of Elis city were all connected with the games, and though we cannot tell the date of those which Pausanias saw, there can be little doubt that they truly indicate the character of the city from the start. The agora was typical of the rest, and Pausanias pointedly contrasts it with the cheerful market-places of Ionian towns. Certainly it cannot have been an attractive place to live in, and the Eleans never took kindly to it; indeed many an old-fashioned country gentleman lived and died without even setting foot in his chief city.[138]

Meanwhile great changes were taking place at Olympia. Its national character was recognized by the dedication in the Altis, from the spoil of Plataea, of a colossal bronze statue of Zeus, on the base of which were inscribed the names of all states which had taken part in the battles. But the new feeling of national unity found a yet worthier monument in the whole series of buildings which the new administration undertook, to render the sacred precinct worthy of its Panhellenic dignity. Hitherto, as we have seen, various states had been allowed to secure for themselves points of vantage at the festival by building, along the foot of the hill of Cronus, treasuries, or communal houses. Three more of these buildings—the last of them—were added shortly after Plataea. All these were at the western end of the terrace. One of them was dedicated by the Syracusans in commemoration of their victory over the Carthaginians at Himera; another was built by the Sicyonians, possibly on the site of an older foundation, containing the great bronze treasure-chests dedicated by Myron; the builders of the third are unknown, but it has been plausibly suggested that they were the Samians. Sicyon had played an important part in the war with Persia both by land and sea, Samos was closely connected with the victory at Mycale, and it is tempting to imagine that both these treasuries were memorials of the national victory. This, however, is mere conjecture; what is certain is, that these treasuries were built shortly after Plataea and that from this date the building of such treasuries ceases abruptly. Henceforth the Eleans took into their own hands the embellishment of the Altis, and their first work was in connexion with the treasuries.[139]

The loose nature of the soil had rendered the building of the westernmost treasuries a matter of considerable difficulty. Accordingly, the Eleans constructed nine rows of stone steps extending continuously from the western end of the Heraeum along the whole length of the treasury terrace. These steps not only served as a retaining wall to the treasuries but furnished a capacious stand from which thousands of spectators could view the games and sacrifices, which still centred round the altar of Zeus. Shortly afterwards was built the additional wing of the Bouleuterion mentioned above.

The next move of the Eleans was to provide a temple worthy of Olympian Zeus, and the money for this work was provided from the plunder gained in Triphylia and Pisatis. The new

---

[138] Polybius iv. 73.
[139] L. Dyer, "The Olympian Theatron" in *J.H.S.* xxviii. p. 265.

temple was begun about the year 468 B.C., and perhaps its buildings suggested to Pindar the opening lines of his 6th Olympian Ode in which he compares the prelude of his song to the façade of a stately fane. The temple must have been completed about the time of the defeat of the Athenians and Argives by Sparta at Tanagra in 457; for the Spartans commemorated their victory by a golden shield which was placed on the summit of the temple. It would be out of place here to attempt any description of the temple: we may notice, however, that while the architect Libon was an Elean, the great chryselephantine statue of Zeus afterwards erected in it was the masterpiece of Pheidias, and Pausanias ascribes some of the sculptural decorations to the Athenian sculptors Paeonius and Alcamenes, though modern authorities generally discredit the statement. And just as Pheidias in his Zeus tried to represent the highest ideal of Greek manhood, so in the lesser works, the mythological scenes of the pediments and metopes, the chariot-race of Pelops and Oenomaus, the battle of the Lapiths and Centaurs, the labours of Heracles, we have in reality various renderings of the theme which inspires all the art of this period, the triumph of the Greek over the barbarian, of trained skill over undisciplined force. Thus the temple of Zeus was truly a national memorial of the Persian wars.

The new temple was built on the site of the ancient grove, and its building had no doubt interfered with anything in the nature of fence or hedge which may have bounded the sacred grove. Perhaps we may assign to this period the idea of marking out the Altis in the rough quadrilateral shape which has been revealed by later ruins. This plan seems to be implied in the building of the first colonnade at the eastern end of and at right angles, to the treasury terrace. This colonnade was built about the middle of the fifth century, and was obviously intended for the convenience of spectators at the festival, commanding, as it did, a full view of the ancient altar and of the east end of the newly built temple of Zeus. Its building necessitated a change in the athletic arrangements.

The foot-races could no longer take place near the altar, and a new permanent "dromos," or race-course, was provided to the east of the colonnade. This may have been partly a concession to the growing demands of professional athletes, but the new race-course was still of the simplest. The ground was approximately levelled, the course was measured and perhaps marked by a permanent line of stone slabs at either end, and water-channels were provided to carry the water from the west of the Altis to the race-course, for the convenience of spectators and athletes alike. Perhaps permanent seats were provided for the Hellanodicae, and for the priestess of Demeter Chamyne, who had a place of honour opposite them. The rest of the spectators had no seats, but reclined or stood on the slopes of the hill of Cronus, or else on the flat plain that stretched between the stadium and the Alpheus.

Whether all the athletic events or only the races were transferred to the new course is uncertain. The only evidence on the point is contained in a passage of Xenophon, describing the battle which took place at Olympia in 364 B.C. In this year the wrestling of the pentathlon undoubtedly took place near the altar as it had done in Pindar's time; but it is not quite clear whether this was the usual thing or exceptional. In the dearth of evidence it is a matter for individual judgment, and my own opinion is that only the foot-races and throwing the diskos and javelin were transferred to the new dromos, and that boxing, wrestling, and the pankration continued to take place in the triangular space commanded by the treasury terrace and the colonnade. The treasury terrace and colonnade formed the theatre of which Xenophon speaks, and certainly offered far better accommodation for spectators of such events than was possible in the stadium proper, at least until it was improved and banked up after the battle of Chaeronea.[140]

About the same time improvements were made in the hippodrome. Hitherto the arrangements for the equestrian events must have been as simple as for the athletics. But now a permanent hippodrome was provided south of the stadium, and an elaborate starting-gate for the chariots was constructed by the artist Cleoetas.[141] The chariots were arranged in pairs opposite each other along the sides of a triangle, the apex of which pointed down the course. In the centre of this triangle was an altar of Poseidon, on which stood a bronze eagle. At the apex was a brazen dolphin. At the moment of starting this dolphin fell to the ground and the eagle rose, thus announcing the start to the spectators. At the same time the ropes in front of the pair of chariots nearest to the base were withdrawn. As they drew level with the next pair, the next ropes were withdrawn, and so on till the whole field were fairly started.

We may notice here a work which, though perhaps of somewhat later date, illustrates the Panhellenic character of Olympia. The old tripod on which the branches of sacred olive tree for the prizes were placed, was replaced by an ivory and gold table, the work of Colotes of Heraclea,[142] a disciple of Pheidias, who assisted the latter in constructing the chryselephantine statue of Zeus. The table was kept in the Heraeum and at the time of the festival was placed beside the seat of the Hellanodicae in the stadium. On one side were representations of Hera and Zeus, of the Mother of the Gods, Hermes, Apollo, and Artemis. On the other side were figures of Pluto and Persephone, recalling those ancient Chthonic cults which had existed at Olympia from time immemorial, and of which many traces survive, especially to the east of the Altis.

The activity of the Eleans had, as we have seen, put an end to architectural dedications by other states; but the piety of the Greek world found expression in the dedication of statues and votive offerings. During the nine Olympiads which followed the Persian wars 476-444 B.C., no less than thirty-five statues of victors were set up on the Altis, while in the next nine Olympiads the number drops to twenty.[143] These statistics bear out the date of the change in Greek athletics which will be discussed in the next chapter.

---

[140] L. Dyer, *l.c.*
[141] Paus. vi. 20, 14. *Vide infra*, Figure 164.
[142] Paus. v. 20, 2; Pliny, *N.H.* xxxv. 54.
[143] These figures are taken from the lists given in Hyde's *De Olympionicarum Statuis*.

Chapter 6

PROFESSIONALISM AND SPECIALIZATION, 440-338 B.C.

Literature and art purified and refined athletics for a while, but at the same time by encouraging competition intensified these very evils which result from excessive competition, and when the Panhellenic movement had spent its force, and strife and faction once more resumed their sway in the Greek world, the decline of athletics was rapid. Nowhere is excess more dangerous than in athletics, and the charm of poetry and art must not blind us to that element of exaggeration which existed in the hero-worship of the athlete. The nemesis of excess in athletics is specialization, specialization begets professionalism, and professionalism is the death of all true sport.

Figure 19. Apoxyomenos. Rome, Vatican.

We have seen how even before the time of Pindar the growth of competition had developed athletics beyond their legitimate sphere of exercise and recreation till they became an end in themselves, and how success in the great games demanded an undue expenditure of time and of money. During the fifth century specialization made rapid progress in the hands of professional trainers, whose business it was to train competitors for the great games.[144]

The earliest trainers were boxers and wrestlers, who probably confined themselves to giving instruction in these exercises. Such training was of course necessary and useful, but shortly after the Persian wars it was discovered that excellence in any particular event could be secured by special training and special diet, and the trainer began to take upon himself the whole direction of his pupil's life. This specialized artificial training was good neither for the athlete nor for the nation.

The aim of the earlier training had been to produce a harmonious development of the whole body. The new training, by prescribing concentration on some particular exercise, produced a one-sided development. "The runner," says Socrates, "has over-developed his legs, and the boxer the upper part of his body,"[145] and he humorously suggests that he finds dancing a better form of exercise than athletics. In another passage of the *Memorabilia*, Socrates compliments a sculptor, whom under the name of Cleiton we may perhaps recognize as Polycleitus,[146] on his power of representing the different physical types produced by different forms of sport. Unfortunately we have not sufficient material to enable us to verify this statement for the sculpture of the end of the fifth century. But some idea of the diversity of type produced may be obtained by comparing two somewhat later works, the Apoxyomenos, formerly ascribed to Lysippus (Figure 19), and the Agias, a genuine work of Lysippus, recently discovered at Delphi[147] (Figure 20). In the former we see the thoroughbred type of the runner with his length of limb and fine ankles, in the latter the sturdier, heavier type of the pankratiast. Neither of these two statues, however, is open to the charge of one-sided development which Socrates brings against the athletes of his time, and which would probably be more noticeable in inferior works of art. For this we must turn to the vases. A Panathenaic vase in the British Museum, dated 336 B.C., shows us the typical boxer of the period, with his clumsy, bulky body and small coarse head[148] (Figure 135). A comparison of these boxers with the athletes on the red-figured vases affords convincing proof of the change which had come over athletics.

The old athlete had lived a simple, natural, open-air life. Training in the strict sense of the word he had none. His diet had been mainly vegetarian. Like the diet of the country-folk in Greece at all times, it consisted mainly of figs and cheese from the baskets, of porridge and meal-cakes with only such meat as occasion offered.[149] It has been often stated that a diet of figs and cheese was prescribed by the law of the Olympic festival, and various fanciful interpretations of this custom have been suggested. It is possible that certain forms of food

---

[144] The first trainer of whom we hear is Tisias, who trained Glaucus of Carystus (Philostratus, *Gym.* 20). Pindar mentions Menander (*N.* v.; cp. Bacchylides xii.), Orseas (*I.* iii.), Ilas (*O.* xi.), Melesias (*O.* viii.; *N.* iv., vi.).
[145] *Symposium*, 2, 17.
[146] *Mem.* iii. 10, 6; iii. 8, 4; cp. P. Gardner, *Grammar of Greek Art*, p. 17.
[147] *Greek Sculpture*, p. 550; and *J.H.S.* 1905, p. 235.
[148] *B.M. Vases*, 607. Quite different is the type of the long-distance runner of B. 611 (328 B.C.) and B. 609 (333 B.C.), and of the Hoplitodromos of B. 608 (336 B.C.). *Vide* Figures. 51, 58.
[149] Paus. vi. 7, 10 τυρὸν ἐκ τῶν ταλάρων. Diogen. Laert. ἰσχάσι ξηραῖς καὶ πυροῖς. Philostrat. *Gym.* 43 αἴ τε μᾶζαι καὶ τῶν ἄρτων οἱ ἄπτιστοι καὶ μὴ ζυμῖται καὶ τῶν κρεῶν τὰ βόειά τε καὶ ταύρεια καὶ τράγεια καὶ δόρκοι. *Vide* Jüthner, *Philostratus*, pp. 268 ff., and Krause, *Gym.* pp. 654 ff.

were forbidden to competitors at particular festivals; thus at Delphi we know that the introduction of wine into the stadium was forbidden, and that any breach of this rule was punished by a fine, half of which was paid to the god, the other half to the informer.[150] But such prohibitions were of the nature of a religious taboo, and there is no reason for supposing that the diet of athletes was otherwise regulated by any law. Indeed we have direct evidence to the contrary, for the introduction of a meat diet in the fifth century is ascribed to two private individuals—to Dromeus of Stymphalus, a runner who twice won the long race at Olympia in Ols. 80 and 81, and to Pythagoras of Samos, who trained Eurymenes, the winner of the boxing in Ol. 77.[151]

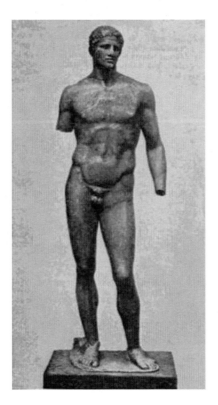

Figure 20. Statue of Agias by Lysippus. Delphi. (*Greek Sculpture*, Figure 141.)

The introduction of a meat diet was a momentous change: it created an artificial distinction between the life of an athlete and the life of the ordinary man, who ate meat but sparingly and only as a relish. Its object, of course, was to produce the bulk of body and weight which are important considerations in boxing and wrestling, and which were especially so in Greece inasmuch as classification by weight was unknown in those

---

[150] *B.C.H.*, 1899, p. 611. I have accepted the rendering of the inscription given by A. D. Keramopoullos in Ἐφ. Ἀρχ., 1906, p. 167. Instead of the name Εὐδρόμου, an utterly unknown hero, of whose shrine not a vestige has been found, he reads δρόμου. He repeats a misstatement made in Dar.-Sagl., Paully-Wissowa, and other dictionaries to the effect that athletes were not allowed to drink any wine. The *only* authority for the statement is a single passage from Galen, *de Salub. vict. rat.*, in which he says that "after exercise athletes do not drink wine but water first, having learnt this from experience!" An egregious example of the absurdities which crowd the pages of our dictionaries!

[151] Paus. vi. 7, 3; Diogen. Laert. viii. 13; Pliny, *Hist. Nat.* xxiii. 7.

competitions. Boxing, wrestling, and the pankration were, as I have stated, the most popular and most honoured of all the events in Greek sport, and it is in these events that specialization and professionalism first made their appearance, and that their results were most fatal. To produce the necessary bulk of body the trainer prescribed for his pupils vast quantities of meat, which had to be counteracted by violent exercise. Eating, sleeping, and exercise occupied the athlete's whole time, and left little time or leisure for any other pursuits.[152] "Socrates," says Xenophon, "disapproved of such a life as incompatible with the cultivation of the soul." Even from a physical point of view this system of training was vicious and unscientific. It might produce weight and strength, but it did so at the sacrifice of activity and health. In the case of the young it tended to stunt the growth and destroy all beauty of form; and Aristotle, speaking no doubt of his own time, remarks on the fact that the boy victors at Olympia rarely repeated their successes as men.[153] Moreover, the athlete's strength was useless for practical purposes. Epaminondas, we are told, when he came of age and began to frequent the palaestra, devoted himself to such exercises as produced activity rather than great strength, considering that the latter was of little use for war. So he exercised himself in running, and in wrestling "only so far as he could stand on his feet," but he spent most of his time in the practice of arms.[154] Equally unsuitable for war was the habit of life produced by athletic training. "The athlete's nature," says Plato, "is sleepy, and the least variation from his routine is liable to cause him serious illness."[155] Such a man is incapable of standing the various vicissitudes of a campaign, and therefore we find athletics condemned not only by philosophers like Plato and Aristotle but by generals such as Epaminondas, Alexander, and Philopoemen.[156] "The athlete," says Euripides, "is the slave of his jaw and of his belly."

Medical science confirmed the verdict of the philosopher and the soldier. Hippocrates of Cos, "the father of medicine," and a contemporary of Herodicus and Gorgias, condemned the high state of training produced by athletics as a dangerous and unstable condition of body.[157] To live in a constant state of training is bad for any man, and especially under a system so unscientific as that of the Greeks.

There was another reason for the condemnation of athletics by military authorities. The old Homeric sports had been practical and military: the system of physical education which had grown out of them had produced that all-round development which made a man fit for all the duties of life in peace or war; but the new specialized education produced only a one-sided development, and at the same time was so exacting as to leave no time for the practice of military exercises. Plato was an ardent advocate of physical training. Trained by his father Ariston, who was a distinguished athlete, he had won victories in wrestling at Delphi, Nemea, and the Isthmus, and is even stated, though with less probability, to have won the Olympic crown. But the philosopher could find no place for the athletics of his day in his ideal state,

---

[152] Xen. *Mem.* i. 2, 4; Aristoph. *Pax*, 33, 34; Aristot. *Eth. Nic.* ii. 6, 7. Eating like a wrestler was proverbial.

[153] *Pol.* v. 1339 a. Krause (*Gym.* p. 645, n. 3), and other writers following him, discredit this statement, not realizing that Aristotle is speaking of professional athletics. Of the eight examples quoted by Krause of athletes who had won victories both as boys and as men, five belong to the sixth or early fifth century, one is later than Aristotle, one is contemporary with him, the date of the eighth is doubtful.

[154] Corn. Nepos, *Epam.* 2.

[155] *Rep.* iii. 404 A; cp. Arist. *Pol.* 1335 b.

[156] Plutarch, *Vit. Alexander* and *Philopoemon*.

[157] Galen, Προτρεπτ. λόγ. ii. ἡ δὲ τῶν ἀθλητῶν ἐπ' ἄκρον εὐεξία σφαλερά τε καὶ εὐμετάπτωτος. Krause, *Gym.* p. 47, n. 1.

and he therefore, in the *Laws*,[158] proposes a new and more practical gymnastic based on the requirements of war. From the age of six, boys, and girls too, are to learn to ride, to learn the use of the bow, the javelin, and the sling, and to learn to use the left hand as well as the right. In wrestling and boxing all tricks invented "out of a vain spirit of competition" are to be eschewed and only such forms practised as are likely to be of service for war. The dances, too, must be military in character, marches and processions in armour and on horseback, or mimic contests like the dances of Crete and Sparta. In another passage[159] he describes the competitions suitable for his ideal state. All foot-races are to be run in armour, there is to be a long-distance race of sixty stades in heavy armour, and a still longer race of 100 stades over mountains and across every sort of country for the light-armed archer. Instead of wrestling and the pankration there are to be conflicts in armour, and for the light-armed troops combats with bows, and javelins, and slings under a code of laws drawn up by military experts. The military character of Plato's scheme indicates the philosopher's opinion on the unpractical character of the existing athletics.

An interesting development of athletic training which has its parallel in our own day was the rise of "medical gymnastics." The valetudinarian school of gymnastic originated with Herodicus of Selymbria, a contemporary of Socrates whom Plato ridicules for corrupting the arts of gymnastic and medicine.[160] "By a combination of training and doctoring he found out a way of torturing, first and chiefly, himself, and, secondly, the rest of the world, by the invention of a lingering death. Having a mortal disease, which he perpetually tended, he passed his whole life as a valetudinarian." By the introduction of elaborate rules for eating and drinking he corrupted athletics, and is justly described by Plato as a gymnastic sophist, a name that might well be applied to many of the advertizing quacks of our own day. In this respect he is coupled by Plato with the somewhat earlier trainer, Iccus of Tarentum, who won the pentathlon at Olympia in Ol. 76, and who was famed for his temperance and self-restraint.[161] These trainers are credited with the invention of medical massage (ἰατραλειπτική), a development of the massage applied to athletes before and after training by the ἀλείπτης. Alexander had in his suite an Athenian Athenophanes, whose duty it was to attend his master in the bath and anoint him with oil.[162]

Of the rich rewards lavished upon successful athletes we have spoken in a previous chapter. In the *Plutus* of Aristophanes Hermes, having deserted the gods, takes service with Plutus as the "presider over contests." "For," says he, "there is no service more profitable to Plutus than holding contests in music and athletics."[163] Plato knows no life more blessed from a material point of view than that of an Olympic victor, and in the myth of Er he describes the

---

[158] *Leg.* 794 ff.
[159] *Leg.* 833 ff.
[160] Rep. 406 B; *Protag.* 316 D; Aristot. *Rhet.* i. 5.
An entirely different view of Herodicus is ably stated by Dr. Jüthner in the introduction to his Philostratus. He regards Herodicus as the father of scientific and medical gymnastic, as applied to the preservation of health and the cure of disease, and he claims that Plato himself shows warm recognition of his merits in the passage in the *Protagoras*, where he classes him with Homer, Hesiod, and others, among the great sophists who beguiled mankind. The passage certainly proves the ability and popularity of Herodicus, but I can see in it no evidence that Plato did not genuinely dislike his system. The strongest proof of the unscientific and useless character of his system is supplied by the deterioration of the athlete and of the national physique, which dates from this period.
[161] Plato, *Leg.* 839 C.
[162] Plutarch, *Vita. Alexand.* 35.
[163] *Plutus*, 1161.

soul of Atalanta choosing the body of an athlete on seeing "the great rewards bestowed on the athlete." Still more significant is the story of the Rhodian Dorieus, one of the famous Diagoridae. Banished from Rhodes by the Athenians he went to Thurii, and, as a commander of a Thurian ship, took part in the war against Athens. Taken prisoner by the Athenians in 407 B.C. he was set free without ransom in consideration of the fame which he and his family had won at Olympia.[164]

The result of specialization is professionalism. There is a point in any sport or game where it becomes over-developed, and competition too severe, for it to serve its true purpose of providing exercise or recreation for the many. It becomes the monopoly of the few who can afford the time or money to acquire excellence, while the rest, despairing of any measure of success, prefer the role of spectators. When the rewards of success are sufficient there arises a professional class, and when professionalism is once established the amateur can no longer compete with the professional.

Before the close of the fifth century the word ἀθλητής had already come to denote the professional athlete as opposed to the amateur or ἰδιώτης. Xenophon relates a conversation between Socrates and an ill-developed youth, in which the philosopher taunts the latter with his very "unprofessional" condition of body.[165] Athletics were out of fashion at that time among the smart young men of Athens, who, like Alcibiades, disdained to compete with their inferiors. "Of course," replies the youth indignantly, "for I am not a professional, I am an amateur." Whereupon the philosopher reads him a lecture on the duty of developing the body to its utmost. "No citizen has a right to be an amateur in the matter of physical training: it is part of his profession as a citizen to keep himself in good condition, ready to serve his state at a moment's notice. The instinct of self-preservation demands it likewise: for how helpless is the state of the ill-trained youth in war or danger! Finally what a disgrace it is for a man to grow old without ever seeing the beauty and strength of which his body is capable!" The ideal of Socrates is the earlier ideal which was already passing away, while the reply of Epigenes illustrates the change which had taken place in the character of the athlete and in the popular attitude towards athletics.

At the time of the Persian wars the Greeks had been a nation of athletes. At the time of the Peloponnesian wars the mass of the people were no longer athletic. Aristophanes bitterly deplores the change.[166] At Athens the young men had deserted the palaestra and gymnasium for the luxurious baths and the market-place; pale-faced and narrow-chested, they had not even sufficient training to run the torch-race. The labour of training was distasteful to the Athenians, who, as Thucydides tells us, preferred to be spectators of the deeds of others rather than doers. Sparta had long taken little part in athletic competitions, with the exception of the foot-race, but her rigorous system of education, brutalizing as it was, saved her at least from the evils of specialized athletics. Of other parts of Greece we know little; in the richer and more progressive cities it is probable that life was much the same as at Athens, while the records of Olympia show that the victors were drawn more and more from the poorer and less progressive country districts, from Thessaly, and particularly from the mountains of Arcadia.[167] It was only when athletics became a profitable profession that the poor but healthy countryman could afford to compete at the great festivals. The large number of competitions

---

[164] Xen. *Hell.* i. 5, 19; Paus. vi. 7, 4.
[165] *Mem.* iii. 12. For the contrast between ἀθλητής and ἰδιώτης cp. *Hieron*, 4, 6; *Mem.* iii. 7, 7.
[166] *Nub.* 961-1023; *Ran.* 1086.
[167] Thus in the present day professional football-players are largely drawn from the country districts of Scotland.

for boys and youths offered the promising boxer or wrestler a source of profit from an early age, and at Olympia these competitions were almost monopolized by the youth of Elis and Arcadia.

The severest indictment of professionalism occurs in the well-known fragment of Euripides' lost play, the *Autolycus*. Euripides was no enemy of sport. His parents had wished to train him as an athlete, and he had won prizes as a boy at the Eleusinian and the Thesean games. He is said to have offered himself as a candidate at Olympia, but to have been disqualified owing to some doubt about his age. Countless allusions in his writings show his appreciation of all manly sports. But athletic success could not satisfy his restless and ambitious spirit, and, like Xenophanes two generations before, he could not be blind to the unreality of the worship of athletics, and to the evils which it was producing. "Of all the countless evils throughout Hellas," he cries, "there is none worse than the race of athletes." The evil is not confined to Athens; it is widespread throughout Hellas. "In youth they strut about in splendour, the pride of their city, but when bitter old age comes upon them they are cast aside like threadbare garments." It is not the athletes themselves but the nation that is to blame for such results. "I blame the custom of the Hellenes who gather together to watch these men, honouring a useless pleasure." And then, echoing the words of Xenophanes, he proceeds: "Whoever helped his fatherland by winning a crown for wrestling or for speed of foot, or hurling the diskos, or striking a good blow on the jaw? Will they fight the foe with diskoi in their hands or, driving their fists through the foemen's shields, cast them out of their land? Crowns should be given to the good and wise, to him who guides his city best, a temperate man and just, or who by his words drives away evil deeds, putting away war and faction." How did the Athenians in the theatre receive this daring denunciation of their idols? Many, at least, with sympathy, and among the number, I believe, would have been the poet's inveterate foe, Aristophanes.

While athletics were passing into the hands of professionals and losing their hold upon the people, the richer classes devoted themselves more and more to chariot and horse races. These had long been the sport of tyrants and nobles; especially brilliant were the victories of the tyrants of Sicily and Italy at Olympia. But the Persian wars gave a fresh impulse to horse-breeding and riding in Greece. Cavalry and light-armed troops played a more and more important part in war. Themistocles, we are told, himself taught his sons to ride, to throw javelins standing on horseback, and perform other equestrian feats.[168] At the Panathenaea, besides a variety of races for chariots and horses, there were parades, processions, and military manœuvres on horseback. The frieze of the Parthenon bears witness to the grace and skill of the Athenian horsemen. The horsiness of the fashionable young Athenian is ridiculed by Aristophanes.[169] He spent large sums on horses, affected horsy names, and talked of horses all the day long. Alcibiades entered no less than seven chariots at Olympia in 416 B.C., and obtained first, second, and fourth places in the race.[170] He celebrated his success by entertaining the whole assembly at a sumptuous banquet.

At Sparta chariot-racing had long been popular; one Euagoras in the sixth century had won the chariot-race in three successive Olympiads with the same team, and King Damaratus himself had won a victory there. After the Persian wars the Spartans gave increased attention

---

[168] Plato, *Meno*, 93 D.
[169] *Nubes*, passim.
[170] Thuc. vi. 16, 2. The epinikion written by Euripides states that he was first, second, and third. So too does Isocrates, *de Bigis*, 34.

to horse-breeding; their victories were frequent, and their enthusiasm for the sport is shown by the story of Lichas. Their victories at the Panathenaea are proved by the recent discovery at Sparta of a number of Panathenaic vases representing the chariot-race,[171] and an inscription detailing the victories of one Damonon in chariot and horse racing records the fact that his horses were got by his own stallion out of his own mares.[172] The addiction of the Spartans to chariot-racing did not meet with the approval of Agesilaus, if we may believe Plutarch's story about his sister Cynisca, who won the chariot-race in Ol. 96, 97.

Chariot-racing was, of course, merely a fashionable amusement, and except so far as it encouraged horse-breeding, of no service for war. Poorer states could not compete in it at all unless, like Argos, they entered public chariots or horses.[173] But the chariot-race was a great attraction to the spectators, and its growing popularity is evidenced by the introduction of two new races at Olympia and at Delphi. A two-horse chariot-race was introduced at Olympia in 408 B.C., at Delphi in 398 B.C., a four-horse chariot-race for colts at Olympia in 384 B.C., and at Delphi in 378 B.C. The introduction of colt-races was of course dictated by the wish to encourage horse-breeding, in which the country gentlemen of Elis were greatly interested.

The evil results of professionalism were not long in showing themselves. When money enters into sport, corruption is sure to follow. It will be remembered how Astylus of Croton had sold his victory for the favour of a Sicilian tyrant. In Ol. 97 or 98 the boys' boxing match was won by Antipater of Miletus, the first Ionian to have his statue erected at Olympia as he recorded in the inscription.[174] Some emissaries of Dionysius of Syracuse had bribed his father to let his son be proclaimed a Syracusan; but Antipater despised the tyrant's bribe and proclaimed himself of Miletus. Not so Sotades of Crete,[175] who, having won the long race in Ol. 99, in the next Olympiad accepted a bribe from the Ephesians to proclaim himself an Ephesian, for which offence he was deservedly banished by his countrymen. Worse, however, than this transfer of victories was their actual sale. The first instance of such bribing occurred in Ol. 98 (388 B.C.) when Eupolus of Thessaly[176] bribed his opponents in boxing to let him win the prize. These were Agenor of Arcadia, Prytanis of Cyzicus, and Phormio of Halicarnassus, who had won the boxing in the previous Olympiad. The offence was discovered, and Eupolus and those who had been bribed by him were heavily fined by the Eleans. From the fines were made six bronze statues of Zeus, called Zanes, which were set up at the entrance to the Stadium, with inscriptions commending the justice of the Eleans, and warning competitors that "not with money but with speed of foot and strength of body must prizes be won at Olympia." The warning apparently had its effect for a time. It was not till 332 B.C. that another case of bribing occurred. On this occasion the Athenian Callippus bribed his opponents in the pentathlon.[177] The guilty parties were fined, but the Athenians despatched the orator Hyperides to beg the Eleans to remit the fine. His mission failed, and the Athenians thereupon, with a high hand, refused to pay, and absented themselves from

---

[171] *vide infra*, Figure 165.
[172] Part of the inscription was found in 1877, and is now in the Museum at Sparta. Tod, *Sparta Mus. Cat.* 440. The rest has been recently discovered during the excavations of the British School, and is discussed in the *B.S.A.* xiii. p. 174. It contains a list of victories won by Damonon and his son, Enymacratidas, in the chariot-race, horse-race, and foot-races at nine local festivals, most of them in Laconia. The inscription belongs to the middle or end of the fifth century. It throws an interesting light on the number of local festivals at this period.
[173] *Ox. Pap.* ii. 222.
[174] Paus. vi. 2, 6.
[175] Paus. vi. 18, 4.
[176] Paus. v. 21, 5.
[177] Paus. v. 21, 5.

Olympia till they were compelled to give in by the Delphic god, who declined to give them any answers until the fines were paid. Six more Zanes were made out of the money, with inscriptions similar to the first. It is a high testimonial to the sanctity of Olympia and the prestige of its authority that cases of corruption were so rare. Yet the Eleans themselves did not escape without reproach. In Ol. 96 (396 B.C.) there was a scandal in connection with the foot-race.[178] Two of the Hellanodicae decided in favour of Eupolemus of Elis, and the third in favour of Leon of Ambracia. The latter appealed to the council, who upheld his appeal and punished the two officials. It seems, however, that an award once given could not be reversed, and Eupolemus therefore retained his victory, and even commemorated it by a statue. A few years later, in Ol. 102, there was a similar scandal with regard to the horse-race which was won by another Elean Troilus, who owed his victory, says Pausanias, partly to the fact that he was a Hellanodicas.[179] In consequence of this incident a regulation was introduced forbidding the Hellanodicae to compete in the chariot or horse races.

The apparent breakdown in the machinery of Olympia during the early years of the fourth century is partly due to political circumstances with which we shall deal shortly. The struggle between Athens and Sparta, involving the whole Greek world in strife, contributed in no small degree to the decay of athletics. But when corruption was possible at Olympia we may be sure that it was rife elsewhere. A class of useless athletes, an unathletic nation of spectators, a corrupt and degraded sport, such were the results which we find in Greece within a century of the glorious 76th Olympiad that celebrated the freedom of Greece. Yet such was the strength and persistency of the old ideal that it was destined to survive for centuries after all freedom had been lost.

The character of the competitions themselves underwent little change during this period. Such changes as took place were due to changes in the conditions of war and to the increased importance of light-armed troops and cavalry.[180] Not only were equestrian events multiplied, but separate competitions were introduced in javelin-throwing and in archery. The javelin had hitherto been confined to the pentathlon. Now we find separate prizes offered for javelin-throwing, both on foot and on horseback, at a target as well as for distance. But such innovations seem to have been confined to local festivals like the Panathenaea, and found no place in the programme of the great festivals. The brutalising effects of professionalism may be traced in the change of the caestus. The soft leather thongs which alone appear on the fifth-century vases were, by the addition of bands of hard leather round the knuckles, developed into the formidable weapon called the σφαῖρα, which we see depicted on the Panathenaic vase in Figure 135. It is curious to find Plato commending the use of the σφαῖρα on account of its brutality as more closely reproducing the conditions of warfare, and so more suitable for training soldiers than the "soft thongs." We are less surprised at the approval with which he and Aristotle regard the pentathlon, the one competition which required the all-round development of the older athletics. But it is to be feared that this event was not really popular. Of the victors in the pentathlon at Olympia during this period we know only three, and of these, two, Stomius and Hysmon, were Eleans, the third the Athenian Callippus, who owed

---

[178] Paus. vi. 3, 7.
[179] Paus. vi. 1, 4.
[180] These changes were particularly connected with the Athenian Iphicrates and Jason of Therae.

his victory to corruption. Of the statues erected at Olympia the vast majority were in honour of boxing, wrestling, and the pankration.[181]

Despite the decline of athletics there was no diminution of the influence and popularity of the athletic festivals. Wealth had increased, means of communication had improved, and with the growing attractions of the festivals and the growing love of sight-seeing among the people the crowds that flocked to the games showed no falling off. It is hardly possible to exaggerate the importance of these gatherings. In an age distracted by civil war and faction they served to remind the Greeks of their common brotherhood and to promote a spirit of good-will.[182] Especially was this true of Olympia, which, under the rigorous administration of the Eleans, had become the chief centre of Panhellenism. The sacred month, jealously guarded by the Eleans, afforded a brief respite from arms and security for all who wished to attend the festival, whether in a public or private capacity. All through the Peloponnesian war the representatives of Athens could travel unmolested to the festival.[183] There all states, unless under the ban of the Eleans, sent embassies, composed of wealthy and prominent citizens, who vied with one another in displaying the wealth and power and culture of their cities.[184] At Olympia the representatives of states at war with one another laid aside their animosities for a time, and opportunity was afforded for the discussion and settlement of many a grievance and dispute.

To these meetings we may partly attribute the growing tendency to the formation of leagues. There, too, the terms of treaties could be proclaimed and made known to the whole Greek world. The terms of the thirty years' truce between Athens and Sparta were recorded on a stele at Olympia;[185] so too was the 100 years' treaty made in 420 B.C. between Athens, Argos, Mantinea, and Elis, and it was ordered that the treaty should be periodically renewed at the Olympia and the Panathenaea.[186] It was to Olympia that the envoys of Mytilene came at the commencement of the Peloponnesian war[187] to protest against the tyranny of Athens and plead for their autonomy before the assembled Greeks. Finally, when Athens and Sparta, false to the cause of Hellenism, were treacherously intriguing with Persia, it was at Olympia that on three occasions a noble appeal for unity was made. In 408 B.C. Gorgias of Leontini, addressing the assembled crowds from the steps of the temple of Zeus, appealed to them to forget their rivalries and unite together in the crusade of Hellenism against Persia.[188] His voice was unheeded at the time, but a later generation appropriately commemorated his appeal by erecting his statue in the Altis.[189] Twenty-four years later Sparta, in alliance with Artaxerxes and the Sicilian tyrant Dionysius, was once more trampling on the liberties of Greece. Dionysius had sent to Olympia a magnificent embassy headed by his brother Thearion; his tents of gold and purple were pitched within the sacred precincts, splendid chariots were entered in his name for the four-horse chariots, while hired rhapsodists recited continually the praises of their master. By a curious chance the winner of the foot-race was

---

[181] Taking the lists given by Hyde, pp. 75-77, we find that between Ols. 84-106 out of 54 statues 20 were in honour of boxers, 6 of pankratiasts, 11 of wrestling, 7 of runners, 2 of pentathletes, and 8 of chariots or horses.
[182] Isocrates, *Panegyric*, 43 ff.; Lysias, *Olymp.*
[183] Thuc. v. 49; cp. viii. 10 of the Isthmia.
[184] Isocrates, *de Bigis*, 32, ὁρῶν τὴν ἐν Ὀλυμπίᾳ πανήγυριν ὑπὸ πάντων ἀνθρώπων ἀγαπωμένην καὶ τοὺς Ἕλληνας ἐπίδειξιν ἐν αὐτῇ ποιουμένους πλούτου καὶ ῥώμης καὶ παιδεύσεως, κτλ.
[185] Paus. v. 23, 4.
[186] Paus. v. 12, 8; Thuc. v. 47.
[187] Thuc. iii. 8 ff.
[188] Phil. *Vita. Soph.* i. p. 209.
[189] Paus. vi. 17, 7; *Ol. Ins.* 293.

Dicon, proclaimed of Syracuse, but in reality a citizen of Caulonia, a city that Dionysius had recently destroyed, transferring its citizens to Syracuse.[190] Such were the circumstances in which the Athenian Lysias, in graceful but vigorous language, warned the Greeks that Artaxerxes and Dionysius were the real enemies of Hellas, and, bidding them lay aside their differences, called on them to unite and show their patriotism by an attack on the tyrant's tents.[191] The appeal was only partially successful, and one cannot but rejoice that the peace of the festival was not broken by such an outrage upon hospitality. Lastly, at the next Olympiad of 380 B.C. Isocrates distributed at the festival copies of his famous Panegyric, a work to which he is said to have devoted ten years' work, in which he once more advocated a Panhellenic crusade against Persia, under the united command of Athens and Sparta.[192]

It was one of the fictions of a later time that no memorial might be set up in the Altis to commemorate the triumph of one Greek state over another. But though Olympia did undoubtedly work for unity, the monuments prove that the ideal was often disregarded, and the Altis bore witness to the divisions as well as to the unity of Greece. Apart from votive offerings of helmets, spears, and shields[193] Pausanias saw at Olympia a statue of Zeus twelve feet high, set up by the Spartans to commemorate the repression of the Messenian revolt.[194] It is doubtful whether this refers to the revolt of 464 B.C. or to an earlier war in the sixth century, but certainly this statue, and probably other statues, mentioned by Pausanias were offerings for wars in which Greeks fought against Greeks.[195] In 424 the Messenians had their revenge, and they commemorated the part which they had played at Pylos by erecting a statue of victory with an inscription stating that it was dedicated by the Messenians and Naupactians from the spoil of their enemy. The statue was the work of the sculptor Paeonius, who is said to have made the sculptures of the eastern pediment of the temple of Zeus.[196] Raised on a lofty triangular pedestal, it must have been the most conspicuous monument in the Altis. The Messenians, says Pausanias, omitted to insert the name of their enemies from fear of the Spartans, but no such fear deterred the Eleans, who celebrated a victory won at Olympia itself in the war at the beginning of the fourth century by setting up a trophy in the Altis with an inscription on the shield that it was dedicated out of the spoils of the Lacedaemonians, and their final triumph over the Arcadians after the 104th Olympiad was commemorated by a colossal monument that rivalled the Victory of the Messenians.[197]

Interest at Olympia was no longer confined to religious ceremonies and sports. It is true that there were no musical or dramatic competitions such as were held at other festivals. The contests for heralds and trumpeters introduced in 396 B.C. had certainly no such character.[198] But the gathering together of crowds from all parts of the Greek world afforded a unique

---

[190] Paus. vi. 3, 11; *Anth. Pal.* xiii. 5; Hyde, *Olymp. Stat.* p. 33.
[191] Lysias, *Olympiakos*; Dionys. Hal. *Jud. de Lysia*, p. 519; Diodor. xiv. 109. A similar tale is narrated by Aelian of Themistocles, who is said to have urged the Greeks in 476 not to allow Hieron of Syracuse to compete, on the ground that he had not shared in the dangers of Greece. Ael. *V.H.* 9. 5.
[192] Isocrates, *Panegyrikos*.
[193] Helmet of Argives (*Ol. Ins.* 250), spears of Sicyonians, Methonii, Tarentines (*Ins.* 245, 247, 254), of Argives and Athenians for Tanagra (Paus. v. 10, 4).
[194] Paus. v. 24; *Ol. Ins.* 252.
[195] Such must certainly have been the statue of Victory by Calamis set up by the Mantineans. Paus. v. 26, 6.
[196] Paus. v. 26, 1.
[197] Paus. v. 27, 11; 24, 4.
[198] They were merely competitions in strength of lung. Herodorus of Megara, a famous trumpeter who won ten times at Olympia, was said to be able to blow two trumpets at once with such force that no one could stand in his neighbourhood. Athen. 10, 7, p. 415.

opportunity for profit and advertisement which appealed to many classes, not only to the huckster and pedlar, who provided for the material wants of the people,[199] to the acrobat and mountebank, who catered for their amusement, but to the man of science, of literature, and of art. The artist, the writer, or the inventor had little means of making himself known outside his own city except by travelling from place to place. All such flocked to Olympia, where all would find an appreciative and critical audience. Lucian[200] tells us that Herodotus was the first to realise the unique possibilities of Olympia for purposes of advertisement, and read his history to the people in the Opisthodome of the temple of Zeus; and another account adds that the youthful Thucydides, who happened to be present, was moved to tears by his recitation. He is also said to have recited his work at Athens, Thebes, and Corinth. Whatever the truth of these stories, it is certain that the practice of public recitation was widely spread in the fifth century, and nowhere could such an audience be found as at Olympia. Moreover, the demand for hymns of victory and athletic statues must have brought thither poets and artists before the day of Herodotus. The practice commended itself especially to the sophists and rhetoricians who travelled about amassing large sums of money by their learning, real or pretended. Some of these have been already mentioned.

Olympia was a meeting-place for all. There one might have seen Socrates listening with polite amusement to the encyclopaedic Hippias of Elis as he proclaimed to an admiring audience his varied knowledge and accomplishments, and told them that everything he had about his person was the work of his own hands, from the shoes on his feet to the girdle of his tunic, fine as the most costly fabric of Persia. There, too, one might have seen many another whose person is familiar to us in Plato's dialogues, the great Gorgias himself, with his pupil, Polus, "impetuous as a runaway colt"; or Prodicus of Ceos declaiming in that fine bass voice of his on subtleties of language or of grammar. Or one might have listened to the mathematician, Oenopides, explaining to a select few the mysteries of the great year, a diagram of which, engraved on a bronze tablet, he had set up in the Altis. There one might have gazed on Zeuxis as he strutted about in his peacock clothes, displaying to the world his vanity and wealth. Every one who had anything to sell, to exhibit, or make known came to Olympia, which thus became a centre from which Hellenic culture was diffused throughout the world.

This expansion of interests is evident in the list of honorary statues which cease in this period to be confined to victors in the games. Thus the Samians commemorated the freedom which they thought they had gained by the victory of Aegospotami by setting up in the Altis a statue of Lysander.[201] The statue of Gorgias has been already mentioned. In Macedonian times the custom spread, while the number of athletic statues steadily declined. Besides kings and princes, the historian Anaximenes of Lampsacus and the philosopher Aristotle received this honour.[202]

Neutrality was the natural and obvious policy of the Eleans. Removed by their geographical situation from the main stress and turmoil of Greek politics, they appreciated to the full the advantages of the position which they had usurped as sole guardians of the Olympian precinct, and lost no opportunity of enforcing and extending the privilege attaching to that position. Thus they claimed for the whole of Elis the sanctity belonging to the sacred

---

[199] Hence the term "Mercatus Olympiacus," Vell. Paterc. i. 8; Cicero, *Tuscul.* v. 3; Krause, *Olympia*, p. 190, n. 2.
[200] Lucian, *Herodotus*.
[201] Paus. vi. 3, 14.
[202] Paus. vi. 18, 2.

plain; their lives were consecrated and their territory immune from war.[203] Elis city was the official headquarters of Olympia, with which it was connected by a sacred road, and there all competitors were forced to assemble to undergo a month's training before the games. Yet the scanty records of history show that the immunity enjoyed by the Eleans was due more to the accident of their position than to a general recognition of their sanctity. Religious scruples, though often convenient as an excuse, were seldom allowed to stand in the way of more practical considerations. Hence the Eleans, however anxious to preserve their neutrality, could not avoid being involved in the complications caused by the Peloponnesian war. Sparta must have regarded with jealousy and suspicion the influence possessed by Athens and the growth of democracy in the new state. In Triphylia and Arcadia the cause of the Pisatans was still popular, and the control of Elis was regarded as an act of usurpation. It was in connection with Lepreum, one of the cities of the old Pisatan league, that difficulties arose.

Sparta had interfered in a quarrel between Elis and Lepreum, which from the commencement of the Peloponnesian war had refused to pay its tribute of a talent to Olympian Zeus, and a Spartan force of 1000 men was despatched in the summer of 424 B.C. to the help of the Lepreates. The Eleans complained that this act was a violation of the Olympic truce which had just been proclaimed, and imposed a fine of 2000 minae—2 minae per head—payable half to Olympian Zeus, half to themselves. The Spartans refused to pay, and after fruitless negotiations the Eleans, unable to obtain satisfaction, excommunicated Sparta, and forbade her to take any part in the forthcoming festival. So, says Thucydides,[204] while all other states were represented the Spartans and Lepreates had no representatives, and offered their sacrifices at home. Alarmed at their own bold action, the Eleans had so little confidence in the protection of sanctity that they put their whole force under arms and summoned assistance from Argos, Mantinea, and Athens. The alarm of the assembly was increased by another insult inflicted on Sparta in the course of the games. Lichas, the son of Arcesilaus, a member of the Spartan royal family, unable to compete in his own name, had entered his team for the chariot-race under the name of the Boeotian commonwealth. When his chariot won, he advanced boldly into the course to bind the fillet of victory on the charioteer's head, but was publicly driven off by the officials and beaten with their rods. Yet in spite of this fresh insult Sparta, deeming the occasion inexpedient to excite the religious susceptibilities of Greece, did nothing, but bided her time, and Elis, three years afterwards, joined the Argive alliance.

Sparta never forgot and never forgave. In 399 Agis led an army against Elis, nominally to force Elis to acknowledge the independence of the Arcadian and Triphylian towns, in reality to wreak vengeance for her conduct during the Peloponnesian war. Agis had also a recent and more personal grievance. Having gone to Olympia to consult the oracle, he had been refused an answer by the Eleans, who invoked an ancient canon forbidding oracles to be given to Greeks engaged in war against Greeks. This time their sanctity could not save them. Frightened away the first year by a providential earthquake,[205] Agis returned in the following summer, and, reinforced by the Triphylian towns, advanced to Olympia, where he offered the

---

[203] Polyb. iv. 73.
[204] Thuc. v. 31 and 49.
[205] From Pausanias, v. 4, 8, and 27, 11; vi. 2, 8, we gather that the Eleans, in the course of this war, obtained a decided success in a fight which took place at Olympia, and erected a trophy for the same in the Altis. Was it really this success which prevented the Spartans from depriving them of the presidency of the games, or have we here the Elean version of the war?

sacrifice which had been forbidden before. He then marched through the rich plains of Elis, the plunder of which attracted to his standard numerous Arcadian and Achaean volunteers. In spite of assistance from Xenias and the oligarchical party he failed to take the city, but finally, by occupying a fortified post on the border and ravaging the country, he reduced the Eleans to complete submission. They were forced to raze their fortifications, surrender their harbour, and acknowledge the independence of all the towns of Arcadia and Triphylia. Only the presidency of the Olympic festival was left to them, for, though the Pisatans claimed it as having belonged to them originally, the Spartans refused to acknowledge their claim, considering, says Xenophon, that they were country bumpkins, and incapable of exercising the presidency, a remarkable testimony to the efficiency of the Elean administration.[206]

The effects of this humiliation were seen in the scandals which disgraced the following Olympiads. The prestige of the festival itself must have suffered. In the next Olympiad, 396 B.C., the competition was so reduced that no less than six events were won by Eleans.[207]

The Spartans had refused to deprive the Eleans of the presidency from no respect for their sanctity, but from disinclination to increase the importance of the country districts of Arcadia and Triphylia. How little real respect they had for religious tradition may be judged from the conduct of Agesilaus at the Isthmia in 390 B.C., when, at the head of an army, he interrupted the games, and, in conjunction with the Corinthian exiles, himself presided at them.[208] The rise of Thebes once more raised the hopes of the disappointed Triphylians.[209] In 371 B.C. Arcadia was consolidated into the Pan-Arcadian league, with its headquarters at the newly founded Megalopolis. The Messenians, who had been so prominent at Olympia in its early days, recovered their liberty. The Messenian exiles from every part flocked to the rising city of Messene, founded by Epaminondas, at the foot of Mount Ithome, and they celebrated their return by winning a victory at Olympia in the boys' foot-race—the first victory, says Pausanias, that they had won since their exile.[210] Everything seemed favourable to the Triphylians. Unfortunately a breach occurred between Thebes and Arcadia, and when Thebes, following the example of Sparta and Athens, sent Pelopidas to Persia to secure the sanction of the great king for her authority, the terms of the imperial rescript reaffirmed the rights of Elis in Triphylia. The Arcadian ambassador, the pankratiast Antiochus, returned home in dudgeon, without even deigning to receive the royal gifts.

The Arcadians refused to accept the king's rescript. When in 365 the Eleans attempted to assert their authority over Lasion, on the Arcadian border, they were driven off by the Arcadians, who followed up their success by overrunning Elis, and occupied Olympia itself, fortifying and garrisoning the hill of Cronus. The next year, under the protection of the whole armed force of Arcadia, the Pisatans at last found themselves presiding over the games. But the festival was not to pass off undisturbed. The Eleans, with some Achaean allies, arrived on the west bank of the Cladeus while the pentathlon was in progress. There was general alarm among the spectators, who had just left the Stadium and were congregated on the steps of the Treasuries and in the Colonnades watching the progress of the wrestling match which took

---

[206] Xenophon, *Hell.* iii. 2, 31.
[207] Förster, *Ol. Sieger*.
[208] Xenophon, *Hell.* iv. 5. 1, 2.
[209] Inscriptions found at Olympia illustrate the political relations of this time. In *Ol. Ins.* 31, Theban, Sicyonian, and Argive benefactors of Olympia are named πρόξενοι of the Arcadians. In *Ol. Ins.* 36, two Sicyonians are named πρόοξενοι and θεαροδόκοι of the Pisatans. Curtius, *Ol.* Text, i. 50.
[210] Compare the triumphant inscription on Sophius of Messene, who won the same events *circa* 300 B.C. Paus. vi. 2, 10, and 3, 2.

place in the open space between the buildings and the great altar. The Arcadian troops advanced to the Cladeus and fell in opposite to the Eleans. But the latter, having crossed the river, charged them with unexpected courage, and drove them back into the Altis, where a desperate fight took place in the space "between the Council House, the shrine of Hestia, and the Theatre adjoining these buildings."[211] There, however, they were exposed to a shower of missiles from the roofs of the Council House, the Colonnades, and the Temple of Zeus. And though they maintained the combat and bore their opponents back towards the altar, their losses were heavy, and Stratolas, their captain, being slain, they drew off to their encampment. During the night the Arcadians, fearful of a renewed attack, occupied themselves in pulling to pieces their elaborately constructed quarters between the Altis and the Cladeus and making a stockade of the material; and in the morning the Eleans, seeing the strength of the fortifications, returned home, leaving the Pisatans to celebrate the festival. Their triumph was only short-lived. The religious feeling of Greece, outraged by the sacrilege at Olympia, was still further scandalized by the appropriation of the sacred treasures of Zeus for the use of the Arcadian league. There was disunion in the league itself, and when, two years later, the Peloponnese was once more threatened by a Theban invasion, the Arcadians made peace with Elis and acknowledged her rights over Olympia.

This was the last attempt of the Pisatans. The Eleans rapidly recovered their power. The 104th Olympiad was expunged from the records and declared an Anolympiad. And the triumph of the Eleans was commemorated by a colossal statue of Zeus, with an inscription truly appropriate to the part which Olympia had played in Greek history—"The Eleans for concord" (Ϝαλείων περὶ ὁμονοίαρ).[212]

---

[211] The view adopted above is that of the late Mr. Louis Dyer, and is fully discussed by him in *J.H.S.* vol. xxviii. pp. 250 ff. The word θέατρον is here used of the arrangements for spectators overlooking the bare north-eastern corner of the Altis, and consisting in (1) the tiers of steps at the foot of the treasuries, (2) the Colonnade and its southward extension by the Hellanodiceon.

[212] *Ol. Ins.* 260.

Chapter 7

THE DECLINE OF ATHLETICS, 338-146 B.C.

From this time onward there is little change to record in the history of athletics. Competitions became more and more the monopoly of professionals and all the evils attendant on professionalism became rampant. The training of the athlete became more artificial and more irrational, rendering him still more unfit for practical life. The degeneration of the physical type and of the artistic ideal is evident in the statue known as the Farnese Heracles, a copy of a Lysippean original exaggerated by the copyist to suit the taste of a later and more decadent age. Those huge bulging muscles,[213] which even repose cannot relax, are a type of clumsy, useless strength, utterly foreign to the ideal of the fifth century, or to that of Lysippus himself as we know it from the Agias. Perhaps it was the type of those professional strong men who called themselves successors of Heracles as having, like Heracles, won the wrestling and pankration at Olympia on the same day.[214] The first of these was Caprus of Elis, who in the year 212 defeated, in the pankration, the redoubtable Cleitomachus of Thebes, who is sometimes supposed to be the original of the boxer of the Terme (Figure 136).

A tale told by Polybius about the latter throws a curious light on the state of sport at the time.[215] He had, it appears, incurred the displeasure of King Ptolemy—presumably Ptolemy IV.—who went to the trouble and expense of training and sending to Olympia a rival boxer, Aristonicus, to compete with him. The contest excited great public interest, and the fickle crowd favoured the new man until Cleitomachus, exasperated at their attitude, taunted them with backing one who was fighting not for the glory of Greece but for King Ptolemy. This appeal caused such a revulsion of feeling that Aristonicus was vanquished, not, says our author, so much by Cleitomachus as by the crowd. With such hired prize-fighters it was only natural that methods became more brutal, and science deteriorated. The increasing weight of the caestus rendered boxing a contest of brute strength and fit to take its place in the Roman gladiatorial shows. The science of wrestling had also suffered. As early as 364 B.C. we read of one Sostratus of Sicyon who won the wrestling at Olympia not by skill in wrestling but by breaking his opponent's fingers.

---

[213] Quintilian aptly contrasts the bulging muscles, "tori," of such athletes with the "lacertus" of soldiers.
[214] Paus. v. 21, 10.
[215] Polyb. 27, 7 A.

Corruption naturally throve under such conditions.[216] Only Olympia, thanks to its ancient prestige and sanctity, maintained the purity of sport, and though even there all sport was professional, cases of corruption were rare.

Figure 21. Farnese Heracles, by Glycon. Naples. (*Greek Sculpture*, Figure 125.)

The decay of athletics was accompanied by an increased activity in the construction and improvement of gymnasia and stadia, which continued all through Hellenistic and Roman times. The stadia at Olympia and Delphi were reconstructed during the fourth century; the Panathenaic stadium at Athens was the work of the Athenian administrator Lycurgus, who also rebuilt the Lyceum Gymnasium, planted it with trees, and built a new palaestra or wrestling-school in it. But this building activity did not denote any improvement of the national athletics. The people took little interest in the games, save as a spectacle, and the improvements made in the stadia were connected solely with the accommodation and comfort of spectators. Some of these buildings were the work of a sort of athletic revival, a temporary demand for physical and military training. Such a movement occurred at Athens in the time of Alexander, under the wise leadership of Lycurgus, who, among the numerous services which he rendered to Athens, reorganized the Athenian epheboi. More often these buildings were the monuments of the generosity or vanity of wealthy princes or ambitious citizens.

But the palaestra and gymnasium, even in the fourth century were no longer devoted principally to gymnastics. The colonnades of the palaestra, the shady walks of the gymnasium were popular resorts and lounging-places. There the Athenian gentleman would betake

---

[216] A third-century inscription from Epidaurus, Dittenb. *Syll.* 2nd Ed., 689, records that three athletes, a stadiodromos, a pentathlete, and a pankratiast, were fined 1000 staters each διὰ τὸ φθείρειν τοὺς ἀγῶνας. The next inscription, 690, records a similar fine on certain actors.

himself in the afternoon to get an appetite for his evening meal; and a whole series of rooms was provided for his accommodation—dressing-rooms, oiling-rooms, dusting-rooms, bath-rooms, cloisters where he could take his exercise in wet weather, rooms for ball-play, and, for the more active, wrestling-rings and running tracks. Many of the rooms and the walks were provided with benches and seats for the convenience of visitors and spectators. Sophists especially resorted there in the hope of attracting pupils; some of them attached themselves to particular gymnasia. Plato delivered his discourses in the Academy; Aristotle took his morning and evening walks in the Lyceum. Gradually the social and educational side of the gymnasium became more important than the athletic. The gymnasium of Cynosarges in the fourth century was the meeting-place of a celebrated club known as the Sixty Wits. The earlier gymnasia of Athens had been outside the walls. The first gymnasium inside the walls was the gift of the versatile Ptolemaeus Philadelphia (285-247 B.C.), the founder of the museum and library of Alexandria. The gymnasium at Athens bore witness to the culture of its founder: it contained a library formed and increased by contributions from the students who attended it. Lectures continued to be given in it by philosophers and men of science down to the time of Cicero, who listened there to the lectures of Antiochus. These gymnasia were intimately connected with the life of the epheboi in whose training philosophy and literature were rapidly taking the place formerly occupied by athletics and military science. From this ephebic training grew up what has been aptly called the University of Athens, to which the young Romans of the time of Cicero resorted to study philosophy.

Our knowledge of the training given to the epheboi is mostly derived from inscriptions of this period or later. The Athenian inscriptions date from the year 334 B.C. to the third century A.D.[217] These inscriptions contain lists of the epheboi and decrees in honour of the epheboi themselves and of their officers. The physical training of the epheboi was largely military in character, and particular attention was paid to those exercises which were likely to be of service in war. This training was under the general supervision of the Kosmetes, one of whose duties was to provide the necessary oil for use in the gymnasium. Under him were subordinate officials, the hoplomachos, a sort of fencing instructor; the akontistes, toxotes, and katapaltaphetes or aphetes, who taught the use of the javelin, bow, and catapult respectively. At the local festivals competitions were held to test the proficiency of men and youths in these and other more purely athletic accomplishments. Many of these competitions, especially those for the younger, were confined to local competitors. Sometimes they took the form of squad competitions between companies representing local tribes and divisions. Torch-races between individuals or teams on foot or on horseback figure frequently on the programme. At Athens cavalry parades formed an important feature of these festivals. The most splendid of these local festivals, the Panathenaea, must be reserved for fuller discussion, but a few examples of the inscriptions dealing with the less-known festivals, will illustrate the character of the festivals and of the physical training of the young in the period.

The Thesea at Athens had been founded shortly after the Persian wars, when, in accordance with the oracle's command, the bones of Theseus were brought from Scyros and reburied at Athens. The programme comprised parades, gymnastic, naval, and equestrian competitions, and a great public sacrifice. We have a list of the victors at this festival in an inscription recording a decree of honour to Nicogenes who held the office of Agonothetes, or

---

[217] Roberts and Gardner, *Greek Epigraphy*, ii. p. 145.

official manager of the games, for the year 161 B.C.[218] Among the services rendered by Nicogenes, it is recorded that he provided prizes and money for other expenses out of his own pocket, and that he took special pains to prevent any competitor in the torch-race from "losing through foul play." For these services, and for his goodwill towards the Council and people of Athens, Nicogenes is to be crowned with a golden crown, and proclamation thereof is to be made at the Dionysia, the Panathenaea, the Eleusinia, and—a strange fourth in such a list—the Ptolemaea!

Similar training and similar competitions are found at many other places, at Ceos, Teos, Chios, Samos, and Tralles.[219] A third-century inscription of Ceos contains arrangements for the holding of a festival at a cost of 65 drachmae. A gymnasiarch is to be chosen to organize the torch-race, take general supervision of the training in the gymnasium, three times a month to take the epheboi out to practise with the bow and javelin and catapult, and to inflict a fine on any who did not attend. The prizes for the men's competitions are: for archery, first prize, a bow and quiver; second prize, a bow;—for the javelin, first prize, three spears and a helmet; second prize, three spears; while the boy victors in these events are to receive a portion of meat. There are prizes also for the use of the catapult and for a torch-race.

At Teos in the third century a patriotic citizen, Polythrous, presented the State with the sum of 34,000 drachmae for the education of boys and girls. The interest on this sum was used to provide salaries for various instructors, including two paidotribai or athletic instructors, at a salary of 500 drachmae each, a hoplomachos at a salary of 300 drachmae, and an instructor in the use of the javelin and the bow at 250 drachmae. The hoplomachos was required to give at least two month's instruction. The highest paid of all the staff was the teacher of music, who received 600 drachmae. The general supervision of this education was in the hands of a paidonomos, who, it is specified, must not be less than forty years of age. In the present day, in making appointments to head-masterships it is commonly specified that candidates must not be over forty. Which is right?

Such training seems to have been universal in Greek states. The instances given suffice to show how entirely it differed from the training of athletes who competed in the great games. Unfortunately education in Greece was, except at Sparta, purely voluntary, and the training afforded only affected, therefore, a small portion of the population.

We have been anticipating; we must now return to the history of Olympia under the Macedonians. It was the policy of the kings of Macedon to encourage and support in every way the Panhellenic festival, and especially Olympia. In the first place, the Macedonians were regarded by the other Greeks almost as barbarians, and it was of supreme importance that their claim to be considered Greeks had been recognized by the most exclusively Hellenic of all festivals. It will be remembered that Alexander, the son of Amyntas, had established this claim for the royal family of Macedon at the close of the sixth century, when he had been allowed to compete in the foot-race at Olympia. A century later Archelaus won a victory in the chariot-race. This able and energetic prince aimed at spreading Greek culture through his dominions. He invited to his court Greek poets, philosophers, and artists; above all, to show his respect for Olympia, he founded at Dium a new Olympic festival of nine days in honour

---

[218] Roberts and Gardner, *Greek Epigraphy*, ii. 61, p. 162 (= *I.G.* ii. 444); cp. *I.G.* ii. 445, 446. Mommsen, *Feste der Stadt Athens*, pp. 278 ff.
[219] Ditt. *Syll.* 2nd Ed., 522, 523, 524, 672, 673, 674.

of Zeus and the nine Muses.[220] The precedent was widely followed during Hellenistic and Roman times, when a host of festivals sprung up bearing the title of the four great Panhellenic meetings. The new Olympia were not confined to athletic contests, which seem to have been less important than dramatic competitions, and their pomp and splendour are indications of the growing taste for spectacular effect.

Philip and Alexander had special reasons for associating themselves with the Panhellenic festivals. Like the tyrants of an earlier age, they realized that if they were to unite Greece under their rule it must be by utilizing those forces which made for unity. Two places in particular represented the spirit of national unity,—Delphi, in Northern Greece, and Olympia in the Peloponnese,—and of both festivals the Macedonians made full use.

Already in 370 B.C. the ambitious tyrant of Thessaly, Jason of Pherae, who dreamt of invading Persia as commander of united Greece, had schemed to consolidate his power by setting himself up as president of the Pythian games. He had made preparation to celebrate the festival with barbarian pomp, sending messengers to all the cities of Thessaly, to bid them provide oxen, sheep, and goats for the sacrifices, and offering a crown of gold as a prize for the finest ox.[221] But his scheme was frustrated by his assassination, which was doubtless partly due to his attempted usurpation of the sacred functions. Fortune was kinder to Philip. The Sacred war gave him an opportunity of posing as the protector and saviour of Delphi. His defeat of the Phocians and restoration of Delphi to the Delphians were rewarded by his election to the place on the Amphictionic Board, of which the Phocians were deprived, and in 346 he received the further honour of being nominated as the president of the approaching games. Thus he stood out the acknowledged head of the most ancient and influential league in Greece. Only Athens protested, but her protest was unavailing, and Philip's newly-acquired dignity was the death-blow to her opposition.

At Olympia Philip had already ingratiated himself with the authorities by a victory in the horse-race in 356 B.C., and two victories in the four-horse chariot-race in the two following Olympiads. The news of his victory in the horse-race reached him, says Plutarch, shortly after his capture of Potidaea, and on the same day he received the news of a victory gained by Parmenio over the Illyrians, and of the birth of Alexander. Following the example of the tyrants of Sicily, he commemorated his victories in the chariot-race by representing a chariot on his coins. After the battle of Chaeronea Philip marched into the Peloponnese, and having ravaged Laconia and reduced Sparta to impotence, summoned a congress of all the Greek states at Corinth. Then he came forward as the champion of united Hellas, declaring his resolve of leading a new crusade against Persia, and was appointed by the congress sole commander of the forces of Greece. It will be remembered how time after time this policy of union against Persia had been preached at Olympia, and nowhere can Philip's proclamation have been more welcome. Did he visit Olympia in person? It is tempting to suppose so. At least we may connect with this time the founding of the Philippeum, a small circular building consisting of a cella surrounded by eighteen Ionic columns, and containing statues in gold and ivory of Philip himself and his ancestors, and even of female members of his family, Eurydice and Olympias. The Philippeum seems to have been an offering similar in character to the treasuries of an earlier age, the founders of which by their erection sought to establish for

---

[220] Krause, *Olymp.* p. 215. Diodorus and Ulpian assign the founding of these games to Archelaus, another account assigns it to Philip II.
[221] Xen. *Hell.* vi. 4, 29.

themselves a right and *locus standi* in the management of the festival. There was no room for further buildings on the treasury terrace itself, and a yet more honourable and unique position was found for Philip's monument to the south-west of the Heraeum within the limits of the Altis itself, the boundary of which had to be moved westward to enclose it. It was the first such building to be placed within the Altis, the first to bear the name of its founder, who was thereby placed on a level with the mythical presidents of Olympia, Pelops and Oenomaus, and acknowledged as the freely-appointed leader of united Greece at the very centre of Panhellenism.

Philip was assassinated in the very act of celebrating the marriage of his daughter Cleopatra with Alexander of Epirus by a magnificent festival at Aegae, where the lavish prodigality of the Macedonian expended itself in banquets, gymnastic and musical contests, dramatic competitions, and every variety of attraction which could appeal to and impress the imagination of the Greek world. Even the name Olympia was given to the games at Aegae, and the statues of the twelve gods of the Olympic pantheon were carried in procession to the theatre followed by the statue of Philip himself who thus anticipated the claim of Alexander to divine honours.

Alexander's ambition was too vast to find satisfaction in victories at Olympia. He treated with contempt the athletics of his day. Though himself vigorous and athletic of body, he had an aversion for the exercises of the palaestra, regarding them as useless for war. When asked whether he would compete in the foot-race at Olympia, he replied, "Yes, if I had kings for my antagonists." There is no doubt that his refusal was fully justified; he could gain no honour by entering into competition with professionals. But though he despised the athletic part of the festivals, he appreciated to the full their social and political importance. He recognized the importance of amusing the people. He celebrated his victories by brilliant Olympic games at Aegae and at Dium, at which he offered prizes for tragic poets, musicians, and rhapsodists, and entertained the people not with athletic competitions but with the hunting of wild beasts, and with fencing or fighting with the staff. Similar entertainments were provided by the king at various places in his triumphal progress through Asia. Olympia itself was to him the true capital of Greece. In spite of his personal aversion to athletic competitions, he is related to have restored to liberty Dionysodorus of Thebes, whom he had taken prisoner at Issus, in consideration of his claims as an Olympic victor.[222] Thither during the course of his eastern campaigns he sent dispatches which were publicly read at the festival. There in 324 Nicanor arrived as bearer of two imperial mandates bidding the cities of Greece receive back their exiles and acknowledge Alexander as a god. This decree was publicly read by the herald in the presence of 20,000 exiles who had mustered for the occasion.

The conquests of Alexander opened the door for the extension of Hellenism over the eastern world, and of this extension, an interesting illustration was discovered at Olympia. It is the monument of Philonides of Crete, who describes himself as courier of King Alexander, and road surveyor of (βηματωτής) of Asia. On one side of the pedestal is a bronze tablet on which Curtius aptly suggests was engraved a map of Asia, enabling visitors to Olympia to trace the course of his master's conquests.[223] Under his successors Asia and Egypt became Hellenized, and this process is illustrated by the appearance in the lists of Olympic victors of

---

[222] Arr. *Anab.* ii. 15.
[223] *Ol. Ins.* 276, 277. Another such courier was Deinosthenes of Sparta, who won the foot-race in Ol. 116, and set up beside his statue a pillar giving the distance from Olympia to Sparta as 630 stades, and from Sparta to the next pillar (at Amyclae) as 30 stades. Paus. vi. 16, 8; *Ol. Ins.* 171.

athletes from the newly-founded cities, and later on from the kingdoms and provinces of Asia. The new cities sought to reproduce the main features of the old Hellenic ideal, and from this ideal athletics and the athletic festivals were inseparable. Everywhere athletic festivals were founded bearing the names of the ancient festivals, everywhere elaborate stadia and gymnasia were erected. The athletic enthusiasm which had died out in the mother country revived in many of her daughter cities: especially was this the case in Alexandria, which under the rule of the Ptolemaei became a stronghold of Hellenism.[224] This revival of athletic interest, if somewhat artificial, must have helped to keep alive the ancient festivals of the mainland.

At Olympia the building of the Philippeum after Chaeronea was the first of a series of improvements, stimulated, no doubt, by Macedonian encouragement, perhaps paid for by Macedonian gold. The choice of a site for the Philippeum had, as we have seen, necessitated a reconstruction of the western boundary of the Altis. A similar reconstruction took place on the east, where the old Stoa was extended and rebuilt, and as part of the same scheme, the west and southern sides of the Stadium were banked up so as to provide better accommodation for the spectators. At the same time a passage was made through the north side of the western embankment on the site of the later Roman tunnelled passage and gateway giving entrance into the Stadium. The use of this entrance was probably confined to officials and athletes: for the latter the sight of the Zanes lining the steps outside the entrance served as a warning only too necessary.

The chronology of the various Olympic buildings is full of difficulty, especially from the fourth century onward. But we are probably justified in assigning to the early period of Macedonian influence the building of the Theocoleon on the west side of the Altis close to the ancient Heroum, to serve as quarters for the Olympic priesthood, and of the Leonidaeum to the south of it. The latter building was the gift of Leonidas of Naxos. The inscription on the pedestal of his statue, which has been found, is apparently contemporary with the inscription on the monument of Philonides, Alexander's courier, which stood close by, and the architectural evidence agrees with this date.[225] In later times the building served as the headquarters of the Roman governors, and this fact renders probable the view that it was originally intended for the use of distinguished visitors. The arrangements for the entertainment of visitors, and for the requirements of the priesthood as provided in the Leonidaeum and the Theocoleon seem entirely in keeping with the pomp and state which were so marked a feature of Macedonian festivities. A record of hospitality shown at Olympia by another islander is preserved on a bronze tablet containing the decree of the Hellanodicae in honour of one Democrates of Tenedos, a wrestler whose strength was such that when he stood behind a line no man could draw him across it. He and his father had taken up their residence in Elis, and the decree, which dates about the first half of the third century, records that in consideration of his services in entertaining guests at the festival, he shall be named Proxenos and Benefactor, and shall have a place of honour in the Dionysian festival and a share in the sacrifices.[226]

On the death of Alexander, Elis joined in the general revolt of the Greek states against Macedon, but on the failure of the revolt found herself once more compelled to acquiesce in the Macedonian supremacy. From this time she seems to have adopted a wise policy of

---

[224] Alexandrian victories in 272, 256, 240, 228, 212 B.C. *Vide* Förster, *op. cit.*
[225] *Ol. Ins.* 294.
[226] *Ol. Ins.* 39.

neutrality, and amid the struggles of rival kings and leagues the sanctity of Olympia was respected and her support courted by all parties. The only occasion on which this sanctity was violated was when Telesphorus, who had revolted from Antigonus, plundered the treasury of Olympia, but the plunder was restored not long afterwards by the unprincipled usurper and murderer Ptolemaeus Ceraunus, who hoped to win the support of Olympia for his ambitious schemes.

The neutrality of Elis is evident in the votive offerings of the period. Side by side with the statues of Antigonus Monophthalmus and his son Demetrius we find the statues of Spartan kings, of Areus who tried to free Greece from the yoke of Macedon, and Cleomenes who attempted to revive the military hegemony of Sparta, of Aratus of Sicyon, the founder of the Achaean league and enemy of Sparta and Macedon alike, of Ptolemaeus Philadelphus of Egypt at whose hospitable court the opponents of Macedon found shelter in defeat; lastly of that brilliant but semi-barbarian conqueror Pyrrhus of Epirus, who in his meteoric career twice occupied the throne of Macedon. Some of these statues were the gifts of the kings themselves, some of the Eleans or other states that wished to show honour to the individual or win favour at Olympia. The statue of Pyrrhus was the gift of the Elean seer Thrasybulus, who took part in the campaigns of Aratus against Sparta, and was himself honoured by a statue in the Altis. Perhaps the honour shown to Pyrrhus was due to his friendship with the Aetolians, whose connexion with Elis dates back to the earliest days of the festival. The Eleans early joined the Aetolian league, and showed their loyalty to their friends by refusing to desert them in spite of the most tempting offers of Philip V. Numerous statues in the Altis bore witness to this friendship. Especial interest attaches to that of the Aetolian Pleistaenus, whose father Eurydamus, as leader of the Aetolian forces, helped in the memorable fight near Delphi, which saved Greece from Brennus and his barbarous horde of Gauls.[227] Lastly, we may notice the significant monument of Antigonus Doson set up after the defeat of Cleomenes at Sellasia in 222 B.C. Greece was represented crowning with one hand Antigonus, with the other Philip Arridaeus the nominal successor of Alexander, while opposite stood a similar group, in which Elis crowned Demetrius Poliorketes and Ptolemaeus the son of Lagus. Both groups it seems probable, as Curtius suggests, were the gift of Antigonus Doson, recalling as they did the earlier group of the personified Ekecheiria crowning Iphitus, and setting forth in emblematic fashion the renewal of Olympic peace and restoration of unity under the beneficent rule of the princes of Macedon.

The period of Macedonian influence is marked by numerous victories gained by Macedonians, or by citizens of Macedonian towns such as Amphipolis or the newly-founded Philippi. But the Macedonian kings had little leisure or peace for competing at festivals, being occupied with more serious contests. And the same is true for the most part of the princes of Asia. From Pergamum, left in peace for a period under the strong rule of Philetaerus, we have an interesting inscription which records the victory in the chariot-race at Olympia of Attalus, brother of Philetaerus and father of Attalus I.[228] But in Egypt life was more settled, and more prosperous, and the Ptolemaei showed themselves devoted supporters of the Hellenic festivals. Ptolemaeus, the son of Lagus, won the chariot-race with a pair of colts in 314 B.C. at Delphi, where he was proclaimed a Macedonian. For, adds Pausanias, the Ptolemaei

---

[227] This victory was commemorated by the founding of a new festival, the Soteria, which is mentioned in various athletic inscriptions of the period.

[228] Fränckel, *Antiq. Pergam.* viii. 1, pp. 8, 10.

delighted to call themselves Macedonians. At Olympia he dedicated statues, one of himself and another of an unnamed athlete. His successor Philadelphus erected the statue of Areus of Sparta as a monument, says his inscription, of his goodwill to himself and to all Greece.[229] Among those who took refuge at his court was Glaucon of Athens, distinguished not only for a victory in the chariot-race 260 B.C., but for his spirited resistance to Antigonus. His statue at Olympia was erected by Ptolemy Euergetes. There, too, was the statue of Belistiche of Macedon, the mistress of Philadelphus, who won the pair-horse chariot-race for colts on the first occasion that this event was introduced, in Ol. 129. The statues of Philadelphus and Arsinoë, his wife and sister, were set up by the Samian Callicrates on lofty pillars placed upon a raised basement of stone in front of the Echo Colonnade.[230]

It has been already mentioned that Philadelphus founded a gymnasium at Athens. Curtius suggests that the palaestra and gymnasium at Olympia were the work of the same benefactor. Neither of these buildings is likely to be earlier than his time, but there is no real proof to connect them with Philadelphus. The fact recorded by Pausanias that Euanoridas, who won the boys' wrestling match in 252 B.C., afterwards as Hellanodicas had the list of Olympic victors inscribed and set up in the gymnasium at Olympia, proves at the most that the gymnasium must have existed at the close of the third century.[231] There is still less evidence for Curtius' view that the founding of the gymnasium and palaestra was an attempt to counteract the one-sided athleticism of Olympia by founding a sort of public school at Olympia where the youth of Greece could receive mental as well as physical instruction. Olympia was not, and was not likely to become, a residential place. This is proved by the story of the eccentric philosopher Alexinus the Litigious, as he was nicknamed, who tried to set up there a school of philosophy but failed, being deserted by all his followers owing to the want of accommodation and difficulty of obtaining supplies. The palaestra of Olympia, which will be described in a later chapter, was of the ordinary Greek type, and the fact that some of the rooms were provided with benches does not prove that the place was intended for a school. Seats and stools are no uncommon accompaniment of athletic scenes on the vases, where they serve, among other purposes, for the athletes to put their clothes upon. That the gymnasium and palaestra were intended for competitors at the festivals and were little used at other times is proved by an inscription at Delphi which contains the contracts for preparing for the festival not only the stadium and hippodrome, but also the gymnasium and palaestra.[232] Before the festival and during it these must have been thronged with athletes practising, and must have been as favourite a resort of visitors interested in their performances as is the paddock to-day at Epsom or Ascot.

I have dwelt at some length on the monuments of this period because they illustrate the extension of Hellenism and therefore of the influence of Olympia over the East. Further, while honorary statues of distinguished men are multiplied the athletic statues gradually fall off in number, ceasing almost entirely after the middle of the second century.[233] Of the thirty-

---

[229] *Ol. Ins.* 308.
[230] *Ol. Ins.* 306, 307.
[231] Little weight can be attached to such a statement. The list may well have been transferred to the gymnasium when it was built. A similar list was set up by the father of Paraballon whose victory in the diaulos is placed by Hyde between Ol. 91-101, when the gymnasium certainly did not exist.
[232] *B.C.H.*, 1899, pp. 565 ff. The inscription is dated by the archonship of Dion, 258 B.C.
[233] Of the statues seen by Pausanias none can be much later than 150 B.C. (*vide* Hyde, *Olymp. Statues*). The Olympic inscriptions show that the custom was revived at the close of the first century B.C. *Ins.* 213, 219, 224, 225, etc.

two statues erected during this period no less than fifteen were erected by the Eleans, a striking testimony to the wealth of Olympia. In the list of Olympic victors the noticeable feature is the almost complete disappearance of names from Sicily and Italy,[234] and also from the old states of the mainland, such as Athens and Sparta. Their place is taken by competitors from the East, from Aetolia and Achaia and the newer cities of the Peloponnese.

Though, as we have said above, athletics were largely neglected by the upper classes, we still as at all times find a few notable exceptions. Such were Aratus, who, though his only victory at Olympia was in the chariot-race, is stated to have won various successes in the pentathlon, the competition which appealed least to professionals; on the other hand, the other great general of the Achaean league, Philopoemen, would have nothing to do with athletics, and even forbade his soldiers to take part in training which only unfitted them for the hardships of a campaign. Another notable pentathlete was Gorgus of Messene, who won considerable renown as a statesman and was sent as ambassador to Philip III of Macedon. Besides the pentathlon he won the diaulos and the race in armour.

The falling off in competition and the growth of professionalism are shown by the number of men who won victories in more than one event at the same festival. Philinus of Cos, who won the stadium race in Ols. 129, 130, is credited with three other victories at Olympia, four in the Pythia, four in the Nemea, and eleven in the Isthmia—twenty-four in all. A still finer record is that of Leonidas of Rhodes, who won all four foot-races in three successive Olympiads 164-156 B.C., thus three times earning the title of τριαστής or triple victor given to those who won the stade-race, diaulos, and dolichos. Besides the professional runner, we have the professional fighter represented by the successors of Heracles already alluded to, with regard to whom we may add that with the exception of Caprus of Elis all holders of the title came from the East. The successors of Heracles are further honoured with the title of παράδοξος or παραδοξονίκης, and in the second century we find for the first time in Olympic inscriptions the term περίοδος or περιοδονίκης used of those who won victories in all the four great festivals which formed the athletic cycle or period. Such terms suggest the age of athletic "records" which was to come under the Romans.

Two more equestrian events were added during this period—the two-horse chariot-race for colts, and the riding-race for colts, introduced in Ols. 129 and 131 respectively. Both these events, introduced obviously with the intention of encouraging horse breeding, had been introduced half a century earlier at Delphi, doubtless owing to Macedonian influence. Lastly in Ol. 145 the athletic programme was completed by the introduction of the pankration for boys, which was won by Phaedimus, described variously as from Alexandria Troas, or from Naukratis in Egypt. The pankration was not a competition suited for boys, and it was a true athletic feeling which had so long excluded it from the boys' events at Olympia. Its introduction is significant of the growing love of sensational and brutal displays which we associate rather with the Romans than the Greeks. It was only a few years later that Antiochus Epiphanes (175-164 B.C.) introduced into Syria the Roman gladiatorial games, and though the innovation at first met with criticism and opposition, the Greeks only too soon became accustomed to such sights.

With the advent of the Romans the history of Greek athletics really ends, though the athletic festivals were destined to survive four centuries or more under their patronage. The Romans posed as the champions and kinsmen of the Greeks, and like the Macedonians fully

---

[234] The only statue from Sicily is that of Hieron II of Syracuse.

realised the importance of these festivals. As early as 228 B.C. they had been admitted to participation in the Eleusinian mysteries and the Isthmian games, in recognition of their services in freeing the Adriatic from Illyrian pirates, though it may be doubtful if Roman citizens deigned to compete in the actual sports. Again in 196 B.C. it was at the Isthmian games that Flamininus proclaimed the liberation of Greece from the tyranny of Macedon. At Olympia Titus Manlius had appeared as ambassador in 208 B.C. to secure the support of the Sicilian and Italian Greeks against their common foe Carthage. Finally Mummius commemorated the defeat of the Achaeans, the destruction of Corinth, and the restoration of unity to Greece by dedicating at Olympia a bronze statue of Zeus and twenty-one golden shields arrayed above the colonnade surrounding the temple of Zeus. But the unity thus commemorated was secured at the cost of liberty.

It was the spirit of independence which had given life to those great athletic meetings where the free citizens of free states contended not for personal glory so much as for the honour of their states. These states were no longer free, and all the pomp and splendour lavished on the festivals by their imperial patrons could not recall to life the spirit that had fled.

Chapter 8

ATHLETICS UNDER THE ROMANS

Greek athletics must have been familiar to the Romans from early times. We have seen how prominent a part the Greek cities of Italy and Sicily had taken in the festivals of Greece during the sixth and fifth centuries. The popularity of athletics among the Etruscans is proved by the numerous scenes painted on the walls of Etruscan tombs, where every variety of sport is represented. The "ludi Maximi" of Rome herself show strong traces of Greek influence. Moreover the Romans, like all vigorous nations, were fond of physical exercises—running, wrestling, throwing the diskos and the spear, and especially games of ball. But they were not fond of competitions. Consequently athletics never acquired at Rome the importance which they possessed in Greece, and their festivals, if originally similar in character to those of Greece, soon became mere spectacles in which the performers, whether actors, riders, or athletes, were professionals belonging to subject races and the lower classes, hired for the amusement of the Roman citizens. Rome recognized no peers among the neighbouring states, and free competition between independent states was therefore impossible at Rome. Moreover, the centuries of struggle during which she step by step extended and consolidated her power had left little time or inclination for less serious contests, and had developed in her citizens a strongly practical type of character that could feel no sympathy with the athletic ideal of Greece. To the Roman as to the Spartan athletics were nothing but a means to an end, and that end military efficiency. To devote to sport the time and energy necessary to secure success at Olympia, to submit for months to the tyranny of a trainer, often a man of no birth or position, and above all to exhibit oneself naked before the eyes of one's fellow-citizens—these were things quite inconsistent with the Roman's idea of his dignity as a citizen. Even as spectacles the Greek sports did not appeal to his taste. Brutalized by incessant war, he preferred more exciting contests, and took more pleasure in the gladiatorial shows of his Etruscan and Campanian neighbours than in musical or gymnastic competitions. It was 186 B.C. that Greek athletes and actors first appeared at the Roman games; but a more pleasing innovation must have been the importation in the same year of lions and panthers from Africa to provide more exciting sport for the spectators in the circus. When in 167 B.C. some famous Greek flute-players who were performing at a festival failed to please the Roman audience, the managers ordered them to box, a performance which caused boundless delight to the spectators.

When in the second century B.C. the Romans were first brought into closer contact with Greece, they found ample justification for their anti-athletic prejudice in the vicious and corrupt state into which athletics had fallen at that period in Greece. The competitions were in the hands of professional athletes, whose training rendered them useless as soldiers; the gymnasia, instead of producing healthy, useful citizens, had become schools of idleness and immorality; from a physical and military point of view the whole nation had degenerated. The athletic festivals were useful political factors, and as such the Romans knew how to utilize them. Some, like Aemilius Paulus, standing before the Zeus of Pheidias might feel something of the beauty and the grandeur of the Greek ideal, or, like Cato, that odd mixture of conservatism and Hellenism, might train their sons in the athletic exercises of Greece; but the mass of the nation was unaffected; for a long time no gymnasia or palaestrae rose in Rome, no Roman deigned to compete in the games of Greece.

The old Roman prejudice died hard. More than a century after the founding of the Empire, in spite of imperial Philhellenism, we find an echo of it in the reign of Nero, in the protests of the old school against the introduction in Rome of a festival on Greek lines. "The youths were degenerating under the influence of foreign tastes, passing their time in athletics, in idling, and low intrigues; what remained for them but to strip themselves naked, put on the caestus, and practise such battles instead of the arms of legitimate warfare?"[235]

Such being the feeling of Rome towards Greek athletics, it is no matter for wonder that in spite of the growing influence of Hellenism, the festivals languished during the century which followed the fall of Corinth. In 80 B.C. Sulla transferred the whole Olympic festival, athletes and all, to Rome, leaving only the boys' foot-race to be decided at Olympia. Perhaps his object was to transfer the festival permanently to Rome; but ere another Olympiad came round Sulla himself was dead, and his purpose was never accomplished. But the prestige of the festival suffered. We possess the list of Olympic victors for the year 72 B.C. In this Olympiad, as in the Olympiad which followed the Spartan invasion of 399 B.C., the falling off in the competition is marked by a series of local victories. Eight, possibly eleven events fell to Elis, Hecatomnus, the winner of three of the foot-races, being variously assigned to Elis and Miletus; two events fell to Sicyon, one to Cyparissia in Messenia, the remaining four events being divided between Alexandria, Mysia, Asia, and Cos. Elis carried off all the equestrian events. In the Olympic inscriptions which belong to this period it is remarkable that nearly all the victors are Eleans and nearly all their victories are gained in the horse-races.[236] This local predominance, coupled with the depression produced by Sulla's invasion, may account for the fact, recorded by Africanus, that the chariot-race and perhaps other equestrian events were discontinued in the year 68 B.C., not to be revived until the time of the Empire.[237]

Meanwhile a change had come over the character of the Roman people. No longer occupied incessantly in war, the dwellers in the capital had become more and more addicted to amusements. Festival after festival was added to their calendar, and ambitious politicians vied with one another in the variety and magnificence of the entertainments which they provided in the hopes of winning the favour of the sovereign people. These entertainments, though containing athletic and equestrian competitions, were, however, purely spectacular,

---

[235] Tacitus, *Annals*, xiv. 20. For the attitude of the Romans towards athletics *vide* Wilkins, *Roman Education*, pp. 31-33.
[236] *Ol. Ins.* 191-210.
[237] Africanus states that the discontinuance of these events lasted from Ol. 178 to Ol. 194, when the chariot-race, after being "long prohibited," was won by Germanicus. The inaccuracy of this statement is proved by the discovery of an earlier inscription recording the victory of Tiberius Claudius Nero. *Ol. Ins.* 220-221.

and it was regarded as a disgrace for a Roman citizen to take part in them personally. The character of these entertainments and their difference from the Greek festivals may be illustrated by the account given by Suetonius of those provided by Julius Caesar.[238] Besides a variety of dramatic and musical performances, there were the games in the circus, athletic displays, and a sea-fight. In these certain Roman citizens of position actually took part. There was a gladiatorial contest between Furius Leptinus, a member of a praetorian family, and Quintus Calpenus, an ex-senator. The Pyrrhic dance was performed by noble youths from Asia and Bithynia; and one Decimus Laberius, a Roman knight, actually performed in a farce of his own composition, for which he was handsomely rewarded by Caesar, and restored to the rank which he had forfeited by his performance. At the games in the circus youths of noble birth took part in the chariot and horse-races. Two companies of boys exhibited the semi-military manœuvres called the Trojan game. Five days were occupied in *venationes*, or combats with wild beasts, and there was a sham fight between two forces consisting each of 500 foot-soldiers, 30 cavalry and 20 elephants. To provide more space for this performance the metae of the circus were removed and a camp was formed at either end. A temporary stand was erected in the field of Mars, where athletic competitions took place lasting three days. Lastly, a huge artificial lake was constructed in which biremes, triremes, and quadriremes from Tyre and Egypt joined in mimic battle. All the neighbouring roads and streets were occupied by the tents of visitors, and so great was the crowd that many were crushed to death. But Caesar himself, the giver of all, cared for none of these things; and his enemies accused him of amusing himself with reading and writing when he ought to have been watching the progress of the games.[239]

With the Empire a new era opened for Greece. As the conquests of Alexander had spread Hellenism throughout the East, so the Roman Empire gradually hellenized the whole civilized world. Though Greece was incorporated in the Roman Empire, cities like Athens and Sparta preserved the outward forms of independence; the bodies which controlled her ancient festivals continued to exercise their hereditary functions, and were treated as a rule with all honour and respect. In the sphere of literature and art Greece had long been recognized as the mistress and teacher of her conqueror. Hence the feeling of subjection disappeared, and so complete was the fusion between conquered and conqueror that in the second century, while the ancient families of Elis or of Sparta bore the names of their Roman patrons, such as the Julii, or the Flavii, and were enrolled in Roman tribes, the Greek language had become the language of communication throughout all the Eastern half of the Empire, and at Rome herself was supplanting Latin as the language of literature. These results were largely due to the Philhellenism of the emperors, and nowhere is this Philhellenism more conspicuous than in connection with athletic festivals. The old festivals were celebrated with increased splendour and ceremony, new festivals were introduced in close imitation of them, sumptuous race-courses and gymnasia were provided not merely in Greece but in Italy and in Rome herself, athletic guilds were formed; and though the athletic revival was purely professional and had little effect on the people, whether of Greece or Rome, the privileges and rewards showered on the successful athletes were certainly no less substantial if less honourable than those bestowed on the victors of the fifth century B.C.

---

[238] *Julius Caesar*, c. 39.
[239] *Octavianus*, c. 45.

The Julii claimed admission to the festivals of Greece as the descendants and heirs of the gods who presided over those festivals. At Olympia their claim was recognized by the re-dedication to their service of the little temple of the Mother of the Gods, in which were placed the statues of Augustus and his successors. Under their patronage the festival recovered much of its ancient glory. The horse-races, which had been discontinued, were revived shortly before our era, when members of the imperial family, emulating the triumphs of the princes of Sicily and Macedon, entered as competitors for the Olympic crown. Inscriptions record the victory of the youthful Tiberius in the chariot-race, and a few years later of Germanicus Caesar in the same event. The building of the arched entrance into the stadium and other improvements possibly belong to the reign of Augustus. The remarkable continuity of Olympic administration is shown by a series of inscriptions recording the names of the various officials connected with the sanctuary.[240] These lists begin in 30 B.C. and continue down to A.D. 265. They include every variety of official, from the seers and heralds of the sacred truce down to the cook and baker who provided the sacrificial feasts, and perhaps catered for the higher officials and for distinguished visitors. One important officer bore the title of official guide or exegetes; his duty doubtless was to explain to the crowds of visitors the historical monuments of the Altis. In the second century, owing to the increasing numbers of visitors a second guide was appointed. It was from these guides that Pausanias derived much of the information contained in his books on Elis. The higher offices seem to have formed a regular scale of honours, a *cursus honorum*, hereditary in the families of the Elean nobility, most of whom bear Roman names. It is curious to find one bearing the name of Flavius Heracleitus, who had the charge of the statue of Zeus, calling himself a descendant of Pheidias. The activity of the administration is shown by the revival of the practice of dedicating honorary statues of athletes and others: perhaps it is to this revival that we may ascribe the rule recorded by Pliny that portrait statues were only allowed in the case of athletes who had won three Olympic victories.[241] It is in the inscriptions of these honorary statues that after a long interval we find mention of the council who seem to have held supreme authority over the sanctuary and whose sanction was necessary for the erection of statues in the Altis.[242] The revival of ancient forms of administration is characteristic of Roman conservatism and love of order.

The Philhellenism of the Caesars and their Roman love of archaism are particularly manifest in the numerous festivals founded by them in various parts of the Empire. Of most of these we know little besides the names which are mentioned in inscriptions and on coins; a few deserve special notice and may be taken as typical of the rest. Augustus celebrated his victory at Actium, not only by holding Actian games at Rome but by instituting at the newly founded Nicopolis an Actian festival intended to rival or even surpass Olympia. A local festival had long been held at Actium every two years. The new festival which, besides athletic, musical, and equestrian competitions, included a regatta, was, like the Olympic festival, held every four years. The victors received crowns and bore the title Actianicae, and the Actiads were intended to form the basis of a new chronology which was to supplant that of the Olympiads. We feel in all this something of that spirit of conscious rivalry between

---

[240] *Ol. Ins.* 59-141.

[241] No satisfactory explanation of this rule has been offered. It certainly does not seem to have been always observed in earlier times. For example, Xenombrotus, *Ol. Ins.* 170, seems to have set up a portrait statue of himself for a single victory in the horse-race.

[242] Louis Dyer, "The Olympian Council House," in *Harvard Studies*, vol. xix. pp. 36 ff.

Rome and Greece which made the Roman poet herald the *Aeneid* as a work greater than the *Iliad*. But though in imperial inscriptions the Actia rank with, or even take precedence of, the Panhellenic festivals, the new games were destined never to acquire the prestige of the old.

The same spirit of conscious rivalry appears again in the proud title "ἰσολύμπια" applied to the Augustalia at Naples. These games, founded in 1 B.C., were reorganized in A.D. 2 as a quinquennial festival with the magniloquent name "Italica Romaia Sebasta Isolympia." The new era which began with them was reckoned by "Italids." The terms ἰσολύμπια and ἰσοπύθια referred originally to the conditions of competition and particularly to the age of competitors. Thus the expressions Olympian, Pythian, Isthmian boys, denote boys within the age-limit for the boys' events at these respective festivals. Under the Empire the terms have often merely an honorary significance, and such apparently is the use of the word here. A long, unfortunately much mutilated, inscription[243] found at Olympia contains regulations for this festival, for the age of competitors, the date of entry, provision for them during the time of training, and the penalties imposed for any breach of these rules. The festival fell into two parts, the first part of which, like the old Olympia, consisted only of equestrian and athletic events. The prize, as at Olympia, was a wreath. The second part, as we learn from another inscription, resembled the Pythian and Nemean festivals in its regulations with regard to ages and prizes. It contained, besides athletic and equestrian events, musical and dramatic competitions, and some of the competitions were confined to citizens of Naples. The prizes consisted in sums of money.

Somewhat similar was the character of the Olympic and Pythian festivals which we find in Rome, Athens, Ephesus, and a number of other places. The right to bestow these titles must originally have rested with the authorities at Olympia and Delphi, but seems later to have been exercised by the emperors.[244] Each new festival founded was the beginning of a new series of Olympiads. At Rome the great Capitolia, founded by Domitian in A.D. 86, bore the title Olympia, and Flavius Archibius, an Olympic victor in Ols. 220, 221, is also described as victor at Rome in the 3rd and following Olympiads. The judges at these festivals were sometimes called Hellanodicae,[245] and doubtless many other features of the original festivals were reproduced. Perhaps the most interesting of all these games are those held at Daphne near Antioch. Founded originally by Antiochus Epiphanes, they obtained from the Eleans the title of Olympia in A.D. 44. Their interest lies in the fact that the model of Olympia was followed in every particular, not only in the programme and administration, but in the relations existing between Daphne and Antioch, which corresponded entirely to these between Olympia and Elis. In the fourth century a fierce dispute arose between a popular party, which wished to transfer the important part of the festival from Daphne to Antioch, and the conservative party headed by Libanius, who characterized the proposed change as sacrilege and a violation of the true Olympia. We have frequent references to the festival in the writings of St. Chrysostom, for a long time presbyter at Antioch; and it continued to be celebrated as late as the reign of Justinus in the sixth century.[246]

Imperial patronage was not at all times an unmixed blessing for the Greeks. Caligula would have carried off to Rome the statue of Olympian Zeus had he not been prevented by the miraculous protest of the statue itself. Nero actually carried off to Rome thousands of

---

[243] *Ol. Ins.* 56; cp. Mie, *Quaestiones Agonisticae*, p. 43.
[244] Krause, *Olympia*, p. 203.
[245] *I.G.* xiv. 739, πρωτελληνοδίκης ἐν Ἐφέσῳ καὶ ἐν Σμύρνῃ.
[246] Curtius, *Ol.* Text, i. 52; Krause, *Olympia*, p. 207.

works of art, and in his jealousy caused the statues of victors at the games to be pulled down and thrown into the sewers. Despite his pretended flattery of the Greeks and desire to win their approbation for his art, he had so little respect for religion that he caused the times of the festivals to be altered so that they might all be celebrated during his visit to Greece.[247] At Olympia contests in tragedy and singing were introduced into the programme at his behest; a house was built for his entertainment at the south-east corner of the Altis, and almost opposite it a magnificent processional entrance was constructed, the Altis wall being at the same time extended southward so as to include the triangular strip between the old wall and the northern line of the council house. The story of his performances at the games is a piteous proof of the degradation of the festivals and of the servility of the Greeks. At Olympia he won crowns in the chariot-races, in the competitions for singing and for tragedy, and in the heralds' competition. For the latter he entered wherever he competed in order to have the privilege of proclaiming his victories with his own voice. In the hippodrome he appeared in a chariot drawn by ten horses; thrown from his chariot, he was picked up and replaced, resumed the race, and was finally awarded the prize by the obsequious officials. Though he was said to be fond of wrestling, he had sufficient respect for Roman prejudice to abstain from exhibiting his skill in the stadium, and contented himself with playing the part of a brabeutes, sitting on the ground during the rounds, and with his own hands pulling the combatants back if they got too far away. The servile Hellanodicae were rewarded with Roman citizenship and with large sums of money, which they had to disgorge in the reign of his successor. Finally, at the end of his tour, he proclaimed himself at the Isthmian games as the restorer of the liberty of Greece. Returning to Italy with 1808 crowns which he had won, he was welcomed at Naples with all the most extravagant honours which were ever recorded to have been paid to an Olympia victor. A breach was made in the city wall through which he entered in a chariot drawn by white horses. The same farce was repeated at Antium and Albanum. He entered Rome in the chariot in which Augustus had triumphed, clothed in purple, with the Olympic crown upon his head, and holding the Pythian crown in his right hand, while before him marched a procession of courtiers carrying the crowns which he had won, and proclaiming to the populace the names and details of his triumphs. No wonder that such as remained of the old Roman stock regarded the competitions of the Greeks with amused contempt, that Seneca and other writers of the first century were unanimous in their condemnation of Greek athletics, and that the Olympic competitor became the butt of the epigrammatist. That Olympia survived even this degradation is perhaps the strongest proof of its vitality.

While the emperors were introducing Greek festivals into Italy, the influence of Rome was degrading and brutalizing the public taste of Greece. Gladiatorial shows had been introduced into the East nearly two centuries before Christ. They had long been popular with the cosmopolitan crowds of Antioch and Alexandria. In Greece they found a congenial home in the equally cosmopolitan crowd of Corinth, which, refounded as a Roman colony by Julius Caesar, quickly regained her commercial supremacy, and eclipsed even the records of her past in wealth and luxury and vice. Athens followed and even improved upon the example set by her rival. For while at Corinth the gladiatorial shows had been held in a ravine outside the city, at Athens they were exhibited in the theatre of Dionysus.[248]

---

[247] Suetonius, *Nero*, c. 23 ff.
[248] Dion of Prusa, *Or.* xxxi.

The growing love of excitement and bloodshed is evident in boxing. The caestus had, as we have seen, become gradually more ponderous and more murderous, and boxing consequently less scientific. Every one is familiar with the description of the boxing match in the *Aeneid*. The brutal, unscientific fight is in perfect keeping with the ponderous character of the weapons, and even the gentle and refined Vergil can only represent a heroic fight by heaping horror upon horror, and by ascribing the heavy caestus to heroic times, he actually reverses the whole history of boxing. We should not perhaps take Vergil's description as typical of Greek boxing even in his day, but only of the feeling at Rome, where scientific boxing was of so little account that even Augustus preferred to watch a fight between two street roughs to a match between trained boxers. But the brutality of boxing even in Greece is strikingly illustrated in a collection of epigrams written by or collected by one Lucilius in the reign of Nero. Their tone of persiflage, so different from that of the early Greek epigrammatist, is just what we should expect from such an age. Some of them are skits upon the athletes or would-be athletes of the age; a whole series are devoted to describing the disfigurement and mutilation of the boxer. Here is an old translation of one of them which may be taken as typical of them all:—

> This victor, glorious in his olive wreath,
> Had once eyes, eyebrows, nose, and ears and teeth.
> But turning cestus champion, to his cost,
> These, and still worse! his heritage he lost,
> For by his brother su'd, disowned, at last
> Confronted with his picture he was cast.[249]

Dion Chrysostom gives us an interesting glimpse of the Isthmia during the first century, in the story he tells of Diogenes' visit to the festival.[250] The scene is laid in the fourth century B.C., but the details are clearly drawn from the orator's own experience. Diogenes the Cynic happens to visit Corinth at the time of the festival. There, at the cross-roads of the world, he finds gathered together visitors from Ionia and Sicily, from Italy and Libya, from Massilia and the Borysthenes. Around the temple of Poseidon are wretched sophists shouting and abusing one another, their pupils are fighting, historians are reading meaningless compositions, poets are reciting verses, miracle-mongers are working miracles, augurs are interpreting omens, thousands of orators are wrangling, and merchants of every sort are bargaining. The crowd, regardless of all other interests, is watching the performances of the athletes, "mere slaves," he calls them, "that run and jump and dance." Here Diogenes sees a band of friends carrying a victor in the foot-race in triumphant procession, while the people shout and cheer and heap upon him fillets and garlands. The Cynic stops him and points out that after all he is not as swift as the hare or the deer, the most cowardly of animals. He himself has won a victory over adversaries that cannot be overcome by men "stuffed and puffed, who spend whole days in eating and snore all night like pigs," for he has won a victory over pain and pleasure. Finally he boldly puts upon his head the celery crown, and when the indignant officials protest, asks them, "Will ye take the crown from me and give it to him who is stuffed with most meat?" The rhetoric is for the most part mere commonplace

---

[249] *Anth. Pal.* xi. 75. The translation is taken from the "Dissertation on the Olympic Games," in a translation of the *Odes of Pindar*, by Gilbert West (London, 1753), vol. ii. p. 92.
[250] *Or.* vii. Διογένης ἢ περὶ ἀρετῆς; *Or.* viii. Διογένης ἢ Ἰσθμικός.

of the schools; yet we cannot doubt that the description is true of the Isthmia and of other festivals, especially of those in the rich cities of the East.

In such soil corruption throve. Philostratus, writing more than a century later, tells us that victories were publicly bought and sold; even the trainers encouraged the traffic, lending money for bribery to athletes at exorbitant rates of interest.[251] At the Isthmia a competitor who had promised his rival 3000 drachmae to let him win, refused to pay on the ground that he had won on his merits. Recourse was had to the oath, and the defeated competitor publicly swore before the altar of Poseidon that he had been promised the money if he allowed himself to be defeated. "What," adds Philostratus, "might not happen in Ionia or in Asia?"

At Olympia the honour of the games was still maintained. Bribery was severely punished. In Ols. 192 (12 B.C.) and 226 (A.D. 125) we read of fines exacted for corruption from which as of old Zanes were erected.[252] In the former case it was a father who bribed his son's opponent, and the fine was therefore exacted from the parents. In Ol. 218 (A.D. 93) one Apollonius of Alexandria was fined for coming too late and thereby disqualifying himself from competition. He pleaded that he had been detained by contrary winds. But it was proved that the plea was false, and that the real cause of his delay was that he had been "pot-hunting" in Ionia. It seems as if the authorities at Olympia even made an attempt to check the arrogant pretensions and self-advertisements of the professional fighter by abolishing the title "Successor of Heracles." The title was won for the last time in Ol. 204 (A.D. 37) by one Nicostratus, after whose victories the Eleans made a secret decree that no one should thereafter be allowed to win in both wrestling and the pankration. The account given by Dion of the Isthmia gathers force from its contrast with the veneration which he expresses for the Olympia, and his charming picture of the youthful Melancomas.[253] He and his father, himself an Olympic victor, seem even in that age of athletic decay to have lived up to the ideal of the best days.

A curious development of professionalism which we now meet with was the growth of athletic guilds resembling the dramatic guilds which had long existed. Victorious athletes at Rome, as in Greece, received certain privileges, including maintenance at the public cost, which privilege Maecenas advised Augustus to confine to winners at Olympia and Delphi and Rome.[254] Augustus, we are told, maintained and increased the privileges of athletes.[255] Guilds were one of the features of the early Empire, and it was therefore natural for athletes to form such combinations. These athletic guilds were called Xystoi from the xystos or covered colonnade which formed part of a gymnasium. The most famous of these clubs was that of the Herculanei,[256] a club which seems originally to have been formed at Sardis. In the reign of Trajan it was dissolved and transferred to Rome. One M. Ulpius came to the emperor as their spokesman to petition for quarters at Rome, and we possess copies of two letters of Trajan granting their petition.[257] He appoints them a house where they may keep their sacred things and records, near the baths built by his grandfather Trajan, and conveniently situated for the great Capitolia. Here they had a gymnasium and a council-chamber in which discussions could take place on all questions affecting the welfare of athletes, the holding of competitions,

---

[251] *Gym.* 45.
[252] Paus. v. 21.
[253] *Or.* xxix., xxx.
[254] Dio Cassius, lii. 30.
[255] Suetonius, *Octavianus* 45.
[256] Krause, *Gym.* p. 131; *I.G.* xiv. 1102-1110.
[257] *I.G.* xiv. 1054, 1055.

and the erection of honorary statues. They were a sacred guild, and within their precinct were statues of emperors and members of the guild. Their president or xystarches was also high-priest of the guild. He was often a distinguished athlete and held the office for life; and with it also the office of overseer of the imperial baths. The religious character of these guilds is a curious survival of the immemorial connexion between religion and athletics. Sometimes there were special competitions for members of certain guilds. At the Augustalia at Naples we find a series of competitions confined to members of the Augustan class, while mention is also made of a pankration for Claudian boys. These expressions seem to denote clubs or guilds bearing the name of Augustus and Claudius.[258] The most important guild at Naples was "the holy itinerant synod of the Alexandrini." The term περιπολιστική, which corresponds to our "nomads" or "wanderers," indicates that they did not confine their attentions to local festivals, but went about from place to place.[259] An Olympic inscription of the year A.D. 85 records the erection of a statue in honour of Lucius Vetulenus Laetus by the whole body of athletes gathered together "from the inhabited world" for the festival, and by the holy synod of the Xystos.[260] This particular xystos was presumably a local Elean guild. The title xystarches is known also at Sparta, and occurs in an inscription recently discovered at Sparta by the British excavators. The inscription contains regulations for a Spartan festival, probably the Leonidaea, a festival held in honour of those who fell at Thermopylae, and confined to Spartan competitors.[261] The xystarches is to place oil in the stadium, and discharge the usual duties of his post. As the president of the local gymnasium, he naturally took an important part in local festivals. He seems generally to have been a man of some importance, often an old athlete. His duties were probably as vague and depended as much on his personal inclination as those of the president of a modern athletic club.

Figure 22. Athletics under the Romans. From a mosaic found at Tusculum.

---

[258] Mie, *Quaestiones Agonisticae*, p. 46.
[259] *I.G.* xiv. 746.
[260] *Ol. Ins.* 436.
[261] *B.S.A.* xii. p. 452.

A mosaic found at Tusculum (Figure 22) gives a vivid picture of the life of these professional athletes under the Empire. A comparison of these scenes with those represented on the Panaetius kylix in Figure 17 will illustrate better than any description the difference between the two ages.

The renaissance of Hellenism which marked the second century brought with it a revival of the Greek athletic festivals and Greek athletics, which, under the patronage of the "Greekling" Hadrian and his successors, attained an outward prosperity and splendour unparalleled since the fifth century. It was the object of these emperors, who were as much at home in Greece as in Italy, to revive the glories of the past, and restore to the mainland of Greece that pre-eminence in the Hellenic world which had been usurped by the great cities of the East. Everywhere splendid buildings testified to the lavish munificence, if not always to the good taste, of the emperors, and of wealthy subjects who emulated their example. Countless monuments and inscriptions throughout Greece bear witness to the activity of Hadrian. At Athens he built a gymnasium and library, at Corinth he provided baths, at Nemea he instituted a winter festival, while at Mantinea and Argos he founded quinquennial festivals in honour of his beloved Antinous, whose cult spread rapidly throughout the Empire. His reverence for Olympia and its ideals is shown by a series of coins bearing on one side the emperor's head, on the other a representation of the Zeus of Pheidias.[262] But Hadrian's monuments sink into insignificance in comparison with the prodigal generosity of Herodes Atticus, who rebuilt in stone the stadia at Delphi and Athens, the latter in marble from Pentelicus. At Olympia he contributed to the comfort of the spectators by providing a new system of water-supply, while he left a more conspicuous if less useful monument of himself in the so-called exedra, a pompous and incongruous semicircular building erected between the Heraeum and the western end of the treasuries, at the only vacant spot commanding a view of the altar of Zeus. The exedra was dedicated to Zeus in the name of his wife Regilla, who held at Olympia the honoured position of priestess to Demeter Chamyne. Statues of Regilla and Herodes were placed by the Eleans in the exedra, which also contained the statues of Hadrian, Antoninus and other members of the imperial family, who from this place of honour seemed to look on for ever as spectators and patrons of the festival. Under such patronage the games attracted crowds from all parts of the "inhabited world," and indeed exercised considerable influence. For the religious idea expressed in the statue of Olympian Zeus fascinated the thought of the age. But for the Greeks themselves regeneration was no longer possible. Physically, morally, politically they were too degenerate. In the Olympic records of the second century there are few names from the mother-country; most of the victors came from the cities of Egypt and the East, especially from Alexandria. The marble stadium of Herodes Atticus at Athens witnessed all the brutalities of the Roman gladiatorial shows.

The artificiality of the athletic revival is nowhere more evident than in the numerous inscriptions of this period, which in their pompous verbosity afford a striking contrast to the severe simplicity of the time when athletics were a real part of the national life. As we read them we feel ourselves in another world, a world of professionalism, of self-advertisement, and of records, which bears no little resemblance to that in which we are living to-day. Compare, for example, the simple inscriptions at Olympia recording the victories of the

---

[262] *Historia Numorum*, p. 357.

Diagoridae[263] with the first-century inscription in honour of Publius Cornelius Ariston of Ephesus, who won the boys' pankration in Ol. 207 (A.D. 49), or better still with the second-century inscriptions found in Italy enumerating the exploits of Titus Flavius Artemidorus of Adana of Cilicia, or of Marcus Aurelius Asclepiades of Alexandria. The very names are significant of the change that has taken place. "Diagoras (son) of Damagetus a Rhodian" such is the simple formula of early days. The only description of the contest vouchsafed is the name of the festival and the event, with the single word ἀκονιτεί added occasionally to denote a "walk over." Occasionally a simple couplet is added. But the pedestal of Ariston's statue[264] had inscribed on it, besides the usual formula, a poem of twenty-four lines describing his powers and his fame, how in a field of seven he won all his heats without having the advantage of a bye, and how his glory was proclaimed not only throughout all Hellas but throughout Asia.

A few examples of these inscriptions will best illustrate the character of the age. They begin with a fulsome list of the victor's honorary titles. That on Asclepiades[265] informs us that he and his father both held for life the office of "high-priest of the whole xystos and overseer of the imperial baths," that he was "chief of the temple guardians of Great Serapis, a citizen of Alexandria, Hermopolis, and Puteoli, and councillor of Neapolis, Elis, Athens, and many other cities." Then follows a glowing description of his unbeaten record as "a pankratiast, a periodonikes invincible, immovable,[266] unrivalled." "I neither challenged any nor did any one in my time dare to challenge me, nor did I divide the crown with any, nor did I decline a contest or enter any protest,[267] nor did I abandon any contest, nor take part in a contest to please royalty, nor did I gain a victory in any new-fangled games, but in all the contests for which I ever entered my name I was crowned in the actual ring and was approved in all the preliminary trials." This emphatic insistence on the cleanness of his record is clearly an answer to those malicious attacks of which he complains at the end of the inscription, and which caused him to abandon athletics.

He proceeds to enumerate his victories in a manner which reminds one of nothing so much as those photographs which we see often in illustrated papers representing some professional athlete with his whole body covered with medals, belts and scarves which he has won, or standing triumphant in the midst of his cups and trophies. "I contended," he says, "among three nations in Italy, in Hellas, and in Asia, and in all the contests mentioned below I was victorious in the pankration,—in the Olympia at Pisa in Ol. 240, in the Pythia at Delphi twice, at the Isthmia twice, in the Nemea twice, at the contest for the shield of Hera at Argos, in the Capitolia at Rome twice, in the Eusebea at Puteoli twice, in the Sebasta at Neapolis twice, five times at Athens in various games, five times at Smyrna, three times at the Augustea at Pergamum, three times at Ephesus, at Epidaurus in the Asclepiea, at Rhodes in the Haliea, at Sardis in the Chrysanthina, besides numerous games for money prizes

---

[263] *Ol. Ins.* 150-153.
[264] *Ol. Ins.* 225.
[265] *I.G.* xiv. 1102-1104.
[266] The word ἀσυνέξωστος recalls the feats recorded of Milo and other athletes, whom no one could move from the place where they had taken their stand.
[267] Such I take to be the meaning of the words μήτ' ἐπεξελθὼν μήτε παραιτησάμενος. But the precise meaning of this and the following phrases μήτε κατὰ χάριν βασιλικὴν ἀγῶνα ἔχων μηδὲ καινὸν ἀγῶνα νεικήσας is hard to determine. ἐπεξελθόντα bears this meaning in the Iobacchi Inscription. Roberts and Gardner, *Epigraphy* ii. 91, l. 92. The antithesis of παραιτησάμενος would rather suggest the rendering "seeking a contest," e.g., "pot-hunting."

(Θεματείτας), including the Heraclea in Lacedaemon, the games at Mantinea and others." In this list Olympia and Adriania are mentioned at Athens, Smyrna, and Ephesus. At Ephesus one of his victories was won at the Balbillea founded by the celebrated astrologer Balbillus in the reign of Vespasian. It is interesting to compare this list of victories with the victories won by Diagoras of Rhodes or Epharmostus of Locrian Opus which are enumerated in the odes of Pindar.[268] With the exception of Rhodes, all their recorded victories were won in festivals of the mother-country, at the four Panhellenic festivals, at Argos, Athens, Pellene, Aegina, Megara, and at various places in Arcadia and Boeotia. The difference may be summed up in the word οἰκουμένη which occurs frequently in late inscriptions. The games are no longer Hellenic, they are Oecumenical, and with this change their whole character is altered. Even at Olympia, most Hellenic of all festivals, athletes and spectators alike are gathered no longer from Hellas only but from "the inhabited world."[269]

In the enumeration of his exploits Asclepiades constantly records that "on various occasions" he brought his opponents to a standstill (στήσας), sometimes without further comment, but usually with the words "from the start, after the first lot, after the second lot." The phrase seems to imply that on these occasions his opponents all withdrew from the competition after the first or second heat, or even before any contest. Such incidents may have been misinterpreted by his enemies, who maliciously accused him of bribing or intimidating his rivals. At all events, he tells us that after six years he retired from athletics at the age of twenty-five, owing "to the dangers and jealousy which beset him." After an interval of some years he was induced to reappear at the Olympic games of his native Alexandria, where he won the pankration in the sixth Alexandrine Olympiad.[270]

It was an age of record-breaking. We see it in the expenditure on magnificent buildings and entertainments, in which each new public benefactor aimed at surpassing the work of his predecessors, and it is no wonder that the same spirit affected athletics. The inscription set up by the itinerant synod of the Alexandrines in honour of Flavius Archibius,[271] and recording his long list of victories, is punctuated by the incessant refrain, "first of mankind." For example, in the Pythian festival he won the pankration at one Pythiad, the pankration and wrestling in the next, the pankration again in the next, "first of mankind." Similarly, Marcus Tullius of Apamea in Bithynia describes himself as "the first boxer from all time"[272] to win a certain series of victories. Such phrases are of constant occurrence. A passage in Pliny's *Natural History*[273] suggests that at Rome records were kept in long-distance running, and that running against time was a popular amusement. After describing various feats of strength, he notes how records in distance-running had been frequently broken. The record of Pheidippides, he says, long held the field until Philonides, and Anystis in Alexander's time ran from Sicyon to Elis and back, a distance of 1300 stades, in a single day. "In the circus," he adds, "we know that some athletes have run 160 miles in a day; and recently in the Consulship of Fonteius and Vipsanius, a youth of eight (surely a mistake for eighteen) ran 75 miles between mid-day and sunset." The accuracy of Pliny's statements on athletics is not beyond question, but the passage is good evidence as to the practice of the times.

---

[268] Pindar, *Ol.* vii., ix.
[269] *Ol. Ins.* 54, 436. Both inscriptions belong to the close of the first century A.D. In two earlier inscriptions of the time of Augustus (53, 366) the distinction between οἱ Ἕλληνες and ἡ οἰκουμένη is still maintained.
[270] The Alexandrine Olympia were probably founded in A.D. 176 by Marcus Aurelius, *I.G.* xiv. 1102.
[271] *I.G.* xiv. 746.
[272] πρῶτος τῶν ἀπ' αἰῶνος πυκτῶν, *I.G.* iii. 128. Cp. πρωτοῦ ἐπὶ τῆς οἰκουμένης, *C.I.G.* 2723.
[273] *N.H.* vii. 20; cp. ii. 73.

The second century was an age of antiquarianism. Conscious of their own inferiority, men thought to make up for their want of originality by studying and reproducing the forms of the past, regardless of the fact that these forms had lost their meaning. The writings of this period abound in allusions to the great athletes of earlier times. Lucian of Samosata sets forth at length the old athletic ideal in his dialogue entitled "Anacharsis," in which he makes Solon defend Greek athletics against the criticism of the barbarian. The gist of his argument is that athletics make a man a better and more useful citizen, and fit him to serve his city in peace and war. But alas! the cosmopolitan Greek of his day had no longer any city to defend, and the appeal to civic patriotism can have carried little weight with men who claimed the citizenship of half-a-dozen cities at the same time. Philostratus, an equally enthusiastic admirer of the old athletes, seeks to find a cure for the athletic degeneracy of his own time by a return to the simpler and more rational methods of training of the past. But his appeal likewise fell on deaf ears. Athletics had become the monopoly of professional trainers and quacks, who regarded them merely as a source of selfish profit.

Olympia, above all, appealed to the antiquarian spirit of the age. It is chiefly to the traveller and antiquarian Pausanias, who visited Elis in 173 A.D., that we owe our knowledge of the festival. The mass of details which he gathered from the official guides of Olympia is sure evidence of the interest which the festival aroused. Phlegon of Tralles, like Aristotle in Macedonian times, revised and edited the Olympic register, making it the chronological basis of his history from 776 B.C. to 137 A.D. One C. Asinius Quadratus carried his zeal for Olympia to such lengths as to place the founding of Rome in the year of the first Olympiad, for which act of flattery he received from the Eleans a monument, "because he had honoured Olympia both in word and deed."[274] Others, not content with a chronology that dated back only to Coroebus, invented a new Olympic era 800 years earlier. On an inscribed diskos dedicated by Publius Asclepiades, a pentathlete of Corinth, the date is given according to the two chronologies, Ol. 255 and Ol. 456! and also by the name of the Alytarch for the year, "Flavius Scribonianus, kinsman of senators and consulars." Archaism took a more practical shape in the minute observance of ceremonies and customs. In the inscription of Claudius Rufus, mentioned in a previous chapter, he is commended especially for having diligently practised in the sight of the Hellanodicae, "in accordance with the ancestral custom of the games." Our knowledge of the usages of the festival is chiefly derived from authors of this period. We have already seen how these usages were reproduced in the new festivals.

No state preserved so large a measure of independence under Roman rule as Sparta. In A.D. 214, when Caracalla appeared in Greece as a second Alexander to lead a new war against the East, he appealed to Sparta for assistance; and Sparta, as a free federate state, sent two regiments of volunteers bearing the time-honoured names of the Laconian regiment, and the regiment of Pitane, as her contribution to what an inscription styles "the most fortunate alliance against the Persians." The excavations conducted by the British School of Athens have shed a flood of light upon the history and condition of Sparta at this period.[275] We see her as a flourishing provincial town with her Roman fortifications, theatre, baths, and suburban villas. But though changed in outward appearance, Sparta clung only the more tenaciously to the traditions and customs which she derived from Lycurgus. The love of archaism characteristic of this period showed itself in an exaggerated revival of the

---

[274] *Ol. Ins.* 356.
[275] The matter of this section is taken from the reports of the *B.S.A.*, vols. xii., xiii.

Lycurgean discipline. Sparta, for centuries, had taken little part in the athletic history of Greece. The one object of her physical education was to produce endurance, and the supreme test of this endurance was the so-called "Contest of Endurance" by means of successive scourgings which took place upon the altar of Artemis. The altar itself has been discovered standing on the site of earlier altars, where from time immemorial this ancient ceremony had taken place. The interest attaching to the contest in Roman times is shown by the numerous references in contemporary writers; and still more by the fact that towards the close of the second century A.D., a large theatre, surrounding the altar, was built for the convenience of spectators. An inscription discovered in the Artemisium records the victory of a boy in this contest. Greek writers represent the contest as a humane substitute for human sacrifice; but Professor Bosanquet[276] has shown that there is good reason for thinking that Greek tradition mistook the meaning of the ceremony, which originated in an ancient ritual practice of whipping away boys who tried to steal cheeses from the altar; and that the "Contest of Endurance" was a brutal exaggeration of the old practice, due to the late and artificial revival of the Lycurgean discipline. It certainly justifies, in part, the contemptuous tone in which Philostratus speaks of Spartan athletics.

If Sparta took little part in the great competitions, she had her own games and her own competitions. One of these, the Leonidaea, was celebrated in honour of those who fell at Thermopylae. Two inscriptions have been discovered containing regulations for this festival which it appears must have been reorganized about the time of Nerva.[277] It was a yearly festival, and only Spartans were allowed to compete. This is perhaps the reason why the programme contained the pankration, an event for which no Spartan might enter at other festivals. The most interesting inscriptions are those referring to certain games in which teams of Spartan boys competed. The late Mr. Kenneth Freeman, in his book, *The Schools of Hellas*, maintained that the prototype of the English public school system was to be found in the Spartan system of education. Certainly the Spartan games resemble our English games more closely than any other games of which we know in the ancient world. The game of Platanistas was played on an island surrounded by a ditch, between two teams of boys who, entering the ground by bridges at either end, strove by fighting, hitting, kicking, and biting, to drive their opponents into the water. But for the absence of the ball, this game bears considerable resemblance to the primitive football scrimmage before any of the existing rules were introduced, and, as we shall see, ball games were of considerable importance at Sparta. The game of Platanistas, like the scourging, may have had its origin in some ritual practice denoted by the sacrifice of a boar, but in the time of Pausanias it was certainly played in the form described.

A series of inscriptions, all with one exception dating from the time of the Antonines, commemorate victories won by teams of ball-players at some yearly competition.[278] The name σφαιρεῖς was given to Spartan youths in their first year of manhood. The competitions took place in the Dromos under the direction of the Bideoi, a board of five officials responsible for the management of the Platanistas and other ephebic games. The teams represented the local districts of Sparta called the Obes, and it seems probable that the expenses connected with the team were provided by a local obe official, the διαβετής, who is

---

[276] *B.S.A.* xii. 314.
[277] *B.S.A.* xii. 445 ff. Another Spartan festival mentioned in inscriptions is the Euryclea founded by Eurycles, a rich and powerful friend of Herod the Great, *C.I.G.* 1378, 1389.
[278] *B.S.A.* x. 63, xii. 212.

mentioned in the inscriptions. Each team was under a captain called the πρέσβυς, but the number of members in a team cannot be decided owing to the mutilation of the inscriptions. It seems not to have been less than fifteen. The competition was arranged on the tournament system, for several inscriptions record the fact that the winning team had not drawn a bye. Unfortunately, we have no clue to the manner of playing the game.

A yet more numerous group of inscriptions found in the Artemisium, and belonging mostly to the same period, consists of dedications to Artemis in honour of victories won by teams of young boys in certain musical and athletic competitions.[279] The competitors seem to be mostly about the age of ten, the age denoted by the term μικιζόμενοι, and each team was under a captain, βοαγός, chosen perhaps for family reasons, who held the title for life. There seem, however, to have been similar competitions for older boys, for one of the inscriptions commemorates a βοαγός whose team was successful in a boys' competition and also in a competition for youths of twenty (εἴρενες). Two musical contests are mentioned, called, respectively, Μῶα and Κελῆα, the precise nature of which cannot be determined. The third competition bears the name Καθθηρατόριν, which seems to describe some rough game resembling the hunting of wild beasts, perhaps some such game as prisoner's base. The victor was crowned with bay and received as a prize a sickle which was affixed to the inscribed tablet and dedicated to Artemis. The presence of musical competitions suggests that the narrowness of Spartan education has been perhaps exaggerated by Greek historians. Much of our knowledge of Sparta is derived from the accounts of her enemies.

In spite of all these outward signs of athletic life, the writers of this period leave us in no doubt as to the real character of the athletic revival. We are no longer forced to draw what inferences we can from the doubtful evidence of casual allusions; we possess in the works of Plutarch, Galen, and Philostratus definite treatises on physical culture and gymnastic. Different as is the point of view of these authors, they agree in condemning the athletics of their day, and prove beyond possibility of doubt how far from realization was the old ideal set forth by Lucian and Dion of Prusa. That old ideal, in which the culture of body and of mind went hand in hand, was inseparable from the ideal of free citizenship that existed when every citizen was both soldier and politician, and when to develop mind and body to the full extent of which each was capable was a duty that the citizen owed to the state. All this had long been changed; war was now the business of paid professional soldiers, politics of the imperial government. The individual, thrown back on self, had no other interest but personal profit and enjoyment. Speculative and mystical philosophy and religion taught men to despise the body, and as a consequence the training of the body no longer maintained its importance in education. Gymnastic, deprived of its proper province in education, found itself confined to the training of professional athletes, who developed the body but neglected the mind. But as life became more sedentary and less active the claims of the body reasserted themselves: hunting was impossible except for the few, games were of little importance in most places, hence there arose a need for artificial exercise, and the need was supplied by the medical gymnastic which aimed at producing health. The Romans, though they despised athletics, realized the importance of exercise for maintaining health. The bath and massage were essential parts of this gymnastic, and the exercises prescribed included walking, gentle running, jumping up and down, the use of halteres as dumb-bells, throwing the diskos and the javelin. Health-culture has its use for men who lead a sedentary, artificial life, but it is not

---

[279] B.S.A. xii. 352, xiii. 182.

athletics; neither is physical training or gymnastics, to use the word in its restricted modern sense—invaluable as such training is in education of the young, especially in thickly populated cities. But health-culture and gymnastics lack the moral value which friendly rivalry gave once to Greek athletics and gives to-day to the games of our public schools. Professional athletics equally lack this moral value; for when livelihood depends on success, rivalry ceases to be friendly, and the door is opened for corruption. Both health-culture and professionalism are poles removed from the true Greek ideal of athletics.

Plutarch's opinion about the athletics of his day is evident from many passages in his Lives, to which reference has already been made. His tract on the Preservation of Health, intended as it is chiefly for the ordinary, middle-aged, business man, hardly concerns us here except so far as it continually condemns by implication the artificial and unhealthy training to which athletes were subjected. Galen and Philostratus are so little known to the ordinary reader, and their works are so important, that some account of them is indispensable.

Born at Pergamum in A.D. 130, Galen studied philosophy and medicine at Alexandria, Smyrna, and Corinth. At Alexandria he was appointed physician to the school of gladiators. At the age of thirty-four he came to Rome, where he became the friend and physician of the Emperor Marcus Aurelius, but after a few years he returned to his native land. His wide experience of men and countries, his knowledge of medicine and anatomy, his breadth of mind and fearless love of truth make his judgment of special value. He wrote numerous works on Health, but the two which are of most importance to us here are his essay on "Exercise with the Small Ball," a masterly statement of the true principles of exercise, and his "Exhortation to the Arts," an attack on professional athletics.

The best of all exercises, he says in his treatise on Ball-play, are those which combine bodily exertion with mental recreation, such as hunting and ball-play. But ball-play has this advantage over hunting that its cheapness puts it within reach of the very poorest, while even the busiest man can find time for it. Moreover, it can be practised with any degree of violence or moderation, at all times and in all conditions. It exercises every part of the body, legs, hands, and eyesight alike, and at the same time gives pleasure to the mind. In contrast with athletic exercises, which make men slow or produce one-sided development, ball-play produces strength and activity, and therefore trains all those qualities which are most valuable for a soldier. Finally, it is free from dangers, and does not expose the player to all those accidents which too often leave the wrestler, "like the Homeric Litai, either halt, or distorted, or altogether bereft of some limb." The practice of games of ball is of particular interest in view of the importance which they possessed at Sparta. These games must have varied in character almost as much as those with which we are familiar to-day, and no better defence of such games has ever been written, though we may doubt whether Galen would have approved of the extent to which they are carried in the present day.

The ostensible object of the "Exhortation" is to urge men to devote themselves to some art or profession which will last them all their life; but the real subject of the discourse is whether athletics deserves the title of an art or profession. τέχνη is defined as having for its aim "the improvement of life," and therefore there can be no art in tumbling or walking the tight-rope. Does the athlete's life benefit the athlete himself or the state? To this question Galen replies emphatically, "No." "The mind is higher than the body, for the mind we share with the gods, the body with the animals. In the blessings of the mind athletes have no share. Beneath their mass of flesh and blood their souls are stifled as in a sea of mud. Nor do they enjoy the best blessings even of the body. Neglecting the old rule of health, which prescribes moderation in all things, they spend their lives in over-exercising, over-eating, over-sleeping, like pigs. Hence they seldom live to old age, and if they do, they are crippled and liable to all sorts of disease. They have not health nor have they beauty. Even those that are naturally well-proportioned become fat and bloated; their faces are often shapeless and unsightly, owing to the wounds received in boxing or the pankration. They lose their eyes and their teeth, and their limbs are strained. Even their vaunted strength is useless. They can dig and plough, but they cannot fight. They cannot endure heat and cold, nor, like Heracles, wear one garment summer and winter, go unshod and sleep on the open ground: in all this they are weaker than new-born babes." Such is the picture which Galen draws of the professional athletes of his day, most of whom, as we have seen, were boxers and wrestlers; and we can judge of the truth of the picture from the mosaics in the baths of Caracalla, where we see represented, in all their brutality and coarseness, the portraits of those professional prizefighters and athletes whom the degraded and unathletic mob and court of Rome delighted to honour (Figure 23).[280] There they stand with their clumsy, ill-proportioned bodies, their scarred and mutilated faces, their small and brainless heads rendered yet more hideous by the top-knot (cirrus) in which their scanty hair is tied. It is the last stage in the decline of athletics, which had begun centuries earlier in the exaggerated honours paid to mere bodily strength, to that lower nature which man shares with the animals, and in which man must remain the inferior of the animals. Galen ends his argument by pressing home this lesson in a parable, in which he imagines an Olympia to which the heralds have summoned all the animals to compete. There man would not win a single event. The horse would win the long race, the hare the short race, the deer the diaulos. None of the successors of Heracles could compete with the lion or the elephant. And I expect, says he, that the bull will win the crown for boxing, and the donkey in a kicking match will carry off the crown. Yes, and in an elaborate history, donkey will record that "once he defeated man in the pankration, and that it was the twenty-and-first Olympiad when Brayer was victorious."

The athletes of the second century must at least be credited with a certain amount of brute strength, but in the generation which succeeded Galen even their strength fell off, if we may believe the statement of Philostratus, who wrote in the first half of the third century. His work on the art of gymnastic reads like an answer to Galen's attack on athletics, and is marked by a strong bias against the medical profession, whom he holds responsible for enervating athletics by the introduction of ridiculous and effeminate rules of diet.[281] By gymnastic, he understands the art of training athletes, which in opposition to Galen he describes as an art inferior to no other and akin to the arts of the doctor and paidotribes. The latter is concerned merely with actual exercises and movements, while the trainer requires a knowledge of the human body which may enable him to prescribe in each case the diet and training necessary to correct any defect. Thus the gymnastes cures by exercise and massage diseases for which the doctor employs potions, plasters, and fomentations. The decline in the athlete's physique Philostratus ascribes to a vicious system of training due in the first instance to the quackery of doctors. The valetudinarianism of the second century had produced, as it always does, a host of impostors with quack systems and rules for health, some of which were imported into

---

[280] The whole mosaic is published by Secchi in his *Musaico Antoniniano*, and a large portion of it in Baumeister's Denkmäler, Figure 174.

[281] Dr. Jüthner, in the introduction to his *Philostratus*, shows that there was a long-standing quarrel between doctors and trainers. The doctors resented the encroachments of the trainers on their domain, and regarded them as ignorant and unscientific quacks.

athletics. Medicine, says Philostratus, has pampered athletics, and rendered athletes dainty and luxurious. They are told to remain seated, stuffed with food, for a long time before taking exercise. Their diet consists of seasoned breads, of fish, and pork. Different kinds of fish are credited with different qualities; their pork must come from pigs fed only on cornel nuts and acorns and not reared in the neighbourhood of the sea or of rivers. We all know this sort of fad; our own age has produced by the score systems no less absurd. The inventors of such systems always insist that their patients must follow their rules without deviating from them a hairbreadth. So the Greek trainers developed hard-and-fast systems of training which they applied indifferently to all alike, to boys as well as men, without any regard to the individual's needs. Boys trained on the same principles as men lost all the buoyancy and activity natural to their age and became lazy, heavy, and sluggish. The most absurd of these systems was that known as the Tetrad, a scheme of work for four days, by which the athlete's life was regulated. Each day had its own work. The first day's work, consisting of light and quick movements, "prepared" the athlete; the second "extended" him and tested all his powers of endurance; the third "relaxed" him by means of gentle movements; the fourth, consisting apparently of movements of defence, left him in a middle state.

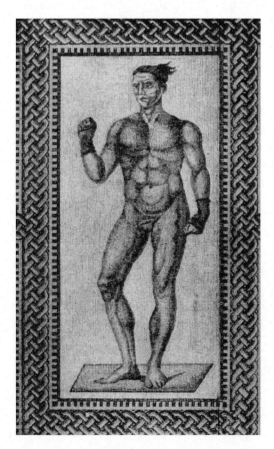

Figure 23. Professional boxer, from mosaic in Thermae of Caracalla. Lateran.

Such is the somewhat obscure account given of the tetrad.[282] It was intended clearly for pankratiasts and boxers who practically formed the whole class of professional athletes. The principle of the gradual increase and diminution of work on which it is founded is absolutely sound, and is one of the essential principles of the "Ling" system of physical training. The fault lay in the ignorant and pedantic application of the principle. No deviation from its routine was permitted, and no account was taken of the individual's actual condition. Philostratus tells a story of a contemporary athlete, Gerenius, who three days after winning an Olympic victory celebrated his success by a banquet at which he ate and drank things to which he was not accustomed. The next day, suffering from indigestion and want of sleep, he repaired to the gymnasium as usual, and being put through a more than usually severe course of exercise by his irritated trainer, actually died under the treatment. The tetrads, says Philostratus, have ruined all athletic training; and the purpose of his book is to show the absurdity of such artificial systems, and by introducing sounder principles of athletics to restore the glory of the stadium. The main principle which he inculcates is the necessity of a thorough knowledge of the human body, and of suiting the training to the individual's requirements. He discusses at length the various physical qualities which are best for different sports,—the qualities of the boxer, the wrestler, or the runner,—and gives a fanciful classification of the different types of athletes, the lion type, the eagle type, the bear type, the plank type, the rope type! He has a profound reverence for the traditions of Olympia, and regards the Eleans as the sole repositories of athletic lore, accepting all that they tell him with childlike simplicity. With much common sense he mingles an amount of rhetoric and fancifulness such as we should expect from the credulous biographer of Apollonius of Tyana, which seriously diminishes the practical value of his work.[283]

With Philostratus our history draws to a close. The Olympic records of Africanus end with Ol. 249 (A.D. 217); the last victor recorded on Olympic Inscriptions is the herald Valerius Eclectus of Sinope, who won the heralds' competition in Ol. 256 and the three succeeding Olympiads; the lists of Olympic officials cease almost at the same time. The Roman empire was now engaged in a desperate struggle with hordes of invading Goths, and in the struggle the Greeks were once more called upon to fight for their country. The Goths were repulsed, but the silence which ensues tells but too clearly of the effects of their ravages. The end was close at hand. Hitherto the Greeks had preserved some semblance of political liberty; but the policy of centralization and unification introduced by Constantine stamped out the last vestiges of the city state. The ancient festivals of Greece were the stronghold of paganism, and therefore recognized as the greatest obstacle of Christianity, now adopted as the Imperial religion. Delphi was dismantled by Constantine, and its treasures removed to adorn his new-built Hippodrome at Constantinople, and in the time of Julian its site was desolate. The Olympic festival was abolished by the emperor Theodosius, though whether by Theodosius I. or Theodosius II is not certain. The generally received tradition is that it was abolished in 393 by Theodosius I. The emperor had set himself to sweep away all vestiges of paganism, but in 390 he had incurred the displeasure of the all-powerful St. Ambrose by his cruel massacre of the Thessalonians, and had been forced to do public penance for his sin.

---

[282] Vide Jüthner, op. cit. pp. 285 ff.
[283] I am glad to find my estimate of Philostratus in substantial agreement with that of Dr. Jüthner. Philostratus had, as he shows, no technical knowledge of gymnastic. He was a rhetorician, writing an essay on what was evidently a burning question, and, like a modern journalist, he naturally derived his knowledge from one of the many technical treatises on gymnastic which existed, and as naturally made mistakes (op. cit. pp. 97-107).

Was the edict that abolished the Olympia a token of his new-born zeal for righteousness? Be this as it may, the last Olympic victor whose name we know was the Armenian prince Varazdates, who won the boxing-match in Ol. 291 (A.D. 385). Varazdates traced his descent from the Arsacidae, and was subsequently placed by Theodosius on the throne of Armenia. There is a pathetic irony in the circumstance that, at the festival linked beyond all others with the cause of Hellenism at war with barbarism, the last-recorded victor came not from Hellas but from the land of her hereditary foes.

Chapter 9

THE OLYMPIC FESTIVAL

Figure 24. Staters of Elis, in British Museum (enlarged). Fifth century. (*a*) Head of nymph Olympia. (*b*) Victory seated, with palm; olive twig below.

Many of the details and regulations connected with the Olympic festival have been already mentioned in previous chapters, where the reader can readily find them by consulting the index. In the present chapter we shall attempt to give some account of the festival itself, as it existed in the fifth century. First we must premise that the details of the festival are involved in the greatest obscurity, largely owing to the fact that the bulk of our information is derived from late writers whose evidence as to what took place five or six hundred years before their time must always be received with a certain amount of reserve. Still, religious conservatism was nowhere stronger than at Olympia, and much that is recorded of the second century of our era existed with little difference in the fifth century B.C. Therefore, though many details remain obscure we can feel fairly certain as to the general outline of the festival.

The festival took place at the second or third full moon after the summer solstice, in the months of Apollonios and Parthenios respectively.[284] Its date was fixed by a cycle of eight years or ninety-nine-months, the divergence between the year of twelve lunar months and the solar year being rectified by the insertion of three intercalary months, one in the first four years, two in the second. Thus it fell alternately after forty-nine or fifty lunar months. The fourteenth day of the month seems to have been reckoned as the day of the full moon, though the actual full moon varied from the 14th to 15th. This day must, from the earliest time, have

---

[284] L. Weniger, *Clio*, 1905, pp. 1-38.

been the central day of the festival.[285] The Greek day was reckoned from sunset to sunset, and as Greek custom demanded that sacrifice to the Olympian gods should be offered in the morning, before mid-day,[286] it follows that the great sacrifice to Zeus was offered on the morning after the full moon. The festival lasted five days. According to Herodotus, a historian of the fifth century, the five days' festival was ordained by Heracles.[287] Certainly it lasted five days in Pindar's time.[288] Scholiasts of various dates, while affirming that it lasted five days, state that it began on the 10th or 11th and lasted till the 15th or 16th.[289] The discrepancy may be due to the variation in the date of the full moon already noticed, more probably to the addition to the festival of one or more preliminary days necessitated in later times by the multiplication of competitions and religious ceremonies. To these days the preliminary business of the festival may have been transferred, but they were not reckoned as part of the actual festival. The seventh ode of Bacchylides, written in honour of Laches of Ceos, who won the boys' foot-race in 452 B.C., proves beyond doubt that in this year the festival ended on the sixteenth day. If then the festival lasted five days, the fourteenth, the day of the full moon, was the central day of the whole festival. The recognition of the importance of this fact is due to Ludwig Weniger, whose conclusions I have in the main adopted in the following pages.

These five days included sacrifices, sports, and feasts. Sacrifices and feasts, both private and public, formed part of each day's programme, especially of the first and last days, which must have been largely, if not entirely, occupied by such ceremonies. How many days were devoted to the actual sports we do not know. A scholiast states that they took place on five days,[290] but the statement is unsupported and certainly was not true of earlier times. The growth of the programme must have necessitated readjustment from time to time, and an extension of the time allotted to competitions. Such an extension took place, according to Pausanias, in Ol. 77, though it did not, of course, take effect till Ol. 78. "The order of the competition," he says,[291] "existing in our time—which is that the sacrifice to the god is offered after the pentathlon and the horse-race—this order was introduced in the 77th Olympiad. Previous to this date, events both for men and horses took place on the same day. But on this occasion the competitors in the pankration were kept on into the night, not having been called in time, and the delay was caused by the horse-races and still more by the pentathlon." This passage gives no countenance to the statement commonly made that at this time the length of the festival, or the number of days allotted to sport was suddenly extended from one day to five. Nor does it prove that before this date *all* events for men took place on the same day as events for horses, and that after this date *none* did. If the literal meaning of the words is pressed, it may be argued, and indeed has been argued, that from this date a separate day was assigned to the horse-races, and a separate day to the pentathlon.

---

[285] L. Weniger, *Clio*, 1904, pp. 126 ff.
[286] *Ib.* p. 127, n. 1.
[287] Quoted in Schol. Pindar, *Ol.* v. 6.
[288] Pindar, *Ol.* v. 6 ὑπὸ βουθυσίαις ἀέθλων τε πεμπταμέροις ἁμίλλαις. The reading and interpretation are much disputed. The scholiasts certainly interpreted πεμπταμέροις "as lasting five days," and even if the reading πεμπταμέροις is correct, the occurrence of the form πεμπτάς for πεμπάσ, and the analogy of forms like ὀγδώκοντα, ἑβδομήκοντα make this meaning at least possible, while there is considerable evidence against the rendering "fifth-day contests." Mie, *Quaestiones Agonisticae*, p. 29.
[289] Schol. Pindar, *Ol.* v. 8, iii. 33.
[290] Schol. vet. Pindar, *Ol.* v. 8 πεμπταμέροις ἁμίλλαις· ἐπεὶ ἐπὶ πέντα ἡμέρασ ᾔγετο αὐτὰ τὰ ἀγωνίσματα.
[291] v. 9, 3.

Unfortunately, we have a definite statement by Xenophon[292] proving that in Ol. 104 the horse-races preceded the pentathlon on the same day. Those who assert that they took place on different days are forced[293] to reject the evidence of a contemporary writer, who lived for years in the neighbourhood of Olympia, in favour of a doubtful interpretation of an obscure and ill-expressed passage written by a traveller who owed his information to a visit paid to Olympia some five hundred years later. The alternative is to assume that after Xenophon's time a separate day was assigned to the horse-races, presumably at the time when the programme of these events was raised to its full complement of six. But this is a mere supposition. All that we can definitely assert is that, after Ol. 77, the pentathlon and horse-races were transferred to the *day before the sacrifice to the god.*

What is "the sacrifice to the god"? and when did it take place? On the answer to these questions depends the interpretation of the passage of Pausanias, and the reconstruction of the order of the festival. There can be little doubt that the sacrifice was the official offering of a hecatomb to Olympian Zeus by the Eleans.[294] It is generally assumed that this took place on the 16th, the last day of the festival, and it is certainly natural to connect it with the official banquet in the Prytaneum which took place on the evening of that day. This arrangement naturally appeals to a modern sentiment which demands a climax. But the Greeks had not this sentiment, and there is a mass of evidence to prove that the usual order of a Greek festival was—sacrifice, sports, feast.[295] That this was the ancient order at Olympia is clear from two odes in which Pindar describes the inauguration of the games by Heracles. In the eleventh *Olympian* we read how Heracles, returning victorious from Cleonae, marked out the Altis, and paid honour to the river Alpheus and the great gods. Then, having first offered sacrifice of his spoil, he ordained the games, and in the evening the precinct resounded, as in Pindar's time, "with songs of festal glee." So, too, in the third ode, first he sanctifies the altars, then he ordains the games. The scholiast, commenting on this ode, explains carefully that the full moon came first, then followed the sacrifice, and "the rest of the competitions." If the games followed the sacrifice, the sacrifice cannot have taken place on the 16th, but rather on the 14th, the morning after the full moon. In speaking of "the rest of the competitions" he is thinking, of course, of the order of the festival in his own time, and this phrase is a strong argument in favour of the views of Weniger.

The meaning of Pausanias is now clear, and there is no need with modern editors to assume that the passage is hopelessly corrupt. Previous to Ol. 78 all the sports followed the sacrifice, mostly on the 15th; but I see no reason why some should not have taken place on the afternoon of the 14th, or even on the 16th. The preceding days were occupied with preliminary business and various religious ceremonies. In Ol. 78 the horse-races and the pentathlon were transferred to the 13th, the day before the sacrifice. Some of the preliminary business may at the same time have been shifted to the 11th day. If at a subsequent date separate days were allotted to the horse-races and pentathlon, or if, as Weniger suggests, the boys' events were after the introduction of the boys' pankration shifted to the 12th, the 10th

---

[292] *Hellen.* vii. 4.
[293] Carl Robert in *Hermes* xxxv.; C. Gaspar in Dar.-Sagl. *s.v.* "Olympia." It had been my intention to discuss Robert's theory in the *J.H.S.*, but I find that nearly all my objections to it have been anticipated by Frederic Mie in *Philologus*, lx. Mie's own theory has in its turn been superseded by Weniger's, which alone offers a satisfactory explanation both of Xenophon and of Pausanias.
[294] Robert's theory of the two sacrifices of thanksgiving offered after the pentathlon and horse-races on the 3rd and 5th days of the festival is pure fiction, and has been conclusively disproved by Mie, *l.c.*
[295] *Clio*, 1904, p. 127; Krause, *Olympia*, p. 84.

day may also have been required for the preliminaries; but there is not sufficient evidence for either of these changes.

The same uncertainty prevails as to the order of the events, and still more as to their distribution into days. The attempts which have been made to prove that the order was the same as that preserved in two fragments of the Olympic register must, in my opinion, be regarded as failures. The order for the fifth century as given in the Oxyrhynchus papyrus is as follows:—(1) Stade-race, (2) Diaulos, (3) Dolichos, (4) Pentathlon, (5) Wrestling, (6) Boxing, (7) Pankration, (8) Boys' foot-race, (9) Boys' wrestling, (10) Boys' boxing, (11) Race in armour, (12) Chariot-race, (13) Horse-race. The list omits the mule chariot-race (ἀπήνη) and the race for mares, which were discontinued after 444 B.C. Phlegon's list for Ol. 177 (72 B.C.) agrees with this except that the boys' pankration is added after the other events for boys, and the four new equestrian events after the horse-race in their order of introduction.

The principle adopted in this list is obvious. The competition is divided into athletic and equestrian. The athletic part is divided into events for men and events for boys. Each division is arranged in the order, real or fictitious, in which the various events were introduced. The only exception is the race in armour, which is placed after the boys' events, owing to its late introduction, its peculiar character, and the fact that it was the last event on the programme. The arrangement is perfectly simple and logical, but it does not follow that it was the order adopted in the sports. We have seen that in 468 B.C. (Ol. 78) a change was made in the order, and we know that the Hellanodicae had power to alter the order under special circumstances. In Ol. 142, at the request of Cleitomachus, who was competing both in boxing and in the pankration, they placed the pankration before the boxing.[296]

From the general uncertainty a few facts emerge:—

1) Plutarch definitely states that at Olympia the boys' competitions took place before any of the men's,[297] and there is no reason for disbelieving his statement. In framing a register it may be natural to place the most important events first; in arranging a programme it would be a ludicrous anti-climax to do so.
2) The foot-races all came on the same day, and probably before any other of the competitions for men. Their order is doubtful. Pausanias in his account of Polites[298] implies that he won the dolichos first, then the stade-race, lastly the diaulos. But practical considerations make this unlikely. Unless a considerable time elapsed between the events it is hard to imagine a three-miler proceeding at once to win a 200 yards and a quarter! Learned writers who have discussed the question all seem to have forgotten that in the stade race and perhaps in the diaulos there was a round of preliminary heats, which may well have complicated the order.[299]
3) Wrestling, boxing, and the pankration took place on the same day and in the same order.[300]
4) The race in armour was the last event of the whole programme.[301] It seems possible from the words of Philostratus that it came on the very last day of the festival.

---

[296] Paus. vi. 15, 5.
[297] *Quaest. Symp.* ii. 5.
[298] Paus. vi. 13, 3. The same order is twice adopted by Philostratus in *Gym.* ch. 4 and 32.
[299] If the final of the stade-race followed the dolichos, the heats would naturally precede it, so as to allow competitors a rest between the heats and the final.
[300] Paus. vi. 6, 5; vi. 15, 4.

5) The pentathlon followed the horse-races, and in Xenophon's time took place on the same day, the day preceding the sacrifice. Previous to Ol. 78 these events may have followed the foot-races.
6) When the competitions for heralds and trumpeters were introduced in Ol. 96, they naturally came off on the first day, seeing that the winners had the privilege of officiating at the festival.

The horse-races and the men's foot-races took place in the morning; the pentathlon, and the heavy events, boxing, wrestling, and pankration, after mid-day.[302] The pentathlon and horse-races, as we know, were in Xenophon's time on the same day, i.e., the 13th. The foot-races and heavy events for men also presumably occupied one whole day, the 15th.[303] There was certainly no time on this day for the boys' events, which were not sufficiently numerous to occupy a whole day. We may conjecture that they took place on the afternoon of the 14th. We arrive therefore at the following probable arrangement for the period beginning 468 B.C.:—

Chariot and horse-races	2nd day of festival (the 13th).
Pentathlon	
Boys' events	afternoon of the 3rd day (the 14th).
Foot-races for men	
Wrestling, boxing, pankration	4th day of festival (the 15th).
Race in armour	

It is uncertain when and where the victors were crowned.[304] The only definite pronouncement on the point is that of a late scholiast, who states that the prizes were distributed on the sixteenth day.[305] In support of this statement is quoted the commencement of the seventh ode of Bacchylides, unfortunately much mutilated, which appears to connect the sixteenth day "with judgment for speed of foot and strength of limb." But it may be noted that the verb ἐγκρίνω here used, like the ἀγνὰ κρίσις of which Pindar speaks, does not necessarily imply the prize-giving, but would be equally applicable to the actual competitions, or to the rejoicings and feast in which all the victors took part on the sixteenth day. At the same time, this passage of Bacchylides may well have given rise to the scholiast's note on Pindar. On the other hand, there are certain allusions which seem to indicate that the victors were crowned by the Hellanodicas immediately after each event. This is certainly the natural inference from the story told by Pausanias of Apollonius, who having been disqualified by the Hellanodicae in the boxing for arriving too late, bound on the boxing thongs, and made a violent attack on Heracleides, to whom the Hellanodicae had already awarded the crown, and who had the olive already on his head.[306] Again, Ageus who won the long-distance race in

---

[301] Plut. *Quaest. Symp.* ii. 5, 2; Paus. iii. 14, 3; Phil. *Gym.* 7; Artemidorus, *Oneirocrit.* i. 65.
[302] Paus. vi. 24, 1.
[303] Lucian, *Timon*, 50.
[304] Robert and Mie hold that the crowns were presented after each event, Weniger that they were all presented on the 16th.
[305] Schol. Pindar, *Ol.* v. 8 τῆς ἑκκαιδεκάτης ἐν ᾗ τὰ ἆθλα ἐδίδοτο. This is possibly a paraphrase of an earlier scholion on *Ol.* iii. 35 καὶ τῇ ἑκκαιδεκάτῃ γίνεται ἡ κρίσις.
[306] Paus. v. 21, 14.

328 B.C. ran straight home to Argos and reported the news of his victory the same day.[307] Surely he must have received the crown first. Otherwise he must have returned that same night from Argos to Olympia in order to receive his prize the next day! Lastly, the picture described by Philostratus of the death of Arrhichion, who died in the moment of victory in the pankration, represents the Hellanodicas in the act of crowning him.[308] The stories themselves are fanciful, and their evidence is by no means conclusive, but, agreeing as they do with the undoubted practice of the heroic age,[309] it seems to me probable that the victor received his crown immediately after his victory.

Let us now try to form some idea of the Olympic festival in the middle of the fifth century, the moment of Olympia's greatest glory, when Libon's temple had been completed, when the stadium and hippodrome had been laid out, when Pindar and Bacchylides were still singing the praises of the victors, and Myron and Polycleitus were immortalizing them in bronze. Some details will be inserted for the sake of convenience which may belong to a later date, but in such cases the fact will be noted.

Some weeks before the actual festival the three truce-bearers of Zeus (σπονδοφόροι), wearing crowns of olive and bearing heralds' staves, set forth from Elis to proclaim the sacred truce to all the states of Greece and bid them to the festival. The truce began from the moment that they left Elis, and lasted probably three months. During this time all competitors and visitors on their way to or from the festival enjoyed its protection, and none might bear arms within the sacred territory.[310]

Competitors were obliged to give in their names by a fixed date. If they failed to do so, they rendered themselves liable to a fine or even to disqualification.[311]

In later times—we do not know when the custom was introduced—they underwent thirty days' training at Elis under the supervision of the Hellanodicae, who had themselves undergone ten months training for their duties. During this period, and during the festival itself, it seems probable that they were lodged and boarded by the authorities of the festival. The training at Elis was noted for its severity: the Hellanodicae exacted absolute obedience to their orders, and punished all infraction with the rod.[312] They tested the capabilities of the athletes, rejecting those who were not fit; they satisfied themselves as to their parentage and claim to compete; above all, they had opportunity for judging the claims of boys and colts to compete as such.[313] Philostratus tells us that at the close of the training they called together the competitors and addressed them[314] in words which well illustrate the high standard which Olympia maintained even under the Empire:—

---

[307] Africanus, 6, 67, R.

[308] *Imag.* ii. 6. This passage is particularly important, as the picture represents the very moment after the contest is over.

[309] In Homer the prizes are set at the finish of the race, or beside the ring, and are awarded immediately afterwards. They are represented similarly on black-figured vases. The same idea is suggested by the well-known epigram on Myron's statue of Ladas, *Anth. Pal.* xvi. 54 πηδήσει τάχα χαλκὸς ἐπὶ στέφος.

[310] Weniger, *Clio*, 1905, pp. 184-218.

[311] Paus. v. 21. 13, 14. Cp. *Ol. Ins.* 56, l. 20-30, regulations for the Augustalia at Naples, which were modelled on those of Olympia. Athletes were required to give in their names to the Agonothetai thirty days beforehand; if they failed to give full information, they incurred a fine; if a competitor arrived late, he had to report the cause to the Agonothetai, and any one might lodge a protest against him; if found guilty, he was disqualified from competing.

[312] Philostr. *Gym.* 11, 18, 54.

[313] *Ib.* 25; Paus. vi. 23, 24.

[314] *Vit. Apoll. Tyan.* v. 43.

"If you have exercised yourself in a manner worthy of the Olympic festival, if you have been guilty of no slothful or ignoble act, go on with a good courage. You who have not so practised, go whither you will."

The whole company quitted Elis a few days before the festival. First came the Hellanodicae and other officials, then the athletes and their trainers, the horses and chariots, their owners, jockeys, and drivers. They went by the sacred way, which, skirting the mountains, followed the coast-line till it entered the valley of the Alpheus. The journey lasted two days. At the fountain of Piera, which marked the boundary between Elis and Olympia, a halt was made, a pig was sacrificed and other rites of purification were performed.[315] The night was passed at Letrini, and the next day the whole procession wound up the valley to Olympia.[316]

Meanwhile, visitors of all classes were flocking to Olympia from every part of the Greek world. Some came to see, some to be seen; some for pleasure, some for profit. Tyrants and statesmen, poets and philosophers, peasants and fishermen, all met at Olympia. The whole Greek world was represented from Marseilles to the Black Sea, from Thrace to Africa. The country folk came on foot along the valleys of the Peloponnese, the richer classes in chariots or on horseback. The river Alpheus was still navigable, at its mouth was a small port, and tyrants and merchant-princes from the West could sail in rich barges up to Olympia itself. Particularly magnificent were the official embassies from the various states, each of them anxious to outshine the rest. For all this crowd there can have been little accommodation or provision at Olympia. Competitors and members of the embassies may have been lodged at the public expense. The rest had to provide for themselves. Some slept in tents or booths of wood in the plain around the Altis, the majority slept on the ground in the open air—no great hardship in summer at Olympia. There was no town, or even village near, and the needs of the assembly must have been supplied by merchants, hucksters, pedlars, who brought in provisions from the country and set up rough stalls and booths such as may be seen to-day at any local fair.

The first day of the festival, perhaps the day preceding the festival, was devoted to preliminary business and sacrifice. There were no competitions, except perhaps those for trumpeters and heralds, which were not introduced till 396 B.C.; they took place near the entrance to the stadium, the competitors taking their stand upon an altar. It was probably on this day that the ceremony in the Council Chamber described by Pausanias took place.[317] There the competitors, their trainers, and their friends underwent a solemn scrutiny. They took their stand before the statue of Zeus Horkios, who was represented with the thunderbolt in his right hand as a warning to evildoers, and there having sacrificed a pig, they swore on its entrails to use no unfair means to secure victory, and further, that they had trained for ten months in a manner worthy of the festival. The ceremony of the oath is represented on a red-figured kylix in Figure 132. Next came the turn of the judges who decided on the eligibility of boys and colts to compete as such. They swore to give their decisions honestly and without

---

[315] Paus. v. 16, 8.
[316] The statement that they quitted Elis a month before the festival is quite inconsistent with the account given by Pausanias vi. 23, 24, and with the narrative in Lucian's *De Morte Peregrini*, ch. 31, 32. The scene of the earlier chapters is laid in Elis, where the Hellanodicae are training the athletes. From Elis Lucian goes straight on to the festival at Olympia. Perhaps the procession from Elis to Olympia took place on the 10th or 11th of the month.
[317] v. 24, 9.

bribes, and not to reveal the reasons for their decision. Then the final list of entries was drawn up and published perhaps on a white board (λεύκωμα).[318] Throughout the day there must have been various sacrifices both public and private, but little is known of their details. All through the year there was daily sacrifice at the great altar of Zeus. Sacrifice was probably offered on this day at the six double altars which Pindar mentions, and an offering of blood was made on the mound of Pelops.[319] Competitors and their friends would offer sacrifices and vows at the altars of the gods or heroes whom they regarded as their patrons, or who were specially connected with the events in which they were competing.[320] The superstitious would consult the oracles and soothsayers as to their chances of success.[321] The crowd of sight-seers would wander through the Altis admiring the statuary of the treasuries or Libon's new-built temple, perhaps listening to some rhapsodist reciting Homer, or to Herodotus as he read the story of the Persian wars, or else visiting the workshop to the west of the Altis where Pheidias was busy on his ivory and gold statue of Zeus. There were friends, too, to be seen and greeted—friends from distant parts of the Mediterranean, who after years spent in the colonies had returned to meet their kinsfolk and acquaintances at Olympia.

The following days were occupied with the sports, on the details of which we need not dwell. These took place in the stadium, or the hippodrome, some of them probably in the open space east of the altar of Zeus. They began early in the morning and lasted all day. Before daybreak every point of vantage was occupied. There were no seats: spectators sat or stood on the banks of the stadium, or hippodrome, on the slopes of the hill of Cronus, on the rows of steps beneath the treasuries, on every point which commanded a view of the games or ceremonies. They were bareheaded, and suffered severely from the sun, and dust, and thirst. Yet nothing could damp their enthusiasm. As they watched the sports they shouted and cheered on their friends and favourites; in their excitement they sprang from their seats, waving their arms, or their clothes, embracing their neighbours in their joy.[322]

A special entrance was reserved for the Hellanodicae and competitors at the north-east corner of the Altis. The vaulted tunnel which served for this purpose in Roman times still exists. Through this the Hellanodicae entered first, robed in purple, with garlands on their heads, and took their places on the seats reserved for them.[323] After them came the competitors, and the herald proclaiming their names asked if any one had any charge against any of them. Each day's proceedings were opened by the herald with a solemn proclamation.[324] Sometimes the Hellanodicas, or some other distinguished person, delivered an address to the assembled competitors. Each event in turn was proclaimed by the herald, together with the names of the competitors, their fathers, and their cities. Possibly the names

---

[318] Dio Cass. lxxix. 10.
[319] Pind. *Ol.* v. 6; i. 90.
[320] Paus. vi. 20, 15; vii. 17, 14.
[321] *Anth. Pal.* xi. 16, 33.
[322] Philostrat. *Im.* ii. 6.
[323] The evidence for most of the statements contained in this paragraph is late. It will be found in Krause, *Olympia*, pp. 138, 139.
[324] Quoted in Julian, p. 318:
Ἄρχει μὲν Ἀγων, τῶν καλλίστων
Ἀθλων ταμίας. καιρὸς δε καλεῖ
μηκέτι μέλλειν. ἀλλὰ κλύοντες
τὰν ἀμετέραν κάρυκα βοάν....
Ἰτ' ἐς ἀντίπαλον ἴστασθε κρίσιν
Νίκης δε τέλος Ζηνὶ μελήσει.
A similar proclamation closed the proceedings, *vide* Lucian, *Demonax*, 65. Cp. *Clio*, 1904, pp. 141, 142.

were written on a white telegraph board (λεύκωμα). In the case of any events requiring heats or ties, lots were drawn in the presence of the Hellanodicae and spectators. The lots marked with letters of the alphabet were thrown into a silver urn; each competitor after uttering a prayer to Zeus drew one in turn, holding it in his hand but not looking at it till all the lots were drawn. Then the Hellanodicas went round and examined the lots, arranging the heats or ties accordingly.[325] Each event was started with a blast of the trumpet, and after each event the herald proclaimed the victor (Figure 37).

We have seen that the olive crowns were probably presented to the victors at once. These crowns were made of branches cut from the sacred olive-tree, "the olive of fair crowns" which stood behind the temple of Zeus. They were cut with a golden sickle by a boy of pure Greek birth whose parents were both living, and were placed on a tripod. At the time of which we are speaking, the old iron tripod had been already replaced by the ivory and gold table made by Colotes, which was kept in the temple of Hera.[326] The table was probably set beside the seats of the Hellanodicae. There, when the herald had proclaimed his name, the victor advanced, having bound his head with fillets of wool, and the chief Hellanodicas set on his head the olive crown, and in later times put in his hand the palm of victory; while the spectators cheered and showered upon him garlands, flowers, and presents of all sorts. The crowning of the victor and the showering him with flowers (φυλλοβολία) are depicted on the interiors of two kylices, in Figures 25, 26.[327] In the case of a tie or dead-heat the crown was not awarded, but was dedicated to the god; hence the phrases ἱερὸν ποιεῖν, ἱερὸν γενέσθαι, *hieram facere*, are used to express a dead-heat or draw.[328]

Figure 25. R.-f. kylix. Bibliothèque Nationale, 532.

---

[325] Lucian, *Hermotim.* 39.
[326] Paus. v. 20, 2.
[327] *Arch. Zeit.*, 1853, 52, 3; Gerl. *A. V.* 274, 1. Cp. Stephani, *O. R. Atlas*, 1874, pl. vii.; Krause, *Olympia*, p. 173.
[328] *Ol. Ins.* 54, and notes thereon.

Figure 26. R.-f. kylix. Canino Coll.

    Then in the evening, beneath the brightness of the mid-month moon, the precinct rang with revelry and song. The victors and their friends in festal attire, with garlands on their heads, went in glad procession round the Altis, while crowds of fellow-citizens chanted to the accompaniment of the flute the old triumphal refrain of Archilochus,[329] or some new hymn of victory written for the occasion by Pindar or Bacchylides. The victors wore the crowns which they had won, but there is no ground for the statement that they dedicated them to Zeus; rather it seems that they took them home and dedicated them in the temples of their own cities. The processionals followed by banquets given by the victors.[330] Alcibiades after his victory in the chariot-race entertained the whole assembly at a feast, and borrowed for the occasion all the plate and vessels belonging to the Athenian theoroi. Anaxilas of Rhegium and his son Leophron celebrated their victories in like manner. Empedocles of Aetna being a Pythagorean, and therefore a vegetarian, had an ox made of costly spices, which he distributed to the spectators. The banquets often lasted all night long, and in the morning the victors paid their vows and offered sacrifices to the gods to whom they owed their victories.

    The most brilliant of all the ceremonies was the great sacrifice to Zeus on the morning after the full moon. The victors, the officials and the representatives of the different states, went in stately procession to the altar, where a hecatomb of oxen was sacrificed by the Eleans. This was the opportunity for the theoroi to display their magnificence and the wealth of their cities. So we can understand the indignation of the Athenians at Alcibiades[331] when instead of returning to the theoroi the vessels which he had borrowed for his banquet the evening before, he used them the next morning for his private offering; so that when a few hours later the Athenian theoroi took part in the public procession, the positions were

---

[329] Pindar, *Ol.* ix. 1, 2.
[330] Krause, *Olympia*, pp. 180, 181.
[331] Pseudo-Andocides, iv. 29, p. 126.

reversed, and the magnificence of the State appeared but as the reflection of the magnificence of a private citizen.

Of the sacrifices, processions, and rejoicings on the last day of the festival we know no details save that in the evening all the victors were entertained at a public banquet in the Prytaneum. The rewards and honours which they received on their return home have been described in a previous chapter.

Chapter 10

THE PYTHIAN, ISTHMIAN, AND NEMEAN FESTIVALS

Figure 27. Imperial coins of Delphi, in British Museum (enlarged). (*a*) Prize table. (*b*) Crown of bay leaves.

THE PYTHIA

We have seen how in 582 B.C. the old local musical festival which had been held at Delphi every eight years was transformed into a Panhellenic four-yearly festival with an athletic and equestrian programme copied from Olympia under the presidency of the amphictyonic league. Delphi now became a second centre of this league, which consisted originally of the twelve tribes dwelling round the shrine of Demeter at Phylae or Anthela. The league was administered by a council composed of two representatives from each tribe, the Hieromnemones, who met twice a year in spring and autumn at Phylae and Delphi alternately. Their autumn meeting must have coincided every fourth year with the Pythian festival which took place in the month of Boukatios, about the end of August. An amphictyonic law of the year 380 B.C.[332] contains full details of the duties of the Hieromnemones. Besides the general care of the sacred territory, precinct, monuments, and revenues, they were responsible for all the preparations necessary for the Pythia. They saw to the repairs of the stadium, hippodrome, and other buildings; they arranged the programme, made provision for the sacrifices and

---

[332] *C.I.G.* 1688.

processions; they saw that the sacred truce was duly proclaimed, and sent invitations to the various states of Greece, while each Hieromnemon was individually responsible for the state of the roads and bridges by which the official theorioi would travel to the festival. At the games themselves certain of their number, with the title of ἐπιμεληταί, acted as stewards and judges, and presented the laurel crowns to the victors. The actual presidency at the games seems usually to have been entrusted to the Thessalians, whose influence predominated in the league.

Though as a festival the Pythia were second only to the Olympia, it may be doubted whether from a purely athletic point of view they equalled in importance the Nemea or even the Isthmia. The Peloponnese was, as we have seen, the real home of Greek athletics, and, moreover, musical competitions seem always to have held the chief place at Delphi, as was but fitting in the precinct of Apollo. The chief event in the musical programme remained throughout all time the ancient Hymn to Apollo, sung to the lyre (κιθαρῳδία), recounting his victory over the Python. Chrysothemis, Philammon, and Thamyris were among the legendary victors in this competition, which was said to have been won in the seventh century four times in succession by Terpander of Lesbos. In 582 two competitions were added: one in singing to the flute (αὐλῳδία)—a competition which was, however, at once discontinued— and a solo on the flute, which, like the ancient hymn, represented the various phases in the contest between Apollo and the Python. This was the celebrated Pythian nome. The prize was won in 582, and on two subsequent occasions, by Sacadas of Argos; and Pythocritus of Sicyon is credited with no less than six successive victories, probably at the close of the sixth century. Pindar's twelfth Pythian ode was written to celebrate the victory of Midas of Agrigentum in flute-playing. The musical programme was completed in 558 B.C. by the introduction of a competition in playing on the lyre, of a somewhat similar character. The first winner was Agesilaus of Tegea. Under the Empire dramatic and poetical competitions took place at the Pythia; but we cannot say whether they existed at an earlier date. If we may trust Pliny's[333] statement, there must have been a competition in painting in the fifth century; for he tells us that Timagoras of Chalcis defeated Panaenus, the brother or nephew of Pheidias.

Next in importance to the musical competitions were the chariot and horse races, which rivalled in popularity even those at Olympia. At first they were confined, as at Olympia, to the four-horse chariot and the horse race. The pair-horse chariot-race (συνωρίς) and the chariot-race for colts were introduced at Delphi in 398 B.C. and 378 B.C., only a few years after their introduction at Olympia. The remaining two events, the synoris for colts and the riding race for colts, which were introduced at Delphi in 338 B.C. and 314 B.C., did not figure at Olympia till the next century. The popularity of horse-racing at Delphi was due to the wide-spread influence of the Delphic oracle among the Greek colonies, and particularly to the intimate connexion between Delphi and the great horse-breeding lands of Northern Greece, which belonged to the Thessalian Amphictyony; at a later time also to the influence of Macedon. Delphi was no less accessible than Olympia to the Greeks on either side of the Corinthian Gulf, and to the colonies of the West, and of Africa. The earliest victor in the chariot-race was Cleisthenes of Sicyon, and in the fifth century we find among the victors Megacles, the Alcmaeonid of Athens; Hieron of Syracuse, twice victor in the horse-race, once in the chariot-race; Xenocrates of Agrigentum, for whom Pindar wrote his earliest hymn of

---

[333] *N.H.* xxxv. 58.

victory; and Arcesilas of Cyrene. The "Charioteer" is supposed by some archaeologists to be part of the monument commemorating the victory of Arcesilas.

Still more significant than these names is the number of competitors. Pindar, in his ode on the victory of Arcesilas, states that in this race no less than forty chariots fell. The entries, then, must have been still more numerous. We may doubt whether such a field was possible at Olympia. The princes of the West can have formed but a small portion of the entries; few of them can have cared to undertake the expense and labour necessary to compete so far from home unless they had a good prospect of success. A field of forty implies large entries from the home district, and the home district of Delphi afforded an abundant supply of competitors. Northern Greece was a land of horses, and therefore, as Aristotle remarks, of oligarchies. Thessaly, in particular, was famed for producing the finest horses in Greece, and Thebes was famous for its chariots.[334] In both countries the power was in the hand of the land-owning classes, whose wealth consisted largely in their studs of horses. In Thessaly cavalry were first organized and employed for war. Thebes was credited with the first victory in the chariot-race, Thessaly with the first victory in the horse-race at Olympia. They had celebrated local festivals. Pindar's second Pythian is in honour of a victory in the chariot-race won by Hieron at some Theban festival, either the Heraclea or the Iolaea, and the thirteenth ode of Bacchylides celebrates the victory of Cleoptolemus of Thessaly in the Thessalian Petraea. Some idea of the proportion of local entries at the Pythia may be formed from the list of competitors given in the description of the chariot-race in the *Electra* of Sophocles. There are ten competitors. One comes from Sparta, one from Achaea; Orestes himself is proclaimed an Argive, but drives a team of Thessalian horses; two are Libyans from Barca, which reminds us of the victory of Arcesilas; the remaining five are an Athenian, a Boeotian, an Aetolian, a Magnesian, and an Aenianian. The Magnetes and Aenianes were Thessalian tribes belonging to the ancient Amphictyony. Thus five came from Northern Greece, two from the colonies, and three from the Peloponnese, if we suppose the Achaean to belong to the Peloponnesian and not to the Thessalian Achaeans. The few records which we possess of the fourth century and later suggest that the competition was now practically confined to Northern Greece, the only exception being the victory of Ptolemaeus, the son of Lagus, in 314 B.C., and he, though king of Egypt, was a Macedonian. In the second century there seem to have been horse-races in connexion with the official deputations, Pythaids, sent from time to time from Athens to Delphi; but these deputations had no necessary connexion with the Pythian games. In Roman times we find no mention of horse or chariot races at Delphi, and we may therefore assume that, owing to the impoverishment of Greece, these competitions had ceased to exist.

The athletic programme was the same as that of Olympia, with the addition of two races for boys, the diaulos and the dolichos. In 498 B.C. the race in armour, which had been introduced at Olympia a few years previously, was introduced at Delphi, and in 346 B.C. the boys' pankration, which did not appear at Olympia till 200 B.C. The strong local element which we have noticed in the horse-races is apparent in athletics, and in the fifth century the festival also attracted numerous athletes from the colonies of the West. Many of those who were victorious at Olympia were also victorious at Delphi. The scanty records do not allow us to draw definite conclusions; but it seems probable that the athletic competition did not reach the same standard as in the festivals of the more athletic Peloponnese. Of individual athletes in the fifth century Phayllus of Croton and Agias of Thessaly deserve especial mention.

---

[334] Pindar, *Fr.* 83.

Phayllus, who served with distinction in the Persian wars, won two victories in the pentathlon and one in the stade-race, which were commemorated by a statue the basis of which still exists. Agias was a pankratiast of the fifth century. Daochus, a member of the same family, two generations later set up in Thessaly a group of bronze statues representing those of his family who had distinguished themselves, including a statue of Agias by Lysippus. A replica of this statue in marble has been found at Delphi (Figure 20).

In Pindar's time the athletic competitions as well as the horse-races took place not at Delphi but in the Crisaean plain below. The horse-races continued to be held there, Delphi itself affording no suitable space for a hippodrome. But in the second half of the fifth century the athletics were transferred to a new stadium constructed above the precinct of Apollo. The change is connected by M. Homolle with an attempt of the Phocians to reassert their rights to the control of the games at the beginning of the Peloponnesian war.[335] The fourth century was one of great activity among the states of Northern Greece, in Thebes, in Thessaly, and in Macedon, and the Pythian festival regained the importance which it had somewhat lost owing to the doubtful part played by Delphi and the Northern States in the struggle with Persia. The Pythian games appealed to the ambitious rulers of Thessaly and Macedon in the same way as the Olympic games had to the tyrants of an earlier age. Jason of Pherae usurped the presidency of the games, and was preparing to celebrate them with extraordinary magnificence when his ambition was cut short by his murder. Philip of Macedon was more politic. By espousing the cause of the Amphictyons against the Phocians in the Sacred war he won their gratitude, and was appointed by them as president of the games. The new activity at Delphi may be seen in the numerous additions to the programme made in this century. The gymnasium was built in this period, and Aristotle undertook the task of drawing up a register of Pythian victors, being assisted in the task by his nephew Callistratus. A copy of this register was placed in the temple of Apollo.[336]

In 290 B.C. during the war between Demetrius Poliorketes and Pyrrhus, the roads leading to Delphi were in possession of the Aetolians, and Demetrius therefore ordered the Pythia to be celebrated at Athens, there being, he said, no more fitting place for the worship of Apollo than Athens, where he was regarded as the father of the race. The intimate relations between Athens and Delphi at this period are proved by the splendid deputations the Pythaids, as they were called, sent to Delphi from time to time.[337] The splendour of the Pythaids reached its height in the second century. Their arrival at Delphi was celebrated by equestrian, musical and dramatic displays and competitions; but these deputations did not necessarily coincide with the Pythian festival, and after the capture of Athens by Sulla in 87 B.C. they practically ceased.

We know little of the Pythian games under the Empire: we have the names of a few victors, many of them in musical or dramatic competitions, others professional periodonikai. Nero won the Pythian crown, and in return for it carried off hundreds of works of art from Delphi to Rome. At a later period Herodes Atticus rebuilt the stadium in the form in which it exists to-day. The Pythian games still existed in the time of the Emperor Julian, and were probably abolished finally at the end of the fourth century when the Olympic games were abolished.

---

[335] *B.C.H.* xxiii. p. 613.
[336] A list of victors in the Pythian games is given in Krause, *Pythien, Nemeen und Isthmien*, pp. 85 ff. Details of the stadium and gymnasium at Delphi will be found below, pp. 257, 483.
[337] *B.C.H.* xxx., 1906, pp. 191-328.

The festival must have lasted several days, but the precise duration is unknown. The musical competitions appear to have come first, then the athletic events, and lastly the chariot and horse races. The boys' events were not, as at Olympia, grouped together; but each boys' competition preceded the corresponding competition for men.[338] The prize was a wreath of bay leaves plucked in the vale of Tempe by a boy whose parents were both living. It is represented on one of the coins in Figure 27, while the other coin shows the prize table and on it a crow, five apples, a vase and a laurel wreath. As at Olympia, the victors had the privilege of erecting their statues in or near the precinct. The chief religious ceremony of the festival must have been the official procession along the sacred way to the temple of Apollo.

Figure 28. Imperial coin of Corinth, in British Museum (enlarged).

THE ISTHMIA

The Isthmian festival, though inferior in athletic standard to the Olympia and in sanctity to the Pythia, was perhaps the most frequented of all the Panhellenic festivals.[339] It was held in the second and fourth year of each Olympiad, under the presidency of Corinth; and though there is some doubt as to the exact date, it seems certain that it was held in the spring, probably in April or early May.[340] No festival was so central and so accessible to all parts of the Greek world, whether by land or sea, and no place offered such innumerable attractions to visitors of every sort as Corinth, the city of commerce and of pleasure. The description which Dion Chrysostom has left of the crowds which flocked to the Isthmia in the first century A.D. has already been quoted. It reminds one of the crowd at a modern race-meeting, where princes, statesmen, millionaires, jostle with beggars, mountebanks, and sharpers. "The Isthmian festival," says Livy,[341] "owed its popularity not only to the national love of witnessing contests of every sort in arts or strength or agility, but especially to the advantageous situation of the Isthmus, which, commanding the resources of two seas, was the

---

[338] Plut. *Quaest. Symp.* ii. 5; Sophocles, *El.* 698.
[339] Strabo viii. 6, 20; Aristid. *Isthm.* 45; Dion of Prusa, Διογ. ἡ Ἴσθμ. etc.
[340] Unger, *Philologus*, xxxvii. p. 1.
[341] xxxiii. 32.

natural meeting-place of the human race, the mart of Greece and Asia." In these words we have, summed up, the essential characteristics of the Isthmia, the attractiveness and variety of their programme, their cosmopolitanism, and last but not least their commercial importance. Livy is speaking of the time in the opening years of the second century, when Flamininus proclaimed the liberty of Greece at the Isthmian festival. We cannot doubt that he had also in his mind the revived splendour of the festival in his own time, since Corinth which had been destroyed by Mummius had been refounded by Julius Caesar and become the capital of Achaia. Of the earlier history of the festival we unfortunately know little; but the few notices which have survived indicate that from the very first the character of the festival differed little from that ascribed to it by Livy and Dion Chrysostom.

The reorganization of the ancient local festival in honour of Poseidon as a Panhellenic trieteris seems to have taken place either during the closing years of the Cypselidae, or shortly after their fall. These princes had laid the foundation of the maritime and commercial greatness of Corinth, which, under their patronage, took the lead in trade and literature and art. From this time her wealth and luxury were proverbial; but wealth and luxury are not the soil on which athletics flourish best. Corinth was not an athletic state; few great athletes hailed from her, and, whatever athletic vigour existed in early times in families such as the Oligaethidae soon died away. The character of the Isthmia cannot fail to have been determined by the character and relations of Corinth.

Corinth, though traditionally Dorian, had little in common with the other Dorian states of the Peloponnese. All her sympathies were Ionian. With the Ionians of the East she was closely connected by that trade which was the basis of her wealth, and by the common worship of Poseidon. The influence of the East is clearly marked in the early art of Corinth, especially in her pottery. Equally close were her relations with Athens. We have seen that Theseus was one of the reputed founders of the Isthmia; and that the Athenian theoroi had a special place of privilege at the festival. Indeed, the Isthmia seem almost to have been regarded as an Attic festival, and were an occasion of merry-making, a sort of public holiday for all classes of Athens, even for slaves. Many an Athenian was debarred from visiting Olympia by the length of the journey, the heat, and other discomforts of the festival itself. The Isthmia suffered from no such drawbacks; it was but a few hours' journey, either by land or sea; the festival took place in the spring; Corinth offered ample accommodation for such as could afford it; those who could not afford it might take their tents with them and encamp in the neighbourhood. Under these circumstances it is reasonable to suppose that the Isthmia bore more resemblance to the Panathenaea, or even to the Delia, both of which festivals were also said to have been founded by Theseus, than they did to the more strenuous Olympia; and such few facts as we know about the programme confirm this idea.

It is perhaps to this essential difference in character that we may ascribe the sort of feud existing between the Olympia and the Isthmia. The Olympia were accounted "the most athletic" of all festivals.[342] The inferiority of the Isthmia in athletic prestige is proved by the fact that Solon assigned only 100 drachmae to a winner at the Isthmia, while he assigned 500 to an Olympic winner.

Of the history of the Isthmia in the fifth and fourth centuries we know practically nothing. The records of victories in the games are too scanty to enable us to form any trustworthy

---

[342] Lucian, *Nero*, 1.

conclusions;[343] as far as they go they indicate that the athletic competition was far more local than at Olympia. There are hardly any names of victors recorded from Sicily and Italy which figure so largely in the Olympic records. With the exception of a few periodonikai the competitors come chiefly from Corinth, Aegina, Thebes, and Athens, and some of the islands of the Aegean. Bacchylides in his Second Ode on Argeius of Ceos mentions that at this date the Ceans had already won seventy victories at the Isthmus, and a Cean inscription, now at Athens, records numerous victories which they had won at the Isthmia and the Nemea, including victories of Argeius.[344] The Oligaethidae of Corinth had, according to Pindar, themselves won sixty crowns at these two festivals, and the Timodemidae of Athens had won eight victories at the Isthmus and seven at the Nemea. We can find no such records as these at Olympia.[345]

During the Peloponnesian war the festival must have suffered greatly from the enforced absence of the Athenians. In the *Peace* of Aristophanes, written shortly after the peace of Nicias, one of the slaves expresses his delight at the prospect of once more taking part in the Isthmia.[346] The Corinthians had probably equal cause for rejoicing; without the Athenians and their allies the festival must have been shorn of half its splendour. A few years later, in 412 B.C., we find the Corinthians insisting vigorously on the observance of the Isthmian truce, and turning a deaf ear to the suggestions of Sparta for a joint expedition to free Chios from the Athenian yoke.[347] They even invited the Athenians to the festival, and thus enabled them to discover the plot of the Chians, and to destroy the fleet which sailed for Chios at the conclusion of the festival. The policy of Corinth was to preserve the balance of power. Her bitter opposition to Athens was the natural result of commercial rivalry, but the supremacy of Sparta was still less to her liking, and within a few years of the humiliation of Athens we find her leagued with Athens, Thebes, and Argos in an anti-Spartan league. The Spartans had no scruples as to the observance of festivals, except when it suited their convenience; and Agesilaus, with certain Corinthian exiles of the Spartan party, actually invaded Corinth during the progress of the Isthmia.[348] The games were being conducted by the Corinthians and Argives, who seem to have been for a time united into one state. On the approach of Agesilaus they took to flight, and Agesilaus himself encamped in the sacred precinct, while the Corinthian exiles offered the customary sacrifice to Poseidon and conducted the games. When Agesilaus withdrew, the Argives returned and celebrated the festival all over again.

From this point we hear no more of the Isthmia till the Romans began to interfere in Greek politics. The cosmopolitanism of the festival and the commercial importance of the Isthmus as the meeting-place of East and West naturally appealed to the Romans, and a new era of prosperity opened for the Isthmia, which for a time seemed likely to eclipse even Olympia. The Corinthians had no narrow national prejudices, and allowed the Romans to take part in the Isthmia as early as 228 B.C.[349] Consequently, it was at the Isthmus and not at Olympia that Flamininus proclaimed the liberty of the Greeks in 196 B.C. Even the destruction of Corinth was not allowed to interrupt the festival which continued to be held

---

[343] Krause, *op. cit.* p. 209.
[344] A full account of this inscription is given in Jebb's *Bacchylides*, pp. 187 ff.
[345] Pindar, *O.* xiii. 98; *N.* ii. 22.
[346] *Pax*, 880. In this play the personified Theoria comes back to earth in the train of Eirene, but Theoria is not confined to the Isthmian theoria.
[347] Thucyd. viii. 9.
[348] Xen. *Hell.* iv. 5.
[349] Polyb. ii. 13.

under the presidency of Sicyon till the rebuilding of Corinth by Julius Caesar.[350] Under the Empire Corinth became richer and more luxurious, and the Isthmian festival more popular than ever. The enthusiasm for athletic spectacles at Corinth seems to have made a deep impression on St. Paul. Preachers are wont to draw glowing pictures of the Isthmian games in this connexion. But few perhaps realize how corrupt and degraded were Greek athletics during St. Paul's lifetime, and nowhere were they more degraded than at the Isthmia. Yet in outward appearance the festival had never been more brilliant. Most of the buildings, which excavations of the sanctuary of Poseidon have revealed, belong to the period of Augustus and his successors.[351] Nero was so deeply impressed with the importance of the site that he conceived the idea of cutting a canal through the Isthmus, and was only prevented from doing so by the opposition of certain ignorant scientists, who maintained that the level of the sea was different in the Gulf of Corinth and in the Aegean.[352] However, he took part in person at the Isthmia, and issued a letter summoning the Greek world to the festival, a copy of which has been recovered.[353] It appears that to suit the emperor's convenience the festival was postponed from the spring to November, or perhaps it was celebrated a second time the same year. He was proclaimed victor in singing to the lyre and also in the heralds' competition; and in obedience to his wishes a competition in tragedy was added to the programme, though, according to Lucian, such competitions were barred by a special Isthmian law. He was forced, moreover, to resort to force in order to secure his victory; for a certain Epirote, possessed of a fine voice and less complaisant than the officials, refused to withdraw from the competition unless the emperor paid him ten talents; and Nero, recognizing that he would be defeated, despatched a band of his creatures, who so battered and ill-treated the Epirote as to spoil his voice. Finally, in imitation of Flamininus, he went through the farce of bestowing freedom on the province, and himself proclaimed his clemency standing in the middle of the stadium.

The venality of athletics at the Isthmia under the Empire is evident from the story already quoted of a disappointed athlete, who actually took proceedings to recover the amount of a bribe, and published his own shame before all the assembled crowds.[354] Such an incident implies a degraded public opinion and the absence of all true love of sport. Indeed, it is evident from Dion Chrysostom that the Corinthians and Athenians had already acquired from the Romans a taste for the more exciting and more brutal exhibitions of the amphitheatre.[355] The festival seems to have survived down to the time of the Emperor Julian; but there was no longer any interest in athletic or musical competitions. The vast sums spent by the Corinthians on their games were spent, the emperor tells us, in the purchase of bears and leopards to be hunted in the arena.[356]

The sanctuary of Poseidon where the Isthmian games were held has been excavated, but the excavations throw little light on the history of the games themselves. It consisted of a small acropolis surrounded by a wall, the north side of which was formed by the great military wall that guarded the Isthmus. The sacred way, according to Pausanias, was lined on one side by a row of pine trees, on the other by statues of athletes who had won victories at the festival. Traces have been found of the temples of Poseidon and Palaemon, of the sacred

---

[350] Paus. ii. 2, 2.
[351] *Gaz. Arch.*, 1884, 1885.
[352] Lucian, *Nero*.
[353] *B.C.H.* xii. 510-528.
[354] *Supra*, p. 174.
[355] *Supra*, p. 172.
[356] Julian, *Epist.* 35.

way, of the theatre, and of the stadium, but all are of late date. The stadium lay in a ravine, formed by a stream which must have been diverted from its course, but has now returned to it. It was about 650 feet long. It was seated with marble; and some traces of the seats survive. An inscription in honour of Publius Licinius Priscus, a Roman citizen of Corinth who lived in the second century A.D., records that he built a stoa adjoining the stadium with vaulted rooms opening into it.[357] The same benefactor provided, at his own expense, buildings for the accommodation of the athletes, who came to the Isthmia from "all the inhabited world," and repaired various buildings which had suffered from the ravages of time and earthquakes including the "judging-rooms" (ἐγκριτηρίους οἴκους), by which phrase, apparently, are meant the rooms where competitors were examined and classified. No traces of these buildings have been found, nor has the site of the hippodrome been discovered.

Figure 29. Silver Vase. Bibliothèque Nationale. Imperial period.

The festival must have lasted several days. It began with a sacrifice to Poseidon,[358] and included athletic, equestrian, and musical competitions, and perhaps also a regatta. The athletic and equestrian events differed little from those at other festivals. There were separate competitions for men, youths, and boys, and the youths' competitions included the pankration.[359] There was also, as at Nemea, a four stades' or hippios foot-race.[360] The multiplication of boys' events here, as at Nemea and at the Panathenaea, indicates the comparatively local character of the competition at these festivals.

From the connexion of the festival with Poseidon we should expect to find that the equestrian events were an important part of the programme. Herodotus of Thebes and

---

[357] *I.G.* iv. 203.
[358] Xen. *Hell.* iv. 5.
[359] Bacchylides i., ii.
[360] *Ib.* ix.

Xenocrates of Agrigentum won the chariot-race in Pindar's time,[361] and somewhat later one Theochrestus of Cyrene and two Spartans, Xenarches and Polycles.[362] A horse named Lycus had in the sixth century won two victories for Pheidolas of Corinth or his sons.[363] These are all the records that we possess; but the occurrence of the two-horse chariot on coins of Commodus may perhaps be an indication that chariot-racing still took place at the Isthmia under the Empire.

There is no mention of musical contests previous to the third century B.C., when a certain Nicocles of Tarentum won six victories as kitharodos.[364] He claims apparently to have been the first victor in this competition, but the existence of musical competitions from the earliest days of the festival is rendered probable by the tradition that in mythical times Olympus was victorious in flute-playing, Orpheus on the lyre, Linus in song, and Eumolpus in singing to the lyre and the flute.[365] In Roman times there were numerous musical competitions. There must also have been poetical competitions. The poetess Aristomacha of Erythrae is stated to have won a prize at the Isthmia, and a pupil of Herodes won a prize for an enkomion.[366] During the Hellenistic age it seems probable that there were dramatic competitions held in connexion with the guilds of Dionysiac players, but these competitions must have disappeared under the Empire. Finally, Pliny asserts that at the Isthmus as at Delphi, a competition in painting existed in the time of Panaenus.[367]

The only evidence for the regatta is the statement that in mythical times the Argo won the boat-race at the Isthmus. The Isthmus was certainly a fitting place for such a race: there were boat-races at the Panathenaea, and the Athenian theoria came to the Isthmia in a ship. But we have no definite information on the point.

Figure 30. Scene from Silver Vase (Figure 29).

---

[361] Pindar, *I*. i., ii.
[362] Paus. vi. 1, 7; 2, 2.
[363] Paus. vi. 13, 10.
[364] *I.G.* ii. 1367.
[365] Hyginus, *Fab.* 165, 173.
[366] Plut. *Quaest. Symp.* ii. 4, v. 2, viii. 4.
[367] *H.N.* xxxv. 58.

In Pindar's time the Isthmian crown[368] was made of wild celery, dry celery, as the scholiast explains, to distinguish it from the fresh celery of which the Nemean crown was made. According to later writers the Isthmian crown was of pine leaves; the pine tree was sacred to Poseidon, and an avenue of pines lined the sacred road at the Isthmus. It seems not unlikely that the original crown was of pine leaves, and this practice was revived under the Empire. On the coins of Augustus and Nero the celery crown is still represented, while on those of Antoninus Pius and Verus, we see the inscription Ἴσθμια encircled by a crown of pine leaves[369] (Figure 28).

A scene connected with the Isthmian games occurs on a silver cup, which was part of an offering dedicated to Mercurius of Canetum by Q. Domitius Tutus (Figures 29, 30). To the left is a victorious athlete crowned, and holding in his hands a palm branch. Before him is a table on which stands a herm, to which he has dedicated a fillet and a crown, which curiously appears to be of oak leaves, not of pine or celery. Beyond the table is seated an Agonothetes; and a woman holding a torch stands next to him. In spite of the crown of oak, the identification of the scene with the Isthmia is rendered certain by the representation of the Acrocorinthus and Pegasus, to whom a nymph gives water from the fountain of Peirene.[370]

Figure 31. Imperial coin of Argos, in British Museum (enlarged).

THE NEMEA

Little is known of the history of the Nemean games. Their importance dates from the year 573 B.C., when they were re-organized as a Panhellenic festival. This year was reckoned as the first Nemead, and from this date the games were held regularly every two years in the

---

[368] Krause, *op. cit.* p. 197.
[369] *B.M. Cat., Coins of Corinth*, 509-512, 564, 602, 624; cp. *I.G.* ii. 1320, where we find Ἴσθμια enclosed in a wreath of pine leaves.
[370] The cup, which forms part of the Bernay treasure, is in the Cabinet des médailles at the Bibliothèque Nationale. Le Prevost, *Mém. sur la collection des vases de Bernay*, Pls. viii., ix.; Schreiber, *Atlas*, xxv. 1, 2.

deep-lying vale of Nemea, "beneath the shadeless hills of Phlious." The presidency of the games belonged to the neighbouring town of Cleonae, until about the year 460 B.C. it was usurped by the Argives, and in spite of rival claims it remained in their hands ever afterwards. The control of a Panhellenic festival was of considerable political importance, and the Argives had no scruple in manipulating the sacred truce to their own interests. On more than one occasion, it seems, a Spartan invasion had been met by sacred heralds proclaiming the sacred truce.[371] At last, Agesipolis in 390 B.C. appealed to Olympian Zeus and Pythian Apollo for leave to disregard the fraudulent truce, and, having obtained their approval, marched through Nemea, and gave such a lesson to the Argives that they never again tried to shelter themselves behind the truce.

At some date between this event and the close of the third century, the festival itself was transferred to Argos. Aratus, when engaged in war with Argos, made an attempt to restore the festival to the Cleonaeans who had joined the Achaean league.[372] The games were once more held at Nemea, and the athletes who had gone to compete at the rival games at Argos were, in defiance of the sacred truce, arrested and sold as slaves by the Achaeans. But the attempt of Aratus failed, and the festival continued to be held at Argos under Argive presidency. It was at Argos probably that musical competitions were first introduced into the festival. Plutarch[373] relates how Philopoemen, after defeating the Spartan tyrant Machanidas in the battle of Mantinea, came to Argos and reviewed his troops before the people assembled for the games. He entered the theatre during the musical competitions at the moment when the musician Pylades was reciting the opening verse of the *Persae* of Timotheus—

The palm of liberty for Greece I won—

and the whole assembly, struck by the coincidence, with one accord hailed him as the saviour of Greece. Philip V. of Macedon had, some years previously, been appointed by the Argives to preside over the games on the ground that the kings of Macedon were of Argive descent, and the same honour was afterwards bestowed on Flamininus.[374] Under the Empire the festival was still celebrated at Argos. Hadrian seems to have revived its glory. He instituted a winter festival, in which the race in armour was a conspicuous feature, and he also revived the hippios or four stades' race which had fallen into disuse at the Nemea and the Isthmia.[375] The Argive coins of Antoninus Pius bear the inscription Νέμεια, surrounded by a celery wreath (Figure 31), and the latter occurs still later on the coins of Gallienus. Meanwhile the old Nemean sanctuary had fallen so far into disuse that when Pausanias visited Nemea, he found the temple of Nemean Zeus roofless and the statue of the god gone.

Little is left to-day of the Nemean sanctuary, nor has the site ever been properly excavated. There was no town at Nemea, merely a sanctuary of Zeus with a stadium and a hippodrome, and we must suppose also a gymnasium. The cypress grove in which the temple of Zeus stood has disappeared, and of the temple itself only three pillars are left, sufficient, however, to show that the temple cannot have been much earlier than the close of the fifth century. The site of the stadium is also visible in a deep ravine some 650 feet long, the end of

---

[371] Xen. *Hell.* iv. 7, 2; v. 1, 29.
[372] Plutarch, *Aratus*, 17.
[373] Plutarch, *Philopoemen*, 11.
[374] Livy xxvii. 30, xxxiv. 41.
[375] Paus. v. 16, 4.

which forms a natural sphendone. There is no trace of hippodrome or gymnasium. There are said to be traces of a theatre, but the statement appears to be doubtful. Possibly the semicircular end of the stadium has been mistaken for a theatre.[376]

The Nemea took place on the 12th day of the month Panemos, which seems to correspond approximately to our July. The old idea that the festival was held alternately in summer and winter is now abandoned, and it is generally agreed that the winter Nemea was a local festival founded by Hadrian. The duration of the festival is unknown; it must certainly have lasted several days. The prize, as has been already stated, was a wreath of wild celery (σέλινον), and the officials, who bore the title of Hellanodicae, wore dusky robes of mourning in commemoration of the funeral origin of the games.

The athletic programme, like that of the Isthmia, included numerous events for boys and youths. The boys' pentathlon was introduced in the 53rd Nemead, and in the next Nemead was won by Sogenes of Aegina; and the boys' pankration, an event not introduced at Olympia till a much later period, was won by Pytheas of Aegina, and probably by Argeius of Ceos, whose victory at the Isthmia has been already noticed.[377] There was also a hippios-race for boys. Races in armour seem to have been a special feature of the Nemea. They were run over the hippios course and were, according to Philostratus, of great antiquity.[378]

We hear little of equestrian competitions. The chariot-race and the horse-race are mentioned in the account of the mythical founding of the games by the Seven Chieftains, and the chariot-race was won in the fifth century by Chromius of Aetna, Alcibiades of Athens, and Xenarches of Sparta; after this we hear no more of it. Nor have we any record of the horse-race which, if we may argue from the mythical tradition, probably existed. The site of the hippodrome is lost; Pausanias tells us that its course was twice the length of the stadium.

There was a competition for trumpeters; but we have no record of musical competitions previous to the transference of the festival to Argos. The absence of any mention of musical competitions in the mythological accounts of the founding of the Nemea, and the association of the Nemea with Zeus and Heracles, makes it improbable that these events existed in early times. The only victors in them known to us belong to the time of the Empire. They are either kitharodoi, singers to the lyre, or Pythaulai, players of the Pythian nome on the flute. In late times there were probably dramatic competitions at Nemea, as at the Isthmus.

From the length of the athletic programme and the scarcity of records of other competitions, we may safely infer that the interest of the Nemea was almost entirely athletic. In fact, if Olympia was "the most athletic of all festivals," Nemea may almost claim second place. At Delphi the musical competitions took precedence of the athletic, at the Isthmus there was a variety of counter-attractions, even at Olympia the chariot-race rivalled athletics in popularity. At the Nemea, previous to their transference to Argos, athletics were supreme.[379]

The scanty records of victors in the Nemea seem to show that in the fifth century competitors came mostly from the Peloponnese, from Athens, and from the islands of the Aegean.[380] Particularly numerous are the victors from Aegina, though the preponderance of this island in the records may be partly due to the fact of its close connexion with Pindar,

---

[376] Frazer, *Pausanias*, iii. 91.
[377] Pindar, *N.* v., vii.; Bacchylides, i. xii.
[378] Phil. *Gym.* 7; Paus. vi. 16, 4.
[379] The athletic character of the Nemea is emphasized in Bacchylides' Twelfth Ode, in which the origin of the pankration is traced to the victory of Heracles over the Nemean lion.
[380] Krause, *op. cit.* p. 147.

most of the Aeginetan victors being known to us from his odes. The Cean inscription, to which reference has already been made, shows that here, as at the Isthmus, the Ceans were constant competitors. The victories of the Oligaethidae of Corinth and the Timodemidae of Athens have been already mentioned. On the other hand, we find few victors at Nemea from either Italy or Sicily. In the succeeding centuries the interest of the festival seems to have declined; the few victors known to us are mostly Peloponnesian; many came from Elis. Under the Empire the only recorded victors are professionals from Alexandria and the powerful cities of Asia Minor.

Chapter 11

THE ATHLETIC FESTIVALS OF ATHENS

It is impossible within the limits of this work to give any account of the various local festivals which existed in every state of Greece. Such an account would too often resolve itself into a barren list of names. With regard to Athens we are more fully informed; and from the fifth century onwards we may regard Athens as typical of the Greek world. A brief account of the Athenian festivals and competitions will enable us to form some idea of the part which such events occupied in the life of the Greeks. Athens was not the most athletic of the states of Greece; but nowhere was the love of festivals more developed, and nowhere were competitions more various and more numerous. The Athenian must have spent a large portion of his life in attending festivals and witnessing competitions. In the following list I shall confine myself to those festivals at which we know that there were competitions, and to the festivals of Athens; but we must remember that there were many other festivals in Athens itself, and that there were numerous competitions, athletic or other, on the borders of Attica, at which Athenians could attend as spectators or competitors.

The Attic year[381] commenced with the month of Hekatombaion (July), and in this month took place the great festival of Athene Polias, the Panathenaea, extending over several days and attracting visitors from the whole Aegean world. The lesser Panathenaea were held yearly; the great Panathenaea of which details will be found below, were held every fourth year, the third year of each Olympiad.

In the next month, Metageitnion, the feast of the Heraclea took place at Marathon. These were athletic games which seem to have been much frequented in Pindar's time.[382] The prize was a silver cup. There were also Heraclea held at Athens in Cynosarges; but we have no evidence of any competitions held there.

Next came the Eleusinia in the month of Boedromion, like the lesser Panathenaea, celebrated yearly; but every second year of the Olympiad they were celebrated as a trieteris, and every fourth year as a pentaeteris. On these occasions there were athletics, horse-races, musical competitions, and a special competition called "the contest of the fathers" (πάτριος ἀγών), which seems to have been equestrian in character. As at the feast of Athene the prize consisted in jars of olive oil, so at Demeter's feast it consisted in measures of corn and barley. Epharmostus of Opous is stated by Pindar to have won a victory in wrestling at Eleusis, and

---

[381] The following section is taken chiefly from A. Mommsen's *Feste der Stadt Athen*.
[382] *O.* ix. 89, xiii. 110; *I.* viii. 79.

Herodotus of Thebes in the chariot-race.[383] The Eleusinia claimed an antiquity greater than that of the Olympia or the Isthmia, and the earliest athletic implement which we possess is an inscribed jumping-weight found at Eleusis which cannot be later than the beginning of the sixth century (Figure 60).

The month of Pyanepsion (October) was a very busy one for the athletic youth of Athens. First came the Oschophoria, a festal race in which two boys, chosen from each tribe, raced, dressed in women's clothes, from the temple of Dionysus to the temple of Athene Skiras at Phalerum. They carried bunches of grapes, and the winner received as his prize a mixed drink, composed of wine, honey, cheese, flour, and oil.[384] On the sixth day of the month began the Thesea, the great athletic festival of the Athenian epheboi, and this was immediately followed by the Epitaphia. The details of the programme will be discussed below. Lastly, in connexion with the Apaturia there were musical competitions and torch-races in honour of Prometheus and Hephaestus.

With October the athletic season seems to have ended. The winter months and early spring were occupied with the dramatic competitions connected with the Dionysia and Lenaea. There may, of course, have been lesser competitions, of which we know nothing. At the "Country Dionysia," for example, there appear to have been various rustic sports, such as the game of Askoliasmos,[385] which correspond to such sports as climbing the greasy pole and other Mayday festivities.

The month of Munychion or April was the beginning of the boating season. At the festival of Munychia there was a procession in honour of Artemis, followed by boat-races in the harbour.[386] At a later date these were replaced by a mimic naval battle, for which prizes were also given.[387] Then the epheboi sailed to Salamis to celebrate the Aiantea. There were more boat-races, and also a long-distance foot-race, in which the youths of Athens competed with the youths of Salamis.

In the same month took place the Athenian Olympia, founded by the Peisistratidae at the time when they commenced to build the temple of Olympian Zeus. There were athletic and equestrian competitions. It is perhaps to this festival that Pindar alludes, when he says that Timodemus won "at home crowns more than may be numbered in the games of Zeus."[388] The festival was apparently a yearly one. It was reorganized on a more magnificent scale by Hadrian.

During the rest of the year there are few important competitions. There were musical competitions at the Thargelia, torch-races on horseback and on foot at the Bendidea, founded in the fourth century, and, lastly, more boat-races at the Diisoteria in the month of Skirophorion.

This list, though probably far from complete, will give some idea of the number of competitions and festivals in Attica. The competitions fall into two divisions, those, like the Panathenaea, which, though not Panhellenic, were open to competitors from all parts of Greece, and those, like the Thesea, which were practically confined to inhabitants of Athens. The character of these festivals will be readily understood from the programme of the

---

[383] *O.* ix.; *I.* 1.
[384] Athen. 495 F.
[385] *Vide* p. 296.
[386] *I.G.* ii. 466, 468, 470, 471.
[387] *I.G.* iii. 1160.
[388] *N.* ii. 23.

Panathenaea and the Thesea, with regard to which we have considerable information from inscriptions and other sources.

The Panathenaic festival undoubtedly occupied several days. According to the highly probable scheme suggested by August Mommsen,[389] it began on the 21st day of Hekatombaion, and lasted nine days. The first three days were occupied by musical competitions, the next two by athletics, the sixth by horse and chariot races, the seventh by the Pyrrhic and other military competitions. The seventh day closed with the torch-races in the evening, which were the beginning of an all-night revel, Pannychis, which preceded the procession and sacrifices on the 28th day of the month—the great day of the festival. A regatta on the last day brought the festival to the end.

The details of the sacrifices and procession do not concern us here. The procession is known to us from the frieze of the Parthenon. Its object was the offering to Athena of the new peplos or mantle wrought by certain selected maidens of Athens, and interwoven with scenes representing the battle between the gods and the giants. In the procession the whole population of Athens was represented, and not only that of Athens but also that of Athenian colonies and allies who sent to the Panathenaea official deputies bearing their offerings and sacrifices.[390] An admirable account of the procession will be found in the British Museum *Guide to the Parthenon Sculptures*, while those who wish for fuller information as to the literary evidence will find it in Michaelis' *Parthenon* or Mommsen's *Feste der Stadt Athen*.

The musical competitions certainly date back to the time of Peisistratus, who reorganized the earlier yearly festival as a pentaeteris, increased the programme, and gave to the festival a wider and more popular scope. It was either Peisistratus himself or his son, Hipparchus, who organized recitations by rhapsodists of the Homeric poems, which had perhaps taken place at a yet earlier date at Brauron. These recitations were confined to Homer, and it is recorded as a special mark of honour that an exception was made in favour of the *Perseis* of Choerilus, which described the triumph of Athens over Xerxes.[391] There seem also to have been competitions in lyric and elegiac poetry.

According to Plutarch[392] Pericles was the first to introduce contests in singing and playing on the lyre and on the flute. The competitions were held in the newly built Odeum, and Pericles himself presided as judge. In the first part of his statement Plutarch is mistaken. Midas of Agrigentum, whose Pythian victory on the flute is celebrated in one of Pindar's earliest odes, is also credited with a victory in the Panathenaea.[393] The existence of musical competitions at a yet earlier date is proved by two small sixth-century Panathenaic amphorae in the British Museum.[394] One represents a citharist playing on the chelys, the other a player on the double flute, standing on a platform before a bearded man, clothed in a long chiton and striped himation, while at the side of the platform is seated a judge similarly clothed and holding a wand. The vase from which our illustration is taken belongs to the class of vase described as imitations of Panathenaic amphorae (Figure 32). The musical competition is represented on both sides. At a later date the musical prizes consisted in a sum of silver and crowns of gold. In any case, the small amphorae cannot have been used to hold oil, and may

---

[389] *Op. cit.* p. 153.
[390] E.g., Priene, *Priene Inschriften*, 5; a decree of the people of Priene not later than 326 B.C. for the sending of two Theoroi to Athens with a panoplia. Similarly Colophon 306 B.C., *I.G.* ii. 164, ii. 5.
[391] Suidas, ii. 2, p. 1691.
[392] *Pericles*, 13.
[393] Schol. to Pindar, *P.* xii.
[394] *B.M. Vases*, B. 139, 141; cp. *Berl. Vas.* 1873.

be regarded as commemorative prizes bestowed on musicians, perhaps in addition to some more substantial prize, on the analogy of the larger amphorae bestowed on victors in athletics or chariot-races.

Figure 32. Small Panathenaic(?) amphora, in British Museum, B. 188. Sixth century.

Figure 33. B.-f. kylix, in British Museum, B. 80.

An early black-figured kylix in the British Museum points to the existence of choral and dramatic competitions at the Panathenaea (Figure 33). The central group represents a sacrifice to Athene, who stands beside her altar armed with shield and spear, much as she is depicted on Panathenaic vases. Advancing towards the altar is a procession formed of a tragic chorus, a comic chorus, and a dithyrambic chorus. Diogenes Laertius[395] states that dramatic competitions existed at the Panathenaea, but we have no further information concerning them.

The musical programme for the fourth century is partly known to us from an inscription, which is unfortunately much mutilated.[396] The opening lines, which apparently referred to the recitations of rhapsodists, are almost entirely wanting. Then come four competitions. For singers to the lyre there are no less than five prizes: a crown of gold valued at 1000 drachmae with 500 drachmae of silver for the winner; prizes of 1200, 600, 400, and 300 drachmae respectively for the next four in order of merit. The "men singers to the flute" receive only two prizes—the first a crown of 300 drachmae, the second a sum of 100 drachmae. For "men players on the lyre" there are three prizes: the first is a crown valued at 500 drachmae; the third is a sum of 100 drachmae; the amount of the second prize is uncertain. Flute-players again have only two prizes, the figures for which are missing in the inscription. There were doubtless many other competitions. The insertion of the word "men" before "singers to the flute" and "players on the lyre" implies that there were also musical contests for boys, as was undoubtedly the case at Aphrodisias.[397] Another competition mentioned in connection with the Panathenaea was called συναυλία,[398] by which perhaps is meant a duet on flutes. The preference shown at Athens for the lyre over the flute is noticeable in the value of the prizes assigned for these events. Playing on the lyre was part of every Athenian's education, but whereas flute-playing had become popular in the early part of the fifth century, it did not commend itself to Athenian educationalists. Its moral effect was considered bad, and it was an ungraceful performance which distorted the face. So it was in the fourth century left for the most part to professional flute-girls.[399] From the number of prizes offered it is obvious that there must have been large entries for the musical competitions, and Mommsen is probably right in assigning three days to these events.

Next came the athletic competitions. The early Panathenaic vases show that all the events of the Olympic programme existed in the Panathenaea in the sixth century, and that there were competitions for men and boys, but there is no evidence as to the division of boys into boys and youths at this period. In the fourth century the inscription already mentioned proves the existence of all three classes.[400] There were five events for boys and youths respectively, the stade-race, the pentathlon, wrestling, boxing, and the pankration. There were two prizes for each event, consisting of so many amphorae of oil; the winner received five times as many amphorae as the second. The following table shows the amounts of amphorae awarded in the different events:—

---

[395] iii. 56.
[396] *I.G.* ii. 965.
[397] *I.G.* ii. 2758.
[398] Pollux, iv. 83.
[399] Plato, *Rep.* 398-399; Aristotle, *Pol.* 1341 a.
[400] *I.G.* ii. 965; cp. 966-970.

	Boys (παῖδες).		Youths (ἀγένειοι).	
	1st Prize.	2nd Prize.	1st Prize.	2nd Prize.
Stadion	50	10	60	12
Pentathlon	30	6	40	8
Pale	30	6	40	8
Pygme	30	6	40	8
Pankration	40	8	50	10

The portion of the inscription referring to men's events is wanting, but we know from Panathenaic vases and other sources that the programme for men included the diaulos, the dolichos, the hippios-race,[401] and the race in armour. When the last two events were introduced we cannot say: the diaulos and dolichos certainly existed in the sixth century. The dolichos is frequently represented on early Panathenaic vases, and a fragment of such a vase found at Athens bears the inscription: "I am a diaulos runner." The prizes for men were of course proportionately higher than those for boys and youths. In inscriptions of the second century we find that the pentathlon has disappeared from the programme for boys; but two races have been added in its place, the dolichos and the diaulos. The programme for youths and men remains unchanged. The whole programme can hardly have taken less than two days. Probably the first day comprised the ten or eleven events for boys and youths, the second day the nine events for men. In the fourth century we learn from Plato that the sports opened with the stade-race, which was followed by the diaulos, the hippios, and the dolichos. The last event was the race in armour—a favourite subject of the Athenian vase-painters, and frequently associated on the red-figured vases with the pankration, which immediately preceded it. In the second century it seems probable from the inscriptions that each day began with a long-distance race; the first day with the boys' dolichos, the second day with the men's.

A noticeable feature in this programme is the large proportion of events for boys and youths. All events were open to competitors from all the Greek states; but events for the young naturally appeal chiefly to local competition. Such being the case, we should expect to find Athens well represented in the lists. But the reverse is the case. Out of more than sixty names only seven are Athenians, and of these five are pankratiasts.[402] These figures show how utterly unathletic Athens became after the fifth century in spite of all her competitions. Watching sports never makes an athletic nation; at Athens it produced a crowd of idle critics and spectators. Nearly half the victors known to us come from Asia Minor and the Aegean: not only Colophon and Ephesus, but Tyre and Sidon figure in the lists. On the mainland Corinth, Sicyon, Argos, Boeotia, and Epirus are best represented.

Previous to the erection of the Panathenaic stadium by Lycurgus the athletic competitions took place in the deme of Echelidae, and this site continued to be the scene of the chariot and horse races. The Hippodrome of Athens is stated to have been of the unusual length of eight stades.[403] The Athenians were at all periods passionately fond of horses. The four-horse chariot-race, the pair-horse chariot-race, and the horse-race are represented on the Panathenaic amphorae of the sixth century. The earliest of these vases which we possess, the

---

[401] Plato, *Leg.* 833 A.
[402] Mommsen, p. 83.
[403] *Etym. M.*, ἐν Ἐχελιδῶν.

Burgon vase in the British Museum, was the prize for the pair-horse chariot-race.[404] The apobates race must have existed in the fifth century, for the apobates is represented on the frieze of the Parthenon.

For the fourth century we have only a portion of the equestrian programme, preserved in the inscription already quoted. We have apparently only the last six events, with the number of measures of oil presented for each of them. The inscription runs as follows:—

	1st Prize.	2nd Prize.
Chariot-race for colts (ἵππων ζεύγει πωλικῷ)	40	8
Chariot-race for full-grown horses (ἵππων ζεύγει ἀδηφάγῳ)[405]	140	40
War (πολεμιστηρίοις), horse-race (ἵππῳ κέλητι νικῶντι)	16	4
War (πολεμιστηρίοις), chariot-race (ἵππων ζεύγει νικῶντι)	30	6
Processional chariot-race (ζεύγει πομπικῷ νικῶντι)	4	1
Javelin throwing on horseback (ἀφ' ἵππου ἀκοντίζοντι)	5	1

In the light of later inscriptions it seems probable that the last four events, if not all six, were confined to Athenian competitors. In this case there must have been other events open to all comers. The introduction of local events of a military type was undoubtedly due to the development of Athenian cavalry in the latter part of the fifth century. According to Photius the war-horse was not really a horse used for war, but merely one equipped as for war in competitions. It is just possible that in the second century the race for war-horses had become a purely artificial event and the war-horse had then as little practical value as the Athenian hoplite of that time. But we can hardly suppose that this was the case in the fourth century, when Athens still possessed a real army. Every Athenian of the first two classes was bound to provide a horse for military service, and the races for war-horses must have been introduced in order to encourage cavalry training, just as the hoplite race had been intended for the benefit of the heavy-armed infantry. But the war-horse was not the same type of animal as the highly-trained and expensive race-horse, and the difference is marked in the amount of the prizes. The team of war-horses receives only 30 amphorae, the team of race-horses 140. The same difference exists in the present day between the prizes given at military or hunt steeple-chases, and those given for race-horses. Still smaller are the prizes for the processional chariots. In this event the chariots and horses may possibly have been provided by the State.

We do not know how many events constituted the full programme in the fourth century; an inscription of the second century enumerates twenty-four events, and another, which is incomplete, contained at least as many.[406] It is possible that on these occasions the programme was exceptionally elaborate, owing to the presence of kings and other distinguished visitors at the festival. Certainly the inscriptions prove that at this period the programme varied considerably from time to time. On one occasion, when four sons of King Attalus were present, it appears that there were three if not four chariot-races for their benefit.

---

[404] *B.M.*, B. 130.
[405] ἀδηφάγος, "eating its full," appears to be a fanciful synonym for τέλειος, perhaps with a special reference to the cost of breeding race-horses. To those familiar with the ordinary type of horse existing in Greece to-day, there is a peculiar appropriateness about the word. In the Thesean inscription, *I.G.* ii. 445, λαμπρός has a similar meaning.
[406] *I.G.* ii. 968, 969.

Three of their names appear as victors in the chariot-race; the name of the fourth also occurs, but the inscription is here broken, and the name of the event which he won is lost. Still, making allowance for such circumstances, we can form a fairly accurate idea of the programme as it existed at this time and probably also in the fourth century.

The programme is divided into open events (ἐκ πάντων) and local events (ἐκ τῶν πολιτῶν). The open events are the six events of the Olympic programme. These take place in the hippodrome. The local events take place partly in the hippodrome, partly in the city in the neighbourhood of the Eleusinium, where perhaps the races ended. Some of the events are ceremonial in character, others military. Of the latter some are confined to soldiers. There are three riding races for officers (ἐκ τῶν φυλάρχων), a straight race (ἄκαμπτον) and a diaulos, and a diaulos ἐν ὅπλοις, i.e., in which the riders wear full armour. Similarly there are three races for cavalry (ἐκ τῶν ἱππέων). In all these races the riders rode their war-horses (ἵππῳ πολεμιστῇ). There are twelve events open to all citizens—five held at the Eleusinium, seven in the hippodrome. These include no less than eleven chariot-races, three ceremonial,—the apobates race, and two races in processional chariots,—four races in racing chariots over the straight and the double course, and four races in war-chariots (ἅρματι πολεμιστηρίῳ, συνωρίδι πολεμιστηρίᾳ) by which perhaps we may understand that, as in Homeric days, there were two men in each chariot, the driver and the soldier. There was only one horse-race, a race ἵππῳ πολυδρόμῳ, by which word I am inclined to understand a war-horse, though it may be merely a variant for fully grown.

The "apobates"[407] was a ceremonial race peculiar to Athens and Boeotia, and recalled, according to tradition, the invention of the chariot by Erechtheus. At the founding of the Panathenaea he had himself appeared as charioteer, having with him in his chariot a companion armed with small round shield and triple-crested helmet, as represented in the frieze of the Parthenon. The event undoubtedly preserves the tradition of Homeric warfare when the chieftain was driven to the scene of action and dismounted to fight, remounting again for pursuit or flight. There is some doubt as to the manner of the race. According to one statement[408] the apobates mounted the chariot in full course, by placing a foot on the wheel, and again dismounted, the performance being repeated apparently at fixed intervals.

Figure 34. Votive Relief. Acropolis Museum. Hellenistic period.

---

[407] Mommsen, *op. cit.* p. 89.
[408] Bekker, *Anecd.* 426.

This account finds some confirmation in one of the groups of the Parthenon frieze, which represents the apobates in the very act of mounting a chariot.[409] Dionysius of Halicarnassus[410] makes no mention of the mounting, but states that at the close of the race, apparently the beginning of the last lap, the apobates dismounted, and from this point chariots and apobatai raced together to the finish. The two accounts are not really irreconcilable if we suppose that Dionysius is thinking merely of the finish, the most interesting part of the race. In most of the groups on the north side of the Parthenon the apobates is represented in the act of dismounting, as he is in Figure 34. In those on the south side he is standing in the chariot or by its side.[411] The latter scene represents the moment before the race, the other scenes different moments in the race, and there is no need to assume with Michaelis two different motives for the south and north frieze. In inscriptions the twofold character of the race is brought out by the mention of charioteer and apobates as two separate victors. The charioteer is described as ἡνίοχος ἐγβιβάζων, the charioteer "who lets his companion dismount," a title which suggests the assistance which the charioteer could render to his fellow by a momentary checking of the pace. The course of the race seems to have been from the Cerameicus to the Eleusinium, on the slopes of the Acropolis.

So extensive a programme required at least two days: in one inscription a torch-race is inserted in the middle of the programme, perhaps as marking the close of the first day. The popularity of the Panathenaea in the second century is proved by the number of distinguished competitors. Besides the sons of King Attalus mentioned already, we find Mastanabas, the son of King Mastanassus, King Antiochus, the son of Antiochus Epiphanes, and Ptolemaeus, king of Egypt, who competed as an Athenian citizen of the Ptolemaid tribe. There are numerous victors from Argos, and the lists include the names of several women. In one list alone we find two victories won by women, or perhaps by the same woman from Argos, and a third won by a woman of Alexandria.

Besides these individual competitions, there seems to have been a cavalry competition between tribes, which took place in the hippodrome, though we do not know on what day. This ἀνθιππασία[412] was a sort of sham-fight between two squadrons, each consisting of the cavalry of five tribes under the command of a hipparchos. Xenophon describes the sight with enthusiasm. They pursued one another in turn, charged, passed through each other's lines, wheeled round, and charging down the whole length of the hippodrome came to a sudden halt, front to front. It seems that prizes were given to the tribe which performed best, or perhaps to their officers.

The day after the horse-races was occupied by a series of competitions between companies or tribes, in which the local and religious character of the festival is yet more clearly manifest. First came the Pyrrhic chorus, an event which took place at the lesser Panathenaea as well as the great.[413] Our inscription enumerates three prizes: one for boys, one for youths, one for men. Each prize is an ox of the value of 100 drachmae, which furnished the victors with a victim for sacrifice and provision for a feast. The composition of the Pyrrhic chorus is known to us from a relief on the basis of a statue set up by Atarbus to commemorate the victories gained at the Panathenaea by a cyclic chorus, and a Pyrrhic

---

[409] *B.M. Guide to Parthenon*, p. 109.
[410] vii. 73.
[411] *Op. cit.* pp. 102 ff., 121.
[412] *I.G.* ii. 1291, 5, 1305b; Xen. *Hipparch.* 3, 11.
[413] Lys. 21. 1, 4.

chorus that he had provided in the archonship of Cephisodorus, i.e., either 366 or 323 B.C.[414] On one side is represented the Pyrrhic chorus (Figure 35): it consists of eight youths linked, and armed with helmets and shields, who move in rhythmic dance under the direction of a trainer, robed in a long mantle and holding in his hand a scroll. The whole Pyrrhic chorus of boys, youths, and men must therefore have numbered twenty-four. Whether they competed as a single chorus or as three is uncertain. On the other side of the relief we see a cyclic chorus, also consisting of eight youths, but clothed in long mantles wrapt close about them, and revolving apparently in a circle. Next came two competitions between tribes, for which the prize again is the sacrificial ox, destined perhaps to be led in the procession of the morrow. The first competition is for εὐανδρία, which in the fourth century seems to mean merely "good looks." In the Panathenaic procession certain old men were selected for their beauty to carry the sacred olive branches. Each tribe chose certain representatives, and this competition was apparently intended to decide which tribe should provide these "handsome old men."[415] The nature of the second competition is not stated in the inscription, but as the next line refers to the torch-race, it is probable that this too was a competition for good looks, to decide which tribe should take part in the evening's torch-race. The torch-race at the Panathenaea was an individual competition, in which the winner received a hydria valued at 30 drachmae.

Figure 35. Relief on monument of Atarbus. Acropolis Museum. Fourth century.

Lastly, the regatta which took place on the last day of the festival was also a competition between tribes. According to the inscription two prizes were offered: the winning tribe received 200 drachmae for a feast besides some other object, possibly three oxen, valued at 300 drachmae. The prize for the second place is also broken off in the inscription, but its value was 200 drachmae. Of the details of the regatta we know nothing. Perhaps we may connect with the Panathenaea a relief found at Athens representing torch-race, wrestling, and boat-race (Figure 36). It forms part of an ephebic inscription of Roman times in the archonship of C. Helvidius.[416]

The prizes in the athletic and equestrian events consisted, as we have seen, in certain quantities of oil. This oil, which was obtained from the sacred olive-trees scattered over Attica, belonged to the state, and none might sell or export it except the victors in the games. The olive-trees were under the care of the Areopagus, and were every year inspected by its

---

[414] Beulé, *L'Acropole d'Athènes*, ii. pl. 4; Schreiber, *Atlas*, xx. 8, 9.
[415] Xenoph. *Quaest. Symp.* iv. 17; Athen. p. 565 F.
[416] Ἐφ. Ἀρχ. 1862, Pl. xxix.

officials, and the oil itself was collected by the archon, who handed it over to the treasurers of the festival. In later time this system was abolished and the land was assessed at a certain number of olive-trees, each proprietor being required to supply a certain quota of oil to the state.[417]

Figure 36. Relief on Stele. Athens, National Museum, 3300. Imperial period.

Besides this the victor received as a memento "a richly painted amphora."[418] In view of the care with which these amphorae were preserved it seems unlikely that the victor received more than one such amphora. A large number of them are still in existence. They date from the middle of the sixth to the close of the fourth century. They are painted in black on a red ground or panel. On one side is an athletic scene, typical of the event for which the amphora was given; on the other, the figure of Athene clothed in her aegis, and brandishing her shield and spear. She stands usually between two Doric pillars surmounted by some emblem, a cock, sphinx, siren, panther, or vase, or in later times by the figure of Victory or Triptolemus. Along the left-hand pillar runs an inscription: "One of the prizes from Athens," ΤΟΝΑΘΕΝΕΘΕΝ.Α.ΘΥΟΝ: to which is added on the Burgon amphora[419] the word EMI, "I am." On the early amphorae the letters are parallel, on the later at right angles to the column. To the inscription is sometimes added the name of the archon. The earliest of these dated vases belongs to the archonship of Polyzelus in 367 B.C., the latest to that of Polemon in 312 B.C.[420] Two fragmentary inscriptions suggest that sometimes the name of the Kosmetes, or Agonothetes, was substituted for that of the archon.[421] The dates of the archon do not always coincide with the years in which the great Panathenaea took place; and Michaelis therefore assigns such vases to the lesser Panathenaea. It seems more likely that, as the oil was collected every year by the archons, the inscription merely records the name of the archon who collected the oil. On two vases we also find the name of the vase-painter.[422]

The scene on the reverse usually represents the actual contest. Occasionally the name of the event is added. On some of the sixth-century amphorae, made perhaps before the tradition was absolutely fixed, the painter seems to have allowed himself more licence in his choice of subject. Thus a British Museum amphora represents the proclamation of a victory in the horse-race (Figure 37).

---

[417] 1-1/2 kotylai for each tree. These details are mostly derived from Aristotle, Ἀθ. πολιτ. 60.
[418] Pindar, N. x. 36.
[419] B.M. Vases, B. 130.
[420] B.M. B. 603; American Journal of Archaeology, ii. p. 332, xii. p. 48.
[421] Cecil Smith in B.S.A. iii. 194 ff.
[422] Sikelos, 5th cent., Kittos, 4th cent., B.M. B. 604.

Figure 37. Panathenaic amphora, in British Museum, B. 144. Sixth century.

The victorious youth is mounted on his horse, and in front of him stands a herald in full official robes, from whose lips issue the words: "The horse of Dyneicetus is victorious": ΔΥΝΕΙΚΕΤΥ: ΗΙΠΠΟΣ: ΝΙΚΑΙ. Behind the rider an attendant bears a wreath and a tripod: we often hear of tripods as prizes; perhaps in early days they may have been given as prizes at the Panathenaea. On another amphora in the British Museum (Figure 38) a seated athlothetes binds a fillet of wool on a youthful victor's head. The latest of the signed vases has a more fanciful representation of victory.[423] Two naked youths have just received palm branches from an athlothetes, by whom a herald stands. One of the youths is standing still, the other, who is perhaps a victor in the foot-race, runs off joyfully. Occasionally the reference to the contest is more obscure. For example, on one early Panathenaic vase in the British Museum the battle of the Giants is depicted, on another an acrobatic scene[424] (Figure 39). The Athenians were intensely fond of acrobatic performances, and, as we know from the story of Hippocleides,[425] even high-born Athenians did not disdain to acquire proficiency in them. The scene is certainly in keeping with all that we know of Athenian festivals, where such side-shows must have been common. Are we, however, to suppose that a sacred prize amphora was actually given as a prize for acrobats? or was this a special mark of honour bestowed on some popular acrobat, like the statue erected at a later age at Athens in honour of a professional ball-player? Perhaps the simplest course is to regard the vase as an imitation Panathenaic amphora. It was found at Camirus in Rhodes, and its provenance, its general character, and the absence of the usual inscription render this explanation probable.[426] Imitation Panathenaic amphorae are numerous: many of them bear representations of musical contests for which, in Aristotle's time at least, a different prize was given. There are also numerous small amphorae, the object of which is uncertain. Were they prizes for boys'

---

[423] *Mon. d. I.* X. 48, g. 11.
[424] B. 145; Salzmann, *Nécropole de Camiros*, lvii.
[425] Hdt. vi. 129.
[426] On either side of Athene is a diminutive figure of a man, a most unorthodox addition. The inscription is wanting on most of the smaller vases.

events, or second prizes? These are some of the numerous questions with regard to these interesting vases which still await solution.

Figure 38. Panathenaic amphora, in British Museum, B. 138. Sixth century.

The painted vases come to a sudden close at the end of the fourth century.[427] The name "Panathenaic vase" occurs occasionally at a later date; but appears merely to denote a particular shape of vase. But a representation of a Panathenaic amphora was found a few years ago on the mosaic floor of a house in Delos, belonging to the early part of the second century.[428] The complete absence of any evidence for their existence in the previous century makes it probable that the vase, which represented a chariot-race, was an heirloom which had been won by some ancestor of the builder of the house. The Panathenaic amphora is, however, still represented on Athenian coins, and on a late relief adorning a marble chair which was probably one of the seats reserved for the judges or agonothetai at the Panathenaea[429] (Figure 40). The vase, which holds a branch, stands on a table, on which are also three crowns. Underneath the table is a palm branch, and by the side of it is represented Athene's sacred olive-tree. The appearance of the vase on the relief and on coins suggests that at this period the earthenware vase had been replaced by a metal vase, but this theory still awaits confirmation.

Though the Panathenaic programme contained a considerable number of local events, these were of quite secondary importance in comparison with the open competitions which, if hardly Panhellenic, were certainly Pan-Ionic. It was for these open competitions that the sacred oil and the Panathenaic amphorae were awarded. In the Thesea, on the contrary, most of the competitions were confined to the youth of Attica, and even in those which were open

---

[427] Cecil Smith in *B.S.A.* iii. 183 ff.
[428] *Ib.* Pl. xvi.
[429] Stuart and Revett, *Antiquities of Athens*, iii. 3, p. 20; Schreiber, *Atlas*, xxv. 9.

to foreigners, the extreme rareness of foreign successes sufficiently indicates the local character of the festival.

Figure 39. Panathenaic (?) amphora from Camirus. Bibliothèque Nationale, 243.

Figure 40. Marble chair of judge at Panathenaea. Imperial period.

The Thesea[430] were instituted in the year 476 or 475 B.C. to celebrate the discovery and restoration to Athens of the bones of the national hero Theseus. The popularity of the worship of Theseus at this period is abundantly attested by the red-figured vases, on which the story of Theseus now takes the place of the labours of Heracles. The Thesea were associated with certain primitive agricultural rites, the Pyanepsia and Oschophoria, ceremonies of the harvest and the vintage, in which the legend of Theseus had been somehow incorporated. They were followed immediately by the Epitaphia, a funeral festival in memory of those who had fallen fighting for their state, which had been held occasionally from the earliest times, but did not take its place as a permanent festival till the time of Pericles, or even later.

Our knowledge of the programme of the Thesea is derived from inscriptions of the second century B.C.,[431] with regard to which I need only repeat that late though they are, such was the religious conservatism of the Greeks, that they may be considered as representing the general character of the festival in the fifth century, and that such changes as had been introduced were merely changes in detail. Theseus was the patron of the Athenian ephebos, and the Thesea were essentially the games of the epheboi. The festival was a yearly one, and included a procession, sacrifice, torch-races, athletics, and horse-races. There was also a banquet provided at the public cost for all free citizens.

The programme of sports opened with the usual competitions for heralds and trumpeters, followed by certain military competitions for general smartness and equipment, εὐανδρία and εὐοπλία. These were divided into three or more classes: first, "the picked troops," οἱ ἐπίλεκτοι; next the foreign troops, οἱ ἐν τοῖς ἔθνεσιν; lastly, the cavalry, οἱ ἱππεῖς, as a subdivision of which we find the Tarantini, so called from their equipment. The competition was between tribes, or, in the case of the foreign troops, regiments (τάγματα), the captain of the successful tribe or regiment being mentioned in the inscriptions. It is evident that εὐανδρία is used here in a slightly different sense to that in which it is used in the Panathenaic inscriptions. There, as we have seen, the object of the competition was purely ceremonial, here it is manifestly military. εὐανδρία like many another word varies in meaning with the object to which it is applied. When used of a regiment, it implies good physique, activity, and general smartness. There is a certain pathos in the existence of these elaborate military reviews and competitions at an age when Athens had no more any freedom to defend, and when her military service was of no practical value. It may be that with the loss of the reality she clung the more closely to the empty form and semblance of an army. But it seems to me more probable that these competitions were not the futile invention of her decadence, but were the survival of the great outburst of patriotism and militarism in the fifth century.

Next came torch-races. At the Thesea these seem to have been contests between teams. There are torch-races for boys, epheboi, and men; sometimes also for young men, νεανίσκοι, who come between the epheboi and the men. The teams are sometimes representatives of a particular palaestra or gymnasium—boys from the palaestra of Timeas or Antigenes, youths or men from the Lyceum. The mention of a torch-race of the Tarantini indicates that there were also torch-races on horseback.

The athletic programme contains the seven ordinary competitions—the dolichos, stade-race, diaulos, wrestling, boxing, pankration, and the race in armour—and in addition certain military competitions, hoplomachia, and javelin-throwing. The hoplomachia, which must

---

[430] Mommsen, *op cit.* p. 278 ff.
[431] *I.G.* ii. 444-450.

have been somewhat similar to our fencing or bayonet competitions, was of two sorts: one with the hoplite's round shield and spear, ἐν ἀσπιδίῳ καὶ δόρατι; the other with the oblong target and sword of the light-armed soldier, ἐν θυρεῷ καὶ μαχαίρα. There are no less than five different classes for these events: there were competitions for boys of the first, second, and third age, open competitions for boys (ἐκ πάντων), and competitions for men. The two younger classes of boys were excluded from the long race, but all classes took part in the five following events. The race in armour was confined to men, javelin throwing to epheboi. The hoplomachia was open to three classes of boys, and to the epheboi. The boys' open competitions and the men's were open to foreign competitors, though few appear to have been successful;[432] the other competitions were confined to the youth of Athens.

The equestrian events are similar in character. A chariot race is only mentioned in one inscription, and there the reference is possibly to an apobates race. The rest of the events are horse-races. There is one race apparently with race-horses (λάμπρῳ ἵππῳ), the rest are military races, either for officers or for men, over the single or the double course. Lastly, there is an open competition (ἐκ πάντων), and javelin throwing on horseback. Not a single foreigner occurs among the names of the victors; but it must not be forgotten how extremely fragmentary is our information.

At the Epitaphia which followed the Thesea there were further competitions, torch-races and military displays. We hear in particular of a race in heavy armour, in which the epheboi ran, starting from the Polyandreum in the Cerameicus.

---

[432] Only four foreigners' names appear, Mommsen, *op. cit.* p. 295, n. 1; F. Mie in *Ath. Mitth.* xxxiv. p. 1. Mie distinguishes the term in ἐκ πάντων, which occurs in athletic and equestrian events, and denotes competitions open to all comers, and the term διὰ πάντων, which occurs only in musical competitions, and appears to denote a final competition in which all the competitors in different musical events took part.

Part 2. The Athletic Exercises of the Greeks with an Account of Their Stadia and Gymnasia

Chapter 12

THE STADIUM

The stadium[433] or racecourse of the Greeks was the natural development of that primitive type of race which is described in Homer, and which we may still see at school treats and rustic meetings. The competitors, drawn up in a line, race to some distant point which is the finish, or, turning round this point, race back again to the starting-point. Here we have the germ of the stade or straight race, and of the diaulos, and other turning races, as the Greeks called them (κάμπειοι). The start is marked by a post (νύσσα) or by a line drawn in the sand (γραμμή), and the finish or turning-point (καμπτῆρες) by a similar post or by some natural object, a stone, or tree-stump.

From this primitive course two types of racecourse are derived. Both differ from the modern oval course in that they are long, narrow, and straight, the runners not describing a curve but running straight up and down the track. The first, which we may call the hippodrome type, is that in which the runners race round two posts placed at either end of the course and connected by one or more intermediate posts, or by a low wall called by the Romans the "spina." One or both ends of the course were rounded off for the convenience of spectators, and this circular end was known as the σφενδόνη. This form was long regarded as the regular type of the Greek racecourse; but recent excavations have rendered it probable that though used by the Greeks for horse-races it was not employed by them for the foot-race, at least until Roman times. The true Greek stadium, as we now know, was strictly rectangular, both starting-point and finish being marked by parallel lines of stone slabs (βαλβίς, βατήρ), and even the seats at the end following the same lines.

For such a course any fairly level plain was suitable; but for the convenience of spectators it was natural to select some level stretch surrounded on one or more sides by some rising ground, along the foot of a hill as at Olympia, or in a dip between two hills as at Epidaurus or Athens. All that was required in such cases was to level the ground for the actual track, and to improve the natural standing-ground by an artificial embankment, which might or might not be afterwards provided with seats. Most of the stadia in Greece, says Pausanias, were formed by such an embankment;[434] it was not till a comparatively late period that the seats were built up on masses of masonry and surrounded by walls and colonnades. The

---

[433] Krause, *Gym.* pp. 131 ff.; *J.H.S.* xxiii. pp. 261 ff.
[434] Paus. ii. 27. 5. The stadium of Epidaurus is στάδιον οἷα Ἕλλησι τὰ πολλὰ γῆς χῶμα. Cp. viii. 47. 4, ix. 23. 1, of the stadia of Tegea and Thebes. That at Corinth in contrast is described as λίθου λευκοῦ, ii. 1. 7; cp. Delphi x. 32. 1, and *infra*.

length of the actual track was always a stade or 600 feet; but, as there was no universal standard of measurement, the length of the stadium varied locally with the length of the foot.

The simplest of all Greek stadia was that at Olympia, and it retained its simplicity throughout its history.[435] We have seen that before the middle of the fifth century all the games were held in the plain commanded by the treasury terrace, and that the permanent running track was first constructed about 450 B.C., after the completion of the first eastern colonnade. At this date the ground at the foot of the hill of Cronus was levelled so as to form a parallelogram some 212 metres long by 29 broad, somewhat broader, however, at the centre than at the ends. This parallelogram was enclosed by a stone sill, and within this sill at a distance of about a metre ran an open stone gutter, opening at regular intervals into stone basins. This gutter, fed from the conduit which ran along the foot of the treasury steps, provided competitors and spectators with the water which they must have sorely needed, exposed as they were all day long, without protection, to the parching rays of the summer sun. The running track lay some 10 feet below the level of the Altis, and slightly below the level of the surrounding plain which sloped gradually upwards to the south towards the bank of the Alpheus. The only accommodation for spectators was afforded by the slopes of the hill of Cronus and this open plain, which it has been calculated would have accommodated from 20,000 to 30,000 people. At a later date, possibly after the battle of Chaeronea in 338 B.C., the ends and southern slope were raised by an artificial embankment. This embankment extended to the south some 40 metres from the actual track, and on it some 40,000 or 45,000 spectators could find standing room. The ends of the embankment were straight, there was no curved theatre or σφενδόνη, nor during the whole history of the stadium did any seats exist. Seats, probably of wood, were provided for a few privileged officials, but the spectators stood or reclined on the banks. At the north-west corner of the stadium a postern gate communicated with the Altis by means of a tunnel through the embankment, which in Roman times was roofed with a stone vault. This was the secret entrance reserved for officials and competitors.[436] The spectators found their way into the stadium over the embankments or along the slopes of Mount Cronius.

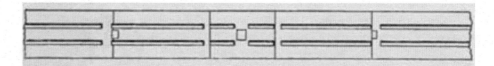

Figure 41. Portion of starting lines at Olympia.

The most interesting discovery at Olympia was that of the actual lines which marked the start and finish of the races (Figure 41). These lines consist of stone sills about 18 inches wide extending nearly the whole breadth of the course. Each sill is divided at intervals of about 4 feet by square sockets obviously intended to hold posts. Between each pair of sockets are two parallel grooves cut in stone about 7 inches apart. Their object was clearly to mark the place for the runners' feet. There are twenty of these sections in the western sill and twenty-one in the eastern sill, one of which is, however, a short one. Each section afforded room for a single runner. The western sill is 11 metres from the end of the stadium, the eastern only 9-1/2. The

---

[435] *Ol.* Text. ii. 63 ff.; Frazer, *Pausanias*, iv. 78.
[436] Paus. vi. 20, 8.

distance between the two sills is 192·27 metres, which gives ·32045 as the length of the Olympic foot. The Olympic foot was said to have been determined by Heracles, who measured out the stadium with his own feet. Hence the stadium at Olympia is slightly longer than other stadia on the mainland.[437]

The discovery of similar stone sills in the gymnasium at Olympia, and subsequently at Delphi and Epidaurus, makes it probable that they were universally employed in Greek stadia, though it is impossible definitely to fix the date at which they replaced the earlier custom of marking the lines in the sand. The reason why the lines are alike at either end is obvious. In the stade-race the finish was at the opposite end from the start, in the diaulos and other races consisting of an even number of stades the runners finished where they started. Hence, as it was clearly desirable that all races should finish at the same point, it was necessary to have starting lines at both ends. At Olympia it seems probable that the finish was at the eastern end of the course. Here were the seats of the Hellanodicae, and opposite them was the seat of the priestess of Demeter Chamyne, the only married woman, possibly the only woman, who was allowed to be a spectator at the Olympia.

Closely resembling the Olympic stadium was that at Epidaurus,[438] where the festival of the Asclepiea was celebrated as early as the time of Pindar. It lies in a shallow trough formed by two low ridges descending into the plain from the hills which encircle the sanctuary of Asclepius. The bottom of the valley has been levelled and its eastern end and part of the sides raised by an embankment. Its western end lies open giving free access to visitors, who here as at all Greek festivals might enter freely without payment. The actual track is 181·30 metres long. Finish and start are alike, marked at either end by a pair of stone pillars between which lies a row of stone slabs with parallel grooves and sockets precisely similar to those found at Olympia, save that there are only eleven divisions and that the parallel grooves are somewhat closer, about four inches apart. The fact that traces of lead were found in some of the sockets confirms the view that iron posts were fastened in them. The pillars possibly belong to an earlier time than the slabs, when start and finish were still marked by lines drawn in the sand between the pillars. The stone slabs seem to have been added in Macedonian times when the stadium was improved, and a record of this reconstruction is preserved in an inscription which states that one Philon of Corinth having undertaken a contract for providing the starting lines (ὕσπλακα) and having failed to fulfil his contract within the specified time was condemned by the Agonothetes and Hellanodicae to pay a fine of 500 drachmae.[439] A still later, possibly Roman arrangement for the start is seen in five half pillars placed at either end in front of the stone sill which they were obviously intended to supersede (Figure 42). On each side these pillars have a shallow groove intended apparently to hold some form of barrier or starting gate, such as we find used in the Roman Circus.[440] A further difficulty is caused by the remains of four small stone platforms which stood immediately in front of the stone sills, two at each end between the outside pillars and the edge of the course. Their use is quite unknown; but the fact that they completely block the grooved starting lines immediately behind them proves that they belonged to some later arrangement. Possibly they are remains

---

[437] The stadium of Pergamum was, however, 210 m. according to Dörpfeld, the standard settled by Philetaerus being higher than that on the mainland. *Ath. Mitth.* xxxiii. 341.
[438] Πρακτικά. 1902, pp. 78-92, Pl. A-D; Frazer, *Pausanius*, v. 576.
[439] Ditt. *Syll.* 2nd Ed., ii. 688.
[440] A drawing from the Codex Ursinianus in the Vatican, published in *Röm. Mitth.* 1890, p. 156, Taf. vii., represents runners standing behind a wooden barrier.

of an intermediate arrangement between the stone sill and the pillars, or possibly they served for starters and judges in later times.

Figure 42. The Stadium of Epidaurus, S.E. corner, showing the starting lines and rectangular end. (From a photograph by Mr. Emery Walker.)

Another interesting feature of the course is that it was marked off on either side at distances of a plethron (100 feet) by small square pillars. These pillars would have been very useful for races in which, as in the girls' race at the Olympic Heraea, only a portion of the course was run. They may also have served for measuring the distance in a javelin or diskos throw. The finish of the course was obviously at the east end, round which alone the rows of seats extend. Between the actual finish and the seats is a further space some 16 metres deep, which may have been used like the curved sphendone of later times for events like wrestling which did not require much room. The three sides of the rectangle were surrounded by a stone border a little less than a yard from the embankment and seats. This contained an open runnel supplied with water by a pipe at the north-east corner of the stadium, and opening out at intervals of 30 yards into oblong basins, like those found at Olympia.

The seating arrangements like the starting lines bear traces of different periods; in contrast to Olympia it seems that from early times a certain number of seats were provided, if we may dignify by the name of seats the five rows of small stones cemented with mud which enclose the eastern end of the course. Beyond the points where these terminate are numerous tiers of seats on either side built of large blocks of dressed stone. The irregularity in the number and dressing of the stones shows that they were not constructed all at the same time. Some of them bear the inscriptions of the dedicators, which seem to date from the Macedonian period to the close of the Roman Republic. But even these seats cease entirely in the western half of the stadium, where as at Olympia spectators can only have stood or reclined on the banks. Staircases give access at intervals to the seats. In the centre of the seats on the northern side is an arched passage communicating with a square enclosure on the other side of the embankment. The enclosure was possibly the place of assembly for officials and competitors who entered the stadium in state through the arch-way. On the southern side of the stadium close to the finish are four stone blocks some 15 feet long and 16 inches high which were probably the seats of the Hellanodicae. Lower down, opposite to the arched passage, there are remains of a curved seat which may also have served for officials. It is rather more than 40 yards from the finish, and if the javelin or diskos were thrown from the finish, would have been a convenient seat for judges in these events. It seems likely too that, at all events after the erection of the later seats, wrestling and other events of the sort took place opposite these seats and not at the east end of the course. Behind this curved seat a broad staircase leads to a platform half-way up the seats. Here, Cavvadias conjectures, stood the table on which the prizes were placed, here the herald proclaimed the victor's name and city, and here the victors received their crowns from the hands of the Hellanodicae. From this point too we may suppose, when the games for the day were finished, the Hellanodicae followed by the victors started in a triumphal procession, and passing through the official entrance on the north side, made their way to the temple of Asclepius to render thanks and pay their vows to the patron of the festival.

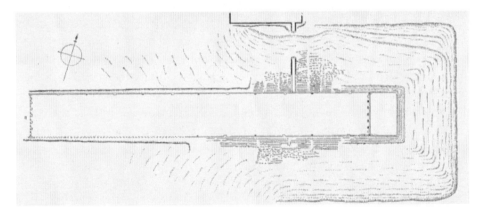

Figure 43. Stadium of Epidaurus.

A further stage in the development of the stadium is seen in the stadium of Delphi, the best preserved and the most romantic in its situation of all Greek stadia. It lies on a rocky shelf to the north-west of the sacred precinct at the foot of the cliffs of Parnassus, which rise sheer above it to a height of 800 feet, and looking down over the valley of the Pleistus and the Crisaean plain. As at Olympia, there seems to have been no permanent stadium till the second half of the fifth century.[441] In Pindar's time the athletic competitions took place in the plain below, where, for want of sufficient room at Delphi itself, the hippodrome must have continued to exist.[442] It seems probable that the change took place between the years 448 and 421 B.C. when the control of the festival was in the hands of the Phocians. To construct a stadium on the steep slope of the mountain it was necessary to build a massive retaining wall, and the date of this wall is approximately fixed by a fifth-century inscription built into it forbidding the introduction of wine into the dromos.[443]

---

[441] *B.C.H.*, 1899, pp. 601-615.
[442] Pindar, *Pyth.* viii. 19-20, x. 15, xi. 21.
[443] *B.C.H. l.c.* p. 611, and *supra*, p. 126.

Figure 44. Stadium of Delphi.

The stadium as we see it to-day is mainly the work of Herodes Atticus, who is said by Pausanias to have reseated it with marble, as he certainly did at Athens.[444] The French excavations, however, show that Pausanias' statement can hardly be accurate. The seats are not of marble but of local stone, and are apparently quite complete. There is no sign of any marble facing having existed, and not a trace of marble has been found in the stadium. If marble was used at all, it can only have been for special parts of the seats. Yet even without marble the appearance of the stadium is sufficiently imposing. The actual track is bounded at either end by a stone sill similar to those found at Olympia and Epidaurus. The stone sill is composed of 17 or 18 sections, and the parallel grooves are about 3-1/2 in. apart. The length of the track is 177·5 metres, and its breadth varies from 25-1/2 metres at the ends to 28-1/2 metres in the centre. The object of this curve, which we find at Athens and in a much less marked degree elsewhere, was to give a better view of the whole course to the spectators. The west end terminates in a shallow curved sphendone 9-1/2 metres deep, and the east end is similarly curved, though the curve is interrupted at the south by the main entrance to the stadium from the precinct below. In this eastern end there stand four pillars of poor and late workmanship which seem to have formed a triumphal entrance for officials and competitors. The two sides and the western sphendone are surrounded by rows of stone seats raised on a stone basement 5 feet high. There are six rows of seats on the south and west, twelve on the north, affording places for some 7000 spectators, though many more could find room on the slopes above the stadium to the north. Flights of steps at the east end gave access to two corridors which ran right round the stadium, above and below the tiers of seats. The latter were further divided by flights of steps placed at regular intervals. There were thirteen of these on either side, dividing the stadium into twelve equal lengths of half a plethron, and these divisions may have served like the similar divisions at Epidaurus for purposes of measurement. Another detail which recalls the stadium of Epidaurus is a seat of honour occupying the centre of the first two rows of seats on the north side.

Such was the Pythian stadium as restored by Herodes Atticus. Before his time it must have been something much simpler. The curved end and the stone seats did not exist. Instead, the northern slope was roughly levelled and an embankment raised above the southern retaining wall, so that the track seemed to lie in a trough, from which fact it derived its popular name the Lakkoma or "hollow." In the intervals between the festivals it can have been used but little; it was overgrown with weeds, perhaps it was used for pasturage. Hence, as the time for the festival approached, the stadium had to be set in order, and the work was let out on contract. We have various records of these contracts. In 338 B.C. one Helixius

---

[444] Pausanias, x. 32, 1.

obtained the contract for work on the Pythian stadium. In the accounts of the Archonship of Dion (258 B.C.) a number of items of work are enumerated in connexion with the gymnasium, stadium, and hippodrome, which throw invaluable light on the details of these institutions.[445]

Figure 45. The starting lines at Delphi. (From a photograph by Mr. Emery Walker.)

First the course itself and the surrounding embankments (τὰ στέφοντα) were thoroughly cleared of weeds and rubbish. This clearing (ἐκκάθαρσις) cost 15 staters. Then the track and the jumping-places (τὰ ἅλματα) were dug up and rolled (σκάψις καὶ ὁμάλιξις) at a further cost of 110 staters, and finally it was covered with 600 medimnoi of white sand, which, at 1-2/3 obols per medimnos, amounted to 83 staters 4 obols. Next a barrier (φράξις) was erected round the course at a cost of 5 staters, and a scaffolding of seats costing 29 staters. The small amount spent on the last item proves that the erection was merely a temporary structure, probably of wood, intended not for the whole body of spectators, but merely for a few distinguished persons. 36 staters were expended on the starting lines and turning posts (καμπτῆρες), and 8 staters on the arrangements for the pentathlon, presumably those for throwing the diskos and the javelin. Further, 77-1/2 staters were spent—if the restoration of the inscription is correct—on arrangements for the boxers, a considerable sum in proportion to other items, which suggests that some sort of raised platform may have been erected to enable as many as possible to view this extremely popular event. A stage, too, was erected for musical competitions, and a triumphal arch, or ψάλις, probably on the site occupied afterwards by the four pillars described above.

The temporary character of these arrangements is indicated sufficiently by their cost. The stater was equal to two Aeginetic drachmae of 96 grains, and equivalent approximately to two shillings of our money, though its purchasing power was considerably greater. In the time of Pericles an Attic drachma of 67 grains was a day's wage for an artisan; in the third century its purchasing power was probably less. Allowing half a drachma as the wage for a labourer, we find that the clearing of the course and embankments took 60 men a day's work.

---

[445] B.C.H., 1899, pp. 564, 613.

Figure 46. The Stadium of Delphi.

The recent restoration of the Panathenaic stadium[446] for the revived Olympic games has enabled us to realize something of the splendour which it owed to its reconstruction by Herodes Atticus in the second century of our era. Previous to the fourth century B.C., the Panathenaic games seem to have been held at some spot in the deme of Echelidae which lay between the Peiraeus and Athens. No traces of this stadium have yet been found, and it is probable that the arrangements were as simple as those existing in early time at Olympia. We gather from Xenophon that there was no artificial barrier to keep spectators off the course; in his treatise on the duty of a cavalry officer he recommends that horsemen should be placed in front of the crowds at reviews and races to keep them in order, but at sufficient intervals not to interfere with the spectators' view.[447] The first permanent stadium was constructed by Lycurgus in the second half of the fourth century, in a deep ravine on the left bank of the Ilissus. The land was the property of a patriotic citizen Demias, who as a mark of respect to Lycurgus presented it to the state. Other citizens followed his example: one Eudemus, who lent a thousand yoke of oxen for the work, was rewarded by a public vote of thanks. The work consisted in closing up the southern end of the ravine by an embankment and levelling the ground for the course, which was further separated from the spectators by a low wall, behind which ran a conduit for carrying off the rain-water. The finish and start were probably marked out as at Olympia by lines of stone slabs, but there were no seats for spectators except for officials and distinguished visitors. We hear of repairs made in the stadium at various times, but it probably maintained substantially its original form till the time of Herodes Atticus. Most of the remains discovered belong to his reconstruction.

The arena which was enclosed by a marble parapet measured something over 205 metres long by 33 metres broad. It ended in a semicircular sphendone which was separated from the actual running track by the stone starting line of which remains have been found. As,

---

[446] Frazer, *Pausanias*, ii. 205; Politis in *The Olympic Games* in 1896, pp. 31 ff.
[447] *Hipparch.* ch. 3.

however, no trace has been discovered of the corresponding line at the other end, it is impossible to determine definitely the length of the course. It must have been approximately 177 metres. At either end of the starting line stood a stone pillar, and between these pillars stood four curious double-headed herms. Two of these have been found almost intact, and portions of the other two have also been found.[448] They consist of square pillars about 6 feet high, on which stand back to back two heads, one bearded, the other beardless, sometimes said to represent a youthful Apollo and a bearded Dionysus. The heads, which are of rude and unfinished workmanship, are probably second-century copies of early originals. The pillars are divided to the height of 3 feet by a narrow slit through which, it has been suggested, may have passed the rope used in starting the races. The position of these herms along the starting line reminds one, however, of the somewhat similar rows of pillars at Epidaurus and Priene. The pillars at Epidaurus, it will be remembered, had likewise grooves on either side, though these did not as at Athens extend right through the pillars. In view of this resemblance it seems probable that both grooves and slits served for fixing either a sort of starting gate or a barrier used to enclose the course when dangerous exhibitions, such as fights of wild beasts, took place. Such shows it is known were exhibited in the stadium. The Emperor Hadrian on one occasion presented 1000 wild animals for this purpose. It was probably to secure the safety of the spectators on such occasions that the seats surrounding the whole arena were raised on a marble basement nearly 6 feet high. Above this rose 46 rows of marble seats, capable of seating at least 50,000 spectators. At the point where the curve of the sphendone began on the northern side a vaulted passage led underneath the seats and through the hill into the valley beyond. This passage may have served originally like the secret entrance at Olympia for the entrance of officials and competitors. In its later and more elaborate form it was probably intended by Herodes for the introduction of wild beasts, like the similar vaults in Roman amphitheatres. The principal entrance was at the other end of the stadium, near the Ilissus, where, it seems, elaborate Propylaea were erected, while the whole effect was greatly enhanced by a marble Doric colonnade which crowned the hills above the upper seats of the sphendone.

The stadium at Priene[449] presents similar difficulties to those at Epidaurus and Athens. It appears to have been constructed at the same time as the lower gymnasium in the second century B.C., but to have been considerably modified in later times. It is built inside the south wall of the town, and is supported along the south side by a massive retaining wall. The ends are square, and the seats are placed along the north side only. There are twelve rows of marble seats, the lowest of which rest on a marble basement 3-1/2 feet high. The marble seats are only found in the centre, extending for a distance of about a third of the course. Beyond them at either end the spectators must have sat on wooden seats or on the embankment. In the absence of any sphendone, the ceremonial part of the games, the proclamation of the victors, and presenting of prizes must have taken place in the centre of the course. Above the seats is a terrace, behind which is a Doric colonnade extending the whole length of the stadium. The starting lines at the west end have been discovered; but excavations at the east end have been fruitless. The western starting line shows traces of an earlier and of a later arrangement. The earlier arrangement is represented by eight square slabs in which are cut sockets for posts of wood or metal, such as are found at Olympia and elsewhere, but there is no sign of the slabs

---

[448] One may be seen in the museum at Athens, another has been re-erected in the stadium.
[449] Wiegand u. Schrader, *Priene*, pp. 258 ff.

marked with parallel grooves between the pillars. Just behind this line of slabs is a row of ten pillar bases standing on a stone sill, in which is cut a runnel extending the whole length of the sill with two short offshoots in the centre. This runnel, which clearly served to carry off some of the water which naturally drained down into the stadium, must have been covered by stone slabs between the pillars. Only small fragments of the pillars have been found; but these seem to indicate that there were longitudinal grooves down the sides which may have served for some form of barrier or starting gate. The total length of the stadium is 191 metres; perhaps the actual course was as at Delphi about 177 metres.

It is unnecessary to describe in detail the remains of the numerous other stadia which have been found in Greek lands; but a few peculiarities which they present may be noted as illustrating the development of the stadium and the way in which the Greeks adapted themselves to the character of the ground. At Messene advantage was taken as elsewhere of a shallow valley.[450] The stadium consists of two parts—an old embanked part, forming the actual racecourse, and an unusually elaborate sphendone. In the former the sides of the valley were carefully banked up into terraces, but no stone seats were provided and no attempt was made to render the two sides parallel. The sphendone was considerably narrower than the actual course and of unusual depth, the sides of the semicircle being continued for some distance in straight parallel lines. It is seated with stone, and the height above is enclosed in an elaborate square court surrounded on three sides by colonnades, which are continued along both sides of the course. A similar narrowing of the entrance of the sphendone occurs at Ephesus,[451] where the curve of the sphendone is produced on either side so as to project into the course. This elaboration of the sphendone is clearly connected with its use for musical and dramatic performances, and marks the declining importance of athletic competitions. At Aezani one end of the stadium was rounded; the other was straight, and formed the stage of an elaborate stone theatre. Finally, the last stage in the evolution of the stadium is reached at Aphrodisias in Caria.[452] Here the course is symmetrical with a sphendone at either end, and the whole is surrounded by a colonnade and wall, through which fifteen openings along one side afford entrance to the spectators' seats, and various underground passages give access through the side of the hill to the arena. It is only in its proportions, its narrowness as compared with its length, that such a stadium differs from the Roman amphitheatre. Indeed, we learn that the large stadium at Laodicea was actually converted into an amphitheatre.[453]

In all the stadia described the essential part is the rectangular course, bounded at either end by a straight line. Not one of the stadia which have been excavated has revealed any trace of the three pillars or metae forming a line down the middle of the course which were the characteristic features of the Greek hippodrome and Roman circus, and which still figure in the descriptions and plans which our handbooks and dictionaries give of the Greek stadium. The only authority for this arrangement is the note of a scholiast on the well-known description of the Pythian games in the *Electra* of Sophocles.[454] He states that there were in the course three stones or square pillars, bearing on one side the respective inscriptions ἀρίστευε, σπεῦδε, κάμψον—"Be stout," "Make speed," "Turn." Now it is by no means

---

[450] Schreiber, *Atlas*, xxvi. 1; Blouet, *Expéd. de Morée*, ii. Pl. xxxix. The stadium is stated to belong to the third century B.C.
[451] Krause, *Gym.* Pl. iv. 5.
[452] *Ionian Antiquities of the Dilettanti*, iii. Pl. xxi.
[453] *Ib.* ii. Pl. lxxxiv. Durm, *Baukunst der Griechen*, gives in his "Register" numerous references to accounts by early travellers of stadia at Aezani, Aphrodisias, Ephesus, Laodicea, Messene, Perga, Pessinus.
[454] *Electra*, 680 ff.

certain that the worthy scholiast is referring to the foot-race at all; the note on the pillars would be far more appropriate in connexion with the horse-race, in which, as every reader will recollect, the pillar is the cause of the supposed catastrophe to Orestes; moreover, practically the same note is repeated in connexion with the chariot-race by another scholiast, who implies that there were several of these square pillars along the course. But even if the passage is intended to refer to the stadium, it does not follow that the posts are in the centre of the course, and the description would apply equally well to the square pillars which are placed along both sides of the course at Epidaurus, if we suppose them to be inscribed. When in 1870 the first of the double herms at Athens was found, it was at once concluded to be one of these three pillars, but the subsequent discovery of portions of the other three herms almost *in situ* along the starting line proves this view to be untenable. At the same time, though we must abandon the idea of any line of metae for the Greek stadium, we shall find that in the long race the runners did probably race round two pillars placed in the centre of the starting lines at either end, but these pillars must have been of metal or wood.

The examples described above enable us to trace with some certainty the history of the Greek stadium. In its simplest form it is a long parallelogram, marked by two lines at either end. The spectators stand along the course on raised banks, natural or artificial. Stone seats occur first perhaps in the fifth century at Epidaurus. In the second half of the third century more elaborate stone seats appear near the centre of the course, which seems to have been usually the place of honour. The curved sphendone with its rows of seats does not appear till the Hellenistic period. Finally, when both ends are curved the stadium approaches the type of the Roman circus, and the resemblance is increased by the addition of colonnades either round the sphendone or round the whole course. The development of the actual racecourse is more rapid: the needs of competitors came before the needs of spectators. The starting lines and finish seem to have been first marked by pillars temporary or permanent on either side. These pillars exist at Epidaurus, and survive at a much later period in the Panathenaic stadium. Pillars are commonly represented in athletic scenes on fifth-century vases.[455] Often they are merely the shorthand symbol used by the vase-painter to denote the buildings of the gymnasium or palaestra. In foot-races and horse-races it is reasonable to suppose that they represent the pillars at the start or finish of the race. They occur chiefly on the red-figured vases, and the usual type is that of a fluted pillar often standing on a square basis. The starting lines with double grooves appear certainly in Macedonian times, though their introduction may well date back to the laying out of the stadia at Olympia and Delphi in the fifth century. The importance attached to the starting lines is proved by their frequent mention in inscriptions. Finally, in Roman times these starting lines were superseded by a row of pillars, between which was fixed some sort of barrier. The details and use of all these arrangements will be more conveniently discussed in connexion with the actual foot-race.

The stadium was used for other events besides the foot-race; but where these took place and what arrangements were made for them we cannot say. The Delphic inscription quoted above proves that special arrangements were made for the jump, for throwing the diskos or javelin, and for boxing. It is reasonable to suppose that the starting lines were utilized for the diskos and the javelin, which must certainly have been thrown along the length of the course. It is probable that at a later period wrestling and boxing matches took place in the sphendone.

---

[455] On earlier black-figured vases the finish is represented by tripods or vases set as prizes (Gerh. *A. V.* 257), or by the seats of the judges as on the Amphiaraus vase (Figure 3).

But in many earlier stadia there was hardly sufficient room at the end for these events, which would have been too far removed from the bulk of the spectators. At Olympia we have seen reason for thinking that they took place not in the stadium but in the Altis. Otherwise it seems likely that they were held in the centre of the stadium, where seats of honour seem often to have been erected. But all this is mere conjecture.

Chapter 13

THE FOOT-RACE

The length of the various foot-races was determined for the Greeks by the length of the stadium. The stade-race, as its name implies, was a single length, approximately 200 yards. The diaulos was twice the length of the stadium, or 400 yards. The length of the dolichos or long race is variously stated as 7, 12, 20, or 24 stades, from seven furlongs to nearly three miles.[456] The divergence of these statements is probably due to the fact that the distances varied at different festivals, and at different periods, as they do at the present day. For Olympia the evidence is slightly in favour of a 24 stades race. These three races seem to have been universal. At the Isthmia, Nemea, and Panathenaea there was also a double diaulos of four stades called the horse diaulos (ἵππιος or ἐφίππιος) from the fact that the length of the course in the hippodrome was two stades, or double that of the stadium.[457] There were different races for different ages, and it is possible that the boys' races were shorter than those for men. Plato, in sketching his ideal scheme of physical education, lays down that boys are to run half the length of the men's course, and the "beardless" two-thirds of the course.[458] We do not know whether his scheme had any foundation in fact, but it is certain that in the girls' races at Olympia the course was one-sixth shorter than the usual course.[459] Besides these purely athletic events, there were races in armour, introduced for military purposes towards the close of the sixth century, and various ceremonial races such as the torch-race, survivals of ancient religious rites.

It will be convenient here to say a few words as to the ages of competitors. What is true of the foot-race holds good, of course, of all other competitions.

The classification of competitors according to age varied at different festivals. At Olympia and Delphi there were only two classes, men and boys. An inscription containing regulations for the Augustalia at Neapolis lays down that competitors in boys' events must be over seventeen and under twenty years of age.[460] As the Augustalia were modelled closely on the Olympia, it seems probable that these were the Olympic limits of age. But it is reasonable to suppose that a certain latitude was allowed, and that the Hellanodicae exercised considerable discretion in their judgment, taking into account not merely a competitor's

---

[456] Krause, *Gym.* p. 348.
[457] Bacchylides, ix. τετραέλικτον ἐπεὶ κάμψεν δρόμον; Eurip. *Electra*, 825; Pausanias, vi. 16, 4; Ditt. *Syll.* 2nd Ed., 676.
[458] *Leg.* viii. 833, C, D.
[459] Pausanias, v. 16, 2.
[460] *Ol. Inschr.* 56.

reputed age, but also his size and strength. Thus we are told that Agesilaus induced the officials to admit as a competitor in the boys' competitions a young Athenian whom they would otherwise have disqualified because he was bigger than the other boys. On the other hand, one Nicasylus of Rhodes, who was eighteen years of age, was actually disqualified, and accordingly entered for and won the men's competition.[461] The possibility of a boy winning among men proves that the upper limit of age was a high one. It is mentioned as a remarkable record that a youth of twenty should be victorious in the open events at all the four Panhellenic festivals.[462] In view of these facts, we may regard with some suspicion the story told by Pausanias that one Damiscus of Messene won the boys' foot-race at the tender age of twelve![463]

At the Nemea and Isthmia we find a threefold division into boys, youths (ἀγένειοι), and men. The ages denoted by these terms varied according to the regulations of different festivals. In later inscriptions we find the expressions "Pythian boys," "Isthmian boys" used to denote boys within the limits of age prescribed at these festivals.[464] Approximately it seems likely that the boys were those between the ages of twelve and sixteen, the beardless those between sixteen and twenty.[465] Elsewhere, especially in local competitions, we have a far more elaborate classification. At the Erotidia in Boeotia the boys were divided into "the younger" and "the older."[466] In Chios we find five classes—boys, younger epheboi, middle epheboi, older epheboi, men.[467] At the Athenian Thesea there are competitions for boys of the first, second, and third ages, confined to Athenians, and an open competition for boys of any age.[468] Similarly, in the girls' foot-races at the Olympic Heraea the girls are divided into three ages.[469]

There is a general but mistaken idea that the stade-race was honoured above all other events among the Greeks.[470] There is no evidence for assigning pre-eminence to the foot-race over other events, or to the stade-race over other foot-races. It is true that Xenophanes speaks of speed of foot as honoured more than strength. The fact that out of the eight athletic events for men existing at Olympia in his day, four were foot-races, while the foot-race also formed part of the pentathlon, is sufficient explanation of such a statement. But an examination of the Epinikia of Pindar and Bacchylides, or the list of athletic statues at Olympia, is sufficient to prove that Xenophanes' words must not be pressed. Out of 25 athletic odes of Pindar, 6 are in honour of victories in the foot-race, including one for a double victory in the pentathlon and stade-race, 19 for other events. In Bacchylides three out of nine odes are for victories in the foot-race. At Olympia 45 statues were erected for victories in the four foot-races, 59 for victories in boxing, 39 for wrestling, 20 for the pankration.[471] These figures are conclusive for Olympia and the Peloponnese. The only evidence to the contrary comes from Athens. At the Panathenaea the winner of the stade-race received 50 amphorae of oil, the pankratiast 40, and

---

[461] Pausanias, vi. 14, 1.
[462] *Ib*. 15, 1.
[463] *Ib*. 2, 10.
[464] Mie, *Quaestiones Agonisticae*, p. 48; Ditt. *Syll*. 2nd. Ed., 677, 678.
[465] Roberts and Gardner, *Greek Epigraphy*, ii. p. 166.
[466] *C.I.G*. 1590.
[467] Ditt. *Syll*. 2nd Ed., 524.
[468] *I.G*. ii. 444.
[469] Pausanias, v. 16, 2.
[470] In *J.H.S*. xxiii. p. 266 I have myself made the mistake.
[471] These figures are drawn up from the tables given in Hyde's *De Olympionicarum Statuis*.

the other winners only 30.[472] The inscription which records these facts refers only to competitions for boys and youths, but probably the same proportion was observed in those for men. The popularity of the foot-race at Athens is shown by the fact that at the Panathenaea in the second century there were no less than nine foot-races, not counting that in the pentathlon. Of the Panathenaic vases which we possess many more belong to the foot-race than to any other event. Most of the victories gained by the Athenians at Olympia were in the short-distance races, the only other event in which they show excellence being the pankration. These facts are in entire accordance with all that we know of the Athenian character, which combined with a certain reckless daring and love of adventure a constitutional dislike of prolonged exertion.[473] But the home of Greek athletics was not Athens but the Peloponnese, and here at least the stade-race enjoyed no pre-eminence. The selection of the winner of this race as eponymos for the Olympiad has been explained already as due to the fact that this race came first in the list; it may also be due in part to the literary supremacy of Athens.

From a very early time the Greeks discarded the use of the loin-cloth in racing, and ran absolutely naked. For this, as for all athletic exercises, the body was carefully oiled. Bacchylides describes how Aglaus of Athens in the double diaulos, as at the finish of the race he rushed on into the cheering crowds, bespattered with oil the garments of the spectators.[474] Competitors ran barefooted and bareheaded. The soft leather boots (ἐνδρομίδες) which Pollux says that they wore, were worn only by couriers and messengers, not by athletes.[475] We see no trace of them on the vases.

Figure 47. R.-f. Amphora. Louvre.

---

[472] *I.G.* ii. 965. *Vide supra*, p. 234.
[473] Mr. R. E. Macnaghten, in a very suggestive paper in the *Classical Review*, xxi. p. 13, attributes to the Athenians the degradation in meaning of all words denoting toil, among which he cites ἄθλιος.
[474] Bacchylides, ix.
[475] Krause, *Gym.* p. 362.

We have seen that the start (ἄφεσις) of the running track was marked by two parallel grooves a few inches apart. Though the evidence of the excavations does not allow us accurately to determine the date of the stone sills in which these lines are cut, the frequent allusions in writers of the fifth century to the starting line (γράμμη) proves beyond all doubt that this was the method of starting in the fifth century and earlier. Here, as an old song tells us, the herald summoned the competitors to "take their stand foot to foot," just as we see them represented on vases.[476] The signal to start was given by the herald calling "Go" (ἄπιτε),[477] or perhaps as in the chariot-race, by a blast of the trumpet.[478] Then, as to-day, runners would try to get a good start, and poach a yard or two. But Greek methods of discipline were more drastic than our own. "Those who start too soon are beaten," says Adeimantus to Themistocles in the historic council before Salamis.[479]

But what was the use of the double line? Here again the parallel grooves can have been no innovation introduced with the stone sills; they must surely represent the practice of an earlier time. Two lines were cut in stone, because two lines had been marked in the sand previously. They certainly cannot have been intended to give a firm foothold for the runners' feet, nor is there a particle of evidence for the natural and attractive suggestion that the Greek started off his hands like the modern sprinter, and that the grooves afforded a grip for his fingers.[480] The lines seem only to have been intended to mark the position for both feet. Why this was done is doubtful. The position implied is somewhat cramped for a starter. Perhaps the object was to render it more difficult to poach at the start. Be this as it may, it is certain that the Greek runner did start with his feet close together in the position required by the lines.[481] The position is depicted on several vases; but the best example of it is the charming bronze statuette of a hoplitodromos from Tübingen (Figure 12).[482] He stands with his right foot a few inches behind the left, the toes of the right nearly level with the left instep. Both knees are slightly bent, the body is leaning forward, and the right arm is advanced to preserve the balance. The whole attitude is that of a man on the alert, ready to start at any moment. The shield on the left arm has been broken away. On a red-figured amphora in the Louvre (Figure 47)[483] a hoplitodromos is represented in an almost identical position. Opposite stands a draped and wreathed official with his right arm extended and his hand turned somewhat upwards and backwards. It is a singularly appropriate gesture, which we often meet with in athletic scenes. We seem almost to hear him say to the runners, "Steady on the mark." Another drawing shows us an unarmed runner standing beside a pillar ready to start, while a youthful official holds over him a forked rod with which to correct him if he leaves the mark too soon (Figure 48). The position of the feet is the same, but the body is inclined more forwards, and having no shield to inconvenience him he holds both arms to the front. A more

---

[476] Pomtow, *Poetae Lyrici Graeci Minores*, ii. p. 154 βαλβῖδι ποδῶν θέντες πόδα παρ πόδα. Julian, 318.
[477] Aristophanes, *Eq.* 1161.
[478] Sophocles, *El.* 711.
[479] Hdt. viii. 59.
[480] The only vase which could possibly represent this position is a r.-f. skyphos reproduced in *J.H.S.* xxiii. p. 283. It represents a hoplitodromos leaning forward, his right hand resting on the ground. But it will be remarked that his feet are in the usual position, level with the pillar where the starting lines should be. Opposite stands an official in the attitude shown in Figure 47, and I am now inclined to think that the runner in practising a start has overbalanced himself, and that the official is telling him to get back to his mark.
[481] *J.H.S.* xxiii. pp. 269 ff.
[482] *Jahrb.* 1886, Pl. ix. Cp. Dr. Hauser in *Jahrb.* 1887 and 1895; M. A. de Ridder in *B.C.H.*, 1897; criticisms on the same in *J.H.S. l.c.*
[483] *Bull. Nap. nouv. sér.* vi. 7; *J.H.S. l.c.* p. 270, Figure 1.

upright position is shown in Figure 49, which is taken from Hartwig's *Meisterschalen*. The attitude illustrated in these examples is in its essence the same as that adopted by many runners in the present day, the chief difference being that the modern runner starts with his feet somewhat wider apart, and his position is therefore less cramped.

Figure 48. R.-f. kylix. Formerly at Naples.

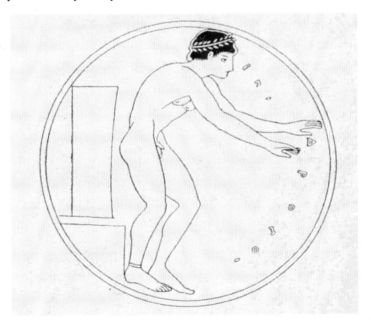

Figure 49. R.-f. kylix. Chiusi.

Such was the position adopted at the start in the fifth century, and it continued as long as and wherever the double-grooved starting lines continued to be used. It seems, however, that sometimes the runners were stationed behind a barrier formed by a rope (ὕσπληξ) or by a wooden bar, and that the signal for the start was given by dropping this rope or bar.[484] Ropes, as we know, were used in the chariot-race, a separate rope being stretched in front of each

---

[484] The passages relating to the ὕσπληξ are collected by me in *J.H.S.* xxiii. p. 263. To these may be added, Bekker, *Anecd.* 220, 31 βαλβίς. Ξύλα δύο τῶν δρομέων ἀφ' ὧν σχοινίον τί διατέταται, ὃ καλεῖται βαλβίς, ἵνα ἐνεῦθεν ἐκδράμωσιν οἱ ἀγωνιζόμενοι; Fränckel, *Antiq. Pergam.* viii. 1, p. 8, 10, epigram on the victory of Attalus in the chariot-race; Schol. to Aristoph. *Eq.* 1159 βαλβίς· ἡ ὑπὸ τὴν ὕσπληγα γενομένη γράμμη.

chariot. Aristophanes uses the phrase "from a single rope" (ὥσπερ ἀπὸ μιᾶς ὑσπλάγιδος) to denote a simultaneous movement "of one accord."[485] The vase paintings do not furnish the faintest indication of the use of a rope in the foot-race. The only possible trace of its use revealed by excavation is the line of herms at Athens, which cannot be earlier than imperial times. The posts, which were placed in the square sockets along the starting line, cannot have been used to support a rope; for such a rope is incompatible with the use of the starting lines. There is no evidence of its use in the foot-race till the third century B.C., when we find reference to the ὕσπληγες in inscriptions relating to the stadia at Epidaurus and Athens,[486] and an undoubted allusion to it in the poet Lycophron, who speaks of a "winged runner bursting through the balbis rope."[487] Even then we may doubt whether its use was ever universal. With a rope a false start is impossible; and yet allusions to runners poaching at the start occur in literature from Herodotus to Plutarch, or even later.[488] Still, it is certain that a rope was sometimes used, that it was raised at some height above the ground and stretched tight in front of the runners, and that the signal to start was given by the dropping of the rope. A late epigram tells us that this was accompanied by an audible sound.[489] In default of definite evidence, it may be suggested that it was worked by a spring, perhaps somewhat after the manner of the modern starting-gate. Some support for this suggestion is afforded by the use of the word ὕσπληξ to denote a spring hunting-trap.

Allusion is also made to a bar of wood placed in front of the runners, the removal of which gave the signal to start.[490] Such a barrier can hardly have been introduced earlier than the time of the Empire, and was probably borrowed from the Roman circus. As stated in the last chapter, it is possible that the grooves in the pillars at Athens and Epidaurus served to hold some solid barrier of this sort.

In the stade-race, the runners were divided into heats (τάξεις), which were drawn by putting into a helmet lots marked with the different letters of the alphabet.[491] If, as seems probable at Olympia, each heat consisted of four, there would be four lots marked A, four B, and so on. It appears that there was no second draw, but that all the winners of heats ran together in the final, so that the final winner had won twice.[492] The starting lines at Olympia provided room for twenty runners at once. In short races the field is often a large one, and we hear of no less than seven Crotoniats winning their heats in a single Olympiad.[493] There is no reason for supposing that the heats were always limited to four. The number would naturally be determined by the number of entries and the length of the starting lines. On the Panathenaic vases representing this race we find usually four, but sometimes two, three, or five runners taking part, though it is unsafe to draw conclusions from this evidence, the number of figures being largely determined in a drawing by considerations of space.[494] Of one thing we may feel sure in spite of assertions to the contrary in modern text-books: the

---

[485] *Lysist.* 1000.
[486] Ditt. *Syll.* 2nd Ed., 688; Ἐφ. Ἀρχ., 1884, 169.
[487] Lycophron 13 βαλβῖδα μηρίνθου σχάσας.
[488] *J.H.S. l.c.* p. 264.
[489] *Anth. Pal.* ix. 557.
[490] Schol. to Aristoph. *Eq.* 1159 βαλβίς δὲ καλεῖται τὸ ἐν τῇ ἀρχῇ τοῦ δρόμου κείμενον ἐγκαρσίως ξύλον, ὃ καὶ ἀφετήριον καλεῖται, ὅπερ μετὰ τὸ ἑτοιμασθῆναι τοὺς δρομέας εἰς τὸ δραμεῖν ἀφαιρούμενοι ἀφίεσαν τρέχειν.
[491] This is the method for drawing the ties for wrestling and boxing described by Lucian, *Hermotim*, 40.
[492] Pausanias, vi. 13, 2. The text of the passage is unfortunately corrupt.
[493] Strabo, vi. 12.
[494] Out of fifteen such vases, one has two runners, three have three, three have five, and eight have four. The number four is more usual also in representations of the longer races.

heats were so arranged as to avoid the necessity of a bye. A single odd runner would be attached to one of the heats, two or more would form a heat by themselves. Whether heats were employed in the longer races we have no evidence to determine.

The runners were separated from one another at the start by posts placed in the stone sill, and in later times by more massive pillars, and similar posts or pillars marked the finish or turning point. It has been suggested that ropes were fastened to these posts, which ran the length of the course and separated the runners from one another. Unfortunately, there is no evidence for this natural and attractive explanation, and such evidence as we do possess is unfavourable. We hear occasionally of runners interfering with one another by holding, tripping, and running across.[495] Such foul practices seem to have been rare, and were of course strictly forbidden. The competitors at Olympia swore a solemn oath to abstain from all foul play. But on a roped course these practices are impossible. They may, of course, have been confined to the long-distance races, in which the course was certainly not roped. But this is mere supposition, and in the dearth of evidence we must look for some other explanation of the posts. In the first place they must have served as guide-posts for the runners, a very necessary aid in a broad track 200 yards long,—in which it is by no means easy to run straight without assistance. Possibly each post was distinguished by some special sign or colour. Then in the diaulos the runners probably turned round these posts, each turning round his own post. Finally, as the use of the tape seems to have been unknown at the finish, they must have given the judges a most useful line for judging a close finish. It is possible that the first who touched his pillar won, and that in the turn the runners had to touch their respective pillars. But this is mere conjecture.

Figure 50. Panathenaic amphora. Sixth century. (*Mon. d. I.* I. xxii. 7 b.)

---

[495] Krause, *Gym.* p. 363. *J.H.S. l.c.* p. 262. In Vergil Nisus trips Salius, *Aen.* v. 335; in Statius, vi. 616, Idas seizes Parthenopaeus by the hair. More important is a passage in Lucian, *Calumn. non temere cred.* 12 ἄναθλος ἀνταγωνιστὴς ἀπογνοὺς τὴν ἐκ τοῦ τάχους ἐλπίδα ἐπὶ τὴν κακοτεχνίαν ἐτράπετο καὶ τοῦτο μόνον ἐξ ἅπαντος σκοπεῖ ὅπως τὸν τρέχοντα ἐπιοχὼν ἢ ἐμποδίσας ἐπιστομιεῖ. Cp. Cicero, *de Officiis*, iii. 10.

In the stade-race each runner ran straight to the post opposite his starting point. The manner of running the other races is more difficult to determine. The centre socket in one of the lines at Olympia is larger than the rest, and Dr. Dörpfeld is of opinion that in the diaulos and dolichos the other posts were removed and only the central one was left, round which all competitors raced. In the diaulos such a system would have put those who started on the outside at a serious disadvantage compared with those who started in the centre, a disadvantage accentuated by the confusion and crowding at the turn. It seems therefore probable that the runners raced each to his own post, and turning round it to the left raced back along the parallel track. In the longer races the objection is less important, and the representations of the dolichos on vases seem to show that all the runners raced round and round the central posts at either end. On an early Panathenaic vase (Figure 50) four runners are shown running to the left towards a rough post. The foremost runner has just reached the post, his left foot just passing it, but he has not yet turned. The style of running shows that the post denotes the turn and not the finish.[496]

Figure 51. Panathenaic amphora, in British Museum, B. 609. Archonship of Niceratus, 333 B.C.

The difference in style between the sprinter and the long-distance runner is clearly marked on Panathenaic vases. The style of the latter is excellent; his arms are held close in to the sides, yet swinging freely without any stiffness; his body is slightly inclined forward, with chest advanced and head erect; and he moves with a long sweeping stride, running on the ball of the foot, but without raising the heel unduly (Figure 51). At the finish he, too, like the sprinter, swung his arms violently in making his spurt, using them as wings, says Philostratus.[497] This idea of the winged runner seems to have influenced the early representation of the stade runner, which at first sight appears almost grotesque. He seems to be advancing by a series of leaps and bounds with arms and fingers spreadeagled (Figure 52).

---

[496] It is unnecessary to repeat here the arguments on which these conclusions are based. They are stated fully in *J.H.S.* xxiii. p. 267.

[497] *Gym.* 32 οἷον πτερούμενοι ὑπὸ τῶν χειρῶν. Winged figures are very frequent in early Greek art: a very beautiful later representation of a winged runner occurs on a r.-f. vase published in *B.C.H.*, 1899, p. 158.

Figure 52. Panathenaic amphora. Munich, 498. Sixth century.

In criticizing these drawings we must not forget that the subjects on the Panathenaic vases are usually treated in a conventional manner. The earliest of these vases are archaic work of the sixth century, the latest archaistic work of the fourth century, and, as is usual in objects connected with religion, the conventions of the earlier period are preserved in the later. Now, if we make allowance for the limitations of the early artist, and the extreme difficulty of the subject, we shall find that the artists have succeeded in reproducing the essential points of a sprint. The runners run well on the ball of the foot, the heel somewhat higher than in the long race; their knees are well raised and their bodies erect. The movement of the arms seems exaggerated at first, till we compare the vase paintings with snapshot photographs of a short-distance race. Then we see that every sprinter uses his arms. The Americans have certainly reduced running to a science, and I will therefore quote a passage from a well-known American trainer and athlete: "The arms are of great service in sprinting, and the importance of this fact is generally under-estimated. They are used in *bent form and moved almost straight forward and back*, not sideways across the body."[498] This is just what we see on the vases. Why, then, is the effect grotesque? Because the vase painter has made the right arm move with the right leg and *vice versa*, whereas, in reality, the right arm moves with the left leg. A similar mistake may often be observed in the drawings of horses. In both cases the mistake is due partly to the difficulty of representing the action accurately; partly, and this is true especially of the finer red-figured vases, to artistic causes. A side view of a sprinter always looks awkward, and the artist therefore tries to improve upon nature. But that the Greek really used his arms just as we do is shown by the fact that on some of the later Panathenaic vases the arms are represented quite correctly (Figure 53), and occasionally even on sixth-century vases, as in the leading runner of Figure 52.[499] The grotesqueness of movement is enhanced by the stiff manner in which the fingers are outstretched—another purely artistic peculiarity, which we need not therefore, as a popular lecturer did recently,

---

[498] *Practical Track and Field Athletics*, by John Graham and Ellery H. Clark (D. Nutt), p. 24. A photograph of two runners (Pl. vi.) taken in an actual race bears a striking resemblance to the pictures on Greek vases.
[499] *C.R.*, 1876, Pl. i.

hold up as an example for the imitation of modern athletes. As a matter of fact, the action of the Greek sprinter is not so violent as that of the modern, and this is natural, seeing that the Greeks had no race shorter than 200 yards.

In the diaulos and hippios the style must have been less violent. Perhaps some of the existing vases represent these events, but owing to the absence of any inscription we cannot say for certain. One fragment found at Athens bears the inscription "I am a diaulos runner"; and the style, as we should expect, is a compromise between that of the sprinter and that of the long-distance runner. The arms are swung, but not as violently as in the sprint, while the stride is long and even, the knees not raised unduly.[500] On another fragment found at Athens we find the position of the arms typical of the dolichos combined with the high action of the sprinter. Unfortunately this fragment is uninscribed.[501]

Figure 53. Panathenaic amphora. Fourth century. (Stephani, *C. R. Atlas*, 1876, Pl. i.)

The physical types represented on these vases vary considerably. On the earlier vases a short, thick-set, bearded type prevails, with powerful shoulders and thighs. On the later vases we see greater length of limb. The thinness of the sprinters is sometimes exaggerated to the point of emaciation. On the other hand, some of the long-distance runners, in spite of their length of limb, seem too heavy in build for the distance. They are of the type of the Apoxyomenos, who, though he might be excellent over 200 yards or quarter of a mile, is too heavy for a three-mile race.

A peculiarity ascribed in our text-books to the Greek runner is the habit of encouraging himself to greater efforts by shouting as he ran, with all the strength of his lungs. The only evidence for so absurd and improbable a practice is a rhetorical passage in Cicero,[502] who can hardly be regarded as an authority on Greek athletics, even on those of his own day, when athletics were at their lowest ebb. Nor need we credit the statement that the Greeks raced in deep sand. Lucian, it is true, describes the youths in the gymnasium practising running in the

---

[500] *National Museum*, 761.
[501] *Mon. d. I.* X. 48 h, 15.
[502] *Tusc. Disp.* ii. 23.

sand as a severe form of exercise,[503] but the account preserved of the careful preparation of the stadium at Delphi proves that the racing track was something very different.

It is difficult to form any estimate of value as to the respective merits of different districts in different branches of athletics. The evidence is too fragmentary and extends over too vast a period. Many of the extraordinary performances which Pausanias records belong to the time of the Empire. For the period of Greek independence it seems safe to say that in the Peloponnese the Spartans and Arcadians were most successful in the foot-race, and outside the Peloponnese, the Crotoniats and Cretans.[504] The excellence of the latter in long-distance running is illustrated by Xenophon's account of the games held by the remnant of the ten thousand at Trapezus, at which no less than sixty Cretans competed in the dolichos.[505] Most of the celebrated runners have been mentioned in the course of our history. To these we may add the names of Phayllus of Croton, a stadiodromos and pentathlete, of whom we shall have more to say, and Ladas of Sparta, a long-distance runner of the fifth century, who must not be confused with a later Ladas of Achaea, who won the stade-race in Ol. 125. The popular idea that Ladas died as he reached the goal, in the very moment of victory, is hardly creditable to the training of the most famous runner of his day. It seems to be a myth, derived from a misunderstanding of the epigram which describes the statue of the runner made by Myron.[506] Pausanias merely tells us that he died shortly after his victory, on his way home. We have no means of comparing the performances of Greek runners with those of our own. We hear of a sprinter who could outrun and catch hares,[507] of another runner who raced a horse from Coronea to Thebes and beat it.[508] Pheidippides, as we all know, ran from Athens to Sparta in two days; Ageus, who won the long race at Olympia in Ol. 113, is reported to have carried the news of his victory to Argos on the same day; and a still better performance is recorded in a fourth-century inscription found at Epidaurus of one Drumos, who records as an "example of manliness," that he brought the news of his Olympic victory from Elis to Epidaurus on the same day. The distance as the crow flies is nearly ninety miles.[509] All this is too vague for comparison. Such scanty evidence suggests that the Greeks obtained a generally high standard of excellence in running, and that such superiority as they may have possessed was shown rather in long races than in short.

The race in armour was first introduced at the close of the sixth century.[510] It was a military exercise, and its introduction was an attempt to restore to athletics that practical character which under the stress of competition was even then in danger of being lost. Its practical character naturally won for it the approval of Plato, who proposed to introduce in his ideal state races in heavy and in light armour. Appealing as it did to the whole body of soldier-citizens rather than to specialized athletes, it was an extremely popular event, and its popularity was enhanced by its picturesqueness, which made it a favourite subject for the vase painter. For the same reason it seems not to have possessed, at all events in later times, the

---

[503] *Anacharsis* 27.
[504] Krause, *Gym.* p. 379.
[505] Xen. *Anab.* iv. 8, 27. The Damonon inscription records the successes of Damonon and his son in local festivals. Damonon won many victories in the stade and diaulos; his son twice won the stade, the diaulos and the long race on the same day. The inscription is a good proof of the athletic ability of the Spartans in the fifth century; specialization in athletics found no favour at Sparta, *B.S.A.* xiii. 179.
[506] *Anth. Plan.* iv. 54; Pausanias, iii. 21.
[507] Philostr. *Gym.* 23.
[508] Diodor. Sic. xiv. 11.
[509] Jul. Africanus, Ol. 113; *I.G.* iv. 1349.
[510] Artemidor. i. 63; Plutarch, *Quaest. Symp.* ii. 5; Pausanias, iii. 14, 3; Philostr. *Gym.* 7; Heliodor. *Aeth.* iv.

same athletic importance as the purely athletic events: it was no race for the specialist; rather it belonged to that class of mixed athletics, such as obstacle races and races in uniform, which are a popular and also a valuable feature in military sports. Hence at Olympia and elsewhere the race in armour was an appropriate close to the athletic programme,[511] marking as it did the connexion between athletic training and real life.

Figure 54. R.-f. kylix ascribed to Euphronius. Paris, Bibliothèque Nationale, 523.

There were many varieties of the armed race, differing from one another in distance, in equipment, and in rules. The most strenuous of all these competitions was that at the Eleutheria at Plataea, partly, Philostratus tells us, owing to the length of the course; partly owing to the completeness of the armour worn, which enveloped the athlete from head to foot; partly owing to a remarkable rule that any competitor who having once won the race entered again and failed incurred the penalty of death. Perhaps this regulation means no more than that no previous winner was allowed to compete a second time.[512] At Nemea the race was over the hippios course of four stades, at Olympia and at Athens it was a diaulos of two stades.[513] Elsewhere the distance may have been different. Similarly the equipment varied. The runners at Olympia originally wore helmets and greaves, and carried round shields, twenty-five of which were kept there for the use of competitors. The wearing of greaves was

---

[511] For a full discussion of the armed race *vide J.H.S.* xxiii. p. 280 ff. On vases this race is frequently connected with boxing and the pankration, the events which probably preceded it in the programme. *Vide* Figures. 54, 151.

[512] Phil. *Gym.* 8, 24. I have already pointed out that Philostratus is somewhat credulous, and too much inclined to accept without investigation the tales poured into his ears by the authorities at Elis and elsewhere. It was the fashion in his time to exaggerate the Spartan severity of Greek athletics.

[513] For Nemea *vide* Philostratus, *l.c.*; for Olympia, Paus. ii. 11, 8; for Athens Aristoph. *Av.* 291, and Scholiast.

discontinued at a later date.[514] The vase paintings, which mostly represent Athenian practice, show that while the usage varied previous to 520 B.C., greaves became general after that date, but disappear entirely after 450 B.C.[515] There is no evidence that the runners ever carried weapons. The danger of such a practice is obvious. We often see processions of hoplites thus armed proceeding at a double, and these are often described as races.[516] It seems safer and more reasonable to regard them merely as military processions, or perhaps competitions such as we know took place at the Athenian festivals.

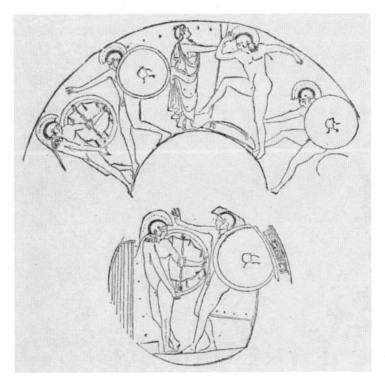

Figure 55. R.-f. kylix. Formerly in Berlin. (*J.H.S.* xxiii. p. 278.)

All the various details of the race are pictured on the vases. On a red-figured vase by Euphronius in Paris we see the preparations for the race (Figure 54). In the centre stands a robed official or trainer with his rod, and around him are various runners practising. One of them is putting on his armour, others, perhaps, are engaged in a preliminary canter such as is described by Statius.[517] The position at the start has already been described. From the number of shields kept for this race at Olympia it would seem that the field was usually a large one, as we should expect, and certain vases representing the turn indicate that whatever was the case in the unarmed diaulos the runners in armour raced, not each round his separate post, but all together round the central post, turning round it to the left. This critical moment is perhaps represented in the left-hand group on the Euphronius kylix, where the runner to the left has just completed the turn, and is starting on his way back, but has not yet got into his stride.

---

[514] Paus. v. 12, 8; vi. 10, 4.
[515] Hauser, *Jahrb.*, 1895, p. 199.
[516] *B.M. Vases*, E. 22; Gerh. *A. V.* 258, 1.
[517] *Theb.* vi. 587.

Another vase shows a pair of runners—one checking his pace before the turn, and another in the very act of turning (Figure 55). Their attitude seems to show that the turn took place round a pillar, and that the runners had not merely to toe the line. The most complete picture of the race is represented on a red-figured kylix in Berlin (Figure 56). On one side we see a group of three. To the right a runner is in the position of the start; to the left another is almost in the act of swinging round the post at the turn. Both these runners move to the left; the central runner, who is already starting back, moves to the right. On the other side we see three runners in full race, one of whom is guilty of the fatal mistake of looking round. Is he protesting against his fellow-runner for some unfairness?

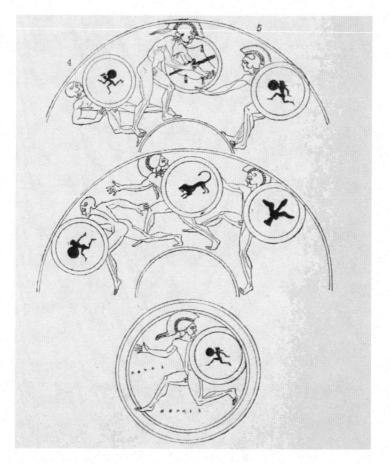

Figure 56. R.-f. kylix. Berlin, 2307.

Finally, on a red-figured vase in the British Museum, we see the finish of the race (Figure 57). A bearded runner who has passed the winning post looks back in triumph on his rival, who, as he reaches the goal, seems to have thrown down his shield in disgust. The winner holds in his hand his helmet, which he has just taken off. This gesture, which occurs on a number of vases, seems to be symbolical of victory. What could be more natural at the finish of a 400 yards' race over the hot sand and beneath the scorching sun of Olympia than to take off the heavy, cumbrous helmet? The action reminds one, too, of a cricketer who after a fine innings takes off his cap as he returns to the pavilion. Of the style of the runners little need be said; it resembles the style of the stade runner in the swinging of the arm, and for obvious reasons of symmetry the vase painter always makes the right arm work with the right leg, the left arm, which holds the shield, being generally stationary. The type of runner represented on Panathenaic vases is, as we should expect, sturdier and heavier than is shown in other races. The hoplites on one in the British Museum exhibit that length of body in comparison with length of leg which Philostratus mentions as a useful quality for this event, and we may further note that they run on a flat foot (Figure 58). Yet in spite of such examples a foreign archeologist has maintained that the hoplitodromos advanced by a series of leaps and bounds, and has deduced therefrom the theory that jumping was the best training for this race, and that therefore the statue of a hoplitodromos practising, described by Pausanias, represented him not running, but jumping! The Greek athlete has certainly been hardly treated by some of his admirers.

Figure 57. R.-f. kylix. British Museum, E. 818.

Figure 58. Panathenaic amphora. British Museum, B. 608. Archonship of Pythodelus, 336 B.C.

The popularity of the armed race in the fifth century is partly due to that spirit of military enthusiasm which animated athletics after the Persian wars, and partly to its attractiveness as a spectacle. There is something amusing in the sight of a body of men racing at full speed in incongruous costume, and the comic element in the armed race is brought out in the *Birds* of

Aristophanes,[518] where Peisthetaerus as he watches the chorus of birds advancing on the stage with their quaint plumage and crests aptly compares them to the hoplites assembling to run the diaulos. Amusing incidents must have been frequent, especially in the crowding at the turning post. On vases, for example, we often see a runner who has dropt his shield, or stoops to pick it up.[519] A race of this kind naturally lends itself to variations, and of these we have evidence on the vases. A red-figured kylix at Munich shows two armed runners racing to the left, holding their shields in front of them in a decidedly quaint style (Figure 59). Three others race in the opposite direction, two of them with helmets only, the third unarmed. The sponge and other implements hanging on the walls indicate that the scene is placed in the gymnasium where athletes are practising; but the idea suggested is undoubtedly that of a race in which the runners at the end of the lap put down their shields and ran the next lap without them, and then, perhaps, doffed their helmets also. No certainty is attainable as to details, but the vases establish the general fact that such variations did exist at different places.[520]

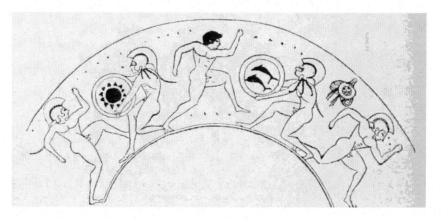

Figure 59. R.-f. kylix. Munich, 1240.

The comic element is still more apparent in the Lampadadromia and in the Oschophoria described above.[521] These old ritual races hardly come within the sphere of true athletics, although connected with the gymnasia and the training of the epheboi. They are of the type of events which we find in the modern gymkhana, and it is therefore unnecessary to describe them here at length.

The torch-race was widely spread throughout Greek lands and its popularity was maintained till Roman times. At Athens there were torch-races at the Panathenaea, at the Epitaphia and the Thesea, and in the time of Socrates a torch-race on horseback was instituted at the festival of Bendis. The torch-race took place at night. There were two principal varieties of it—one a race between individuals, the other between teams. In the former the runners started from the altar of Prometheus in the Academy, and raced into the city, the one who arrived first with his torch lighted being proclaimed victor. The efforts of the runners to

---

[518] *Av.* 291.
[519] *J.H.S. l.c.* pp. 284-287.
[520] *J.H.S. l.c.* pp. 282-284. The argument which I drew from the use of the epithet ποικίλοι in the passage of Philostratus must be abandoned. Dr. Jüthner's recent edition of the *Gymnastik* proves that there is no authority for this reading; he himself suggests πάλαιοι. The general conclusions drawn in my article are not really affected by the change.
[521] P. 228.

keep their torches alight as they ran along stooping like boys in an egg and spoon race caused endless amusement among the spectators, and as they passed through the narrow gateway into the city, the ribald dwellers in the potters' quarter sped them on their way with loud resounding slaps.[522] The team-race is familiar to all from the famous simile in the *Agamemnon*. The members of the teams were posted at intervals along the way; the first runner handed it to the second as he reached him, and so on till it came to the last. The team that brought their torch still lighted to the finish first was declared the winner. The teams must have been originally representative of the tribes. In the first century B.C. we find teams mentioned from various palaestrae; thus victories are recorded of boys from the palaestra of Timeas, and of Antigenes, or from the Lyceum.[523] The training of the teams was a voluntary service (λειτουργία) performed by the Gymnasiarchoi, or by special officials, the Lampadarchoi, whose names are mentioned on inscriptions when their teams won. There were torch-races for boys and youths of various ages. Aristophanes speaks of torch-racing and hunting as the fashionable amusements of a smart youth.[524] At a later time the torch-race is mentioned in inscriptions as one of the duties expected from the epheboi, rather as a ceremonial duty than as an athletic exercise.[525] The religious character of the race was maintained in Roman times. An inscription from Scyros prescribes penalties for any one, whether slave or freeman, found guilty of unfair practices in the torch-races of the tribes. If a slave, he is to be scourged and his master fined; if a freeman or one of the runners, he is not only to be fined but considered a "sacrilegious person and accursed."[526]

Little is known of the methods of training employed by Greek runners. The gymnasia at Olympia and Delphi were provided with running tracks corresponding in length to the actual stadia, and that at Olympia was provided with grooved starting sills. Thus the runners could practise the start, and, what was equally important, the turn, under the same conditions as obtained in competition. To gain endurance they ran in heavy sand. Aristotle mentions as an exercise practised in the palaestra running or rather waddling on the knees![527] At a later date we learn from Epictetus that the training for the long-distance runner was different from that of the sprinter in its regulations for diet, massage, and food; but he gives us no details.[528] Philostratus tells us that the long-distance runner instead of training over the whole course would run eight or ten stades only, a practice quite in accord with that of the present day.[529] In those degenerate days athletes had also recourse to quack medicines and charms. A concoction of equisetum was recommended as a cure for the stitch, and some runners for a similar purpose wore a girdle of horses' teeth. Athletes have always been superstitious.[530]

---

[522] Aristophanes, *Ran.* 1087; *Lysistr.* 1002.
[523] *I.G.* ii. 444, 446.
[524] *Vesp.* 1203.
[525] *I.G.* 444.
[526] Ditt. *Syll.* 2nd Ed., 680.
[527] *De Gressu Animal.* p. 709.
[528] Arrian, iii. 22.
[529] *Gym.* 11.
[530] Pliny, *H. N.* xxvi. 13, 83; xxviii. 19, 78. The spleen was supposed to cause stitch; Plautus, *Merc.* i. 2, 14.

Chapter 14

THE JUMP AND HALTERES

Jumping is not a military exercise but an amusement of peace. It is useful, of course, at times for a soldier to be able to leap over any obstacle in his way. But the Homeric chieftain was not suitably dressed for such feats of agility, whether he went to war in Mycenaean style with his long-shadowing spear and towerlike shield reaching down to his feet, or like the later hoplite arrayed in panoply of bronze. For flight or pursuit he trusted in his chariot and horses. Hence jumping was no part of his training, and it is mentioned in Homer only as an accomplishment of the peaceful Phaeacian traders. Pindar, true to Homeric tradition, does not include it among the sports introduced by Heracles in the first Olympic games, and Plato has no use for it in the training of his soldier-citizens. In athletic festivals the jump was one of the events of the pentathlon, but never existed as an independent competition. Yet it must have been always a popular exercise and amusement, and its popularity during the sixth and fifth centuries is shown by the frequency with which it is depicted on vases. Pentathletes were sometimes represented with jumping weights in their hands, and the jump seems to have been regarded as the typical event of the pentathlon.[531] Perhaps it owed its importance to the part which the jumping weights played in physical training, at least in later times. They were used much in the same way as the modern dumb-bells, and many of the modern dumb-bell exercises were known to the Greeks and freely practised, especially in medical gymnastics.

The only form of jumping that had any place in athletic competitions was the long jump. The explanation of this is obvious. Greece was not a land of fences or hedges, and the only natural obstacles which it afforded were streams and ditches. There is no ground for the statement frequently made that the Greeks practised also the high jump, and the deep jump, much less that they practised the pole jump. They certainly used a spear or a pole in vaulting on horseback (Figure 174), but the so-called jumping poles are now universally recognized as either javelins or measuring rods. A certain number of vase paintings may possibly represent the high jump, but they may just as well represent a standing long jump; none represent jumping from a height, or the deep jump.

It would be rash to say that such exercises were never practised; but certainly they were unknown in athletic competitions. In the daily life of the palaestra and gymnasium there must have been countless exercises and feats practised, of which no record survives. Lucian describes the athletes in the gymnasium jumping up and down like runners, but without

---

[531] *J.H.S.* xxiii. p. 60; Paus. v. 27, 8; vi. 3, 10.

moving from their places, and kicking the air.[532] The exercise is that known in the modern gymnasium as "knees up," and is apparently the same as that described by Seneca as "the fuller's jump,"[533] from its resemblance to the action of a fuller jumping up and down on the clothes in his tub. The Spartan Lampito in the *Lysistrata* of Aristophanes ascribes her complexion and figure to her athletic training, and mentions an exercise, not unknown in foreign gymnasia and dancing-schools, of jumping up and down and kicking the buttocks with alternate feet.[534] Another Spartan lady claims to have made a record by repeating this feat a thousand times. But these tricks belong rather to the sphere of dancing than to that of athletics, though we must remember that dancing was an important part of Greek physical training. Its value consisted chiefly in graceful and rhythmic movement; but its practice also involved a variety of jumps, hops, flings, and kicks. Hopping (ἀσκωλιασμός)[535] was a favourite amusement, but can hardly claim to be classed under athletics, unless we suppose that the Greek jump was a hop, skip, and jump.[536] At the Dionysia there was a popular competition in which the competitors had to hop on to a greased wine-skin full of wine. He who succeeded in hopping on to it and staying there took it as a prize, while the falls of the unsuccessful were a source of boundless amusement to the populace. Mr. Henry Balfour informs me that the game still exists in Northern Greece.

The Greeks jumped into a pit (σκάμμα)[537] the ground of which had been carefully dug up and levelled. The same term skamma is also used of the wrestling ring. The picks (σκαπάναι) used for loosening the ground are frequently represented on athletic scenes on the vases, and the exercise of digging with them was regarded as a valuable means of training, especially for wrestlers and boxers.[538] The ground of the skamma was soft, so as to take the impress of the jumper's feet. No jump was allowed to be measured unless the impress of the feet was regular, says Philostratus, meaning thereby that if the jumper fell or stumbled or landed with one foot in advance of the other, the jump was not counted.[539] In all athletics the Greeks attached great importance to style. If we are to believe the legends recorded by scholiasts and lexicographers about Phaÿllus, the length of the skamma was 50 feet. One version of this story is that Phaÿllus having jumped 5 feet beyond the skamma, on to the hard ground, broke his leg—a contingency by no means unlikely if such a jump were possible.[540]

The take-off (βατήρ) was at one end of the skamma. It is marked in vase paintings, sometimes by spears or poles placed in the ground, sometimes by pillars similar to those that mark the start of the running track.[541] Possibly the stone starting-lines of the stadium may have served as the bater. The word merely denotes a stepping-place or threshold. We know that the bater must have been hard and firm,[542] but whether it was made of wood or stone we cannot say. There is no evidence for the use of any kind of spring-board in athletics.[543]

---

[532] *Anacharsis*, 4.
[533] *Ep.* xv.
[534] *Lysistrata*, 82; cp. Krause, *Gym.* p. 398, n. 11.
[535] Aristoph. *Plut.* 1129; Plato, *Symp.* 190 D; cp. Krause, *Gym.* p. 399.
[536] Vide *J.H.S.* xxiv. pp. 74 ff.
[537] *J.H.S.* xxiv. pp. 70 ff., where I have shown that there is no distinction between σκάμμα and τὰ ἐσκαμμένα.
[538] Theocrit. iv. 10.
[539] *Gym.* 55 οὐ γὰρ συγχωροῦσι διαμετρεῖν τὸ πήδημα ἢν μὴ ἀρτίως ἔχῃ τοῦ ἔχνους.
[540] All the evidence about Phaÿllus is collected and discussed in *J.H.S.* xxiv. *l.c.*
[541] Figure 65; cp. *J.H.S.* xxiv. p. 186.
[542] This is clear from the proverb κέκρουκα τὸν βατῆρα.
[543] The bater is perhaps represented on a vase reproduced by Krause, *Gym.* ix. 23, as a small raised platform. We may remark that in this case the jump is a standing one and without halteres.

The jumps were measured by rods (κανόνες),[544] and the individual jumps were marked either by pegs or by lines drawn in the sand. On a vase in the British Museum (Figure 67) three vertical lines are drawn beneath the figure of a jumper in mid-air, and three similar lines occur under a jumper depicted on an Etruscan carnelian. They mark the jumps of previous competitors, but may equally well be interpreted as pegs or as lines in the sand. Certainly they are not, as has been sometimes suggested, spikes or arrows set there to give zest and danger to the sport. The acrobat might turn somersaults over swords and spikes, but the acrobat was a slave-girl usually, not a free citizen, and the Greeks fully appreciated the difference between acrobatics and athletics.

Figure 60. Leaden halter found at Eleusis. Athens, National Museum, 9075.

The Greek jumper generally used jumping weights (ἁλτῆρες). These halteres were of stone or metal, and differed considerably in shape and weight. We cannot say when their use came in. Homer does not mention them, but we find them already in existence at the very beginning of the sixth century, if not earlier. To this period belongs an inscribed halter of lead found at Eleusis, perhaps one of a pair, dedicated by a certain Epaenetus to commemorate his victory in the jump (Figure 60).[545] It is merely an oblong piece of lead about 4-1/2 inches long, 1-1/2 broad, and with the sides slightly concave, varying in depth from 1-1/4 inch at either end to less than an inch in the centre. It weighs 4 lbs. 2 oz. (1·888 kg.).

Figure 61. Halteres in the British Museum. (*a*) Cast of halter found at Olympia, L. 11-1/2 in. (*b*) Limestone halter found at Camirus, L. 7-1/2 in. (*c*) Leaden halter, L. 8 in.

---

[544] Pollux, iii. 151. The so-called measuring ropes and compasses have been shown by Jüthner to be merely boxing thongs and amenta.

[545] Ἐφ. Ἀρχ., 1883, 190. Roberts and Gardner, ii. 391, give the inscription Ἀλ(λ)όμενος νίκησεν Ἐπαίνετος οὕνεκα τοῦδε ἁ.

The vase paintings show that a large variety of shapes existed during the sixth and fifth centuries. There are two main types. On the earliest black-figured vases the halter appears as a nearly semicircular piece of metal or stone with a deep recess on the straight or lower side, which affords a convenient grip. The two club-like ends are equal, and the effect is that of a curved flattened dumb-bell. This type does not occur after the sixth century, towards the close of which the halter is improved by an increase in the size of the end projecting to the front, and a decrease in the hinder part. Numerous modifications of this type appear on the vases, differing mainly in the size and shape of the club-like ends. The British Museum possesses a pair of these halteres (Figure 61). They are of lead about 8 inches long, affording a comfortable grip for the hand in the centre. One of the pair is damaged, the other weighs about 2 lbs. 5 oz. (1·072 kg.). A similar pair found at Athens are in the Museum at Copenhagen. They are somewhat shorter and heavier (1·610 and 1·480 kg. respectively), and the recess is so narrow that they can only have been held by the smaller end, and not in the centre.

Side by side with this club-like type we find in the fifth century another type consisting of an elongated, roughly semispherical block of metal or stone, thickest in the middle, with the ends pointed or rounded, the upper side being pierced or cut away, so as to furnish a grip for the thumb and fingers. These are the "old-fashioned" dumb-bells which Pausanias describes as held by a statue of Agon, which was dedicated by Micythus in the second half of the fifth century. Of this type we possess two interesting examples both of stone, a pair of halteres found at Corinth, and now in the Museum at Athens, and a single halter found at Olympia, and now at Berlin, a cast of which may be seen in the British Museum. Those from Corinth (Figure 62) are nearly 10-1/4 inches long, and 4 inches deep by 3 broad. A little distance behind the centre they are cut through, the depression on one side affording a hold for the thumb, that on the other side for the four fingers. The Olympic halter (Figure 61) is larger and more primitive. It is a right-handed halter 11-1/2 inches long, and weighs over 10 lbs., or four times as much as the leaden halteres in the British Museum. The surface of the stone is left rough, and the grip is formed by cutting away the stone on either side, so as to enable the hand to grasp it.

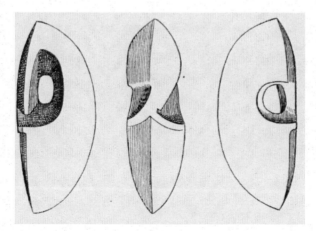

Figure 62. Stone halter found at Corinth (10 inches).

After the fifth century there is no evidence as to the form of the halteres until Roman times. On Roman copies of athletic statues a new cylindrical type of halter is represented, and the same appears on mosaics and wall paintings.[546] It is merely a cylinder slightly narrower at the centre than at the ends, like a dice-box, and though very useful for dumb-bell exercises, can hardly have been as handy for jumping as the earlier types. We do not know when this type came in. The British Museum possesses a curious example of it, found at Camirus in Rhodes (Figure 61). It is made of limestone, 7-1/2 inches long, and carefully grooved, so as to afford grips for the thumb and each of the fingers. References in late authors indicate that the halteres were usually not of stone, but of lead.

Philostratus distinguishes two kinds of halteres: "the long," which "exercise shoulders and hands"; the spherical, which "also exercise the fingers."[547] It is clear that these cannot correspond to the two types which we found prevalent in the fifth century. For Pausanias regards one at least of these types as "old-fashioned," and Philostratus is speaking of the halteres in use in his own day. Though he describes the halteres as an "invention of the pentathlon, and invented, as its name denotes, for the jump," his ideas of their use for this purpose are of the vaguest,[548] and he regards them principally as a means of training, employed, he says, by all athletes alike, "whether heavy or light." It seems, therefore, that his "long halteres" are those used by the heavy athletes, the boxer or the wrestler, while the spherical ones are those used by light athletes, the runner or the spear-thrower. The former may be identified with the cylindrical halteres; the latter are perhaps little more than balls of wood or lead, such as are recommended by a medical writer in the early fifth century A.D., for the use of those suffering from gout in their hands.[549]

Figure 63. R.-f. pelike, in British Museum, E. 427.

---

[546] E.g., *supra*, Figure 22; cp. Jüthner, *Antike Turngeräthe*, pp. 10, 11.
[547] *Gym.* 55. Dr. Jüthner in his *Antike Turngeräthe*, p. 11, identifies them, wrongly as I think, with the two early types. It is hard to see how either of these types could exercise the fingers.
[548] "They lighten the jump, serving as a guide to the hands, and enabling the jumper to land firmly and evenly."
[549] Caelius Aurelianus, *De morb. acut. et chron.* v. 2, 38. Such sufferers are to be given "wax to mould, or *manipuli*, which athletes call halteres, to hold, and to move, either of wax or of wood, at first with only a little lead, afterwards gradually increased in weight."

The manner of using the halteres is clearly shown on the vases. The principle is the same as that of a standing jump, the utilization of the swing of the arms to assist the spring of the legs. The jumper swings the halteres forwards and upwards till they are level with, or higher than, his head, and then swings them vigorously downwards, at the same time bending his body till his hands are just below his knees. The actual jump takes place on the return swing. As the hands swing to the front, and the centre of gravity is shifted forward, the knees, which have been bent on the back swing, are vigorously straightened, and the swing of the halteres combines with the push of the legs to propel the body forwards. In the case of a standing jump the preliminary swing may be repeated two or three times.

It is this preliminary swing which is most frequently depicted on vases. On a red-figured pelike in the British Museum (Figure 63) we see a youth preparing to jump. The right leg, which is advanced, is straight, and he is just in the act of swinging the halteres to the front. Opposite him stands a flute-player in a long striped and spotted robe, playing the double flute. The jump was always accompanied by music. But why the jumper especially required this assistance is not clear. Philostratus gives as the reason that the Greeks regarded the jump as the most strenuous of all exercises. But this is hardly satisfactory. It seems probable that in early days flute-playing was a common accompaniment of all athletic exercises. The Argives wrestled to the accompaniment of the flute. On the chest of Cypselus, Admetus, and Mopsus were represented boxing to music, on vases the flute-player accompanies the diskos-thrower in his exercise, and less frequently the spear-thrower.[550] Possibly the rhythmical swing of the diskos and the halteres may have been assisted by the strains of music. But I suspect that the special connexion between the jump and the flute dates from the time when the halteres had already begun to be used as dumb-bells, and it was found that music was of great assistance as an accompaniment of physical drill for large classes.

The two typical moments in the swing, and those therefore which the artist usually selects, are the top of the upward swing and the bottom of the downward swing, though the two types are connected by a closely graduated series of intermediate types.[551]

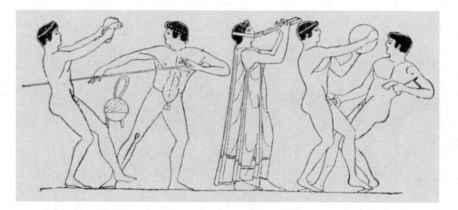

Figure 64. R.-f. krater. Copenhagen (?). (*Annali*, 1846, M.)

---

[550] Plutarch, *De musica*, 1140; Paus. v. 17, 10.
[551] For vase paintings representing jumpers in various positions vide *J.H.S.* xxiv. pp. 184 ff.

A good example of the upward swing occurs on a red-figured krater presented by Campana to the King of Denmark (Figure 64). It is a scene from the life of the gymnasium, and represents youths practising the exercises of the pentathlon. A diskos in its case hangs on the wall. In the centre stands a flute-player. To the left a youth has swung the halteres vigorously upward; his body is thrown well back, and its weight rests on the right leg, which is behind, the left foot being lifted off the ground by the swing. Next to him stands a javelin-thrower, who has just adjusted the thong of his javelin, and is drawing back his arm to throw. Beyond the flute-player a diskos-thrower prepares to throw the diskos. All three are depicted at similar stages in their respective exercises. They seem to be moving in time to the music. The fourth figure is also that of a jumper: he is in the attitude of a runner suddenly checking his pace; perhaps he is practising a long jump, and after a short run checks himself in order to swing the halteres before the spring. The upward swing is also represented on black-figured vases, but less vigorously, and with the arms raised slightly higher and somewhat bent.

Figure 65. R.-f. kylix. Bologna. (Jüthner, *Ant. Turn.* 16.)

The downward swing is represented on a red-figured kylix found at Bologna (Figure 65). The same motive is repeated in a number of red-figured vases, though it does not occur on earlier vases. The scene takes place in a gymnasium, as the strigils and other objects hanging on the walls show. A robed trainer in the centre is resting on his staff and directing the practice of two jumpers. The pillar and javelins on either side mark the bater from which the jumpers take off. The impression produced is of an exercise performed in time to music, or by word of command. Perhaps the Greek trainer taught his pupils jumping "by numbers" as the modern instructor teaches vaulting. At all events, the position shown is one essential to a jumper swinging the halteres before his spring, and is not a mere gymnastic exercise. Nor does the scene represent jumpers jumping from a height, as one writer has suggested. A jumper doing so in this position with weights would probably perform a somersault or land on his head.

Figure 66. R.-f. kylix. Bourguignon Coll. (*Arch. Zeit.*, 1884, xvi.)

On another red-figured kylix we see an excellent picture of a jumper in mid-air (Figure 66). The style is perfect: he has jumped high, and arms and legs are extended to the front and almost parallel. This vase also represents a practice-scene from the gymnasium. To the right stands a trainer ready to correct any mistake with his rod, and to the left another jumper is swinging his halteres in a somewhat curious style, to which we shall refer again. On the other side of the kylix we see another trainer, a diskobolos, and another jumper, while a pick lies on the ground.

Immediately before alighting the jumper quickly forces his arms backwards, a movement which increases the length of the jump and enables him to land firmly and securely. This moment is admirably represented on a black-figured imitation Corinthian amphora in the British Museum (Figure 67). The three lines underneath the jumper represent the jumps of other competitors, as has been already explained. A somewhat later moment is shown in an Etruscan wall-painting in a tomb at Chiusi.[552] The jumper is in the very act of alighting and his body is almost straight.

---

[552] Inghirami, *Mus. Chius.* cxxv.; Krause, ix. c. 25.

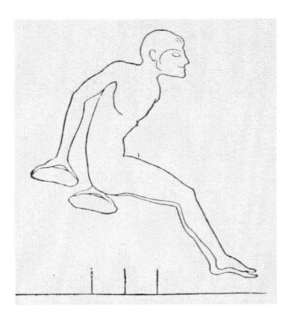

Figure 67. B.-f. amphora. British Museum, B. 48.

The method of swinging the halteres and the positions depicted on the vases seem at first sight more suitable for a standing jump than a running jump, and the Greek jump has therefore been described usually as a standing jump. A representation of a jumper running with halteres occurs, however, on a number of vases both black-figured and red-figured.[553] The realism of the earlier vases despite their grotesqueness makes their evidence very valuable. The run as represented on these vases is by no means incompatible with the use of the halteres. It is not like the run of the modern long-jumper who uses his pace to increase his spring, but like that of the high-jumper, consisting of a few short, springy steps, intended to prepare the limbs and muscles for the final spring. A somewhat exaggerated picture of such a run is seen on a Panathenaic amphora at Leyden,[554] representing the pentathlon (Figure 108), and a later picture of it occurs on the interior of a red-figured kylix by Euphronius (Figure 68). A jumper running appears as the device of a shield on a kylix in the British Museum, representing a hoplitodromos arming for the race.[555] The run in all these cases is similar, and is quite reconcilable with the upward and downward swings of the halteres. The jumper starts with arms close to the side and takes a short run, holding the halteres to the front. As he nears the bater he checks himself in the manner represented in Figure 64. As he does so he swings the halteres upwards, and then with a slow stride forwards swings them down again, and on the return swing takes off. Such a run is in accordance with the practice of modern professionals who use jumping weights.[556]

---

[553] *J.H.S.* xxiv. p. 187.
[554] *J.H.S.* xxvii. p. 260.
[555] *J.H.S.* xxiii. p. 288, Figure 15.
[556] Mr. George Rowdon, who formerly held the championship for the high jump, once gave me the following description of the method of using weights in the high jump: "The jumper starts about 14 yards from the posts, taking two-thirds of the distance with short, quick steps, scarcely swinging the weights at all, after which he takes one or two comparatively long, slow strides, swinging the bells together twice, and on the second swing taking off from the ground as the bells come to the front." The weights used are usually 5 lb. dumb-bells or even heavier. The run for the long jump with such weights would be very similar, the chief difference being

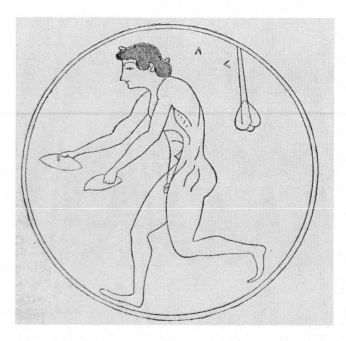

Figure 68. R.-f. kylix. (Klein, *Euphronius*, p. 306.)

It seems, then, that the Greeks certainly practised the running jump, and probably also the standing jump. In the pentathlon the somewhat doubtful evidence of the Panathenaic amphorae is in favour of a running jump.

The pentathlete in competition seems always to have used the halteres, but in the gymnasia jumping was also practised without weights. Sometimes the jumper is represented swinging his arms in the same way as he does with the halteres, but on several vases a totally distinct type occurs.[557] The jumper stands with both feet together, knees well bent, and arms stretched to the front. On one vase he seems to be standing on a low bema or platform, and opposite him is a short pillar, over which Krause supposes he is preparing to jump. The attitude is, however, quite as appropriate to the long jump as to the high jump, and on the interior of a red-figured kylix in Munich we see an almost identical figure, but with the pillar behind and not in front of him. The best example of this attitude is found on a red-figured pelike belonging to Dr. Hauser (Figure 69). Opposite to the jumper stands a robed trainer, stretching out his hand with a familiar gesture of command. There can be no doubt that these figures represent jumpers, but whether long jumpers or high jumpers we cannot say for certain. What is certain is that the jump is a standing jump.

The use of jumping weights adds considerably to the length of jump possible. The present record for the long jump without weights is 24 feet 11-3/4 inches, whereas with jumping weights and off a board 29 feet 7 inches has been cleared by a jumper, who unassisted could probably not have jumped more than 21 feet. But neither weights nor spring-board can explain the discrepancy between these figures and the feats ascribed to the Greeks. Till recently it was commonly stated, and perhaps believed, that the Greeks jumped 50 feet or more. Even if we make the fullest allowance for the fact that jumping was a national exercise

---

that while in the high jump the weights are thrown away at the moment of jumping, in the long jump they are retained.

[557] *J.H.S.* xxiv. pp. 193, 194.

of the Greeks, a single jump of 50 feet is a physical impossibility. Two explanations are possible. Either the Greek jump was not a single jump or the record is pure fiction.

Figure 69. R.-f. pelike, belonging to Dr. Hauser. (*J.H.S.* xxiii. p. 272.)

It has been suggested that the Greek jump was a hop, step, and jump, in which case the jump of 55 feet ascribed to Phaÿllus would be a very fine performance, but not perhaps impossible. Unfortunately there is absolutely no evidence in support of this suggestion. For the suggestion that the jump was a triple jump some evidence may be found in the fact that a triple jump is known in the present day in parts of Northern Greece. By itself this fact can hardly be regarded as adequate proof, and there is, I believe, good reason for discrediting all the evidence on which the supposed record rests. The evidence consists in (1) the well-known epigram on Phaÿllus, which states that he jumped 55 feet;[558] (2) various statements of scholiasts and lexicographers of late and mostly uncertain date; (3) a passage in Africanus, who states that one Chionis, an Olympic victor in Ol. 29 (i.e., seven or eight hundred years before the time of Africanus), jumped 52 feet.

The 52 feet of Africanus is probably a simple mistake for 22 feet, which is the reading of the Armenian Latin text. The various statements of scholiasts and others can all be traced back to the epigram on Phaÿllus, and to an explanation given by some collector of proverbs on the use of the phrase "to jump beyond the pit,"[559] to denote something extraordinary or excessive, and they have no independent value apart from the epigram.

The Phaÿllus of the epigram is identified by the scholiasts with Phaÿllus of Croton, who in the first half of the fifth century won two victories in the pentathlon and one in the foot-race at Delphi, but won no victory at Olympia. He fought at Salamis in a ship equipped at his own expense. Aristophanes alludes to one Phaÿllus, probably the same man, as a noted runner. He had a statue at Delphi which Pausanias saw, and Alexander the Great is said to

---

[558] *Anth. Pal.* App. 297—
πέντ' ἐπὶ πεντήκοντα πόδας πήδησε Φάϋλλος
δίσκευσεν δ' ἑκατὸν πέντ' ἀπολειπομένων.
The argument in the following passage is stated more fully in *J.H.S.* xxiv. pp. 77 ff., where the reader will find full references.
[559] ἄλλεσθαι ὑπὲρ τὸ σκάμμα. *J.H.S.* l.c. p. 71.

have honoured his memory by sending a portion of his Asiatic spoils to Croton. He was evidently a popular hero, just the sort of man about whose exploits all sorts of tales arise. But though Herodotus, Aristophanes, Plutarch, and Pausanias all mention him, they know nothing of the epigram or of the jump. Moreover, according to one statement the epigram was inscribed on the basis of his statue. Parts of this basis and of the inscription have been recently found at Delphi, but, needless to say, there is no trace of the epigram. When the epigram was written we cannot say. Certainly it is not a contemporary commemorative epigram. We meet with it first in Zenobius, a collector of proverbs who lived in the time of Hadrian, and the artificiality of its style is characteristic of the epigrams of this period. But whatever its date it can hardly be regarded as serious evidence. The sporting story is notorious, and the sporting epigram is even less trustworthy than the sporting story. The pages of the *Anthology* abound in epigrams on famous athletes such as Milo and Ladas, some of them no less incredible. Milo, we are told in one epigram, picked up a four-year-old heifer at Olympia, and after carrying it round the Altis in triumph, killed it and ate it all in a single day. Nobody has yet elaborated a theory to account for this extraordinary gastronomic feat, and yet it rests upon just as good evidence as Phaÿllus' jump. The mere fact that the numbers five and ten were used by the Greeks proverbially, just as we use the terms "half a dozen" or "a dozen," sufficiently explains why an epigrammatist wishing to describe a prodigious jump should select such a number as fifty-five.

In Roman times the halteres were used as dumb-bells. The details of such exercises preserved in medical writings prove that they were very similar to those in use at the present day.[560] Antyllus describes three kinds of this "halter-throwing" (ἁλτηροβολία). The first consists in bending and straightening the arms, an exercise which strengthens the arms and shoulders. In the other two exercises the arms are extended and take little part in the movement, which consists in lunging with the arms advanced as in boxing, or in alternately bending and straightening the trunk. The former strengthens the legs chiefly, the latter the back. Galen adds a variety of the latter exercise for strengthening the side muscles of the body. The performer places the halteres 6 feet apart, and standing between them picks up first the left-hand halter with his right hand, next the right-hand halter with his left, and then replaces them, repeating the movement. The prominence given to exercises for developing the important muscles of the trunk is interesting, because the careful representation of these muscles in Greek sculpture and on vases shows that they were developed to a marked degree by the athletic exercises of the Greeks. Wrestling, jumping, and throwing the diskos all helped to develop these muscles. The absence of light clothing round the waist contributed to the same result, and, above all, the fact that the Greek stood and walked, but seldom sat. In the present day these muscles are the worst developed of all muscles in the ordinary man, a result due partly to the character of our games, partly to our clothing, chiefly to our habit of sitting, and sitting in a radically wrong position. It is to these causes that we may ascribe the general absence in the modern figure of the roll of flesh above the iliac crest which is so prominent in all ancient sculpture, and the difference in the form of the iliac line.[561]

---

[560] In Oribasius, vi. 14. 34, the passages from Antyllus and Galen are quoted. The chapter of Oribasius on exercises contains a variety of interesting quotations from earlier medical writers.

[561] On this subject *vide* Ernst Brücke, *The Human Figure*, translated by William Anderson, pp. 115 ff.

Figure 70. R.-f. oinochoe. British Museum, E. 561.

When were the halteres first used as dumb-bells? We have no definite evidence, but I venture to suggest as probable that the practice began about the time of the Persian wars, when the Greeks first consciously realized the national importance of athletic training. The first signs of such a use of the halteres occur on the red-figured vases. It began, I conjecture, in connexion with the jump. We have seen how certain vase paintings suggest that the various movements of the jump and the swinging of the halteres were practised in classes and in rhythmical time. Take the swing of the halteres and make of it a separate exercise, and you have at once a familiar and valuable dumb-bell exercise. Not that this exercise was practised by the Greeks at this period consciously as a physical exercise; it was an exercise for jumpers, and practised for the sake of the jump. It was soon found that the swinging of halteres was useful for other exercises. In Figure 66 we see to the left a youth swinging the halteres sideways, his head is turned towards his extended left arm, and his right arm is bent, the hand being level with the breast. The type occurs on several vases, sometimes the left, sometimes the right arm being extended, but the head is always turned towards the extended hand. Now, if we compare this type with the type of the javelin-thrower drawing back his javelin to throw, we shall find that the position of body, arms, legs, and head is identical in the two types. Does it not seem, then, that we have here a halter exercise suggested by javelin-throwing, perhaps invented by the javelin-thrower to develop the special muscles and practise the special positions required for the throw? Perhaps we may recognize an intermediate position of this swing on a red-figured oinochoe in the British Museum (Figure 70). In this sideways swing of the halteres we have another familiar exercise of the modern gymnasium. Such exercises intended originally for the jumper or javelin-thrower were subsequently adopted by trainers and medical men, and were incorporated by them in their systems of physical training. This conjectural history of the use of the halteres is confirmed by the fact that on later vases, when athletic scenes have given place to groups of idle epheboi, the halteres are still frequently seen hanging on the wall as the symbol of athletic training.

Chapter 15

THROWING THE DISKOS

It will be remembered that while frequent reference is made in the Homeric poems to throwing the diskos,[562] the weight thrown at the games of Patroclus was a lump of unwrought iron described as "solos." The word diskos seems already to have acquired its special athletic meaning, but there is in Homer nothing distinctively athletic about "solos," which probably meant originally a boulder, then a mass of iron. Later writers occasionally use "solos" as equivalent to diskos, and scholiasts and lexicographers are much exercised in distinguishing the two terms.[563] Their arbitrary and often contradictory distinctions still find a place in our dictionaries and commentaries. The diskos, they tell us, is flat, the solos round and ball-shaped; the diskos of stone, the solos of metal; the diskos has a hole in it and is thrown by means of a cord; the solos is solid. The first distinction is fairly accurate: the diskos is more or less flat, the solos is a mass which may be roundish. As to material, we know that the diskos was made in stone and in metal; the solos might also be stone or metal. As to the hole and cord, authorities differ: some assign them to the diskos, some to the solos. That they belonged to the solos is disproved by every passage in which the word is used; that they belonged to the diskos is still more conclusively disproved by the monuments. The origin of this blunder, which is ascribed to Eratosthenes, may perhaps be found in some popular game in which a round object is bowled along by means of a cord wound round it. A game of this sort called "ruzzola" is still played in parts of Italy on the roads, much to the danger of pedestrians.[564] It is played with round stones about a foot in diameter, or sometimes with cheeses, which are believed to be improved by the treatment. A more probable explanation of the mistake is that suggested to me by Mr. J. L. Myres, and already accepted in Chapter II., that the scholia to *Iliad* xxiii have become dislocated, and that the hole and string belong not to the diskos or the solos, but to the word καλαῦροψ mentioned in the same passage. This word, usually interpreted as a shepherd's staff, is explained by Mr. Myres as a kind of bolas, an implement formed by a string to which one or more perforated stones are attached, which is used in the present day in South America for catching cattle, and is still a plaything with boys in the country districts of Greece. Whatever the explanation, the hole and string have nothing to do either with diskos or with solos, nor is there any ground for the statement that the solos was

---

[562] For this chapter *vide J.H.S.* xxvii. 1-36, where full references will be found; and Jüthner's *Antike Turngeräthe*, pp. 18 ff.
[563] References collected by Jüthner, pp. 19-21.
[564] Dodwell, *Tour through Greece*, 1819, ii. p. 39.

an athletic implement distinct from the diskos. The popular translation of diskos as "quoit" is erroneous and most misleading.

Figure 71. B.-f. amphora, in British Museum, B. 271.

The diskos of the fifth century was of bronze, but the Homeric diskos was of stone, and Pindar, therefore, makes the heroes Niceus and Castor hurl the older stone diskos rather than the bronze diskos of his own day.[565] The stone diskos is clearly represented on the black-figured vases of the sixth century as a thick white object (Figure 71), but the metal diskos must have been introduced before the close of this century. The British Museum possesses a bronze diskos found at Cephallenia which bears a sixth-century inscription (Figure 73).

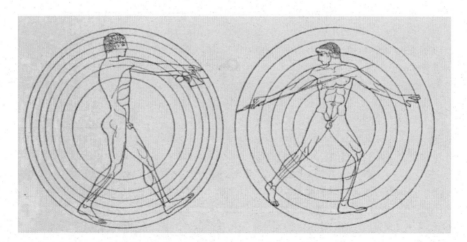

Figure 72. Bronze diskos found at Aegina. Berlin.

---

[565] *Ol.* x. 72; *Isthm.* i. 23.

There exist in our museums various inscribed and carved marble diskoi.[566] But though in size and shape they differ little from the bronze specimens, they are too fragile and thin for actual use, and their inscriptions prove clearly that they are merely votive offerings. The practice of inscribing and dedicating diskoi was an ancient one, as we see from the diskos of Iphitos dedicated at Olympia. With regard to the metal diskos we are more fortunate. Of the fifteen specimens which we possess, four are probably votive offerings, but one of these certainly, possibly three, had also been used; the rest were certainly intended for use. Their weights and measurements can be best seen from the following table:—

Finding-place.	Museum.	Weight in kilos.	Diameter in cms.	Thickness in mms.
1. Olympia	Olympia, *Inv.* 7567	5·707	34	5-13
2. Corfu	B.M. 2691	3·992	23	6-13
3. Gela	Vienna	3·800	28	7
4. Amyclae	Athens, De Ridder, *Cat.* 530	3·349	19	
5. Olympia	Olympia, *Inv.* 4257	2·945 (?)	22	6-12
6. Olympia	Olympia, *Inv.* 12,892	2·775	18	11-12
7. Olympia	Rome, Museo Kircheriano	2·378	21, 21·5	
8. Olympia	Olympia, *Inv.* 2859	2·083	19, 22·5	3 at edge
9. Sicily	B.M. 248	2·075	21	5
10. Olympia	Berlin	2·023	17·5	9-10
11. Aegina	Berlin	1·984	21	
12. Olympia	Berlin	1·721	20	7
13. Olympia	Berlin, *Inv.* 2286	1·353 (?)	20·5	4
14. Olympia	Olympia, *Inv.* 12,891	1·268	17	4-12
15. Cephallenia	B.M. 3207	1·245	16·5	5

Of these diskoi No. 1 is ornamented with concentric circles and bears on one side a dedication by the Corinthian pentathlete Publius Asclepiades, on the other side the name of the alytarch. The difference in the date, which is given respectively as Ol. 255 and 456, has been already explained.[567] From its style and weight it is probable that it was purely a votive offering and was never intended for use. Nos. 9 and 11 are of cast bronze, engraved on one side with the figure of a jumper, on the other with that of a javelin-thrower (Figure 72). The engraving belongs to the best period except that of the javelin-thrower on the British Museum diskos, which, if not actually spurious, is probably a late addition. Though in weight and size they approximate closely to Nos. 8 and 10, their flatness and the sharpness of their edges makes it doubtful if they were ever actually used. No. 11 is also ornamented with concentric circles. No. 3 had originally an inlaid dolphin, possibly of silver. No. 12 is of lead and has probably lost considerably in weight. No. 15, which is very badly worn, must also have been considerably heavier (Figure 73). It bears the following inscription in archaic letters of the sixth century:[568] "Exoïdas dedicated me to the twin sons of Great Zeus, the bronze diskos wherewith he conquered the high-souled Cephallenians."

---

[566] Cambridge, *Fitzwilliam Museum*, 70, 72; Καββαδίας Ἰλυπτὰ τοῦ Ἐθνικοῦ Μους. 93; Salzmann, *Nécropole de Camiros*, Pl. viii.
[567] *supra*, p. 183.
[568] Ἐχσοίδα(ς) μ' ἀνέθηκε ΔιFὸς Φο(ύ)ροιν μεγάλοιο χάλκεον ᾧ νίκασε Κεφαλ(λ)ᾶνας μεγαθύμους.

The dimensions of the diskos as represented in art correspond with those given in our table. On the vases, too, the diskos is often ornamented with concentric circles, as in Nos. 1 or 2, or with various forms of crosses and dots; while the dolphin on the diskos from Gela has its counterpart in the owl, the symbol of Athens, which is frequently depicted on Attic vases.[569]

When not in use, the diskos was kept in a sort of sling, the two ends of which were tied in a knot. In such a sling the diskos is often represented hanging on the wall or carried in the hands of some youth (Figure 17).

Figure 73. Diskos of Exoïdas. British Museum, 3207.

It is difficult to form any definite conclusion as to the size and weight of the diskos used in competitions. The diskoi are all more or less worn, and the weights are therefore only approximate. They seem, however, to fall into certain groups. The best marked group is formed by Nos. 8-11 and perhaps 12, which suggest a standard of about 2·1 kilos. Heavier standards are suggested by Nos. 2 and 3, and by Nos. 4 and 5, say 4·0 and 2·8 kilos respectively, while Nos. 14 and 15 point to a standard of 1·3. The difference between these standards is partially due to the fact, vouched for by Pausanias, that boys used a smaller and lighter diskos than men.[570] No doubt the standard varied greatly at different times and places. At Olympia three bronze diskoi were kept in the treasury of the Sicyonians[571] for the use of competitors in the pentathlon, and it seems probable that the diskos used there was heavier than that in use elsewhere.[572] Unfortunately, though there was only one competition with the diskos at Olympia, there are great differences in the eight diskoi found there, and no conclusion is possible even for Olympia. If any inference can be drawn from the heavy votive

---

[569] Jüthner, pp. 28, 29; Figures. 21, 22, 23.
[570] Paus. i. 35, 3.
[571] Paus. vi. 19, 3.
[572] Philostratus, *Heroic.* p. 291.

diskos dedicated by Publius in the third century A.D., it would be that in later times the weight of the diskos was greatly increased, much, of course, to the detriment of the sport. Certainly the lightest diskos which we possess is the sixth-century diskos from Cephallenia.

The scanty records which we possess give us little help towards determining the weight used. Phaÿllus is said to have thrown the diskos 95 feet, and Philostratus speaks of the hero Protesilaus throwing beyond a hundred cubits, and that with a diskos twice the size of the Olympian.[573] Statius, again, describes Phlegyas as hurling a diskos across the Alpheus at its widest.[574] As far as they go, these data agree with the one fact emphasized by ancient writers that the diskos was a heavy object. In the revived Olympic games a diskos is used weighing 2 kilos. It is made of wood with a metal core, and is a clumsy, ugly object for which there is absolutely no authority, infinitely inferior in every way to the ancient diskos. J. Sheridan threw it 135 ft. 8 in. at Athens in 1906, throwing in the free style, while in the cramped and artificial Greek style he succeeded in throwing 124 ft. 8 in. in the games of 1908. It would seem then that the men's diskos was probably heavier than 2 kilos; usually but not always, for Exoïdas, as we have seen, used one much lighter.

The place from which the diskos was thrown was called the βαλβίς. Our knowledge of the balbis is derived entirely from an obscure and much misunderstood passage in Philostratus,[575] describing the death of Hyacinthus who was accidentally killed by Apollo with a diskos. "The balbis," he says, "is small and sufficient for one man, marked off except behind, and it supports the right leg, the front part of the body leaning forward while it takes the weight off the other leg which is to be swung forward and follow through with the right hand." Then follows a description of the method of throwing the diskos, evidently based on Myron's diskobolos, perhaps an extract from some handbook of gymnastics. "The thrower is to bend his head to the right and stoop so as to catch a glimpse of his (right) side, and to throw the diskos with a rope-like pull, and putting all the force of the right side into the throw."

All that we learn from this passage is, that the balbis was marked off by a line in front, and by lines on the side, but not behind, so that the thrower could take as many preliminary steps as he chose. There is nothing to show that it was in any way a raised platform, much less a sloping platform such as has been adopted by the modern Greeks for the so-called "Hellenic style."[576] This extraordinary platform is 80 cm. long by 70 cm. wide, with a height of not more than 15 cm. behind and not less than 5 cm. in front. The only authority for this platform is Dr. Kietz' interpretation of an old, corrupt reading of the passage in Philostratus just quoted. Even if the old text were correct its evidence would be worthless in face of the manifest absurdity of the idea, and the fact that in all the numerous representations of the diskobolos there is not the slightest trace of such a platform. Again, the following words, as has been pointed out, are an obvious reminiscence of Myron's diskobolos. Can any one conceive of Myron's statue tilted forward on a sloping platform? Were it so, there would be indeed some excuse for Herbert Spencer's criticism that he is about to fall on his face.

It is natural to suppose that in the stadium the diskos and spear were thrown from the line of stone slabs which mark the start, and which are also called βαλβῖδες. The stone pillars

---

[573] *l.c.*
[574] *Theb.* vi. 675.
[575] *Im.* i. 24 (Benndorf and Schenkl). Fully discussed in *J.H.S.* xxvii. 9; cp. Jüthner in *Eranos Vindob.* p. 317; Pernice in *Jahrb.*, 1908, p. 95.
[576] Cp. G. S. Robertson, "On throwing the Discos," in *Official Handbook of the Olympic Games, 1908*, pp. 79-85.

placed along the sides of the course at regular intervals would have been useful for measuring the distance of the throw. But there is no direct evidence for identifying the balbis with the starting lines. In the Delphic inscription, containing contracts for the Pythian festival,[577] we find mention of "the arrangements for the pentathletes," the contract for which was eight staters. These would seem to refer to arrangements for the diskos and spear competitions, i.e., the balbis and means for measuring the throws.

The throw was measured from the front line of the balbis to the place where the diskos or spear fell, and it is obvious that the competitor might not overstep this line under penalty of disqualification.[578] In the gymnasia this line might be marked out temporarily by means of spears stuck in the ground on either side, or, as Dr. Pernice has suggested, by a line traced on the sand, though I cannot agree with his interpretation of certain vases on which he fancies the tracing of this line to be represented.[579] The place where the diskos fell was marked by a peg or arrow as described by Statius,[580] and on several vases we see a diskobolos in the act of putting down or taking up such a mark (Figure 74).

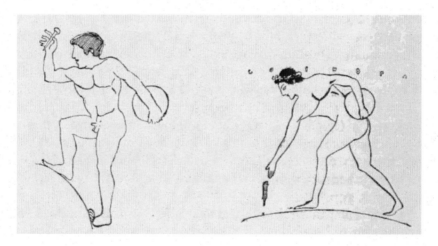

Figure 74. (*a*) R.-f. kylix. Chiusi. (*b*) R.-f. kylix. Würzburg, 357, A.

In the modern "free style" the diskos is thrown from a circular area 2-1/2 metres in diameter, and the method of throwing is a modification of throwing the hammer, the thrower's body making two or three complete turns. There is no trace in ancient times of such a method or of a circular area and, effective as it is, we may doubt if it would ever have been invented but for the experience acquired in hammer-throwing or in slinging weights.

Throwing the diskos has acquired a practical interest of late years owing to the revival of this event in the modern Olympic Games. Unfortunately neither of the styles at present in vogue can be regarded as satisfactory from an archaeological standpoint. For our knowledge of the ancient method of throwing we depend almost entirely on the monuments. The scanty literary evidence has no independent value. Fortunately the monumental evidence is

---

[577] *vide* p. 261.
[578] This is the obvious meaning of μὴ τέρμα προβάς in Pindar, *Nem.* vii. 70.
[579] In *Jahrb.*, 1908, pp. 95 ff., he enumerates Gerh. *A. V.* 22, Naples 3084, *B.M. Vases*, E. 256. On the B.M. vase we see a familiar type of a youth preparing to throw a javelin; the vase in Gerh. represents the same type, but left-handed, whether by accident or intention; the Naples vase is equally inconclusive.
[580] *Theb.* vi. 679-712.

exceptionally rich and varied. The two statues—the Standing Diskobolos and Myron's Diskobolos—are of first-rate importance, such works being independent of the accidents which affect the types in the lesser arts. Besides these we have a multitude of vases, bronzes, coins, and gems connected with this subject. Most of the schemes based upon this evidence are, however, more or less unsatisfactory, because the authors have failed to recognise two important factors.[581] In the first place, apparent divergence of type is often due not to a difference in motive but to artistic causes, to differences in material, or space, or to the age or style of the artists. Secondly, though the principle of the Greek throw appears to have been always the same, there can be no doubt that the styles of individual performers were as varied as the styles of modern golfers, and these differences of style were naturally reflected in art. Hence the absurdity of endeavouring, as so many writers have done, to force all the attitudes depicted on the vases into a single series of movements.

Figure 75. The Standing Diskobolos. Vatican. Copy of fifth-century original. (From a photograph by Anderson.)

The principle of the throw is clearly shown in Myron's Diskobolos (Figure 13). The thrower, taking his stand with the right foot forward, swings or lifts the diskos to the front in his left hand, and then grasping it with his right hand, swings it vigorously downwards and backwards, turning both head and body to the right until he reaches the position represented by Myron. The right foot is the pivot on which the whole body swings. This swing of the body round a fixed point is of the essence of the swing of the diskos as it is of the swing of a

---

[581] Vide Kietz, *Diskoswurf*, Munich, 1892. Six in *Gaz. Archéolog.* 1888, 291. Jüthner *l.c.* Chryssaphis, *Bulletin du Comité des Jeux Olympiques 1906*, p. 57. Criticisms of these schemes will be found in *J.H.S. l.c.*

golf club. The force comes not from the arms, which merely connect the body and the weight, but from the lift of the thighs and the swing of the body.

If we confine ourselves to the two statues, we see that no movement of the feet is necessary in the preliminary movements; but this simple scheme fails to explain a number of vase paintings and bronzes representing intermediate positions in which the diskobolos has his left foot forward. There are two types of such frequent occurrence that we may feel sure that they belong to the usual method of throwing the diskos.

Figure 76. R.-f. kylix, in *British Museum*, E. 6.
1. The diskobolos holds the diskos in front of him in both hands (Figure 76).
2. He holds the diskos flat in his right hand which is turned outwards so that the diskos rests against the forearm. The left hand is usually raised above the head.[582]

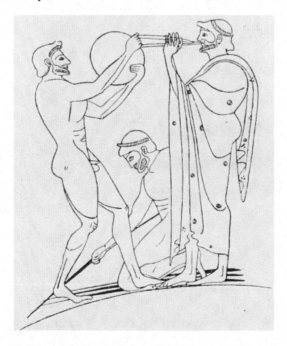

Figure 77. B.-f. kelebe. British Museum, B. 361.

---

[582] A full list of the vases and bronzes representing these two types is given in *J.H.S. l.c.* pp. 14-24.

The first of these positions is the natural connecting link between the preliminary stance and Myron's statue. If no movement of the feet took place, we should expect to find that the right foot was always advanced. In many cases this is so, but in the majority the left foot is advanced (Figure 77). This circumstance can hardly be due to accident, or carelessness, or even to the tendency general in Greek sculpture to put the left foot forward. The uniformity of other details is remarkable. The advanced leg is always straight or nearly so, the other leg more or less bent. The right hand always grasps the diskos, the left merely supports it. We are forced to conclude, therefore, either that the thrower took up his stand with the left foot forward, or that, as the diskos swung forward in the left hand, the left foot was advanced. How then did he pass from this position with the left foot forward to the position of Myron's statue? The change of feet may be effected in two ways—either by making another step forward with the right foot, or by drawing back the left foot. The former was the method adopted by some of the competitors in the Olympic games of 1896. Starting with the left foot forward, the thrower raised the diskos in both hands to a level with the shoulders and at the moment of swinging it back advanced the right foot, stepping forward again with the left in making the actual throw. This method requires room for three steps, the impetus being helped by this forward movement. The other method requires room only for one step, and the pendulum-like swing of the left leg, first forward, then back, and finally forward again, seems at least equally effective as helping the swing of the body, like the preliminary waggle of a golf club. Both methods are effective and it seems probable from the vases that both were employed. The former method is suggested by Figure 79, the latter by Figure 78.

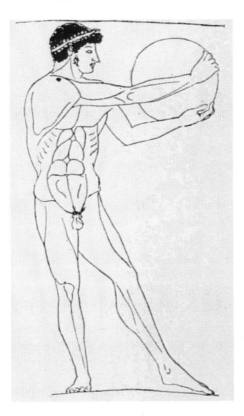

Figure 78. R.-f. krater of Amasis. Corneto.

Figure 79. R.-f. pelike, in British Museum, E. 395.

An examination of the second type with the diskos flat in the right hand confirms these conclusions. This type is an excellent illustration of differences due to artistic causes. The attitude of the body varies from the stiff upright pose of archaic bronzes and vases to the graceful curves of the stooping figure on a vase assigned to Euphronius (Figure 80). Sometimes the body is inclined forward, sometimes it is upright, sometimes it is thrown well back. The essential point, however, is the position of the arms, and this is always constant. The diskos rests against the right forearm, and the left hand is raised above the head or stretched to the front. There can be little doubt that in all these cases the moment represented is the backward swing of the diskos. The position of the right hand turned outward is necessary to prevent the diskos from slipping while the left arm is raised to balance the body as it swings. The best example of this type is a beautiful little bronze, exhibited at the Burlington Fine Arts Club in 1903 (Figure 81). Here the right foot is well advanced, the right knee bent, and the weight, as in Myron's statue, rests entirely on the right leg, the left foot touching the ground only with the toes. This is the normal position of the right leg: but just as in the first type when the normal position was with the left foot forward we found numerous exceptions with the right foot advanced, so here the left foot is occasionally in front.[583] This variation points to a variation in the style of throwing. A thrower who has advanced the left foot in the forward swing, must, as we have seen, either advance the right foot, or draw back the left to reach the position of Myron's statue. If he draws back the left foot, he may let go the diskos with the left hand first, in which case we have the diskos swinging back in the right hand and the left leg still advanced. If, however, he draws back the left leg first, he will for a moment be still holding the diskos in both hands but the right leg will be still advanced, and it is noticeable that on vases which show this attitude, the left foot rests very lightly on the ground and the body is slightly inclined forward. The precise moment at which the change takes place is just one of those details in which we should expect to find a difference in style.

---

[583] *J.H.S. l.c.* p. 18.

Figure 80. Interior of Figure 66.

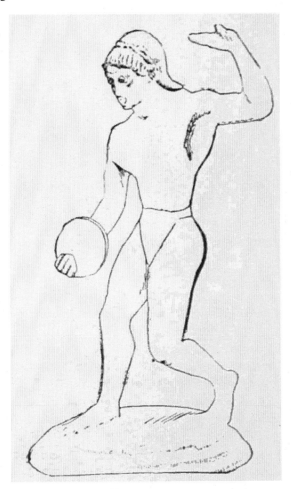

Figure 81. Fifth-century bronze. (*J.H.S.* xxvii. p. 18.)

We see then that while the principle observed in Myron's statue remained constant, considerable latitude was allowed as to the movements of the feet and the style of throwing. Bearing this in mind, we may proceed to reconstruct the method of throwing.

THE STANCE AND PRELIMINARY MOVEMENTS

After first rubbing the diskos with sand to secure a firm grip as described by Statius, the thrower takes his stand on the balbis, which is marked out by a line in front, and possibly at the sides, but not behind, so that he may take as many steps as he pleases. He takes his stand a little behind the front line, carefully measuring with his eye the space which he requires, so as not to overstep the line before the diskos has quitted his hand. This is the precise moment represented in the Standing Diskobolos (Figure 75).

Figure 82. B.-f. lekythos, in British Museum, B. 576.

The care with which the thrower is planting his right foot, the firm grip which the toes are taking of the ground, and the consequent contraction of the muscles of the calf, all indicate that though for the moment the weight may rest on the left leg, it will immediately be transferred to the right. The position is one of rest; but it is the rest which precedes action, and every line of the figure betokens the readiness for action. Particularly noticeable is the direction of the head and eyes. The head is inclined to the right and slightly downwards, and the eyes are fixed on the ground a few feet in front; he is, as I said, measuring his distance. The right forearm is said to be modern; if so, the restoration is particularly happy; the position of the arm is found in certain bronzes resembling the statue, and the nervous curl of the fingers appropriately suggests the alertness which characterises the whole figure.

Starting, then, in this position, the thrower swings the diskos forward. He may either keep the left leg stationary or bring it forward. In the latter case he will be in the position depicted on the exterior of the Panaetius kylix in Munich (Figure 17). The left leg is advanced and straight, the body leans forward, and the right hand is extended to the front, ready to grip the diskos as it swings to the front. The completion of the movement is shown on the interior of the same kylix where the thrower grasps the diskos in both hands, his body leaning backward with a pendulum-like movement preparatory to the swing backwards.

Figure 83. Bronze statuette. New York.

The position of the standing diskobolos is reproduced in certain bronzes but does not occur on the vases. The latter suggest an alternative method of starting, the diskos being swung forward not in the left hand but in both hands. Such is perhaps the explanation of the figure on a black-figured lekythos in the British Museum (Figure 82) and of certain other vases.

A totally distinct stance is represented by a fine bronze in the Metropolitan Museum of Art in New York (Figure 83). The thrower stands with the right foot forward and the diskos raised in the left hand level with the head. A similar type occurs on several vases, the best of which is a red-figured krater in the Ashmolean at Oxford.[584] From this position the diskos is raised above the head in both hands. This moment is represented in a bronze in the National Museum at Athens.[585] The thumb of the left hand is turned inwards on the inside of the diskos, whereas on the vases it is usually on the outside. The thumb could not be on the inside if the diskos was swung upwards in the manner first described. There can therefore be no doubt that we have here a totally distinct style. A British Museum bronze (Figure 84) carries

---

[584] No. 561.
[585] No. 7412. Cp. r.-f. amphora, Munich, 374, published in Hoppin's *Euthymidês*.

the movement a little further and shows the moment of transition to the downward swing. The diskos, instead of being upright, lies flat on the palm of the right hand, while the left hand only touches it lightly and is on the point of letting go. Here, too, the thumb is on the inside. In all these bronzes the right leg is advanced, and it seems probable, therefore, that there has been no movement of the feet.

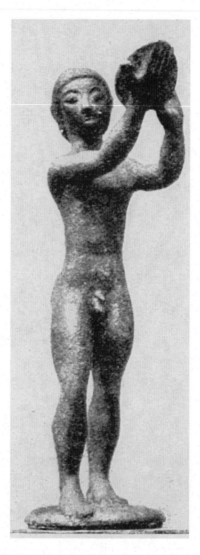

Figure 84. Bronze diskobolos, in British Museum, 675.

THE BACKWARD SWING

At this point the left hand releases its hold and the diskos is swung back in the right hand. If the right foot is in front, no change of feet is necessary; if the left is in front, either the left must be drawn back or the right foot advanced. The body, which at the end of the swing forward was upright or inclined backwards, is bent first forwards and then sideways, the head following the movements of the body. The diskos is held flat in the hand and the hand turned outwards till it passes the body. We have already seen several representations of the early part of the swing. The later part is finely represented on a red-figured kylix in the Louvre (Figure 85), and a fragment of an alabastron at Würzburg shows an interesting back view of the same movement.

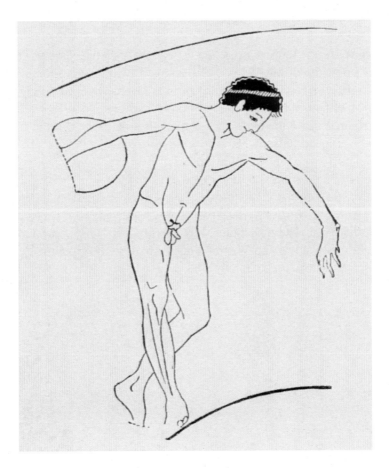

Figure 85. R.-f. kylix. Louvre.

The top of the swing is, of course, represented in Myron's statue. An interesting variation of the top of the swing occurs on a number of coins of Cos belonging to the early part of the fifth century (Figure 86). These coins have been often misinterpreted and supposed to represent a distinct moment either before or after the top of the swing. A few experiments would convince any one that no one but a contortionist could pass from this position to that of Myron's statue or *vice versa*. An examination of a series of these coins leads to the conclusion that the peculiarities which they present are due to artistic causes. The maker of the coin die has tried to represent the top of the swing from the front, and the difficulty of the task has been too much for him. The amount of foreshortening required to represent the forward bend of the body was far beyond him, and even if it had not been, the success of the result on a coin would be more than doubtful. He therefore adopted the obvious expedient of bending the body to the right instead of forwards. The bend of the right arm which is noticeable on some of the coins is clearly due to considerations of space. The diskos is represented at right angles to the body, because, if drawn parallel, it would appear from the front as a thin line, which in so small a space would be almost unrecognisable. The position of the unemployed left hand may point to a difference in the style of throwing.

THE THROW

"The diskobolos," says Lucian, speaking of Myron's statue, "seems as if he would straighten himself up at the throw."[586] At the beginning of the swing forward the extensor muscles come into play, and by a vigorous lift from the right thigh the whole body is raised and straightened. This momentary but most important movement is cleverly represented on two vases, a Panathenaic vase in Naples and a black-figured hydria in the British Museum (Figures 87, 88).[587] The attitude depicted is unique in Greek athletic art, which prefers positions of comparative rest and equilibrium. But here we have a sort of snapshot, an impressionist picture of a position almost too momentary to be seen, too unstable to maintain. On the Panathenaic vase especially, the thrower seems to be flying from the ground in a way which recalls the figures of winged Victory so strongly as to suggest the idea that the attitude is borrowed from that type. The diskobolos, however, has no wings, and unless he quickly recovers his equilibrium by advancing one foot, he must fall to the ground.

Figure 86. Coins of Cos, in British Museum (enlarged).

---

[586] *Philopseud.* 18.
[587] Dr. Jüthner deduces from these vases his theory of the *Kreisschwung*, an impossible method of throwing the diskos by whirling the arm right round, for a criticism of which *vide J.H.S. l.c.* p. 33.

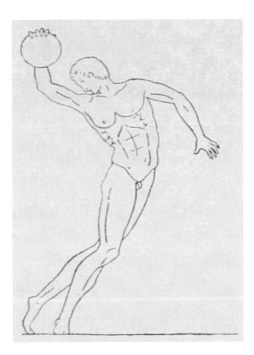

Figure 87. Panathenaic amphora. Naples, Racc. Cum. 184.

The modern thrower in the Hellenic style does contrive to rid himself of the diskos in this attitude without advancing the left foot, but the throw inevitably suffers, and there is no evidence that the ancients ever imposed such a restriction. Moreover, in the modern style the downward swing of the diskos almost precedes the straightening of the body; on the vase the body is already lifted while the diskos remains behind. The inevitable conclusion is that the actual throw takes place off the left foot which is advanced before the diskos leaves the hand. This is the only rational method of throwing, and that this was the method of the Greeks is proved by the evidence of literature and art. "The left foot," says Philostratus in the passage already quoted, "must be swung forward and follow through with the right hand." These words are confirmed by the less definite language of Lucian and Statius, and by the vases. A red-figured kylix at Boulogne (Figure 89) shows the early part of the movement, and the continuation is seen on a black-figured hydria in Vienna (Figure 90). On both vases the diskobolos strides forward with the left leg.

The so-called bronze diskoboloi of Naples are said to represent the movement after the throw, but this interpretation seems impossible, in view of the position of the arms and the alertness and expectancy expressed both by the figures and the heads, and I have no doubt that they are really wrestling boys. Moreover, as the diskos leaves the hand, the natural tendency is to advance the right foot to prevent the thrower from falling forward, and in the bronzes the left foot is advanced. The attitude of the follow through must have been somewhat similar to that of the youth on the right hand in Figure 89, but it is impossible with certainty to identify such figures with diskos throwers.

In modern throwing competitions it is generally the rule that the thrower may not overstep the line till the object has quitted the hand. If this was the rule of the Greeks, the diskos thrower was not allowed to overstep the line with the left foot; such a rule offers a natural explanation of the position of the head in the Standing Diskobolos described above.

Figure 88. B.-f. hydria. British Museum, E. 164.

Figure 89. R.-f. kylix. Boulogne.

Dr. Pernice has recently tried to prove that the diskos thrower took his stand with the right foot immediately behind the line, and that it was this foot which was not allowed to cross the line. There is little difference between his view and mine, seeing that in any case the right foot is stationary till the throw is completed, and only follows through after the diskos has left the hand. In support of his view Dr. Pernice cites certain vases where, as he says, a figure is seated on the ground carefully watching the thrower's right foot.[588] This evidence seems to me far from conclusive, seated figures being commonly introduced in early art for the sake of variety or to fill empty spaces. Moreover, this view does not explain the position of the statue. In the dearth of further evidence no certainty is attainable.

A summary of the movements described may be useful—

---

[588] Gerh. *A. V.* 260, Naples 3084, *B. M. Vases*, B. 361 (Figure 77), and a lekythos in Boulogne (*J.H.S. l.c.* Figure 22).

1. The stance.
    (*a*) Position of standing diskobolos (Figure 75), or
    (*b*) Diskos held in both hands level with the waist (Figure 82), or
    (*c*) Diskos raised in left hand level with the head (Figure 83).
From these positions, with or without a change of foot, the diskos is raised to
2. Position with left foot forward (usually) and diskos in both hands,
    (*a*) Extended horizontally to the front (Figure 76, etc.), or
    (*b*) Raised above the head.
3. The diskos is swung downwards, resting on the right forearm. If the left foot is forward, either before or in the course of the swing,
    (*a*) The left foot is drawn back (Figure 78), or
    (*b*) The right foot is advanced (Figure 79), so that we reach
4. The position of Myron's diskobolos (Figure 13).
5. At the beginning of the swing forward the body is straightened (Figures 87, 88).
6. And as the diskos swings down, the left foot is vigorously advanced (Figures 89, 90).
7. Finally after the diskos has left the hand, the right foot is again advanced.

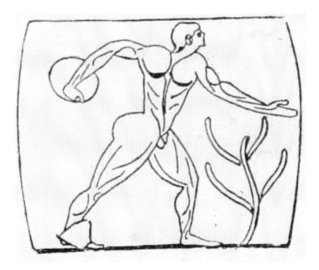

Figure 90. B.-f. hydria. Vienna, 318.

We see then that the principle contained in Myron's statue remains fixed, while there is room for considerable diversity in style and detail, especially in the movement of the feet. This scheme differs essentially from both the styles employed in the modern Olympic games. The "free style" abandons the principle; the so-called Hellenic style demands a slavish adherence to an artificial model. When diskos-throwing was first revived in Athens in 1896, the Greeks and other competitors, taking for model Myron's statue and untrammelled by theories, naturally developed a style which certainly approximated to the true style of the ancients. A new method was invented shortly afterwards by foreign athletes, particularly Americans, who applied to the diskos the principles employed in throwing the hammer and the heavy weight, in which the force is gained by one or more complete turns of the body. This method was certainly effective, but it was not Greek, and it destroyed the distinctive character of the exercise. This annoyed the Greeks, and to check such innovations they devised the so-called "Hellenic style," and in the last two Olympic games there were separate competitions in the two styles. Unfortunately "the Hellenic style" is as far removed from the true style as the free style. The throw is made from the ridiculous sloping balbis already described, and it is ordained that because Myron's diskobolos has his right foot forward, the right foot must be kept forward till the completion of the throw. A more senseless restriction it is hard to imagine. Not only is it fatal to all grace and freedom of movement, but it shows a complete misunderstanding of the statue, and is, as we have seen, contrary to all the evidence of literature and art. The mistake is much to be regretted. Diskos-throwing is a valuable and graceful exercise, which well deserves to find a place in our modern sports; but if ever it is to regain its popularity, it must be by a return to the true methods of the ancients.

In heroic times throwing the diskos was a separate event, and various gods and heroes excelled therein; in historical times it only occurs as part of the pentathlon, and as such it was accompanied by the flute as represented in Figure 77. The only separate competition with the diskos was at Olbia, a Milesian colony in Scythia, at the festival of Achilles Pontarches.[589] The diskos, however, seems to have played an important part in the life of the gymnasium and palaestra if we may judge from the frequent allusions to it in literature and the countless representations of it in art. It even won favour with the Romans, who despised most Greek sports, and Horace mentions throwing the diskos and the javelin as manly exercises fit for a young soldier.[590] As a physical exercise it was certainly valuable. According to Lucian it strengthened the shoulders and gave tone to the extremities.[591] Doctors approved of it, and Aretaeus recommends it as a cure for chronic headache and dizziness.[592]

---

[589] *C.I.G.* i. 2076.
[590] *Carm.* i. 8, 10.
[591] *Anacharsis*, 27.
[592] Krause, *Gym.* p. 464, n. 9.

Chapter 16

THROWING THE JAVELIN

The javelin used in Greek sports is called variously ἄκων, ἀκόντιον, μεσάγκυλον, ἀποτομάς.[593] The latter term appears to denote merely a lath or stick, and accurately describes the javelin as represented on the vases. A straight pole, in length nearly equal to the height of a man, though occasionally longer, and about the thickness of a man's finger, it is one of the commonest objects in palaestra scenes, whether in use or planted in the ground singly or in pairs, perhaps to mark a starting-line for jump or throw. These rods were formerly described as jumping-poles, but the fact that the throwing-strap or ankyle is often attached to them proves that they are nothing more than javelins. At the same time there is no reason why they should not have served as measuring rods (κανόνες) for measuring the jump, a use which is perhaps represented on the British Museum kelebe (Figure 77).

The athletic javelin is in the vast majority of cases pointless. On early black-figured vases such as the kelebe just mentioned, it is represented by a black line which seems to taper, but this is a mere accident of technique, the natural result of a line drawn with a single rapid stroke of brush or pen. On the red-figured vases the rod is usually square at the end, and often appears to have a blunt cap or ferule, indicated by a thickening of the end, or by a black patch or by lines which represent the binding by which it is attached. Such, we may suppose, were the javelins which Xenophon recommends cavalry soldiers to use in practice, provided with a round end (ἐσφαιρωμένα) like the button on the modern foil or bayonet.[594] These caps served not only for protection, but to give to the head of the javelin the necessary weight, without which it would not fly properly. Blunt javelins were naturally used for practice, especially for distance throws.

Pointed javelins are rarely represented in athletic scenes; but their use even in practice is shown by the speech of Antiphon in defence of a youth who accidentally hit and killed a boy who ran across the range as he was throwing.[595] On the vases which represent javelin throwing on horseback at a target, the javelins are all pointed, and in two cases have long leaflike heads such as we see in hunting scenes.[596] For throwing at a target, pointed javelins were necessary, at all events in competitions: but the enormous preponderance of the blunt

---

[593] Jüthner, *Antike Turngeräthe*, p. 37; *J.H.S.* xxvii. pp. 249-273.
[594] *De re equestri*, viii. 10.
[595] *Tetralogia*, ii. 4. An example of the pointed javelin occurs in Figure 150.
[596] *Vide infra*, p. 358.

javelins justifies the conclusion that these were generally used for practice, and that, down to the close of the fifth century distance-throwing was more usual than throwing at a target.

Whether pointed or blunt, the athletic javelin was evidently a light weapon, and Anacharsis contemptuously contrasts it with more formidable weapons which are not carried about by the wind.[597] It was thrown by means of a thong, called ἀγκύλη or amentum, fastened near the centre of the javelin, which was therefore called μεσάγκυλον. The amentum was a leather thong, a foot or eighteen inches in length, if we may judge from the numerous representations of a javelin thrower (ἀκοντιστής) holding the javelin in one hand, and the thong in the other.[598] It was detachable, but before use was firmly bound round the shaft, in such a way as to leave a loop three to four inches long, in which the thrower inserted his first, or his first and middle fingers. The point of attachment was near the centre of gravity, in the lightheaded javelins of athletics almost in the centre of the shaft, in the heavier javelins of war or the chase generally nearer to the head. Possibly, too, its place varied, according as the javelin was to be thrown for distance, or at a mark. By putting the amentum behind the centre of gravity, it is possible to increase the distance thrown, but at a sacrifice of accuracy. Hence the athlete fastened it to suit his taste shortly before use. On the British Museum hydria shown in Figure 88 a youth is seated on the ground in the act of attaching the amentum. On a red-figured kylix at Würzburg (Figure 91) we see a youth winding the amentum round the shaft, while he holds the other end tight with his foot. Some of the ways in which the amentum was fastened can be seen in the accompanying illustration. The clearest example is that from the Alexander Mosaic in Naples (Figure 92e). In every case it is only the actual loop which is left free.

Figure 91. R.-f. kylix. Würzburg, 432.

The amentum was no invention of the gymnasium but was adopted by the gymnasium from war and the chase. Whether it was used in Homeric times we cannot say. The principle of the sling was certainly known to the Homeric shepherd, and besides the long-shadowing spear of the chieftain, there was a lighter and shorter weapon (αἰγανέη) which like the bow

---

[597] Lucian, *Anacharsis*, 32.
[598] Jüthner, *l.c.*, Figures . 34, 35, 36. Jüthner proves conclusively that the objects represented on the Panaetius kylix and elsewhere (Figure 17) are not compasses, but amenta misdrawn.

was used for hunting, and by the common soldiery in war and in sport. The warrior vase from Mycenae[599] shows two types of spear, a long spear clenched firmly in the hand, and a short spear raised almost at arm's length behind the head, the hand being pointed as if the fingers were extended as they are in holding the amentum.

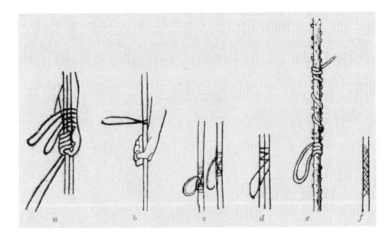

Figure 92. Various methods of attaching the amentum. (*J.H.S.* xxvii. p. 250.)

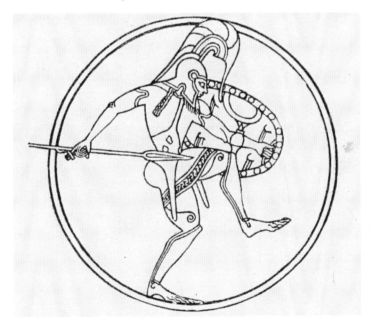

Figure 93. B.-f. kylix. British Museum, B. 380.

From the sixth century onwards the amentum was used for throwing the javelin in war, in hunting, and in the chase. It is frequently represented on early black-figured vases. Its use is admirably shown on the interior of a Chalcidian kylix in the British Museum, where a fully armed warrior with his fingers inserted in the thong, prepares to throw a javelin with a sort of underhand throw, a throw in which certain savages to-day are said to be extraordinarily

---

[599] Schliemann-Schuchardt (Eng. Trans.), Figures . 284, 285.

skilful (Figure 93). The more usual overhand throw is employed by some of the warriors on the François vase (Figure 94), who advance to the attack with arms drawn back and fingers inserted in the thong in the manner which Xenophon recommends to his peltasts.[600] The fingering and the whole attitude are precisely the same as we find in athletic scenes, except that in the latter the head is usually turned backward, a position obviously ill-suited to the warrior or hunter. In a boar-hunting scene, depicted on a Corinthian vase in the British Museum, B. 37, javelins fitted with amenta are seen sticking in the boar's back, a clear proof that they were fixed to the shaft and did not remain in the thrower's hand.

Figure 94. François vase. Florence.

The light javelin, fitted with the amentum, was primarily intended for throwing; but the vases show that it could also be used for thrusting or stabbing, in which case the thong served as a convenient handle or grip. It also marked the proper place to grasp the javelin, and is therefore occasionally represented on the long spear, which, though generally used for thrusting, could on occasions be thrown. These long spears were the weapons of the Homeric chieftains and of the hoplites who formed the chief strength of the Greek forces at the time of the Persian wars. The light javelin was the weapon of the common soldiery and light-armed troops, and its real importance dates from the closing years of the Peloponnesian War, when the value of light-armed troops and cavalry began to be realized. These light-armed troops were mostly mercenaries, Lydians, Mysians, Arcadians, Aetolians, Thessalians, Thracians. All these races were skilled in the use of the javelin. At Athens, where the cavalry were recruited from the ranks of the young nobles, the javelin was the special weapon of the ephebos, who is frequently represented on horseback, holding in his hand a pair of javelins. Javelin throwing was an important part of his training; competitions in it were multiplied, and in the third century B.C. we find special teachers of the javelin, ἀκοντισταί, engaged by the state to train the epheboi at Athens and elsewhere.[601]

---

[600] *Anab.* v. 2, 12.
[601] Ditt. *Syll.* 2nd Ed., ii. 520, 521, 522, 523.

The distribution of the amentum[602] is a point of some interest and importance. It does not seem to have been a Greek invention. It was known at an early date in Italy, and was freely used by Etruscans, Samnites, and Messapians, but it does not appear to have been used in the Roman army till after the Punic Wars. The tragula, the weapon of the Spanish in the second Punic War, was thrown with an amentum. In Caesar's time it was the weapon of the Gallic cavalry. From this time it was widely used by the light-armed mercenaries. There are traces of the amentum on the Roman weapons found at Alise Sainte Reine, and we even find it attached to the heavy spear of the legionary. Going yet further afield, we find it represented on an embossed sword-belt discovered at Watsch in Austria, and there is reason to suppose that the light javelins found at La Tène were thus thrown. Undoubtedly the amentum was known in Denmark in the early Iron Age. Remains of it have been found at Nydam. The spears found there are 8 to 10 feet long. On the middle of the shaft are often visible certain small bronze rivets, between which a cord was fastened. In some cases the cord was found still fastened between the rivets. Lastly, we find the amentum frequently mentioned in old Irish story. Thus in the battle of Moyreth "Cuanna, pressing his foot on the solid earth, put his finger in the string of his broad-headed spear and made a cast at Congal." This loop, called *suanem* or *suaineamh*, was made of silk or flax, and the laigan or spear to which it was attached is said to have been brought to Ireland by Gaulish mercenaries in the fourth century B.C. An interesting survival of this old Irish spear with its loop is seen in a picture of Captain Thomas Lee, painted in 1594, now in the possession of Lord Dillon.

We see, then, that the amentum was known throughout Greece and Italy, in Spain and Gaul, in Central Europe, in Denmark, and Ireland. The light javelin to which it belongs is the weapon of the less highly civilized peoples. It is a weapon of the chase and of the common people, but it plays little part in the heavily-equipped citizen armies of Greece and Rome. In both lands it comes into prominence with the organization of light-armed troops, and then chiefly as the weapon of subject states and mercenaries. Hence we are forced to the conclusion that the amentum was the invention of the tribes of Central Europe, and in the course of their wanderings was carried throughout the southern and western portions of the Continent.

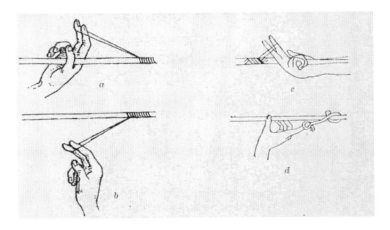

Figure 95. Illustrations of the use of the throwing-thong. *a*, *b*, Jüthner, Figures 47, 48. Reconstruction of throw. *c*, Detail from *B.M. Vases*, B. 134. *d*, The ounep of New Caledonia.

---

[602] For fuller details *vide J.H.S.* xxvii. p. 255.

The fixed amentum does not appear to be known outside Europe, but somewhat similar contrivances exist to-day among savage tribes. Such is the ounep used by the people of New Caledonia and the New Hebrides. It is a thickish cord, 6 or 8 inches long, with a loop at one end and a knot at the other. The spears are 9 to 12 feet long, with a slight projection just behind the centre of gravity, behind which the cord is placed and twisted over the knot in such a way as to untie as the spear is thrown, remaining itself in the thrower's hand. Examples of it can be seen in the Ethnographical Gallery of the British Museum, and our illustration is taken from a drawing exhibited there (Figure 95). A combination of this thong with the throwing-stick is found in New Zealand. The throwing-stick is by far the commonest contrivance for increasing the throw of a spear. It is widely used in Australia, Melanesia, Central America, and among the Eskimos, but is unknown in Europe, although throwing-sticks made of bone appear to have been used by Palaeolithic man in France.

The working of the amentum can be easily understood from our illustration. In preparing for an overhand throw the spear rests on the web between the thumb and fingers, but is really held by the two fingers inserted in the loop and projecting above the shaft. At the moment of throw the position is reversed; the pull on the amentum gives a half-turn to the shaft, and the javelin is held only by the amentum, the fingers being below the shaft. The action of the amentum is similar to that of the rifling of a gun. By imparting a rotatory movement to the missile it not only helps it to keep its direction but also increases its carry and penetrating power. The carry is further increased by the additional leverage given to the thrower's arm. It is obvious that, as Philostratus points out,[603] length of finger was a considerable advantage to a javelin thrower.

The effect of the amentum on a light javelin has been demonstrated by practical experiments carried out by General Reffye for the Emperor Napoleon. It was found that a javelin which could only be thrown 20 metres by hand could, after a little practice, be thrown 80 metres, with the help of an amentum. Jüthner further records that an inexperienced thrower increased his throw from 25 to 65 metres by its use. The meaning of these figures can be realised from the fact that the record for javelin throwing made by Lemming, the winner at the Olympic games, was only 57·33 metres. It must be noted, however, that the javelin used in these games was a heavy one, weighing 800 grammes (about 2 lbs.), whereas the Greek javelin was very much lighter.[604]

The method of throwing the javelin is clearly shown on the vases. Two things are necessary: the amentum must be firmly fastened to the shaft, and the loop must be drawn tight by the fingers before the throw. The fastening of the amentum has been already described. On a red-figured psykter (Figure 96) we see the next stage in the preparation. A group of youths are preparing to practise under the supervision of a paidotribes and his assistant, while two other paidotribai are occupied with a pair of wrestlers. Two of the youths are testing the bindings; resting one end of the javelin on the ground, and holding it firm with their left hand, they pass the right hand along the shaft to see that the binding is secure. A third in the same position is passing his fingers through the loop, the lines of which have disappeared. A fourth

---

[603] *Gym.* 31, and Jüthner's note, p. 249.
[604] The lightness of the Greek javelin is illustrated by Xenophon. In the passage of the Ten Thousand through the mountainous territory of the Carduchi, the Greeks picked up the long arrows of the enemy, and, fitting thongs to them (ἐναγκυλῶντες), used them as javelins. By means of a thong it is possible to throw a dart too light to be thrown effectively by hand alone. *Anab.* iv. 2, 28.

has already inserted his fingers in the loop, and, raising the javelin breast-high, presses it forward with his left hand so as to draw the thong tight.

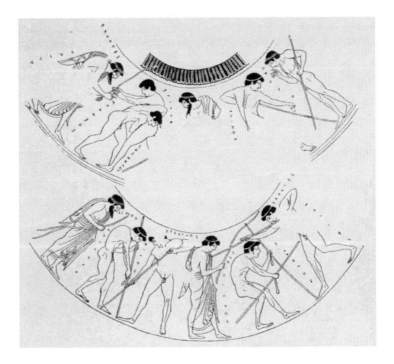

Figure 96. R.-f. psykter. Bourguignon Coll.

Two styles of javelin throwing can be distinguished, one in which the javelin is horizontal, the other in which it is pointed more or less upwards. The horizontal style is the practical style of war or the chase, the other the style of pure athletics. In the latter distance is the one and only object, and the thrower may take his time; in the former distance is only a secondary consideration compared with force and accuracy, and everything depends on rapidity of action. It is the difference between throwing in a cricket ball from the long field and throwing it in competition.

THE PRACTICAL STYLE

The soldier or hunter must have his javelin ready for use at a moment's notice. He therefore carries it with his fingers passed through the loop (διηγκυλισμένος). He may carry it horizontally at his side, as does the warrior in Figure 93, but a freer and more natural position is with the arm bent and the javelin sloped over the shoulder and pointed downwards. From this position he can draw his arm straight back for the throw, or raise the elbow so that the javelin is level with his head, the natural position for taking aim. This manner of holding the javelin is implied or represented in numerous scenes of war or the chase, and is equally serviceable on horseback or on foot. Perhaps the best examples of it occur on two Panathenaic vases representing the pentathlon, one in the British Museum, the other in Leyden (Figures 107, 108). On the Leyden vase the akontistes carries his javelin still on the slope; so does the athlete who heads the procession on the British Museum vase, but the other akontistes has raised it horizontally. This position with the javelin poised on a level with the head is the natural position for starting, whether the thrower uses an amentum or not. The javelin may remain in this position during the run, or may be at once drawn back. Where time was no object, the thrower might, before starting to run, adjust the javelin by pressing the point back with the left hand, in the manner represented on a black-figured stamnos in the Museo Gregoriano (Figure 97).

Figure 97. B.-f. stamnos. Vatican.

Figure 98. B.-f. vase. Acropolis, Athens, 606.

From the carry the arm is drawn back to its full extent, as shown on the François vase (Figure 94). In the actual throw the movement is reversed, arm and spear travelling back through the same positions, except that when the amentum is used the hand at once releases the shaft of the spear, which is merely held by means of the thong. A realistic picture of this moment is shown on an early black-figured vase from the Acropolis, the lower zone of which contains a cavalry fight between archers and javelin throwers (Figure 98).

This style of throw is typical of the black-figured vases, and quite distinct from that which we find general on the red-figured vases of the fifth century. It is the practical style of the chase and of war adapted to sport. It is, of course, the natural style for throwing at a target, and at first sight one is tempted to suppose that this is what the artists wish to represent; but the care with which they emphasize the bluntness of the javelins is conclusive for a distance throw.

THE ATHLETIC STYLE

The purely athletic character of the style depicted on the red-figured vases is obvious from the most casual inspection. Till the actual moment of the throw the head is turned backwards, the eyes fixed on the right hand, a position equally absurd for war, or the chase, or aiming at any sort of mark. After carefully adjusting and testing the amentum in the manner described, and inserting one or two fingers in the loop, the thrower extends his right arm backwards to its full extent, while, with his left hand opposite his breast, he holds the end of the spear, and pushes it backwards to draw the thongs tight. The spear is sometimes horizontal, sometimes pointed downwards, as we see it on the British Museum amphora, E. 256 (Figure 99). On this vase it will be noticed that the little finger and the third finger, which play no part in the practical style in which the spear is poised above the shoulder, are required to keep the javelin steady when the right hand is dropped.

Figure 99. R.-f. amphora, in British Museum, E. 256.

Figure 100. R.-f. kylix. Munich, 562 A.

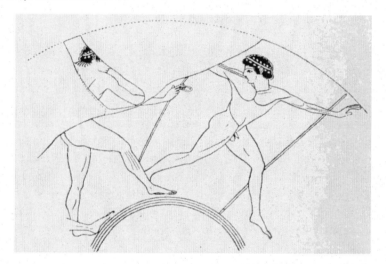

Figure 101. R.-f. kylix. Berlin, 3139 inv.

As the thrower starts to run, he draws his right hand still further backwards, turning his body sideways, and extends his left arm to the front. On a Munich kylix (Figure 100) we see two consecutive positions; the youth on the left still steadies the javelin with his left hand, the youth on the right has just let go. The next moment, with the left hand fully extended to the front, is represented on a kylix in Berlin (Figure 101). From the position of the head and arm it is obvious that the violent, rapid run, of which some authors speak, is an impossibility. Just as in throwing a cricket ball, the run consists of a few short, springy steps. Immediately before the throw a further turn of the body to the right takes place, the right knee being well bent and the right shoulder dropped, while the hand is turned outwards, so that the shaft almost rests on the palm of the hand. This attitude is vividly depicted on a Torlonia kylix (Figure 102).

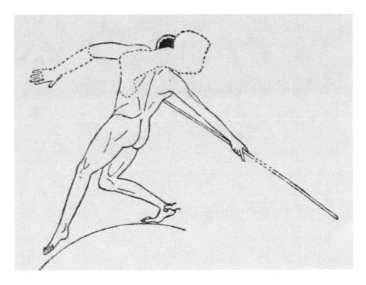

Figure 102. R.-f. kylix. Torlonia, 270 (148).

The actual throw is very rarely shown, and the artists who attempt it fall into hopeless confusion. For example, on the Munich kylix (Figure 100) the youth in the centre is intended to be throwing a javelin to the right, but the fingering of the right hand is only compatible with a throw to the left. Not much better is the drawing of the javelin thrower on the Panaetius kylix (Figure 17). Here, as in a red-figured amphora in Munich (Figure 103), though the general attitude is vigorous and lifelike, the position of the hand is hopeless, the wrist being curved over the shaft instead of bent back under it. The amentum too is conspicuous by its absence. The carelessness of the painters of red-figured vases in such details is in marked contrast to the carefulness of the earlier painters. This is partly due to the fact that the athletic types have become conventional, partly to the fact that, whereas in the black-figured vases the amentum was painted black like the spear itself, on the red-figured vases it had to be added in some other colour, usually white or purple, after the rest of the drawing was finished. Hence this detail was often omitted altogether, or if inserted, was the first to be obliterated.

Figure 103. R.-f. amphora. Munich, 408.

The javelin was usually thrown with a short run, but one or two vase paintings suggest that a standing throw was also practised. Such is the figure on a kylix in Rome (Figure 104), the attitude being evidently borrowed from that of the diskobolos. Possibly the Torlonia kylix may also represent a standing throw.

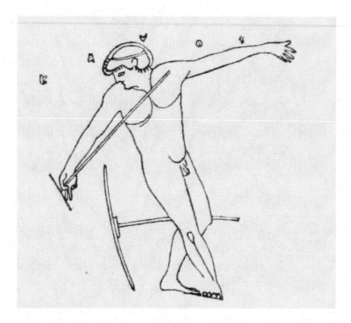

Figure 104. R.-f. kylix. Rome(?) (Jüthner, *Ant. Turn.* Figure 43.)

Was the javelin thrown with the left hand as well as the right? Plato recommends the training of both hands alike, and the fact that the Greek always carried two javelins, often one in either hand, renders the suggestion possible. But the only direct proof of a left-handed throw is a figure on a kylix of Nicosthenes in Berlin.[605] Even if a left-handed throw was practised in the gymnasia, there is no evidence of it in competitions. Nor is there any evidence to show that the Greeks ever threw the javelin without the amentum. The omission of the amentum on the vases is a detail too untrustworthy to warrant us in drawing any definite conclusion from it.

It is hardly necessary to point out that the vases in which the spear is pointed upwards offer no support at all to the remarkable theory that the Greeks practised high throwing "le tir en haut," as it is described by a French writer. To obtain the maximum of distance it is, of course, absolutely necessary to throw high. A similar theory has been put forward for the diskos. One wonders how "le lancement en haut" of the diskos was measured.

In the games of Patroclus javelin throwing was a separate event. Here, and wherever it is mentioned in Homer as a sport, the competition is for distance only. Throwing at a mark may be implied in the association of javelin throwing with the bow, which meets us again in fourth-century inscriptions, and Pindar definitely refers to such a competition when he describes how at the founding of the Olympic games "Phrastor with the javelin hit the mark."[606] On a fragment of a large vase found on the Acropolis which represents the funeral

---

[605] *Berlin Vas.*, 1805.
[606] *Ol.* x. 71.

games of Pelias a javelin competition is shown. The prize is a tripod, and the javelins are not the blunt weapons of the palaestra, but have broad metal points. On one of them the amentum is clearly shown.[607]

As the weapon of the chase, every Greek boy must from boyhood have practised throwing the javelin both for distance and at any improvised target. At an early date its use was taught in the gymnasia, and its popularity is shown by the numerous representations of it in art, and by the frequent metaphors which Pindar borrows from it. But in the Greek games, at least, the javelin, like the diskos, only figured as part of the pentathlon, and with the exception of the competition on horseback at Athens, there is no evidence for any separate competition for javelin throwing, either for distance or at a target, till the fourth century.

Towards the close of the fifth century increased importance was given to the javelin as the weapon of light-armed troops and of the epheboi; and from the fourth century onwards we find ἀκοντισμός quoted in inscriptions as a separate competition at Athens and elsewhere.[608] The association of the javelin and the bow suggests that in these competitions some sort of target was used, and the case cited by Antiphon proves the use of a target and pointed javelins in practice. But the only direct evidence for such a competition, apart from that on horseback, is furnished by two later inscriptions from Larisa of the time of Hadrian which mention victors σκοπῷ πεζῶν and σκοπῷ ἱππέων.[609]

What was the character of the competition in the pentathlon? The question has been discussed at wearisome length by commentators on Pindar and others, but Dr. Jüthner's conclusion seems to me incontestable, namely, that the competition in the pentathlon was one for distance only.

On this point the evidence of the vases seems conclusive. The javelins are blunt, the head is turned backward just before the throw, and there is no sign of any target. The last point is particularly convincing because in the competition on horseback the target is always represented. Certain archaeologists, it is true, have discovered evidence of targets in the badly-drawn amenta held in the hand of the javelin thrower on the Panaetius kylix and other vases. These have been interpreted as compasses for drawing circles on the ground at which the throwers aimed; or again as a sort of croquet-hoop stuck in the ground to serve as target! The authors of these delightful suggestions forget that the hunter or soldier does not aim at his opponent's feet but at his body, and that if a target is used it is at a reasonable height.

The literary evidence agrees with that of the vases. The passages of Pindar referring to a mark, with the exception of the passage already quoted on the Olympic games, have no necessary connexion with any competition, certainly none with the pentathlon. They are metaphors borrowed from the practice of everyday life. One passage in Pindar certainly refers to the pentathlon, two others possibly; all three indicate a distance-throw.[610] Lastly, Lucian, in a passage referring to Olympia and therefore to the pentathlon, definitely states that in throwing the javelin athletes compete for distance.[611]

---

[607] *Vasen von d. Acrop.* 590, Pl. xxvii.
[608] Ceos, Sestos, Samos, Tralles, Larisa. Vide *J.H.S. l.c.* notes 21 and 53.
[609] Ditt. *Syll.* 2nd Ed., ii. 670, 671.
[610] *Nem.* vii. 70; *Isthm.* ii. 35; *Pyth.* i. 44.
[611] Lucian, *Anacharsis*, 27.

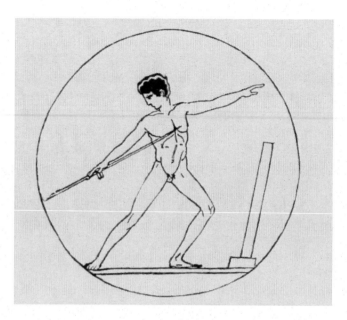

Figure 105. R.-f. kylix. Berlin, 2728.

The conditions for throwing the javelin must have been similar to those for the diskos. The competitors threw from behind a line which they were not allowed to overstep. This line was perhaps the starting-line of the stadium; it is certainly the τέρμα of Pindar's Seventh Nemean Ode. It appears probable from this ode that a competitor who overstepped the line was disqualified from taking any further part in the competition. On a kylix in Berlin the line is marked by a pillar in front of, or perhaps on a level with, the thrower (Figure 105). Further, common-sense and the safety of the spectators required that the throw should keep within certain limits as regards direction; and this is implied by Pindar when in the first Pythian he prays that his throw may not fall "outside the lists," ἔξω ἀγῶνοσς, but that with a far throw he may surpass all his rivals.

The javelins which we see so frequently sticking in the ground in palaestra scenes have been adduced as an argument to prove that no throw counted unless the javelin stuck in the ground; clearly an impossible condition with blunt javelins on the hard-baked ground of Greece. How the throw was measured we know no more than in the case of the diskos. Nor do we know how many throws were allowed. Various scraps of evidence have been brought forward to prove that two or three throws were allowed, but the evidence is quite inconclusive.

We have seen that from an early date the javelin was employed by horsemen, both in war and in the chase. At Athens, especially, horsemanship, was the duty and also the recreation of the richer classes. Plato tells us that Themistocles himself taught his son Cleophantus not only to ride but to throw the javelin standing on horseback, and in the *Laws* he recommends javelin throwing on horseback as a useful accomplishment.[612] Xenophon,[613] in his treatise on the duties of a cavalry officer, urges the latter to encourage his men to practise the javelin and to stir up emulation among them by offering prizes. In his treatise on horsemanship he gives further instructions. Velocity and distance are the most important points for war. To secure

---

[612] *Meno* 93 D; *Leg.* 834 D.
[613] *Hipparch.* i. 6; *De re equest.* viii. 10.

these, he tells us, the thrower must advance the left side of the body and draw back the right, straightening himself from the thighs and holding the javelin pointed slightly upwards. If, however, the object is accuracy, the javelin must point straight at the mark. At Athens there were competitions in this sport as early as the fifth century. At the Panathenaea five amphorae of oil were given for the first prize, and one for the second. In the second century this competition is mentioned in inscriptions relating to the Thesea. The Larisa inscription already referred to makes it probable that it still existed in Thessaly in the time of Hadrian.

Figure 106. Panathenaic amphora. British Museum.

Fortunately we are able to supplement these scanty details from the vases. A fifth-century aryballos from Eretria, now at Athens, a fourth-century krater in the Louvre,[614] and a Panathenaic amphora in the British Museum (Figure 106), give vivid pictures of the competition. The target is a shield with a crown forming a sort of bull's-eye in the centre, raised on a post to a level with the horses' heads. The competitors gallop past this target, hurling their javelins at it as they pass. The javelins are pointed, and are held a little above the shoulder with the point directed slightly downwards towards the target. The riders on the Panathenaic vase wear the typical dress of the Athenian ephebos, a flat, broad-brimmed hat called petasos, and a bright-bordered chiton fastened over the shoulder. On the Eretria vase they also wear high boots, and on the krater in the Louvre the hats are replaced by wreaths, and winged victories hover over the riders bearing wreaths.

The Panathenaic amphora of course refers to the Panathenaic festival, and the festal character of the other vases suggests a definite connexion with some other festival or festivals, but we can say no more. The sport was probably a common one in Attica, Thessaly, and other horse-breeding lands, and formed an attractive feature of other festivals besides the Thesea and Panathenaea. There is certainly no ground for connecting it with the Argive Heraea.

---

[614] Collignon, 1478; Millin, i. 45. Both vases are reproduced by P. Wolters, *Zu griechischen Agonen* (Würzburg Programm, 1901).

Chapter 17

THE PENTATHLON

The pentathlon was a combined competition in five events, running, jumping, throwing the diskos, throwing the javelin, and wrestling. This is one of the few facts regarding the pentathlon which may be regarded as absolutely certain. These five events are vouched for by three epigrams, one of them assigned to Simonides, and by the repeated testimony of Philostratos in his *Gymnastike*.[615] Nothing proves more conclusively the utter unreliability of the statements on athletics made by late scholiasts and lexicographers, than the mistakes which they contrive to make on a matter so clearly established. The lexicon of Phavorinus, following certain late scholia, substitutes boxing for throwing the javelin; and Photius quotes certain writers as substituting the pankration for the jump. Stranger still, such mistakes survive in the present day; and our own standard Greek Lexicon by Liddell and Scott contains, in the latest edition, the appalling statement that the five exercises were the jump, the diskos, running, wrestling, boxing, the last being afterwards exchanged for javelin throwing. After this we are not surprised to find quoted the antiquated theory of Böckh, that "no one received a prize unless he was winner in all five events," a theory that was disproved by Philip, years before the first edition of Liddell and Scott was published. The introduction of boxing into the pentathlon is due to the mischievous habit of using such inaccurate expressions as "the Homeric pentathlon."[616] In heroic days, as Pindar tells us, there was no pentathlon, "but for each several feat there was a prize."[617]

Of these five events, three—the jump, the diskos, and the javelin—were peculiar to the pentathlon, and formed its characteristic feature. These three events were regarded as typical of the whole competition; on the Panathenaic vases given as prizes for the competition one or

---

[615] Epigram of Simonides on Diophon—
    Ἴσθμια καὶ Πυθοῖ Διοφῶν ὁ Φίλωνος ἐνίκα
    ἅλμα, ποδωκείην, δίσκον, ἄκοντα, πάλην.
    Epigram quoted by Eustathius, *Il.* Ψ 621, p. 1320—
    ἅλμα ποδῶν δίσκου τε βολὴ καὶ ἄκοντος ἐρωὴ
    καὶ δρόμος ἠδὲ πάλη· μία δ' ἔπλετο πᾶσι τελευτή.
      cp. Epigram of Lucilius, *Anth. Pal.* xi. 84; Philostratus, *Gym.* 3, 11, 31, 55; Artemidorus, *Oneir.* i. 55; and numerous scholia.

[616] E.g., of the games at the court of Alcinous. No argument can be based on the accidental occurrence on vases of boxing together with some of the events of the pentathlon, e.g., Figure 150.

[617] *Isthm.* i. 26.

more of these three events, on two vases all three of them, are represented[618] (Figures 107, 108). The same events are among the commonest on other vases, especially red-figured vases; but we are not justified in connecting these with the pentathlon, or using them as evidence in discussing the pentathlon. These scenes for the most part represent the daily life of the gymnasium, and all that they prove is the important part which these sports played in that life. They were the only three events which required any form of apparatus; the exercises seem to have been taught in classes, and were performed both in practice and in competition to the accompaniment of the flute. If any of the three was regarded as more representative than another, it was the jump, which perhaps owed its importance partly to the extensive use of halteres in the gymnasium. The halteres were the special symbol of the pentathlon, and were frequently represented on statues of victorious pentathletes.[619]

Figure 107. Panathenaic amphora, in British Museum, B. 134. Sixth century.

Figure 108. Panathenaic amphora. Leyden. Sixth century.

---

[618] Three events, *B.M.* B. 134. *Arch. Zeit.*, 1881, ix.; diskos and javelin, *B.M.* B. 142, *Mus. Greg.* xliii. 2 b; jump and javelin, *Munich*, 656; diskos, *B.M.* B. 136, 602, etc.; javelin, *B.M.* 605, etc.
[619] *J.H.S.* xxiii. p. 60.

These three events, together with running and wrestling, were representative of the whole physical training of the Greeks, and the pentathlete was the typical product of that training. Inferior to the specialised athletes in his special events he was superior to him in general development, in that harmonious union of strength and activity which produces perfect physical beauty; and this beauty of the pentathlete won him the special commendation of thinkers such as Aristotle, who condemned all exaggerated or one-sided development.[620]

A combined competition like the pentathlon is obviously later than any of the individual events of which it is composed, and implies a considerable development in athletics and physical education. Not that we are to regard it with certain German writers as an elaborate scheme based on abstract physiological principles evolved with much expenditure of midnight oil out of the brain of some athletic student. The pentathlon was the natural product of a number of exercises which had been familiar for centuries. But before the idea could originate of combining these exercises into a single competition to find the best all-round athlete, these exercises must have become part of the national education. The combination implies a certain amount of thought and conscious reflexion. There is in it an artificiality of which we find no trace in the Homeric sports. In view of this it is remarkable that, according to Greek tradition, the pentathlon was introduced at Olympia as early as the 18th Olympiad.

No importance need be attached to the statement of Philostratus that the pentathlon was invented by Jason. The Greeks always loved to trace their institutions back to heroic times. As, however, the passage which contains the statement is of considerable importance in discussing the method of deciding the pentathlon, it will be useful to quote it in full:—

> "Before the time of Jason there were separate crowns for the jump, the diskos, and the spear. At the time of the *Argo's* voyage Telamon was the best at throwing the diskos, Lynceus with the javelin, the sons of Boreas were best at running and jumping, and Peleus was second in these events but was superior to all in wrestling. Accordingly, when they were holding sports in Lemnos, Jason, they say, wishing to please Peleus combined the five events, and thus Peleus secured the victory on the whole."[621]

The order of the events and the method of deciding the pentathlon have given rise to a literature equally extensive and inconclusive.[622] Almost every combination of events has been tried, and every conceivable method has been devised. Many of the systems proposed are so utterly unpractical that they have only to be stated to be rejected by anyone with a rudimentary knowledge of practical athletics. None can be regarded as established. The evidence is too scanty and too contradictory. It consists largely in extracts from scholiasts and lexicographers, and we have seen in considering the constitution of the pentathlon the untrustworthiness of this class of evidence. It is well, therefore, to recognise from the outset that whatever solutions we may accept are only provisional, and that it is therefore in the highest degree unsafe to use such theories as evidence in the interpretation of Pindar or other poets.

---

[620] Aristot. *Rhet.* i. 5; cp. Plato, *Amatores* 135 D, E.
[621] Phil. *Gym.* 3.
[622] To the works enumerated by me in *J.H.S.* xxiii. pp. 55 ff., I may add K. E. Heinrich, *Über das Pentathlon d. Gr.*, Würzburg, 1892; C. A. M. Fennell in *Pindar: Isthm. and Nem. Odes*, 1883; Ph. E. Legrand in Dar.-Sagl. *s.c.* "Quinquertium," 1907.

First, as to the order of events, it must be premised that we are not certain that the order was fixed, and did not vary at different times and places. Still, the conservatism of the Greeks in such matters certainly makes it probable that there was a fixed order at Olympia, and that this order was generally adopted elsewhere. At all events we shall assume that this was so. The one fact which we know for certain about the order is that wrestling came last. Bacchylides definitely describes it as last, and the evidence of Bacchylides is confirmed by Herodotus and Xenophon.[623] Describing the attack on Olympia by the Eleans in Ol. 104, when the Arcadians had usurped the presidency of the games, Xenophon says: "They had already finished the horse-race and the events of the pentathlon held in the dromos (τὰ δρομικὰ τοῦ πεντάθλου) and those who had reached the wrestling were no longer in the dromos but were wrestling between the dromos and the altar." It is generally agreed that τὰ δρομικά are the first four events, which were held in the stadium, whereas according to the view set forth in a previous chapter wrestling took place in the open space in front of the treasury steps.[624] At all events, it is clear from Xenophon's words that wrestling came last, and common sense tells us that this was the only possible position for it consistent with fairness. After several hard bouts of wrestling no competitor could do himself justice in the other events.

For the order of the first four events we have to fall back on the uncertain and contradictory evidence of various passages in which the events of the pentathlon are enumerated. Now in none of these passages is the order of events of any importance to the writer; in the case of an epigram it is obvious that the order is likely to be modified by metrical considerations. Still, the probability remains that such passages will in spite of metre and carelessness reflect more or less the actual order.[625] Thus we find that in five passages wrestling comes last, in two passages it comes first, and in both of these the order of events is merely reversed, in one passage it comes second. The epigram of Simonides gives the following order: Jump, foot-race, diskos, javelin, wrestling. The epigram quoted by Eustathius gives the same order except that the foot-race comes fourth instead of second. Now, except in the epigram of Simonides, the three events peculiar to the pentathlon are always grouped together. It is probable, therefore, that they were grouped together in practice, and that the foot-race cannot have occupied the second place. Why Simonides put it after the jump is obvious, neither δρόμος nor ποδωκεῖν could possibly begin a hexameter. The foot-race, therefore, came either first or fourth. Once more, if we examine the lists we find the foot-race first in two lists, last in the two reversed lists, while two scholia follow the epigram and place it fourth. As the order in these scholia is identical with that of the epigram, it is

---

[623] Bacch. ix. 30-36 τελευταίας ἀμάρυγμα πάλας; Hdt. ix. 33; Xen. *Hellen.* vii. 4. 29.
[624] *Vide* p. 120.
[625] The following are the orders given in the various lists:—

1. Simonides	jump, race, diskos, javelin, wrestling.
2. Epigram quoted by Eustathius	jump, diskos, javelin, race, wrestling.
3. Schol. Pind. *Isthm.* i. 26	
4. Schol. Soph. *El.* 631	
5. Artemidorus, *Oneirocrit.* i. 55	race, diskos, jump, javelin, wrestling.
6. Schol. Plato, *Amat.* 135 E (reversed)	race, diskos, jump, javelin, wrestling.
7. Phil. *Gym.* 3 (reversed)	race, jump, javelin, diskos, wrestling.
8. Schol. Aristid. *Pan.* p. 112	race, wrestling, diskos, javelin, jump.
9. Epigram *Anth. Pal.* xi. 84	wrestling, race, diskos, jump, javelin.

In 6 and 7 the order of the text is obviously reversed, and I have therefore reversed again. No. 9 is of very little value and may be disregarded.

doubtful whether they have any independent authority. The evidence, therefore, is slightly in favour of first place for the foot-race, and this order receives some slight support from the passage in Philostratus already quoted concerning the pentathlon of Peleus, and the passage of Herodotus discussed below about Tisamenus and Hieronymus.

For the remaining events the lists appear to support the order of the two epigrams—jump, diskos, javelin, though there is not much to show whether the diskos or the javelin came first. Certain passages in Bacchylides and Pindar have been quoted to prove that the diskos preceded the javelin.[626] On the two Panathenaic vases reproduced above, the javelin comes between the jump and the diskos. This is the position assigned to it by Philostratus when he enumerates the events of the pentathlon. Unfortunately the value of this passage is lessened by the distinction which he introduces between light events and heavy events. The heavy events, he says, are wrestling and throwing the diskos; the light events, the javelin, the jump, and the foot-race. The order is obviously reversed, but whether all three light events preceded both heavy events or not cannot be decided from this passage. Such distinctions give us no clue to the actual order, and all attempts to discover the system on which the order of events depended are absolutely futile. It is easy enough to argue that all the exercises were arranged in an ascending scale, or that easy exercises alternated with difficult, that similar exercises were grouped together, or that leg exercises alternated with arm exercises, and if we were constructing an ideal pentathlon such arguments might be of some use. As it is, we are not concerned with an ideal pentathlon but with that of the Greeks, and there is not a particle of evidence to prove that the Greeks arranged their pentathlon on any abstract principle however plausible. All we can do is to confine ourselves to the actual evidence, and the order which this evidence renders *probable* is foot-race, jump, diskos, javelin, wrestling.

It is unnecessary to discuss in full the various systems that have been suggested for deciding the pentathlon. These systems for the most part fall into certain well-defined groups based on certain hypotheses, and it will be sufficient briefly to examine these hypotheses.

The old hypothesis perpetuated by Liddell and Scott, that victory in all five events[627] was necessary, may be briefly dismissed as not only unpractical but contrary to the little evidence which we possess. On such a system a victory in the pentathlon must have been an extremely rare event; for it can seldom have happened that one competitor won all five events. The idea seems to have arisen from the epigram of Simonides, and from a misunderstanding of an important passage in Herodotus (ix. 33), which is in reality a conclusive proof against it.

"Tisamenus," says Herodotus, "came within a single contest or fall (πάλαισμα) of victory, being matched against Hieronymus of Andros." Pausanias confirms the victory of Hieronymus (vi. 14), and says of Tisamenus (iii. 11, 6), "In two events he was first, for he was superior to Hieronymus in running and jumping, but he was defeated by him in wrestling and so failed to win the victory." The true interpretation of the passage is obvious. "Tisamenus came within a single contest of victory," i.e., he won two events but lost the odd; or perhaps we may go farther still and give to πάλαισμα its literal meaning, "a fall in wrestling." He came within a "single fall" of winning.

---

[626] Bacch. ix. 30-36; Pind. *Nem.* v. 72; *Isthm.* ii. 30. Little value can be attached to these passages or to the vases.
[627] The system adopted by Böckh, Hermann and Dissen.

Each had won two events, each had scored two falls in wrestling, and the whole contest depended on the last fall![628] just as we talk of winning a golf match by a single putt, or winning a rubber by the odd trick.

Yet obvious as this interpretation is, Hermann and other more recent German writers have asserted that, according to Herodotus, Tisamenus won the first four events, and only missed the victory because he was defeated in wrestling. It is more than doubtful whether the words of Herodotus can bear the meaning "he missed victory by wrestling only"; but apart from this, Hermann's theory is absolutely contradicted by the very circumstantial statements of Pausanias. If Tisamenus won all four events, why should Pausanias expressly state that he won two? If victory in all five events was necessary, how can Hieronymus have won the pentathlon, seeing that on Hermann's showing he only won one event? If victory in five events was not necessary, is it not ridiculous to suppose that a solitary victory in wrestling should have not only cancelled the four victories of Tisamenus, but secured the prize for Hieronymus?

The only inference which we are justified in drawing from the story of Tisamenus is that victory in three out of the five events was sufficient. This is expressly stated by a scholiast to Aristides, and is implied in a highly metaphorical passage in Plutarch describing the different points in which the letter A is superior to all the other letters of the alphabet.[629] It has been further inferred that victory in three events was not only sufficient but necessary. The writers who have taken this view generally assume that with several competitors competing against one another it would be unusual for any individual to win three events, and various elaborate theories have been devised to get over this difficulty. Of these theories by far the most reasonable was that suggested by Professor Percy Gardner in the first volume of the *Journal of Hellenic Studies*. He supposed that the pentathlon was treated as a single event, and the competition was conducted as a tournament, the competitors being arranged in pairs, and each pair competing against each other in all five contests. The winner of each pair, and therefore the final winner, must necessarily have won three out of the five events. This plan has the conspicuous merit of fairness and simplicity, but it is open to several serious objections. In particular, the passage of Xenophon quoted above seems decisive against it, for Xenophon's words naturally mean that all the events in the dromos took place before any of the wrestling. There are many practical objections. The length of such a competition would have made it tedious to spectators and competitors alike, and it must have degenerated into a mere test of endurance, in which the elements of skill, activity, and grace which made the pentathlon so popular would have been lost. I need not dwell on the hopelessly unpractical modifications of this theory proposed by Dr. Marquardt, nor on the ludicrously unfair systems suggested by Fedde, and more recently by Legrand in Daremberg and Saglio, the principle of which is the arrangement of all competitors in groups of three. It will be sufficient to examine the two assumptions on which these theories rest, viz. that in an open competition it would be unusual for any competitor to win three events, and that victory in three events was necessary. If these assumptions prove to be unfounded, the *raison d'être* of all these theories disappears at once; for they have no merit whatsoever except that they satisfy these supposed conditions.

---

[628] This interpretation is, I am glad to find, adopted by Dr. Jüthner in his recent edition of Philostratus.

[629] Schol. Aristid. *Pan.* p. 112 οὐκ ὅτι πάντως οἱ πένταθλοι πάντα νικῶσιν· ἀρκεῖ γὰρ αὐτοῖς γ' τῶν ἓ πρὸς νίκην. Plut. *Symp.* ix. 2 διὸ τοῖς τρισὶν ὥσπερ οἱ πένταθλοι περίεστι καὶ νικᾷ.

In considering the first point we must remember that the pentathlete was not a specialist in any one exercise, but an all-round athlete who combined strength and activity. Among competitors of this sort it is not unusual to find one or two men surpassing their fellows not in one event but in several, especially if most of the events require much the same qualities and physique. This was undoubtedly the case with the pentathlon. It is obvious that the same man might often win the foot-race and the long jump, or the diskos and the spear. Though less obvious it is equally probable that the diskos and the long jump might fall to the same man. It is not uncommon to find a hammer-thrower who is also a good long-jumper. The reason is that weight-throwing and jumping both require a harmonious well-timed effort of every part of the body. The use of jumping weights increased the resemblance between the two exercises; for the swing of the weights was not unlike the swing of the diskos. The general development and complete control of the muscles necessary for these events would give an equal advantage in wrestling, especially with men of the same weight, for the heavy-weight wrestler would be excluded by the very nature of the pentathlon. These considerations make it probable that the five events would commonly be divided between two or at most three competitors, and the few details which we know of actual winners confirms this view. Phayllus of Croton must have won the jump, the diskos, and the foot-race, for he won the stade-race at Delphi. Hieronymus won the diskos, spear, and wrestling. So apparently did Automedes of Phlius.[630] Diophon, the subject of Simonides' epigram, apparently won all five events. The only example to the contrary is the mythical pentathlon of Peleus, in which none of the heroes won more than one event.

The pentathlon of Peleus is fatal to the second assumption that victory in three events was necessary. We must either reject the evidence of the story, or abandon the assumption. And inasmuch as there is absolutely no proof of the assumption, the latter is the only course. The principal evidence on which the assumption is based has already been stated. The utmost that we can infer is that victory in three events was sufficient, and was by no means an unfamiliar result. We may further add the statement of Pollux that the term used for victory in the pentathlon was ἀποτριάξαι, "to win a treble," a statement confirmed by a quite unintelligible scholion on the Agamemnon. The word τριάσσειν is properly a wrestling term, meaning "to win three falls," "to win in wrestling," and so generally "to win a victory" or "conquer." The cognate words τριάκτηρ and ἀτρίακτος mean no more than "conqueror," "unconquered." There is no evidence of the connexion of the word in early times with the pentathlon; but the fact that wrestling was the last event in the pentathlon is itself sufficient explanation of the late use of the word ἀποτριάξαι to denote victory in the pentathlon, especially if, as was frequently the case, the final victory was decided by the wrestling. It is, of course, possible that the word contained some allusion to a victory in three events, but this supposition is unproved and unnecessary, and certainly does not warrant the assumption that victory in three events was necessary.[631] Such being the case we may reject all theories based upon this assumption. Above all, there is no longer any necessity for dividing competitors into heats of two or three.

---

[630] Bacchylides, *l.c.*
[631] For a fuller treatment of this point *vide J.H.S.* xxiii. p. 63, and Jüthner, *Philostratus*, p. 207. The passage quoted by me from Philostratus on p. 65 n. 47, γυμνάζεταί τι τῶν τριῶν, appears to be corrupt and cannot be used as evidence for speaking of τριαγμός as applied to the three events of the pentathlon which secured victory, or the three events peculiar to the pentathlon, and Jüthner seems to me correct in his criticism that this use of the word is "mehr als unsicher."

A common feature in the systems proposed is the gradual reduction of the number of competitors at each stage of the competition, so that in the final wrestling only two or three competitors were left. The only evidence for the theory in this form is the rhetorical passage in Plutarch already noticed—evidence as untrustworthy as it is possible to conceive. There is, however, more evidence for a modified form of the theory, viz. that only those who had qualified in the first four competitions were allowed to compete in the wrestling. This appears to me now the only possible conclusion from the words of Xenophon already quoted:[632] "The events in the dromos were already finished, and *those who had reached the wrestling* were no longer in the dromos, etc." Such a system would give an advantage to the all-round athlete, and exclude the specialised wrestler. But what constituted qualification? It certainly was not confined to the winners in the first four events, otherwise Peleus would have been excluded; nor does it seem to me probable that only the two or three who had obtained the best averages in the first four competitions were permitted to wrestle. Speculation is useless; we must be content for the present to accept Xenophon's words, and hope that some inscription or papyrus may be discovered to enlighten us.

Much has been written by archaeologists about the bye (ἔφεδρος) in the pentathlon. It is not a little curious that there is absolutely no evidence for a bye in the pentathlon at all. We hear of a bye in wrestling, in boxing, and in the pankration, but in no other competitions. Of course, if all competitors competed in wrestling a bye was unavoidable. But a bye necessarily introduces an element of luck, especially in a long competition, and we may be sure that the Greeks avoided it as far as possible. If only a certain number of competitors were admitted to the wrestling, the necessity for a bye could be easily avoided. German archaeologists, with a strange perverseness, seem to delight in introducing compulsory byes at every turn.

So far, then, we have established the principle that *victory in three events was sufficient* but not necessary. If no competitor won three events, or two won two events, how was the victory decided? The pentathlon of Peleus supplies the answer. Each of the heroes won one event. Peleus, besides winning the wrestling, was second in the other four events. Only two explanations of the victory of Peleus are possible. Either wrestling counted more than other events, an assumption adopted by various writers, but contrary to the whole spirit of the pentathlon, or *in case of a tie at least, account was taken of second or third places*, i.e., the result was decided by marks. These two principles, that the result was decided in the first place by victories in the separate events, and in the case of a tie by some system of marks, are sufficient to explain all possible cases, though the details of their application are uncertain. Let us try to see how the competition would work out on these lines.

The pentathlon began with the foot-race. The distance was a stade. The race might be run in heats if necessary; but there is no evidence for them in the pentathlon. The starting lines at Olympia could accommodate twenty starters, and it does not seem probable that there were often so many entries. The competitions in jumping, throwing the diskos and the javelin, were conducted as in the present day, all competing against all. The jump was a long jump; the diskos and the javelin were thrown for distance, not at a mark. Wrestling was conducted on the tournament principle. "Upright wrestling" only was allowed, and three falls were required for victory. Only those who had qualified in the first four events took part in the wrestling. If

---

[632] In *J.H.S.* xxiii. p. 65 I was mistaken in rejecting this conclusion. I cannot, however, accept as proved either Holwerda's or Heinrich's application of it. Holwerda in particular, like many of the Germans, attaches an altogether undue importance to wrestling, which was certainly not the most important of the five events.

there were only two competitors, one of them must have won three events. Suppose there were more, at least five, A, B, C, D, E; there is no evidence that it was possible to win the pentathlon without being first in at least one event, and, therefore, what holds good of five will hold good of any smaller or larger number. There are only four possible cases.

1) A 3, B 2, or B 1, C 1.—A wins by the first principle.
2) A 2, B 2, C 1.—The victory would depend on the result of the fifth event which C won. If this event were wrestling, it would be reasonable to suppose that other competitors would drop out, and A and B would be matched together. If the event won by C was one of the earlier events, the issue must have been decided by the performances of A and B in that event, or perhaps by marks, i.e., by their performances in all the events.
3) A 2, B 1, C 1, D 1.—This is a very doubtful case: the victory might be awarded to A as having won more firsts than any of the others, or it might be decided by marks.
4) A 1, B 1, C 1, D 1, E 1.—In this highly improbable case victory can only have been decided by marks.

Complications may have been introduced by dead heats or ties: all such cases would, no doubt, have been settled by the same common-sense principles. This scheme, which I stated more fully in vol. xxiii. of the *Journal of Hellenic Studies*, is not affected by the modification which I have since adopted about admission to the wrestling. It is in entire accordance with modern athletic experience, and there is no passage in any ancient author which contradicts it.

Chapter 18

WRESTLING

Wrestling is perhaps the oldest and most universal of all sports. The wall-paintings of Beni Hassan show that almost every hold or throw known to modern wrestlers was known to the Egyptians 2500 years before our era. The popularity of wrestling among the Greeks is proved by the constant metaphors from this sport, and by the frequency with which scenes from the wrestling ring appear not only in athletic literature and art but also in mythological subjects. Despite the changes in Greek athletics caused by professionalism, which affected wrestling and boxing more than any other sports, the popularity of wrestling remained unabated. On early black-figured vases Heracles is constantly represented employing the regular holds of the palaestra not only against the giant Antaeus but against monsters such as Achelous or the Triton, or even against the Nemean lion, and centuries later the language in which Ovid and Lucan describe these combats is in every detail borrowed from the same source. Still more is this the case with the wrestling match between Cercyon and Theseus which occurs so often on the red-figured vases of Athens. On coins wrestling types survive into imperial times. The fight with the Nemean lion is represented on the fourth-century gold coins of Syracuse, and that with Antaeus on imperial coins of Alexandria (Figure 109).

These fights are one of the many forms under which Greek imagination loved to picture the triumph of civilization and science over barbarism and brute force. To the Greek wrestling was a science and an art. Theseus, the reputed discoverer of scientific wrestling, is said to have learnt its rules from Athena herself.[633] The greatest importance was attached to grace and skill; it was not sufficient to throw an opponent, it had to be done correctly and in good style.[634] Hence even when athletics had become corrupted by professionalism, wrestling remained for the most part free from that brutality which has so often brought discredit on one of the noblest of sports. Pausanias records the case of a certain Sicilian wrestler, Leontiscus, who defeated his opponents by trying to break their fingers.[635] But such tactics did not commend themselves to the Greeks, although it does not seem that they were formally prohibited, and Pausanias expresses his disapproval by the comment that he did not understand how to throw his opponents.

---

[633] Schol. Pindar, *Nem.* v. 49.
[634] Aelian, *Var. Hist.* ii. 4. Cp. *J.H.S.* xxv. p. 19, n. 27.
[635] vi. 4, 2.

Figure 109. Wrestling types on coins, in British Museum. *a, b, c*, Aspendus, fifth and fourth centuries. *d*, Heraclea in Lucania, fourth century. *e, f*, Syracuse, *circa* 400 B.C. *g*, Alexandria, Antoninus Pius. (*J.H.S.* xxv. p. 271.)

The very name palaestra sufficiently indicates the early importance of wrestling in Greek education, an importance which it maintained even during the Empire. The method of instruction was strictly progressive.[636] There were separate rules for men and boys; the different movements, grips, and throws were taught as separate figures, the simpler movements first, then the more complicated. In learning them the pupils were grouped in pairs, and more than one pair could be taught at the same time. In the early stages a beginner would be paired with a more advanced pupil, who would help him. Later on the movements were combined, and practice was allowed in free play. The paidotribes seems to have enforced his instruction with a free use of the rod. In Figure 96 a vivid picture of a wrestling lesson is seen. A pair of paidotribai are engaged in instructing a pair of youthful wrestlers. One of the latter has seized his opponent round the waist and prepares to give him the heave; the other has allowed him to obtain his grip and stands with outstretched hands waiting for the paidotribes to give his next order.

There were doubtless numerous text-books of drill in wrestling and other sports for the use of paidotribai. A fragment of such a text-book has been found on a papyrus of the second century A.D.[637] It contains orders for executing a number of different grips and throws, and each section ends with the order "complete the grip" (πλέξον) or "throw him" (ῥεῖψον). The sections dealing with the throws are hopelessly mutilated, but considerable portions of four sections dealing with the grips remain. Unfortunately, the brevity of the commands, characteristic of all drill books, makes them extremely difficult to understand accurately, and the interpretation is too technical to deal with here.

---

[636] *J.H.S. l.c.* p. 15. Freeman, *Schools of Hellas*, p. 130.
[637] *Ox. Pap.* iii. 466. For a full discussion of it *vide* Jüthner, *Philostratus*, p. 26. With the papyrus may be compared a curious passage in Lucian's *Asinus*, c. 9, and an epigram in *Anth. Pal.* xii. 206. The latter, like the passage in Lucian, is probably erotic. Such a metaphorical use of wrestling terms is common. Cp. Aristoph. *Pax* 895, *Av.* 442, and the expressions ἀνακλινοπάλη, κλινοπάλη.

Competitions in wrestling, boxing, and the pankration were conducted in the same way as a modern tournament. Lucian's description of the manner of drawing lots has already been quoted. In case of an odd number of competitors one of them drew a bye. This of course gave him a considerable advantage in the next round over a less fortunate rival, who had perhaps been exhausted by his previous contest. Thus the crown may sometimes have depended on the luck of the lot. It is to such an accident that Pindar refers at the close of the sixth Nemean Ode when he says that Alcimidas and his brother were deprived of two Olympic crowns by the fall of the lot. So it is mentioned as an additional distinction for an athlete to have won a crown without drawing the bye, and Pausanias speaks with some contempt of such as have ere now won the olive by the unreasonableness of the lot and not by their own strength.[638] There is, of course, no ground for the idea that one who had drawn a bye in the first round remained a bye till the final. To draw a bye in a single round is quite sufficient advantage, and archaeologists should really credit the Greeks with a certain amount of practical common-sense.

The number of competitors varied. Lucian, in the passage referred to, speaks of five or twelve competitors,[639] and this statement agrees generally with our other evidence. Pindar's heroes, the Aeginetan wrestlers Alcimedon and Aristomenes,[640] were each victorious over four rivals, that is, in four rounds. The same number is mentioned in the Olympic inscriptions on the wrestler Xenocles and the boxer Philippus.[641] Four rounds imply nine to sixteen competitors. A long epigram on Ariston,[642] who won the pankration in Ol. 207, tells us that there were seven competitors, and that he took part in all three rounds and did not owe his crown to the luck of the lot.

Sometimes a famous athlete was allowed a walk over, in which case he was said to have won ἀκονιτεί, without dust, that is, without having even dusted his body with the fine sand which athletes used before exercise. Such a victory is recorded of Milo at some unknown festival when he was the only competitor in wrestling.[643] The first victory of this sort recorded at Olympia is that of Dromeus in the pankration of Ol. 75.[644] An inscription found at Olympia enumerating the victories of the Diagoridae at Rhodes records that Dorieus won a victory in boxing (ἀκονιτεί) at the Pythia.[645] These instances, which could be multiplied, are sufficient to prove that Philostratus is mistaken when he asserts that no crown was awarded at Olympia without competition (ἀκονιτεί).[646] The case of Dorieus disproves the similar statement made by Heliodorus with regard to the Pythia.[647] There can hardly have been any necessity for such a rule in early times, but a rule requiring more than one competitor may well have been introduced at the time of the athletic revival under the Empire, if not at the Olympia or Pythia, at some of the many festivals which bore their names. A rule to this effect might be reasonably expected at festivals where valuable prizes were offered.

---

[638] *Ol. Ins.* 225, 226, 54; Paus. vi. 1, 2.
[639] *Hermotim.* 40.
[640] *Ol.* viii. 68; *Pyth.* viii. 81.
[641] *Ol. Ins.* 164, 174.
[642] *Ib.* 225, 226.
[643] *Anth. Pal.* xi. 316.
[644] Paus. vi. 11, 4.
[645] *Ol. Ins.* 153.
[646] *Gym.* 11; *vide* Jüthner's note, p. 206.
[647] *Aethiop.* iv. 2.

The Greeks distinguished two styles of wrestling, one which they called "upright wrestling" or wrestling proper (ὀρθὴ πάλη, or σταδιαία πάλη,[648] or simply πάλη) in which the object was to throw an opponent to the ground (καταβλητική), the other "ground wrestling" (κύλισις or ἀλίνδησις) in which the struggle was continued on the ground till one or other of the combatants acknowledged defeat. The former was the only wrestling admitted in the pentathlon and in wrestling competitions proper; the latter did not exist as a separate competition, but only as part of the pankration, in which hitting and kicking were also allowed.[649]

In the practice of the palaestra ground wrestling as well as wrestling proper was freely indulged in. We gather from Lucian that separate places were assigned to the two exercises. Ground wrestling took place in some place under cover, and the ground was watered till it became muddy.[650] The mud rendered the body slippery and difficult to hold, and so rendered accidents less likely; while wallowing in the mud was supposed to have a most beneficial effect on the skin. Wrestling proper took place on the sandy ground in the centre of palaestra. This was called the skamma, the same word that is used for the jumping pit. It denotes a place dug up, levelled and sanded so as to form a smooth soft surface. For actual competitions a skamma must have been provided somewhere in the stadium, probably, where such existed, in the semicircular theatre at the end.

In heroic times boxers and wrestlers wore a loin-cloth (περίζωμα), such as is occasionally depicted on black-figured vases (Figure 128), but this loin-cloth seems to have been usually discarded even in the sixth century. Wrestlers, especially boys, sometimes wore ear-caps (Figure 17), but there is no evidence of their use in competitions. For obvious reasons they always wore their hair short.[651] Professional athletes under the Empire wore the little hair that was left uncut, tied up in an unsightly little topknot called the "cirrus."[652]

In the present chapter we are concerned only with wrestling proper. Before discussing its rules let me utter an emphatic protest against the slanderous fallacy implied in the use of the term Graeco-Roman to describe a style of wrestling in vogue in some of the Music Halls at the present day. There is nothing in Greek wrestling proper, or in the pankration, which bears any resemblance to, or can offer any justification for, this most useless and absurd of all systems, which, as Mr. Walter Armstrong remarks, might have been invented for the express purpose of bringing a grand and useful exercise into disrepute.

We have no definite statement as to the rules of Greek wrestling, and are forced to infer them from the somewhat fragmentary evidence of literature and art. The two essential points which distinguish one style of wrestling from another are the definition of a fair throw and the nature of the holds allowed.

In most modern styles a man is considered thrown only when both shoulders, or one shoulder and one hip touch the ground at the same time; in the Cumberland and Westmorland style he is thrown if he touches the ground with any portion of his body, or even with his knee. A throw may be either a clean throw or the result of a struggle on the ground. With the Greeks it is practically undisputed that only clean throws counted; if one or both wrestlers fell to the ground the bout was finished. Further, it is certain that a fall on the back, on the

---

[648] Philostrat. *Vit. Soph.* 225, perhaps a mistake for σταδαία.
[649] *Vide* Jüthner, *Philostratus*, p. 212.
[650] *Ib.* pp. 206, 297. This place was called ἀλινδήθρα, Aristoph. *Ran.* 904. Cp. Lucian, *Anacharsis*, 2, 28, 29.
[651] Euripides, *Bacchae*, 455.
[652] Krause, *Gym.* p. 541, n. 6.

shoulders, or the hip counted as a fair throw.[653] An epigram on one Damostratus is conclusive evidence for the back, an epigram on Cleitomachus for the shoulders.[654] Another epigram relates how Milo, advancing to receive his crown after a "dustless" victory, slipped and fell on his hip, whereupon the people cried out not to crown a man who had fallen without an adversary.[655] The question of a fall on the knee is more difficult. The passages quoted from Aeschylus are doubtful, and capable of being interpreted either way. So is the epigram on Milo ascribed to Simonides, which states that he won seven victories at Pisa without ever falling on his knee.[656] The evidence of the monuments is divided. We have a group of bronzes, apparently copies of some well-known Hellenistic original, which represent a wrestler who has fallen on one knee (Figures 130, 131). His victorious opponent stands over him with one hand pressing down his neck, with the other forcing back his arm. There can be no doubt that he is in a position to throw him on his back if necessary, but he seems to make no effort to do so. On the other hand, we have a group of vases and wall-paintings representing the throw known as "the flying mare," in which the wrestler as he throws his opponent over his head sinks on one knee (Figures 114, 115). Various explanations are possible, the most plausible being that these scenes really belong to the pankration; but none of them is quite convincing. Where the evidence is so evenly balanced, certainty is impossible. On the whole I am inclined to abandon the view which I formerly held and to accept Jüthner's view that a fall on the knee did not count.

What happened if both wrestlers fell together? The only evidence for this is the wrestling match in the *Iliad*, described in our second chapter. There it will be remembered that in the first bout Odysseus fell on the top of Ajax, in the second they both fell sideways, after which Achilles declared the contest drawn. From this we inferred that if both wrestlers fell together no fall was counted. The accounts of wrestling in later writers are merely literary imitations of Homer, and of little independent value.

One fall did not decide the victory; three falls were necessary. There are numerous allusions in literature to the three throws.[657] The technical word for winning a victory in wrestling was τριάσσειν, "to treble," and the victor was called τριακτήρ. At first sight it seems uncertain whether the reference is to three bouts or three falls. But the latter interpretation is the only one which suits every passage, and is rendered certain by the categorical statement of Seneca that a wrestler thrice thrown lost the prize.[658]

So much for the actual throw and the number of throws necessary for victory. We pass on to the question of the means employed by the Greek wrestler to throw his opponent. In particular, was tripping allowed, and were leg-holds allowed? In the artificial "Graeco-Roman" style of to-day tripping is forbidden and no holds are allowed below the waist. Tripping is seldom represented in art; but the frequent references to it in literature from the time of Homer to that of Lucian leave no doubt that it played an important part in Greek wrestling, as it has in every rational system in every age.[659] The evidence for leg-holds is less definite, but it seems certain that in practice at least the Greeks made little use of them. This is

---

[653] *J.H.S.* xxv. 21. Cp. Jüthner, *Philostratus*, p. 212.
[654] *Anth. Plan.* iii. 25; *Anth. Pal.* ix. 588. Cp. Aristoph. *Eq.* 571; Aeschylus, *Suppl.* 90.
[655] *Anth. Pal.* xi. 316.
[656] *Agamemnon* 63; *Persae* 914; *Anth. Plan.* iii. 24.
[657] Collected in my article on the Pentathlon, *J.H.S.* xxiii. p. 63; cp. xxv. p. 26. Jüthner, *Philostratus*, 207.
[658] "Luctator ter abjectus perdidit palmam." Cp. Sophocles, *Fr.* 678.
[659] *J.H.S.* xxv. 29. where I have somewhat understated the evidence for tripping.

the natural inference from a passage in the *Laws*,[660] where Plato contrasts the methods of the pankration in which leg-holds and kicking played a conspicuous part with the methods of upright wrestling. The latter is the only form of wrestling which he will admit as useful in his ideal states, and he defines it as consisting in "the disentangling of neck and hands and sides," a masterly definition showing a true understanding of wrestling, for the wrestler's art is shown more perhaps in his ability to escape from or break a grip than in his skill in fixing one. The vases show that the omission of leg-holds in Plato's definition is no accident. In the pankration one competitor is frequently represented in the act of seizing another's foot in order to throw him; Antaeus and Cercyon, whose methods Plato in the above passage strongly condemns, are commonly depicted as grabbing at the feet of Heracles and Theseus. But in wrestling proper, though arm, neck, and body-holds occur constantly, we never see a leg-hold. It is probable that this is the result not so much of a direct prohibition as of the practical riskiness of such a hold under the conditions of upright wrestling. A wrestler who stoops low enough to catch an opponent's foot is certain to be thrown himself if he misses his grip. On the other hand, there is no practical objection when once the wrestlers are engaged to catching hold of an opponent's thigh whether for offence or defence. Indeed, one of the commands of the papyrus implies that it was lawful to take a grip between an opponent's legs, or round the thigh.[661] In wrestling groups which represent the heave we sometimes see a wrestler trying to save himself by seizing the other's legs. Perhaps we may recognize as a wrestling scene a group which occurs on an Etruscan tomb.[662] One man has lifted another on to his shoulder, with his right arm clasped round his right thigh, and his left hand holding his right hand. He may intend to throw him, or he may merely be carrying him. Further, we must remember that upright wrestling formed part of the pankration, and such groups may therefore belong to the pankration.

The conditions of Greek wrestling may be summed up as follows:—

1) If a wrestler fell on any part of the body, hip, back or shoulder, it was a fair fall.
2) If both wrestlers fell together, nothing was counted.
3) Three falls were necessary to secure victory.
4) Tripping was allowed.
5) Leg-holds, if not actually prohibited, were rarely used.

The positions of the Greek wrestler, the grips and the throws which he employed, are known to us from numerous monuments. In view of the number of the monuments and the complexity of the subject it is impossible within the limits of this work to treat them exhaustively, and I must confine myself to the most important and most interesting of the types represented.

The attitude adopted by the Greek wrestler before taking hold was very similar to that of the modern wrestler. Taking a firm stand with his feet somewhat apart and knees slightly bent, rounding (γυρώσας) his back and shoulders, his neck advanced but pressed down into the shoulder blades, his waist drawn in (σφηκώσας), he tried to avoid giving any opening (λαβή) himself, while his outstretched hands were ready to seize any opportunity offered by

---

[660] 796 A, B, discussed more fully *op. cit.* p. 27.
[661] l. 26, σύ κατὰ τῶν δύο πλέον, for the interpretation of which see Jüthner, p. 28.
[662] *Mus. Greg.* i. 103.

his opponent.[663] This position is frequently represented in art; but no better illustration of it can be found than the Naples wrestling-boys, generally miscalled Diskoboloi (Figure 110).

Figure 110. One of a pair of bronze wrestling boys, generally known as Diskoboloi. Naples. (Photograph by Brogi.)

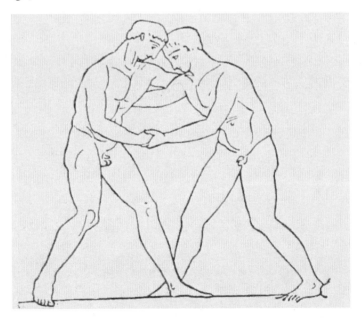

Figure 111. Panathenaic amphora, in British Museum, B. 603. Archonship of Polyzelus, 367 B.C.

---

[663] Heliodorus, *Aethiop.* x. 31.

Generally the wrestlers stand square to one another, and prepare to take hold somewhat in the style of Westmorland and Cumberland wrestlers, "leaning against one another like gable rafters of a house," or "butting against each other like rams," or "resting their heads on each other's shoulders."[664] This position, known apparently as σύστασις, is frequently depicted on the vases (Figure 111). Needless to say, this type does not represent a preliminary "butting-match," as a certain foreign archaeologist seems to imagine, it is the natural position of two wrestlers engaging. Sometimes their heads do crash together as they meet. I read recently an account of a wrestling match in which the heads of the two wrestlers met with a noise which could be heard through the whole house.

Sometimes instead of taking hold from the front the wrestlers try to obtain a hold from the side as in preparing for "the heave," and in such a case the bodies are turned sideways to one another, a position described as παράθεσις.[665] A not very satisfactory illustration of such a position is shown on a British Museum kylix representing Theseus and Cercyon[666] (Figure 112), with which we may compare the group of Heracles and Antaeus on the frieze of the theatre at Delphi,[667] where the sideways position is more clearly marked. Theseus and Heracles seem in both cases to have avoided the ponderous rush of their foes by stepping sideways.

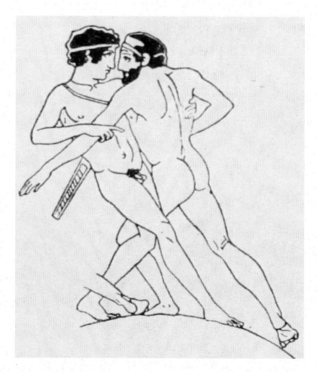

Figure 112. R.-f. kylix, in British Museum, E. 84.

---

[664] Homer, *Il.* xxiii. 712; Lucian, *Anacharsis*, 1; Philostrat. *Vit. Soph.* 225.
[665] Plutarch, *Symp.* ii. 4, enumerates as wrestling terms συστάσεις, παραθέσεις, ἐμβολαί, παρεμβολαί. Jüthner in his interesting account of the Oxyrhynchus Papyrus appears to deny this interpretation, but suggests no satisfactory alternative.
[666] On the interior of this kylix the same group is repeated, but the moment is not quite the same. Cercyon appears to be trying to draw back.
[667] Homolle, *Fouilles de Delphes*, iv. 76.

Figure 113. Group from British Museum amphora, B. 295 (Figure 143).

In endeavouring to obtain a hold wrestlers frequently seize one another by the wrist. This action which is probably denoted by δράσσειν is often a purely defensive movement to prevent an opponent from obtaining a hold on the neck or body. Sometimes, as on a Munich amphora (Figure 123), each wrestler holds the other by the wrist. Sometimes one wrestler holds both his opponent's wrists. Such holds are merely momentary and of little importance. A more effective hold was obtained by seizing an opponent's arm with both hands, one hand seizing the wrist, the other gripping him at the elbow or under the armpit (Figure 113). This seems to have been a very favourite hold and led to one very effective fall of which we have many illustrations.

It is the throw known in modern wrestling as the flying mare and is probably what Lucian describes as εἰς ὕψος ἀναβαστάσαι.[668] Having seized his opponent's arm in the manner described the wrestler rapidly turns his back on him,[669] draws his arm over his own shoulder, using it as a lever by which to throw him clean over his head, at the same time he stoops forward, sometimes sinking on one knee or both. The beginning of the throw is seen on an Etruscan wall painting.[670] One wrestler has swung his opponent off his feet and hoisted him over his shoulder. His right hand still grasps his left wrist, and his left hand has been transferred to his neck, and he leans forward in order to complete the throw. A somewhat later moment occurs on a British Museum kylix (Figure 114). The drawing is rough and careless, and the stoop of the legs is probably exaggerated because otherwise the group would be too high for the vase space. Two wonderfully life-like pictures of this throw occur on a kylix in the Bibliothèque Nationale of Paris (Figures 54, 115). On the interior we see the victor kneeling on one knee; he has let go with his right hand, and his opponent, left unsupported, is about to fall on his back. The exterior, which is unfortunately much mutilated, shows the same fall a moment later, the falling wrestler tries to save himself by placing his right hand on the ground. This throw was undoubtedly common to wrestling proper and to the pankration. A black-figured amphora in the British Museum, B. 193, represents Heracles employing it against the Nemean lion.

---

[668] *Anacharsis*, 24.
[669] A small ivory statuette of two boys wrestling, recently acquired by the British Museum, perhaps represents the moment of the turn.
[670] Dar.-Sagl. 4624.

Figure 114. R.-f. kylix, in British Museum, E. 94.

Figure 115. R.-f. kylix. Paris. (Interior of Figure 54.)

Returning to the arm-hold which leads to this throw, we find several methods of meeting it represented. On the Amphiaraus vase (Figure 3) Peleus has seized with both hands the left arm of Hippaleimus. The latter with his free right hand grips Peleus under the right arm-pit, and thus weakens his grip and prevents him from turning round. A similar defence is shown on the black-figured amphora in the British Museum, B. 295, where the attack is made on the right arm. A Berlin amphora by Andocides (Figure 116) shows another style of counter. The wrestler to the left grasps his opponent's left wrist, but the latter, by a quick move forward, has rendered useless the right hand which should have grasped his upper arm, and passing his own right hand behind his back grasps his right arm just above the elbow. In all these cases the object is to prevent the opponent turning round or to loosen his grip. The latter object is noticeable on the coins of Aspendus (Figure 109), where the left-hand wrestler grasps with both hands his opponent's left, while the latter with his right hand grasps his right wrist or left upper arm. We may remark how on some of the coins the right-hand wrestler's hand hangs down helplessly as if rendered powerless by the grip.

Figure 116. R.-f. amphora. Berlin, 2159.

Greek wrestling was governed, it would seem, more by a tradition of good form than by actual rules. Thus, though it was not regarded as good form to seize an opponent's fingers and break them, as Leontiscus did, such practices do not appear to have been actually prohibited. They were well enough in the pankration, where the object was to force an opponent, by any means to acknowledge defeat, but they could hardly be regarded as legitimate means for throwing an opponent, which was the object of true wrestling.

The neck is an obvious and effective place by which to obtain a hold, and strength of neck is essential to a wrestler.[671] Pindar, in the seventh Nemean ode, speaks of the wrestler's "strength and neck invincible," and Xenophon, describing the training of the Spartans, says that they exercised alike legs and arms and neck. In the *Knights* of Aristophanes Demos advises the sausage-seller to grease his neck in order to escape from Cleon's grip. The technical word for obtaining a neck-hold is τραχηλίζειν. Neck-holds were freely used in the pankration, but rather for the purpose of choking an opponent than of throwing him.

Several varieties of neck-hold are exhibited on the vases. On a red-figured krater in the Ashmolean (Figure 117) one wrestler seizes the other's wrist with his left hand, his neck with his right. The wrestler so attacked defends himself by seizing the other under the left arm-pit with his left hand. An interesting feature of this vase is the figure of winged Victory seated upon a pillar watching the contest. A different defence is shown on the black-figured amphora in the British Museum, B. 295 (Figure 118). Here the left-hand wrestler grasps with his left hand his opponent's right which is seizing his neck. We may notice that he grasps it at one of the weakest points just below the elbow. Yet another means of defence is to seize the opponent's neck.

---

[671] Phil. *Gym.* 35; Xen. *Lac. Rep.* 5, 9; Aristoph. *Eq.* 491.

Figure 117. R.-f. krater. Oxford, Ashmolean, 288.

Figure 118. Reverse of Figure 143. British Museum, B. 295.

Perhaps the best illustration of a neck-hold occurs on a black-figured amphora in Munich, representing the wrestling match between Peleus and Atalanta, which took place at the funeral games of Pelias (Figure 119). Peleus has apparently tried to seize Atalanta's right arm with both hands, but Atalanta, moving forward, seizes him by the back of the neck, very much in the style of a modern wrestler. The picture reminds us how in the gymnasia of Chios young men and maidens might be seen wrestling with one another.[672]

---

[672] Athenaeus xiii. p. 566.

Figure 119. B.-f. amphora. Munich, 584.

The neck-hold is commonly employed by Heracles in his fight with the Nemean lion. Sometimes his left arm is round the animal's neck, while his right hand grasps its left paw, sometimes both hands are clasped round its neck. The interlocking of the hands is the same as that employed by Westmorland and Cumberland wrestlers to-day, the hands being turned so that the palms face one another and the fingers hooked together. On an amphora in Munich Heracles employs this same grip against Antaeus, who, sinking on one knee, grabs characteristically but vainly at the hero's foot.[673]

Of the actual throws to which a neck-hold led we have little evidence in the monuments. On a psykter of Euthymides Theseus has secured a powerful hold on Cercyon with one arm passed over his left shoulder, the other under his right arm-pit and swings him off his feet.[674] Tripping was doubtless freely employed with these holds, but the only illustration of this combination occurs in a group of bronzes discussed below. Similarly the movement described as ἕδραν στρέφειν, to turn one's buttocks towards an opponent was certainly combined with neck-holds. A good illustration of this occurs on a Panathenaic vase in Boulogne (Figure 120).

Passing on to body-holds we find a preliminary position represented on a Panathenaic vase in the British Museum (Figure 111). The wrestlers have each one hand round the other's back, and one of them with his other hand grasps the other's wrist.

A very effective body-hold is obtained by seizing the opponent round the waist with both hands: he can then be lifted off his feet and swung to the ground. The hold may be obtained from the front, from behind, or from the side, and all three forms are constantly represented.

---

[673] Munich, 3; Gerh. *A. V.* 114. In *J.H.S.* xxv. I have dealt more fully with the fights of Heracles.
[674] Schreiber, *Atlas*, xxiv. 10.

There are various technical terms for such grips,[675] and the effectiveness of the grip is shown by the proverbial use of the expression μέσον ἔχειν, to hold by the waist.

Figure 120. Panathenaic amphora. Boulogne, Musée Municipale, 441.

Figure 121. B.-f. amphora. Munich, 1336.

The body-hold from the front is difficult to obtain, but when obtained is extremely effective. It is the hold by which Hackenschmidt, a few years ago, gained his sensational victory over Madrali. But clumsiness and slowness are fatal, for, as the wrestler stoops to obtain the under grip, his opponent can either, by a sideways movement, obtain a hold for the heave, or falling on him may force him to the ground. This is the fate which continually befalls Cercyon and Antaeus as they rush in blindly, head down, in hope of obtaining this

---

[675] *J.H.S.* xxv. p. 280, διαλαμβάνειν, μεσοφέρδειν, μεσοφέρδην, μέσον ἔχειν; διαλαμβάνειν means to clasp both hands round an opponent's waist; περιτιθέναι means rather to put one arm round an opponent as in taking a grip for the heave, but does not necessarily imply that the hands are clasped. *Vide* Jüthner, *Philostratus*, p. 28.

hold.[676] The danger of it is well illustrated by a pair of groups from a black-figured amphora in Munich (Figure 121). In both cases a bearded athlete rushes in to seize his opponent by the waist: the upper group is merely preliminary; in the lower group his opponent, unable to secure a hold for the heave owing to the grip on his right hand, seems to be pressing on him with all his weight to bear him to the ground. Perhaps a further stage is represented on a red-figured kylix in the Museum at Philadelphia (Figure 122). One wrestler has already lost his balance, and is supporting himself with both hands on the ground. The other with his left hand holds his right arm down, and with the other prepares to take a body-hold and roll him over. Usually then the body-hold from the front is unsuccessful. On the Berlin amphora (Figure 116) we see a youth who has successfully obtained this hold on a bearded athlete, and lifts him off his feet in order to throw him.

Figure 122. R.-f. kylix. Philadelphia.

Figure 123. B.-f. amphora. Munich, 495.

---

[676] *Vide J. H. S.* xxv. pp. 281 ff., and Figures 18, 19, 20.

More commonly the hold is secured from behind in the manner represented on a black-figured amphora in Munich (Figure 123). We may notice that the wrestler in mid air has, in defence, hooked his right foot round his opponent's leg. The hands are interlocked in the manner already described. But despite of these realistic touches the drawing as a whole is stiff and lifeless, and contrasts strangely with the much more vigorous portrayal of the same type on gems and coins. The type is particularly connected with Heracles and Antaeus. The lifting of Antaeus is first represented on the fourth century coins of Tarentum. From this time it is constantly repeated in bronzes and statues, and especially on coins and gems.[677] Roman poets said that Antaeus being the son of earth derived fresh force from his mother each time he touched earth, and that Heracles therefore lifted him from earth and squeezed him to death in midair. This version of the story is, however, unknown to the literature and art of Greece; and though it may have originated in a mistaken interpretation of the type which we are considering, cannot possibly be regarded as its motive. With a few doubtful exceptions Heracles is always represented as lifting Antaeus, not to crush him, but to swing him to the ground, and nowhere is this motive clearer than on some of the imperial coins, such as the coin of Antoninus Pius shown in Figure 109.

For no throw have we such abundant evidence as for "the heave," the hold for which is obtained from the side by passing one hand across and round the opponent's back, and the other underneath him. This is the hold which is being practised in the wrestling lesson shown in Figure 96. It is a hold sometimes employed by Heracles against Antaeus, but is particularly characteristic of Theseus. Two kylikes in the British Museum (Figures 124, 125) will sufficiently illustrate it. On the one Cercyon has endeavoured vainly to save himself by applying a similar hold to Theseus, but too late; on the other vase he has already been swung off the ground, one arm still clasps Theseus' back, the other hand reaches for the ground or grabs at the foot of his adversary. The popularity of "the heave" among the Greeks is shown by a far more important monument. A metope from the Theseum shows Theseus in the very act of turning Cercyon over to throw him (Figure 126). A yet later moment is represented in a well-known bronze statuette now in Paris (Figure 127). The victor here has turned his opponent completely over, and standing upright prepares to drop him on the ground. On an Attic stele already mentioned, representing Athenian sports, a wrestler is in the act of falling headlong to the ground, and as he slips through his opponent's hands clasps his leg to save himself (Figure 36). The heave and the holds necessary for it are clearly described in the late epics of Quintus Smyrnaeus and Nonnus.[678]

Some of the holds described must have been combined with various turns of the body. Thus to obtain a hold from behind a wrestler must either force his opponent to shift his position (μεταβιβάζειν), or shift his own position so as to get behind him (μεταβαίνειν), while the wrestler so attacked will naturally turn round himself (μεταβαλέσθαι). The last two terms occur in two consecutive lines of the Oxyrhynchus papyrus. One pupil is told to get behind his fellow and grip him, the other is ordered at once to turn round himself.[679] The use of the preposition μετά in these compounds suggests the "afterplay" of Cornish wrestling.

---

[677] For references see *J.H.S.* p. 283, n. 76.
[678] Quintus iv. 215; Nonnus xxxvii. 553-601. For a brief account of these *vide J.H.S.* xxv. p. 25.
[679] l. 25 σὺ αὐτὸν μεταβὰς πλέξον· σὺ μεταβαλοῦ.

Figure 124. R.-f. kylix. British Museum, E. 48.

Figure 125. B.-f. kylix, in British Museum, E. 36.

A sudden turn of the body is often used when a hold has been already obtained, in order to twist an opponent off his feet. The modern throws known as the "buttock" and "cross-buttock" find their Greek equivalent in the phrase ἕδραν στρέφειν, to turn the buttock. The cross-buttock differs chiefly from the buttock in that the legs come more into play, and we may therefore infer that this is the special throw whereof Theocritus speaks when he relates how Heracles learnt from Harpalacus "all the tricks wherewith the nimble Argive cross-buttockers (ἀπὸ σκελέων ἑδροστρόφοι) give each other the fall."[680] It was evidently a favourite throw. Theophrastus, in his character of the late learner who wishes to be thought

---

[680] xxiv. 111.

thoroughly accomplished and up-to-date, remarks that "in the bath he is continually giving the cross-buttock as if wrestling."[681] Cannot we picture this athletic fraud strutting about the bath cross-buttocking imaginary opponents, just as his modern counterpart bowls imaginary balls, or with his walking-stick wings imaginary birds?

These movements may be illustrated by a group on a black-figured vase in the Museo Gregoriano (Figure 128). The wrestler to the left has obtained a hold round his opponent's waist, either from in front or from behind. In the former case his opponent must have immediately turned round. Anyhow, by throwing his weight well forward, he frustrates the attempt to lift him, and puts himself in an advantageous position for swinging the other off his feet. Somewhat similar must have been the motive of a much mutilated group on a metope of the treasury of the Athenians at Delphi, representing the exploits of Theseus, except that the figures are more upright.[682]

A throw somewhat resembling the cross-buttock is represented in a recently acquired bronze of the British Museum (Figure 129). As two other replicas[683] exist it seems probable that it is a copy of some well-known Hellenistic group in bronze or marble. A thick-set bearded man is wrestling with a powerful youth, and with his back turned to him twists him off his feet by a most curious arm-lock. With his right hand he forces his opponent's right arm back across his own thigh, while he has slipped his left arm under his left armpit and gripped his neck, thus rendering the imprisoned arm quite useless, and obtaining a leverage similar to that of our half Nelson. Perhaps the grip was obtained in the following way. The man seizes the youth's right arm, and by a quick movement pulls him towards him and turns him round, μεταβιβάζει, at the same time stepping himself to the left so as to be behind him. He then slips his left hand under his left armpit so as to grasp his neck and force it down. The grip obtained he turns round to the right and twists him over.

Figure 126. Metope of Theseum. Theseus and Cercyon. (*Greek Sculpture*, Figure 66.)

---

[681] *Char.* xxvii.
[682] *Fouilles de Delphes*, iv. 46, 47.
[683] *Collection Philip*, Paris, 1905, No. 484; de Ridder, *Collection de Clercy*, Paris, 1905, iii. 253, Pl. xli. 3.

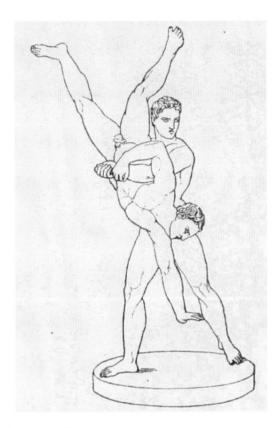

Figure 127. Bronze wrestling group. Paris.

Figure 128. B.-f. amphora. Vatican.

Figure 129. Bronze group, in the British Museum.

We have seen that tripping (ὑποσκελίζειν) was at all times an essential part of Greek wrestling. There are various technical terms for the different chips, but their interpretation is very uncertain and the monuments give little help. The words βάλλω, βολή, and their compounds, are used to denote both arm and leg movements. Perhaps we may recognise in ἐμβολή the modern "hank" and in παρεμβολή the "back heel," the foot being hooked round the opponent's leg from the inside and the outside respectively. The latter term occurs in an amusing passage of Lucian's *Ocypus*.[684] Ocypus, who is suffering from gout but will not acknowledge it, alleges, among various excuses for his lameness, that he hurt his foot in trying a back heel. By analogy the term διαβολή, if used of a leg movement, may mean the "outside stroke." The chip by which Odysseus threw Ajax is described by Eustathius as μεταπλασμός or παρακαταγωγή. From the Homeric account these terms ought to correspond to the "inside click" or "hank." Some such click is perhaps intended on the vases in Figures 116, 123, where one wrestler, lifted from the ground, clicks his foot round his opponent's leg.

---

[684] *Ocypus*, 60.

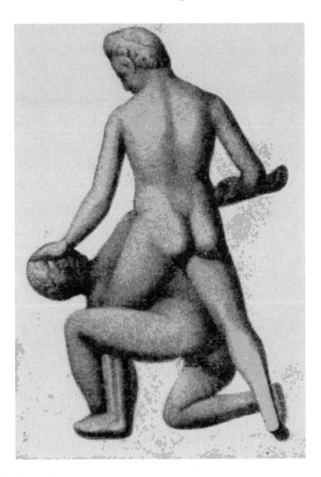

Figure 130. Bronze. St. Petersburg.

The best illustration of tripping is furnished by a group of bronzes representing a wrestler fallen on one knee and supporting himself on his left arm, while his opponent stands over him with his left leg still hooked round his, and his right foot behind. So far all the bronzes agree, but in the position of the arms there are two varieties. In the St. Petersburg bronze (Figure 130) the victor forces the other's head down with his left hand, and with his right presses his right arm back in the same way as in the bronze in the British Museum (Figure 129). In the Constantinople bronze (Figure 131) he holds his opponent's neck with his right hand, while with his left he has twisted backwards his arm and shoulder. In both cases he makes the attack from behind. In the first case he seizes his opponent's right hand with his own right, places his arm across his neck, and at the same time hooks his left leg round the other's left leg; then pressing his neck forward he forces his right arm backwards, using it as a lever to twist him off his feet. The other as he falls puts out his left hand to save himself and falls with his left hand and right knee on the ground. In the other type he seizes the other's left hand with his own left and pulls it across his back, at the same time forcing his head forwards and downwards with his right hand, and hooking his left leg. The fall is still more inevitable. All the bronzes seem to represent the fall as completed, and the victor has no appearance of continuing his attack. If a fall on the knee was a fair fall no further explanation is wanted. In any case the fallen man's position is hopeless, and he can at any moment be rolled over on the ground.

Figure 131. Bronze. Constantinople.

These bronzes are probably copies of some well-known Hellenistic group. The number of replicas which exist of it attest the importance of the original statue and the popularity of the throw represented. It is the sort of attack that must naturally have commended itself to boys playing tricks on one another, or street roughs attacking innocent passers-by from behind. And it is, I believe, the very trick by which Aristophanes, in the *Knights*, describes the way in which Cleon cheated simple old country gentlemen. "Whenever you find such a one," say the chorus, "you fetch him home from the Chersonese, and as the old gentleman is walking along unsuspectingly star-gazing you suddenly throw your arm across his neck (διαβαλών), hook his leg (ἀγκυρίσας), and, pulling his shoulder back, kick him in the stomach (ἐνεκολήβασας)."[685] Horse-play of this character was not unknown among the fashionable youth of Athens. Demosthenes relates how Conon and his sons set upon Ariston, tripped him up, threw him in the mud, and jumped upon him; and several of the terms which the orator uses are, like those of Aristophanes, terms familiar in the wrestling school.

In no sport is there greater variety of styles and rules than in wrestling. Almost every country has a style of its own. In Greece the Panhellenic festivals helped to preserve uniformity of rule, but there was still room for much diversity of style.[686] The Sicilians in particular had a style of their own, the rules for which had been drawn up by one Oricadmus.[687] There was also a "Thessalian chip,"[688] but in what the Sicilians or Thessalians

---

[685] *Equites*, 261-3; Demosthenes *in Cononem*, 8. For a full discussion of this passage and of the bronzes *vide J.H.S.* xxv. pp. 289-293.
[686] Krause, *Gym.* 428.
[687] Aelian, *Var. Hist.* xi.

excelled we do not know. The Argives, who were specially famed for their skill in wrestling, are described by Theocritus as "cross-buttockers." On the other hand, the Spartans disdained the science of wrestling and the teaching of trainers, and relied on mere strength and endurance.[689] Plutarch ascribes the victory of the Thebans at Leuctra to their superiority over the Spartans in wrestling.[690] Individuals, too, had their favourite chips. It is recorded of Cleitostratus of Rhodes who won the wrestling at Olympia in Ol. 147 that he owed his victories to the use of the neck-hold.

---

[688] Eustathius, *Il.* ii. p. 331, 18, 39.
[689] Epigram on a Spartan by Damagetus, *Anth. Plan.* i. 1.
[690] *Quaest. Symp.* ii. 5, 2.

Chapter 19

BOXING

No sport was older, and none was more popular at all periods among the Greeks than boxing. Its antiquity and its popularity are manifest in their mythology.[691] Apollo himself is said to have defeated Ares in boxing at Olympia, and the Delphians sacrificed to Apollo the Boxer (πύκτης), a conclusive proof that boxing was regarded by the Greeks as a contest of skill rather than of brute strength. Heracles, Tydeus, and Polydeuces were all famous boxers, and the invention of boxing is ascribed to Theseus. Both in the *Iliad* and the *Odyssey* boxing appears as a common accomplishment and a popular sport; it was represented, according to Hesiod, on the shield of Heracles. The discoveries of Cnossus have shown that boxing was known in the Aegean centuries before the arrival of the Greeks. The survival of the tradition in these parts may perhaps explain the extraordinary popularity of boxing in the East, and particularly among the Ionians. Boxing formed part of the ancient Delian festival, and the laws of boxing in use at Olympia were ascribed to Onomastus of Smyrna. It was also extremely popular among the Arcadians, but found less favour with the Spartans who, though claiming to have invented boxing at first as a military exercise, abandoned it at an early date and took no part in boxing competitions.[692]

The early inhabitants of Crete are thought to have worn some kind of glove or caestus. But the boxing of historic times was far more nearly akin to fighting with bare fists, from which, of course, all boxing originated. The fight between Odysseus and Irus in the *Odyssey* proves that fights with bare fists were frequent in Homeric times. But the competitors in the funeral games of Patroclus had their hands covered with well-cut thongs of ox-hide, such as we find represented later on the vases. The use of some sort of covering or protection for the hand necessarily determines the whole system of fighting, and it will be convenient, therefore, before we consider the style of Greek boxing, to trace the history and development of what for convenience we may call the Greek gloves.[693] The simplest form of glove consisted in long, thin thongs wound round the hands. They were made of ox-hide, raw or simply dressed with oil or fat so as to render them supple. Later writers described them as "soft gloves," ἱμάντες μαλακώτεροι or μείλιχαι in contrast with the more formidable implements in use in

---

[691] For mythological references *vide* Krause, pp. 498 ff.
[692] Philostr. *Gym.* 9, 12.
[693] For a fuller account of this subject the reader is referred to the admirable chapter in Dr. Jüthner's *Antike Turngeräthe*, pp. 66-95, where he will find full references both literary and monumental.

their own time.[694] In reality they must have been far from soft, and like the light gloves used sometimes in modern fights they served to protect the knuckles from swelling, and so to increase the power of attack rather than to deaden the force of the blow. From the vase paintings they appear to be ten or twelve feet long, and the number of windings represented require at least that length.

These thongs are among the commonest objects on the vases. Sometimes we see them gathered into a bundle; and carried in the hand. A fragment of a red-figured kylix in the British Museum, E. 63, shows a procession of youthful boxers standing before an official (Figure 132). They appear to be competitors taking the preliminary oath to observe all the laws of the games. Their right hands are raised, and in their left they carry bundles of thongs. Similarly on the interior of another British Museum kylix, E. 39, a youthful boxer with the thongs in his left hand stands over an altar (Figure 133). His attitude expresses surprise and excitement at something which he sees upon the altar, perhaps, as Dr. Jüthner suggests,[695] at the appearance of the victim, from the burning of which he seeks an omen of his success in the games (μαντεῖον δί ἐμπύρων). On the exterior of the same kylix the artist has drawn a series of boxing scenes. On one side two youths are preparing or waiting their turn to box, one holds in his hands a pair of thongs, one of which he is handing to his fellow. The latter holds a thong outstretched with both hands. At either end the thong is gathered into a loop. This type, which is of very frequent occurrence, is often misinterpreted, the thong being regarded either as a jumping rope, or as a rope used in a sort of pulling match or tug-of-war, which was a familiar boys' game in Plato's time.[696] But Dr. Jüthner has proved conclusively that the objects represented are boxing thongs.[697]

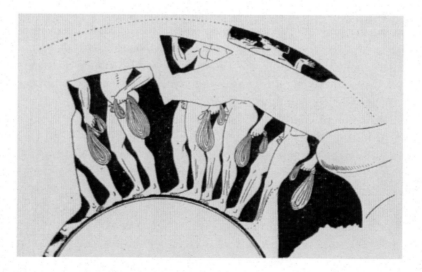

Figure 132. R.-f. kylix, in British Museum, E. 63.

---

[694] Paus. vi. 23, 4; viii. 40, 3. Plato, *Leg.* viii. 830 B.

[695] *Ant. Turn.* p. 67.

[696] Plato, *Theaet.* 27. Krause, p. 323, distinguishes two games, one described as διελκυστίνδα or διὰ γραμμῆς παίζειν, a tug-of-war between teams, the other called σκάπερδα or ἑλκυστίνδα, a game in which two youths tried to lift one another off the ground by means of a rope passed through a hole in a pillar. Roulez was the first to suggest this explanation of the thongs shown on vases. His explanation is adopted in a recent article on a fine r.-f. kylix representing wrestling and boxing scenes, Pl. xxxv. in the *Transactions of the University of Pennsylvania*, 1907, p. 140.

[697] *Op. cit.* p. 69.

Boxing

Figure 133. R.-f. kylix, in British Museum, E. 39.

Very frequently, as in the vase with which we are dealing, we see one or both ends of the thong gathered into a loop. This arrangement is clearly connected with the method of fastening the thong. Philostratus, in describing the meilichai, says that the four fingers were inserted into a loop in such a way as to allow the hand to be clenched, and were held tight by a cord fastened round the forearm.[698] Cord and loop are merely parts of the leather thong. The act of binding the thong is frequently pictured on the red-figured vases, but the drawing of the thongs is too small and usually too sketchy to allow us to form any conclusion as to the precise method.[699] Probably there were various methods in use. The thumb is always free and usually uncovered, though occasionally the thong is wound round the thumb separately.[700] As a rule the thong is wound several times round the four fingers and knuckles, passed diagonally across the palm and back of the hand, and wound round the wrist, the binding

---

[698] *Gym.* 10 ὥπλιστο δὲ ἡ ἀρχαία πυγμὴ τὸν τρόπον τοῦτον· ἐς στρόφιον οἱ τέτταρες τῶν δακτύλων ἐνεβιβάζοντο καὶ ὑπερέβαλλον τοῦ στροφίου τοσοῦτον ὅσον, εἰ συνάγοιντο, πὺξ εἶναι, συνείχοντο δὲ ὑπὸ σειρᾶς ἣν καθάπερ ἔρεισμα ἐβέβληντο ἐκ τοῦ πήχεος. Cp. Paus. viii. 40, 3.

[699] Sometimes the thongs are drawn only on the hand, sometimes only on the wrist, sometimes they are completely wanting. This is probably due to nothing but carelessness, but in some cases these lines, which were usually painted in after the rest of the figure was finished, may have simply worn off.

[700] Jüthner, Figure 59.

sometimes being carried some distance up the forearm. The interior of a British Museum kylix, E. 78 (Figure 134), shows a youth in the act of binding the thong on his right arm, pulling the end tight with his left hand. In this case it seems that the fingers are bound first, and the thong is fastened round the wrist. On a B.M. amphora (Figure 135) representing a later type of glove the order appears to be reversed.

Figure 134. Interior of Figure 151. British Museum, E. 78.

Figure 135. Panathenaic amphora, in British Museum, B. 607. Archonship of Pythodelus, B.C. 336.

The meilichai were the only form of boxing glove used in the sixth and fifth centuries, and they continued in use, at all events for practice in the palaestra, during the fourth century. Early in this century, however, they seem to have been superseded in competition by more formidable gloves which Plato describes as σφαῖραι, and which he recommends for use in his ideal state as more closely reproducing the conditions of actual warfare. These σφαῖραι or balls have been identified by Dr. Jüthner with a type of glove represented on certain Panathenaic vases of the fourth century, and also on some Etruscan cistae which belong to the early part of the third century. On the latter the ball-like appearance to which they owed their name is clearly marked. On the well-known Ficoroni cista[701] the hand appears to be covered by a glove which leaves the fingers free but extends almost the whole length of the forearm; and the glove is bound on by triple thongs, crossing and recrossing each other, and finally gathered together into a bunch, and secured by passing through a loop at the back of the hand. Very similar is the type represented on the B.M. amphora (Figure 135) which bears the name of the Archon Pythodelus, 336 B.C. The glove seems to be formed of thick bands of some soft substance stretching along the arm, and bound round by stout, stiff leather thongs fastened apparently between the fingers and the thumb. The youth to the left, who is waiting to fight the winner, is drawing the end tight with his teeth. On the right is represented, in place of the usual judge, a draped and winged figure of Victory bearing in her hand a palm. A similar glove is represented on another Panathenaic vase, in the Louvre, belonging to the Archonship of Hegesias in 324 B.C.

Figure 136. Boxer. Terme Museum, Rome. (From a photograph by Anderson.)

---

[701] Jüthner, Figure 66.

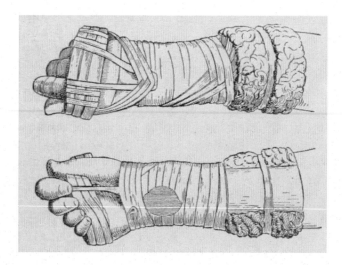

Figure 137. Right hand of boxer, from Sorrento. Naples.

To bind on the hand these complicated thongs must have been a troublesome and lengthy process. And the introduction of the sphairai was followed almost immediately by the invention of gloves which could be drawn on or off more readily. These gloves, which are appropriately described as ἵμαντες ὀξεῖς, are familiar to us from the seated boxer in the Terme at Rome (Figure 136). They occur also in a marble figure of a boxer from Sorrento which is now at Naples (Figure 137), on an arm also at Naples, and on a hand found at Verona.[702] They consist of two parts, a glove and a hard leather ring encircling the knuckles. The glove extends half-way down the forearm and ends in a thick strip of fleece serving doubtless to protect the arm, which might easily be broken by a blow from so formidable a weapon; the glove itself appears from the way in which the straps cut into it to have been padded; the ends of the fingers are cut off and there is an opening on the inside. On the knuckles the glove is provided with a thick pad which prevents the ring in which the fingers are inserted from slipping down. This ring is formed of three to five strips of hard, stiff leather, bound together by small straps, and held in its place by thongs bound round the wrist. It is about an inch wide and half an inch thick, and its sharp, projecting edges must have rendered it a weapon of offence fully as effective as the modern knuckle-duster. Under these circumstances it is amusing to learn from Philostratus that the thumb was not allowed to take any part in the blow for fear of causing severe and unsightly wounds (ὑπὲρ συμμετρίας τῶν τραυμάτων) and that for the same reason the use of pigskin was forbidden.[703] In later writers the term "sphairai" seems to be used of these ἵμαντες ὀξεῖς, and inasmuch as they were too dangerous for use in practice, soft, padded gloves were used in the palaestra called ἐπίσθαιρα.[704]

These gloves continued in use with but little variation till the second century A.D. at least. Indeed it is doubtful if any other form was ever used in the true Greek festivals. The latest representation of them in art is a relief now in the Lateran supposed to represent the fight between Entellus and Dares.[705] The influence of Roman feeling is seen in the fact that both combatants instead of being naked wear a chiton tucked up so as to leave the right

---

[702] Jüthner, p. 79, Figures . 62-64.
[703] *Gym.* 10.
[704] Plutarch, *Mor.* 825 E.
[705] Jüthner, Figure 68. Helbig, 619.

shoulder bare.[706] The gloves differ little from those described above, except that the thumb is protected by leather thongs, though not bound up with the fingers. Pausanias, Plutarch, and Philostratus know no other form of glove, and none of these writers makes any reference to the masses of lead and iron with which, according to Roman poets, the caestus was loaded. The ἱμάντες ὀξεῖς were certainly capable of inflicting all the injuries on which the writers of epigrams in the *Anthology* delight to dwell.[707] The use of metal to render the caestus heavier and more dangerous is a purely Roman invention, utterly barbarous and entirely fatal to all science in boxing. The Roman caestus may have figured in some of those gladiatorial shows which found favour in some parts of Greece under the empire, but the silence of Philostratus and others proves that it was never used at Olympia, or indeed at any place when any vestige of the athletic tradition of Greece yet lingered.

The caestus has really no place in the history of Greek athletics except in so far as it is a development of the ἱμάντες ὀξεῖς or σφαῖραι of the Greeks. Completely ignorant of true boxing, the Romans assumed that the power of attack could be increased by additional weight. They did not understand that in boxing a quick, sharp blow is far more dangerous and effective than a slow, heavy blow, and that the more the hand is weighted, the slower the blow is, and therefore the easier to guard against or avoid. According to the poets they increased the weight by sewing pieces of lead and iron into the glove. In the existing representations of the caestus the hand seems to be encased in a hard ball or cylinder, from the back of which over the knuckles is a toothed protection presumably of metal, which sometimes takes the form of two or three spikes. These spikes have been sometimes mistaken for the fingers, but their true nature has been conclusively shown by Dr. Jüthner. At the same time the owner was protected by a padded sleeve extending almost to the shoulder. This sleeve is usually made of a skin or fleece with the rough side turned outwards and is secured by straps. On the Lateran Mosaic the whole arm appears to be encased in a hard sheath (Figure 138).[708]

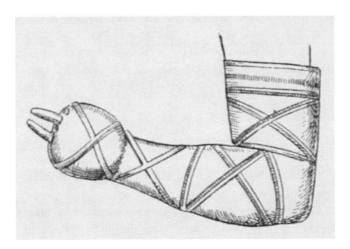

Figure 138. Caestus, from mosaic in the Thermae of Caracalla. Lateran Museum.

---

[706] Cp. *Inschr. v. Priene*, 112, l. 91, where mention is made of boxing ἐν εἵμασι.
[707] The word μύρμηκες, which is used by the epigrammatists (*Anth. Pal.* xi. 78), appears to be merely a humorous designation of these weapons, but to have no special significance.
[708] Jüthner, pp. 87 ff., Figures. 69-74; cp. Hans Lucas, *Jahrbuch*, 1904, pp. 127-136.

Figure 139. Bronze situla. Watsch.

In the preceding sketch no mention has been made of a very curious form of caestus represented on the bronze situlae found at Bologna and in the Tyrol, because, as Dr. Jüthner has pointed out, this form finds no place in the development of the Greek boxing glove.[709] So-called boxing scenes are of common occurrence on these situlae; the form of the weapon is most clearly shown on the well-known situla from Watsch (Figure 139), on which two boxers are depicted fighting over a helmet placed on a stand between them and holding in their hands objects exactly resembling modern dumb-bells. In fact one is tempted to suppose that they really are halteres shaped like dumb-bells, and that the scene depicted is not so much a boxing match as some sort of athletic dance. Certainly the style of the performance has as little connexion with true boxing as these objects have with boxing gloves. But the composition of the group seems to show that it really is a crude and barbarous representation of boxing. The helmet placed between the two figures is, of course, the prize for which they are fighting, and cannot possibly represent any sort of barrier between the two combatants as a recent writer has suggested.[710] In archaic art the tripods, cauldrons, or helmets which are the objects of competition are frequently represented. In a race the prize is naturally placed at the finish; in a combat it is no less naturally placed between the combatants. The same scheme of composition occurs on the walls of tombs at Tarquinii and Clusium,[711] and on the fragment of a black-figured vase in the British Museum found at Daphnae in Egypt (Figure 140).[712] On the Etruscan tombs the scheme is not confined to boxers. In the Tomba degli Auguri at Tarquinii a pair of wrestlers[713] are wrestling over three large bowls placed between them; but no one could suppose for a moment that the bowls were in reality so placed. The numerous athletic scenes on those tombs bear witness to the popularity of athletics and especially of boxing among the Etruscans; but they do not justify us in assuming any connexion between Etruscan art and that of the situlae, nor between Etruscan athletics and the athletics of the Tyrol. The athletic scenes on Etruscan tombs are nothing but imitations of the athletic scenes

---

[709] Jüthner, Figure 61, pp. 75, 76.
[710] R. M. Burrows, *Discoveries in Crete*, p. 35. As far as the athletic argument is concerned, the connexion which Professor Burrows suggests between Crete and Central Europe and Etruria appears to me entirely without foundation.
[711] Dennis, *Cities and Cemeteries of Etruria, passim*.
[712] *Tunis*, ii. 30.
[713] *Mon. d. I*. XI. Pl. 25.

on the Greek vases which we know were from an early period imported into Etruria. The diskoi, halteres, and himantes differ little from those on the vases, such differences as do occur being possibly due to the fact that the Etruscan artist did not quite understand what he was copying. The scheme of composition is usually Greek; that the particular boxing scheme which we are discussing is Greek is proved by the vase from Daphnae. Such resemblance then as exists between the Etruscan scheme and that on the situlae is clearly due to the fact that both were imitated from the Greeks, unless we are to maintain that the situlae were the original for both Etruscans and Greeks. But if the scheme of composition on the situlae is Greek, what shall we say of the form of caestus? It certainly cannot have been derived from or even suggested by anything that Greek boxers ever wore. Two explanations alone are possible. Either we have a picture of some barbarous form of combat belonging to the Tyrol in which such weapons were used,[714] or the makers of the situlae, ignorant of Greek athletics, have mistaken the halteres of the Greeks for weapons used in boxing.

Figure 140. Fragment of b.-f. situla, in British Museum, B. 124.

The history of Greek boxing may be divided then into three main periods. The first is the period of the soft thongs or meilichai, and extends from Homeric times to the close of the sixth century; the second is that of the "sharp thongs" and sphairai, extending from the fourth century into late Roman times; the third is that of the weighted caestus, though as has been shown it is doubtful whether this was really Greek. The changes in the form of the glove must have greatly modified the style of boxing and even the scanty evidence which we possess allows us to trace to some extent the change in style. For the first period we have the evidence of Homer, and of the painted vases of the sixth and fifth centuries: for the second period we have the evidence of a few Panathenaic vases, and of Theocritus and Apollonius Rhodius, both of whom have left us descriptions of fights which doubtless reflect the practice of their own day: for the last period we have the extremely unreliable evidence of Vergil and other

---

[714] Athenaeus quotes Poseidonius as saying that the Celts were addicted to fights with arms, wounding and even killing one another. ἐν γὰρ τοῖς ὅπλοις ἀγερθέντες σκιαμαχοῦσι καὶ πρὸς ἀλλήλους ἀκροχειρίζονται, Athen. 154 A.

Roman poets. There is also much scattered information referring to different periods contained in the writings of Plutarch, Pausanias, Lucian, and Philostratus. These writers for the most part derive their information from earlier records, and it is often difficult to estimate the value of their evidence. It is, therefore, extremely important to consider first of all in its proper order such evidence as can be dated with certainty. The neglect of this precaution has led to many ill-considered and misleading statements about the Greek boxer. Thus in a well-known dictionary, I find a paragraph constructed with sublime indifference to dates from some sixteen authors, Greek, Latin, and Byzantine, from the time of Homer to that of Eustathius. The events referred to in this miscellaneous collection of writers cover a period of at least a thousand years, and from this farrago of evidence the author has produced a generalised picture of the Greek boxer equally applicable or inapplicable to a Homeric warrior or a Roman gladiator. The result is still worse when a writer like Professor Mahaffy[715] bases a wholesale condemnation of Greek boxing on Vergil's description of the fight between Dares and Entellus and a few stories of uncertain date. Before we consider such criticism in detail we will first see what we can learn from a chronological study of the evidence.

In Homer boxing, like wrestling, is already a specialised sport, though the pankration, which combined the two, did not yet exist. The art of boxing was hereditary in certain families, and custom had already evolved a body of tacitly accepted rules for the regulation of a fight. This is evident not merely from the description in the *Iliad*, but still more so in the ease with which the suitors arrange all the preliminaries for the impromptu fight between Odysseus and Irus. In the latter bare fists are used; but otherwise the conditions of the two fights are precisely similar. These conditions, which seem never to have altered during the long history of Greek boxing, determined the whole history of the sport, and are largely responsible for the differences which distinguish Greek boxing from modern.

In the first place, there was no regular ring, beyond what was formed by the spectators. Greek boxers had ample space and there was therefore no opportunity for cornering an opponent. The only reference to any such thing is in Theocritus' account of the fight between Polydeuces and Amycus, where the Greeks were afraid for the moment lest "the giant's weight might crush their champion in a narrow place."[716] The narrowness of the place is evidently noted here as something unusual. The scene of the fight is the wooded dell at the foot of a lofty cliff where Amycus makes his abode and waits to waylay strangers. A fitting place for a robber but very different from the open ground where sports were wont to be held, and where brute strength could have no chance against the trained skill of the boxer. It was only the "narrow place" which gave the bully a momentary advantage, and the passage, therefore, really confirms the view that the boxing ring was wide and open. These conditions tend to discourage close fighting and to encourage defensive and waiting tactics.

Other circumstances contributed to the same result. There were no rounds in Greek boxing. The opponents fought to a finish. It might happen that both were too exhausted and by mutual consent paused to take breath; but usually the fight went on until one of the two was incapable of fighting any more, or acknowledged himself defeated (ἀπειπεῖν) by holding up his hand. This signal of defeat is often depicted on vase paintings. A good example of it occurs on the amphora in the British Museum, reproduced in Figure 141. In such fights

---

[715] *Rambles in Greece*, 2nd Ed., p. 314. There is no foundation at all for his description of the meilichai as weights held in the hand and fastened by thongs.
[716] xxii. 93.

forcing tactics do not pay, the boxer who makes the pace too fast exhausts himself to no purpose; in the descriptions of fights which we possess it is usually the clumsy, untrained boxer who forces the pace and tries to rush his opponent, with disastrous effects to himself. Caution was therefore the rule of the Greek boxer; and the fighting was therefore usually slow. We shall see to what absurd lengths this caution was carried in later times.

Figure 141. B.-f. amphora, in British Museum, B. 271.

Lastly, classification by weights was unknown to the Greeks. Their competitions were open to all comers whatever their weight, and under the conditions described, weight had perhaps even greater advantage than it has to-day. Consequently boxing became more and more the monopoly of heavy weights and became less and less scientific.

These conditions were not unlike those existing in the early days of the English prize-ring, except that in the latter bare fists were used and wrestling was allowed. The use of gloves or thongs renders wrestling impracticable, and it appears, therefore, never to have been allowed in Greek boxing. But there is an element of artificiality about all fighting with covered hands. Modern boxers tell us that the use of gloves has corrupted the true art of self-defence because the boxer with gloves may expose himself to blows which would effectually end the fight with bare fists. I doubt whether such a thing could be said of the Greek thongs, which certainly can never have deadened the blow in the least. Consequently boxing remained with the Greeks essentially the art of "defence." In late times we hear of boxers winning competitions without even being hit by their opponents, a feat which would be quite impossible under modern conditions.[717] But though the true tradition of fighting was preserved in the pankration, and though in Homer we find the same tactics employed whether with bare fists or with boxing thongs, it is undoubtedly true that an artificial style was at an early date developed in Greek boxing, and the artificiality was increased by the changes which converted the simple boxing thongs into a formidable weapon both for offence and defence. So the style of fighting employed by the boxer diverged more and more from that of

---

[717] Dion Chrysostom, *Orat.* 29.

the pankratiast, and whereas in the fifth century it is not infrequent to find families like the Diagoridae distinguished in both boxing and the pankration, this combination becomes rarer, and the so-called successors of Heracles of a later age were those who won the pankration and wrestling.

The two Homeric fights have been already fully described in a previous chapter. They give us little information as to the style of Greek boxing, except that both fights were decided by knock-out blows on the jaw or thereabouts, delivered presumably with the right hand much in the same way as in modern boxing. Nor are the vase paintings as enlightening as we should expect from the number of vases on which boxing is indicated. The fact is that a boxing match is a supremely difficult subject for an artist, as may be readily realised by a glance at the illustrations in modern books on athletics. The Greek vase painter instinctively avoided violent movement, and often preferred to represent a sport not by the actual performance but by some preliminary scene. Hence the large number of vases on which he has represented boxing by groups of men holding or adjusting the himantes.[718] Even when he did depict the actual fight he confined himself to a small number of conventional types. There is less conventionality and more originality shown on the early black-figured than on the red-figured vases; but the crowding of figures on these early vases was incompatible with a true representation of open fighting, and consequently on many of these vases the boxing is confined to short arm punching and chopping, the grotesque effect of which is frequently heightened by the blood which flows copiously from the noses of the combatants. A good example of this style is seen in Figure 142, taken from a black-figured stamnos in the Bibliothèque Nationale in Paris, where, it will be observed, the athletes all wear the archaic loin-cloth. On the red-figured vases a more open style of fighting prevails. We are not, however, justified thereby in assuming any change of style in the actual fighting; the difference is due chiefly, if not entirely, to artistic causes. In spite, however, of this lack of variety on the vases we can, I think, draw certain conclusions from them as to the attitude and methods of the Greek boxer.

Figure 142. B.-f. stamnos. Bibliothèque Nationale, 252.

---

[718] Jüthner, p. 71.

There can be no doubt as to the position assumed by the Greek boxer when he first "puts up his hands." It is the moment most frequently depicted on the vases. He stands with body upright and head erect, the feet well apart, and the left foot advanced. The left leg is usually slightly bent, the foot pointing straight forwards, while the right foot is sometimes at right angles to it, pointing outwards in the correct position for a lunge with the left. The left arm, which is used for guarding, is extended almost straight, the hand sometimes closed, sometimes open. The right arm is drawn back for striking, the elbow sometimes dropped, but more usually raised level with or even higher than the shoulder. This position is clearly shown on a series of vases from the British Museum, from which our illustrations are taken, extending from the sixth century to the fourth century B.C. They are a black-figured amphora by Nicosthenes (Figure 143), two red-figured kylikes one of which is signed by Duris (Figures 133, 151), and two Panathenaic vases of the latter half of the fourth century (Figures 135, 148).

Figure 143. B.-f. amphora, in British Museum, B. 295.

On all these vases and on most other vases containing boxing scenes the left leg is vigorously advanced. Mr. Frost, in his article on Greek boxing in the *Journal of Hellenic Studies*, vol. xxvi., to which I am indebted for many useful hints, maintains that this is merely a conventional rendering, and that the Greek boxer really stood with his feet nearly level, like the early pugilists of the English prize-ring. Little evidence is adduced for this statement, and he seems to me to have been misled by the analogy of the prize-ring, forgetting that our knowledge of Greek boxing begins at the point where the history of the prize-ring ends. In the prize-ring bare fists were used, and clinching, wrestling, and throwing were allowed; whereas in Greek boxing the hand always had some form of covering, and no clinching or wrestling was allowed. Moreover, Mr. Frost's theory does not seem to me to explain the facts. If both feet were approximately level we should expect to find that in a fair proportion of cases the right foot was advanced, especially as symmetry, which exercised a strong influence over the Greek painter, would naturally prompt him to represent one boxer with the right foot, the other with the left foot in advance, an arrangement by no means uncommon in wrestling groups. In boxing, however, such symmetrical groups are extremely rare, and the left foot is nearly always advanced, and in several cases is shown in the very act of lunging. Indeed, so far from holding the body square, it would appear from the vases that the Greeks exaggerated the sideways position. For frequently the left foot and left arm of one boxer are represented as outside or to the right of the left foot and arm of his opponent (Figure 143).[719]

This sideways position with the left arm extended was an elective guard for the head and kept an opponent at a distance, but it left the body quite unprotected, a mistake which would be fatal in the confined space of the modern ring with a strong and active opponent. This exposure of the body is, as Mr. Frost has pointed out, characteristic of all Greek boxing as depicted on the vases, and this peculiarity is connected with a fact which, as far as I know, has not been observed before, that the Greek boxer confined his attention almost exclusively to his opponent's head. Whether it was that he did not realise the use of body blows, or that he considered them bad form, or that they were prohibited, it is certain that he made little or no use of them. There is not, as far as I know, a single representation of a body blow; the injuries inflicted are all injuries to the head; in the few cases where body blows are mentioned they are delivered by unscientific fighters, such as Irus and Amycus, and appear to be ill-aimed or short blows, which, missing the head, have fallen on the shoulder or chest. The only exception which I know is the fatal blow by which Damoxenus, according to Pausanias, slew Creugas at the Nemean games;[720] but though there was doubtless some foundation for the story the details are so manifestly fabulous that they are valueless as evidence. On the other hand a passage in Philostratus affords a strong presumption that boxing was practically, if not formally, confined to head blows. He tells us that boxing was invented by the Spartans because they did not wear helmets, considering the shield the only manly form of protection.[721] They practised boxing in order to learn to ward off blows from the head and to harden the face. Further, in describing the physical qualities of the boxer he regards a prominent stomach as a possible advantage, because it renders it less easy for an opponent to reach the face! Nor does he anywhere make any reference to body blows. Boxing like fencing is governed by artificial laws, and it is just possible that the laws of Greek boxing prohibited intentional blows on the body, just as blows below the belt are prohibited to-day. Perhaps they were forbidden by the unwritten law of tradition. Whatever the explanation, the fact seems fairly established that body hitting was not practised, and consequently the body was left unguarded; and this peculiarity is perhaps the most important difference between Greek and modern boxing, and had important results on the history of the sport.

It would appear at first sight from the vases that the left hand was used almost exclusively for guarding, and the right for attack. Though the actual blow with the right is never represented, the right fist is almost invariably clenched and drawn back for the blow. But this statement requires considerable modification. In the first place, so long as a boxer kept his left

---

[719] Cp. Figures. 142, 145.
[720] Paus. viii. 40, 3.
[721] *Gym.* 10, 23.

arm extended as guard, it was only possible to reach his head with the right hand either by stepping to the right so as to get outside his guard, or by breaking down his guard. In the first case it was possible to deliver a swinging blow on the left side of the chin—the knock-out blow described in Homer and Theocritus. But as the opponent naturally met the movement by himself moving to the right, the result was usually that the fighters circled round each other ineffectively. This is perhaps the reason why the left foot and hand of the boxer are so commonly represented to the right of his opponent's left foot and hand. But it can seldom have been possible to bring off such a blow as a lead, and therefore an opening had to be made for the use of the right hand by sparring with the left somewhat in the style of fencers. In this sparring which is commonly depicted on the vases, the hands are usually open. An instance of it occurs in Figure 151, where a pair of boxers are seen sparring with open hands apparently for practice. Still better is the scene on a Panathenaic vase in Berlin (Figure 144). Here the left-hand boxer having made his opening prepares to follow up the attack with his right, while his opponent draws back his head out of reach and guards with both hands. Sometimes in such sparring an opportunity occurred for delivering a blow with the left. On a Panathenaic vase published by Stephani (Figure 145) the right-hand boxer in pressing the attack has exposed his head, and his opponent has shot out his left hand without even closing it and hit him on the nose. This leads us to a second point. Wherever the actual blow is represented, or one boxer is represented as in the act of being knocked down, or having been knocked down, the blow is delivered with the left hand. We may therefore conclude that the Greek boxer used his left hand as much as the right for attack, and that some of the most effective blows could be delivered with the left. This conclusion is borne out by the descriptions in Homer, Theocritus, and other writers, who with one consent represent the Greek as a two-handed fighter.

Figure 144. Panathenaic amphora. Berlin, 1831. Sixth century.

The position of the right arm indicates that it was employed chiefly for round or hook hits, upper cuts, and chopping blows, and a consideration of the general attitude and guards of the Greek boxer shows that only such blows were as a rule possible with the right. Sometimes the right hand is swung back in preparation for the knock-out blow (Figure 133), sometimes it is raised slightly above the shoulder as if for a downward chopping blow (Figure 143), sometimes it is held on a level with or below the shoulder, in which case a straight hit may be intended (Figure 148). But a straight hit was impossible unless the opponent's guard had been previously broken down or knocked aside with the left. With the left hand, however, straight hits appear to be the rule, as indeed we should expect from the position with the left leg advanced, and, as the heel of the right foot is usually lifted from the ground, it appears that the force of the blow was obtained correctly from a lunge. An excellent illustration of such a blow is found on a kylix of Pamphaeus (Figure 146). The falling boxer raises his left hand to guard his head; but it is in vain; for he lifts the forefinger of his right hand in acknowledgment of defeat. Still better is the scene on a Panathenaic amphora in the Louvre (Figure 147) which represents a boxer knocking his opponent down with a blow on the point of the chin. A further stage is depicted in one of the groups on the Duris kylix (Figure 133) where one boxer has already been knocked down by his opponent's left. He too raises his finger as a sign that he is beaten. Sometimes a vigorous lunge with the left foot is represented.[722]

Figure 145. Panathenaic amphora. Campana. Sixth century (?).

Figure 146. R.-f. kylix of Pamphaeus. Corneto.

---

[722] Benndorf, *Gr. Sic. Vasenb.* xxxi. 2; Gerhard, *A.V.* 177 (= Munich 584); *Le Musée*, ii. p. 276, Figure 24 (b.-f. vase at Boulogne). Other examples of a blow with the left hand are: a Fragment in the Louvre (Hartwig, *Meisterschalen*, Figure 31); *Mus. Greg.* ii. 17 (very similar to B.M. B. 271); Krause, *Gym.* xviii. d. 66 f.; Brussels 336. In the Benndorf vase and some others the blow seems to be somewhat downward, which is probably due to the fact that the opponent is in the act of falling.

Figure 147. Panathenaic amphora. Louvre, F. 278.

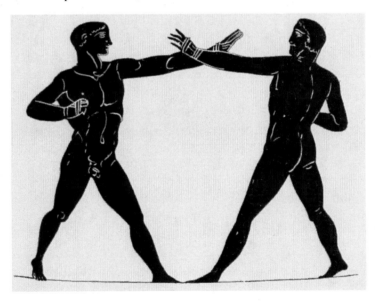

Figure 148. Panathenaic amphora, in British Museum, B. 612. Fourth century.

The view stated in the last paragraph is at variance with that put forward by Professor Mahaffy and supported with some modification by Mr. Frost. These writers maintain that the straight hit from the shoulder was practically unknown to the Greek boxer. They argue partly from the description of the fights in Theocritus and Vergil, which will be discussed later; but their main argument is that the wounds received in Greek boxing were chiefly on the side of the head and on the ear, and that the Greek boxer was known throughout all Greek history as "a man with the crushed ear." The latter statement is absolutely erroneous. The earliest reference to the crushed ear is in Plato, who uses the term to describe those who aped Spartan manners and practised fighting like the Spartans.[723] Now it is well known that scientific boxing was unknown at Sparta: fighting there was in plenty with bare fists and no regulations; but science in boxing and also in wrestling was despised by the Spartans. Moreover, it seems that the crushed ear was quite as much the sign of the pankratiast or even of the wrestler;[724] it appears to have been very similar to the swollen ear which is so common among Rugby football players. When we come to consider the literary evidence we shall find that the crushed ear plays but little part; eyes, nose, mouth, teeth, chin, come in for far more punishment than the ears, and the vase paintings agree with the literary evidence. Bleeding at the nose, cuts on the cheek, blows on the chin are freely depicted; but I do not know a single vase which represents the crushed ear. So far as the crushed ear is concerned, the charge against the Greek boxer of neglecting straight hitting breaks down completely.

Nor does it seem to me at all easy to substantiate the statement also made that the Greeks had no knowledge of foot-work, and that having taken up their position they stood practically still. Naturally the vases throw little light on such a point; but they do prove undoubtedly that the Greeks understood how to give force to a blow by lunging, and inasmuch as the lunge is always with the left foot, it seems probable that they understood the importance of not changing feet. Further, in all the descriptions of fights the value of quick foot-work is clearly recognised. This appears even in late writers like Statius.[725] His victor Alcidamas defeats his heavier opponent Capaneus by his greater activity. Capaneus drives him round the ring but Alcidamas "avoids a thousand deaths which flit around his temples by quick movement and by the help of his feet." When we find the value of foot-work recognised in a writer like Statius, whose ideas of boxing are vitiated by the brutalities of the Roman caestus, we are surely justified in assuming that the Greeks of a better period were at least equally skilful. Still more convincing is the evidence of Philostratus. "I do not approve," he says, "of men with big calves in any branch of athletics, and especially in boxing. They are slow in advancing, and easily caught by an opponent's advance."[726] Philostratus, it will be remembered, though writing in the time of the Empire, aims at reviving the practice of the old Greek athletes, and much of his material is derived from earlier treatises on athletics. In describing the ideal boxer he lays particular stress on activity and suppleness. So Bacchylides describes the youthful Argeius of Ceos,[727] a victor in the boys' boxing at the Isthmia, as "stout of hand, with the spirit of a lion and light of foot."

---

[723] *Gorgias*, 516 A; *Protag.* 342 B; cp. Theocritus xxii. 45. For full references *vide* Krause, *Gym.* pp. 516, 517, and *J.H.S.* xxvi. p. 13.

[724] Philostratus, *Heroic.* 180 τὰ δὰ ὦτα κατεαγὼς ἤν οὐκ ὑπὸ πάλης.

[725] *Theb.* vi. 731-825.

[726] *Gym.* 34 προσβῆναι ταῖς τῶν ἀντιπάλων κνήμαις ἄργοι καὶ εὐάλωτοι τῷ προσβάντι. Cp. c. 11 ὁ πύκτης τρωθήσεται καὶ τρώσει καὶ προσβήσεται ταῖς κνήμαις. Το προσβῆναι I have given the somewhat wider sense of "advancing" or "lunging" which is undoubtedly implied in the following words, ὁρμητικώτερον τὸ σχῆμα τοῦ πυκτεύοντος ἤν μὴ συμβαίνωσιν οἱ μηροί. The addition of the words ταῖς τῶν ἀντιπάλων κνήμαις is a difficulty. There can be no question of "kicking" which was certainly not allowed in boxing, nor are any of the vases quoted by Jüthner in his note on the passage appropriate. The words can only mean "advancing against an opponent's shins." Shoving an opponent backwards in this way may occur in "in-fighting," in which case his only remedy is "slipping." But the tactics are not particularly effective, and shoving is not allowed in modern boxing. I have a suspicion that Philostratus was very vague in his ideas about boxing. As Jüthner has shown in his recent edition, Philostratus was a rhetorician, not a practical athlete, and he owed his athletic knowledge to some technical treatise on gymnastics, which he did not always quite understand.

[727] Bacchylides i.

Such appear to be the general characteristics of the Greek boxer as depicted on the vases. He used both hands freely, was active on his feet, and had a considerable variety of attack. His style resembled the freer style of American boxing which has recently become popular rather than the somewhat conventional almost one-handed style which so long prevailed in England. From later literature we learn that he was an adept at dodging, "ducking," and "slipping." The defect of his style appears to me to be the stiff, high guard with the left hand, which is best explained on the supposition that he hit only at the head. This guard is stiffer, and the arm straighter on the red-figured vases than on the earlier black-figured vases, and this is still more the case on the Panathenaic vases of the fourth century (Figures 135, 148). The use of the left hand for guarding cramped the attack and encouraged the use of downward chopping blows, of which there are some traces on the vases. This is probably the reason why the forearm was protected by leather thongs. The introduction of the hard, cutting rims round the hand at the close of the fifth century rendered the style of fighting still more artificial, and necessitated still further protection for the forearm. How difficult it must have been to get within the guard of a big boxer with a long reach armed with these weapons will be realised from the figure on the Panathenaic vase in Figure 135. Thus a thoroughly vicious style of boxing sprang up which accentuated the natural advantages of the heavy-weight boxer. Instead of relying on activity and skill he relied more and more on his stiff defence. He even practised holding up his arm for long periods in order to weary his opponent, and the absurdity of his style reaches its climax in the highly rhetorical tales of Dion Chrysostom. Describing Melancomas, the favourite of the emperor Titus, he says that he could keep up his guard for two whole days and so forced his opponents to yield not merely before he had been struck himself but even before he had struck them.[728] The story is sufficiently remarkable; but, nothing daunted, Eusebius succeeds in improving upon it and asserts that Melancomas by these tactics "killed all his opponents," an illustration of the growth of sporting stories which may well make us sceptical of the evidence of late commentators. Dion, however, is writing of a man who was his own contemporary, and, making allowance for rhetorical exaggeration, we may therefore safely accept his evidence as to the style of boxing in vogue at his time. Such a defence explains the employment of those slogging, downward blows which figure so largely in the descriptions of late Greek and Latin poets. In these descriptions we can trace the decay of Greek boxing; but the faults which were developed in Hellenistic and Roman times should not be ascribed to the boxers of the fifth century. The changes in the boxing thongs altered the whole character of the boxing.

Incomparably the best description of a fight which we possess is that between Amycus and Polydeuces in the 22nd Idyll of Theocritus. It illustrates the changes in Greek boxing; for it is a fight between a boxer of the old heroic school who relies on science and activity, and the coarse braggart prize-fighter with whom the poet was perhaps familiar in Alexandria. We see the bully sitting in the sunshine beside the spring, the muscles on his brawny arms standing out like rounded rocks, just as they do in the Farnese Heracles. His ears are bruised and crushed from many a fight. There he sits sulkily guarding the spring, and when Polydeuces approaches and with courtly grace craves hospitality he challenges him to battle. The boxing thongs are all ready to hand, not soft thongs but hard (στερεοῖς). "Then," says the poet, "they made their hands strong with cords of ox-hide, and wound long thongs about their arms." Here we have the σφαῖραι depicted on the Ficoroni cista in a picture of this very fight.

---

[728] Dion. *Orat.* xxix.; cp. Eustath. *Il.* Ψ 1322, 1324. Eusebius, *Histor. Syn.* p. 350, quoted in Krause, p. 510.

A keen struggle ensued for position—which should have the sun's rays on his back—and the more active Polydeuces naturally outwitted his clumsy opponent. Writers on athletics are wont to dwell on this incident as typical of boxing at Olympia, and to expatiate on the glare of the sun in the eyes, forgetful of the fact that at midday, the hour at which it seems boxing took place, the rays of the summer sun at Olympia must be too nearly vertical to make much difference. Amycus, exasperated at the advantage gained, made a wild rush at Polydeuces, attacking with both hands, but was promptly stopped by a blow on the chin. Again, he rushed in head down, and for a time the Greeks were afraid that he would crush Polydeuces by sheer weight in the narrow space; but each time Polydeuces stopped his rushes with blows right and left on mouth and jaws, till his eyes were swollen and he could hardly see, and finally knocked him down with a blow on the bridge of the nose. He managed, however, to pick himself up and the fight began again; but his blows were short and wild, falling without effect on the chest, or outside the neck, while Polydeuces kept smashing his face with cruel blows. At last in desperation he seized Polydeuces' left hand with his left and tried to knock him out with a swinging right-hander, "driving a huge fist up from his right haunch." It is an admirable description of a knock-out blow, but he was too slow; the very act of seizing his opponent's hand, an obvious illegality, spoilt his effort. Polydeuces slipped his head aside and with his right struck him on the temple "putting his shoulder into the blow," and he followed up this advantage by a left-hander on the mouth, "so that his teeth rattled." After this he continued to punish his face with quickly repeated blows "till Amycus sank fainting on the ground, and begged for mercy."

In this masterly description Theocritus shows an intimate knowledge of boxing. It is a fight between science and brute strength. Amycus has the advantage of height and weight, but he has no science and blunders hopelessly. He rushes in head down, hits wildly with both hands, neglects his guard, and finally commits a glaring breach of the rules of boxing by seizing his opponent's hand. Polydeuces acts on the defensive, husbanding his strength by allowing the bully to exhaust himself, while he avoids his rushes by dodging, or ducking, or stops them by well-aimed blows on the face. Did he stop his rushes by swinging hits only, or by straight hitting from the shoulder? The description appears to me conclusive proof that even in the third century some of the Greeks understood the art of hitting straight. I do not dwell on the evidence of the words ἐμέεμπεσεν ὠμῷ, though I confess that the only interpretation which is to me intelligible, is the ordinary one "he put his shoulder into the blow." It is rather the whole character of the fight which implies straight hitting. Polydeuces is the smaller man, and time after time he stops the other's rushes with blows which fall on chin, mouth, nose, eyes, forehead, in fact everywhere except on the ears or side of the heads, the parts which should have suffered most according to the argument of those who maintain that the Greeks did not hit from the shoulder. As for the faults of Amycus, Theocritus is quite aware that he is no trained boxer, and it is hardly fair to judge the Greek boxer by him.

The account of this same fight in the *Argonautica* of Apollonius Rhodius[729] is somewhat similar, and though infinitely inferior as a whole presents certain details of interest. The himantes are carefully described; they are manufactured by Amycus himself; "rough and dry with hard ridges round them" like the gloves worn by the boxer of the Terme. Amycus makes the fighting; Polydeuces retreats and dodges his rushes, but at last he stands his ground and a fight ensues so fast and furious that both men, utterly exhausted, pause and separate by

---

[729] ii. 25-97.

mutual consent. After a moment they spring at one another again, and Amycus, rising on tiptoe to his full height, aims a swinging downward blow at Polydeuces "like one that slays an ox." Polydeuces slips aside, and, before his opponent has time to recover his balance or his guard, steps past him and deals him a swinging blow above the ear which not only knocks him out but kills him. The conclusion of the fight is an obvious imitation of Homer. But the poet has introduced a feature of his own which finds no place in Homer, when he describes Amycus as rising on tiptoe. The detail is copied by Vergil who probably knew no better. But Apollonius has more knowlege of athletics; it is the action not of a boxer but of "one that slays an ox." And yet, in spite of this, we find it stated by modern writers, on the authority of these two poets, that the boxer habitually rose on tiptoe to increase the weight of his blow! If we would learn the principles of Greek boxing it must be from the practice not of Amycus but of Polydeuces.

The boxing match between Entellus and Dares in the fifth *Aeneid* need not detain us long. Its character is obvious from the first in the description of the caestus. Entellus throws into the ring the caestus of the hero Eryx; they are made of seven ox-hides stiff with iron and lead, and still stained with blood and brains, and at their sight Dares and all the host tremble. "What!" cries Entellus, "do these frighten you? What if you had seen the weapons of Hercules?" Finally by the advice of Anchises these murderous weapons are rejected, but the point of interest in this scene is that the poet's Roman ideas have led him to reverse the whole history of boxing. In reality the heavy caestus had developed slowly from the simple leather thongs. But to the Roman murder and bloodshed were the essence of a fight. And therefore as the heroes of the past excelled in physique the men of the present, they must have excelled them also in the bloodiness of their fights and the murderous brutality of their weapons. The fight itself is in accordance with this beginning.

Both men rise on tiptoe and hammer each other as hard as they can. Entellus is the bigger man and for a long time acts on the defensive, keeping his more active opponent at a distance. At last, tired of such tactics, he makes a big effort; rising on tiptoe to his full height he ostentatiously lifts his arm on high, thus giving Dares full warning of what is coming. The latter is not slow to take advantage of the warning; he dodges the ponderous blow, and Entellus, unable to recover his balance, falls to the ground. Exasperated by his fall, he picks himself up and chases Dares all round the ring till Aeneas in mercy ends the fight. Baulked of his vengeance on Dares he vents his rage and exhibits his strength by killing with a single blow the ox which is his prize. What a contrast to the finish in the *Iliad* when the great-hearted Epeius picks up his fallen opponent and gently sets him on his feet! What a contrast even to the fight in Theocritus! There science is matched against strength and science deservedly wins. Here both men are as devoid of science as Vergil himself is devoid of all knowledge of boxing; if either of the two has any claim to skill it is the defeated Dares. Entellus owes his victory simply to brute strength. A still more absurd result occurs in Statius; the lighter and more skilful boxer is declared the victor, but is only saved from the fury and vengeance of his defeated opponent by the intervention of Adrastus, who separates them. But the brutalities and absurdities out of which these later fights are concocted need no discussion.

Little is known of the laws regulating Greek boxing. The competitions were conducted in the same manner as wrestling competitions, on the tournament system, and to obtain a bye must have been a very great advantage. We learn from Plutarch that no wrestling or clinching was allowed.[730] It appears from the vases that there was no rule against hitting a man who was down. The successful boxer is frequently depicted as preparing to hit his fallen opponent, who under the circumstances naturally gives in at once.[731] On the other hand, in Theocritus and Vergil the fallen boxer certainly manages to rise again, either by his own dexterity or his opponent's forbearance. It appears also from the story of Creugas and Damoxenus[732] that when a fight had continued long without any result, the combatants sometimes agreed to exchange free hits without guarding. A similar practice in wrestling was called κλῖμαξ. It is further argued from this story that cases of fatal injury inflicted on an opponent were severely punished; but the evidence seems insufficient to justify a general statement. In the cases quoted in support of such a law the offence appears to have consisted in some unlawful and intentional act of violence.[733] Fatal accidents were certain to occur occasionally; but there is no evidence that they were at all frequent, nor do they seem to have been punished. It is not clear what the offence was for which Damoxenus was dishonoured and deprived of his victory. Pausanias seems to imply that because he hit Creugas with his fingers extended, he hit several blows at the same time. Was hitting with the hand open prohibited? It is certainly a reasonable prohibition. Or can it be that hitting in the stomach was prohibited? We have no evidence for deciding.

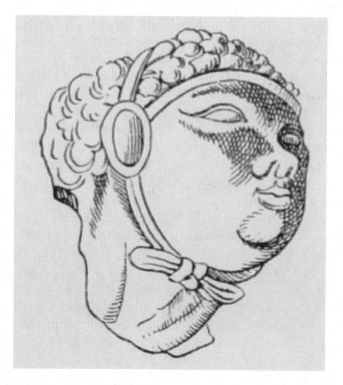

Figure 149. Marble head of boxer, with ear-lappets.

---

[730] *Symp.* ii. 4.
[731] Figures 133, 141.
[732] Pausanias viii. 40.
[733] Paus. vi. 9, 6; Pindar, *Ol.* v. 34 Schol.

Boxing

Figure 150. B.-f. hydria, in British Museum, B. 326.

We are not told how the Greeks taught boxing; perhaps it was in the same way as they taught wrestling, by a sort of drill. Boys in the palaestra had their ears and heads protected with ear-lappets (ἀμφωτίδες or ἐπωτίδες)[734] or caps. The former are represented on a marble head formerly in possession of Fabretti (Figure 149).[735] They closely resemble the ear-caps worn by modern football players, and were probably made of padded leather. On the vases a close-fitting cap is often represented (Figure 17). Such protection was used both in wrestling and boxing, but only, it seems, for practice and by boys, never in public competitions. Boxers kept themselves in training by light sparring with open hands, which was therefore known as ἀκροχειρισμός.[736] An example of such sparring may be seen on an early black-figured hydria in the British Museum (Figure 150), or on the kylix in Figure 151. In default of an opponent they practised "shadow-fighting" (σκιαμαχία),[737] just as a modern athlete will practise in front of a looking-glass. The statue of the famous Glaucus represented him "shadow-fighting" because of his skill in the use of his hands.[738] This form of practice was also known as χειρονομία, or hand drill. Sometimes a κώρυκος or punch-ball was employed (Figure 179).[739] An exercise much recommended for boxers was digging, and the pick (σκαπάνη) was therefore regarded as the badge of a boxer.[740]

---

[734] Krause, p. 517.
[735] Fabretti, *De Columna Trajani*, p. 267. The evidence for these lappets is all late, but the caps belong to the fifth century B.C.
[736] Aristotle, *Nic. Eth.* iii. 1; Plato, *I. Alcib.* 107 E. For further references *vide* Krause, p. 510, and *J.H.S.* xxvi. p. 14.
[737] Plato, *Legg.* viii. 830 C.
[738] Paus. vi. 10, 1.
[739] *Vide infra*, p. 478.
[740] Theocritus, iv. 10.

Chapter 20

THE PANKRATION[741]

The combination of boxing and wrestling known as the pankration was a development of the primitive rough and tumble. To get his opponent down, and by throttling, pummelling, biting, and kicking, to reduce him to submission, is the natural instinct of the savage or the child. But this rough and tumble was too undisciplined for athletic competition. Competitions require law, and in the growth of law the simpler precedes the more complex. Hence it was only natural that particular forms of fighting such as boxing and wrestling should be systematized first, and so made suitable for competition, before any attempt was made to reduce to law the more complicated rough and tumble of which they both formed part. Wrestling and boxing were known to Homer, but not the pankration, and Greek tradition was following the natural order of development in assigning the introduction at Olympia of wrestling to the 18th, of boxing to the 23rd, and of the pankration to the 33rd Olympiad. In the pankration as in boxing the contest continued till one or other of the parties held up his hand in sign of defeat. At Sparta, where for this reason the laws of Lycurgus forbade citizens to compete in these events, the primitive rough and tumble unrestricted by law and unrefined by science was allowed and encouraged as a test of endurance and a training for war. The pankration at the great festivals was something quite different; it was governed by the law of the games (νόμος ἐναγώνιος), and was, at all events in the best period, a contest no less of skill than of strength.

Modern writers turn up their eyes in holy horror at the brutality of the pankration, and marvel that a race so refined as the Greeks could have tolerated so brutal a sport. Undoubtedly the pankration might degenerate into brutality, and perhaps sometimes actually did. So may football, boxing, wrestling, unless they are controlled by rules, and unless the rules are enforced. But the pankration was controlled by rules, and the rules were enforced in the wrestling school and in the games by trainers and officials under public control, and enforced with the rod in a practical way which the modern umpire or referee may well envy, and the rod was certainly not spared. Further, the rules were enforced by a public opinion and tradition that in the best times certainly placed skill and grace far above brute strength in all athletics. No branch of athletics was more popular than the pankration. Philostratus describes it as the fairest of all contests.[742] Mythology ascribed its invention to Heracles and Theseus,[743]

---

[741] *J.H.S.* xxvi. pp. 4-22.
[742] *Im.* ii. 6.

the typical representatives of science as opposed to brute strength. What the pankration was in the fifth century we can learn from Pindar. No less than eight of his odes are in praise of pankratiasts, and from these odes can be illustrated every feature of the poet's athletic ideal. There was, of course, an element of danger, but danger does not make a sport brutal. Serious injuries, even loss of life, sometimes occurred, but these accidents were rare, rarer probably than in football or in the hunting-field, and the Greeks certainly regarded the pankration as less dangerous than boxing.[744] Finally, the example of jiujitzu proves that such contests may be conducted without any brutality as contests of pure skill.

Figure 151. R.-f. kylix. British Museum, E. 78.

The fullest account of the pankration occurs in Philostratus' description of the death of Arrhichion, a famous pankratiast of the sixth century, who expired at the very moment when his opponent acknowledged himself beaten.[745] After describing the scene and the excitement of the spectators, Philostratus adds a characteristic account of the pankration. "Pankratiasts," he says, "practise a hazardous style of wrestling (κεκινδυνευμένῃ τῇ πάλῃ). They must employ falls backward (ὑπτιασμῶν) which are not safe for the wrestler, and grips in which victory must be obtained by falling (οἷον πίπτοντα). They must have skill in various methods of strangling (ἄγχειν); they must also wrestle with an opponent's ankle (σφυρῷ προσπαλαίουσι) and twist his arm (στρεβλοῦσι), besides hitting and jumping on him, for all these practices belong to the pankration, only biting and gouging (ὀρύττειν) being excepted. The Spartans admit even these practices, but the Eleans and the laws of the games exclude them, though they commend strangling."

It would be difficult to give a more concise description. Wrestling, hitting, and kicking are employed; the style of wrestling is hazardous; victory is usually obtained by strangling;

---

[743] Heracles, according to Bacchylides, xiii., first employed the art of the pankration against the Nemean lion; according to another tradition, Theseus employed it against the Minotaur.
[744] Paus. vi. 6, 5; 15, 5; Artemidor. *Oneir.* i. 64.
[745] *Im.* ii. 6.

biting and gouging are alone prohibited. The prohibition of gouging and biting is evidently a quotation from the actual rules of Olympia. It is twice quoted by Aristophanes.[746] Biting needs no comment. The meaning of the word translated "gouging" is clear from Aristophanes. It means digging the hand or fingers into the eyes, mouth, and other tender parts of the body. A vivid illustration of "gouging" occurs on a British Museum kylix (Figure 151). One of the pankratiasts has inserted his thumb and finger into his opponent's eye as if to gouge it out, and the official is hastening up with his rod uplifted to interfere and punish such foul play. A somewhat similar scene is represented on a kylix in Baltimore (Figure 152), where a pankratiast inserts his thumb into the mouth of an opponent whom he has thrown head over heels.

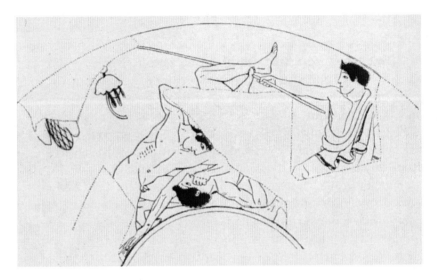

Figure 152. R.-f. kylix. Baltimore.

Figure 153. R.-f. kylix. Berlin.

---

[746] *Aves*, 442; *Pax*, 899.

The pankration naturally divides itself into two parts, the standing pankration (τὸ ἄνω παγκράτιον) and the struggle on the ground (τὸ κάτω παγκράτιον). In the former the opponents endeavoured to throw one another heavily to the ground, by wrestling or kicking or hitting. There was much preliminary sparring, appropriately described as ἀκροχειρισμίς.[747] The hands were unprotected by thongs or other covering, and, as is natural in a combination of wrestling and boxing, the open hand and the fist were both used. Both are represented on the fragment of a kylix in Berlin (Figure 153). The fallen youth bleeds freely from the nose, and bears on his back the imprint of his opponent's fingers. At the same time, his fist is clenched ready to strike. The relative importance of wrestling and boxing in the pankration depended much on the individual. The man with a long reach naturally preferred to utilize his advantage in hitting; the short, thickset boxer generally depended for victory on his wrestling.[748] The struggle was usually decided on the ground. It is commonly stated that when one or other opponent had fallen, hitting was no longer allowed. This purely modern idea is conclusively disproved by such vases as the one just quoted. Neither in boxing nor in the pankration was it forbidden to strike a man who was down. As a rule, when both men were down hitting was of little use, and the contest was usually decided by wrestling, especially by twisting a limb, or by strangling. If, however, one opponent had been knocked down by a heavy blow, he was usually at his opponent's mercy, and he commonly holds up his hand in sign of defeat, or else the official is represented interfering to stop the contest.

The epithet "hazardous" by which Philostratus characterizes the wrestling of the pankration is appropriate to such throws as "the flying mare" and the various foot and leg holds which, though too risky for the wrestler proper, were freely employed in the pankration, where it was not sufficient only to throw an opponent, but he must be thrown heavily. The use of the flying mare is illustrated on the Baltimore kylix (Figure 152), where the left-hand wrestler proceeds to pummel his fallen opponent. A much mutilated group on the kylix illustrated in Figure 54 represents a throw from a leg-hold. A wrestler kneeling on one knee has seized his opponent between the legs and lifts him up, bending forwards as if to hurl him on to the ground. The scene is described by Anacharsis in Lucian.[749] "Look," he cries, "that fellow has picked up the other by the legs and flung him to the ground, and falling on him, will not suffer him to rise, but forces him into the mud, and at last, winding his legs round his stomach, with his arm placed under his throat, he strangles the poor wretch."

A favourite trick of the pankratiast was to catch his opponent by the foot, and lifting it up, to tilt him backwards. Antaeus is frequently depicted grabbing thus at the foot of Heracles, but without success.[750] The manœuvre is excellently illustrated on two Panathenaic vases (Figures 154, 155), and on the coins of Aspendus (Figure 109). On a gem in the British Museum (Figure 162) a somewhat similar hold is adopted by way of defence by a wrestler who has his head in chancery.

---

[747] *J.H.S.* xxvi. p. 14.
[748] Phil. *Gym.* 36. I do not agree with Jüthner's division of the text. He makes the account of οἱ ἐν μικρῷ μεγάλοι the beginning of the classification of athletic types which follows. Kayser rightly connected it with the account of wrestling and the pankration which preceded.
[749] *Anacharsis*, 1.
[750] *J.H.S.* xxv. pp. 283 ff., Figures. 19, 20.

Figure 154. Panathenaic amphora. Sixth century. (*Mon. d. I.* I. xxii.)

Figure 155. Panathenaic amphora. Sixth century. (*Mon. d. I.* I. xxii.)

Sometimes a wrestler, having thrown his opponent, would lift him up by the legs, and the other, to save himself from a heavy fall, would balance himself on his hands and head. Philostratus, speaking of the short, thickset athletes, whom he calls οἱ ἐν μικρῷ μεγάλοι[751]— the type of the "pocket Hercules"—says, "They are quick and active, and able to extricate themselves from the most hopeless grips, standing on their heads as on a pedestal." This manœuvre, quite familiar in modern wrestling, is not represented in Greek art, but occurs on the wall paintings of Beni-Hassan.

A wrestler who was thrown on his back was defeated. But a pankratiast might intentionally throw himself on his back in order to throw his opponent more heavily, or to

---

[751] *Gym.* 36.

throw him in a worse position. A manœuvre of this sort called τὸ ἀποπτερνίζειν was invented, according to Philostratus,[752] by a Cilician pankratiast, nicknamed for the smallness of his stature, Halter or the Dumbbell. On his way to compete at Delphi, he stopped at the shrine of the hero Protesilaus to ask him how he should conquer his opponents. The hero replied, "By being trampled upon" (πατούμενος). At first he was disconcerted by this ambiguous answer, but after a little thought he understood that the hero's advice meant "that he was not to let go the foot of his opponent; for the man who wrestles with the opponent's foot must be constantly trampled on and be underneath his opponent." So he devised the "heel trick," by means of which he remained undefeated and won great renown. This is probably the same method as that described in the passage of Philostratus already quoted as "wrestling with the ankle." Such a hold ensures a heavy fall; but the peculiarity of the "Dumbbell's" method was, that instead of releasing the foot after throwing his opponent, he preserved his hold, and by twisting or bending the foot forced him to yield. This use of the ankle hold is well known in Japanese wrestling. Arrhichion, we are told, forced his opponent to succumb by twisting his foot out of its socket.

Another throw in which the thrower throws himself on his back is the "stomach throw." A wrestler seizes his opponent by the shoulders or arms and throws himself backward, at the same time planting his foot in the other's stomach and thus throwing him heavily clean over his head, while he himself falls lightly. This favourite throw of the Japanese is depicted on the tombs of Beni-Hassan. It is accurately described by Dio Cassius in his account of a fight between the Romans and Iazyges:[753] "Whenever any of them fell backwards, he would drag his opponent after him, and with his feet hurl him backwards as in wrestling." Pindar in his third Isthmian Ode is referring to tactics of this sort when he says of Melissus: "In craft he is as the fox that spreadeth out her feet and preventeth the swoop of the eagle." The only representation which I know of such a throw is on a black-figured hydria in Munich (Figure 156), where Antaeus lies on his back with his right hand grasping Heracles' left foot and his left leg kicking him in the stomach. As usual, Antaeus has failed to execute the throw and Heracles has regained the advantage.

The throws described in the last two paragraphs sufficiently illustrate those "backward falls unsafe for the wrestler, and grips in which victory must be obtained by falling," which made the wrestling of the pankration particularly hazardous.

Wrestling and boxing combined are depicted in a highly conventional manner on two Panathenaic vases in the British Museum (Figures 157, 158) representing respectively the contest for youths and for men. On B 604 a pankratiast has rushed in head down, allowing his opponent to catch his head in the bend of his arm. It is not quite clear what the latter intends to do, whether to complete the neck hold or to pummel him. In B 610 there is no doubt: the left-hand wrestler lifts his fist to pummel the other's head, which he still holds in the bend of his arm. Why he allows his head to remain unnecessarily in such a position is not quite clear. Perhaps he has really had his head in chancery, and unable to break the grip, has bitten the other's arm. A favourite Greek story told by Plutarch of Alcibiades, and in another place of a Spartan wrestler, illustrates this suggestion.[754] Being hard pressed and about to be thrown, he bit his opponent's hand. Letting go his hold, the latter exclaimed, "You bite, Alcibiades, like a

---

[752] *Heroic.* 53, 54. The word πτερνίζειν is used in the LXX. of Jacob supplanting Esau (Gen. xxvii. 36, cp. xxv. 26). *J.H.S.* xxvi. 20.
[753] lxxi. 7.
[754] *Alc.* 2; *Apophthegm. Lac.* 234 D, 44.

woman." "No," he replied, "like a lion." Biting, as we know, was strictly forbidden, and some confirmation of the explanation of the vase may be found in the attitude of the official on the right, who seems to be awarding the palm to the other pankratiast. Other examples of biting in the pankration, whether standing or on the ground, will be found in our illustrations.

Figure 156. B.-f. hydria. Munich, 114.

Figure 157. Panathenaic amphora, in British Museum, B. 604. Fourth century. Signed by the artist "Kittos."

Figure 158. Panathenaic amphora, in British Museum, B. 610. Archonship of Nicetes, 332 B.C.

Kicking was also a distinctive feature of the pankration. In Theocritus,[755] Polydeuces being challenged to fight by Amycus, inquires if it is to be a boxing match or whether kicking too was allowed; and Galen,[756] in his skit on the Olympic games, awards the prize for the pankration to the donkey, as the best of all animals in kicking. A combination of kicking and boxing is represented on the two Panathenaic vases in Figures 154, 155. At least it seems to me probable that the pankratiast on the left has caught his opponent's foot in mid-air as he was trying to kick him in the stomach. Kicking in the stomach (γαστρίζειν)[757] appears to have been a favourite trick in the pankration, as it is in the French *savate*. It is depicted in one of the groups in the Tusculan mosaic (Figure 22), and in a relief in the Louvre. On another Panathenaic vase (Figure 159) one pankratiast appears in the act of catching the other's leg as he lifts it in his onset. The action of the latter rather resembles that described as jumping on an opponent (ἐνάλλεσθαι) than of kicking. A better illustration of this term is seen in Figure 153, where one pankratiast is jumping on his fallen opponent.

Figure 159. Panathenaic amphora. Lamberg Coll.

---

[755] xxii. 66.
[756] Προτρεπτ. ἐπὶ τέχνας, 36.
[757] Lucian, *Anachars*. 9; Aristoph. *Eq.* 273, 454; Pollux, iii. 150.

Twisting an opponent's arm or fingers (στρεβλοῦν) and strangling him (ἄγχειν) are tricks belonging principally to the later stage of the contest, when both opponents are on the ground, but opportunities for them also occurred in standing wrestling. Twisting the arm has already been illustrated in our chapter on wrestling (Figures 129-131). Similarly in the Uffizi group (Figure 163) the upper wrestler twists his opponent's arm across his back, and the same motive occurs in one of the groups on the frieze of Lysicrates' monument. Pausanias tells us of one Sostratus, a pankratiast of Sicyon, who, like Leontiscus in wrestling, forced his opponents to yield by twisting and breaking their fingers.[758] At first sight we are apt to condemn such practices as brutal and unsportsmanlike, but the principle of twisting an opponent's limb so as to incapacitate him has been reduced to a science in Japanese wrestling. The same may be said of "strangling," the method of finishing a contest of which the Eleans much approved. Almost any neck hold can be used to throttle an opponent. Reference has already been made to the familiar hold known as "getting the head in chancery," illustrated on the gems in Figure 162. The most effective and favourite method of strangling an opponent is that known as κλιμακισμός,[759] which consists in mounting on an opponent's back, winding the legs round his stomach, and the arms round his neck. The klimakismos can be employed both in the standing pankration and on the ground. On the Tusculan mosaic both types are represented (Figure 22), and we have references to both types in literature. It is the favourite method of attack employed by Heracles in his contests with the Triton and Achelous (Figure 160), and is best known to scholars from the account of the latter contest given in the chorus of the *Trachiniae*, 407-530. In the standing pankration, in order to execute the klimakismos it was necessary to get behind one's opponent either by making him turn round or by springing round him. This may be illustrated from the humorous picture which Anacharsis draws of the Greeks advancing to meet their foe like boxers with clenched fists.[760] "And the enemy," he says, "naturally cower before you and take to flight for fear lest, as they stand gaping, you fill their mouth with sand, or jumping round to get on their backs, twist your legs round their bellies and strangle them to death, placing your arm beneath their helmets." A similar description of the klimakismos on the ground has already been quoted.

Ground wrestling must have been the most distinctive, as it certainly was the most decisive, part of the pankration. It was probably as complicated if not as long as it is at the present day, the combatants sometimes sprawling at full length, sometimes on their knees,[761] sometimes on the top of one another. It is this part of the pankration to which Plato objected and which led him to exclude it from his ideal state as useless for military training, because it did not teach men to keep their feet.[762] Perhaps in Plato's time the pankratiast, like the modern Graeco-Roman wrestler, was apt to neglect the preliminary contest and go down on the ground at once. Such grovelling, if it existed, was a sign of the decay of these antagonistic sports, which, as we have seen, had set in before Plato's time; it was unknown to Pindar, who specially emphasizes the importance of boxing in the pankration.[763] Ground wrestling is seldom represented on the vases, except in the contest of Heracles and Antaeus (Figure 161); but groups of the kneeling type are frequent on later gems, being particularly suitable for

---

[758] Paus. vi. 4, 2.
[759] *J.H.S.* xxvi. 15.
[760] Lucian, *Anachars.* 31.
[761] From Lucian's *Asinus* we gather that knee wrestling (τὰ ἀπὸ γονάτων) was systematically taught in the palaestra. Cp. Aristoph. *Pax*, 895.
[762] *Legg.* 795, 834.
[763] *Nem.* iii. 29; *Isthm.* v. 60.

oblong or oval spaces. The examples given in Figure 162 from gems in the British Museum explain themselves.

Figure 160. Heracles and Triton. B.-f. amphora, in British Museum, B. 223.

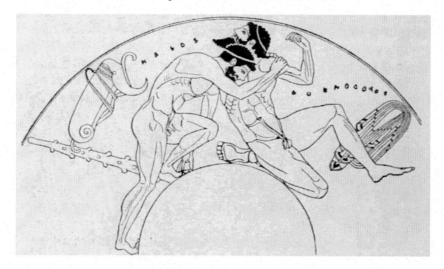

Figure 161. Herakles and Antaeus. R.-f. kylix. Athens.

Figure 162. Graeco-Roman gems in British Museum.

Figure 163. Group of pankratiasts. Uffizi Palace, Florence. (From a photograph by Brogi.)

The most important and interesting of all the monuments connected with the pankration is the group of wrestlers in the Uffizi gallery in Florence (Figure 163). Unfortunately, it is considerably restored, but in spite of recent criticism there seems to be no reason for doubting the general correctness of the restoration.[764] The underneath wrestler supports himself on his left arm, and his opponent's immediate object is to break down this support. This can be

---

[764] *J.H.S.* xxv. 30, xxvi. 19.

effected by a blow. For the underneath wrestler's right arm being secured, he can only guard his head with his left. The situation can be illustrated by the description in Heliodorus of the match between Theagenes and the Aethiopian champion.[765] Theagenes forces the latter on to his knees, twines his legs round him, and then knocks away his wrists, with which he is keeping his chest off the ground. Having broken down this support, he forces him down on his stomach on the ground. While a wrestler is supporting himself on his hands and knees, his position is far from hopeless, and he may by a quick and vigorous movement often overturn his adversary and reverse matters. Such is the moment selected by the sculptor; the victory is still undecided, the uppermost wrestler is anxious to make sure of victory, the other is eagerly watching to take advantage of any carelessness on his opponent's part. How fatal any such carelessness may be we learn from the story of Arrhichion.[766] Arrhichion was being strangled by his opponent, who was on the top with arms and legs entwined round him; but even as he was expiring he took advantage of a momentary relaxation of the grip to kick his right leg free, and rolling over so as to crush his opponent's left side, he seized his right foot and twisted it out of its socket with such violence as to force him to yield, and so even with his last breath he secured the victory.

There are numerous technical terms of wrestling and the pankration known to us only from scholiasts and lexicographers. These are of very doubtful interpretation and of no practical importance, and it is therefore unnecessary to discuss them here.[767]

---

[765] *Aeth.* x. 31, 32.
[766] Phil. *Im.* ii. 6; Paus. viii. 40, 2.
[767] Many of them are discussed in my articles in the *J.H.S.* xxv., xxvi. Cp. Grasberger, 349-374; Krause, 400-438, 534-556.

Chapter 21

THE HIPPODROME

Chariot and horse races were so important a part of most Greek festivals that, though we cannot strictly describe them as athletics, a brief account of the hippodrome and the events which took place there will not be out of place.

Hippodromes must have abounded in all parts of Greece which offered any facilities for riding or driving. The fifth-century inscription of the Spartan Damonon[768] enumerates sixty-eight victories won by himself and his son in the chariot-race and the horse-race at no less than eight distinct festivals, all of them in Laconia or in the immediate neighbourhood. The plains of Argos, Athens, Euboea, and Thessaly were famed for their breeds of horses, while the passionate devotion of the Sicilian and Italian Greeks to horse-racing is proved by the constant occurrence of the racing-chariot or the race-horse on the coins of various cities from the beginning of the fifth century onwards.[769]

Yet of all the hippodromes which must have existed hardly a trace is left, and we are forced to fall back on the scattered notices of Pausanias and other writers. The fact is that the Greek hippodrome as a rule was a very simple affair, hardly more elaborate than the course selected on the plains of Troy for the funeral games of Patroclus or the course of a local race meeting to-day. All that was necessary was a fairly smooth open plain, if possible, in a valley or at the foot of some hill, the slopes of which formed a natural stand for spectators.

At either end of the track a pillar was erected to mark the place where chariots and horses turned. These pillars are generally represented on coins and vases as Ionic or Doric columns; sometimes, it appears, movable pillars[770] were used, perhaps for safety, like the posts used in modern driving competitions. Occasionally we see a pillar which has been knocked over by a chariot.[771] But usually the pillars were fixed, and then it was the chariot that suffered. There is not a particle of evidence for the existence in any Greek hippodrome of the low wall (spina) which ran down the middle of the course between the pillars in the Roman circus, though this wall regularly appears in the fanciful plans of the hippodrome which adorn our works of

---

[768] *B.S.A.* xiii. pp. 174 ff.
[769] The four-horse chariot occurs on coins of Agrigentum, Camarina, Catana, Eryx, Gela, Himera, Leontini, Panormus, Segesta, Syracuse; the two-horse chariot on coins of Messana; the mule car on coins of Rhegium and Messana; numerous riding types on coins of Tarentum. In the early coinage of Syracuse the tetradrachm bears a four-horse chariot, the didrachm a horseman leading another horse, the drachma a horseman, and the obol a chariot-wheel. *Vide* Hill, *Coins of Sicily*, pp. 43-46 and *passim*.
[770] Gerh. *A.V.* 267.
[771] *Mus. Greg.* ii. xxii. 1 A.

reference. There were no stone seats, and as a rule no permanent structures of any kind.[772] Given the ground, the necessary arrangements for the start or the turn could be readily made in a few days whenever required. In the intervals between one festival and another the ground might be let out for pasturage, as it was at Delos.

The only hippodrome of which any remains exist, almost the only one which can be located, is that mentioned by Pausanias on Mount Lycaeus in Arcadia.[773] It is 240 metres long by 105 broad. Possibly the actual course was exactly a stade in length. It seems likely that the usual course was two stades long, and that from this circumstance the four-stades foot-race was called the "horse-race" (hippios).[774]

The hippodrome at Olympia was larger and more elaborate than the ordinary hippodrome. Unfortunately, the floods of the Alpheus and other catastrophes have removed every trace of its remains, and we must be content with what we learn from Pausanias and other writers.[775] The hippodrome lay between the stadium and the river. On its north side it was bounded by the southern embankment of the stadium, and farther east by a projecting spur of Mount Cronius. To the south a long embankment protected it from the floods of the Alpheus. The western end was formed by the portico of Agnaptus, but we do not know whether this portico extended along the whole end. Here presumably was the official entrance; there was another entrance at the south-east end of the course through the embankment.

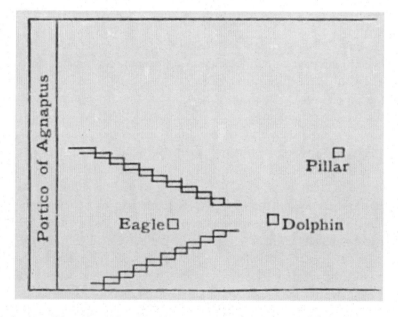

Figure 164. Aphesis at Olympia. (After Weniger.)

---

[772] In Roman times both stadium and hippodrome merge into the circus. The hippodrome at Constantinople is a purely Roman structure and does not concern us; so is the hippodrome at Pessinus (Texier, *Asie Mineure*, Pl. lxii.).

[773] Paus. viii. 38, 5; *Expédition en Morée*, ii. p. 37, Pls. xxxiii.

[774] Paus. vi. 16, 4; Plut. *Sol.* 23; Photius, p. 296.

[775] Paus. vi. 20. Many of the details are much disputed. I have followed in the main the account given by A. Martin in Dar.-Sagl. *s.v.* "Hippodrome."

The dimensions of the hippodrome are given in a manuscript discovered in the old Seraglio at Constantinople.[776] The circuit of the course was 8 stades (1538·16 m.), or nearly a mile. The width was 1 stade 4 plethra (320·45 m.), and the length of the sides was 3 stades 1 plethron (608·85 m.). It is not clear how the circuit is measured, but the fact that twice the long side + the short side gives the desired result suggests that half the short sides only are counted, and that 1 stade 4 plethra is the outside measurement, 5 plethra the inside measurement. The actual course traversed by the horses measured from pillar to pillar and back was, however, only 6 stades (1153·62 m.).

The elaborate starting gate (ἄφεσις), devised by Cleoetas probably in the fifth century, and improved at a later date by Aristides, has been described in a previous chapter (Figure 164). It consisted of a triangular structure like the prow of a ship, the apex pointing down the course.[777] The base joined the portico of Agnaptus. Along the two sides of the triangle which pointed down the course a number of stalls were arranged in pairs on either side. In these stalls the chariots were placed with a rope in front of each. At the signal the ropes in front of the pair of chariots nearest the base were dropped or withdrawn; in what way, we do not know. As these chariots drew level with the next pair, the next pair of ropes were withdrawn, and so on till the whole field was started. It is obvious, of course, that if the whole number of stalls was not required, the unoccupied ones were those nearest the base. The length of each side was 400 feet; we do not know how many stalls there were. At Delphi, Pindar speaks of forty competitors in the chariot-race. This must surely have been an exceptional field, and we are not surprised to hear that of the forty the chariot of Arcesilas alone reached the goal in safety. Still, the size of the aphesis at Olympia implies large fields,[778] and if the base of the triangle was 400 feet, there would have been ample room for twenty stalls on either side.

The general arrangement of the aphesis is clear enough, but the absence of all details renders it impossible to reconstruct the hippodrome with any certainty. In view of its great width we may certainly reject the old view that the base of the aphesis extended the whole width of the course. We cannot for a moment imagine the pair of chariots near the base starting at a distance of some 300 or even 150 yards from one another. But if the inside measurement of the width of the hippodrome was 5 plethra (168 yards), the base of the aphesis may quite well have extended over half this distance, and a base of this width agrees well with the length of the sides. We may assume, then, that the aphesis occupied the whole or part of the southern half of the course. Positions were, of course, assigned by lot, and undoubtedly the chariots on the left had a slight advantage in point of distance, but this advantage seems to have been greatly exaggerated, and was perhaps more than compensated by the wider sweep which the outside chariots could take in turning at the farther end of the course. Still, it is possible that, as Pollack[779] suggests, the apex of the aphesis was turned slightly to the left, so as to equalize the distance for all. In the circus of Maxentius, where the *carceres* occupy the whole breadth, they are for a similar reason inclined towards the right. There is no proof that this arrangement was adopted at Olympia, much less that the imaginary line joining the two pillars was inclined like the spina at the circus, so that the pillar nearest

---

[776] Quoted in Dar.-Sagl., *s.v.* "Olympia," p. 177, n. 5; cp. Frazer, *Pausanias*, v. p. 616, and Schoene in *Jahrb.* xii. p. 150. Schoene's conclusions as to the distances of the races seem to me quite impossibly long.
[777] Martin's statement that the part of the aphesis near the base was open, and the apex covered in, is hardly warranted by the words of Pausanias, and seems improbable.
[778] Alcibiades on one occasion entered no less than seven chariots of his own. Thuc. vi. 16, 2.
[779] Ervinus Pollack, *Hippodromika*. Leipsic, 1890.

the start was farther from the south side of the hippodrome than from the north, and thus more room was provided at the points where the chariots were most crowded. The width of the Olympic course made such an arrangement quite unnecessary.

This elaborate aphesis prevented the confusion and delay inevitable in starting a large field all together; but it is hard to see how it secured a fairer start than the ordinary plan of starting in a straight line.[780] Probably, as Martin suggests, its object was chiefly spectacular. At all events, though it was one of the wonders of Olympia, it does not seem to have been imitated anywhere else.

Another notable feature of the hippodrome at Olympia was the altar called Taraxippus—the terror of horses—which was supposed to inspire horses as they passed it with a sudden panic, and so to cause the numerous accidents for which the chariot-race was notorious. A mass of superstition grew up about this altar, which was held to be the home of some unfriendly demon. The altar seems to have been near the turn, where accidents were most frequent. Some writers have supposed that, as the horses turned the goal, they were frightened at the sight of their own shadows cast in front of them by the morning sun. If so, the Greek horse must have been a far less intelligent animal than the modern, which has shown an extraordinary faculty of becoming accustomed rapidly to trains, bicycles, motors,—sights far more disturbing than a shadow! Really, there is no need for any such theory to explain the numerous accidents which happened at the turn, and which superstition naturally ascribed to some spirit; and we may therefore accept the rationalistic explanation of Pausanias that Taraxippus was merely a name of Poseidon Hippios. There was also, he tells us, a Taraxippus at the Isthmus, the spirit of Glaucus the son of Sisyphus who was killed by his horses at the games of Adrastus, while at Nemea the panic of the horses was caused by a gleam like fire reflected from a red stone near the turn. But nowhere was there any Taraxippus which inspired such terror as the Taraxippus at Olympia!

The Olympic aphesis was something exceptional. Usually horses and chariots were started much in the same way as runners. Lots were drawn for places, and they drew up in line.[781] It appears that a rope (ὕσπληξ) was stretched in front of the whole line, which was dropped, or removed at the moment of starting. How this rope was dropped without risk of entangling the horses' feet, is a mystery; there is no record of any accident caused at the start. The signal for the start was given by a trumpet. The horse-races, being mostly of the diaulos type, finished at the start. The only place where we hear of straight races is at Athens. The starting-line, as in the stadium, was probably marked by pillars at either end. The pillars represented on coins and vases may be either these pillars or the pillars round which the horses turned. On a fine Panathenaic vase (Figure 165) recently discovered at Sparta there is a spirited drawing of a four-horse chariot passing a pillar on its right. As the turn always took place to the left, it is clear that unless the artist has made a mistake, the pillar represents the finish.

---

[780] It can hardly have been as fair; for the outside chariots had the enormous advantage of a flying start. I conjecture, however, that the chariots did not really start racing till they were all in line, and that the object of the aphesis was partly to facilitate the getting them into line, no easy matter with a large field.

[781] Sophocles, *El.* 709.

Figure 165. Panathenaic amphora found at Sparta. Sixth century.

We have seen that the fully developed programme comprised six events, three for full-grown horses (τέλειοι), three for colts, for each class a four-horse chariot-race (ἅρμα, τέθριππον), a horse race (κέλης), and a pair-horse chariot-race (συνωρίς). The last event, which was really perhaps the oldest of all, was not revived at Olympia till Ol. 93 (408 B.C.), but we learn from the Panathenaic vases that it existed as well as the other two races in the sixth century; indeed the earliest of these vases existing, the Burgon vase in the British Museum, was a prize for this event. The three events for colts were not introduced either at Olympia or Delphi till the fourth century. In 500 B.C. a mule chariot-race (ἀπήνη) was introduced at Olympia, and four years later a race for mares (κάλπη), in which the rider dismounted and finished the race on foot. Both events were abolished in 444 B.C., perhaps from lack of competition. At Athens we find a far more elaborate programme, including races for war-horses and processional horses, the apobates' race (Figure 34), and a torch-race on horseback.

The four-horse chariots ran twelve times round the course, the pair-horse chariots and colts' four-horse chariots eight times, the colts' synoris three times. These are the figures given by the Constantinople Manuscript, and they agree with what we learn from Pindar and the scholia.[782] The four-horse chariot-race at Olympia was therefore no less than seventy-two stades, nearly nine miles. The length of the course, which at first sight seems excessive, undoubtedly checked the pace, and thereby made for safety, but it makes it extremely improbable that heats were ever allowed in chariot-races. All equestrian events took place on the same day, and no team could be expected to race seventy-two stades twice on a day. The riding races consisted of only a single lap or six stades. This is the obvious conclusion of the story told by Pausanias of the Corinthian mare Aura, who, having thrown her rider at the start,

---

[782] Pindar, *Ol.* ii. 50, iii. 33, vi. 75; *Pyth.* v. 30. The passages referring to the measurements are collected by Pollack, *op. cit.* pp. 103 ff.

continued her course, turned the pillar, and on hearing the sound of the trumpet, spurted and came in first, and then knowing that she had won, stopped.[783] There is of course nothing remarkable in the story; indeed, I recollect seeing a very similar incident on the Totnes racecourse, but modern racing rules do not allow a horse thus to get rid of its rider's weight.

From this story we learn that at some point, perhaps at the turn of the last lap, a trumpet was blown. Perhaps the number of laps were marked by a blast of the trumpet. Some means must certainly have been employed for the information of the drivers. In the Roman circus the laps were marked by figures of dolphins and eggs set upon pillars at either end. At each lap one of the dolphins was turned round and one of the eggs probably removed, but we know of no such arrangement in the hippodrome.

Two distinct types of chariot were used in Greek racing. The four-horse chariot was a modification of the Homeric war-chariot. This war-chariot consisted of a low car mounted on two wheels with a high framework in front and at the sides, iii which the chieftain and the driver stood side by side. It was open behind, so that the chieftain could readily dismount to fight, and remount when he found it desirable. The racing car was very similar, but was usually drawn by four horses instead of two, had a lighter framework, and had only room for the charioteer. One of the earliest representations of a racing car occurs on an eighth-century vase in the British Museum.[784] The artist probably intended to represent a two-horse car, but finding this too difficult contented himself with one horse. The drivers are standing and wear the regulation dress of the Greek charioteer, a long white chiton such as is worn by the Delphi charioteer (Figure 18). The type of racing car remains the same, with but little difference, on Panathenaic vases from the sixth to the fourth century, and on coins of Macedon and Sicily. On some of the later vases, such as a Panathenaic vase B. 606 in the British Museum, the car seems to be decidedly lighter, and the wheels higher than on earlier vases. The driver has usually a whip or goad, and he holds the reins with his left hand or with both hands. The two middle horses (ζύγιοι) were harnessed to the yoke, which was attached to the pole, and further supported by a strap fastened to the front rim of the car. The other two horses were the trace-horses (σειραφόροι). The details of the harness and of the chariot do not concern us here.

The two-horse chariot (συνωρίς) as represented on Panathenaic vases is not really a chariot at all, but a sort of cart, the body of which has been reduced so that nothing is left but the driver's seat and a square open framework on either side. The driver sits with his feet resting on a footboard suspended from the pole. On the Burgon vase he wears a short, sleeveless, purple chiton, and carries in one hand a goad, in the other a long curved rod like a fishing-rod, to the end of which are fastened certain pieces of metal, which we may suppose made a jingling noise like bells.[785] On the two other Panathenaic vases in the Museum connected with this race the drivers wear short, tight-fitting drawers, which are not visible in our illustration (Figure 166).

---

[783] Paus. vi. 13, 9.
[784] *J.H.S.* xix. p. 8. *B.M. Guide to Greek and Roman Life*, p. 200.
[785] In the catalogue this instrument is described as a καλαῦροψ, but I can find no authority for this use of the word.

Figure 166. Panathenaic amphora, in British Museum, B. 132. Sixth century.

Figure 167. Silver tetradrachm and gold stater of Philip II. of Macedon, in the British Museum (enlarged).

This type of synoris seems to have been peculiar to Athens, for on coins the two-horse chariot is similar to the four-horse chariot, and the driver stands. Such a chariot appears on the gold coins of Philip II. of Macedon (Figure 167). Philip won victories at Olympia, in the riding-race and in the four-horse chariot-race. The two-horse chariot must, therefore, refer to some other victory, perhaps at the games of Dium, or it may be merely an allusion to his name.

The mule car (ἀπήνη) differs little from the Athenian synoris. It is represented on the coins of Rhegium and Messana. Sicily was famous for its mules; and the introduction of this event at Olympia was probably due to Sicilian influence. Of the four winners whose names we know one was a Thessalian, three were Sicilians. The event evidently found no favour with the Eleans, who abolished it at the first opportunity, perhaps alleging as an excuse an ancient curse which prevented mules from being bred in Elis.[786] The coin in our illustration (Figure 168) commemorates the victory of Anaxilas of Rhegium early in the fifth century. On it the mule-car appears as little more than a box-seat perched above two wheels.

---

[786] Paus. v. 5, 2.

Figure 168. Silver tetradrachm of Rhegium, in British Museum (enlarged). Early fifth century.

Figure 169. Panathenaic amphora, in British Museum, B. 133. Sixth century.

In the horse-races the jockeys rode without stirrups or saddle. On the Panathenaic vase (Figure 169) in the British Museum they appear as naked youths with long hair; those on the Amphiaraus vase (Figure 3) wear a short chiton girt in closely. In a red-figured vase-painting in Munich[787] one of the jockeys has been thrown from his horse in making the turn, and is being dragged along still holding the rein. The victories of Philip II. of Macedon have already been mentioned. His victory in the horse-race at Olympia is commemorated by a coin bearing on one side the figure of his victorious jockey holding in his hand the palm (Figure 167).

---

[787] Munich, 805; Schreiber, *Atlas*, xxiv. 9.

Of the Olympic κάλπη I know no illustration, but something very similar to it occurs on the coins of Tarentum. The didrachms of Tarentum,[788] from the fifth century to the end of the third century B.C., present a wonderful variety of equestrian types which, as Dr. Evans says, "give artistic expression to the passionate love of the turf which was so distinguishing a feature of Tarentine public life." The coin in our illustration (Figure 170), which belongs to the beginning of the third century, represents a common type, a naked youth armed with a small round shield in the act of vaulting off his horse. As was pointed out in a previous chapter, the exercises of the apobates, whether in chariot or on horseback, are really military; and this military character is marked on the Tarentum coins by the addition of a shield. Another type represented on the coins of Tarentum is the torch-race on horseback. The coin selected (Figure 170) is slightly later than the last, and is ascribed by Dr. Evans to the hegemony of Pyrrhus.

Figure 170. Silver staters of Tarentum, in the British Museum (enlarged).

Horses and mares were admitted alike to all races except the κάλπη, which was confined to mares. The distinction between colts and horses was one of the points decided by the Hellanodicae in the preliminary dokimasia before the games. Pausanias cites the case of a Spartan Lycinus, who had entered a team for the colts' race, but as one of his team was rejected by the judges, he entered them for the open chariot-race, and won it.[789] The story is open to suspicion, because the statue of Lycinus was made by Myron, and in Myron's time the colts' race had not been introduced.

Women, even if they could not be present in person at Olympia, were allowed to enter their horses for the races. Cynisca, the sister of Agesilaus, won two victories in the chariot-race about the year 380 B.C. Horse-breeding and racing were growing very fashionable among the Spartan nobles, and according to Plutarch, Agesilaus, wishing to read his countrymen a lesson, persuaded his sister to try her fortune in the chariot-race. "This he did to show the Greeks that a victory of that kind did not depend upon any extraordinary spirit or abilities, but only upon riches and expense." It is to be feared that this lesson failed of its effect, if we may judge from the honours paid to Cynisca. A bronze representation of her horses was dedicated in the Heraeum, and her own statue stood in the Altis, while at Sparta she was worshipped at a heroum built in her honour. Shortly after her another Spartan lady,

---

[788] *The Horsemen of Tarentum, passim.*
[789] Paus. vi. 2, 1.

Euryleonis, was victorious with the two-horse chariot. Belistiche, the mistress of Philadelphus, was the first to win the two-horse chariot-race for colts in 264 B.C. An Olympic inscription of the first century mentions, among the victories won by Antiphanes of Elis and his family, the victory of his daughter Theodota in the four-horse chariot-race for colts. Numerous victories of women are recorded in Athenian inscriptions.

Horses and chariots were sometimes entered not in the name of individuals, but of states. In 480 B.C. the public horse of the Argives (Ἀργείων δημόσιος) was successful at Olympia, and two Olympiads later their public chariot won.[790] An Olympic victory not only shed honour on the state, but must have been an excellent advertisement for all who were interested in horse-breeding.

The drivers and jockeys were usually paid servants; but sometimes we hear of the owner himself, or one of his family acting in this capacity. Damonon, in the inscription referred to above, records with pride certain races where he was his own charioteer. Pindar, in the first Isthmian Ode, congratulates Herodotus of Thebes on not entrusting his chariot to the hands of strangers. Thrasybulus probably drove his father's chariot in the victory commemorated in the sixth Pythian ode. Carrhotus, the charioteer of Arcesilas of Cyrene, was his brother-in-law. Next to the statue of Timon at Olympia was the statue of his youthful son, Aepytus, who had ridden his horse to victory.[791] Though the owner took the prize, the victory was due in no small degree to the skill of the charioteer, and the latter was not undeservedly sometimes associated with his master in the hymn of victory, or represented in the monument which commemorated the victory.

No event could compare in brilliance or in excitement with the four-horse chariot-race, the sport of kings in the Greek world. Each turn in the course was fraught with danger, and there were twenty-three turns. Every reader is familiar with the description of the chariot-race, with its shifting fortunes, and its catastrophes, in the *Electra* of Sophocles. The danger of the turn was twofold, there was the danger of striking the pillar with the chariot wheel in trying to turn too close, there was the danger of collision with other chariots. Both dangers are illustrated in the *Electra*. The first accident occurred at the turn between the sixth and seventh round; "The Aenian's hard-mouthed horses bolt, and at the turn dash headlong into the Barcaean car." The Barcaean car was leading on the outside; to make the turn, it had to sweep round in front of the Aenian car, thereby forcing the latter to check its pace for fear of collision. Unfortunately, the Aenian horses had bolted, and could not be checked, and therefore charged into the back of the other chariot. The accident is perfectly intelligible if we realise that the chariots were not racing in a line, one behind the other, but were often side by side. The chariot on the inside would naturally make a wide sweep after the pillar; the outside chariot would make the sweep first, and try to turn close to the pillar on the other side.[792] One accident leads to others. All the chariots came to grief except that of Orestes, who drove last, keeping himself for the finish, and the chariot of the Athenian, who cleverly pulled aside, and checked his pace, letting the crowd of chariots rush on to their destruction. Orestes started off in quick pursuit of him, but in making the last turn he was too quick. The left-hand trace-horse had been reined in to make the turn; the horses had already turned round the pillar, but the chariot itself was not yet clear when Orestes gave the rein to the left-hand horse. The

---

[790] *Oxyrhynchus Papyri*, ii. 222.
[791] Paus. vi. 2, 8.
[792] M. A. Bayfield in *Class. Rev.* xxii. p. 45.

horses dashed off down the straight, and the wheel of the chariot caught the pillar, Orestes was thrown from the chariot, and dragged along by the horses still entangled in the reins.

Accidents of a milder character are often depicted on coins and vases. On a red-figured hydria in Würzburg, one of the horses has broken his traces and runs away.[793] A broken rein tangled round the forefoot of a horse is a favourite motive on the fifth-century coins of Syracuse, bearing the signature of Euaenetus.[794] It occurs also on one of the coins of Catana shown in Figure 171. The other coin has in the exergue an object which seems to represent a broken chariot-wheel.

Figure 171. Silver tetradrachms of Catana, in the British Museum (enlarged). Fifth century.

The chariot-race is depicted on the François vase, and also in the Amphiaraus vase (Figure 3). The scene on the latter is a particularly fine picture of the crowding and confusion of the race. It represents the finish. Three tripods are set for the prizes, and beyond them sit the three judges.

Figure 172. Decadrachm of Agrigentum, 413-406 B.C. Decadrachm of Syracuse, 400-360 B.C.

The finest representations of the chariot occur on the coins of Sicily (Figure 172). It is impossible to dwell on them in detail, and interesting as they are artistically, they add little to our knowledge of the race. Two examples must suffice; two decadrachms of Agrigentum and Syracuse respectively. The former shows a spirited rendering of a four-horse chariot, as the

---

[793] Gerh. *A.V.* 267.
[794] Hill, *Coins of Sicily*, p. 63.

driver reins in his horses. The driver, contrary to usual custom, is almost naked, probably he is the personification of the river Acragas. Above him is an eagle flying away with a serpent in its claws; below is the city emblem, a crab. Still more interesting is the coin of Syracuse belonging to the series of medallions connected with the defeat of the Athenians at the river Assinarus. This defeat was commemorated by the festival of the Assinaria, which was celebrated for the first time in 412. The coin in our illustration is the work of an unknown artist, usually called "the New Artist." The chariot is represented in full career, and above the chariot floats a figure of Victory holding a crown. The most interesting feature of the coin is the group of objects in the exergue. They are a shield and helmet on either side, in the middle a cuirass flanked by a pair of greaves. These form the panoply of a heavy-armed soldier. Above the shield on the left is the word ἆθλα, prizes, and there can be little doubt that these arms are the spoils taken from the Athenian hoplites, which were offered as prizes at the Assinarian games.

Chariot-racing was a costly amusement, and in the century before our era it disappeared from the programme of Olympia, doubtless because of want of competitors. It was restored spasmodically under the Empire, but never recovered its old position in Greece. The racing of the hippodrome had given place to the races of the rival factions in the Roman circus. The account of the circus and its games belongs not to Greek history but to Roman.

Chapter 22

THE GYMNASIUM AND THE PALAESTRA

In Homeric times the gymnasium and the palaestra did not exist. The broad runs in Ithaca,[795] which are sometimes quoted as the prototype of the Greek gymnasia, were not running-tracks but cattle-runs. The need for special places for exercise first arose with the growth of city life. At first these were no more than open spaces in some grove or plain where the ground had been cleared for running or for wrestling. Such were the "runs and wrestling rings" which Cleisthenes of Sicyon prepared for his daughter's suitors.[796] The place where the Spartan youth exercised retained its ancient name the "Dromos" or run, even in the time of Pausanias. The runs developed into the gymnasium, the wrestling-ring into the palaestra.

The word "gymnasium" means, properly, an athletic exercise. By a natural transference it comes to be used first in the plural, afterwards collectively in the singular for a place set apart for such exercises. It is a general term. The gymnasium is merely an athletic ground, or playing-field, where all sorts of sport take place. It contains "runs and wrestling-rings." It may serve as a riding-school. Euripides speaks of "gymnasia resounding with the tramp of horses."[797] It may contain buildings for the comfort of those who use it, but the essential part of the gymnasium is the running-ground. On the other hand, the palaestra is a special term for the wrestling-school. In its simplest form it is a square enclosure, containing some provision for undressing and washing. It is essentially a building. The palaestra may exist without a gymnasium, but no gymnasium can exist without a palaestra. Moreover, in a gymnasium the necessary buildings are naturally centred round the palaestra. Hence the palaestra being architecturally the most important part of the gymnasium, the two terms are in practice often used synonymously. Yet the original distinction is never wholly obliterated; in Pausanias the gymnasium is still the athletic ground, the palaestra the wrestling-school.[798]

Gymnasia probably existed in most Greek states in the sixth century or even earlier. Shade and water being essential for the comfort of those who used them, the site selected was usually a grove beside some stream outside the city. Such was the Platanistas at Sparta, an island formed by the windings of the river, and taking its name from the plane trees which surrounded it. Such were the three ancient gymnasia at Athens: the Academea, the Lyceum, and the Cynosarges. All three were sacred groves outside the walls of the city, the Academea

---

[795] *Od.* iv. 605.
[796] Hdt. vi. 126. Cp. Eur. *Andromache*, 599.
[797] Eur. *Hipp.* 229; *Hec.* 207.
[798] Paus. v. 15, 8; vi. 21, 2.

on the west side, on the banks of the Cephisus, the other two on the east near the Eridanus and Ilissus. All three probably existed in the sixth century. The Academea was first enclosed with a wall by Hipparchus, and was afterwards improved by Cimon into a well-watered grove with trim avenues and walks. The origin of the Lyceum was variously ascribed to Peisistratus, Pericles, and Lycurgus. As it certainly existed in the time of Socrates, it was probably founded by Peisistratus, if not earlier, and underwent various improvements at the hands of Pericles and Lycurgus. The gymnasium of Cynosarges was reserved for bastards, and those whose parents were not both Athenian. Themistocles being the son of a Carian mother, and resenting his exclusion from the other gymnasia, succeeded in persuading some prominent young Athenians to accompany him to the Cynosarges. Slaves were not allowed to take any part in athletics, which were regarded as the distinctive mark of freeborn Greeks. The Academea and Lyceum were large enough to serve as riding-schools and parade-grounds for cavalry. The Athenian gymnasia were open to Athenians of all ages; boys were certainly not excluded, though, as we shall see, they were usually sent to the palaestra for education;[799] men of all ages resorted to them for their daily exercise; competitors for the games trained in them; above all, they were the training-school of the epheboi, at all events from the fifth century onwards. "When a boy is enrolled among the Epheboi," says Socrates, in the Pseudo-Platonic dialogue called *Axiochus*,[800] "then come the Lyceum and the Academea, the rule of the gymnasiarchos, beatings with rods and ills innumerable." Consequently, the gymnasia were the favourite resort of sophists and philosophers in search of pupils. Some philosophers habitually frequented certain gymnasia, which thereby became connected with particular schools of philosophy. In course of time literary studies prevailed over athletics, and the gymnasium developed into a sort of university.

The existence of palaestrae at Athens in the sixth century is attested by the speech of Aeschines against Timarchus. In this speech the orator refers to certain laws ascribed to Solon for the regulation of schools and palaestrae. The paidotribai were not to open the palaestrae before sunrise, and were to close them before sunset. There were regulations as to the class of boys to be admitted, their numbers and age, their discipline and the conduct of the Hermaea, a boy's festival celebrated in the palaestrae. The actual text of the laws is spurious, but there is no reason for doubting the existence of the regulations mentioned by Aeschines, and their antiquity. But we must not confound the palaestrae referred to with those which formed part of the gymnasia. The latter were public institutions, mostly outside the city; the palaestrae for which Solon laid down regulations were such of the private palaestrae as were used for the physical education of boys. There were numerous private palaestrae, some perhaps built by rich individuals for their own use,[801] others kept by paidotribai[802] for profit. The publicity of the gymnasia and their remoteness rendered them unsuitable for the training of young boys. Parents and teachers naturally preferred the comparative privacy of the palaestra in the city. Some of these may have been attached to schools, others may have been reserved for boys of certain ages, or special times may have been reserved in them for different ages. Certainly it is at these palaestrae that the Athenian boys received their physical training. But it is no more

---

[799] Aristoph. *Av.* 141; Antiphon, *Tetr.* ii.
[800] *Axioch.* 366 C, 367 A.
[801] Xen. *Rep. Ath.* 2, 10.
[802] E.g., Taureas (Plato, *Charm.* 153), Timagetus (Theocrit. ii. 8), Sibyrtius (Plut. *Alcib.* 3), Hippocrates (Plut. *Vit. dec. or.* 837), Timeas and Antigonus in second century (*I.G.* ii. 444, 445, 446). Cp. Staseas at Delos (*B.C.H.*, 1891, p. 255).

correct to say that the palaestrae generally were reserved for the education of boys under the age of eighteen, than it is to say that no boys under that age were admitted to the gymnasia. Some of the palaestrae were certainly used by older pupils. In Plato's *Lysis* the sophist Miccus is stated to have established himself in a newly built palaestra. Boys of different ages are trained there at different times, but the pupils of Miccus are not boys, but epheboi or grown-up men, and these at all events had free entry there at certain times. The fact is that there were palaestrae of various sorts just as there are schools and colleges of various sorts in England to-day. To treat all the palaestrae as similar, and to endeavour to lay down hard and fast rules for all alike, is as ridiculous as it would be to write a treatise on the schools of England in which no distinction was made between primary schools and secondary schools, or between a college which forms part of a university and a college which is really a school.

Our knowledge of Greek gymnasia down to the fourth century is practically confined to Athens. The earliest existing gymnasium is that of Delphi, which belongs to the fourth century. The gymnasium at Olympia cannot be earlier than the third century. The only contemporary evidence for the fifth century is derived from the vase-paintings which give a vivid picture of the life of the gymnasium at Athens in the first half of this century, but yield only fragmentary evidence as to the arrangements of the gymnasium. Yet this evidence agrees so well with the remains discovered at Olympia and Delphi, and also with such scattered allusions as we find in literature, especially in Plato's dialogues, that we may feel sure that the gymnasia and palaestrae of the fifth century throughout Greece were substantially of the type which we find in these places.[803]

The essential parts of the gymnasium or palaestra are clearly stated in the treatise on the Athenian Republic,[804] which if not written by Xenophon was probably written in the second half of the fifth century. The writer, speaking of the progress of the Athenian democracy, says: "As for gymnasia and baths and undressing-rooms some rich people have their own, but the people have built for their own use many palaestrae, dressing-rooms, and bath-rooms, and the mob has far more advantages in these respects than the fortunate few." In this passage we notice, first, that there is no real distinction between gymnasium and palaestra; if there is any distinction, it is merely that the palaestra is somewhat more elaborate than the gymnasium, as the bath-room is more than the bath. Both are merely places for exercise. Secondly, the dressing-rooms and bath-rooms are clearly not independent buildings, but are connected with the gymnasia. Bath-rooms might exist separately, but what would be the use of separate undressing-rooms? Every gymnasium and every palaestra must contain, besides the actual "runs and wrestling-rings," some place where those who use them may undress and oil themselves before exercise, and may wash themselves afterwards. These are the three essential parts of every such building, and all the complicated arrangements of the gymnasia at Ephesus and Pergamum are merely elaborations of these three requirements.

The dialogues of Plato illustrate alike the similarity and difference in the arrangements of a gymnasium and palaestra. The scene of the *Lysis* is laid in the new-built palaestra to which reference has already been made. In general plan it resembles an ordinary one-storied Greek house. It is surrounded by a wall (περίβολος), the only opening in which is a door giving

---

[803] M. Fougères (Dar.-Sagl., *s.v.* "Gymnasium") considers the earliest gymnasium to be that of Messene, which he identifies with the colonnade surrounding the sphendone of what is usually considered to be the stadium. The identification and the date of the building must be regarded as very doubtful in the absence of more systematic excavation.

[804] ii. 10.

access to the street. Around this wall, on the inside, are placed the various rooms which all open out into the central court (αὐλή) which in the palaestra is considerably larger than in an ordinary house. On entering, the visitor finds himself in a sort of ante-chamber, from which he passes into a large hall called the apodyterion (ἀποδυτήριον). The front of this hall is open, so that it commands a view of the court, which is used for exercise. This hall, as its name denotes, is the undressing-room. But, like the modern cricket pavilion, it serves as a general meeting-place for all who frequent the palaestra. There are seats around the walls for their convenience. A group of boys are playing knuckle-bones when Socrates enters, and Socrates retreats to the farther corner to find a seat. Probably, if there were no other rooms, it was in the apodyterion that Miccus used to hold his classes. There may, of course, have been other rooms around the court, certainly there must have been some accommodation for washing, but as the bath-room is not conducive to serious conversation it naturally plays no part in these dialogues.

Now let us pass on to the Lyceum gymnasium.[805] The arrangement is similar, but on a larger scale. Close to the entrance is the apodyterion where Socrates takes his seat and watches people come and go. But besides the court, there is a covered track (κατάστεγος δρόμος), probably a colonnade running round one or more of the four sides of the court. This covered dromos is the place where Athenian gentlemen take their daily constitutional. As Socrates is waiting, two such enter, take two or three turns in this dromos, and then return to the apodyterion. Acumenos[806] indeed recommends a walk in the country as less fatiguing, but the gymnasium is a more sociable place, there is more life and amusement to be found there, and so the Athenian prefers it. But these covered runs are not for athletes or epheboi except in the worst of weather. For them tracks are provided in the park outside (ὁ ἔξω δρόμος) where, as in the Academy, they may run races "mid a fragrance of smilax, and leisure, and white poplar in the spring-season when the plane tree whispers to the elm."[807]

The pictures on the red-figured vases enable us to fill in these outlines. These vases, manufactured mostly at Athens, between the years 520 and 440 B.C., represent the life of the Athenian epheboi, that is to say, life in the public gymnasia. On them we see scenes from the gymnasia proper, where youths are exercising, scenes from the apodyterion, and scenes from the bath-room.

We will first take a kylix in the Munich Museum, which gives a general picture of exercises in the gymnasium (Figure 17). The scene takes place within a walled enclosure. The background represents this wall, or perhaps the wall of the apodyterion; for on it are hanging all the paraphernalia of the gymnasium, diskoi in their slings, halteres fastened together by a cord, strigils, oil-flasks, sponges. A pair of Ionic pillars frame the picture suggesting, perhaps, a covered colonnade. Sometimes these pillars are surmounted by a large flat block, which clearly indicates a roof. The actual exercises take place in the court in front, or the dromoi outside. In the ground are planted poles and picks. The poles are used as javelins for practice, and perhaps as measuring-rods; or as posts to mark the lines from which the jump is practised, or the diskos and javelin thrown. The two bearded men are instructors—paidotribai or gymnastai. Usually these are clothed in a long mantle; here they are naked, probably because they are teaching by example. One of them leans on the usual official staff and holds

---

[805] Plato, *Euthydemus*.
[806] *Phaedr.* 227 A.
[807] *Theaetet.* 144 C; Aristoph. *Nub.* 1005.

in his right hand a jumping-weight; the other holds in one hand a rod or javelin, in the other a thong for throwing the javelin, but it is not quite clear what his attitude means. The youth who looks on, leaning upon a pole, may be either a youthful assistant or a spectator.

Figure 173. R.-f. kylix. Canino Coll.

Another kylix gives a vivid picture of the discipline of the gymnasium (Figure 173). On one side are a pair of wrestlers, and looking on at them is an instructor wearing his robe, leaning on his staff with his right hand, while in his left he holds the forked rod with which he enforces discipline. On the other side is an instructor in the act of using this rod on some boxers. The youth who stands behind the first instructor with the pick may be another boxer taking this form of exercise, but the mantle rolled up round his waist suggests rather that he is an assistant who is loosening the ground of the skamma used by wrestlers and jumpers. On the interior of this vase is a third instructor, and a youth who seems to be measuring the ground with his feet, perhaps measuring the throw of a javelin, for he holds in his hands a javelin and its thong. The careless drawing of this amentum caused it to be misinterpreted formerly as a pair of compasses. Another figure frequently depicted in these scenes is the flute-player,[808] who is usually dressed in a long, gaudy robe, and wears round his head a curious sort of muzzle called φορβεία. These flute-players were probably slaves attached to the gymnasium.

Many of the exercises depicted require considerable space. The javelin and diskos could hardly be thrown with safety in the court of an ordinary palaestra. The open dromoi were the places for such sports. Here, too, it seems riding-lessons were given. Sometimes a group of athletes and a riding scene are placed on opposite sides of the same vase.[809] In these riding

---

[808] Gerh. *A. V.* 272, and *supra*, Figures 63, 64.
[809] Gerh. *A. V.* 272, 294.

scenes pillars[810] are sometimes depicted, oil-flasks and other objects hang on the walls, and the instructors are the same as in athletic scenes. A good example of such a scene occurs on a kylix in Munich (Figure 174). There are three naked epheboi, one already mounted, one leading a horse and holding in his hand the familiar forked rod, the third is being instructed in the art of vaulting on to his horse by means of a spear or pole. An oil-flask indicates the building, while a tree suggests the groves of the gymnasium.

Figure 174. R.-f. kylix. Munich, 515.

Figure 175. R.-f. kylix. Copenhagen.

---

[810] Hartwig, *Meisterschal.* liii.; Freeman, *Schools of Hellas*, Pl. x.

Scenes in the Apodyterion are very numerous, especially on later vases. We will first take a kylix in the Museum at Copenhagen (Figure 175). The broad tops of the pillars suggest the roof of the room. Hanging or leaning against the wall are the usual paraphernalia; one object seems curious, it is a hare. Perhaps one of the epheboi has just caught it, or he has brought it as a present to his trainer, or received it as a present or prize.[811] A group of youths and trainers are standing about or seated on stools. Some are fully dressed, others naked; one is scraping himself with a strigil, another is just about to put on his mantle; his walking-stick rests against the wall behind him. Some clothes are placed on one of the stools. We can quite understand the necessity of severe laws against theft in the gymnasia. A law attributed to Solon imposed the penalty of death on any one who stole from the Lyceum, or Acadamea, or Cynosarges a himation, or an oil-flask, or any other object worth more than ten drachmae.[812]

After divesting himself of his clothes and placing them in as safe a place as possible, the athlete next proceeded to anoint himself with oil and carefully rub the oil into the skin. He might do so himself or obtain the services of an attendant, the aleiptes. The terms aleiptes and paidotribes indicate the importance which the Greeks attached to the oiling and massaging of the body both before and after exercise. These processes were afterwards developed into elaborate arts, and special rooms were set apart for them, but in the fifth century they were comparatively simple and took place either in the apodyterion or else in the open air.[813] The oil was contained in little narrow necked flasks of various shapes, lekythoi, aryballoi, alabastra. Each person probably brought his own flask of oil and his strigil. At times of festival oil was supplied free to all competitors, and in later times gymnasiarchoi and other high officials showed their generosity by providing at their own expense the oil required for the epheboi using the gymnasia. A krater in Berlin (Figure 176) shows a group of epheboi undressing and preparing for exercise. One of them has just taken off his himation and folded it up and is about to hand it to a slave-boy, either his own slave or one attached to the gymnasium. Another has laid his himation on a stool, and is pouring some oil from an aryballos into his left hand. To his left stands a third ephebos resting on his stick, with his mantle thrown loosely across his shoulders, while a small slave removes a thorn from his foot. The other side of the vase illustrates the curious custom of infibulation. Massaging is, as far as I know, not depicted on any vases; but a drawing of an aleiptes rubbing down a boxer occurs on a bronze cist in the Vatican[814] (Figure 177).

It may have been in the Apodyterion, or else in some other corner of the gymnasium, that the korykos (κώρυκος) was fixed up. In later times a special room was provided for the korykos, but its use at this time is proved by the caricature of a pankratiast using it which occurs on a vase in St. Petersburg (Figure 178). The korykos was a sort of punchball, a leathern bag or skin filled with fig grains, meal, or sand, and suspended from the branch of a tree or a beam. It varied in size. The larger sort which was used by pankratiasts was about the size of a sack of coals, and was hung so that the bottom of it was on a level with the athlete's waist. The boxer used a smaller korykos about the size of a punchball hung on a level with his head, to judge from the picture of it on the Ficoroni cist, a work of the third century B.C. (Figure 179).[815] In the later gymnasia a special room was set apart for ball-play; but popular

---

[811] The hare was frequently offered as a present. Gerh. *A. V.* 275, 276, 280, 290.
[812] Demosth. *in Timocr.* 114.
[813] Plato, *Theaet.* 144 C.
[814] *Mus. Greg.* i. 37: Schreiber, *Atlas*, xxiii. 9.
[815] Helbig, *Führer*, p. 388.

as ball games always were they seem to have been of little or no importance in the gymnasia of the fifth century.

Figure 176. R.-f. krater. Berlin, 2180.

Figure 177. Bronze cista. Vatican.

Figure 178. R.-f. amphora. St. Petersburg, Hermitage, 1611.

Figure 179. Ficoroni cista. Kirchner Museum, Rome. Third century B.C.

The bathing arrangements in the gymnasium were severely simple. There existed, indeed, even in the time of Herodotus and Aristophanes, separate bathing establishments (βαλανεῖα) where hot baths and even vapour baths were to be obtained.[816] But these balaneia had nothing to do with the gymnasia, and are indeed sharply contrasted with them. To frequent them was considered, at all events among old-fashioned folk, to be a sign of effeminacy. Aristophanes bitterly complains that the effect of the new-fashioned education was to empty the wrestling schools and fill the balaneia, and Plato considers hot baths only suitable for the old and feeble.[817] In later times elaborate baths of this type were attached to the gymnasia, and became so important that the athletic part of the building was little more than an apanage of the baths. But there is no sign of such baths in connexion with the gymnasia of the fifth century, nor do they exist in the later gymnasia at Delphi and Olympia. The epheboi of the fifth century washed in cold water after exercise. The simplest form of washing is represented on a black-figured hydria in Leyden which dates from the close of the sixth century (Figure 180).[818] A group of men and boys are washing at a fountain which stands in the grove of the gymnasium. Their clothes hang on the branches of the trees. The fountain itself is under a portico, and the water issues from two panthers' heads under which a man and a boy are taking a douche and rubbing themselves. On either side stand others preparing for the bath. One on the left lifts in his right hand what is probably an oil-flask, while on the right we see a youth engaged in powdering himself. Various powders were used, a sort of lye obtained from wood ashes, an alkali called litron and somewhat similar to nitre, and a kind of fuller's earth.[819] After oiling and powdering his body the bather rubbed himself till a lather was obtained.

---

[816] Hdt. iv. 75; Aristoph. *Eq.* 1060; *Nub.* 835, 991, 1045.
[817] Plato, *Legg.* vi. 761.
[818] Roulez, *Vases peints du Musée de Leyde*, Pl. 19. A similar scene in a woman's bath occurs on a b.-f. amphora in Berlin 1843. Vide Schreiber, *Atlas*, xxi. 9, lvii. 4.
[819] Aristoph. *Ran.* 710.

Figure 180. B.-f. hydria. Leyden, 7794b.

Figure 181. Scene on r.-f. vase. (Tischbein, i. 58).

On the red-figured vases the washing takes place in a bath-room forming a part of the gymnasium and probably adjoining the apodyterion. In the centre of this room is set a large stone or metal basin placed on a stand. Close to it a cistern is sometimes represented, and on one vase we see a youth pouring water into the basin from a bucket which he has drawn up from the cistern by means of a rope and windlass[820] (Figure 181). The inscription on the basin (δημόσια) shows that it is a public bath. One youth is splashing the water over himself, but a more satisfactory way of washing is to get a friend or assistant to swill a bucket of water over you in the manner represented on a kylix in the British Museum (Figure 182). On the other side of this kylix is seen a group of youths scraping themselves with strigils (στλεγγίδες). The strigil was in constant use in the gymnasium to remove dirt and sweat after exercise or remove moisture and lather after the bath. It was made of iron or bronze, sometimes of silver or even of gold; the handles are sometimes highly ornamental. Many of them exist in the

---

[820] Tischbein, i. 58; Schreiber, *Atlas*, xxiii. 3.

British Museum and elsewhere. Their shape will be best understood from the accompanying illustration of a fifth-century strigil from the British Museum, on which the owner's name is inscribed (Figure 183). A youth scraping himself with a strigil is the motive of the well-known statue, the "Apoxyomenos," formerly ascribed to Lysippus.

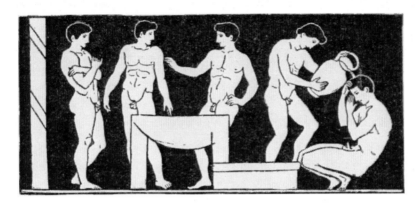

Figure 182. R.-f. kylix. British Museum, E. 83.

Figure 183. Strigil, in British Museum, inscribed κέλων. Fifth century.

Plunge baths (κολυμβήθραι) certainly existed at this period. A red-figured amphora[821] in the Louvre signed by Andocides (c. 500 B.C.) shows a group of women bathing in a swimming bath. One is swimming, while another is preparing to dive into the water. We shall find plunge baths both at Delphi and Olympia, but we have no evidence for their existence in the gymnasia of the fifth century.

In passing on to the gymnasia at Delphi and Olympia we must bear in mind the essential difference which distinguishes them from the gymnasia at Athens, which we have been considering. The latter were intended for the regular use of a large resident population. At Delphi, and still more at Olympia, the resident population was small and scattered; and though they doubtless took advantage of the gymnasia, these buildings were primarily erected, not for their use, but for the use of the competitors in the four-yearly festivals. Hence there was no need for the shady walks and avenues which formed so prominent a feature of the early gymnasia at Athens, nor for the lecture-rooms and libraries which were provided for the literary training of the epheboi in the gymnasia of Ptolemaeus Philadelphus or Hadrian. The gymnasia at Delphi and Olympia were strictly practical and athletic.

---

[821] Dar.-Sagl., Figure 747; Schreiber, *Atlas*, lvii. 5.

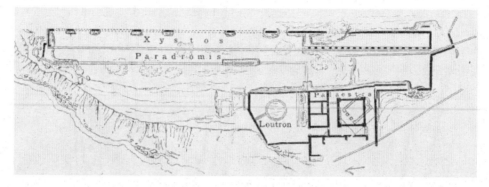

Figure 184. Plan of gymnasium at Delphi. (*B.C.H.*)

The gymnasium at Delphi[822] is a good example of the skill with which the Greeks adapted their buildings to the nature of the ground (Figure 184). It lies a little to the southwest of the precinct of Apollo below the road which runs from Itea to Arachova and on the steep slopes which overhang the valley of the Pleistus. It is built on two terraces, the upper of which forms a rectangle some 180 metres long by 25 or 30 metres deep, and contains the running tracks, while the lower terrace contains the palaestra proper and the baths. The fine retaining wall which divides the two terraces, and other architectural remains point to the existence of the gymnasium in the early part of the fourth century, and most of the parts which have been excavated are mentioned in an inscription containing the official accounts for repairing the stadium and gymnasium in the year 258 B.C.

The upper terrace was bounded above by the outer wall of the gymnasium. It contained a covered running-track 7 metres broad, and a double uncovered track 20 metres broad. These are the ξυστόν and παραδρομίς of the inscription. They are divided from one another by a stone water channel which, besides carrying off rain water, provided water for the athletes when training. Another channel, which divided the paradromis into two unequal parts, carried water from the Castalian stream to the baths in the lower terrace. The Ionic pillars which formed the colonnade (περίστυλος) of the xystos are of poor and late workmanship, and seem to have replaced an earlier Doric colonnade. Neither xystos nor paradromis was paved; but, as we learn from the accounts of Dion's archonship, they were dug up, rolled, and covered with fine white sand. Six picks (ἐπισκαφεῖα) were provided either for this work or for the use of the athletes.[823] The length of the xystos, 180 metres, is approximately that of the Delphic stadium, which was 177 metres.

The lower terrace contains an irregular enclosure forming the baths, and a small palaestra 32 metres square. The latter consists of a small court nearly 14 metres square, surrounded by a colonnade (περίστυλος) on to which several rooms open on the north and west sides. The uses of these rooms cannot be determined. The inscription mentions an apodyterion, a κόνιμα, and two σφαιριστήρια. The κόνιμα is probably another name for the skamma or wrestling ring which is also called κονίστρα, and if so may be identified with the central court.[824] The

---

[822] Homolle, *B.C.H.*, 1899, pp. 560 ff.
[823] The purchase of a pick (σκαφεῖον) and rollers (τροχιλείαι) for the palaestra is mentioned in the Delian accounts for 279 B.C., *B.C.H.*, 1890, p. 397, ll. 98, 99; cp. p. 488 note 2, for similar purchases in other years.
[824] Similarly in *Ath. Mitth.* v. 232 τὸ πυριατήριον καὶ τὸ κόνισμα; Lebas Waddington, *Inscr. As. Min.* 1112 λουτρῶνα καί κόνισμα. The open court for exercise was an essential part of every bath. The κόνισμα must not be confused with the konisterion or powdering-room of Vitruvius.

wrestling ring was covered with fine sand, and the contract appropriately mentions the "sifting of the earth" in the konima (τᾶς γᾶς τὰν σάσιν) at a cost of ten drachmae. The sphairisteria were rooms, or perhaps open courts, for ball play. In one of them the ground was to be dug up and rolled, then carefully raked over and levelled, and finally covered with black earth. A wall, too, is mentioned in the sphairisterion. Among the various games of ball practised by the Greeks we find mention of one which consisted in bouncing the ball on the ground or against a wall, and striking it back with the flat of the hand as it rebounded. The object was to keep it up as many times as possible; the first to miss was called the donkey, and had to submit to any penalty imposed by the winner or "king," as he was called.[825] The palaestra at Delphi was not spacious enough for games in which the balls were thrown with any violence, but the carefully prepared floor and the wall may well have served for the games described, which seem to have been quite familiar in Plato's time. As athletics became professional, ball play seems to have become increasingly popular, and the ball alley probably became a recognized part of the palaestra. The little private palaestra owned by the "Man of Petty Ambitions" (μικροφιλότιμος) in Theophrastus contains "a wrestling arena and a sphairisterion,"[826] the two parts mentioned in the Delphic inscription. Alexander the Great was specially fond of ball play, and one Aristonicus of Carystus, described as his "sphairistes," received at the hands of the Athenians the citizenship and an honorary statue[827]

The baths lay in an irregular enclosure to the north of the palaestra. The washing arrangements are particularly interesting from their resemblance to what we have seen pictured on the vases. The whole enclosure was uncovered. The east side of it was formed by the retaining wall of the upper terrace, and in this wall a series of fountains were arranged precisely similar to those illustrated in Figure 180. The water was supplied from the conduit in the upper terrace and issued through eleven bronze spouts in the shape of animals' heads, placed at such a height as to fall conveniently over the head and shoulders of the bathers beneath. It was caught below in eleven basins, which were used for washing in the manner represented on the vases, and from the basins it fell into large stone troughs by which it was carried outside the building to fall into the Castalian ravine. In the centre of the enclosure was a circular plunge bath (κολυμβήθρα) 10 metres in diameter, and 1·80 metres in depth, the sides of which sloped downwards towards the centre in a series of stone steps. There were no warm baths in the old gymnasium, but these seem to have been added in Roman times, and their remains exist to the north of the older building.

The gymnasium and palaestra at Olympia[828] (Figure 185), situated on the left bank of the Cladeus to the north-west of the Altis, are far more symmetrical in plan and more elaborate than those at Delphi. The palaestra appears to be somewhat older than the gymnasium, and was built in the third century B.C. It is a building 66 metres square enclosing an open court 41 metres square, surrounded by a colonnade of Doric columns on which numerous rooms open. There are two entrances at the corners of the southern wall, and a third door in the middle of the northern wall gives access to the gymnasium proper. The two chief entrances consist of pillared vestibules leading into small anterooms which open on to the covered

---

[825] Plato, *Theaet.* 146 A, and Schol. on the same. The game of bouncing the ball on the ground was called ἀπόρραξις.

[826] *Char.* xxi. αὐλίδιον παλαιστριαῖον κόνιν ἔχον καὶ σφαιριστήριον. This palaestra he lends to philosophers, sophists, fencing-masters (ὁπλόμαχοι) and musicians for their displays, at which he will himself appear on the scene rather late in order that the spectators may say one to another, "This is the owner of the palaestra."

[827] Athen. i. 34, p. 19 A.

[828] *Ol.* Text. ii. pp. 113, 127.

colonnade. In the eastern anteroom are remains of a hearth or altar. Between the two anterooms is a long narrow room or gallery only separated from the colonnade by a row of pillars, in which we may certainly recognize the apodyterion. In the north-eastern corner is a bathroom, and in it were found remains of a brick-lined bath of Roman date 4 metres square and 1·38 metres deep. There is another basin in the adjacent corner of the gymnasium at the point where the southern corridor opens on to the street. There are no signs in the palaestra or gymnasium of the warm baths which are so important a feature of the gymnasium described by Vitruvius. In Roman times warm baths were installed at Olympia not in the palaestra but in a separate building to the south-west. It is impossible to determine the uses of the various rooms surrounding the court. Some of them are closed with doors, and doubtless served for storing the oil, sand, and other requisites of the palaestra. The larger rooms are open in front. In five of the rooms there are remains of stone seats round the walls, and the floor is paved with concrete. Such rooms must have been used as exedrai or galleries for the spectators, but hardly, as it is sometimes stated, as lecture rooms for philosophers and other teachers, who would certainly have preferred the greater publicity afforded by the opisthodome of the temple of Zeus or by the stoai. The palaestra and gymnasium at Olympia must have been practically confined to the use of competitors, and the practice of these competitors naturally drew thither crowds of friends and interested spectators. In some of the rooms there are traces of altars and bases of statues. Such buildings were always under the patronage of certain gods and heroes. Hermes was in a special sense the patron of the palaestra, and at Athens festivals were held there in his honour. At Elis one of the gymnasia contained altars to Idaean Heracles, to Eros and Anteros, to Demeter and Persephone, and the statues of the first three were placed in the gymnasium called Maltho which was specially reserved for wrestlers. Honorary statues were also sometimes placed in the gymnasia, and at Olympia there were tablets inscribed with the lists of Olympic victors.

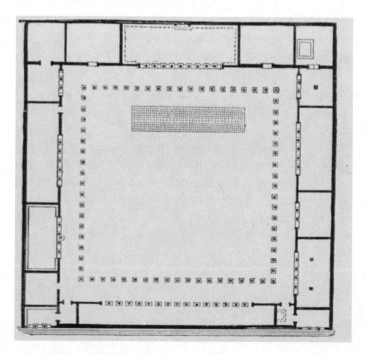

Figure 185. Plan of palaestra at Olympia.

The most curious feature in the palaestra at Olympia is a strip of tiled pavement along the north side of the court. It is 24 metres long by 5 metres broad, and consists of two bands of rough ribbed tiles 1·60 metres in breadth divided by a band of smooth tiles 1 metre broad, while a double row of these same tiles runs along the upper edge of the pavement. The edges of these smooth tiles are raised so as to form continuous ridges running the whole length of the pavement. The purpose of this curious pavement is unknown; it certainly cannot have been intended as a wrestling ring, or as a jumping ground, as certain learned writers have with unconscious humour suggested. The most plausible hypothesis is that it was used for some unknown game of ball, and this hypothesis finds some support from the existence of a somewhat similar bowling alley in the larger Thermae at Pompeii, on which two large heavy stone balls were actually found.[829]

Of the gymnasium proper which lay to the north of the palaestra nothing remains but portions of the southern and eastern colonnades. All the western side has been destroyed by the floods of the Cladeus. The southern colonnade consisted of a single row of pillars parallel to the north wall of the palaestra, with which it communicated by a door in the centre of the wall. The eastern colonnade was not, however, continuous with the east wall of the palaestra, but, to avoid the slope of Mount Cronius, was diverted so as to form a slightly acute angle with the southern colonnade. It was 210 metres long by nearly 12 metres broad, and divided into two tracks by a row of Doric pillars. The similar row of pillars which formed its western front began only on a level with the third of the central pillars from the south, and ended with the third pillar from the north. At these two points are traces of the attachment of stone sills such as were found in the stadium, and the distance between these two points, 192·27 metres, is exactly the distance of the Olympic stadium. This double track was the xystos, or covered running-track, and athletes could practise there under precisely the same conditions as in the actual stadium. On the western side of the gymnasium were rooms for the accommodation of competitors during the festival, and possibly in front of them another xystos. In the centre of the open court was constructed a sort of stone stand for the spectators described by Pausanias as κρηπίς, the term which he uses for the rows of stone steps below the treasury terrace in the Altis. But of this and of the lodgings of the athletes, and of the paradromides or uncovered tracks which doubtless existed here, not a trace is left.

The gymnasia at Epidaurus and Delos belong apparently to the same period, and as far as can be judged from their scanty remains were very similar in type. They bear a much closer resemblance to the buildings described by the Roman architect Vitruvius, who lived in the time of Augustus, than do the elaborate gymnasia of later times, which we find at Ephesus and Pergamum. They differ, however, from the Vitruvian type in the absence of hot baths. In Lucian's time the Lyceum at Athens certainly possessed a hot bath and a plunge bath, and perhaps these existed in Hellenistic times. It is probable that such gymnasia, which were the daily resort of the inhabitants of Athens, resembled the Vitruvian type more closely than did the gymnasia of Olympia and Delphi, which were chiefly used at the seasons of the festivals by competitors. Now that excavation has revealed to us the actual plans of so many gymnasia and palaestrae, the descriptions of Vitruvius are of only secondary importance, and it is needless to discuss the various reconstructions of his plans which the reader will find fully treated in all books of reference. It will be sufficient here to discuss briefly such of the various parts of the building mentioned by him as have not already been noticed.

---

[829] Overbeck, *Pompeii*, 4th Ed., p. 219.

The palaestra of Vitruvius is of the same type as that at Olympia, a square court surrounded by colonnades on to which the various rooms enter. On three sides the colonnades are single, and the rooms are provided with benches for the use of philosophers, rhetoricians, and men of letters, who can sit there and converse with one another, or lecture to their pupils. The colonnade on the fourth side, which faces south in the ideal palaestra, is double, and the rooms behind it are devoted to the needs of those who take exercise in the palaestra. These rooms are elaborations of the simple apodyterion and bathroom. In the centre is a large hall provided with seats called the ephebeion,[830] which probably served rather as a general club-room for the epheboi than as a dressing-room. For dressing and washing, full provision is made in the rooms to left and right.

To the right are the elaiothesion, and a series of rooms connected with the hot baths. The elaiothesion is the room where the oil was stored, and perhaps also where athletes and bathers oiled themselves. Oil was used not only before exercise, but both before and after the bath. A large supply was required, and, as has been already mentioned, there was no better way in which a gymnasiarchos could show his liberality than by providing oil for the use of the epheboi at his own expense. We even hear of cases where a sum of money was left to form an endowment for this purpose.[831] The oil was kept in amphorae or tanks. A picture of such a tank occurs on the funeral stele found at Prusa of one Diodorus, a gymnasiarchos, who, we may suppose, had celebrated his term of office by himself providing the oil (Figure 186). It is a large circular tank, somewhat resembling a font, supported on three elaborately wrought legs. On its side hang three ladles (ἀρυτῆρες), which were used for measuring out the oil. Each perhaps held a kyathos, a small liquid measure equal to about 1/12 of a pint. A Spartan inscription referring to some athletic contest, perhaps the Leonidaea, directs that the gymnasiarchos shall provide daily four kyathoi for each man, three for each ageneios, and two for each boy.

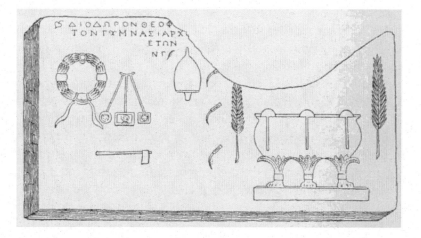

Figure 186. Stele of Diodorus. Prusa. (Imperial period.)

---

[830] For the sake of uniformity I have kept the Greek spelling of the names of different rooms instead of the Latin forms actually used in Vitruvius.

[831] For references to the numerous inscriptions connected with the provision of oil *vide* Dar.-Sagl., *s.vv.* "Gymnasiarchia," p. 1682, "Gymnasium," p. 1689.

Next to the elaiothesion comes the frigidarium, a term usually denoting the cold bath, but here apparently corresponding to the tepidarium of the Roman baths, a room kept at a moderate temperature, heated if necessary by a brazier, where bathers were oiled and scraped and massaged before or after the bath.[832] A passage separates this room from the propnigeion, a hot-air chamber connected with the furnace, and adjoining this is the large vaulted sweating-room (*concamerata sudatio*) which contains the hot-water bath (*calda lavatio*) and the hot-air bath (*laconicum*). It is curious to find one of the principal parts of those luxurious hot baths bearing a name which denotes its Spartan origin. Perhaps the Spartans employed this means of reducing weight in training. Exposure to the heat of the sun's rays was a recognized part of athletic training, and helped to give the skin the rich brown tone which the Greeks so greatly admired. Philostratus in the chapter in which he deals with this point ridicules the use of the sweating-bath (πυριατήριον) and rubbing with oil without a bath (ξηραλοιφεῖν) as parts of the unscientific system of training adopted by the Spartans, the object of which was merely to produce the power of endurance.[833]

On the other side of the ephebeion are three rooms, the korykeion, the konisterion, and the cold bath. The korykeion can hardly mean anything else than the room of the korykos, or punch-ball. Some writers have objected to this interpretation on the ground that the korykos was not of sufficient importance to have a room especially allotted to its use, and they have therefore suggested that the korykos referred to in this term was not a punch-ball but a basket or string bag, in which visitors to the palaestra brought their luncheon. The explanation is ingenious, but hardly satisfactory. The punch-ball, as we have seen, was known in the fifth century, and is represented on works of art. It was used by boxers and pankratiasts, and, as has been made clear in the first part of this work, boxing and the pankration were by far the most popular events, especially in Hellenistic and Roman times. Hence it is not evident that the korykos was of secondary importance. Moreover, it is a most significant coincidence that the chapter in Philostratus describing the korykos follows immediately on the chapter on the various kinds of konis, and in Vitruvius the korykeion and konisterion are next to one another.

If the above view is correct, the konisterion of Vitruvius is obviously the powdering-room, where athletes powdered themselves before exercise. This powder (κόνις) which they used must not be confused with the lye (κονία) which was used in washing to form a lather. Indeed, its effects were just the opposite; instead of forming a lather with the oil it helped to dry it, and thus counteracted the excessive slipperiness which the oil produced. Its effects on the body were regarded as no less beneficial than those of the oil. It closed the pores of the skin, checked excessive perspiration, and kept the body cool, thus protecting it from chills and rendering it less susceptible to fatigue.[834] There were also special sorts of powder credited

---

[832] In inscriptions we find mention of a special room called ἀλειπτήριον, which is sometimes used as synonymous with palaestra or gymnasium, just as οἱ ἀλειφόμεινοι is equivalent to οἱ γυμναζόμενοι. Vide *Hermes*, vii. 42; *C.I.G.* 2782, l. 25; *B.C.H.* xii. p. 326.

[833] Phil. *Gym.* 58. I am pleased to find the explanation of ξηραλοιφεῖν given above, which had occurred to me independently, anticipated and confirmed by Jüthner in his recent edition of Philostratus. The word occurs in a decree of Solon quoted by Aeschines. Galen defines it as rubbing with pure oil as opposed to χυτλοῦσθαι, rubbing with oil mixed with water. But this distinction can hardly be ascribed to Solon or to the Spartans. The latter appear to have used a primitive kind of sweating-bath in the open air (Strabo, iii. 3, 6), and the rubbing connected with such a bath might well be described as ξηραλοιφεῖν in contrast with the rubbing usual in other parts of Greece, which was associated with bathing or washing in water. Jüthner, pp. 181, 182.

[834] Lucian, *Anachars.* 2, 29.

with special virtues.[835] One of a clayey nature (πηλώδης) was supposed to be particularly cleansing; another resembling brick dust (ὀστρακώδης) produced perspiration in bodies which were over-dry; a third of bituminous character (ἀσφαλτώδης) warmed the skin. Two sorts, a black and a yellow, both of an earthy character, were especially prized for making the body supple and sleek, the yellow in particular imparting to the skin the glossiness which was the sign of good training. The powder was kept in baskets (σπυρίδες). Philostratus describes how it should be applied, thrown on with a supple wrist and the fingers slightly opened so as to fall like fine dust. But these are refinements for the few. The ordinary youth contented himself with the ordinary earth or sand. Lucian in his *Anacharsis* describes the youths in the court of the gymnasium picking up the sand and throwing it over one another. Sometimes it seems the earth was mixed with water into a sort of mud, and then the simplest plan was to roll in it. Under the Empire a special sort of ointment (κήρωμα) was used, and the term ceroma was applied to part of the palaestra; but the ceroma belongs to Rome, not to Greece.

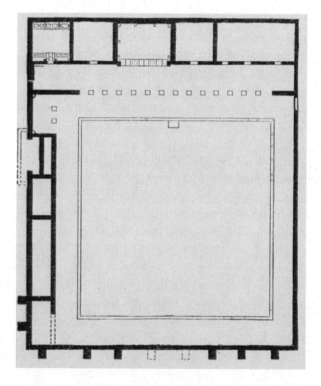

Figure 187. Plan of lower gymnasium, Priene. (*Priene*, Figure 271.)

The gymnasium of Vitruvius occupies an intermediate position between the true Greek gymnasium and the type which was prevalent under the Empire. The prominent feature of the latter is the elaboration of the buildings, especially of those connected with the warm baths. Indeed, as every bath had its court for exercise, it is sometimes difficult to decide whether some particular building was a bathing establishment or a gymnasium. The most familiar example of these later gymnasia is that at Ephesus; but as the plans of it are to be found in every text-book it is unnecessary to discuss it at length. It consists of a rectangular block of buildings some 80 by 100 metres, standing in the centre of a large enclosed court. Of this

---

[835] Philostr. *Gym.* 56.

outer enclosure very few traces are left, and the imaginary restoration of its courts commonly reproduced rests on no other foundation than the desire of early archaeologists to accomplish the absolutely impossible task of reproducing in it all the features of the Vitruvian gymnasium. The central block of buildings, however, which we may call the palaestra, is fairly well preserved, although the identification of most of the rooms is extremely doubtful. Its plan is almost exactly the reverse of the earlier palaestra. Round three sides of the interior, if not all four sides, there runs a vaulted colonnade (*cryptoporticus*), while the great central courtyard is almost entirely occupied by the hot baths and buildings connected with them, the ancient wrestling ring being reduced to a narrow strip along one side.

The two gymnasia excavated by the Germans at Priene[836] illustrate the earlier and the later types. The lower gymnasium (Figure 187) which adjoins the stadium near the south wall of the town appears to have been built between the years 130 and 120 B.C. It is very similar in plan to the Vitruvian palaestra, consisting of a court about 35 metres square surrounded by a colonnade. On the north side, facing south, the colonnade is double, as recommended by Vitruvius. On this side and on the west a number of rooms open into it; on the other two sides there are none. The entrance is in the centre of the west side, and is in the form of an Ionic propylaion. To the north of it is an exedra fitted with stone benches, and in the north-west corner is the Loutron or bathroom, which is in excellent preservation and extremely interesting. Along the north side is placed a row of stone troughs into which water flows from a row of lions' heads about 3 feet from the ground (Figure 188). On either side of the doorway in the south wall are remains of stone benches, in front of which are troughs in the floor, so that people could sit there and bathe their feet. There is no trace of any hot baths in this gymnasium. In the centre of the north wall is the ephebeion, a large lofty room, open in front save for two massive pillars. There are stone benches round the walls, the upper part of which was decorated by an elaborate arrangement of half pillars and architraves, on either side of a round arched niche containing a large statue of a draped man. The walls and pillars are covered with names of those who used the hall, usually in the form ὁ τόπος Νέστορος τοῦ Νέστορος, "the place of Nestor, the son of Nestor." Another large hall at the north-east corner has some traces of shelves, and may have been used as a place for undressing and leaving clothes. The northern side of the gymnasium is cut out of the slope of the hill, and was evidently two-storied. Above the ephebeion seems to have been a large square room cut still farther back into the hill. Perhaps there was an entrance from the street above into this upper story. These upper rooms may have served as class-rooms. In Hellenistic times the gymnasium was often a school where training was given for mind as well as body.

The upper gymnasium at Priene stood in the middle of the town. It was the older of the two, for we learn from an inscription that it already existed at the time when the lower gymnasium was being built. In its original plan it seems to have been very similar; but so many alterations have been made in it, and so much subsequent building has taken place on the site, that we cannot be certain of its details. What is certain is that in Roman times it was provided with hot baths. These baths are referred to in an interesting inscription detailing the services rendered by one Zosimus, who lived perhaps in the first century B.C. "From a desire that every young man might attend the gymnasium for the culture of his body, he had the furnace lighted all through the winter."[837]

---

[836] *Priene*, pp. 265 ff.
[837] *Priene Inschriften*, 112. The authors date the inscription after 84 B.C.

Figure 188. Bathroom in gymnasium at Priene. (*Priene*, Figure 278.)

Zosimus seems to have been an enthusiastic educationalist. Not only did he provide for the physical training and recreation of the young "a punch-ball, and hoops, and also balls and weapons," he also provided for the students a teacher in literature. He instituted competitions in all accomplishments of mind and body, and showed the most lavish generosity in furnishing oil and unguents in the gymnasium and in the bath, for all visitors to the festivals of Priene. Among the competitions which he instituted were a "squill fight" (σκιλλομαχία), and boxing in clothes (ἐν εἵμασι). For the former he gave a heifer as a prize, while each successful boxer received a golden fillet. The precise meaning of the "squill fight" is uncertain; it was perhaps some sort of ceremonial contest connected with the worship of Pan. The wearing of clothes in boxing was possibly a concession to the Roman prejudice against nudity.

Equally interesting are the extensive remains of the gymnasia at Pergamum recently excavated by the German archaeologists.[838] These remains belong mostly to the second century A.D., but many traces of earlier buildings survive. Built originally in the second century B.C., or earlier, under the early kings of Pergamum, the gymnasia underwent various modifications and reconstructions in the succeeding centuries, and may be regarded as typical of the gymnasia existing in Hellenistic and Roman times in these rich cities of the East, which, after the loss of Greek independence, became the chief centres of athletic activity. Like the gymnasium at Delphi, they bear witness to the ingenuity of the Greeks in adapting their buildings to the exigencies of the ground, while the magnitude of the work involved is a striking proof of the wealth of the Attalidae. They were built on a series of three terraces cut out of the steep face of the hill above the road which led up to the upper city. The lowest terrace at its western end is some twelve metres above the road, and the other terraces are about the same height above one another. The terraces are supported by numerous retaining walls, strengthened by buttresses and cross walls forming a series of compartments filled up

---

[838] *Ath. Mitth.* xxix. pp. 121 ff., xxxii. pp. 190 ff., xxxiii. pp. 327 ff.

with earth and rubble. Each terrace formed a separate gymnasium, devoted respectively to the use of boys, epheboi, and young men. It seems that there were originally four terraces, corresponding perhaps to the four gymnasia mentioned in an inscription of the time of Attalus III. (146 B.C.).[839] In the time of Tiberius, Pergamum possessed five gymnasia, and at a later period six, but the site of these additional gymnasia is unknown at present. Elder men, and foreigners too, had the privilege of using the gymnasia. An inscription in honour of Metrodorus,[840] a gymnasiarchos who lived at the close of the second century B.C., records that besides offering prizes for boys and epheboi he spent a considerable sum in providing "elder men" with "all things necessary for their health." The generosity of these gymnasiarchoi is frequently recorded in inscriptions. The office seems to have been held by the most distinguished citizens. The general direction of education was in the hands of four Paidonomoi.

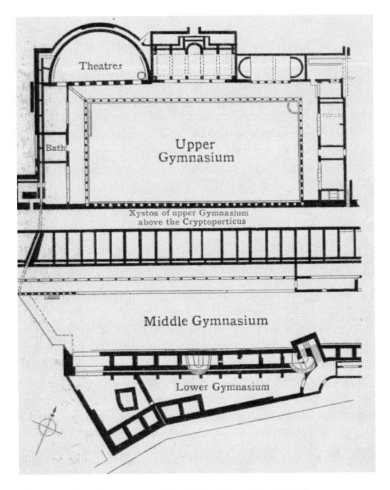

Figure 189. Plan of gymnasia at Pergamum. (Simplified from *Ath. Mitth.*)

---

[839] *Op. cit.* xxix. p. 158.
[840] *Op. cit.* xxxii. p. 273, 10.

The general arrangement of the buildings will be sufficiently clear from the accompanying plan (Figure 189). The lowest terrace, which was the gymnasium of the boys, consists of a narrow triangle, about 80 metres long and 25 broad at its widest point, divided into two parts by a wall. Its northern side is formed by the retaining wall of the middle terrace, the buttresses of which form niches containing long stone bases on which were placed statues and stelai. One of these stelai contains a list of boys who have passed out into the ranks of the epheboi. The middle terrace forms the gymnasium of the latter. It measures 150 by 36 metres, and contains at its eastern end a small Corinthian temple, the walls of which seem to have been covered with lists of epheboi. The northern side is formed by a long double colonnade, and beyond it to the east a series of rooms, one of which is an exedra open to the front. This double colonnade, which is two metres above the level of the court, seems to have replaced an earlier single colonnade.

The upper terrace is far the most extensive. It contains the gymnasium of the young men, and to the east the thermae or hot baths. This gymnasium is identified on account of its size with what is called in an inscription "The Panegyric Gymnasium," where doubtless public festivals and competitions were held. It consisted of an open court 36 by 74 metres, surrounded by a Corinthian colonnade of the time of Hadrian, which replaced an earlier Doric building. In front of the pillars are bases on which statues were placed. Numerous rooms opened on to the colonnade, those on the north being especially spacious. One of these, a large hall with an apse at either end, is named by the excavators the Imperial Hall, on account of an inscription which it has on the architrave, "To the Emperors and the Fatherland." The floor of the court is unpaved, but at the north-east corner is a small circular pavement which may mark the site of a washing-fountain. Along the south side of the gymnasium is a long corridor extending a considerable distance beyond the gymnasium on either side to a total length of 200 metres, which was obviously the xystos or running track, and behind this track are some thirty or more small rooms which may have served as lodgings for competitors. These rooms must have been a late addition; for in the original building there ran underneath the half-open corridor a second vaulted corridor, the windows of which must have been blocked by the later buildings. This covered running track (crypto-porticus) seems originally to have looked out on a fourth terrace dividing the upper and middle terraces, the northern half of which was subsequently occupied by the foundations of the rooms described, while the southern half was dug away so as to form part of the new double colonnade of the middle terrace. From this date the vaulted corridor became useless for athletic purposes. The eastern half of the terrace is occupied by the thermae, with the details of which we are not concerned.

Pending the final publication of the results of the excavations, it is useless to try to determine the uses of the various buildings. Some of these are mentioned in inscriptions. Diodorus, the son of Heroidas,[841] a distinguished citizen who filled the office of gymnasiarchos about the year 127 B.C., restored the gymnasium of the young men, and repaired the covered colonnade, περίπατος, surrounding the court. Further, finding that the konisterion or dusting-room was quite unworthy of the gymnasium, he built another at his own expense with a marble exedra in front, and rebuilt in marble the cold bath adjoining it. Metrodorus, whom we have already mentioned, placed several public basins (ληνοί) in the bathroom and improved the water-supply. He placed in the sphairisterion two public basins described as λουτῆρας, which seem to have been used to hold oil, and he also made suitable

---

[841] *Op. cit.* xxxii. p. 257, 8.

provision for the safe keeping of clothes. In recognition of these gifts his statue was erected in the paradromis of the gymnasium.

Athletics being an essential part of Greek education, the gymnasia were naturally under the control of the various magistrates charged with the education and discipline of the young. The titles and functions of these magistrates and also of the officials who formed the staff of the gymnasia varied considerably at different times and places, and the differences between them are therefore very ill-defined. To discuss them fully is impossible within the limits of this book, nor would it be profitable, most of the details which we know about them belonging to Hellenistic and Roman periods. I shall, therefore, confine myself to a brief general account of the most important of these officials, referring the reader for fuller details to special works dealing with the subject.

The gymnasiarchos[842] must have been originally the magistrate in charge of the gymnasium, and it can only be an accident that the earliest officials of this name whom we know of, the gymnasiarchoi of Athens in the fifth and fourth centuries, had no such general control of the gymnasia and were little more than lampadarchoi, responsible for the training of teams for the various torch-races which were one of the favourite amusements of the Athenian populace. Perhaps the reason for this narrow use of the term was that from the time of Solon, the discipline and education of the young, and consequently the supervision of the gymnasia, was in the hands of a board of ten called sophronistai, while at the close of the fourth century we find a single magistrate, the kosmetes, apparently taking over their functions and exercising supreme control over the epheboi. Hence there was at Athens no room for a special gymnasiarchos such as we find in many Greek states from the third century onwards, and such as must undoubtedly have existed at a much earlier date, if we may trust the obvious meaning of the title.

The gymnasiarchia at Athens was one of the regular leitourgiai or public services exacted from rich citizens for the benefit of the sovereign people. The duty of the gymnasiarchos in early days was to train a team of youths or of boys, or sometimes two teams, for one of the many torch-races. These teams represented the different tribes, each one of which selected a certain number of names of rich tribesmen and submitted them to the King Archon to make the final choice. The selected gymnasiarchos had to collect and train a team, find their instructors, provide oil and torches, and pay for all other expenses. If his team was successful he dedicated a memorial of the victory to the gods, and in return for all his trouble his name figured alone or at the head of his epheboi in the official list of victors, and in records of the victory. He doubtless exercised some authority over the epheboi in his tribe, or at least over those in his team, but had no general control over the public gymnasia.

In Hellenistic and Roman times the gymnasiarchos appears as a sort of minister of education, maintaining discipline among the young, exercising control over the gymnasia, and generally providing out of his own pocket many of the expenses incurred. Sometimes the gymnasiarchia is still a voluntary service. Such was the case at Athens, and in many other states especially in Asia Minor under the Empire. Among the distinguished men who undertook this office we find Marcus Antonius at Athens and at Alexandria, Tiberius and Germanicus at Salamis in Cyprus, Titus at Naples, Hadrian at Eleusis, and, needless to say,

---

[842] For the Gymnasiarchia *vide* the article by G. Glotz in Dar.-Sagl., where a full bibliography of the subject and copious references to inscriptions are given. For the Gymnasiarchia at Athens *vide* also Freeman's *Schools of Hellas*, p. 155.

Herodes Atticus at Athens. The office was usually held for a year, but was sometimes voluntarily renewed and even continued for life and handed down from father to son. We even hear of women serving as gymnasiarchoi.

Generally in the last three centuries B.C. the gymnasiarchia is not a leitourgia but a public magistracy. The gymnasiarchos is appointed by the assembly and holds office for one year. At Ceos[843] he has to be over thirty years of age. An inscription from Phintia[844] tells us that he has charge of the epheboi, the neoteroi, and generally of those who use the gymnasia, and of all business connected with the gymnasia. He is assisted by subordinates, sometimes by a hypogymnasiarchos, sometimes by a paidonomos who looks after the younger boys, sometimes by other gymnasiarchoi responsible for youths of different ages. At Teos[845] he is charged with the appointment and payment of the hoplomachos and the instructor in the use of the bow and the javelin. He is responsible for the discipline of the young, checks rioting or disorder among them, supervises their education in literature as well as athletics, above all he personally superintends the military training of the epheboi, and organises competitions to test their efficiency, He maintains discipline sometimes with the rod, sometimes by means of fines.

Whether the gymnasiarchia was a leitourgia or a public magistracy it involved considerable expense. The sums allotted by the state for the service of the gymnasia were often ludicrously inadequate, and the gymnasiarchos had usually to supplement them out of his own pocket; often indeed, disdaining to use the public money at all, he provided for all expenses himself. The chief expense was the provision of oil. Even in a small state like Iasos the supply of oil for a single gymnasium cost 450 denarii a month.[846] During the Empire the number of competitions, and consequently the expenses for oil and other purposes, were multiplied at an extraordinary rate. At Tauromenium the number of competitions rose from twenty-four a year in A.D. 69 to eighty-one in A.D. 92.[847] Sacrifices, processions, feasts, prizes afforded ample scope to the liberality of the gymnasiarchos, which often took a more permanent form in costly repairs and additions to the buildings of the gymnasia and baths.

The gymnasiarchoi described above must not be confused with the ephebic gymnasiarchoi at Athens, officers elected by the epheboi from their own ranks. The expenses of training were borne to a great extent by the epheboi themselves, and they seem, therefore, often to have elected as captains rich youths who were willing to provide wholly or in part for the public expenses, for any period from a month to a year.

The actual teachers were the paidotribes and the gymnastes. The paidotribes, as his name denotes, was properly the teacher of boys, who trained their bodies as the schoolmaster did their minds; the gymnastes was the trainer of athletes for athletic competitions. This is the original distinction between the two, and though in practice their functions often overlapped, and though in Plato the terms are practically synonymous, the original distinction never entirely disappeared.

The paidotribes existed long before the gymnastes, for athletic exercises formed part of the national education long before the demand for specialised athletic training arose. From the

---

[843] Ditt. *Syll.* 2nd Ed., 522.
[844] *I. G.* xiv. 256.
[845] Ditt. *Syll.* 2nd Ed., 523.
[846] Th. Reinach, *Rec. des études gr.* vi. p. 164, n.
[847] *I. G.* xiv. 422?

time of Solon education was in the hands of the paidotribes and the schoolmaster.[848] In most states education was voluntary, and the paidotribai were usually private teachers, who received fees for their services. In the fourth century the fee seems to have been a mina (about £4) for the whole course.[849] Many of the paidotribai had palaestrae of their own; failing that, they must have taken their pupils to the public palaestrae and gymnasia, which they must in any case have used for such exercises as required more space than could be found in the ordinary palaestra.[850] Besides those private paidotribai who took pupils from the age of seven upwards, there were others who were paid by the state to superintend the training of the epheboi. At Teos the paidotribes received in the third century 500 drachmae a year.[851] The training of the epheboi was practical and military and had no connexion with professional athletics, and the paidotribes regularly figures in the ephebic inscriptions down to the latest times.

Thus the paidotribes had charge of boys from their seventh to their twentieth year. But the training which he gave was not of course sufficient for those who aspired to win prizes in the great games. These required special natural abilities and special practice for the development of their natural abilities; and the special practice they required was supplied by the gymnastai.[852] There was, however, nothing to prevent a successful paidotribes if he possessed the necessary skill and knowledge employing them in training athletes. It was not everyone who could afford the services of a champion boxer or wrestler. Further, the paidotribes might also devote himself to medical gymnastics.[853] Herodicus of Selymbria, the founder of medical gymnastics, is said to be have been a paidotribes who suffered from ill-health, and discovered from personal experience the means of treating disease by diet and exercise. Hence the paidotribes might be also a gymnastes. But such training and such knowledge were really outside his sphere, which was that of the drill sergeant, whose duty it is to teach certain definite movements and exercises to boys of various ages. As athletics became more and more professional, and medical gymnastics developed, the difference between the paidotribes and the gymnastes increased, till in Galen and Philostratus we find the paidotribes subordinated to the gymnastes as the mere drill sergeant to the professor of physical culture. Galen compares them respectively to the cook and the physician.[854]

The gymnastes can hardly have come into existence much before the beginning of the fifth century.[855] His work consisted partly in perfecting his pupils in some particular form of athletics, partly in developing their strength and training them into proper condition. The earlier gymnastai, such as those whom we read of in Pindar and Bacchylides, devoted themselves chiefly to practical instruction. They were often themselves successful athletes, especially boxers and wrestlers, who having retired from competition took to teaching, and were doubtless richly rewarded by their patrons. Such was Melesias the trainer of thirty

---

[848] Aeschines *in Timarch.* 10; Aristoph. *Nub.* 973; *Eq.* 1238.
[849] Athen. 584 C.
[850] Antiphon. *Tetr.* ii.
[851] Ditt. *Syll.* 2nd Ed., 523.
[852] Isocr. Περὶ ἀντιδόσεως, 181-185.
[853] Plato, *Rep.* 406.
[854] Philostr. *Gym.* 14; Galen, *De San.* ii. 86, 90.
[855] The word first occurs in Xenophon, *Mem.* ii. 1, 20. But the fact that it does not occur in literature earlier is no proof that it was not in use; for the cognate words γυμνάζομαι and γυμνάσιον were in use at a much earlier date.

victors in wrestling and the pankration;[856] Iccus of Tarentum, a winner in the pentathlon at Olympia in Ol. 76, the most celebrated trainer of his day; Dromeus of Stymphalus and Pythagoras of Samos, to whom were attributed the introduction of a meat diet. These trainers, like other teachers, went wherever they could find a market. Menander of Athens trained Pytheas of Aegina to victory.[857] We cannot for a moment suppose that men like these descended to the work of the ordinary paidotribes, though, as I have suggested, the reverse must often have been the case. It was an age of science, and in the hands of gymnastai and paidotribai there arose in the middle of the fifth century a new science of gymnastic which aimed not at the performance of particular exercises but at the production of certain physical conditions (ἕξις),[858] especially the condition required for athletic success. Its professors in the fourth century are in ordinary speech called paidotribai, and Isocrates[859] describes it as a branch of the art of the paidotribes, undoubtedly because so many paidotribai professed it. The new science was closely allied to medicine. The trainer, like the doctor, required some knowledge of diet and the effects on the body of different kinds of food;[860] he required, too, some knowledge of the body itself, and the effect on it of various exercises; he required, too, to be a judge of the human animal, and to be able to tell in what form of athletics any individual had most chance of excelling, and what particular form of training he required.[861] The ideal gymnastes, according to Aristotle,[862] should know what is the ideally best condition for the ideally best man, what is the best for the average man, and what is the best for any particular man. Unfortunately the art of the gymnastes was almost from the first connected with the training of professional athletes, and the condition which they aimed at was that artificial condition required for success in some particular form of athletics. At the same time medical gymnastics was corrupted by the quackery which from the fourth century was rampant in all departments of knowledge.[863]

There were also other officials connected with the gymnasia. The xystarches was the president of one of those guilds of professional athletes which we find under the Empire. The aleiptes was properly the person who oiled and rubbed people who exercised in the gymnasia. This was part of the work of the paidotribes or the gymnastes, and it is doubtful whether there were special officials for the purpose. In Aristotle aleiptes is merely another name for gymnastes.[864] In Roman times we find slaves (*unctores*) performing this work in the public baths, and possibly these existed in the Greek gymnasia. Subordinate officials are also mentioned, the hypopaidotribes or assistant, and others who had charge of the palaestra and its contents, variously described as palaistrophylax, epimeletes, epistates. Besides these there were in Hellenistic times special instructors for special exercises, the sphairistes who taught

---

[856] Pindar, *Ol.* viii.; *Nem.* iv., vi.
[857] Pindar, *Nem.* v.
[858] Xenophon, *Mem. l.c.*; Aristotle, *Pol.* 1338 b.
[859] *l.c.*
[860] Plato, *Protag.* 313 E.
[861] Plato, *De virtute*, 378 E.; *Amator.* 134 E.
[862] *Pol.* 1288 b.
[863] The account of the paidotribes and gymnastes was written before I had read Jüthner's learned discussion of the subject in the introduction to his *Philostratus*, but I see no reason to alter my views. Jüthner regards the gymnastes as from the first "the professor of physical culture," but himself inadvertently applies the term to Pindar's Melesias (p. 22), who was merely a teacher of boxing. Further Jüthner seems to me vastly to overrate the value of the medical gymnastics and the science of health based on the teaching of Herodicus of Selymbria.
[864] *Nic. Eth.* ii. 6, 7.

ball-play, the akontistes and toxotes who gave instruction in the use of the javelin and the bow, and the hoplomachos who gave lessons in the use of arms.

Of the special training prescribed for athletes little is known beyond a few details as to diet which have been noticed in the earlier chapters of this book, and a few other details noticed under the special exercises with which they are connected. There were manuals of athletic training, but all are lost except the late treatise by Philostratus to which we have so often referred. With regard to athletics as a branch of education we are somewhat better informed, and it is instructive to compare the physical training given in the fifth and fourth centuries B.C. with the system described by Galen in the second century A.D.

The training given in the earlier period was based on those athletic exercises which at all times formed the programme of Greek athletic meetings. To these we may add ball-play, which is enumerated by Plautus among the exercises which formed a young Greek's training till the age of twenty.[865] These exercises were taught progressively, at first the simple movements or positions (σχήματα) separately, then combinations of these movements which involved more exertion.[866] Many of these movements admitted of being taught to classes as drill to the accompaniment of music. Such drill, especially with halteres, is sometimes represented on vases.[867] The various holds and throws of wrestling were taught in this way, and we possess on the Oxyrhynchus papyrus, to which we have already referred, a portion of such a wrestling lesson.[868] Dances could be utilised in the same way: the movements of wrestling were imitated in a dance performed by Spartan boys called the gymnopaidike[869] just as the movements of war were imitated in the Pyrrhic and other war dances. In the fourth century particular attention was given to exercises of a military character, the use of weapons of all sorts, and riding, but these exercises must have been confined chiefly to older pupils of the age of the epheboi. Proficiency in all the various exercises taught was encouraged by numerous festivals and local competitions where prizes were offered for boys of various ages. The training of teams for the torch-races and choirs for dancing competitions, though not formally a part of the education given by the paidotribes, must have afforded those who took part in them a considerable amount of healthy and agreeable exercise.

Life in this period was spent mostly in the open air, and the formal training of the palaestra was supplemented by hunting, swimming, rowing, and other forms of exercise. Cities in Greece were small, and hunting was as a rule easily obtainable. In Attica, owing to the increase of population and the spread of cultivation, game was scarce, and sport had therefore declined in Xenophon's time; but the red-figured vases prove its popularity in the fifth century. Swimming and diving were common recreations. Every Greek could swim, and not to know how to swim was as much a sign of an uneducated person as ignorance of letters.[870] Rowing must also have been a universal accomplishment, at least among the Greeks who lived near the sea; but we know nothing of the teaching of rowing or swimming. Probably the Greek boy taught himself to swim and row or picked it up from his fellows.

---

[865] *Bacch.* iii. 3, 24.
[866] Isocrates, *l.c.*
[867] Cp. Figure 65.
[868] *Supra*, p. 374.
[869] Athen. 631 B.
[870] Plato, *Legg.* 689 D.

Here too the element of competition came in. At Hermione we hear of a competition in diving (or perhaps swimming[871]), and also boat-races.[872] We have seen that boat-racing took place at the Isthmia and at various Athenian festivals. There was also a boat-race at the Actian festival in the time of Augustus; and Professor Percy Gardner has shown that there is a possible reference to this contest on the coins of Corcyra and Nicopolis, on which a victorious galley is sometimes represented. The coins suggest a race between galleys such as that described in the *Aeneid*, but the boats used in the Athenian races were probably not triremes, but small boats with a single bank of oars, tender-boats (ὑπηρετικά) such as always accompanied a fleet. A boat of this description is depicted on a stele in the Museum of Athens of Hellenistic or Roman period (Figure 190). It is a long narrow boat with a pointed beak in front, and a curved aplustre at the stern, and in it there sit eight oarsmen. There is no sign of the oars. The men are naked and are sitting at ease, and bow, who is the smallest of the crew, holds a palm-branch. The number eight is of course a pure accident. There is no cox in the boat, but on the upper part of the stele are three figures standing, a draped figure in the centre, probably the gymnasiarchos who fitted out and trained the crew, on his left a naked youth bearing a palm, on his right a youth in a chlamys crowning the man in the centre. These two Professor Gardner identifies with the stroke and cox of the victorious crew.

Figure 190. Stele representing victorious crew. Athens. (Hellenistic period?)

When we come to Galen, we seem to pass from the free and open atmosphere of the playing-field and the country into the artificial air of the town gymnasium. The simple exercises of the earlier period, so inseparably bound up with the lives and habits of the people, have given place to a scientific system of physical training based on the teaching of generations of gymnastai. In his treatise on Health[873] he describes at length the exercises suited for youths between the ages of fourteen and twenty-one. He distinguishes exercises for the legs, the arms, and the trunk. He further classifies exercises into those which exert the muscles and give them tone without violent movement (τὰ εὔτονα), quick movements which promote activity (τὰ τάχεα), and violent exercises (τὰ σφόδρα). As examples of the first class he mentions digging, driving, carrying heavy weights, rope-climbing, and exercises of resistance such as holding the arms extended while another person tries to pull them down.

---

[871] Paus. ii. 35, 1.
[872] *Vide* three papers in the *J.H.S.* by Prof. Percy Gardner, vol. ii. p. 90 and p. 315, vol. xi. p. 146.
[873] *De San. Tu.* ii. 8-11. Oribasius, vi. 14.

Among quick exercises he enumerates running, sparring, the use of the korykos or punch-ball, ball-play, rolling on the ground "either alone or with others," an exercise which seems to resemble "tackling" at football, and a variety of leg and arm movements. Many of these movements are well known in our modern physical drill. That known as ἐκπλεθρίζειν is the familiar running figure in which the runner runs in an ever-decreasing circle till he comes to the centre. Another exercise (πιτυλίζειν) consisted in marching on the toes, and at the same time swinging the arms. The leg exercises include jumping up and down, and raising the legs alternately backwards and forwards. The arm exercises are the usual dumb-bell movements performed rapidly without dumb-bells, with the hands either open or clenched. Finally, any of the exercises of the first class may become violent if practised rapidly and without interruption, and quick exercises become so if practised with weights or in heavy armour. Besides prescribing exercises Galen lays down elaborate rules for the time of exercise, and for massage both before and after exercise. The actual teaching of these exercises must have been in the hands of paidotribai, but the direction of the training and the arrangement of the exercises is, according to Galen, the work of the gymnastes, who alone has a scientific knowledge of physical training.

The details of this training are full of interest to the student of education and hygiene. There is, indeed, little in our modern systems of physical education which he will not find anticipated in Greek medical writings. We do not know how far Galen's principles were ever carried into practice, though we may suspect that it was only in the case of individuals, and that they had little influence on the nation. But of this we may be certain, that physical training did not, and could not, do for Galen's contemporaries what athletics had done for their ancestors. Nor can physical training ever take the place of our own games. For it lacks the element of competition and cannot inspire. There is no antagonism between the two. Both are valuable, but their spheres are different. Physical training is a branch of education—a most important branch, and one hitherto shamefully neglected in England—and it must therefore be carried out under discipline: it is a matter of compulsion. Athletics and games are, or ought to be, a matter of free choice, and compulsion tends to kill the spirit of joy which is their essence. Physical training develops the body and imparts habits of discipline, but it cannot impart those still higher qualities, courage, endurance, self-control, courtesy, qualities which are developed by our own games, or by such manly sports as boxing and wrestling when conducted in the true spirit of friendly rivalry: it cannot teach boys "to play the game" in the battle of life; it could never have inspired the poetry of Pindar, or the art of Myron.

BIBLIOGRAPHY

N.B.—No references are given to articles or sections on athletics or athletic festivals in the following books of reference:—

Baumeister, A. Denkmäler des klassischen Altertums.
Daremberg et Saglio. Dictionnaire des antiquités.
Frazer, J. G. Pausanias.
Iwan von Müller. Handbuch der klassischen Altertumswissenschaft.
Pauly-Wissowa. Real-Encyclopädie.
Schreiber-Anderson. Atlas of Classical Antiquities.
Smith, W. Dictionary of Antiquities.
etc. etc.

ATHLETIC FESTIVALS

Olympia

General

Bötticher, A. *Olympia: das Fest und seine Stätte.* 2nd edition. Berlin, 1866. [*Olympia: the festival and its site*]
Flash, A. *Olympia, in Baumeister's Denkmäler,* ii. p. 1053. Munich and Leipsic, 1887.
Gardner, P. *Olympia, in New Chapters in Greek History.* London, 1892. On the Ancient Olympic Games, in the Official Handbook of the Olympic Games. London, 1908.
Hachtmann, K. *Olympia u. seine Festspiele.* Gütersloh, 1899. [*Olympia and his festival*]
Krause, J. H. *Olympia.* Vienna, 1838.
Leonardos, B. *Ὀλυμπία.* Athens, 1901.
Olympia. *Die Ergebnisse der von dem deutschen Reich veranstalteten Ausgrabung.* Edd. E. Curtius and F. Adler. Berlin, 1892-1897. [*The results of the excavation organized by the German Reich*]
S. P. Lambros and N. G. *Politis. Οἱ Ὀλυμπιακοὶ ἀγῶνες.* Athens, 1896. [*Political. The Olympic Games*]

West, G. A *Dissertation on the Olympick Games*, in his translation of The Odes of Pindar. London, 1753.

Chronology and Lists of Victors

Diehl, C. Olympische Sieger. *Hermes*, xxxvi. p. 71. [*Olympic winner. Hermes*]
Förster, H. *Sieger in den olympischen Spielen*. 2 parts. Zwickau, 1891, 1892. [*Winner in the Olympic Games*]
Guttmann, W. *De Olympionicis apud Minae Philostratum*. Breslau, 1865. [*Threats at the Olympic Philostratus*]
Hyde, W. *De Olympionicarum statuis a Pausania commemoratis*. Halle, 1903. [*The Olympic establish a report by Pausanias*]
Körte, A. Die Entstehung der Olympionikenliste. *Hermes*, xxxix. p. 224. [*The emergence of the Olympics list. Hermes*]
Mahaffy, J. P. On the Authenticity of the Olympic Register. *J.H.S.* ii. 164.
Robert, C. Die Ordnung der olympischen Spiele und die Sieger der 75-83 Olympiade. *Hermes*, xxxv., 1900. p. 141. [*The order of the Olympic Games and the winners of the 75-83 Olympiad. Hermes*]
S. Julii Africani Ὀλυμπιάδων ἀναγραφή (Eusebii Chronic. (Schoene), i. 193) rec. J. Rutgers. Leyden, 1862. [*Olympiad Recording*]

Miscellaneous

Dissen, L. *De ordine certaminum Olympicorum*. Göttingen, 1841. [*The order of the conflict Olymick*]
Dörfeld, W. Alter des Heiligtums von Olympia. *Ath. Mitth.* xxxi. p. 205. Tiryns, Olympia, Pylos. *Ib*. xxxii. p. 1. Pisa bei Olympia. *Ib*. xxxiii. p. 318. Olympia in prähistorischer Zeit. *Ib*. p. 185.
Dyer, L. Olympian Treasuries and Treasuries in General. *J.H.S.* xxv. p. 294. Details of Olympian Treasuries. *Ib*. xxvi. p. 46. The Olympian Theatron and the Battle of Olympia. *Ib*. xxviii. p. 250. The Olympian Council-House and Council. *Harvard Studies in Classical Philology*, xix. p. 1.
Förster, H. *De Hellanodicis Olympicis*. Leipsic, 1879.
Hermann, G. *De Hippodromo Olympico*. Leipsic, 1839.
Holwerda, J. Olympische Studien. *Arch. Zeit.*, 1880, pp. 169-172. (1) Die Folgenreihe der Festspiele. (2) Ἔφεδρος and ἐφεδρεία. [Olympic studies.]
Mie, F. *Quaestiones agonisticae, imprimis ad Olympia pertinentes*. Rostock, 1888. [*Agonisticae issues, especially relevant for the Olympics*]
Mommsen, A. *Über die Zeit der Olympien*. Leipsic, 1891. [About the time of the Olympics]
Puchstein, O. Altar des olympischen Zeus. *Jahrb.*, 1896, p. 53. [Altar of the Olympian Zeus]
Robert, C. Sosipolis in Olympia. *Ath. Mitth.*, xviii. p. 37.
Scherer, C. *De Olympionicarum statuis*. Göttingen, 1885. [*The Olympic statues*]
Schöne, H. Neue Angaben über den Hippodrom zu Olympia. *Jahrb.*, 1897, p. 150. [New information about the Hippodrome at Olympia]

Weniger, L. Das Hoch Fest des Zeus in Olympia. *Klio*, 1904, p. 125; 1905, pp. 1, 184. Olympische Forschungen. *Ib.*, 1906, pp. 1, 259; 1907, p. 145; 1909, p. 291. [*The high feast of Zeus in Olympia*]

Wernicke, K. Olympische Beiträge. *Jahrb.*, 1894, pp. 88, 127, 191; 1897, p. 169. (1) Altäre, (2) Heraion, (3) Proedria u. Hellanodikeon, (4) Gymnasien, (5) Hippodrom, (6) Ostgiebel des Zeustempels. [*Olympic contributions*]

The Panhellenic Festivals

Bury, J. B. Pindar. Nemean Odes. (*Vide* Appendix.) London, 1890.

Corsini, E. *Dissertationes IV. agonisticae quibus Olympiorum, Pythiorum, Nemeorum atque Isthmiorum tempus inquiritur ac demonstratur.* Florence, 1747. [*Et 4. agonisticae to whom the Olympian, the Pythian, Nemean Games and the Isthmian games is shown, and the time for so doing*]

Droysen, J. G. Die Festzeit der Nemeen. *Hermes*, xiv., 1879, p. 1. [*The festive season of the Nemeen*]

Homolle, T. *Les Fouilles de Delphes.* Paris, *in progress.* [*The excavations of Delphi*]

Jebb, Sir Richard C. Bacchylides. (*Vide* Introduction.) Cambridge, 1905.

Krause, J. H. *Die Pythien, Nemeen und Isthmien.* Leipsic, 1841. [*The Pythias, Nemeen and Isthmien*]

Monceaux, P. Fouilles et recherches archéologiques au sanctuaire des jeux isthmiques. *Gazette archéologique*, 1884, ix. pp. 273-285, 352-365; 1885, x. pp. 205-214, 402-412. [*Excavations and archaeological research at the shrine of the isthmic games. Archaeological Gazette*]

Pomtow. *Studien zu den Weihgeschenken und der Topographie von Delphi.* Ath. Mitth. xxxi. p. 437. [*Studies on the dedications and topography of Delphi*]

Unger, G. T. Die Zeit der nemeischen Spiele. *Philologus*, xxxiv., 1874, pp. 50-64. Die Winter Nemeen. *Ib.* xxxvii., 1877, pp. 524-566. Die Isthmien und Hyacinthien. *Ib.* xxxvii., 1877, p. 1. [*The time of the Nemean Games*]

Villoison. Recherches historiques sur les jeux néméens. (*Hist. de l'Acad. des Inscr. et Belles-Lettres*, xxxviii. p. 29.) [Historical research on nemean games. (*History of the Academy of Inscriptions and Belles-Lettres*)]

The Panathenaea

Böckh, A. *De ludis Panathenaicis.* Berlin, 1832. [*The sports panathenaicon*]

Michaelis, A. *Der Parthenon.* Leipsic, 1871. [*The Parthenon*]

Mommsen, A. *Feste der Stadt Athen.* Leipsic, 1898. [*Festivals of the city of Athens*]

Smith, A. H. *Sculptures of the Parthenon* (Part of British Museum Catalogue of Sculpture).

GREEK ATHLETICS

General

Daremberg, Ch. *Philostrate. Traité sur la gynmastique.* Paris, 1858. [*Philostratus. Treatise on gymnastics*]

Fabri, P. *Agonisticon.* Lugduni, 1592.

Grasberger, L. *Erziehung und Unterricht im klassischen Altertum.* Würzburg, 1864. [*Education in Classical Antiquity.*]

Jaeger, O. *Die Gymnastik der Hellenen.* Stuttgart, 1878. [*The Gymnastics of the Hellenes*]

Jüthner, Julius. *Philostratos über Gymnastik.* Leipsic and Berlin, 1909. [*Philostratos about gymnastics*]

Kayser, G. L. *Philostratei libri de Gymnastica quae supersunt.* Heidelberg, 1840. Flavii Philostrati opera. Leipsic, 1870. [*Philostratos books that are left out of the gymnast*]

Krause, J. H. *Die Gymnastik und Agonistik der Hellenen.* Leipsic, 1841. [*The gymnastics and agonistic Hellenes*]

Mercurialis. *De arte gymnastica.* Venetiis, 1573. [*Gymnastic art*]

Meursii, J. *De ludis Graecorum.* Elzevir, 1662. [*From the games*]

Paciaudi, P. M. *De athletarum κυβιστήσει in palaestra Graecorum.* Rome, 1756. [*On the athletic Greek athletes κυβιστήσει*]

Philostratus. For full Bibliography of the *Gymnastike*, *vide* Jüthner's edition, p. 84.

Special

Burette, M. In *Mémoires de l'Académie des Inscriptions et Belles-Lettres,* 1736. *Mémoire pour servir à l'histoire de la sphéristique ou de la paume des anciens,* i. p. 153. *Mémoires pour servir à l'histoire des athlètes,* i. pp. 211, 237, 258. *Mémoire pour servir à l'histoire de la lutte des anciens,* iii. p. 228. *Mémoire pour servir à l'histoire du pugilat des anciens,* iii. p. 255. *Mémoire pour servir à l'histoire de la course,* iii. p. 280. *Dissertation sur ce qu'on appelle pentathle,* iii. p. 318. *Dissertation sur l'exercice du disque ou palet,* iii. p. 330. [*Memoirs of the Academy of Inscriptions and Fine Letters,* 1736. *Memory for use in the history of the spherical or the palm of the ancients,* i. p. 153. *Memories for the Use of Athlete History,* i. pp. 211, 237, 258. *Memory to serve in the history of the struggle of the ancients,* iii. p. 228. *Memory for the History of the Boxing of the Ancients,* iii. p. 255. *Memory for the Use of Race History,* iii. p. 280. *Dissertation on the so-called pentathle,* iii. p. 318. *Dissertation on disc or pallet exercise,* iii. p. 330.]

Gardiner, E. N. The Method of deciding the Pentathlon. *J.H.S.* xxiii. p. 54. Notes on the Greek Foot-race. *Ib.* xxiii. p. 261. Phayllus and his Record Jump. *Ib.* xxiv. p. 70. Further Notes on the Greek Jump. *Ib.* xxiv. p. 179. Wrestling, I., II. *Ib.* xxv. pp. 14, 263. The Pankration and Wrestling. *Ib.* xxvi. p. 4. Throwing the Diskos. *Ib.* xxvii. p. 1. Throwing the Javelin. *Ib.* xxvii. p. 249.

Jüthner, Julius. *Antike Turngeräthe.* (Halteres, Diskos, Akontion, Himantes.) Vienna, 1896. Also in Pauly-Wissowa, *passim.* [*Antique gym equipment*]

Boxing

Fabretti. *Columna Trajani*, p. 260. Rome, 1683. [*Trajan's column*]
Frost, K. T. Greek Boxing. *J.H.S.* xxvi. p. 213.
Hülsen. Il Cesto dei pugili antiqui. *Röm. Mitth.* iv. 175. [*The Basket of anti-boxers*]

The Diskos

Chryssaphis, J. E. Ἡ Ἑλληνικὴ δισκοβολία in *Bulletin du comité des jeux olympiques*, No. 3, p. 59. Athens, 1906. [*Bulletin of the Olympic Games Committee*]
Kietz, G. Der Diskoswurf bei der Griechen. *Agonistische Studien*, i. Munich, 1892. [*The discos throw at the Greeks. Agonistic studies*]
Pernice, E. Zum Diskoswurf. *Jahrb.*, 1908, p. 95.
E. R. The Diskos Thrower. *Bulletin of the Metropolitan Museum of Art, New York*, 1908, iii. 2, p. 31.
Robertson, G. S. On Throwing the Discus, in the *Official Handbook of the Olympic Games*. London, 1908.
Six. Vases polychromes sur fond noir. Appendice au sujet du discobole. *Gaz. Arch.*, 1888, 291.

The Hippodrome, etc.

Helbig, W. *Les Hippeis athéniens*. Paris, 1902.
Martin, A. *Les Cavaliers athéniens*. Paris, 1886. Also in Dar.-Sagl., *s.v.* Hippodrome.
Pollack, E. *Hippodromica.* Leipsic, 1890.

The Javelin and the Amentum

Bertrand, A. L'Amentum et la cateia sur line plaque de ceinture en bronze. *Revue arch.*, 1884, 104 f. [*L'Amentum and the cata on a bronze belt plate.*]
Köchly. *Opuscula*, ii. 351 ff.
Krause, F. Schleudervorrichtungen für Wurfwaffen. *Internationales Archiv*. Leyden, 1902, pp. 121 ff. [*Launcher for throwing weapons. International Archive*]
Mérimée, P. *Revue arch.*, 1860, 2nd Ed., 210 f.

The Jump

Küppers. *Arch. Anz.*, 1900, 104 ff.
Pinder, E. *Arch. Anz.*, 1864, 230 f.
Roulez, M. *Mémoire sur une coupe de Vulci*. Brussels, 1842. [*Memory on a cut of Vulci*]

The Race in Armour

Hauser. Zur Tübinger Bronze, i., ii. *Jahrb.* 2, 1887, p. 95; 1895, p. 182. [*To Tübingen bronze*]
De Ridder, A. L'Hoplitodrome de Tübingen. *B.C.H.*, 1897, p. 211.

Wrestling Groups

Förster. *Jahrb.*, 1898, p. 178; 1901, pp. 49-51.
Perclüzet. *Rev. arch.*, 1903, sér. 1, pp. 396-397.

The Pentathlon

Blümner. In *Baumeister's Denkmäler*, i. p. 1592.
Böckh, A. Adnotationes criticae, in his edition of Pindar, 1811. Über die kritische Behandlung der pindarischen Gedichte. *Abhandlungen d. Berl. Akad.*, 1822-1823, p. 391. [On the Critical Treatment of Pindaric Poems]
Faber, Martin. Zum Fünfkampf der Hellenen. *Philologus*, 1891 (L), p. 469. [The Pentathlon of the Hellenes]
Fedde, F. *Der Fünfkampf der Hellenen.* Breslau, 1888. Über den Fünfkampf d. Hell. Leipsic, 1889. [*The Pentathlon of the Hellenes.*]
Fennell, C. A. M. *The Pentathlon*, in his edition of Pindar's Nemean and Isthmian Odes. Cambridge Press, 1883.
Gardner, P. The Pentathlon. *J.H.S.* i. p. 210.
Haggenmüller. Die *Aufeinanderfolge der Kämpfe im Pentathlon.* Berlin, 1892. [*Sequence of Fights in the Pentathlon*]
Heinrich, K. E. *Über das Pentathlon der Griechen.* Würzburg, 1892. [*About the Pentathlon of the Greeks*]
Hermann, G. *Commentationes de metris Pindari.* Ed. Heyne, iii. 225. De Sogenis Aeginetae victoria quinquertii. Lips., 1822. [*Perspectives on Pindar meters.*]
Holwerda. Zum Pentathlon. *Arch. Zeit.*, 1881, pp. 205-216.
Legrand, Ph. E. In *Dar.-Sagl.*, *s.v.* Quinquertium. 1907.
Marquardt, H. *Zum Pentathlon der Griechen.* Güstrow, 1886. [*To the Pentathlon of the Greeks*]
Myers, E. The Pentathlon. *J.H.S.* ii. p. 217.
Philipp, G. F. *De Pentathlo.* Berlin, 1827.
Pinder, E. *Über den Fünfkampf der Hellenen.* Berlin, 1867. [*About the Pentathlon of the Hellenes.*]

Miscellaneous

Basiades, C. *De vet. Graecorum gymnastice.* Berlin, 1858.
Becker, W. A. *Charikles.* Leipsic, 1840.
Bintz, J. *Die Gymnastike d. Hellenen.* Gütersloh, 1878.
Egger, J. B. *Begriff der Gymnastik bei den alten Philosophen und Medizinern.* Freiburg (Switz.), 1903. [*Term of gymnastics among the ancient philosophers and medics*]
Freeman, K. J. *Schools of Hellas.* Macmillan & Co., 1907.
Gardner, P. Boat-races among the Greeks. *J.H.S.*, ii. p. 90. Boat-races at Athens. *Ib.* p. 315. A Stele commemorating a Victory in a Boat-race. *Ib.* xi. p. 146.
Girard, P. *L'Éducation athénienne.* Paris, 1889. [*Athenian Education*]

Gutch, C. *The Greek Games*. Cambridge, 1900.

Joubert, L. *De gymnasiis et generibus exercitationum apud antiquos*. Sallengre Thes., i. [*The types of exercise and sports centers in the ancient*]

Jüthner, J. *Gymnastisches in Philostrat's Eikones*. Eranos Vindob. p. 310. Vienna, 1893. [*Gymnastics in Philostratus Icons*]

Lindemann, F. *De utilitate artis gymnasticae apud Graecos*. Zitt., 1841. [*The utility of art gymnastics in Greece.*]

Mie, F. Über die διὰ πάντων καὶ ὁ ἐπινίκιος in agonistischen Inschriften. *Ath. Mitth.* xxxiv. p. 1.

Petersen, Chr. *Das Gymnasium der Griechen*. Hamburg, 1858. [*The Gymnasium of the Greeks*]

Polke. *Artis gymnasticae apud Graecos origo atque indoles*. Gleiw., 1851. [*Among the Greeks, and the nature of the origin of the art of gymnastics*]

Richter, W. *Die Spiele der Griechen und Römer*. Leipsic, 1840. [*The games of the Greeks and Romans.*]

Stallbaum, G. *De vet. gymnasiorum disciplina et institutione*. Leipsic, 1856, 1858. [*The vet. schools for training and education*]

Tarbell, F. B. The Palm of Victory. *Classical Philology*, iii. p. 264.

Wilkins, A. S. *Roman Education*. Cambridge Press, 1905.

P. Wolters. *Zu griechischen Agonen*. Würzburg, 1901. [*To Greek agones*]

ATHLETIC ART

N.B.—The following section lays no claim to completeness. The references are as a rule too scattered and fragmentary to be included in a bibliography. Much information will be found in all histories and handbooks of athletic art.

Coins (for Equestrian Types)

Evans, A. *The Horsemen of Tarentum*. London, 1889.

Hill, G. F. *Historical Greek Coins*. London, 1906.

Mosaics

Lucas, Hans. Athleten-Typen. *Jahrb.* xix., 1904, pp. 127-136.

Secchi, P. *Musaico antoniniano*. [*Antoninian mosaic*]

Sculpture

Furtwängler, A. *Die Bedeutung der Gymnastik in der griechischen Kunst*. Leipsic, 1905. [*The importance of gymnastics in Greek art*]

Gardner, P. The Apoxyomenos of Lysippus. *J.H.S.* xxv. p. 234.
Kalkmann, A. Die Statue von Subiaco. *Jahrb.*, 1895, p. 46.
Pater, Walter. *The Age of Athletic Prizemen*, in Greek Studies. London, 1895.
Waldstein, C. Pythagoras of Rhegium and the Early Athletic Statues. *J.H.S.* i. p. 168; ii. p. 332.

Vases

References to the most important Athletic vases will be found in our list of illustrations. The following list is confined to Panathenaic vases.

Böckh, A. *De vasorum Panathenaicorum generibus*. Berlin, 1831. [*The types of vessels panathenaicon*]
Dickins, G. Panathenaic Amphorae found at Sparta. *B.S.A.* xiii. p. 150.
Heermance, T. W. Fragment of dated Panathenaic Amphora. *Amer. Journ. Archaeology*, 1896, p. 331.
Heinze, F. *Eine panathenäische Amphore des akademischen Kunstmuseums zu Bonn*. Bonner Studien R. Kekulé gewidmet. Berlin, 1890, p. 240. [*A panathenaic amphora of the academic art museum in Bonn*. Bonn studies dedicated to R. Kekulé]
Hoppin, J. C. A Panathenaic Amphora. *Amer. Journ. Archaeology*, 1906, p. 385.
Pottier, E. Amphora panathénaïque. *B.C.H.* vi. p. 168.
Robinson, D. M. Fragment of Panathenaic Amphora. *Amer. Journ. of Philology*, 1908, p. 47.
Smith, Sir C. Panathenaic Amphorae. *B.S.A.* iii. p. 182.
Stephani. *Compte rendu*, 1876, p. 18.
Tarbell, F. B. Fragment of a dated Panathenaic Amphora. *Cl. Review*, 1900, p. 474.
Walters, H. B. *History of Ancient Pottery*, ii. p. 388.
Witte, J. de. *Annali dell' Instituto*, 1877, p. 294; 1878, p. 276. [*Annals of the Institute*]

INDEX

A

Achaeans, 7, 9, 10, 13, 14, 17, 22, 25, 26, 27, 36, 105, 141, 150
acrobats, 20, 164
Actia, 111
Adriania, 118
Aeginetan pediments, 59
Aezani, 180
Agias, ix, 80, 81, 95, 141
Aglaus of Athens, 185
Agonothetes, 97, 149, 163, 173
Aiantea, 154
Alcibiades, 69, 84, 85, 136, 151, 314, 323
Alexander, 5, 21, 29, 31, 52, 82, 83, 96, 98, 99, 100, 101, 102, 109, 118, 119, 211, 236, 345
Alexander the Great, 211, 345
Alexandria, xii, 97, 101, 104, 108, 112, 114, 116, 117, 118, 122, 152, 161, 261, 262, 303, 355
Alexandrian victories, 101
Alexandrini, 115
altar of Zeus, 27, 35, 45, 76, 116, 134
Altis wall, 112
amentum, xi, 236, 237, 238, 239, 240, 242, 243, 245, 246, 247, 337, 367
Amentum, 367
Amphiaraus vase, ix, 20, 21, 181, 270, 328, 331
Anaxilas of Rhegium, 136, 327
Anolympiads, 30
Antioch, 111, 112
Antiochus, 92, 97, 104, 111, 161
Antiphon, 235, 247, 334, 357
Anystis, 118
aphesis, xiii, 322, 323, 324
Aphrodisias, 157, 180
apobates, 159, 160, 161, 168, 325, 329
apodyterion, 336, 339, 342, 344, 346, 348

Apollo, ix, 12, 21, 23, 41, 42, 55, 58, 59, 78, 140, 142, 143, 150, 179, 219, 285, 344
Apollonius, 114, 125, 131, 293, 304
Apollonius Rhodius, 293, 304
Apoxyomenos, ix, 79, 80, 192, 343, 370
Aratus of Sicyon, 102
Arcesilas of Cyrene, 72, 141, 330
Archilochus of Paros, 37
Argeius of Ceos, 145, 151, 302
Argos, x, 11, 30, 36, 44, 46, 47, 52, 64, 86, 88, 91, 116, 117, 132, 140, 145, 149, 150, 151, 158, 161, 193, 321
Aristomenes of Aegina, 69
Aristonicus of Carystus, 345
Aristophanes, 68, 83, 84, 85, 145, 186, 188, 198, 199, 202, 211, 271, 282, 311, 341
Aristotle, 29, 33, 37, 52, 82, 87, 90, 97, 119, 141, 142, 157, 163, 164, 199, 253, 307, 358
armed combat, 15
armed race, 194, 197
artificial training, 80
Assinaria, 332
Atarbus, x, 161, 162
Athenian festivals, 153, 164, 195, 360
Athenian successes, 48
Athens, vii, x, xi, xiii, xiv, xv, 21, 34, 36, 37, 39, 42, 47, 48, 49, 50, 60, 64, 68, 70, 75, 84, 85, 87, 88, 90, 91, 92, 96, 97, 98, 99, 103, 104, 109, 111, 112, 116, 117, 119, 140, 141, 142, 144, 145, 151, 153, 154, 155, 157, 158, 159, 160, 162, 163, 164, 165, 167, 168, 171, 176, 178, 179, 181, 184, 188, 192, 193, 194, 198, 203, 204, 217, 218, 219, 227, 233, 238, 242, 247, 248, 249, 261, 282, 318, 321, 324, 325, 327, 333, 334, 335, 336, 343, 346, 347, 355, 356, 360, 363, 365, 367, 368
athletic, vii, xvii, 1, 3, 4, 5, 6, 7, 8, 9, 10, 11, 12, 13, 16, 17, 19, 20, 21, 22, 23, 25, 27, 31, 32, 33, 34,

35, 36, 37, 39, 40, 41, 42, 44, 45, 46, 47, 48, 50, 52, 53, 55, 57, 59, 61, 64, 65, 66, 67, 68, 69, 70, 71, 72, 73, 74, 75, 77, 82, 83, 84, 85,88, 90, 96, 97, 98, 99, 100, 101, 102, 103, 104, 105, 107, 108, 109, 110, 111, 114, 116, 119, 120, 121, 122, 125, 130, 139, 140, 141, 142, 143, 144, 145, 146, 147, 151, 153, 154, 157, 158, 162, 163, 167, 168, 169, 175, 180, 181, 183, 184, 185, 186, 193, 194, 199, 201, 202, 205, 206, 212, 213, 215, 230, 235, 236, 238, 243, 245, 253, 259, 261, 263, 278, 291, 292, 302, 309, 310, 312, 333, 338, 341, 343, 348, 349, 352, 354, 356, 358, 359, 363, 366, 369, 370
athletic art, 4, 19, 57, 61, 64, 69, 230, 369
athletic character, 25, 27, 151, 243
athletic events, 17, 39, 42, 72, 75, 77, 111, 143, 183, 184, 194
athletic games, 4, 41, 153
athletic guilds, 109, 114
athletic ideal, vii, 3, 5, 23, 55, 57, 64, 66, 69, 107, 119, 310
athletic revival, 96, 109, 116, 121, 263
athletic statue, 46, 59, 65, 69, 90, 103, 184, 205, 370
athletic style, 243
athletic training, 4, 40, 53, 55, 60, 64, 69, 82, 83, 125, 194, 202, 213, 349, 356, 359
athletic types, 61, 67, 68, 245, 312
Augustalia at Neapolis, 183
Augustea, 117
Aurelius Asclepiades, 117
Automedes of Phlius, 257
Azan in Arcadia, 21

B

Bacchylides, 26, 27, 45, 53, 69, 70, 80, 128, 131, 132, 136, 141, 145, 147, 151, 183, 184, 185, 254, 255, 257, 302, 310, 357, 365
backward swing, 224, 228
Balbillea, 118
balbis, 188, 219, 220, 226, 234
ball games, 120, 340
bater, 202, 207, 209
bath-room, 97, 335, 336, 342
battle of Olympia, 364
beauty, 4, 35, 57, 59, 64, 65, 66, 69, 71, 74, 82, 84, 108, 123, 162, 253
Belistiche, 103, 330
Bendidea, 154
Beni-Hassan, 8, 313, 314
boat-races, 148, 154, 360, 368
body-holds, 266, 273
Bouleuterion, 75, 76

boxer, ix, xii, xiii, 9, 13, 51, 54, 59, 73, 80, 85, 95, 113, 118, 124, 125, 205, 263, 285, 286, 289, 290, 294, 295, 296, 297, 298, 299, 301, 302, 303, 304, 305, 306, 307, 312, 337, 339, 352, 357
boys, xii, 3, 4, 10, 15, 31, 34, 37, 38, 42, 46, 52, 65, 71, 82, 83, 85, 86, 92, 98, 103, 104, 108, 109, 111, 115, 117, 120, 121, 124, 128, 129, 130, 131, 132, 133, 141, 143, 147, 151, 154, 157, 158, 161, 164, 167, 168, 183, 184, 185, 199, 215, 218, 231, 262, 264, 267, 269, 282, 286, 302, 307, 334, 336, 341, 353, 354, 355, 356, 357, 359, 361
bronze situlae, 292
Burgon vase, 159, 325, 326
Bybon, 54

C

caestus, xii, 9, 87, 95, 108, 113, 285, 291, 292, 293, 302, 305
Capitolia at Rome, 117
Caprus of Elis, 95, 104
Carnea, 47
Ceos, 51, 69, 90, 98, 247, 356
charioteer, ix, 12, 26, 47, 72, 91, 141, 160, 161, 326, 330
chariot-race, 7, 11, 12, 14, 17, 19, 21, 22, 26, 31, 34, 37, 39, 42, 43, 47, 48, 49, 53, 69, 72, 77, 85, 86, 91, 98, 99, 102, 104, 108, 110, 112, 130, 136, 140, 141, 148, 151, 154, 156, 158, 159, 160, 165, 181, 186, 187, 321, 323, 324, 325, 327, 329, 330, 331
chariot-races, 11, 19, 21, 47, 53, 112, 156, 159, 160, 325
Chilon, 48
Chios, 98, 145, 184, 272
Choiseul-Gouffier Apollo, ix, 59, 60
Chromius of Aetna, 42, 73, 151
Chrysanthina, 117
Cleisthenes of Sicyon, 42, 44, 140, 333
Cleitomachus of Thebes, 95
Cleitostratus of Rhodes, 283
clothes, 90, 103, 134, 154, 202, 339, 341, 351, 352, 355
Cnossus, ix, 8, 10, 17, 285
coins, x, xi, xii, xv, xix, 47, 66, 99, 110, 116, 139, 143, 148, 149, 150, 165, 221, 229, 230, 261, 262, 270, 276, 312, 321, 324, 326, 327, 329, 331, 360, 369
Colonnades, 92
Colotes, 78, 135
competition, 4, 6, 9, 11, 15, 16, 18, 22, 34, 38, 39, 40, 41, 45, 49, 52, 53, 71, 75, 79, 80, 83, 84, 87, 92, 100, 104, 107, 108, 111, 112, 114, 118, 120,

121, 125, 128, 130, 140, 141, 143, 145, 146, 147, 148, 151, 153, 155, 157, 158, 161, 162, 167, 168, 184, 193, 199, 201, 202, 210, 218, 234, 241, 246, 247, 248, 249, 251, 253, 256, 258, 263, 264, 289, 292, 309, 325, 357, 360, 361
Corinth, x, 23, 25, 36, 39, 42, 43, 44, 49, 90, 99, 105, 108, 112, 113, 116, 119, 122, 143, 144, 145, 147, 148, 149, 158, 171, 173, 204
corruption, 5, 73, 86, 87, 88, 96, 114, 122
council, xviii, 27, 29, 45, 46, 75, 87, 93, 98, 110, 112, 114, 133, 139, 186, 364
Cretans and Phoenicians, 25
Crete, 8, 9, 33, 36, 83, 285, 292
cross-buttock, 277, 278, 283
Croton, 36, 38, 50, 53, 54, 73, 86, 211
crushed ear, 301
Cynisca, 86, 329
Cynosarges, 97, 153, 333, 339
Cypselus, 21, 26, 35, 39, 43, 206

D

Damaretus, 46
Damostratus, 265
dead heats, 259
Deinosthenes of Sparta, 100
Delia, 144
Delos, 23, 31, 41, 50, 165, 322, 334, 347
Delphi, ix, x, xiv, xviii, 21, 24, 27, 36, 40, 41, 42, 43, 44, 46, 49, 58, 59, 72, 80, 81, 82, 86, 96, 99, 102, 103, 104, 111, 114, 116, 117, 125, 139, 140, 141, 142, 148, 151, 171, 173, 175, 176, 177, 178, 180, 181, 183, 193, 199, 211, 257, 268, 278, 314, 323, 325, 326, 335, 341, 343, 344, 345, 347, 352, 365
Delphi charioteer, 326
Democrates of Tenedos, 101
Diadumenos of Polycleitus, 61
Diagoras of Rhodes, 73, 118
Diagoridae of Rhodes, 23, 36
Diaulos, 130
diet of athletes, 81
Diisoteria, 154
Dioclea at Megara, 4
Dion, 103, 112, 113, 114, 121, 143, 146, 177, 295, 303, 344
Dion Chrysostom, 113, 143, 146, 295, 303
Dionysia, 98, 154, 202
Diophon, 251, 257
discipline, 40, 64, 65, 120, 186, 334, 337, 355, 356, 361
Diskos, vii, xi, 215, 218, 233, 234, 366, 367
Dium, 98, 100, 327
Dolichos, 130

Dorian invasion, 23, 25
Dromeus of Stymphalus, 81, 358
Dromos, 120, 333
dual control, 29, 30, 75
dumb-bells, 121, 201, 204, 206, 209, 212, 213, 292, 361

E

Eastern Aegean, 23
education, xvii, 3, 4, 5, 9, 10, 13, 37, 41, 57, 66, 68, 69, 70, 82, 84, 98, 108, 120, 121, 157, 183, 253, 262, 334, 341, 353, 355, 356, 359, 361, 366, 368, 369
Eleans, 26, 27, 28, 29, 33, 35, 36, 43, 45, 47, 74, 75, 76, 78, 86, 87, 88, 89, 90, 91, 92, 93, 102, 104, 108, 111, 114, 116, 119, 125, 129, 136, 254, 310, 317, 327
Eleans and Pisatans, 29
Eleusinia, 98, 153
Elis, ix, 11, 18, 24, 25, 26, 28, 30, 31, 33, 35, 36, 45, 74, 75, 85, 86, 88, 90, 91, 92, 101, 102, 108, 109, 110, 111, 117, 118, 119, 127, 132, 133, 152, 193, 194, 327, 330, 346
Elis and Arcadia, 85
Empedocles of Aetna, 136
Epaenetus, 203
Epaminondas, 82, 92
Epharmostus of Opous, 153
ephebic inscription, 162, 357
Epheboi, 8, 16, 334
Ephesus, 111, 117, 158, 180, 335, 347, 350
Epicharinus, 60
Epidaurus, x, xviii, 36, 96, 117, 171, 173, 174, 175, 176, 179, 181, 188, 193, 347
epigram, 32, 52, 55, 132, 187, 188, 193, 211, 251, 254, 255, 257, 262, 263, 265, 283
Epinikia, 184
Epitaphia, 154, 167, 168, 198
equestrian, 4, 42, 44, 78, 85, 87, 97, 104, 108, 110, 111, 130, 139, 142, 147, 151, 153, 154, 159, 162, 168, 325, 329, 369
equestrian events, 78, 87, 104, 108, 111, 130, 147, 162, 168, 325
equestrian programme, 139, 159
Erotidia, 184
Eumastas, 54
Eumelus, 23
Eupolemus of Elis, 87
Eupolus of Thessaly, 86
Euripides, 6, 51, 69, 71, 82, 85, 264, 333
Eusebea at Puteoli, 117
Euthymus of Locri Epizephyrii, 50

Exaenetus of Agrigentum, 50
exercises, vii, 3, 4, 10, 13, 17, 18, 20, 31, 52, 57, 65, 70, 80, 82, 97, 100, 107, 108, 121, 122, 123, 169, 185, 201, 205, 206, 207, 212, 213, 234, 251, 252, 253, 255, 257, 264, 329, 333, 336, 337, 356, 357, 358, 359, 360
Exoïdas, xi, 217, 218, 219

F

Farnese Heracles, ix, 95, 96, 303
fees, 357
festivals, vii, xvii, xviii, 1, 3, 4, 5, 7, 15, 18, 19, 20, 21, 22, 23, 30, 41, 43, 44, 46, 47, 50, 52, 66, 73, 81, 84, 86, 87, 88, 89, 97, 98, 99, 100, 101, 102, 103, 104, 105, 107, 108, 109, 110, 111, 112, 114, 115, 116, 118, 119, 120, 125, 139, 141, 144,145, 147, 151, 153, 154, 173, 176, 183, 184, 193, 201, 249, 263, 290, 309, 321, 343, 346, 347, 352, 354, 359, 363, 365
first Olympiad, 22, 24, 33, 34, 37, 119, 123
first Sacred war, 21, 42
flute-player, 107, 157, 206, 207, 337
flying mare, 265, 269, 312
foot-race, vii, 7, 11, 14, 26, 33, 34, 50, 52, 67, 77, 83, 84, 86, 87, 88, 92, 98, 100, 104, 108, 113, 128, 130, 131, 147, 154, 164, 171, 181, 183, 184, 188, 193, 211, 254, 255, 257, 258, 322, 366
foot-work, 302
four-horse chariot, 26, 34, 37, 50, 86, 88, 99, 140, 158, 321, 324, 325, 326, 327, 330, 331
François vase, xi, 238, 243, 331
funeral games, 11, 19, 21, 22, 27, 34, 43, 247, 272, 285, 321

G

Galen, 81, 82, 121, 122, 123, 212, 316, 349, 357, 359, 360, 361
games, xvii, 3, 4, 5, 6, 7, 8, 9, 10, 11, 15, 17, 18, 19, 20, 21, 22, 23, 25, 26, 27, 28, 29, 31, 33, 34, 35, 38, 39, 40, 41, 42, 43, 44, 45, 46, 47, 48, 50, 51, 52, 57, 65, 67, 70, 71, 74, 76, 80, 85, 88, 90, 91, 92, 96, 98, 99, 100, 104, 105, 107, 108, 109, 110, 111, 112, 113, 114, 116, 117, 118, 119, 120, 121, 122, 129, 134, 140, 141, 142, 144, 145, 146, 149, 150, 151, 154, 162, 167, 172, 175, 178, 179, 180, 193, 201, 212, 215, 219, 220, 223, 233, 240, 246, 247, 251, 254, 286, 309, 310, 316, 324, 327, 329, 332, 334, 345, 357, 361, 363, 364, 365, 366, 367, 369
gems, xiii, 8, 66, 221, 276, 317, 319

Germanicus Caesar, 110
gladiatorial shows, 9, 95, 107, 112, 116, 291
Glaucon of Athens, 103
Glaucus of Carystus, 51, 53, 80
guilds, 114, 148, 358
gymnasia, vii, xiv, 15, 16, 37, 40, 41, 48, 76, 96, 97, 101, 108, 109, 169, 198, 199, 202, 210, 220, 246, 247, 272, 333, 334, 335, 336, 339, 341, 343, 346, 347, 350, 351, 352, 353, 355, 356, 357, 358
gymnasium, viii, xiv, xvii, 3, 10, 16, 70, 76, 84, 96, 97, 98, 103, 114, 116, 125, 142, 150, 167, 173, 177, 179, 181, 192, 198, 201, 207, 208, 213, 234, 236, 252, 333, 334, 335, 336, 337, 338, 339, 341, 342, 344, 345, 347, 348, 349, 350, 351, 352, 354, 355, 356, 360, 369

H

Hadrian, 33, 74, 116, 150, 151, 154, 179, 212, 247, 249, 343, 354, 355
Halter, 314
Halteres, vii, x, 201, 203, 366
heats, 117, 130, 135, 188, 257, 258, 325
Hellanodicae, 26, 29, 31, 44, 45, 75, 76, 77, 78, 87, 101, 111, 112, 119, 130, 131, 132, 133, 134, 135, 151, 173, 175, 183, 329
Helvidius, 162
Heraclea, xii, 78, 118, 141, 153, 262
Heracles, xiii, 7, 10, 13, 23, 24, 26, 27, 37, 38, 43, 55, 67, 72, 77, 95, 104, 114, 123, 128, 129, 151, 167, 173, 201, 261, 266, 268, 269, 273, 276, 277, 285, 296, 309, 310, 312, 314, 317, 318, 346
Heraea, 30, 31, 35, 174, 184, 249
Heraeum, 21, 27, 28, 31, 35, 38, 40, 76, 78, 100, 116, 329
heralds, 34, 35, 89, 110, 112, 123, 125, 131, 132, 133, 146, 150, 167
Herculanei, 114
Hermes, 19, 35, 70, 78, 83, 129, 346, 349, 364, 365
Herodes Atticus, 116, 142, 176, 178, 356
Herodicus of Selymbria, 83, 357, 358
Herodotus of Thebes, 72, 147, 154, 330
Heroum, 101
Hieromnemones, 139
Hieron of Syracuse, 89, 140
Himantes, 366
Hippeis, 47, 367
Hippias of Elis, 33, 90
Hippocrates of Cos, 82
Hippodamium, 26
Hippodrome, viii, xvii, 125, 158, 321, 322, 364, 367
Hippomachus, 74

Homer, vii, 7, 9, 10, 11, 12, 13, 14, 15, 16, 17, 19, 21, 27, 40, 83, 132, 134, 155, 171, 201, 203, 215, 246, 265, 268, 293, 294, 295, 299, 305, 309
horse-races, 19, 20, 43, 49, 53, 75, 108, 109, 110, 128, 129, 131, 141, 142, 153, 161, 167, 168, 171, 181, 324, 328

I

Iasos, 356
Iccus of Tarentum, 83, 358
immorality, 65, 108
Iphitus, 23, 27, 28, 29, 33, 34, 35, 102
Ireland, 19, 239
Isthmia, 42, 43, 44, 49, 88, 92, 104, 113, 114, 117, 140, 143, 144, 145, 146, 147, 148, 149, 150, 151, 154, 183, 184, 302, 360
Italy, 25, 36, 47, 50, 51, 53, 85, 104, 107, 109, 112, 113, 116, 117, 145, 152, 215, 239

J

Jason of Pherae, 99, 142
javelin, vii, 17, 26, 68, 77, 83, 87, 97, 98, 121, 159, 167, 168, 174, 175, 177, 181, 207, 213, 217, 220, 234, 235, 236, 237, 238, 239, 240, 241, 243, 244, 245, 246, 247, 248, 251, 252, 253, 254, 255, 258, 336, 337, 356, 359, 366, 367
jockeys, 133, 328, 330
Julius Caesar, 109, 112, 144, 146

K

Kosmetes, 97, 163

L

Laches of Ceos, 128
Lampito, 202
Lampon of Aegina, 73
Laodicea, 180
Larisa, 247, 249
law, 20, 69, 80, 139, 146, 298, 306, 309, 330, 339
Leon of Ambracia, 87
Leonidaeum, 101
Leonidas of Naxos, 101
Leonidas of Rhodes, 104
Licinius Priscus, 147
Ligourio bronze, 59
loin-cloth, 32, 185, 264, 296
long jump, 201, 207, 209, 210, 257, 258

love names, 65
Lyceum at Athens, 347
Lycurgus of Sparta, 28
Lygdamis of Syracuse, 38
Lysander, 90

M

Macedon, xiii, 52, 98, 101, 102, 103, 104, 105, 110, 140, 142, 150, 326, 327, 328
marathon, 6, 68, 69, 153
massage, 54, 83, 121, 123, 199, 361
medical gymnastics, 83, 201, 357, 358
medicine, 82, 83, 122, 124, 358
Melancomas, 114, 303
Melesias, 80, 357, 358
Menander of Athens, 358
Messene, 92, 104, 180, 184, 335
Midas of Agrigentum, 140, 155
military competitions, 155, 167
Milo of Croton, 53
mosaic, ix, xii, 115, 116, 123, 124, 165, 236, 291, 316, 317, 369
mud, 122, 174, 264, 282, 312, 350
mule car, 321, 327
mule chariot-race, 47, 130, 325
musical contests, 49, 100, 121, 148, 157, 164
musical events, 42, 168
musical festival, 139
Mycenae, 9, 44, 237
Myron, ix, 38, 39, 42, 61, 63, 64, 66, 76, 132, 193, 219, 221, 223, 224, 226, 229, 230, 233, 329, 361

N

neck-holds, 271, 273
Nemea, 40, 41, 42, 43, 44, 49, 82, 104, 116, 117, 140, 145, 147, 149, 150, 151, 183, 184, 194, 324
Nemean games, 149, 298, 365
Nero, 108, 111, 112, 113, 142, 144, 146, 149
new buildings, 46
Nicasylus of Rhodes, 184

O

oath, 45, 114, 133, 189, 286
Oenomaus, 7, 22, 26, 77, 100
officials, 15, 29, 30, 75, 87, 91, 97, 101, 110, 112, 113, 120, 125, 133, 136, 146, 151, 163, 172, 175, 176, 178, 179, 184, 199, 309, 339, 355, 358

oil, 47, 49, 67, 83, 97, 115, 153, 154, 155, 157, 159, 162, 163, 165, 184, 185, 249, 253, 285, 335, 336, 338, 339, 341, 346, 348, 349, 352, 354, 355, 356
Oligaethidae of Corinth, 145, 152
Olympia, ix, x, xiii, xiv, xv, xvii, xviii, xix, 4, 5, 6, 7, 21, 22, 23, 24, 25, 26, 27, 28, 29, 30, 31, 33, 35, 36, 37, 38, 39, 41, 42, 43, 44, 45, 46, 48, 49, 50, 52, 53, 54, 55, 57, 65, 66, 69, 70, 74, 75, 76, 77, 78, 81, 82, 83, 84, 85, 86, 87, 88, 89, 90, 91, 92, 93, 95, 96, 98, 99, 100, 101, 102, 103, 104, 105, 107, 108, 110, 111, 112, 114, 116, 117, 118, 119, 123, 125, 126, 127, 129, 130, 132, 133, 134, 135, 136, 139, 140, 141, 143, 144, 145, 151, 154, 171, 172, 173, 174, 175, 176, 178, 179, 181, 182, 183, 184, 188, 189, 190, 193, 194, 195, 196, 199, 203, 204, 211, 217, 218, 247, 253, 254, 258, 263, 283, 285, 291, 304, 309, 311, 322, 323, 324, 325, 327, 328, 329, 330, 332, 335, 341, 343, 345, 346, 347, 348, 358, 363, 364, 365
Onomastus, 23, 36, 47, 285
Orsippus of Megara, 32
Oschophoria, 154, 167, 198
Oxyrhynchus Papyrus, 33, 130, 268, 276, 359

P

paidotribes, 123, 240, 262, 339, 356, 357, 358, 359
palaestra, viii, xiv, 52, 57, 67, 68, 70, 82, 84, 96, 100, 103, 167, 181, 199, 201, 234, 235, 247, 248, 261, 262, 264, 289, 290, 307, 317, 333, 334, 335, 337, 344, 345, 346, 347, 348, 349, 350, 351, 357, 358, 359, 366
Palaestra, viii, 333
palm of victory, 135
Panathenaea, x, 32, 40, 49, 85, 86, 87, 88, 97, 98, 144, 147, 148, 153, 154, 155, 157, 160, 161, 162, 163, 164, 165, 166, 183, 184, 198, 249, 365
Panathenaic, x, xi, xii, xiii, 48, 49, 59, 80, 86, 87, 96, 155, 156, 157, 158, 162, 164, 165, 166, 167, 178, 181, 185, 188, 189, 190, 191, 192, 197, 209, 210, 230, 231, 241, 249, 251, 252, 255, 267, 273, 274, 288, 289, 293, 297, 299, 300, 301, 303, 312, 313, 314, 315, 316, 324, 325, 326, 327, 328, 370
Panathenaic amphorae, 155, 158, 164, 165, 210, 370
Panathenaic stadium, 96, 158, 178, 181
Panhellenic festivals, 5, 40, 44, 45, 46, 48, 49, 69, 74, 99, 111, 118, 143, 184, 282, 365
Panhellenism, 43, 88, 100
pankratiast, 46, 54, 74, 80, 92, 96, 117, 142, 184, 296, 302, 310, 311, 312, 313, 314, 316, 317, 339
Pankration, viii, 130, 158, 309, 366
Parthenon, 47, 62, 66, 85, 155, 159, 160, 161, 365
Patroclus, 9, 11, 12, 17, 22, 215, 246, 285, 321

Peisistratus, 47, 48, 49, 155, 334
Peleus, 253, 255, 257, 258, 270, 272
Pelias, 21, 247, 272
Peloponnese, 7, 22, 23, 24, 25, 26, 27, 28, 36, 37, 38, 44, 47, 51, 55, 75, 93, 99, 104, 133, 140, 141, 144, 151, 184, 193
Pentathlon, viii, 130, 131, 158, 251, 253, 265, 366, 368
Pergamum, xiv, xviii, 102, 117, 122, 173, 335, 347, 352, 353
Petraea, 141
Phaedimus, 104
Phanas of Pellene, 54
Phayllus of Croton, 141, 193, 257
Pheidon of Argos, 36, 39
Pherenice, 31
Philinus of Cos, 104
Philip II, xiii, 99, 104, 327, 328
Philip V, 102, 150
Philippeum, 99, 101
Philippus, 50, 263
Philippus of Croton, 50
Philon, 173
Philonides of Crete, 100
Philopoemen, 82, 104, 150
Philostratus, xviii, 33, 35, 53, 54, 80, 83, 114, 119, 120, 121, 122, 123, 125, 130, 132, 151, 190, 194, 197, 198, 199, 202, 205, 206, 218, 219, 231, 240, 251, 253, 255, 256, 257, 262, 263, 264, 265, 274, 287, 290, 291, 294, 298, 302, 309, 310, 312, 313, 314, 349, 350, 357, 358, 359, 364, 366, 369
Phintia, 356
Phlegon of Tralles, 33, 119
physical training, xvii, 7, 10, 52, 65, 69, 82, 84, 97, 122, 125, 201, 202, 213, 253, 334, 352, 359, 360, 361
Pindar, 9, 13, 21, 22, 23, 26, 27, 34, 35, 37, 41, 42, 43, 44, 47, 48, 53, 55, 66, 69, 70, 71, 72, 73, 77, 80, 113, 118, 128, 129, 131, 132, 134, 136, 140, 141, 142, 145, 148, 149, 151, 153, 154, 155, 163, 173, 175, 184, 201, 216, 220, 246, 247, 248, 251, 253, 255, 261, 263, 271, 306, 310, 314, 317, 323, 325, 330, 357, 358, 361, 364, 365, 368
Pisa, 27, 28, 29, 30, 51, 117, 265, 364
Pisatae, 27, 29
Pisatis, 30, 75, 76
Platanistas at Sparta, 333
Plato, 15, 16, 29, 82, 83, 85, 87, 90, 97, 157, 158, 183, 193, 201, 202, 246, 248, 253, 254, 266, 286, 289, 302, 307, 317, 334, 335, 336, 339, 341, 345, 356, 357, 358, 359

Plutarch, 22, 33, 53, 82, 83, 86, 99, 121, 122, 130, 150, 155, 188, 193, 206, 212, 256, 258, 268, 283, 290, 291, 294, 305, 314, 329
poaching at the start, 188
Polites, 130
political importance, 39, 48, 100, 150
Polycleitus, ix, 59, 61, 63, 64, 66, 80, 132
Polydamas of Scotussa, 51
Polydeuces, 13, 51, 285, 294, 303, 304, 316
Polymnestor, 38
pot-hunting, 114, 117
Praxidamas of Aegina, 46
Praxiteles, 35
pre-Dorian times, 27
Priene, xiv, xviii, 155, 179, 291, 350, 351, 352
prize, x, 9, 11, 12, 13, 14, 15, 16, 17, 21, 26, 33, 35, 41, 42, 43, 44, 47, 49, 86, 95, 98, 99, 111, 112, 121, 123, 131, 139, 140, 143, 148, 151, 153, 154, 156, 157, 158, 159, 161, 162, 164, 202, 247, 249, 251, 256, 265, 292, 295, 297, 303, 305, 316, 325, 330, 339, 352
prize table, x, 139, 143
processional entrance, 112
professionalism, vii, 5, 6, 53, 74, 79, 82, 84, 85, 86, 87, 95, 104, 114, 116, 122, 261
Prytaneum, 35, 46, 50, 129, 137
Ptolemaea, 98
Ptolemaeus Philadelphus, 102, 343
Publius Asclepiades, 119, 217
Pyrrhic chorus, 161
Pythagoras of Samos, 81, 358
Pythaids, 141, 142
Pytheas of Aegina, 70, 151, 358
Pythia, 21, 42, 44, 104, 117, 139, 140, 141, 142, 143, 263

R

record-breaking, 118
religion, 4, 5, 19, 22, 26, 42, 50, 57, 74, 112, 115, 121, 125, 191
rewards, 33, 48, 50, 52, 71, 83, 84, 109, 137
riding, 38, 47, 50, 72, 85, 104, 140, 160, 321, 325, 327, 333, 334, 337, 359
Roman games, 107
Roman prejudice, 108, 112, 352
Romans, vii, ix, 19, 97, 104, 107, 108, 115, 121, 145, 146, 171, 234, 291, 314, 369
Rowing, 359

S

sanctuary, 27, 28, 42, 50, 110, 146, 150, 173
Scholiasts, 128
sculptor, ix, 57, 58, 59, 64, 68, 69, 80, 89, 320
sculpture, ix, xii, xv, xix, 7, 8, 44, 46, 55, 58, 59, 61, 63, 64, 67, 69, 72, 80, 81, 96, 212, 223, 278, 365, 369
Sicilian, 86, 88, 105, 261, 321, 327
Sicily, 25, 36, 39, 47, 51, 53, 66, 69, 85, 99, 104, 107, 110, 113, 145, 152, 217, 321, 326, 327, 331
Simonides, 32, 51, 52, 69, 70, 251, 254, 255, 257, 265
Smyrna, 8, 23, 36, 74, 117, 122, 285
Socrates, 80, 82, 83, 84, 90, 198, 334, 336
Sogenes of Aegina, 151
Solon, 37, 41, 42, 48, 49, 50, 119, 144, 334, 339, 349, 355, 357
Sophius of Messene, 92
Sostratus of Sicyon, 95
Sotades of Crete, 86
Soteria, 102
Sparta, xiii, 7, 21, 27, 29, 34, 36, 37, 41, 47, 50, 52, 53, 77, 83, 84, 85, 86, 87, 88, 91, 92, 98, 99, 100, 102, 103, 104, 109, 115, 119, 120, 121, 122, 141, 145, 151, 193, 302, 309, 324, 325, 329, 370
Spartan, 31, 36, 37, 38, 39, 46, 47, 48, 53, 70, 75, 91, 102, 107, 108, 115, 120, 121, 145, 150, 194, 202, 283, 302, 314, 321, 329, 333, 348, 349, 359
spectators, 9, 12, 14, 29, 35, 39, 52, 71, 76, 77, 78, 84, 86, 87, 92, 93, 96, 97, 101, 107, 116, 118, 120, 134, 135, 136, 153, 158, 171, 172, 174, 176, 177, 178, 179, 180, 181, 182, 185, 199, 248, 256, 294, 310, 321, 345, 346, 347
sphairai, 290, 293
stadium, vii, x, xvii, 10, 26, 31, 35, 38, 42, 46, 74, 77, 78, 81, 86, 92, 101, 103, 104, 110, 112, 115, 116, 125, 132, 133, 134, 139, 142, 146, 147, 150, 151, 171, 172, 173, 174, 175, 176, 178, 179, 180, 181, 183, 193, 202, 219, 248, 254, 264, 322, 324, 335, 344, 347, 351
Statius, 189, 195, 219, 220, 226, 231, 302, 305
stone-throwing, 16
strangling, 310, 312, 317
Strigil, xiv, 343
Sulla, 108, 142
sweating-bath, 349
swimming, 54, 343, 359, 360
Sybaris, 36, 38, 46, 53
synoecism of Elis, 74
Syracuse, xii, xiii, 21, 36, 86, 89, 104, 261, 262, 321, 331

T

Taraxippus, 324
Tarentum, xiii, 148, 276, 321, 329, 369
Tauromenium, 356
Temple of Zeus, 93
Teos, 98, 356, 357
Theagenes of Thasos, 51, 53
Thebes, 17, 36, 37, 69, 90, 92, 100, 141, 142, 145, 154, 171, 193
Themistocles, 75, 85, 89, 186, 248, 334
Theocoleon, 101
Theocritus, 277, 283, 293, 294, 299, 301, 302, 303, 304, 305, 306, 307, 316
Theodota, 330
Theophrastus, 277, 345
Theoroi, 155
Thesea, 15, 97, 154, 165, 167, 168, 184, 198, 249
Thessaly, 8, 11, 69, 84, 99, 141, 142, 249, 321
Timodemidae of Athens, 145, 152
Titormus, 54, 55
torch-races, 49, 97, 154, 155, 167, 168, 198, 355, 359
trainers, 31, 53, 54, 67, 72, 80, 83, 114, 119, 123, 124, 133, 213, 283, 309, 339, 358
training, 3, 4, 6, 15, 16, 18, 37, 38, 40, 41, 52, 53, 54, 55, 65, 67, 70, 71, 73, 74, 75, 80, 82, 83, 84, 87, 91, 95, 96, 97, 98, 104, 108, 111, 119, 121, 122, 123, 125, 132, 133, 159, 193, 197, 198, 199, 201, 202, 205, 213, 238, 246, 253, 271, 307, 309, 317, 334, 343, 344, 349, 350, 351, 355, 356, 357, 359, 361, 369
treasuries, 36, 38, 39, 40, 45, 46, 76, 92, 93, 99, 116, 134, 364
tripping, 189, 265, 266, 273, 280, 281
truce, 20, 29, 30, 31, 33, 35, 39, 88, 91, 110, 132, 140, 145, 150
truce of Iphitus, 29, 30
trumpet, 135, 186, 324, 326
trumpeters, 34, 89, 131, 133, 151, 167
two-horse chariot, 37, 86, 104, 148, 321, 326, 327, 330
Tydeus, 285
Tyrtaeus, 53, 57

V

Valerius Eclectus, 125
Varazdates, 126
vases, xi, xv, xviii, xix, 13, 21, 32, 47, 49, 55, 57, 59, 62, 67, 68, 70, 80, 86, 87, 103, 132, 149, 155, 157, 158, 163, 164, 165, 167, 181, 185, 186, 188, 190, 191, 192, 194, 195, 196, 198, 201, 202, 204, 206, 207, 209, 210, 212, 213, 216, 218, 220, 221, 222, 223, 224, 227, 230, 231, 232, 235, 237, 238, 239, 240, 241, 243, 245, 246, 247, 249, 251, 255, 261, 264, 265, 266, 268, 271, 280, 285, 286, 287, 289, 293, 296, 297, 298, 302, 303, 306, 307, 312, 314, 316, 317, 321, 324, 325, 326, 331, 336, 339, 341, 342, 345, 359, 367, 370
Vergil, 113, 189, 293, 301, 305, 306
Vide, 24, 29, 65, 66, 70, 78, 80, 101, 125, 154, 185, 194, 202, 221, 235, 247, 254, 264, 274, 275, 307, 321, 341, 349, 360, 365
Vitruvius, 344, 346, 347, 348, 349, 350, 351
votive offerings, 19, 27, 35, 78, 89, 102, 217

W

Watsch, xii, 239, 292
weight-lifting, 54
winter Nemea, 151
women, 4, 20, 23, 26, 31, 58, 65, 154, 161, 329, 343, 356
wooden barrier, 173
wrestler, 13, 14, 54, 59, 82, 85, 101, 122, 125, 205, 257, 258, 261, 263, 265, 266, 269, 270, 271, 272, 274, 276, 278, 280, 281, 302, 310, 312, 313, 314, 317, 319, 357

X

Xenarches, 148, 151
Xenocles, 263
Xenocrates, 140, 148
Xenophanes, 6, 51, 53, 85, 184
Xenophon, 24, 30, 77, 82, 84, 92, 129, 131, 161, 178, 193, 235, 238, 240, 248, 254, 256, 258, 271, 335, 357, 358, 359
Xystos, 115

Z

Zanes, 86, 101, 114

INDEX OF GREEK WORDS

α

ἀγένειοι, 52, 65, 158, 184
ἀγκύλη, 236
ἀγκυρίσας, 282
ἄγχειν, 317
ἀγὼν ἐπιτάφιος, 21
ἀθλητής, 84
ἄθλιος, 185
αἰγανέη, 236
αἰδώς, 66, 73
ἄκαμπτον, 160
ἀκονιτεί, 117, 263
ἀκοντισμός, 247
ἀκροχειρισμός, 307
ἀλεγεινός, 12
ἅλματα, 177
ἁλτῆρες, 203
ἁλτηροβολία, 212
ἀνακλινοπάλη, κλινοπάλη, 262
ἀνθιππασία, 161
ἀπειπεῖν, 294
ἀπήνη, 47, 130, 325, 327
ἀποβατής, 47
ἀποδυτήριον, 336
ἀποπτερνίζειν, 314
ἀπόρραξις, 345
ἀποτομάς, 235
ἀποτριάξαι, 257
ἅρμα, 325
ἀρυτῆρες, 348
ἀσκωλιασμός, 202
ἄφεσις, 186, 323

β

βαλβίς,, 171, 187
βάλλω, βολή, 280
βατήρ, 171, 202
βοαγός, 121

Γ

γαστρίζειν, 316
γραμμή, 171
γυμνάσιον, 357

Δ

διαβολή, 280
διαλαμβάνειν, 274
δίαυλος, 34
διηγκυλισμένος, 241
δράσσειν, 269
δρόμος, 251, 254, 336

ε

ἐκεχειρία, 29
ἐκπλεθρίζειν, 361
ἐναγκυλῶντες, 240
ἐνάλλεσθαι, 316
ἐνδρομίδες, 185
ἐνεκολήβασας, 282
εὐανδρία, 162, 167
ἔφεδρος, 258

Index of Greek Words

ἡ

ἡμεροδρόμοι, 59
ἡνίοχος ἐγβιβάζων, 161

Θ

θεωρίαι, 39

Ι

ἰδιώτης, 84
ἱερομηνία, 29
ἱερὸν ποιεῖν, 135
ἱμάντες μαλακώτεροι, 285

κ

Καθθηρατόριν, 121
καλαῦροψ, 17, 215, 326
κάλπη, 47, 325, 329
καμπτῆρες, 171, 177
κατωμαδίοιο, 17
κελῆα, 121
κέλης, 325
κήρωμα, 350
κλιμακισμός, 317
κλῖμαξ, 306
κολυμβήθρα, 345
κύλισις, 264
κώρυκος, 307, 339

Λ

λαβή, 266
λαμπρός, 159
ληνοί, 354

μ

μείλιχαι, 285
μεσάγκυλον, 235, 236
μεσοφέρδειν, 274
μεταπλασμός, 280
μικιζόμενοι, 121
μύρμηκες, 291
μῶα, 121

ν

νεανίσκοι, 167
νύσσα, 171

Ξ

ξηραλοιφεῖν, 349

ὀ

ὀξεῖς, 290, 291
ὀρύττειν, 310

π

πάλαισμα, 255
παραδρομίς, 344
παράθεσις, 268
παρακαταγωγή, 280
παρεμβολή, 280
περίζωμα, 264
περίπατος, 354
περιπολιστική, 115
περιτιθέναι, 274
πιτυλίζειν, 361
προεδρία, 43
πυριατήριον, 344, 349

σ

σκαπάναι, 202
σκιαμαχία, 307
σκιλλομαχία, 352
σπονδοφόροι, 29, 132
στρεβλοῦν, 317
συναυλία, 157
συνωρίς, 140, 325, 326
σύστασις, 268
σφαῖραι, 289, 291, 303
σφαιρεῖς, 120
σφαιριστήρια, 344
σφενδόνη, 171, 172
σχήματα, 359

Τ

τάξεις, 188
ταυροκαθαψία, 8
τέθριππον, 325
τέρμα, 220, 248
τραχηλίζειν, 271
τριαστής, 54, 104

Υ

ὑποσκελίζειν, 280
ὕσπληξ, 187, 324

Φ

φορβεία, 337
φράξις, 177
φυλλοβολία, 135

Χ

χειρονομία, 307

Ψ

ψάλις, 177

Related Nova Publications

A Crucible of Modern Sport: The Early Development of Football in Sheffield

Editor: Graham Curry

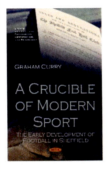

Series: Sports and Athletics Preparation, Performance, and Psychology

Book Description: This book examines in detail the early development of the game of football in and around Sheffield, England. When the first football club, Sheffield FC, was founded on 24 October 1857, it began a chain of events which would see the emergence of the earliest modern footballing subculture.

Hardcover ISBN: 978-1-53613-090-4
Retail Price: $195

The Science of Swimming and Aquatic Activities

Editor: Ricardo J. Fernandes, Ph.D.

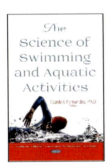

Series: Sports and Athletics Preparation, Performance, and Psychology

Book Description: This volume gathers important research from around the globe in the field of swimming and aquatic activities. Readers will be able to better grasp the science behind the sport and related physical activities, with approaches from physiology, biochemistry, immunology, biomechanics, pedagogy, didactics and history.

Hardcover ISBN: 978-1-53614-028-6
Retail Price: $230

To see a complete list of Nova publications, please visit our website at www.novapublishers.com

Related Nova Publications

An In-Depth Guide to Sports

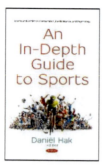

Editor: Daniël Hak

Series: Sports and Athletics Preparation, Performance, and Psychology

Book Description: An *In Depth Guide to Sports* opens with a review of the study of different biochemical profiles, through the analysis of the results obtained in different works carried out by a biochemical group and based on the literature reviewed.

Hardcover ISBN: 978-1-53613-910-5
Retail Price: $160

Soccer: The Physical and Cultural Effects of the World's Most Popular Sport

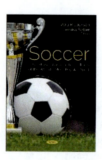

Editors: Vera R. Jackson and Jessika Farber

Series: Sports and Athletics Preparation, Performance, and Psychology

Book Description: This collection investigates the time-motion characteristics of collegiate soccer games, repeated-sprint ability in female players, and skill-based assessments of collegiate male and female players.

Softcover ISBN: 978-1-53613-220-5
Retail Price: $82

To see a complete list of Nova publications, please visit our website at www.novapublishers.com